Microsoft® Visual C#® 2008

An Introduction to Object-Oriented Programming

Third Edition

Joyce Farrell

COURSE TECHNOLOGY
CENGAGE Learning™

Australia • Brazil • Japan • Korea • Mexico • Singapore • Spain • United Kingdom • United States

**Microsoft® Visual C#® 2008
An Introduction to Object-Oriented
Programming**
Joyce Farrell

Executive Editor: Marie Lee

Acquisitions Editor: Amy Jollymore

Managing Editor: Tricia Coia

Developmental Editor: Dan Seiter

Editorial Assistant: Patrick Frank

Marketing Manager: Bryant Chrzan

Senior Content Project Manager: Cathie
DiMassa

Art Director: Marissa Falco

Manufacturing Coordinator:
Julio Esperas

Proofreader: Harold Johnson

Indexer: Alexandra Nickerson

Compositor: International Typesetting
and Composition

Microsoft® is a registered trademark of the Microsoft Corporation.

International Student Edition:
ISBN-13: 978-0-538-74708-0

ISBN-10: 0-538-74708-0

Course Technology
20 Channel Center Street
Boston, MA 02210
USA

Cengage Learning is a leading provider of customized learning solutions with
office locations around the globe, including Singapore, the United Kingdom,
Australia, Mexico, Brazil, and Japan. Locate your local office at:
international.cengage.com/region

Cengage Learning products are represented in Canada by Nelson Education, Ltd.

For your lifelong learning solutions, visit **course.cengage.com**

Visit our corporate Web site at **cengage.com.**

Some of the product names and company names used in this book have
been used for identification purposes only and may be trademarks or
registered trademarks of their respective manufacturers and sellers.

Course Technology, a part of Cengage Learning, reserves the right to
revise this publication and make changes from time to time in its content
without notice.

Printed in Canada
1 2 3 4 5 6 7 12 11 10 09

BRIEF CONTENTS

CONTENTS

CONTENTS

CONTENTS

CHAPTER 6 USING METHODS — 199

CONTENTS

CONTENTS

CHAPTER 10   USING GUI OBJECTS AND THE VISUAL STUDIO IDE   415

CONTENTS

PREFACE

Microsoft Visual C# 2008: An Introduction to Object-Oriented Programming, Third Edition provides the beginning programmer with a guide to developing programs in C#, a language created by the Microsoft Corporation as part of the .NET Framework and Visual Studio platform. The .NET Framework contains a wealth of libraries for developing applications for the Windows family of operating systems. With C#, you can build small, reusable components that are well suited to twenty-first century Web-based programming applications. Although similar to Java and C++, many features of C# make it easier to learn and ideal for the beginning programmer. You can program in C# using a simple text editor and the command prompt, or you can manipulate program components using Visual Studio's sophisticated Integrated Development Environment. This book provides you with the tools to use both techniques.

This textbook assumes that you have little or no programming experience. The writing is non-technical and emphasizes good programming practices. The examples are business examples; they do not assume mathematical background beyond high school business math. Additionally, the examples illustrate one or two major points; they do not contain so many features that you become lost following irrelevant or extraneous details. This book provides you with a solid background in good object-oriented programming techniques and introduces you to object-oriented terminology using clear, familiar language.

ORGANIZATION AND COVERAGE

Microsoft Visual C# 2008: An Introduction to Object-Oriented Programming, Third Edition presents C# programming concepts, enforcing good style, logical thinking, and the object-oriented paradigm. Chapter 1 introduces you to the language by letting you create working C# programs using both the simple command line and the Visual Studio environment. In Chapter 2 you learn about data and how to input, store, and output data in C#. In Chapters 3, 4, and 5, you learn about the classic programming structures and how to implement them: making selections, looping, and manipulating arrays. Chapter 6 provides a thorough study of methods, including passing parameters into and out of methods and overloading them.

Chapter 7 introduces the object-oriented concepts of classes, objects, data hiding, constructors, and destructors. After completing Chapters 8 and 9, you will be thoroughly grounded in the object-oriented concepts of inheritance and exception handling, and you will be able to take advantage of both features in your C# programs. Chapters 10 and 11 introduce you to GUI objects. You will learn about controls, how to set their properties, and how to make attractive, useful, graphical, and interactive programs. Chapter 12 takes you further into the intricacies of handling events in your interactive GUI programs. In Chapter 13, you learn to save data to and retrieve data from files. In Chapter 14, you learn how to interact with databases in C# programs—an increasingly valuable skill in the information-driven business world. C# 3.0 supports LINQ (Language Integrated Query) statements, which allow you to integrate SQL-like queries into C# programs. Chapter 14 provides you with the fundamentals of this important technology.

FEATURES

Microsoft Visual C# 2008: An Introduction to Object-Oriented Programming, Third Edition is a superior textbook because it also includes the following features:

NEW! » *C# 3.0 in Visual Studio 2008*—This edition is written and tested using the latest edition of C#.

NEW! » *Database queries*—This edition includes a new chapter on database management and LINQ.

» *Objectives*—Each chapter begins with a list of objectives so you know the topics that will be presented in the chapter. In addition to providing a quick reference to topics covered, this feature provides a useful study aid.

» *Notes*—These tips provide additional information—for example, an alternative method of performing a procedure, another term for a concept, background information on a technique, or a common error to avoid.

» *Figures*—Each chapter contains many figures. Code figures are most frequently 25 lines long or shorter, illustrating one concept at a time. Frequently placed screen shots show exactly how program output appears. In this edition, all C# keywords that appear in figures are blue to help them stand out from programmer-created identifiers.

» *Summaries*—Following each chapter is a summary that recaps the programming concepts and techniques covered in the chapter. This feature helps you to recap and check your understanding of the main points in each chapter.

» *Key Terms*—Each chapter includes a list of newly introduced vocabulary, shown in the order of appearance in the text. The list of key terms provides a mini-review of the major concepts in the chapter.

» *You Do It*—In each chapter, step-by-step exercises help the student create multiple working programs that emphasize the logic a programmer uses in choosing statements. This section enables students to achieve success on their own—even students in online or distance learning classes.

NEW! » *Two Truths and a Lie*—These true-false mini-quizzes appear throughout each chapter, with answers provided. The quiz contains three statements from the preceding section of text—two true and one false. Over the years, students have requested answers to problems, but we have hesitated to distribute them in case instructors want to use problems as assignments or test questions. These true-false mini-quizzes provide students with immediate feedback as they read, without "giving away" answers to the existing multiple choice and programming problem questions.

» *Review Questions*—Each chapter contains 20 multiple-choice review questions that provide a review of the key concepts in the chapter.

» *Exercises*—Each chapter concludes with meaningful programming exercises that provide additional practice of the skills and concepts you learned in the chapter. These exercises increase in difficulty and allow you to explore logical programming concepts.

» *Debugging Exercises*—Each chapter contains four programs that contain syntax and/or logical errors that you fix. Completing these exercises provides valuable experience in locating errors, interpreting code written by others, and observing how another programmer has approached a problem.

NEW! » *Glossary*—This edition includes a glossary that contains definitions for all key terms in the book, presented in alphabetical order.

» *Up for Discussion*—Each chapter concludes with a few thought-provoking questions that concern programming in general or C# in particular. The questions can be used to start classroom or online discussions, or to develop and encourage research, writing, and language skills.

» *Program code*—The Student Disk provides code for each full program presented in the chapter figures. Providing the code on disk allows students to run it, view the results for themselves, and experiment with multiple input values. Having the code on disk also enables students to experiment with the code without a lot of typing.

» *Quality*—Every program example in the book, as well as every exercise, case project, and game solution, was tested by the author using Visual Studio 2008 Express Edition, and then tested again by a Quality Assurance team using Visual Studio 2008 Professional Edition, the most recent version available.

TEACHING TOOLS

The following supplemental materials are available when this book is used in a classroom setting. All of the instructor resources for this book are provided to the instructor on a single CD-ROM.

Electronic Instructor's Manual. The Instructor's Manual that accompanies this textbook includes additional instructional material to assist in class preparation, including teaching tips, quick quizzes, class discussion topics, and additional projects.

ExamView®. This textbook is accompanied by ExamView, a powerful testing software package that allows instructors to create and administer printed, computer (LAN-based), and Internet exams. ExamView includes hundreds of questions that correspond to the topics covered in this text, enabling students to generate detailed study guides that include page references for further review. The computer-based and Internet testing components allow students to take exams at their computers, and save the instructor time by grading each exam automatically.

PowerPoint Presentations. This book comes with Microsoft PowerPoint slides for each chapter. These slides are included as a teaching aid for classroom presentation; teachers can make them available on the network for chapter review, or print them for classroom distribution. Instructors can add their own slides for additional topics they introduce to the class.

Solution Files. Password-protected solutions to all Review Questions, end-of-chapter programming exercises, debugging exercises, Up For Discussion questions, and "You Do It" exercises are provided on the Instructor Resources CD-ROM and on the Course Technology Web site at *www.course.com*.

Distance Learning. Course Technology is proud to present online test banks in WebCT and Blackboard to provide the most complete and dynamic learning experience possible. Instructors are encouraged to make the most of the course, both online and offline. For more information on how to access the online test bank, contact your local Course Technology sales representative.

ACKNOWLEDGMENTS

I would like to thank all of the people who helped to make this book a reality, especially Dan Seiter, the developmental editor, who once again worked against multiple, aggressive deadlines to make this book into a superior instructional tool. Thanks also to Tricia Coia, managing editor; Amy Jollymore, acquisitions editor; and Cathie DiMassa, senior production editor. I am grateful to be able to work with so many fine people who are dedicated to producing good instructional materials.

I am also grateful to the many reviewers who provided helpful comments and encouragement during this book's development, including Albert Arnold, Ozarks Technical Community College; I-Ping Chu, DePaul University; Phil Jalowiec, Maricopa County Community Colleges; Richard Mowe, St. Cloud State University; and Paul Rosenberg, DePaul University.

Thanks, too, to my husband, Geoff, for his constant support and encouragement. Finally, this book is dedicated to my goddaughter Robin.

Joyce Farrell

READ THIS BEFORE YOU BEGIN

TO THE USER

To complete the exercises in this book, you will need data files that have been created specifically for the book. Your instructor will provide the data files to you. You also can obtain the files electronically from the Course Technology Web site by connecting to *www.course.com* and then searching for this book title. Note that you can use a computer in your school lab or your own computer to complete the exercises in this book.

The data files for this book are organized such that the examples and exercises are divided into folders named Chapter.*xx*, where *xx* is the chapter number. You can save these files in the same folders unless specifically instructed to do otherwise in the chapter.

USING YOUR OWN COMPUTER

To use your own computer to complete the steps and exercises, you will need the following:

- » **Software**. Microsoft Visual C# 2008 Express Edition or Professional Edition, including the Microsoft .NET Framework. If your book came with a copy of the software, you may install it on your computer and use it to complete the material.
- » **Hardware**. *Minimum*: 1.6-GHz CPU, 192 MB of RAM, 1024 × 768 display, 5400-RPM hard disk. *Recommended*: At least a 2.2-GHz CPU, at least 384 MB of RAM, 1280 × 1024 display, at least a 7200-RPM hard disk. *On Windows Vista*: 2.4-GHz CPU, 768 MB of RAM, 1.3 GB available disk space for full installation.
- » **Operating system**. Windows Vista or XP.
- » **Data files**. You will not be able to complete the exercises in this book using your own computer unless you have the data files. You can get the data files from your instructor, or you can obtain them electronically from the Course Technology Web site by connecting to *www.course.com* and searching for this book title.

TO THE INSTRUCTOR

To complete all the exercises and chapters in this book, your users must work with a set of data files. These files are included on the Instructor Resources CD. You can also obtain these files electronically through the Course Technology Web site at *www.course.com*. Follow the instructions in the Help file to copy the user files to your server or stand-alone computer. You can view the Help file using a text editor such as WordPad or Notepad.

Once the files are copied, you can make copies for the users yourself or tell them where to find the files so they can make their own copies.

LICENSE TO USE DATA FILES

You are granted a license to copy the files that accompany this book to any computer or computer network used by people who have purchased this book.

1

A FIRST PROGRAM
USING C#

In this chapter you will:

Learn about programming
Explore object-oriented programming concepts
Learn about the C# programming language
Write a C# program that produces output
Learn how to select identifiers to use within your
  programs
Add comments to a C# program
Eliminate the reference to `Out` by using the `System`
  namespace
Write and compile a C# program using the command
  prompt and using Visual Studio
Learn alternate ways to write the `Main()` method

Programming a computer is an interesting, challenging, fun, and sometimes frustrating task. It requires you to be precise and careful as well as creative. If you do this, you will find that learning a new programming language expands your horizons.

As new programming languages are developed and introduced, your job becomes easier and more difficult at the same time. Programming becomes easier because built-in capabilities are added to every new language that is developed, and tasks that might have taken you weeks or months to develop 20 years ago are now included in the language so you can add them to a program with a few keystrokes. Programming becomes more difficult for the same reason— new languages have so many features that you must devote a significant amount of time to learning them.

C# (pronounced "C Sharp") is a relatively new language that provides you with a wide range of options and features. As you work through this book, you will master many of them, one step at a time. If this is your first programming experience, you will learn new ways to approach and solve problems and to think logically. If you know how to program but are new to C#, you will be impressed by its capabilities.

In this chapter, you will learn about the background of programming that led to the development of C#, and you will write and execute your first C# programs.

PROGRAMMING

A computer **program** is a set of instructions that you write to tell a computer what to do. Internally, computers are constructed from circuitry that consists of small on/off switches; the most basic circuitry-level language that computers use to control the operation of those switches is called **machine language**. Machine language is expressed as a series of 1s and 0s—1s represent switches that are on, and 0s represent switches that are off. If programmers had to write computer programs using machine language, they would have to keep track of the hundreds of thousands of 1s and 0s involved in programming any worthwhile task. Not only would writing a program be a time-consuming and difficult task, but modifying programs, understanding others' programs, and locating errors within programs all would be cumbersome. Additionally, the number and location of switches vary from computer to computer, which means you would need to customize a machine-language program for every type of machine on which the program had to run.

Fortunately, programming has evolved into an easier task because of the development of high-level programming languages. A **high-level programming language** allows you to use a vocabulary of reasonable terms such as "read," "write," or "add" instead of the sequence of on/off switches that perform these tasks. High-level languages also allow you to assign reasonable names to areas of computer memory; you can use names such as "hoursWorked" or "payRate," rather than having to remember the memory locations (switch numbers) of those values.

Each high-level language has its own **syntax**, or rules of the language. For example, to produce output, you might use the verb "print" in one language and "write" in another. All languages have a specific, limited vocabulary, along with a set of rules for using that vocabulary. Programmers use a computer program called a **compiler** to translate their high-level language statements into machine code. The compiler issues an error message each time a programmer commits a **syntax error**—that is, each time the programmer uses the language incorrectly. Subsequently, the programmer can correct the error and attempt another translation by compiling the program again. The program can be completely translated to machine language only when all syntax errors have been corrected. When you learn a computer programming language such as C#, C++, Visual Basic, or Java, you really are learning the vocabulary and syntax rules for that language.

> **»NOTE** In some languages, such as BASIC, the language translator is called an interpreter. In others, such as assembly language, it is called an assembler. These translators operate in different fashions, but the ultimate goal of each is to translate the higher-level language into machine language.

In addition to learning the correct syntax for a particular language, a programmer must understand computer programming logic. The **logic** behind any program involves executing the various statements and procedures in the correct order to produce the desired results. For example, you might be able to execute perfect individual notes on a musical instrument, but if you do not execute them in the proper order (or execute a B-flat when an F-sharp was expected), no one will enjoy your performance. Similarly, you might be able to use a computer language's syntax correctly, but be unable to execute a logically constructed, workable program. Examples of logical errors include multiplying two values when you should divide them, or attempting to calculate a paycheck before obtaining the appropriate payroll data.

> **»NOTE** Programmers call some logical errors **semantic errors**. For example, if you misspell a programming language word, you commit a syntax error, but if you use a correct word in the wrong context, you commit a semantic error.

To achieve a working program that accomplishes the tasks it is meant to accomplish, you must remove all syntax and logical errors from the program. This process is called **debugging** the program.

> **»NOTE** Since the early days of computer programming, program errors have been called "bugs." The term is often said to have originated from an actual moth that was discovered trapped in the circuitry of a computer at Harvard University in 1945. Actually, the term "bug" was in use prior to 1945 to mean trouble with any electrical apparatus; even during Thomas Edison's life, it meant an "industrial defect." In any case, the process of finding and correcting program errors has come to be known as debugging.

»TWO TRUTHS AND A LIE: PROGRAMMING

Two of the following statements are true, and one is false. Identify the false statement and explain why it is false.

1. A high-level programming language allows you to use a vocabulary of reasonable terms such as "read," "write," or "add" instead of the sequence of on/off switches that perform these tasks.
2. Each high-level programming language has its own syntax, or rules of the language.
3. Programmers use a computer program called a compiler to translate machine code into a high-level language they can understand.

The false statement is #3. Programmers use a computer program called a compiler to translate their high-level language statements into machine code.

OBJECT-ORIENTED PROGRAMMING

Two popular approaches to writing computer programs are procedural programming and object-oriented programming.

When you write a **procedural program**, you use your knowledge of a programming language to create and name computer memory locations that can hold values, and you write a series of steps or operations to manipulate those values. The named computer memory locations are called **variables** because they hold values that might vary. In programming languages, a variable is referenced by using a one-word name (an **identifier**) with no embedded spaces. For example, a company's payroll program might contain a variable named `payRate`. The memory location referenced by the name `payRate` might contain different values at different times. For instance, an organization's payroll program might contain a different value for `payRate` for each of 100 employees. Additionally, a single employee's `payRate` variable might contain different values before or after a raise or before or after surpassing 40 work hours in one week. During the execution of the payroll program, each value stored under the name `payRate` might have many operations performed on it—for example, reading it from an input device, multiplying it by another variable representing hours worked, and printing it on paper.

> **» NOTE** When programmers do not capitalize the first letter of an identifier but do capitalize each new word, as in `payRate`, they call the style **camel casing**, because the identifier appears to have a hump in the middle. When programmers adopt the style of capitalizing the first letter of all new words in an identifier, even the first one, as in `PayRate`, they call the style **Pascal casing**. Most C# programmers use camel casing when creating variable names, but this convention is not required to produce a workable program.

> **» NOTE** Depending on the programming language, methods are sometimes called *procedures*, *subroutines*, or *functions*. In C#, the preferred term is *methods*.

For convenience, the individual operations used in a computer program often are grouped into logical units called **procedures** or **methods**. For example, a series of four or five comparisons and calculations that together determine an employee's federal tax withholding value might be grouped as a method named `CalculateFederalWithholding()`. A procedural program defines the variable memory locations, then **calls** or **invokes** a series of procedures to input, manipulate, and output the values stored in those locations. A single procedural program often contains hundreds of variables and thousands of procedure calls.

> **» NOTE** In C#, methods conventionally are named using Pascal casing, and all method names are followed by a set of parentheses. When you pronounce a method name, you ignore the parentheses. When this book refers to a method, the name will be followed with parentheses. This practice helps distinguish method names from variable and class names.

Object-oriented programming is an extension of procedural programming. Object-oriented programs contain variables, methods, and six other features:

» Objects

» Classes

» Encapsulation

» Interfaces
» Polymorphism
» Inheritance

> **NOTE** Although procedural and object-oriented programming techniques are somewhat similar, they raise different concerns in the design and development phase that occurs before programs are written.

The components called **objects** are similar to concrete objects in the real world. You create objects that contain their own variables and methods, and then you manipulate those objects to achieve a desired result. Writing object-oriented programs involves both creating objects and creating applications that use those objects.

If you've ever used a computer that has a command-line operating system (such as DOS), and if you've used a GUI (a graphical user interface, such as Microsoft Windows), then you already have an idea of the difference between procedural and object-oriented programs. If you want to move several files from a CD to a hard disk, you can accomplish the task using either a typed command at a prompt or command line (as in DOS), or using a mouse in a graphical environment (as in Windows). The difference lies in whether you issue a series of sequential commands to move the files (in DOS) or drag icons representing the files from one screen location to another (in Windows). You can move the files using either operating system, but the GUI system allows you to simulate the way you would move their real-world paper counterparts. In other words, the GUI system allows you to treat files as objects.

> **NOTE** The **command line** is the line on which you type a command in a system that uses a text interface. The **command prompt** is a request for input that appears at the beginning of the command line. In DOS, the command prompt indicates the disk drive and optional path, and ends with >.

Objects in both the real world and in object-oriented programming are made up of attributes and methods. The **attributes** of an object represent its characteristics. For example, some of your `Automobile`'s attributes are its make, model, year, and purchase price. Other attributes describe whether the `Automobile` is currently running, its gear, its speed, and whether it is dirty. All `Automobile`s possess the same attributes, but not the same values, or **states**, for those attributes. For example, some `Automobile`s currently are running, but some are not. The value of an attribute can change over time; for example, some `Automobile`s are running now, but will not be running in the future. Therefore, the states of an `Automobile` are variable. Similarly, your `Dog` has attributes that include its breed, name, age, and shot status (that is, whether its shots are current); the states for a particular dog might be "Labrador retriever", "Murphy", "7", and "yes".

> **NOTE** Programmers also call the values of an object's attributes the **properties** of the object. The **state of an object** is the collective value of all its attributes at any point in time.

A **class** is a category of objects or a type of object. A class describes the attributes and methods of every object that is an **instance**, or example, of that class. For example, `Automobile` is a class whose objects have a year, make, model, color, and current running status. Your 2005 red Chevrolet is an instance of the class that is made up of all `Automobile`s; so is my supervisor's 2009 black Porsche. Your Collie named Bosco is an instance of the class that is made up of all Dogs; so is my Labrador named Murphy. Thinking of items as instances of a class allows you to apply your general knowledge of the class to its individual members. The particular instances of these objects contain all of the attributes that their general category contains; only the states of those attributes vary. If your friend purchases an Automobile, you know it has some model name; if your friend gets a Dog, you know it has some breed. You probably don't know the current state of the Automobile's speed or exact contents of the Dog's shots, but you do know that those attributes exist for the Automobile and Dog classes. Similarly, in a GUI operating environment, you expect each window you open to have specific, consistent attributes, such as a menu bar and a title bar, because each window includes these attributes as a member of the general class of GUI windows.

> **»NOTE** By convention, programmers using C# begin their class names with an uppercase letter. Thus, the class that defines the attributes and methods of an automobile would probably be named Automobile, and the class that contains dogs would probably be named Dog. However, following this convention is not required to produce a workable program.

Besides attributes, objects possess methods that they use to accomplish tasks, including changing attributes and discovering the values of attributes. Automobiles, for example, have methods for moving forward and backward. They also can be filled with gasoline or be washed; both are methods that change some of an Automobile's attributes. Methods also exist for ascertaining the status of certain attributes, such as the current speed of an Automobile and the status of its gas tank. Similarly, a Dog can walk or run, eat, and get a bath, and there are methods for determining whether it needs a walk, food, or a bath. GUI operating system components, such as windows, can be maximized, minimized, and dragged; depending on the component, they can also have their color or font style altered.

Like procedural programs, object-oriented programs have variables (attributes) and procedures (methods), but the attributes and methods are encapsulated into objects that are then used much like real-world objects. **Encapsulation** is the technique of packaging an object's attributes and methods into a cohesive unit that can be used as an undivided entity. Programmers sometimes refer to encapsulation as using a "**black box**," a device you use without regard for the internal mechanisms. If an object's methods are well written, the user is unaware of the low-level details of how the methods are executed; in such a case, the user must understand only the **interface** or interaction between the method and object. For example, if you can fill your Automobile with gasoline, it is because you understand the interface between the gas pump nozzle and the vehicle's gas tank opening. You don't need to understand how the pump works or where the gas tank is located inside your vehicle. If you can read your speedometer, it does not matter how the display figure is calculated. In fact, if someone produces a new, more accurate speedometer and inserts it into your Automobile, you don't have to know or care how it operates, as long as the interface remains the same as the previous one. The same principles apply to well-constructed objects used in object-oriented programs.

Object-oriented programming languages support two other distinguishing features in addition to organizing objects as members of classes. One feature, **polymorphism**, describes the ability to create methods that act appropriately depending on the context. For example, you are able to "fill" both a Dog and an Automobile, but you do so by very different means. A friend would have no trouble understanding your meaning if you said "I need to fill my Automobile" and distinguishing that process from the process of "filling" your `Dog`, your `BankAccount`, or your `AppointmentCalendar`. Older, non-object-oriented languages could not make such distinctions, but object-oriented languages can.

Object-oriented languages also support inheritance. **Inheritance** provides the ability to extend a class so as to create a more specific class. The more specific class contains all the attributes and methods of the more general class and usually contains new attributes or methods as well. For example, if you have created a `Dog` class, you might then create a more specific class named `ShowDog`. Each instance of the `ShowDog` class would contain all the attributes and methods of a `Dog`, along with additional methods or attributes. For example, a `ShowDog` might require an attribute to hold the number of ribbons won and a method for entering a dog show. Using polymorphism, you might need to specialize the `Dog`'s methods to be appropriate for a `ShowDog`. For example, the fill method might be different (perhaps using more expensive food). The advantage of inheritance is that when you need a class such as `ShowDog`, you often can extend an existing class, thereby saving a lot of time and work.

»TWO TRUTHS AND A LIE: OBJECT-ORIENTED PROGRAMMING

1. Procedural programs use variables and tasks that are grouped into methods or procedures.
2. Object-oriented programming languages do not support variables or methods, but they do contain objects and classes.
3. In object-oriented programming, a class is a category of objects or a type of object, and each object is an instance of a class.

The false answer is #2. Object-oriented programs contain variables and methods just as procedural programs do.

THE C# PROGRAMMING LANGUAGE

The **C# programming language** was developed as an object-oriented and component-oriented language. It is part of Microsoft Visual Studio 2008, a package designed for developing applications that run on Windows computers. Unlike other programming languages, C# allows every piece of data to be treated as an object and to employ the principles of object-oriented programming. C# provides constructs for creating components with properties, methods, and events, making it an ideal language for twenty-first-century programming, where building small, reusable components is more important than building huge, stand-alone applications.

C# contains a GUI interface that makes it similar to Visual Basic. C# is considered more concise than Visual Basic, and is modeled after the C++ programming language, but some of the most difficult features to understand in C++ have been eliminated in C#. For example, pointers are not used in C#, object destructors and forward declarations are not needed, and using `#include` files is not necessary. Multiple inheritance, which causes many C++ programming errors, is not allowed in C#.

»NOTE
Technically, you can use pointers in C#, but only in a mode called unsafe, which is rarely used.

C# is very similar to Java, because Java was also based on C++. In Java, simple data types are not objects; therefore, they do not work with built-in methods. In C#, every piece of data is an object, providing all data with the functionality of true objects. Additionally, in Java, simple parameters (also called primitive parameters) must be passed by value, which means a copy must be made of any data that is sent to a method for alteration, and the copy must be sent back to the original object. C# provides the convenience of passing primitive parameters by reference, which means the actual object can be altered by a method without a copy being passed back. If you have not programmed before, the difference between C# and other languages means little to you. However, experienced programmers will appreciate the thought that the developers of C# put into its features.

»NOTE Microsoft Corporation refers to the current version of C# as C# 3.5. You can find Microsoft's C# specifications at *msdn.microsoft. com/vcsharp/ programming/ language.*

»NOTE **Primitive data** is simple data, such as a number, as opposed to complex data, such as an `Employee`, a `BankAccount`, or an `Automobile`. In Chapter 2, you will learn about C#'s simple data types—those that are intrinsic to the language. In Chapter 7, you will create complex objects that are composed of primitive data types.

»NOTE The C# programming language was standardized in 2002 by Ecma International. You can read or download this set of standards at *www.ecma-international.org /publication /standards/Ecma-334.htm.*

T T F

»TWO TRUTHS AND A LIE: THE C# PROGRAMMING LANGUAGE

1. The C# programming language was developed as an object-oriented and component-oriented language.
2. C# contains several features that make it similar to other languages such as Java and Visual Basic.
3. C# contains many advanced features, so the C++ programming language was created as a simpler version of the language.

The false statement is #3. C# is modeled after the C++ programming language, but some of the most difficult features to understand in C++ have been eliminated in C#.

WRITING A C# PROGRAM THAT PRODUCES OUTPUT

»NOTE Some words appear in blue in Figure 1-1. These are C# keywords. A complete list of keywords appears in Table 1-1.

At first glance, even the simplest C# program involves a fair amount of confusing syntax. Consider the simple program in Figure 1-1. This program is written on seven lines, and its only task is to display "This is my first C# program" on the screen.

```
public class FirstClass
{
    public static void Main()
    {
        System.Console.Out.WriteLine("This is my first C# program");
    }
}
```

Figure 1-1 `FirstClass` console application

The statement that does the actual work in this program is in the middle of the figure:

```
System.Console.Out.WriteLine("This is my first C# program");
```

The statement ends with a semicolon because all C# statements do.

The text "This is my first C# program" is a **literal string** of characters—that is, a series of characters that will be used exactly as entered. Any literal string in C# appears between double quotation marks.

The string "This is my first C# program" appears within parentheses because the string is an argument to a method, and arguments to methods always appear within parentheses. **Arguments** represent information that a method needs to perform its task. For example, if making an appointment with a dentist's office was a C# method, you would write the following:

```
MakeAppointment("September 10", "2 p.m.");
```

Accepting and processing a dental appointment is a method that consists of a set of standard procedures. However, each appointment requires different information—the date and time— and this information can be considered the arguments of the `MakeAppointment()` method. If you make an appointment for September 10 at 2 p.m., you expect different results than if you make one for September 9 at 8 a.m. or December 25 at midnight. Likewise, if you pass the argument "Happy Holidays" to a method, you will expect different results than if you pass the argument "This is my first C# program."

> **NOTE** The words *argument* and *parameter* are closely related. An argument is the expression used when you call or invoke a method, while a **parameter** is an object or reference that is declared in a method definition, where the method instructions are written. You will learn more about the terms *call* and *invoke* in Chapter 6. Do not worry if you do not understand arguments and parameters at this point; their uses will become clearer when you write methods in Chapter 6.

> **NOTE** Although a string can be an argument to a method, not all arguments are strings. In this book, you will see and write methods that accept many other types of data.

Within the statement `System.Console.Out.WriteLine("This is my first C# program");`, the method to which you are passing the argument string "This is my first C# program" is named `WriteLine()`. The **WriteLine() method** displays output on the screen and positions the cursor on the next line, where additional output might be displayed subsequently.

> **NOTE** In C#, you usually refer to method names by including their parentheses, as in `WriteLine()`. This practice makes it easy for you to distinguish method names from variable names.

> **NOTE** The **Write() method** is very similar to the `WriteLine()` method. With `WriteLine()`, the cursor is moved to the following line after the message is displayed. With `Write()`, the cursor does not advance to a new line; it remains on the same line as the output.

Within the statement System.Console.Out.WriteLine("This is my first C# program");, Out is an object. The Out object represents the screen on the terminal or computer where you are working. Of course, not all objects have a WriteLine() method (for instance, you can't write a line to a computer's mouse, your Automobile, or your Dog), but the creators of C# assumed that you frequently would want to display output on the screen at your terminal. For this reason, the Out object was created and endowed with the method named WriteLine(). Soon, you will create your own C# objects and endow them with your own methods.

Within the statement System.Console.Out.WriteLine("This is my first C# program");, Console is a class. It defines the attributes of a collection of similar "Console" objects, just as the Dog class defines the attributes of a collection of similar Dog objects. One of the Console objects is Out. (You might guess that another Console object is In, which represents the keyboard.)

Within the statement System.Console.Out.WriteLine("This is my first C# program");, System is a namespace. A **namespace** is a scheme or mechanism that provides a way to group similar classes. To organize your classes, you can (and will) create your own namespaces. The **System namespace**, which is built into your C# compiler, holds commonly used classes.

The dots (periods) in the statement System.Console.Out.WriteLine("This is my first C# program"); are used to separate the names of the namespace, class, object, and method. You will use this same namespace-dot-class-dot-object-dot-method format repeatedly in your C# programs.

In the FirstClass class in Figure 1-1, the statement System.Console.Out.WriteLine ("This is my first C# program"); appears within a method named Main(). Every method in C# contains a header and a body. A **method header** includes the method name and information about what will pass into and be returned from a method. The **method body** of every method is contained within a pair of curly braces ({ }) and includes all the instructions executed by the method. The program in Figure 1-1 includes only one statement between the curly braces of the Main() method. Soon, you will write methods with many more statements. In Figure 1-1, the statement within the Main() method (the WriteLine() statement) is indented within the curly braces. Although the C# compiler does not require such indentation, it is conventional and clearly shows that the WriteLine() statement lies within the Main() method.

For every opening curly brace ({) in a C# program, there must be a corresponding closing curly brace (}). The precise position of the opening and closing curly braces is not important to the compiler. For example, the method in Figure 1-2 executes exactly the same way as the one shown in Figure 1-1. The only difference is in the amount of whitespace used in the method. In general, whitespace is optional in C#. **Whitespace** is any combination of spaces, tabs, and carriage returns (blank lines). You use whitespace to organize your program code and make it easier to read; it does not affect your program. Usually, vertically aligning each pair of opening and closing curly braces and indenting the contents between them, as in Figure 1-1, makes your code easier to read than the format shown in Figure 1-2.

```
public static void Main(){System.Console.Out.WriteLine
  ("This is my first C# program");}
```

Figure 1-2 A `Main()` method with little whitespace

The method header for the `Main()` method contains four words. Three of these words are **keywords**—predefined and reserved identifiers that have special meaning to the compiler. In the method header `public static void Main()`, the word `public` is an access modifier. When used in a method header, an **access modifier** defines the circumstances under which the method can be accessed. As opposed to cases in which a method is **private**, the access modifier **public** indicates that other classes may use this method.

>> **NOTE** If you do not use an access modifier within a method header, then by default the method is `private`. Other classes cannot use a `private` method. You will learn more about public and private access modifiers in Chapter 7.

In the English language, the word *static* means "showing little change" or "stationary." In C#, the reserved keyword **static** has a related meaning. It indicates that the `Main()` method will be executed through a class—not by a variety of objects. It means that you do not need to create an object of type `FirstClass` to use the `Main()` method defined within `FirstClass`. In C#, you will create many nonstatic methods within classes that are executed by objects. For example, you might create a `display()` method in an `Automobile` class that you use to display an `Automobile`'s attributes. If you create 100 `Automobile` objects, the `display()` method will operate differently and appropriately for each object, displaying different makes, models, and colors of `Automobiles`. (Programmers would say a nonstatic method is "invoked" by each instance of the object.) However, a `static` method does not require an object to be used to invoke it. Only one version of the `static Main()` method for `FirstClass` will ever be executed. Of course, other classes eventually might have their own, different `Main()` methods. You will learn the mechanics of how `static` and nonstatic methods differ in Chapter 4.

In English, the word *void* means empty. When the keyword **void** is used in the `Main()` method header, it does not indicate that the `Main()` method is empty, but rather that the method does not return any value when called. This doesn't mean that `Main()` doesn't produce output—it does. Instead, it means the `Main()` method does not send any value back to any method that calls it. You will learn more about return values when you study methods in greater detail in Chapter 3.

In the method header, the name of the method is `Main()`. All C# applications must include a method named `Main()`, and most C# applications will have additional methods with other names. When you execute a C# application, the `Main()` method always executes first.

> **»NOTE** You will write many C# *classes* that do not contain a `Main()` method. However, all executable *applications* (runnable programs) must contain a `Main()` method.

> **»NOTE** You also can write the `Main()` method header as `public static int Main()`, `public static void Main(string[] args)`, or `public static int Main(string[] args)`. You will learn more about these alternative forms of `Main()` at the end of this chapter.

»TWO TRUTHS AND A LIE: WRITING A C# PROGRAM THAT PRODUCES OUTPUT

1. Strings are information that methods need to perform their tasks.
2. The `WriteLine()` method displays output on the screen and positions the cursor on the next line, where additional output might be displayed.
3. Many methods such as `WriteLine()` have been created for you because the creators of C# assumed you would need them frequently.

The false statement is #1. Strings are literal values represented between quotation marks. Arguments represent information that a method needs to perform its task. Although an argument might be a string, not all arguments are strings.

SELECTING IDENTIFIERS

Every method that you use within a C# program must be part of a class. To create a class, you use a class header and curly braces in much the same way you use a header and braces for a method within a class. When you write `public class FirstClass`, you are defining a class named `FirstClass`. A class name does not have to contain the word "Class" as `FirstClass` does. You can define a C# class using any identifier you need, as long as it meets the following requirements:

> **»NOTE**
> In this book, all identifiers begin with a letter.

> **»NOTE**
> An identifier with an @ prefix is a **verbatim identifier**.

> » An identifier must begin with an underscore, the at sign (@), or a letter. (Letters include foreign-alphabet letters such as Π and Ω, which are contained in the set of characters known as Unicode.)
> » An identifier can contain only letters or digits, not special characters such as #, $, or &.
> » An identifier cannot be a C# reserved keyword, such as `public` or `class`. Table 1-1 provides a complete list of reserved keywords. (Actually, you can use a keyword as an identifier if you precede it with an "at" sign, as in `@class`. This feature allows you to use code written in other languages that do not have the same set of reserved keywords. However, when you write original C# programs, you should not use the keywords as identifiers.)

abstract	float	return
as	for	sbyte
base	foreach	sealed
bool	goto	short
break	if	sizeof
byte	implicit	stackalloc
case	in	static
catch	int	string
char	interface	struct
checked	internal	switch
class	is	this
const	lock	throw
continue	long	true
decimal	namespace	try
default	new	typeof
delegate	null	uint
do	object	ulong
double	operator	unchecked
else	out	unsafe
enum	override	ushort
event	params	using
explicit	private	virtual
extern	protected	void
false	public	volatile
finally	readonly	while
fixed	ref	

Table 1-1 C# reserved keywords

> **»NOTE** The following identifiers have special meaning in C# but are not keywords: add, alias, get, global, partial, remove, set, value, where, and yield. For clarity, you should avoid using these words as your own identifiers.

A programming standard in C# is to begin class names with an uppercase letter and use other uppercase letters as needed to improve readability. Table 1-2 lists some valid and conventional class names you might use when creating classes in C#. Table 1-3 lists some class names that are valid, but unconventional; Table 1-4 lists some illegal class names.

Class Name	Description
`Employee`	Begins with an uppercase letter
`FirstClass`	Begins with an uppercase letter, contains no spaces, and has an initial uppercase letter that indicates the start of the second word
`PushButtonControl`	Begins with an uppercase letter, contains no spaces, and has an initial uppercase letter that indicates the start of all subsequent words
`Budget2010`	Begins with an uppercase letter and contains no spaces

Table 1-2 Some valid and conventional class names in C#

Class Name	Description
`employee`	Begins with a lowercase letter
`First_Class`	Although legal, the underscore is not commonly used to indicate new words
`Pushbuttoncontrol`	No uppercase characters are used to indicate the start of a new word, making the name difficult to read
`BUDGET2010`	Appears with all uppercase letters
`Public`	Although this identifier is legal because it is different from the keyword `public`, which begins with a lowercase "p," the similarity could cause confusion

Table 1-3 Some unconventional (though legal) class names in C#

Class Name	Description
`an employee`	Space character is illegal
`Push Button Control`	Space characters are illegal
`class`	"class" is a reserved word
`2011Budget`	Class names cannot begin with a digit
`phone#`	The # symbol is not allowed; identifiers consist of letters and digits

Table 1-4 Some illegal class names in C#

In Figure 1-1, the line `public class FirstClass` contains the keyword `class`, which identifies `FirstClass` as a class. The reserved word `public` is an access modifier. Similar to the way an access modifier describes a method's accessibility, when used with a class, the access modifier defines the circumstances under which the class can be accessed; `public` access is the most liberal type of access.

The simple program shown in Figure 1-1 has many pieces to remember. For now, you can use the program shown in Figure 1-3 as a shell, where you replace the identifier `AnyLegalClassName` with any legal class name, and the line `/*********/` with any statements that you want to execute.

```
public class AnyLegalClassName
{
    public static void Main()
    {
        /*********/;
    }
}
```

Figure 1-3 Shell program

»TWO TRUTHS AND A LIE: SELECTING IDENTIFIERS

1. In C#, an identifier must begin with an underscore, the at sign (@), or an uppercase letter.
2. An identifier can contain only letters or digits, not special characters such as #, $, or &.
3. An identifier cannot be a C# reserved keyword.

The false statement is #1. In C#, an identifier must begin with an underscore, the at sign (@), or a letter. There is no requirement that the initial letter be capitalized, although in C#, it is a convention that the initial letter of a class name is capitalized.

ADDING COMMENTS TO A PROGRAM

As you can see, even the simplest C# program takes several lines of code and contains somewhat perplexing syntax. Large programs that perform many tasks include much more code. As you write longer programs, it becomes increasingly difficult to remember why you included steps and how you intended to use particular variables. **Program comments** are nonexecuting statements that you add to document a program. Programmers use comments to leave notes for themselves and for others who might read their programs in the future.

» NOTE As you work through this book, you should add comments as the first few lines of every program file. The comments should contain your name, the date, and the name of the program. Your instructor might want you to include additional comments.

Comments also can be useful when you are developing a program. If a program is not performing as expected, you can **comment out** various statements and subsequently run the program to observe the effect. When you comment out a statement, you turn it into a comment so that the compiler will ignore it. This approach helps you pinpoint the location of errant statements in malfunctioning programs.

There are three types of comments in C#:

» **Line comments** start with two forward slashes (//) and continue to the end of the current line. Line comments can appear on a line by themselves, or at the end of a line following executable code.

» **Block comments** start with a forward slash and an asterisk (/*) and end with an asterisk and a forward slash (*/). Block comments can appear on a line by themselves, on a line before executable code, or after executable code. When a comment is long, block comments can extend across as many lines as needed.

» C# also supports a special type of comment used to create documentation from within a program. These comments, called **XML-documentation format comments**, use a special set of tags within angle brackets (< >). (XML stands for Extensible Markup Language.) You will learn more about this type of comment as you continue your study of C#.

>> **NOTE** The forward slash (/) and the backslash (\) characters often are confused, but they are distinct characters. You cannot use them interchangeably.

Figure 1-4 shows how comments can be used in code. The program covers 12 lines of type, yet only seven are part of the executable C# program, and the only line that actually *does* anything is the shaded one that displays "Message".

```
public class ClassWithOneExecutingLine
/* This class has only one line that executes */
{
   public static void Main()
   {
      // The next line writes the message
      System.Console.Out.WriteLine("Message");   // Comment
   }
/* This program serves
   to demonstrate that a program
   can "look" a lot longer than it really is */
}
```

Figure 1-4 Using comments within a program

»TWO TRUTHS AND A LIE: ADDING COMMENTS TO A PROGRAM

1. Line comments start with two forward slashes (//) and end with two backslashes (\\).
2. Block comments can extend across as many lines as needed.
3. XML-documentation format comments use a special set of tags within angle brackets (< >).

The false statement is #1. Line comments start with two forward slashes (//) and continue to the end of the current line.

ELIMINATING THE REFERENCE TO Out BY USING THE System NAMESPACE

A program can contain as many statements as you want. For example, the program in Figure 1-5 produces the three lines of output shown in Figure 1-6. A semicolon separates each program statement.

```csharp
public class ThreeLines
{
    public static void Main()
    {
        System.Console.Out.WriteLine("Line one");
        System.Console.Out.WriteLine("Line two");
        System.Console.Out.WriteLine("Line three");
    }
}
```

Figure 1-5 A program that produces three lines of output

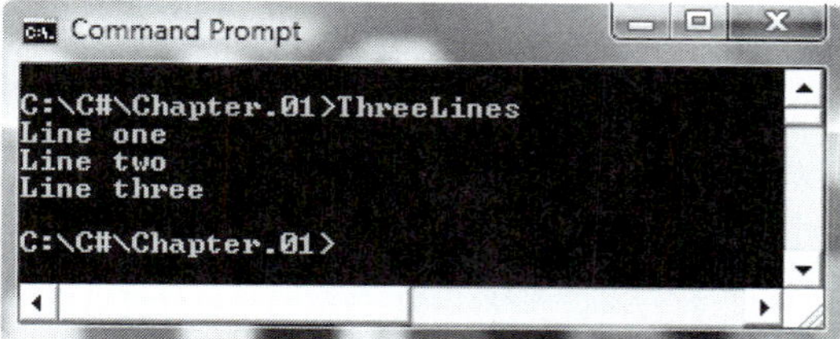

Figure 1-6 Output of ThreeLines program

The program in Figure 1-5 shows a lot of repeated code—the phrase System.Console.Out. WriteLine appears three times. When you use the name of the object Out, you are indicating the console screen. However, Out is the default output object. That is, if you write System.Console.WriteLine("Hi"); without specifying a Console object, the message "Hi" goes to the default Console object, which is Out. Most C# programmers usually use the WriteLine() method without specifying the Out object.

When you need to repeatedly use a class from the same namespace, you can shorten the statements you type by using a clause that indicates a namespace where the class can be found. You use a namespace with a **using clause**, or **using directive**, as shown in the shaded statement in the program in Figure 1-7. If you type `using System;` prior to the class definition, the compiler knows to use the `System` namespace when it encounters the `Console` class. The output of the program in Figure 1-7 is identical to that in Figure 1-5, in which `System` and `Out` were both repeated with each `WriteLine()` statement.

```
using System;
public class ThreeLines
{
    public static void Main()
    {
        Console.WriteLine("Line one");
        Console.WriteLine("Line two");
        Console.WriteLine("Line three");
    }
}
```

Figure 1-7 A program that produces three lines of output with a `using System` clause and no explicit reference to the `Out` object

NOT RECOMMENDED: USING AN ALIAS

At this point, the clever programmer will say, "I'll shorten my typing tasks even further by typing `using System.Console;` at the top of my programs, and producing output with statements like `WriteLine("Hi");`." However, `using` cannot be used with a class name like `System.Console`—only with a namespace name like `System`. Another option is to assign an alias to a class with a `using` clause. An **alias** is an alternative name for a class. You might assign one as a convenience when a fully qualified class name is very long. For example, Figure 1-8 shows a program that uses an alias for `System.Console` (see shaded statement). The lines of code within the program are shorter, but more difficult for another programmer to read. In general, and especially while you are learning C#, you should avoid using aliases if your intention is simply to reduce typing.

```
using SC = System.Console;
public class ThreeLines
{
    public static void Main()
    {
        SC.WriteLine("Line one");
        SC.WriteLine("Line two");
        SC.WriteLine("Line three");
    }
}
```


Figure 1-8 Using an alias for `System.Console`—a technique that is not recommended

»TWO TRUTHS AND A LIE: ELIMINATING THE REFERENCE TO Out BY USING THE System NAMESPACE

1. Most C# programmers usually use the WriteLine() method without specifying the Out object.
2. You use a namespace with a using clause, or using directive, to shorten statements when you need to repeatedly use a class from the same namespace.
3. Whenever possible, you should use aliases to make your programs as concise as you can.

The false statement is #3. You might assign an alias as a convenience when a fully qualified class name is very long. However, using an alias makes your programs more difficult for other programmers to read. In general, and especially while you are learning C#, avoid using aliases if your intention is simply to reduce typing.

WRITING AND COMPILING A C# PROGRAM

After you write and save a program, two more steps must be performed before you can view the program output:

1. You must compile the program you wrote (called the **source code**) into **intermediate language** (**IL**).

2. The C# **just in time** (**JIT**) compiler must translate the intermediate code into executable code.

> **»NOTE** When you compile a C# program, you translate your source code into intermediate language. The JIT compiler converts IL instructions into native code at the last moment, and appropriately for each different type of computer on which the code might eventually be executed. In other words, the same set of IL can be JIT-compiled and executed on any supported architecture.

> **»NOTE** Some developers say that languages like C# are "semi-compiled." That is, instead of being translated immediately from source code to their final executable versions, programs are compiled into an intermediate version that is later translated into the correct executable statements for the machine on which the program is running.

You can perform these steps from the command line or within the Integrated Development Environment (IDE) that comes with Visual Studio. Both methods produce the same results; the one you use is a matter of preference. You might prefer the simplicity of the command line because you do not work with multiple menus and views. Additionally, if you want to pass command-line arguments to a program, you must compile from the command line. On the other hand, many programmers prefer using the IDE because it provides features such as color-coded keywords and automatic statement completion.

COMPILING CODE FROM THE COMMAND PROMPT

To compile your source code from the command line, you first locate the command prompt. For example, in Windows Vista, you click Start, All Programs, Accessories, and Command

Prompt. As shown in Figure 1-9, you type `csc` at the command prompt, followed by the name of the file that contains the source code. The command `csc` stands for "C Sharp compiler." For example, to compile a file named ThreeLines.cs, you would type `csc ThreeLines.cs` and then press the Enter key. One of three outcomes will occur:

» You receive an operating system error message such as "Bad command or file name" or "csc is not recognized as an internal or external command, operable program or batch file".

» You receive one or more program language error messages.

» You receive no error messages (only a copyright statement from Microsoft), indicating that the program has compiled successfully.

```
Command Prompt
C:\>csc ThreeLines.cs
Microsoft (R) Visual C# 2008 Compiler Beta 2 version 3.05.20706.1
for Microsoft (R) .NET Framework version 3.5
Copyright (C) Microsoft Corporation. All rights reserved.

error CS2001: Source file 'ThreeLines.cs' could not be found
fatal error CS2008: No inputs specified

C:\>
```

Figure 1-9 Attempt to compile a program from the root directory at the command line, and error message received

If you receive an operating system message such as "csc is not recognized . . . ," or "Source file . . . could not be found," it may mean that:

» You misspelled the command `csc`.

» You misspelled the filename.

» You forgot to include the extension .cs with the filename.

» You didn't use the correct case. If your filename is ThreeLines.cs, then `csc threelines.cs` will not compile.

» You are not within the correct subdirectory or folder on your command line. For example, Figure 1-9 shows the `csc` command typed in the root directory of the C drive. If the ThreeLines.cs file is stored in a folder on the C drive, then the command shown will not work.

» The C# compiler was not installed properly.

» You need to set a path command.

To set a path command, you must locate the C# compiler on your hard disk. To locate the C# compiler whose name is csc.exe, use one of the following techniques:

» In either Vista or Windows XP, double-click Computer (or My Computer), double-click the C drive, double-click the Windows folder, double-click the Microsoft.NET folder, double-click the Framework folder, double-click the v3.5 folder, and confirm that csc.exe is a program listed there. C# should be installed in this location if the program was installed using the default options.

» If the compiler can't be found in the default location, click Start in Vista, click Search, click the button to the right of Advanced Search, and then click the list box next to Location. From the drop-down list, click OS (C:) or the name of your local hard drive. Check the box next to "Include non-indexed, hidden, and system files." In the Name dialog box, type csc.exe, then click Search.

» If the compiler can't be found in the default location, click Start in Windows XP, click Search, and choose All Files or Folders to look for the file named csc.exe.

» If your search fails to find csc.exe, you need to obtain and install a copy of the C# compiler. For more information, visit *http://msdn2.microsoft.com/en-us/vcsharp/default.aspx*.

If you do find the csc.exe file, type `path =` at the command line, followed by the complete path name that describes where csc.exe is stored; then try to compile the `ThreeLines` program again. For example, if C# was stored in the default location, you might type the following:

```
path = c:\Windows\Microsoft.NET\Framework\v3.5
```

Press Enter. Next, type `csc ThreeLines.cs` and press Enter again.

>> **NOTE** In Windows XP, you also can change the path command if you are the System Administrator on the local computer. Click Start, click Control Panel, and then double-click System. In Vista, click Advanced system settings, then click Continue. In either Vista or Windows XP, click Environment Variables on the Advanced tab, then scroll through the list of variables for the path command. If it is there, click it and click Edit; if not, click New. Either way, type the new path variable value in the dialog box that appears. Then click OK twice and close the System Properties window.

If you receive a programming language error message, it means that the source code contains one or more syntax errors. A syntax error occurs when you introduce typing errors into your program. For example, if the first line of your program begins with "Public" (with an uppercase *P*), you will get an error message such as "`A namespace does not directly contain members such as fields or methods`" after compiling the program, because the compiler won't recognize `ThreeLines` as a class with a `Main()` method. If this problem occurs, you must reopen the text file that contains the source code, make the necessary corrections, save the file, and compile it again.

>> **NOTE** The C# compiler issues warnings as well as errors. A warning is less serious than an error; it means that the compiler has determined you have done something unusual, but not illegal. If you have purposely introduced a warning situation to test a program, then you can ignore the warning. Usually, however, you should treat a warning message just as you would an error message and attempt to remedy the situation.

If you receive no error messages after compiling the code, then the program compiled successfully and a file with the same name as the source code—but with an .exe extension—is created and saved in the same folder as the program text file. For example, if ThreeLines.cs compiles successfully, then a file named ThreeLines.exe is created.

To run the program from the command line, you simply type the program name—for example, `ThreeLines`. You can also type the full filename, ThreeLines.exe, but it is not necessary to include the extension.

COMPILING CODE FROM WITHIN THE VISUAL STUDIO IDE

As an alternative to using the command line, you can compile and write your program within the Visual Studio IDE. This approach has several advantages:

» Some of the code you need is already created for you.

» The code is displayed in color, so you can more easily identify parts of your program. Reserved words appear in blue, comments in green, and identifiers in black.

» If error messages appear when you compile your program, you can double-click an error message and the cursor will move to the line of code that contains the error.

» Other debugging tools are available. You will become more familiar with these tools as you develop more sophisticated programs.

Figure 1-10 shows a program written in the editor of the Visual Studio IDE. You can see that the environment looks like a word processor, containing menu options such as File, Edit, and Help, and buttons with icons representing options such as Save, Copy, and Paste. You will learn about some of these options later in this chapter and continue to learn about more of them as you work with C# in the IDE.

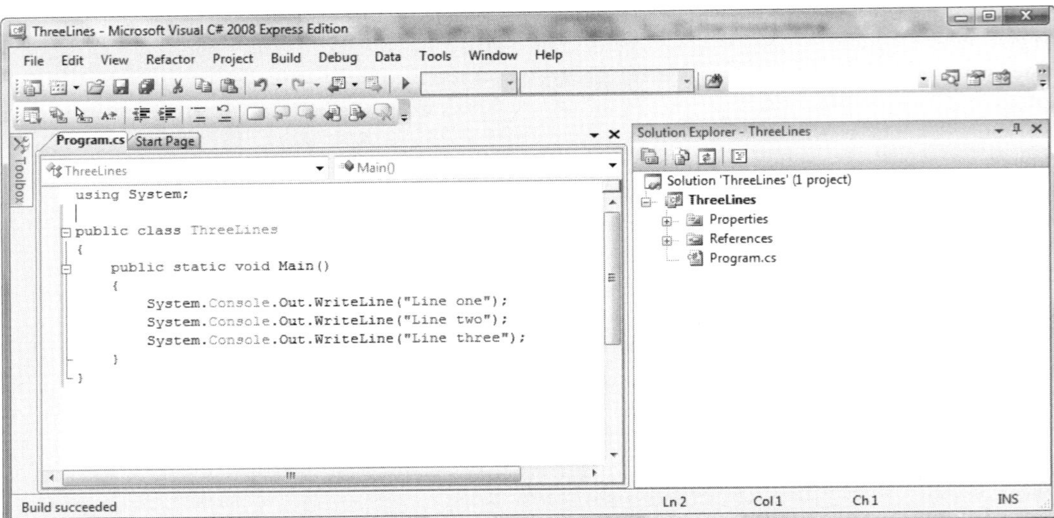

Figure 1-10 `ThreeLines` program as it appears in Visual Studio Express Edition

»TWO TRUTHS AND A LIE: WRITING AND COMPILING A C# PROGRAM

1. After you write and save a program, you must compile it into intermediate language and then the C# just in time (JIT) compiler must translate the intermediate code into executable code.

2. You can compile and execute a C# program from the command line or within the Integrated Development Environment (IDE) that comes with Visual Studio.

3. Many programmers prefer to compile their programs from the command line because it provides features such as color-coded keywords and automatic statement completion.

The false statement is #3. Programmers who prefer the command line prefer its simplicity. Programmers who prefer the Visual Studio IDE prefer the color-coded keywords and automatic statement completion.

ALTERNATE WAYS TO WRITE A `Main()` METHOD

Figures 1-8 and 1-10 show a `Main()` method with the following header:

```
public static void Main()
```

Using the return type `void` and listing nothing between the parentheses that follow `Main` is just one way to write a `Main()` method header in a program. (However, it is the first way listed in the C# documentation, and it is the convention that this book uses.)

Figure 1-11 shows an alternate way to write the `Main()` method header in the `ThreeLines` class. The shaded phrase `string[] args` is a parameter to the `Main()` method. A **string** is a data type that can hold a series of characters. The square brackets indicate that you can include a list or array of those strings. In Figure 1-11, `args` is a programmer-chosen name for the memory location where the list of `strings` is stored. Although you can use any

> **» NOTE**
> In Chapter 6, you will create other methods that can accept parameters.

> **» NOTE**
> You will learn more about the `string` data type in Chapter 2. You will learn more about how to use command-line arguments in Chapter 5 when you study arrays.

```
using System;
public class ThreeLines
{
    public static void Main(string[] args)
    {
        Console.WriteLine("Line one");
        Console.WriteLine("Line two");
        Console.WriteLine("Line three");
    }
}
```

Figure 1-11 A `Main()` method with a `string[] args` parameter

identifier, `args` is traditional. Use this format for the `Main()` method header if you need to access command-line arguments passed in to your application. For example, if you issued the following command, then the `string`s "yes", "no", and "maybe" would be stored at the memory location named `args`:

```
cs ThreeLines yes, no, maybe
```

> **▶▶ NOTE** In particular, Java programmers might prefer the version of `Main()` that includes the `string[] args` parameter because, conventionally, they write their main methods with the same parameter.

Even if you do not need access to command-line arguments, you can still use the version of the `Main()` method header that references them. You should use this form for your `Main()` method headers if your instructor at school or supervisor at work indicates you should follow this convention.

Some programmers prefer to write the `ThreeLines` class `Main()` method as shown in Figure 1-12. The shaded keyword `int` replaces `void` in the method header, indicating that the method returns an integer value. If you use this form of method header, then the last statement in the `Main()` method must be a return statement that returns an integer. By convention, a return value of 0 means an application ended without error. The value might be used by your operating system or another program that uses your program.

```
using System;
public class ThreeLines
{
    public static int Main(string[] args)
    {
        Console.WriteLine("Line one");
        Console.WriteLine("Line two");
        Console.WriteLine("Line three");
        return 0;
    }
}
```

Figure 1-12 A `Main()` method with an `int` return type

> **▶▶ NOTE** You will learn more about the `int` data type in Chapter 2. You will learn more about how to return values from methods in Chapter 6.

> **▶▶ NOTE** In particular, C++ programmers might prefer the version of `Main()` that returns an `int` because, conventionally, they write their main methods with an `int` return type.

Even if you do not need to use a return value from a `Main()` method, you can still use the version of the `Main()` method header that uses a return value. You should use this form for your `Main()` method headers if your instructor at school or supervisor at work indicates you should follow this convention.

»TWO TRUTHS AND A LIE: ALTERNATE WAYS TO WRITE A `Main()` METHOD

1. In C#, a `Main()` method header can be written `public static void Main()`.
2. In C#, a `Main()` method header can be written `public static void Main(string[] args)`.
3. In C#, a `Main()` method header can be written `public static int main(string args)`.

The false statement is #3. In C#, a `Main()` method header can be written as shown in either of the first two examples, or as `public static int Main(string[] args)`. That is, `Main()` must be capitalized and string must be followed by a pair of square brackets.

YOU DO IT

Now that you understand the basic framework of a program written in C#, you are ready to enter your first C# program into a text editor so you can compile and execute it. It is a tradition among programmers that the first program you write in any language produces "Hello, world!" as its output. You will create such a program now. To create a C# program, you can use the editor that is included as part of the Microsoft Visual Studio IDE. (The C# compiler, other language compilers, and many development tools also are contained in the IDE, which is where you build, test, and debug your C# application.) Alternatively, you can use any text editor. There are advantages to using the C# editor to write your programs, but using a plain text editor is simpler when you are getting started.

ENTERING A PROGRAM INTO AN EDITOR
To write your first C# program:

1. Start any text editor, such as Notepad, and open a new document, if necessary.

2. Type the class header **public class Hello**. In this example, the class name is `Hello`.

3. Press the **Enter** key and type the class-opening curly brace **{**. Press **Enter** again to start a new line.

4. Type three spaces to indent, and write the `Main()` method header:

    public static void Main()

    Press **Enter** to start a new line.

5. Type three spaces to indent, type **{**, and then press **Enter**.

6. Type six spaces so the next statement will be indented within the curly braces of the `Main()` method. Type the one executing statement in this program:

   `System.Console.Out.WriteLine("Hello, world!");`

7. Press **Enter**, type three spaces, type a closing curly brace for the `Main()` method, press **Enter**, and type a closing curly brace for the class. Your code should look like Figure 1-13.

```
public class Hello
{
   public static void Main()
   {
      System.Console.Out.WriteLine("Hello, world!");
   }
}
```

Figure 1-13 The `Hello` class

8. Choose a location that is meaningful to you to save your program. For example, you might create a folder named C# on your hard drive. Within that folder, you might create a folder named Chapter.01 in which you will store all the examples and exercises in this chapter. If you are working in a school lab, you might be assigned a storage location of your school's server, or you might prefer to store your examples on a USB drive or other portable storage media. Save the program as **Hello.cs**. It is important that the file extension be .cs, which stands for *C Sharp*. If the file has a different extension, the compiler for C# will not recognize the program as a C# program.

> **⏵⏵ NOTE** Many text editors attach their own filename extension (such as .txt or .doc) to a saved file. Double-check your saved file to ensure that it does not have a double extension (as in Hello.cs.txt). If the file has a double extension, rename it. If you type quotes surrounding a filename (as in "Hello.cs"), most editors will save the file as you specify, without adding their own extension. If you use a word-processing program as your editor, select the option to save the file as a plain text file.

COMPILING AND EXECUTING A PROGRAM FROM THE COMMAND LINE

To compile and execute your `Hello` program from the command line:

1. Go to the command prompt on your system. For example, in Vista or Windows XP, click **Start**, click **All Programs**, click **Accessories**, and click **Command Prompt**. Change the current directory to the name of the folder that holds your program.

   If your command prompt indicates a path other than the one you want, you can type `cd\` and then press Enter to return to the root directory. You can then type `cd` to change the path to the one where your program resides. For example, if you stored your program file in a folder named Chapter.01 within a folder named C#, then you can type the following:

   `cd C#\Chapter.01`

   The command `cd` is short for *change directory*.

2. Type the command that compiles your program:

```
csc Hello.cs
```

If you receive no error messages and the prompt returns, it means that the compile operation was successful, that a file named Hello.exe has been created, and that you can execute the program. If you do receive error messages, check every character of the program you typed to make sure it matches Figure 1-13. Remember, C# is case sensitive, so all casing must match exactly. When you have corrected the errors, repeat this step to compile the program again.

3. You can verify that a file named Hello.exe was created in several ways:

   » At the command prompt, type **dir** to view a directory of the files stored in the current folder. Both Hello.cs and Hello.exe should appear in the list. See Figure 1-14.

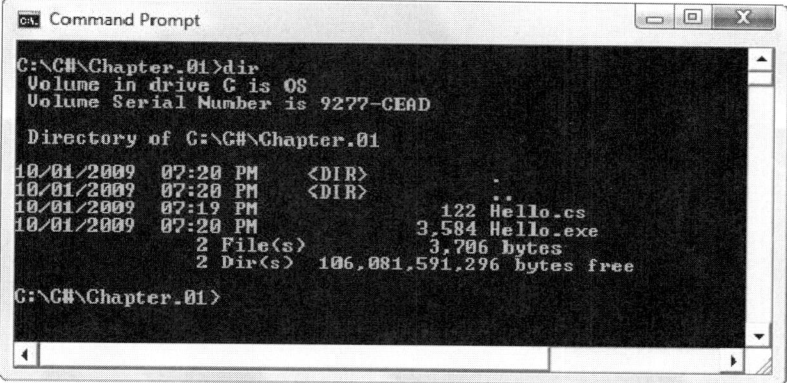

Figure 1-14 Directory of Chapter.01 folder after compiling Hello.cs

   » Use Windows Explorer to view the contents of the Chapter.01 folder, verifying that two Hello files are listed.

   » Double-click the **My Computer** icon, find and double-click the **Chapter.01** folder, and verify that two Hello files are listed.

4. At the command prompt, type **Hello**, which is the name of the program (the name of the executable file), and then press **Enter**. Alternatively, you can type the full filename **Hello.exe**, but typing the .exe extension isn't necessary. The output should look like Figure 1-15.

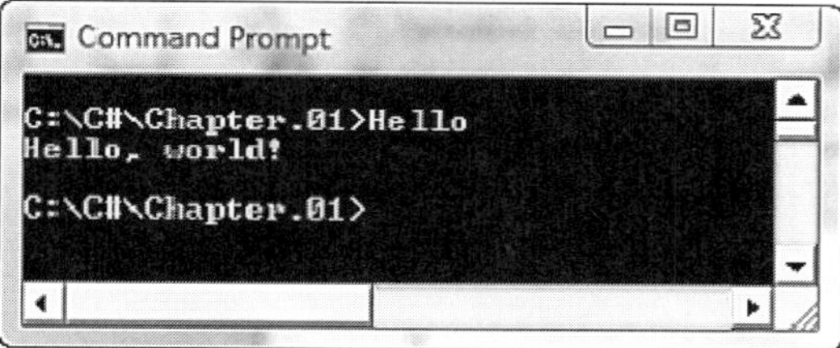

Figure 1-15 Output of the `Hello` application

COMPILING AND EXECUTING A PROGRAM USING THE VISUAL STUDIO IDE

Next, you will use the C# compiler environment to compile and execute the same Hello program you ran from the command line.

To compile and execute the Hello program in the Visual Studio IDE:

1. Within the text editor you used to write the Hello program, select the entire program text. In Notepad, for example, you can highlight all the lines of text with your mouse (or press **Ctrl+A**). Next, copy the text to the Clipboard for temporary storage by clicking **Edit** on the menu bar and then clicking **Copy** (or by pressing **Ctrl+C**). You'll paste the text in a few steps.

2. Open Visual Studio. If there is a shortcut icon on your desktop, you can double-click it. Alternatively, in Vista or Windows XP, you can click the **Start** button and then click **All Programs**. Then you can click **Microsoft Visual C# 2008 Express Edition**.

3. On the Start Page, click **File** on the menu bar, then click **New Project**, as shown in Figure 1-16.

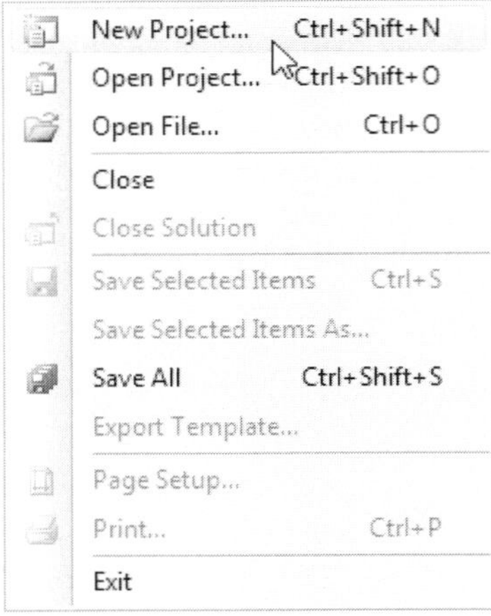

Figure 1-16 Selecting a new project

4. In the New Project window, click **Console Application**. Enter **Hello** as the name for this project (see Figure 1-17). Click **OK**. Visual C# creates a new folder for your project named after the project title.

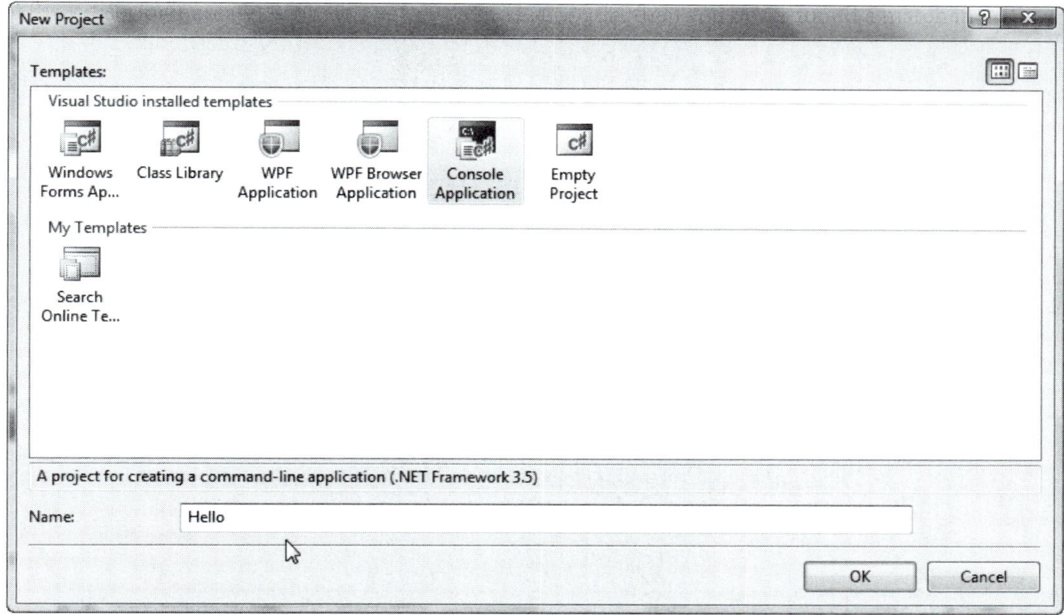

Figure 1-17 Entering the project name

5. The `Hello` application editing window appears, as shown in Figure 1-18. A lot of code is already written for you in this window, including some `using` statements, a namespace named `Hello`, a class named `Program`, and a `Main()` method. You could leave the class header, `Main()` method header, and other features, and just add the specific statements you need. You would save a lot of typing and prevent typographical errors. But in this case, you have already written a functioning `Hello` program, so you will replace the prewritten code with your `Hello` code. Select all the code in the editor window by highlighting it with your mouse (or by pressing **Ctrl+A**). Then press **Delete**. Paste the previously copied `Hello` program into the editor by pressing **Ctrl+V** (or by clicking **Edit** on the menu bar and then clicking **Paste**).

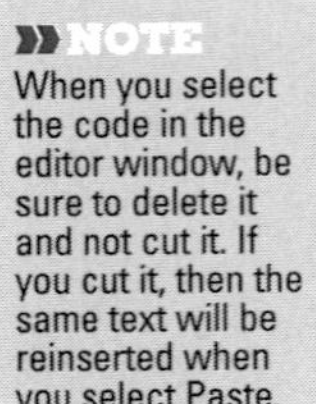

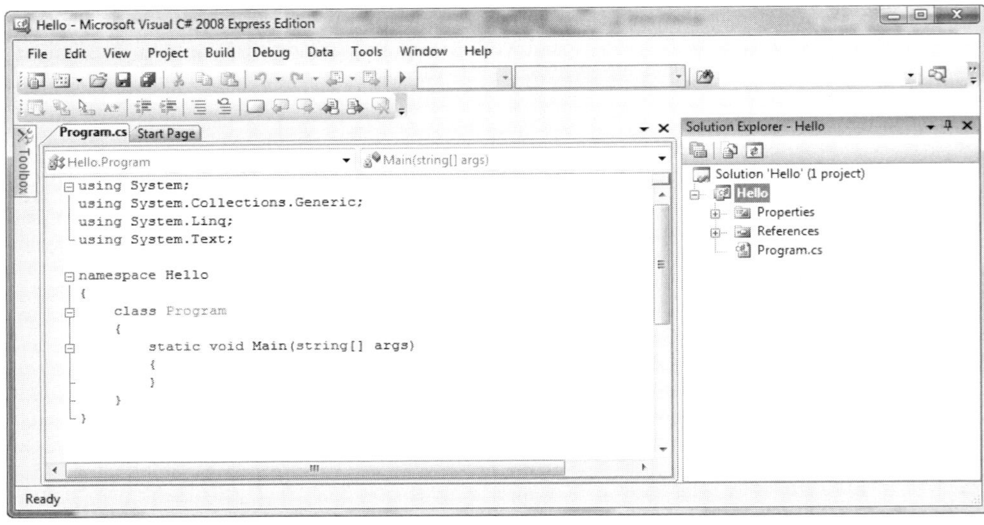

Figure 1-18 The `Hello` application editing window

6. Save the file by clicking **File** on the menu bar and then clicking **Save Hello**, or by clicking the **Save** button on the toolbar. Your screen looks like Figure 1-19.

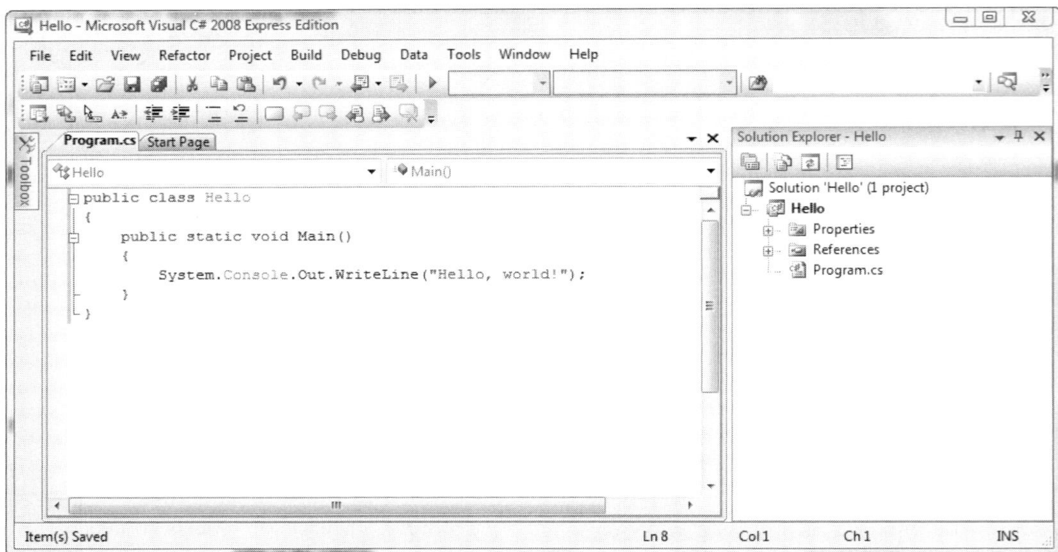

Figure 1-19 The `Hello` application in the IDE

> **NOTE** The tab that contains Program.cs does not contain an asterisk if your program has been saved. As soon as you change even one character in the editor, an asterisk appears in the Program.cs tab, indicating that a change has been made but not yet saved.

7. To compile the program, click **Build** on the menu bar and then click **Build Solution**. (Alternatively, you can press **F6**.) You should receive no error messages, and the words "Build succeeded" should appear near the lower-left edge of the window.

8. Click **Debug** on the menu bar and then click **Start Without Debugging**. Figure 1-20 shows the output; you see "Hello, world!" followed by the message "Press any key to continue". Press any key to dismiss the output screen.

> **NOTE** If the output appears but quickly disappears before you can read it, you can add a statement to the program to hold the output screen until you press Enter. Position your insertion point at the end of the `WriteLine()` statement, press Enter to insert a new line, and type `System.Console.ReadLine();`. Then build and start the program again.

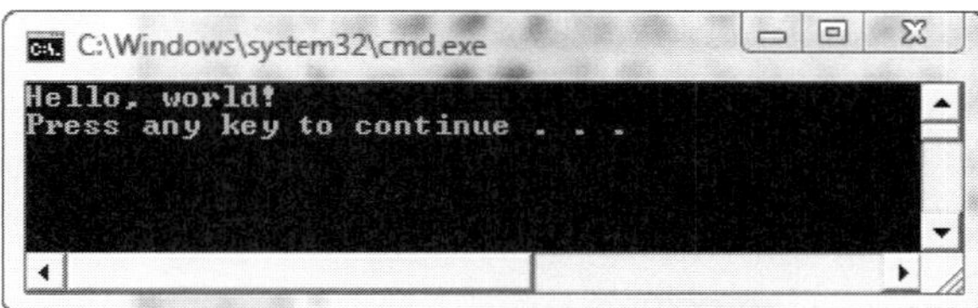

Figure 1-20 Output of the `Hello` application in Visual Studio

9. Close Visual Studio by clicking **File** on the menu bar and then clicking **Exit**, or by clicking the **Close** box in the upper-right corner of the Visual Studio window. When you receive a message "Do you want to save or discard changes to the current solution?", click **Save**. In the Save Project window, you can select a folder location to save the project, as shown in Figure 1-21.

Figure 1-21 The Save Project window

10. When you create a C# program using an editor such as Notepad and compiling with the `csc` command, only two files are created—Hello.cs and Hello.exe. When you create a C# program using the Visual Studio editor, many additional files are created. You can view their filenames in several ways:

» At the command prompt, type **dir** to view a directory of the files stored in the folder where you saved the project (for example, your Chapter.01 folder). Within the folder, a new folder named Hello has been created. Type the command **cd Hello** to change the current path to include this new folder, then type **dir** again. You see another folder named Hello. Type **cd Hello** again, and **dir** again. Figure 1-22 shows the output using this method; it shows several folders and files.

» Double-click the **Computer** icon (or My Computer in Windows XP), find and double-click the correct drive, select the **C#** folder and the **Chapter.01** folder (or the path you are using), double-click the **Hello** folder, and view the contents. Double-click the second **Hello** folder and view the contents there too. Figure 1-23 shows the second Hello folder contents.

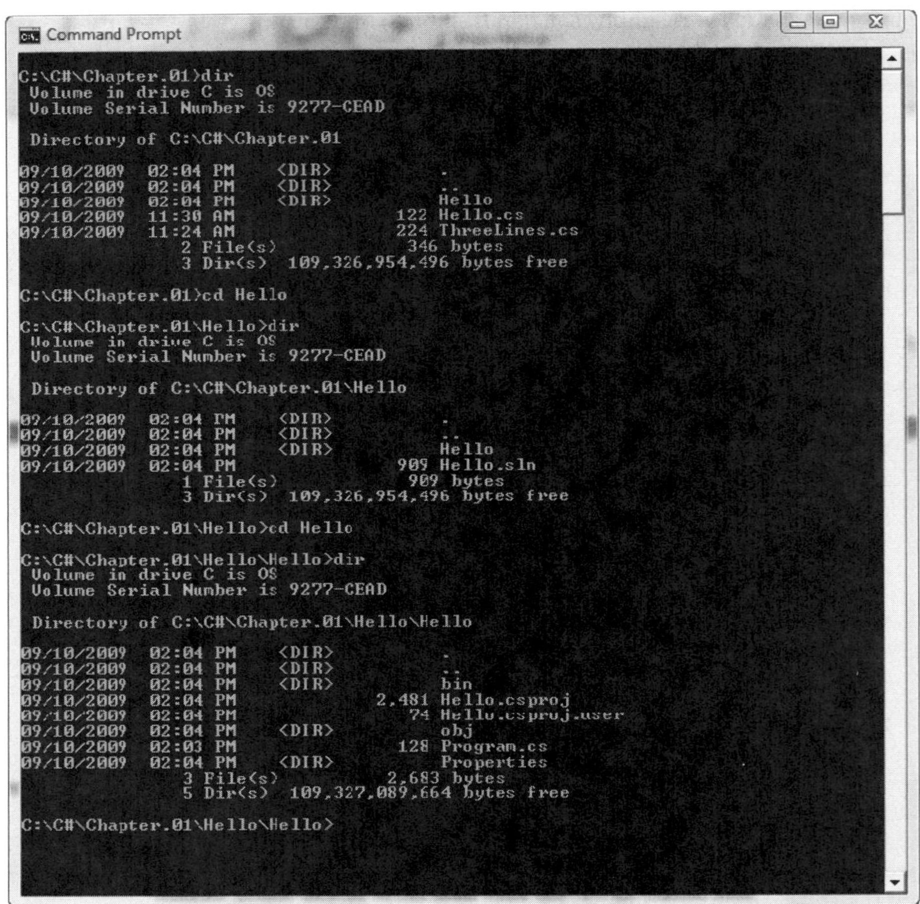

Figure 1-22 Directory listing for Hello folder

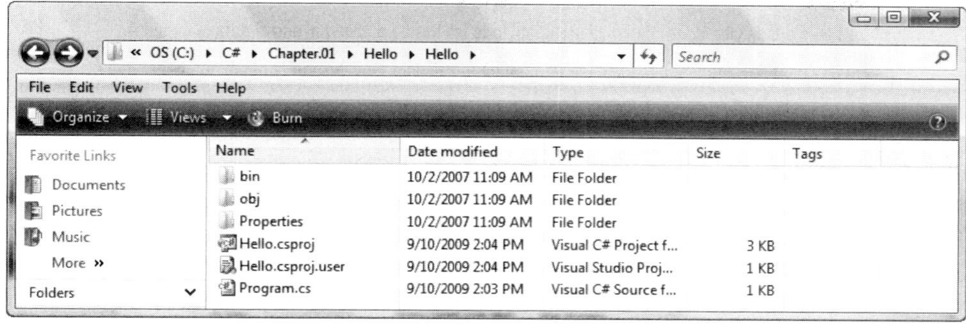

Figure 1-23 Contents of the C#/Chapter.01/Hello/Hello folder

» Use Windows Explorer to view the contents of the Hello folders within the Chapter.01 folder. In Vista, click **Start**, **All Programs**, **Accessories**, and **Windows Explorer**. Then, in the left panel, select **Desktop** and **Computer**. The remaining navigation steps are the same as using **Computer** from the desktop in the last bullet.

The innermost Hello folder contains a bin folder, an obj folder, a Properties folder, and additional files. If you explore further, you will find that the bin folder contains Debug and Release folders, which include additional files. Using the Visual Studio editor to compile your programs creates a lot of overhead. These additional files become important as you create more sophisticated C# projects. For now, while you learn C# syntax, using the command line to compile programs is simpler.

»NOTE If you are using a version of Visual Studio other than 2008 Express, your folder configuration might be slightly different.

»NOTE If you followed the earlier instructions on compiling a program from the command line, and you used the same folder when using the IDE, you will see the additional Hello.cs and Hello.exe files in your folder. These files will have an earlier time stamp than the files you just created. If you were to execute a new program from within Visual Studio without saving and executing it from the command line first, you would not see these two additional files.

DECIDING WHICH METHOD TO USE

When you write, compile, and execute a C# program, you can use either the command line or the Visual Studio IDE. You would never need to use both. You might prefer using an editor with which you are already familiar (such as Notepad) and compiling from the command line because only two files are generated, saving disk space.

On the other hand, the IDE provides many useful features, such as automatic statement completion. For example, if you type `System` and a dot, then a list of choices is displayed, and you can click `Console` instead of typing it. Similarly, after the dot that follows `Console`, a list of choices is displayed from which you can select `Out`. Additionally, in the IDE, words are displayed using different colors based on their category; for example, one color is used for C#-reserved words and a different color for literal strings. It is also easier to correct many errors using the IDE. When compiler errors or warnings are issued, you can double-click the message, and the cursor jumps to the location in the code where the error was detected.

Another advantage to learning the IDE is that if you use another programming language in Visual Studio (C++ or Visual Basic), the environment will already be familiar to you.

The C# language works the same way, no matter what method you use to compile your programs. Everything you learn in the next chapters about input, output, decision making, loops, and arrays will work the same way, regardless of the compilation technique you use. You can use just one technique, or compile some programs in each environment as the mood strikes you. You can also mix and match techniques if you prefer. For example, you can use an editor you like to compose your programs, then paste them into the IDE to execute them.

Although any program can be written using either compilation technique, when you write graphical user interface (GUI) applications that use existing objects such as message boxes and buttons, you will find that the extensive amount of code automatically generated by the IDE is very helpful. For the first nine chapters of this book, you are encouraged to use whichever compilation technique you prefer. In Chapter 10, you will be encouraged to use the IDE to take advantage of its many time-saving features.

ADDING COMMENTS TO A PROGRAM
To add comments to your program:

>> NOTE
In Visual Studio Professional, you click **File**, point to Open, and click **Project/Solution**.

1. If you prefer compiling programs from the command line, then open the **Hello.cs** file in your text editor. If you prefer compiling programs from within Visual Studio, then open Visual Studio, click **File**, click **Open Project**, browse for the correct folder, double-click the **Hello** folder, and then double-click the **Hello** file. In the Solution Explorer at the side of the screen, double-click **Hello.cs**, as shown in Figure 1-24.

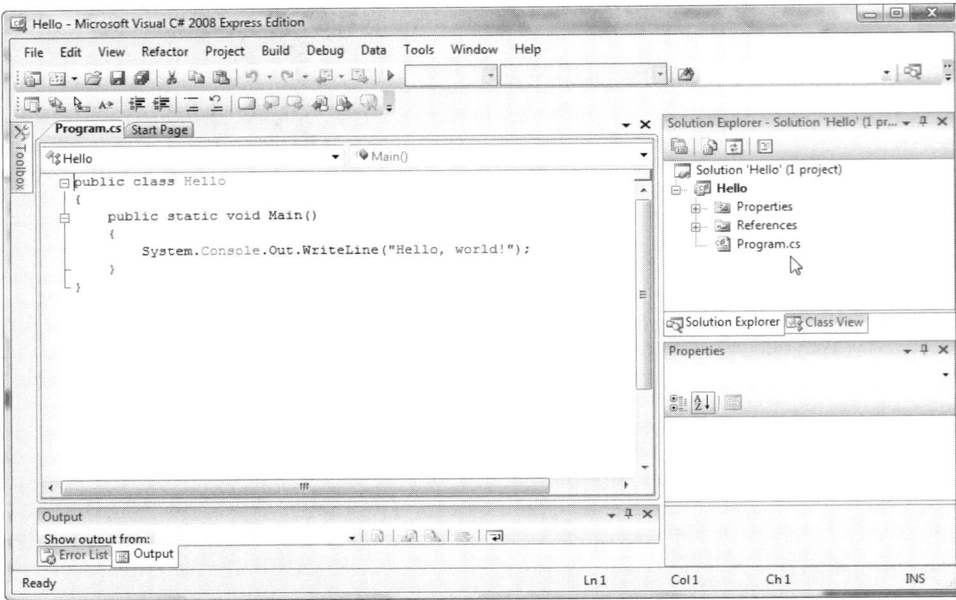

Figure 1-24 Visual C# and the Solution Explorer window

> **»NOTE** If you do not see the Solution Explorer window in Visual Studio, click the Solution Explorer icon on the toolbar (shown at right). Alternatively, from the main menu, choose **View** and then **Solution Explorer**. The Solution Explorer displays the various files that make up a project.

2. Position your cursor at the top of the file, press **Enter** to insert a new line, press the **Up** arrow key to go to that line, and then type the following comments at the top of the file. Press **Enter** after typing each line. Insert your name and today's date where indicated.

```
// Filename Hello.cs
// Written by <your name>
// Written on <today's date>
```

3. Scroll to the line that reads `public static void Main()` and press **Enter** to start a new line. Then press the **Up** arrow; in the new blank line, aligned with the start of the `Main()` method header, type the following block comment in the program:

```
/*  This program demonstrates the use of
the WriteLine() method to print the
message Hello, world!  */
```

4. Save the file, replacing the old Hello.cs file with this new, commented version.

5. If you prefer to compile programs from the command line, type **csc Hello.cs** at the command line. When the program compiles successfully, execute it with the command **Hello**. If you prefer compiling and executing programs from within Visual Studio, click **Debug** and **Start Without Debugging**. Adding program comments makes no difference in the execution of the program.

CHAPTER SUMMARY

» A computer program is a set of instructions that you write to tell a computer what to do. Programmers write their programs, then use a compiler to translate their high-level language statements into intermediate language and machine code. A program works correctly when both its syntax and logic are correct.

» Procedural programming involves creating computer memory locations, called variables, and sets of operations, called methods. In object-oriented programming, you envision program components as objects that are similar to concrete objects in the real world; then you manipulate the objects to achieve a desired result. Objects exist as members of classes and are made up of states and methods.

» The C# programming language was developed as an object-oriented and component-oriented language. It contains many features similar to those in Visual Basic, Java, and C++.

» To write a C# program that produces a line of console output, you must pass a literal string as an argument to the `System.Console.Out.WriteLine()` method. `System` is a namespace, `Console` is a class, and `Out` is an object. The `WriteLine()` method call appears within the `Main()` method of a class you create.

» You can define a C# class or variable by using any name or identifier that begins with an underscore or a letter, contains only letters or digits, and is not a C#-reserved keyword.

» Program comments are nonexecuting statements that you add to document a program or to disable statements when you test a program. There are three types of comments in C#: line comments that start with two forward slashes (//) and continue to the end of the current line, block comments that start with a forward slash and an asterisk (/*) and end with an asterisk and a forward slash (*/), and XML-documentation comments.

» When you need to repeatedly use a class from the same namespace, you can shorten the statements you type by using a clause that indicates a namespace where the class can be found.

» To create a C# program, you can use the Microsoft Visual Studio environment. You can also use any text editor, such as Notepad, WordPad, or any word-processing program. After you write and save a program, you must compile the source code into intermediate and machine language.

» You have multiple options for writing the `Main()` method header; the format you use depends on your need for command-line arguments and the conventions you prefer in your working environment.

KEY TERMS

A computer **program** is a set of instructions that you write to tell a computer what to do.

Machine language is the most basic circuitry-level language.

A **high-level programming language** allows you to use a vocabulary of reasonable terms such as "read," "write," or "add" instead of the sequence of on/off switches that perform these tasks.

A language's **syntax** is its set of rules.

A **compiler** is a computer program that translates high-level language statements into machine code.

A **syntax error** is an error that occurs when a programming language is used incorrectly.

The **logic** behind any program involves executing the various statements and methods in the correct order to produce the desired results.

Semantic errors are the type of logical errors that occur when you use a correct word in the wrong context.

Debugging a program is the process of removing all syntax and logical errors from the program.

A **procedural program** is created by writing a series of steps or operations to manipulate values.

Variables are named computer memory locations that hold values that might vary.

An **identifier** is the name of a program component such as a variable, class, or method.

Camel casing is a style of creating identifiers in which the first letter is not capitalized, but each new word is.

Pascal casing is a style of creating identifiers in which the first letter of all new words in a variable name, even the first one, is capitalized.

Procedures or **methods** are compartmentalized program units that accomplish tasks.

A program **calls** or **invokes** methods.

Object-oriented programming is a programming technique that features objects, classes, encapsulation, interfaces, polymorphism, and inheritance.

Objects are program elements that are instances of a class.

The **command line** is the line on which you type a command in a system that uses a text interface.

The **command prompt** is a request for input that appears at the beginning of the command line.

The **attributes** of an object represent its characteristics.

The **states** of an object are the values of its attributes.

The **properties** of an object are its values.

The **state of an object** is the collective value of all its attributes at any point in time.

A **class** is a category of objects or a type of object.

Each object is an **instance** of a class.

Encapsulation is the technique of packaging an object's attributes and methods into a cohesive unit that can be used as an undivided entity.

A **black box** is a device you use without regard for the internal mechanisms.

An **interface** is the interaction between a method and an object.

Polymorphism is the ability to create methods that act appropriately depending on the context.

Inheritance is the ability to extend a class so as to create a more specific class that contains all the attributes and methods of a more general class; the extended class usually contains new attributes or methods as well.

The **C# programming language** was developed as an object-oriented and component-oriented language. It exists as part of Visual Studio 2008, a package used for developing applications for the Windows family of operating systems.

Primitive data is simple data, such as a number.

A **literal string** of characters is a series of characters that is used exactly as entered.

An **argument** or a **parameter** to a method represents information that a method needs to perform its task. An argument is the expression used when you call a method, while a parameter is an object or reference that is declared in a method definition; that is, where the method instructions are written.

The **WriteLine() method** displays a line of output on the screen, positions the cursor on the next line, and waits for additional output.

The **Write() method** displays a line of output on the screen, but the cursor does not advance to a new line; it remains on the same line as the output.

A **namespace** is a scheme that provides a way to group similar classes.

The **System namespace**, which is built into your C# compiler, holds commonly used classes.

A **method header** includes the method name and information about what will pass into and be returned from a method.

The **method body** of every method is contained within a pair of curly braces ({ }) and includes all the instructions executed by the method.

Whitespace is any combination of spaces, tabs, and carriage returns (blank lines). You use whitespace to organize your program code and make it easier to read.

Keywords are predefined and reserved identifiers that have special meaning to the compiler.

An **access modifier** defines the circumstances under which a method or class can be accessed; public access is the most liberal type of access.

In a method header, **public** is an access modifier that indicates other classes may use the method.

In a method header, **private** is an access modifier that indicates other classes may not use the method.

The reserved keyword **static** indicates that a method will be executed through a class and not by an object.

In a method header, the keyword **void** indicates that the method does not return any value when called.

A **verbatim identifier** is an identifier with an @ prefix.

Program comments are nonexecuting statements that you add to document a program.

When you **comment out** a statement, you turn it into a comment so that the compiler will not execute its command.

Line comments start with two forward slashes (//) and continue to the end of the current line. Line comments can appear on a line by themselves, or at the end of a line following executable code.

Block comments start with a forward slash and an asterisk (/*) and end with an asterisk and a forward slash (*/). Block comments can appear on a line by themselves, on a line before executable code, or after executable code. They can also extend across as many lines as needed.

XML-documentation format comments use a special set of tags within angle brackets to create documentation from within a program.

You use a namespace with a **using clause**, or **using directive**.

An **alias** is an alternative name for a class.

Source code is the statements you write when you create a program.

Intermediate language (**IL**) is the language into which source code statements are compiled.

The C# **just in time** (**JIT**) compiler translates intermediate code into executable code.

A **string** is a data type that can hold a series of characters.

REVIEW QUESTIONS

1. A computer program written as a series of on and off switches is written in ___________ .

   a. machine language

   b. a low-level language

   c. a high-level language

   d. a compiled language

2. A program that translates high-level programs into intermediate or machine code is a(n) ___________ .

   a. mangler

   b. compiler

   c. analyst

   d. logician

3. The grammar and spelling rules of a programming language constitute its ___________ .

   a. logic

   b. variables

   c. syntax

   d. vortex

4. Variables are ___________ .

   a. procedures

   b. named memory locations

   c. grammar rules

   d. operations

5. Programs in which you create and use objects that have attributes similar to their real-world counterparts are known as ___________ programs.

   a. procedural

   b. logical

   c. authentic

   d. object-oriented

6. Which of the following pairs is an example of a class and an object, in that order?

   a. robin and bird

   b. chair and desk

   c. university and Harvard

   d. oak and tree

7. The technique of packaging an object's attributes into a cohesive unit that can be used as an undivided entity is __________ .

   a. inheritance

   b. encapsulation

   c. polymorphism

   d. interfacing

8. Of the following languages, which is least similar to C#?

   a. Java

   b. Visual Basic

   c. C++

   d. COBOL

9. A series of characters that appears within double quotation marks is a(n) __________ .

   a. parameter

   b. interface

   c. argument

   d. literal string

10. The C# method that prints a line of output on the screen and then positions the cursor on the next line is __________ .

   a. `WriteLine()`

   b. `PrintLine()`

   c. `DisplayLine()`

   d. `OutLine()`

11. Which of the following is an object?

   a. `System`

   b. `Console`

   c. `Out`

   d. `WriteLine`

12. In C#, a scheme that groups similar classes is a(n) __________ .

   a. superclass

   b. method

   c. namespace

   d. identifier

13. Every method in C# contains a __________ .

   a. header and a body

   b. header and a footer

   c. variable and a class

   d. class and an object

14. Which of the following is a method?

   a. `namespace`

   b. `public`

   c. `Main()`

   d. `static`

15. Which of the following statements is true?

   a. An identifier must begin with an underscore.

   b. An identifier can contain digits.

   c. An identifier must be no more than 16 characters long.

   d. An identifier can contain only lowercase letters.

16. Which of the following identifiers is not legal in C#?

    a. `per cent increase`

    b. `annualReview`

    c. `HTML`

    d. `alternativetaxcredit`

17. The text of a program you write is called ____________ .

    a. object code

    b. source code

    c. machine language

    d. executable documentation

18. Programming errors such as using incorrect punctuation or misspelling words are collectively known as ____________ errors.

    a. syntax

    b. logical

    c. executable

    d. fatal

19. A comment in the form `/* this is a comment */` is a(n) ____________ .

    a. XML comment

    b. block comment

    c. executable comment

    d. line comment

20. If a programmer inserts `using System;` at the top of a C# program, which of the following can the programmer use as an alternative to `System.Console.Out.WriteLine("Hello");`?

    a. `System("Hello");`

    b. `WriteLine("Hello");`

    c. `Console.WriteLine("Hello");`

    d. `Console.Out("Hello");`

EXERCISES

1. Indicate whether each of the following C# programming language identifiers is legal or illegal.

    a. `WeeklySales`

    b. `last character`

    c. `class`

    d. `MathClass`

    e. `myfirstinitial`

    f. `phone#`

    g. `abcdefghijklmnop`

    h. `23jordan`

    i. `my_code`

    j. `90210`

    k. `year2008Budget`

    l. `abfSorority`

2. Name at least three attributes that might be appropriate for each of the following classes:

    a. `TelevisionSet`

    b. `EmployeePaycheck`

    c. `PatientMedicalRecord`

3. Name a class to which each of these objects might belong:

   a. your red bicycle

   b. Albert Einstein

   c. last month's credit card bill

4. Write, compile, and test a program that displays your first name on the screen. Save the program as **Name.cs**.

5. Write, compile, and test a program that displays your full name, street address, and city and state on three separate lines on the screen. Save the program as **Address.cs**.

6. Write, compile, and test a program that displays your favorite quotation on the screen. Include the name of the person to whom the quote is attributed. Use as many display lines as you feel are appropriate. Save the program as **Quotation.cs**.

7. Write, compile, and test a program that displays a pattern similar to the following on the screen:

```
    X
   XXX
  XXXXX
 XXXXXXX
    X
```

Save the program as **Tree.cs**.

8. Write a program that displays your initials in a pattern on the screen. Compose each initial with six lines of smaller initials, as in the following example:

```
        J       FFFFFF
        J       F
        J       FFF
        J       F
J       J       F
JJJJJJ          F
```

Save the program as **Initials.cs**.

9. From 1925 through 1963, Burma Shave advertising signs appeared next to highways all across the United States. There were always four or five signs in a row containing pieces of a rhyme, followed by a final sign that read "Burma Shave." For example, one set of signs that has been preserved by the Smithsonian Institution reads as follows:

```
Shaving brushes
You'll soon see 'em
On a shelf
In some museum
Burma Shave
```

Find a classic Burma Shave rhyme on the Web and write a program that displays it. Save the program as **BurmaShave.cs**.

DEBUGGING EXERCISES

Each of the following files in the Chapter.01 folder on your Student Disk has syntax and/or logical errors. In each case, determine the problem and fix the program. After you correct the errors, save each file using the same filename preceded with "Fixed". For example, DebugOne1.cs will become FixedDebugOne1.cs.

a. DebugOne1.cs

b. DebugOne2.cs

c. DebugOne3.cs

d. DebugOne4.cs

UP FOR DISCUSSION

1. Using an Internet search engine, find at least three definitions for *object-oriented programming*. (Try searching with and without the hyphen in *object-oriented*.) Compare the definitions and compile them into one "best" definition.

2. What is the difference between a compiler and an interpreter? What programming languages use each? Under what conditions would you prefer to use one over the other?

3. What is the image of the computer programmer in popular culture? Is the image different in books than in TV shows and movies? Would you like a programmer image for yourself, and if so, which one?

2

USING DATA

In this chapter you will:

Learn about declaring variables
Display variable values
Learn about the integral data types
Learn about floating-point data types
Format floating-point values
Use standard binary arithmetic operators
Use shortcut arithmetic operators
Learn about the `bool` data type
Learn about numeric type conversion
Learn about the `char` data type
Learn about the `string` data type
Define named constants
Accept console input

In Chapter 1, you learned about programming in general and the C# programming language in particular. You wrote, compiled, and ran a C# program that produces output. In this chapter, you build on your basic C# programming skills by learning how to manipulate data, including variables, data types, and constants. As you will see, using variables makes writing computer programs worth the effort.

DECLARING VARIABLES

You can categorize data as variable or constant. A data item is **constant** when it cannot be changed after a program is compiled—in other words, when it cannot vary. For example, if you use the number 347 within a C# program, then 347 is a constant, and every time you execute the program, the value 347 will be used. You can refer to the number 347 as a **literal constant**, because its value is taken literally at each use.

> **» NOTE** You will learn to create named constants later in this chapter.

On the other hand, when you want a value to be able to change, you can create a variable. A **variable** is a named location in computer memory that can hold different values at different points in time. For example, if you create a variable named `heatingBill` and include it in a C# program, `heatingBill` might contain the value 347, or it might contain 200. Different values might be used when the program is executed multiple times, or different values might even be used at different times during the same execution of the program. Because you can use a variable to hold `heatingBill` within a utility company's billing system, you can write one set of instructions to compute `heatingBill`, yet use different `heatingBill` values for thousands of utility customers during one execution of the program.

Whether it is stored as a constant or in a variable, each data item you use in a C# program has a data type. A **data type** describes the format and size of (amount of memory occupied by) a data item. C# provides for 14 basic or **intrinsic types** of data, as shown in Table 2-1. Of these built-in data types, the ones most commonly used are `int`, `double`, `char`, `string`, and `bool`. Each C# intrinsic type is an **alias**, or other name for, a class in the `System` namespace.

> **» NOTE** You learned about the `System` namespace in Chapter 1.

Type	System Type	Bytes	Description	Largest Value	Smallest Value
byte	Byte	1	Unsigned byte	255	0
sbyte	Sbyte	1	Signed byte	127	−128
short	Int16	2	Signed short	32,767	−32,768
ushort	UInt16	2	Unsigned short	65,535	0
int	Int32	4	Signed integer	2,147,483,647	−2,147,483,648
uint	UInt32	4	Unsigned integer	4,294,967,295	0
long	Int64	8	Signed long integer	Approximately 9×10^{18}	Approximately -9×10^{18}
ulong	UInt64	8	Unsigned long integer	Approximately 18×10^{18}	0
float	Single	4	Floating-point	Approximately 3.4×10^{38}	Approximately -3.4×10^{38}
double	Double	8	Double-precision floating-point	Approximately 1.8×10^{308}	Approximately -1.8×10^{308}
decimal	Decimal	16	Fixed precision number	Approximately 7.9×10^{28}	Approximately -7.9×10^{28}
string	String	NA	Unicode string	NA	NA
char	Char	2	Unicode character	0xFFFF	0x0000
bool	Boolean	1	Boolean value (true or false)	NA	NA

Table 2-1 C# data types

>>**NOTE** The highest `char` value, 0xFFFF, represents the character in which every bit is turned on. The lowest value, 0x0000, represents the character in which every bit is turned off. Any value that begins with "0x" represents a hexadecimal, or base 16, value.

>>**NOTE** For any two `string`s, the one with the higher Unicode character value in an earlier position is considered higher. For example, "AAB" is higher than "AAA". The `string` type has no true minimum. However, you can think of the empty string "" as being the lowest.

>>**NOTE** Although the `bool` type has no true maximum or minimum, you can think of `true` as the highest and `false` as the lowest.

You name variables using the same rules for identifiers as you use for class names. Basically, variable names must start with a letter, cannot include embedded spaces, and cannot be a reserved keyword. You must declare all variables you want to use in a program. A **variable declaration** is the statement that names a variable and reserves storage for it; it includes:

» The data type that the variable will store
» The identifier that is the variable's name
» An optional assignment operator and assigned value when you want a variable to contain an initial value
» An ending semicolon

>> NOTE   Variable names usually begin with lowercase letters to distinguish them from class names. You should follow this convention when naming your variables. However, variable names *can* begin with either an uppercase or lowercase letter.

>> NOTE   You learned the rules for creating identifiers in Chapter 1. The C# reserved keywords are listed in Table 1-1 in Chapter 1.

For example, the variable declaration `int myAge = 25;` declares a variable of type `int` named `myAge` and assigns it an initial value of 25. In other words, four bytes of memory are reserved with the name `myAge` and the value 25 is stored there. The declaration is a complete statement that ends in a semicolon. The equal sign (=) is the **assignment operator**; any value to the right of the assignment operator is assigned to, or taken on by, the variable to the left. An assignment made when a variable is declared is an **initialization**; an assignment made later is simply an **assignment**. Thus, `int myAge = 25;` initializes `myAge` to 25, and a subsequent statement, such as `myAge = 42;`, assigns a new value to the variable. Note that the expression `25 = myAge;` is illegal because assignment always takes place from right to left. By definition, a constant cannot be altered, so it is illegal to place one (such as 25) on the left side of an assignment operator.

>> NOTE   The assignment operator means "is assigned the value of the following expression." In other words, the statement `myAge = 25` can be read as "`myAge` is assigned the value of the following expression: 25".

>> NOTE
The number 32 in the name `System.Int32` represents the number of bits of storage allowed for the data type. There are 8 bits in a byte, and an `int` occupies 4 bytes.

Instead of using a name from the Type column of Table 2-1, you can use the fully qualified type name from the `System` namespace that is listed in the System Type column. For example, instead of using the type name `int`, you can use the full name `System.Int32`. It's better to use the shorter alias `int`, however, for several reasons:

» The shorter alias is easier to type and read.
» The shorter alias resembles type names used in other languages such as Java and C++.
» Other C# programmers expect the shorter type names.

The variable declaration `int myAge;` declares a variable of type `int` named `myAge`, but no value is assigned at the time of creation. You can make an assignment later in the program, but you cannot use the variable in an arithmetic expression or display the value of the variable until you assign a value to it.

You can declare multiple variables of the same type in separate statements on different lines. For example, the following statements declare two variables. The first variable is named `myAge` and its value is 25. The second variable is named `yourAge` and its value is 19.

```
int myAge = 25;
int yourAge = 19;
```

You also can declare two variables of the same type in a single statement by using the type once and separating the variable declarations with a comma, as shown in the following statement:

```
int myAge = 25, yourAge = 19;
```

Some programmers prefer to use the data type once and break the declaration across multiple lines, as in the following example:

```
int myAge = 25,
    yourAge = 19;
```

> **NOTE** When a statement occupies more than one line, it is easier to read if lines after the first one are indented a few spaces. This book follows that convention.

> **NOTE** A statement and a line of code are not synonymous. In C#, a statement might occupy multiple lines or a single line might contain multiple statements. Every statement ends with a semicolon.

When you declare multiple variables of the same type, a comma separates the variable names and a single semicolon appears at the end of the declaration statement, no matter how many lines the declaration occupies. However, when declaring variables of different types, you must use a separate statement for each type. The following statements declare two variables of type `int` (`myAge` and `yourAge`) and two variables of type `double` (`mySalary` and `yourSalary`), without assigning initial values to any of them:

```
int myAge, yourAge;
double mySalary, yourSalary;
```

Similarly, the following statements declare two `int`s and two `double`s, assigning values to two of the four named variables:

```
int     numCarsIOwn = 2,
        numCarsYouOwn;
double  myCarsMpg,
        yourCarsMpg = 31.5;
```

»TWO TRUTHS AND A LIE: DECLARING VARIABLES

1. A constant cannot be changed after a program is compiled, but a variable can be changed.
2. A data type describes the format and size of a data item.
3. A variable declaration is the statement that names a variable and assigns a value to it.

The false statement is #3. A variable declaration names a variable and reserves storage for it; it includes the data type that the variable will store, an identifier, an assignment operator and assigned value can be included, but they are not required.

DISPLAYING VARIABLE VALUES

You can display variable values by using the variable name within a `WriteLine()` method call. For example, Figure 2-1 shows a C# program that displays the value of the variable `someMoney`. Figure 2-2 shows the output of the program.

```
using System;
public class DisplaySomeMoney
{
    public static void Main()
    {
        double someMoney = 39.45;
        Console.WriteLine(someMoney);
    }
}
```

Figure 2-1 Program that displays a variable value

Figure 2-2 Output of `DisplaySomeMoney` program

The output shown in Figure 2-2 is rather stark—just a number with no explanation. The program in Figure 2-3 adds some explanation to the output; the result is shown in Figure 2-4. This program uses the `Write()` method to display the string "The money is $" before displaying the value of `someMoney`. Because the program uses `Write()` instead of `WriteLine()`, the second output appears on the same line as the first output.

```
using System;
public class DisplaySomeMoney2
{
    public static void Main()
    {
        double someMoney = 39.45;
        Console.Write("The money is $");
        Console.WriteLine(someMoney);
    }
}
```

Figure 2-3 Program that displays a string and a variable value

Figure 2-4 Output of `DisplaySomeMoney2` program

If you want to display several strings and several variables, you can end up with quite a few
`Write()` and `WriteLine()` statements. To make producing output easier, you can combine
strings and variable values into a single `Write()` or `WriteLine()` statement by using a
format string. A **format string** is a string of characters that optionally contains fixed text
and contains one or more format items or placeholders for variable values. A **placeholder**
consists of a pair of curly braces containing a number that indicates the desired variable's
position in a list that follows the string. The first position is always position 0. For example,
if you remove the `Write()` and `WriteLine()` statements from the program in Figure 2-3
and replace them with the shaded statement in Figure 2-5, the program produces the output

```
using System;
public class DisplaySomeMoney3
{
    public static void Main()
    {
        double someMoney = 39.45;
        Console.WriteLine("The money is ${0} exactly",
            someMoney);
    }
}
```

Figure 2-5 Using a format string

shown in Figure 2-6. The placeholder {0} holds a position into which the value of someMoney is inserted. Because someMoney is the first variable after the format string (as well as the only variable), its position is 0.

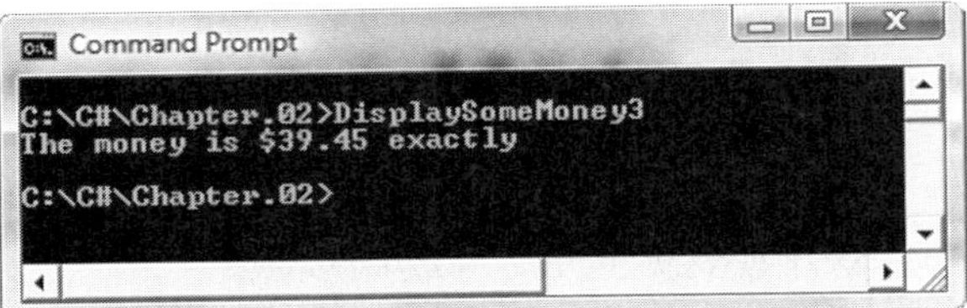

Figure 2-6 Output produced using format string

To display two variables within a single call to Write() or WriteLine(), you can use a statement like the following:

```
Console.WriteLine("The money is {0} and my age is {1}",
    someMoney, myAge);
```

The number within the curly braces in the format string must be less than the number of values you list after the format string. In other words, if you list six values to be displayed, valid format position numbers are 0 through 5. You do not have to use the positions in order. For example, you can choose to display the value in position 2, then 1, then 0. You also can display a specific value multiple times. For example, if someMoney has been assigned the value 439.75, the following code produces the output shown in Figure 2-7:

```
Console.WriteLine("I have ${0}. ${0}!! ${0}!!",
    someMoney);
```

Figure 2-7 Displaying the same value multiple times

When you use a series of WriteLine() statements to display a list of variable values, the values are not right-aligned as you normally expect numbers to be. For example, the following code produces the output shown in Figure 2-8:

```
int num1 = 4, num2 = 56, num3 = 789;
Console.WriteLine("{0}", num1);
Console.WriteLine("{0}", num2);
Console.WriteLine("{0}", num3);
```

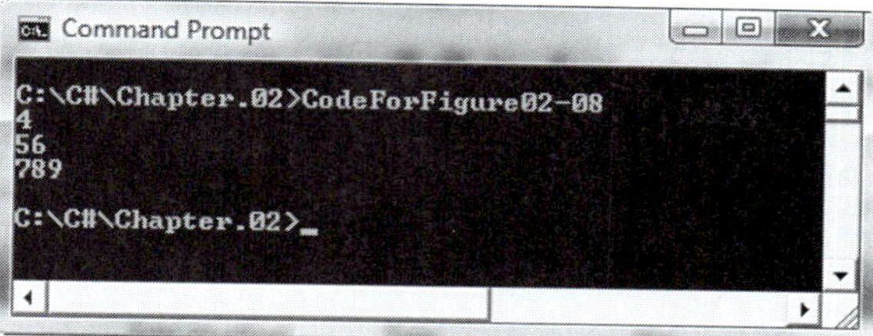

Figure 2-8 Displaying values with different numbers of digits without using field sizes

If you use a second number within the curly braces in a number format, you can specify alignment and field size. For example, the following code produces the output shown in Figure 2-9. The output created by each `WriteLine()` statement is right-aligned in a field that is five characters wide.

```
int num1 = 4, num2 = 56, num3 = 789;
Console.WriteLine("{0, 5}", num1);
Console.WriteLine("{0, 5}", num2);
Console.WriteLine("{0, 5}", num3);
```

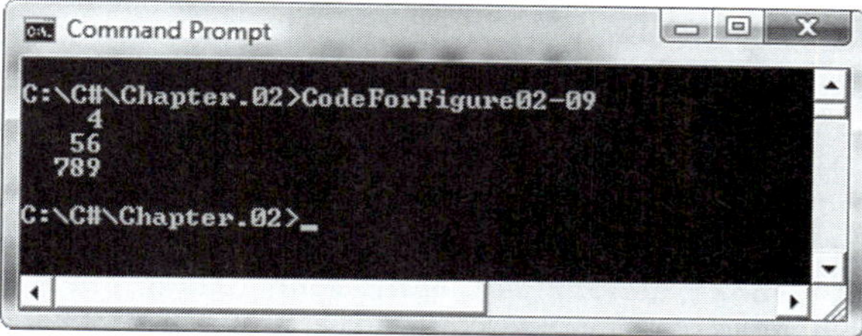

Figure 2-9 Displaying values with different numbers of digits using field sizes

> **»NOTE** By default, numbers are right-aligned in their fields. If you use a negative value for the field size in a `Write()` or `WriteLine()` statement, the value displayed will be left-aligned in the field.

When you include a format string in a `Console.WriteLine()` statement, you cannot extend the string across multiple lines by pressing Enter. Instead, you can **concatenate** (join together in a chain) multiple strings into a single entity using a plus sign (+). For example, the following two statements produce identical results. In the second, the format string is broken into two parts and concatenated.

```
Console.WriteLine("I have ${0}. ${0} is a lot.",
    someMoney);
Console.WriteLine("I have ${0}. " +
    "${0} is a lot. ", someMoney);
```

» NOTE In this example, the + could go at the end of the first code line or the beginning of the second one. If the + is placed at the end of the first line, someone reading your code is more likely to notice that the statement is not yet complete. Because of the limitations of this book's page width, you will see examples of concatenation frequently in program code.

» TWO TRUTHS AND A LIE: DISPLAYING VARIABLE VALUES

1. Assuming number and answer are legally declared variables, then the following statement is valid:

```
Console.WriteLine("{1}{2}", number, answer);
```

2. Assuming number and answer are legally declared variables, then the following statement is valid:

```
Console.WriteLine("{1}{1}{0}", number, answer);
```

3. Assuming number and answer are legally declared variables, then the following statement is valid:

```
Console.WriteLine("{0}{1}{1}{0}", number, answer);
```

The false statement is #1. When two values are available for display, the position number between any pair of curly braces in the format string must be 0 or 1.

USING THE INTEGRAL DATA TYPES

In C#, nine data types are considered **integral data types**—that is, types that store whole numbers. The nine types are **byte**, **sbyte**, **short**, **ushort**, **int**, **uint**, **long**, **ulong**, and **char**. The first eight always represent whole numbers, and the ninth type, char, is used for characters like 'A' or 'a'. Actually, you can think of all nine types as numbers because every Unicode character, including the letters of the alphabet and punctuation marks, can be represented as a number. For example, the character 'A' is stored within your computer as a 65. Because you more commonly think of the char type as holding alphabetic characters instead of their numeric equivalents, the char type will be discussed in its own section later in this chapter.

The most basic of the other eight integral types is int. You use variables of type int to store (or hold) **integers**, or whole numbers. An int uses four bytes of memory and can hold any whole number value ranging from 2,147,483,647 down to -2,147,483,648. If you want to save memory and know you need only a small value, you can use one of the shorter integer types— byte, sbyte (which stands for signed byte), short (short int), or ushort (unsigned short int). For example, a payroll program might contain a variable named numberOfDependents that is declared as type byte, because numberOfDependents will never need to hold a negative value or a value exceeding 255; for that reason, you can allocate just one byte of storage to hold the value.

> **NOTE** When you declare variables, you always make a judgment about which type to use. If you use a type that is too large, you waste storage. If you use a type that is too small, your program won't compile. Many programmers simply use `int` for most whole numbers.

When you assign a value to any numeric variable, you do not use any commas; you type only digits. You can also type a plus or minus sign to indicate a positive or negative integer. For example, to initialize a variable named `annualSalary`, you might write the following:

```
int annualSalary = 20000;
```

»TWO TRUTHS AND A LIE: USING THE INTEGRAL DATA TYPES

1. C# supports nine integral data types, including the most basic one, `int`.
2. Every Unicode character, including the letters of the alphabet and punctuation marks, can be represented as a number.
3. When you assign a value to any numeric variable, it is optional to use commas for values in the thousands.

The false answer is # 3. When you assign a value to a numeric variable, you do not use commas, but you can type a plus or minus sign to indicate a positive or negative integer.

USING FLOATING-POINT DATA TYPES

A **floating-point** number is one that contains decimal positions. C# supports three floating-point data types: `float`, `double`, and `decimal`. A **float** data type can hold as many as seven significant digits of accuracy. A **double** data type can hold 15 or 16 significant digits of accuracy. A value's number of **significant digits** specifies the mathematical accuracy of the value. For example, a `double` given the value 123456789.987654321 will appear as 123456789.987654 because it is accurate to only the fifteenth digit (the sixth digit to the right of the decimal point). Compared to `float`s and `double`s, the **decimal** type has a greater precision and a smaller range, which makes it suitable for financial and monetary calculations. For example, a `decimal` given the value 123456789.987654321 will appear as 123456789.987654321 (notice that it is accurate to the rightmost digit). A `decimal` cannot hold as large a value as a `double` can, but the `decimal` will be more accurate to more decimal places.

Just as an integer constant such as 178 is an `int` by default, a floating-point number constant such as 18.23 is a `double` by default. To explicitly store a constant as a `float`, you place an *F* after the number, as in the following:

```
float pocketChange = 4.87F;
```

You can use either a lowercase or uppercase *F*. You can also place a *D* (or *d*) after a floating-point value to indicate that it is a `double`; even without the *D*, however, it will be stored as a `double` by default. To explicitly store a value as a `decimal`, use an *M* (or *m*) after the number. (*M* stands for monetary; *D* can't be used for `decimal`s because it indicates `double`.)

If you store a value that is too large in a floating-point variable, you will see output expressed in **scientific notation**. Values expressed in scientific notation include an *E* (for exponent). For example, if you declare `float f = 1234567890f;`, the value will appear as 1.234568E9, meaning that the numeric constant you used is approximately 1.234568 times 10 to the ninth power, or 1.234568 with the decimal point moved nine positions to the right.

»TWO TRUTHS AND A LIE: USING FLOATING-POINT DATA TYPES

1. A floating-point number is one in which the decimal point varies each time you reference it.
2. C# supports three floating-point data types: `float`, `double`, and `decimal`.
3. To explicitly store a constant as a `float`, you may place an *F* after the number, but to store a constant as a `double` you need no special designation.

The false statement is #1. A floating-point number is one that contains decimal positions.

FORMATTING FLOATING-POINT VALUES

By default, C# always displays floating-point numbers in the most concise way it can while maintaining the correct value. For example, if you declare a variable and display it as in the following statements, the output will appear as "The amount is 14".

```
double myMoney = 14.00;
Console.WriteLine("The amount is {0}", myMoney);
```

The two zeros to the right of the decimal point in the value will not appear because they add no mathematical information. To see the decimal places, you can convert the floating-point value to a string using a standard numeric format string.

Standard numeric format strings are strings of characters expressed within double quotation marks that indicate a format for output. They take the form *X0*, where *X* is the format specifier and *0* is the precision specifier. The **format specifier** can be one of nine built-in format characters that define the most commonly used numeric format types. The **precision specifier** controls the number of significant digits or zeros to the right of the decimal point. Table 2-2 lists the nine format specifiers.

You can use a format specifier with the `ToString()` method to convert a number into a string that has the desired format. For example, you can use the *F* format specifier to insert a decimal point to the right of a number that does not contain digits to the right of the decimal point, followed by the number of zeros indicated by the precision specifier. (If no precision

Format Character	Description	Default Format (if no precision is given)
C or c	Currency	$XX,XXX.XX ($XX,XXX.XX)
D or d	Decimal	[-]XXXXXXX
E or e	Scientific (exponential)	[-]X.XXXXXXE+xxx [-]X.XXXXXXe+xxx [-]X.XXXXXXE-xxx [-]X.XXXXXXe-xxx
F or f	Fixed-point	[-]XXXXXXX.XX
G or g	General	Variable; either with decimal places or scientific
N or n	Number	[-]XX,XXX.XX
P or p	Percent	Represents a numeric value as a percentage
R or r	Round trip	Ensures that numbers converted to strings will have the same values when they are converted back into numbers
X or x	Hexadecimal	Minimum hexadecimal (base 16) representation

Table 2-2 Format specifiers

specifier is supplied, two zeros are inserted.) For example, the first `WriteLine()` statement in the following code produces 123.00, and the second produces 123.000:

```
double someMoney = 123;
string moneyString;
moneyString = someMoney.ToString("F");
Console.WriteLine(moneyString);
moneyString = someMoney.ToString("F3");
Console.WriteLine(moneyString);
```

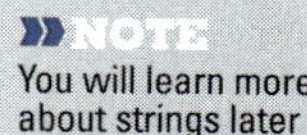

You use *C* as the format specifier when you want to represent a number as a currency value. Currency values appear with a dollar sign and appropriate commas as well as the desired number of decimal places, and negative values appear within parentheses. The integer you use following the *C* indicates the number of decimal places. If you do not provide a value for the number of decimal places, then two digits are shown after the decimal separator by default. For example, both of the following `WriteLine()` statements produce $456,789.00:

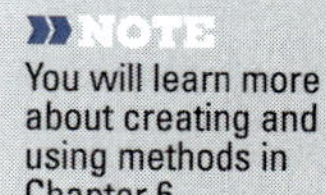


```
double moneyValue = 456789;
string conversion;
conversion = moneyValue.ToString("C");
```

```
Console.WriteLine(conversion);
conversion = moneyValue.ToString("C2");
Console.WriteLine(conversion);
```

> **NOTE** Currency appears with a dollar sign and commas in the English culture. A **culture** is a set of rules that determines how culturally dependent values such as money and dates are formatted. You can change a program's culture by using the `CultureInfoClass`. The .NET framework supports more than 200 culture settings, such as Japanese, French, Urdu, and Sanskrit.

To display a numeric value as a formatted string, you do not have to create a separate string object. You also can make the conversion in a single statement; for example, the following code displays $12,345.00:

```
double payAmount = 12345;
Console.WriteLine(payAmount.ToString("c2"));
```

»TWO TRUTHS AND A LIE: FORMATTING FLOATING-POINT VALUES

1. If `gpa` contains the value 4, then the value of `gpa.ToString("F")` is "4.00".
2. If `gpa` contains the value 4, then the value of `gpa.ToString("F")` is the same as `gpa.ToString("F0")`.
3. If `gpa` contains the value 4, then the value of `gpa.ToString("C")` is "$4.00".

The false statement is #2. If gpa contains the value 4, then the value of gpa.ToString("F") is the same as gpa.ToString("F2").

USING THE STANDARD BINARY ARITHMETIC OPERATORS

> **NOTE** Several shortcut arithmetic operators will be discussed in the next section.

Table 2-3 describes the five most commonly used binary arithmetic operators. You use these operators to manipulate values in your programs. The operators are called **binary operators** because you use two arguments with each—one value to the left of the operator and another value to the right of it. The values that operators use in expressions are called **operands**; binary operators are surrounded by two operands.

Operator	Description	Example
+	Addition	45 + 2: the result is 47
−	Subtraction	45 − 2: the result is 43
*	Multiplication	45 * 2: the result is 90
/	Division	45 / 2: the result is 22 (not 22.5)
%	Remainder (modulus)	45 % 2: the result is 1 (that is, 45 / 2 = 22 with a remainder of 1)

Table 2-3 Binary arithmetic operators

The operators / and % deserve special consideration. When you divide two integers using the / operator, whether they are integer constants or integer variables, the result is an integer; in other words, any fractional part of the result is lost. For example, the result of 45 / 2 is 22, not 22.5. When you use the remainder (modulus) operator with two integers, the result is an integer with the value of the remainder after division takes place—so the result of 45 % 2 is 1 because 2 "goes into" 45 twenty-two times with a remainder of 1.

>> **NOTE** In older languages, such as assembler, you had to perform division before you could take a remainder. In C#, you do not need to perform a division operation before you can perform a remainder operation. In other words, a remainder operation can stand alone.

>> **NOTE** Even though you define a result variable as a floating-point type, integer division still results in an integer. For example, the statement `double d = 7 / 2;` results in d holding 3, not 3.5, because the expression on the right is evaluated as integer-by-integer division before the assignment takes place. If you want the result to hold 3.5, at least one of the operands in the calculation must be a floating-point number, or else you must perform a cast. You will learn about casting later in this chapter.

>> **NOTE** As with `int`s, you can add, subtract, multiply, and divide with floating-point numbers. Unlike with `int`s, however, you cannot perform modulus operations with such numbers. (Floating-point division results in a floating-point answer, so there is no remainder.)

When you combine mathematical operations in a single statement, you must understand **operator precedence**, or the rules that determine the order in which parts of a mathematical expression are evaluated. Multiplication, division, and remainder always take place prior to addition or subtraction in an expression. For example, the following expression results in 14:

```
int result = 2 + 3 * 4;
```

The result is 14 because the multiplication operation (3 * 4) occurs before adding 2. You can override normal operator precedence by putting the operation that should be performed first in parentheses. The following statement results in 20 because the addition within parentheses takes place first:

```
int result = (2 + 3) * 4;
```

In this statement, an intermediate result (5) is calculated before it is multiplied by 4.

>> **NOTE** Operator precedence is also called **order of operation**. A closely linked term is **associativity**, which specifies the order in which a sequence of operations with the same precedence are evaluated. Appendix A contains a chart that describes the precedence and associativity of every C# operator.

>> **NOTE** You can use parentheses in an arithmetic expression even if they do not alter the default order of operation. You can do so to make your intentions clearer to other programmers who read your programs, and so they do not have to rely on their memory of operator precedence.

»TWO TRUTHS AND A LIE: USING THE STANDARD BINARY ARITHMETIC OPERATORS

1. The value of 26 % 4 * 3 is 18.
2. The value of 4 / 3 + 2 is 3.
3. The value of 5 + 6 / 4 is 6.

The false statement is #1. The value of 26 % 4 * 3 is 6. The value of the first part of the expression, 26 % 4, is 2, because 2 is the remainder when 4 is divided into 26. Then 2 * 3 is 6.

USING SHORTCUT ARITHMETIC OPERATORS

Increasing the value held in a variable is a common programming task. Assume that you have declared a variable named `counter` that counts the number of times an event has occurred. Each time the event occurs, you want to execute a statement such as the following:

```
counter = counter + 1;
```

This type of statement looks incorrect to an algebra student, but the equal sign (=) is not used to compare values in C#; it is used to assign values. The statement `counter = counter + 1;` says "Take the value of `counter`, add 1 to it, and assign the result to `counter`."

Because increasing the value of a variable is so common, C# provides several shortcut ways to count and accumulate. The following two statements are identical in meaning:

```
counter += 1;
counter = counter + 1;
```

The += operator is the **add and assign operator**; it adds the operand on the right to the operand on the left and assigns the result to the operand on the left in one step. Similarly, the following statement increases `bankBal` by a rate stored in `interestRate`:

```
bankBal += bankBal * interestRate;
```

Besides the shortcut operator +=, you can use –=, *=, and /=. Each of these operators is used to perform an operation and assign the result in one step. For example:

» `balanceDue -= payment` subtracts a payment from `balanceDue` and assigns the result to `balanceDue`.

» `rate *= 100` multiplies `rate` by 100. For example, it converts a fractional value stored in `rate`, such as 0.27, to a whole number, such as 27.

» `payment /= 12` changes a payment value from an annual amount to a monthly amount due.

When you want to increase a variable's value by exactly 1, you can use either of two other shortcut operators—the **prefix increment operator** and the **postfix increment operator**. To use a prefix increment operator, you type two plus signs before the variable name. For example, these statements result in someValue holding 7:

```
int someValue = 6;
++someValue;
```

The variable someValue holds 1 more than it held before the ++ operator was applied. To use a postfix ++, you type two plus signs just after a variable name. Executing the following statements results in anotherValue holding 57:

```
int anotherValue = 56;
anotherValue++;
```

You can use the prefix ++ and postfix ++ with variables, but not with constants. An expression such as ++84 is illegal because 84 is constant and must always remain as 84. However, you can create a variable as in int val = 84;, and then write ++val or val++ to increase the variable's value to 85.

The prefix and postfix increment operators are **unary operators** because you use them with one operand. Most arithmetic operators, like those used for addition and multiplication, are binary operators that operate on two operands.

When you only want to increase a variable's value by 1, there is no apparent difference between using the prefix and postfix increment operators. However, these operators function differently. When you use the prefix ++, the result is calculated and stored, and then the variable is used. For example, in the following code, both b and c end up holding 5. The WriteLine() statement displays "5 5". In this example, 4 is assigned to b, then b becomes 5, and then 5 is assigned to c.

```
b = 4;
c = ++b;
Console.WriteLine("{0} {1}", b, c);
```

In contrast, when you use the postfix ++, the variable is used, and then the result is calculated and stored. For example, in the second line of the following code, 4 is assigned to c; then, *after* the assignment, b is increased and takes the value 5.

```
b = 4;
c = b++;
Console.WriteLine("{0} {1}", b, c);
```

This last WriteLine() statement displays "5 4". In other words, if b = 4, then the value of b++ is also 4, and that value is assigned to c. However, after the 4 is assigned to c, b is increased to 5.

Besides the prefix and postfix increment operators, you can use a prefix or postfix **decrement operator** (--) that reduces a variable's value by 1. For example, if s and t are both assigned the value 34, then the expression --s has the value 33 and the expression t-- has the value 34, but t then becomes 33.

»TWO TRUTHS AND A LIE: USING SHORTCUT ARITHMETIC OPERATORS

1. If price is 4 and tax is 5, then the value of ++price + tax is 10.
2. If price is 4 and tax is 5, then the value of price++ * tax is 25.
3. If price is 4 and tax is 5, then the value of price - tax++ is -1.

The false statement is #2. If price is 4 and tax is 5, then the value of the expression price++ * tax is 20. The value of the expression price++ is only 4 when it is multiplied by tax, although after the operation occurs, the value of price becomes 5. The value of ++price * tax would be 25.

USING THE bool DATA TYPE

Boolean logic is based on true-or-false comparisons. An int variable can hold millions of different values at different times, but a **Boolean variable** can hold only one of two values—true or false. You declare a Boolean variable by using type **bool**. The following statements declare and assign appropriate values to two bool variables:

```
bool isItMonday = false;
bool areYouTired = true;
```

»NOTE If you begin a bool variable name with a form of the verb "to be" or "to do," such as "is" or "are," then you can more easily recognize the identifiers as Boolean variables when you encounter them within your programs.

»NOTE When you use "Boolean" as an adjective, as in "Boolean variable," you usually begin with an uppercase B because the data type is named for Sir George Boole, the founder of symbolic logic, who lived from 1815 to 1864. The C# data type bool, however, begins with a lowercase "b."

You also can assign values based on the result of comparisons to Boolean variables. A **comparison operator** compares two items; an expression containing a comparison operator has a Boolean value. Table 2-4 describes the six comparison operators that C# supports.

Operator	Description	`true` Example	`false` Example
<	Less than	3 < 8	8 < 3
>	Greater than	4 > 2	2 > 4
==	Equal to	7 == 7	3 == 9
<=	Less than or equal to	5 <=5	8 <= 6
>=	Greater than or equal to	7 >= 3	1 >= 2
!=	Not equal to	5 != 6	3 != 3

Table 2-4 Comparison operators

When you use any of the operators that require two keystrokes (==, <=, >=, or !=), you cannot place any whitespace between the two symbols.

Legal (but somewhat useless) declaration statements might include the following, which compare two values directly:

```
bool isSixBigger = 6 > 5;  // Value stored would be true
bool isSevenSmallerOrEqual = 7 <= 4;
   // Value stored would be false
```

Using Boolean values is more meaningful when you use variables (that have been assigned values) rather than constants in the comparisons, as in the following examples:

```
bool doesEmployeeReceiveOvertime = hoursWorked > 40;
bool isEmployeeInHighTaxBracket = annualIncome > 100000;
```

» NOTE
Boolean variables become more useful after you learn to make decisions within C# programs. You learn about decision making in Chapter 3.

In the first statement, the `hoursWorked` variable is compared to a constant value of 40. If the `hoursWorked` variable holds a value less than or equal to 40, then the expression is evaluated as false. In the second statement, the `annualIncome` variable value must be greater than 100000 for the expression to be true.

» NOTE When you display a `bool` variable's value with `Console.WriteLine()`, the displayed value is `True` or `False`. However, the values within your programs are `true` and `false`.

» TWO TRUTHS AND A LIE: USING THE `bool` DATA TYPE

1. If `rate` is 7.5 and `min` is 7, then the value of `rate >= min` is false.
2. If `rate` is 7.5 and `min` is 7, then the value of `rate < min` is false.
3. If `rate` is 7.5 and `min` is 7, then the value of `rate == min` is false.

The false statement is #1. If `rate` is 7.5 and `min` is 7, then the value of `rate >= min` is true.

UNDERSTANDING NUMERIC TYPE CONVERSION

When you perform arithmetic with variables or constants of the same type, the result of the arithmetic retains the same type. For example, when you divide two `int`s, the result is an `int`; when you subtract two `double`s, the result is a `double`. Often, however, you need to perform mathematical operations on different types. For example, in the following code, you multiply an `int` by a `double`:

```
int hoursWorked = 36;
double payRate = 12.35;
double grossPay = hoursWorked * payRate;
```

When you perform arithmetic operations with operands of dissimilar types, C# chooses a **unifying type** for the result and **implicitly** (or automatically) converts nonconforming operands to the unifying type, which is the type with the higher **type precedence**. The conversion is called an **implicit cast**—the automatic transformation that occurs when a value is assigned to a type with higher precedence.

For example, if you multiply an `int` and a `double`, the result is implicitly a `double`. This requirement means the result must be stored in a `double`; if you attempt to assign the result to an `int`, you will receive a compiler error message like the one shown in Figure 2-10.

Figure 2-10 Error message received when trying to compile a program that attempts to store a `double` in an `int`

The implicit numeric conversions are:

» From `sbyte` to `short`, `int`, `long`, `float`, `double`, or `decimal`
» From `byte` to `short`, `ushort`, `int`, `uint`, `long`, `ulong`, `float`, `double`, or `decimal`
» From `short` to `int`, `long`, `float`, `double`, or `decimal`
» From `ushort` to `int`, `uint`, `long`, `ulong`, `float`, `double`, or `decimal`
» From `int` to `long`, `float`, `double`, or `decimal`
» From `uint` to `long`, `ulong`, `float`, `double`, or `decimal`
» From `long` to `float`, `double`, or `decimal`
» From `ulong` to `float`, `double`, or `decimal`
» From `char` to `ushort`, `int`, `uint`, `long`, `ulong`, `float`, `double`, or `decimal`
» From `float` to `double`

> **NOTE** Implicit conversions are not always the result of arithmetic calculations; simple assignments often result in implicit conversions. For example, if `money` is declared as a `double`, then the following statement implicitly converts the integer 15 to a `double`:
>
> ```
> money = 15;
> ```

> **NOTE** A constant expression of type `int`, such as 25, can be converted to `sbyte`, `byte`, `short`, `ushort`, `uint`, or `ulong`. For example, `sbyte age = 19;` is legal. However, you must make sure that the value of the constant expression is within the range of the destination type, or the program will not compile.

> **NOTE** Conversions from `int`, `uint`, or `long` to `float` and from `long` to `double` may cause a loss of precision, but will never cause a loss of magnitude.

The error message in Figure 2-10 asks "are you missing a cast?" You may **explicitly** (or purposefully) override the unifying type imposed by C# by performing an explicit cast. An **explicit cast** involves placing the desired result type in parentheses followed by the variable or constant to be cast. For example, two explicit casts are performed in the following code:

```
double bankBalance = 189.66;
float weeklyBudget = (float) bankBalance / 4;
        // weeklyBudget is 47.415, one-fourth of bankBalance
int dollars = (int) weeklyBudget;
        // dollars is 47, the integer part of weeklyBudget
```

The value of `bankBalance / 4` is implicitly a `double` because a `double` divided by an `int` produces a `double`. The `double` result is then converted to a `float` before it is stored in `weeklyBudget`, and the `float` value `weeklyBudget` is converted to an `int` before it is stored in `dollars`. When the `float` value is converted to an `int`, the decimal-place values are lost.

> **NOTE** It is easy to lose data when performing a cast. For example, the largest `byte` value is 255, and the largest `int` value is 2,147,483,647, so the following statements produce distorted results:
>
> ```
> int anOkayInt = 345;
> byte aBadByte = (byte)anOkayInt;
> ```

> **NOTE** If you attempt to store 256 in a `byte`, you will receive an error message unless you place the statement in a section of code preceded by the keyword `unchecked`, which tells the compiler not to check for invalid data. If you use the unchecked mode and store 256 in a byte, the results will look the same as storing 0; if you store 257, the result will appear as 1. You will see 89 when you store 345 in a `byte` variable and display the results, because the value 89 is exactly 256 less than 345.

T T F

» TWO TRUTHS AND A LIE: UNDERSTANDING NUMERIC TYPE CONVERSION

1. If `deptNum` is an `int` with a value of 10, then `double answer = deptNum` is a valid statement.
2. If `deptNum` is an `int` with a value of 10, and `answer` is a `double` with a value of 4, then `deptNum = answer` is a valid statement.
3. If `deptNum` is an `int` with a value of 10, and `answer` is a `double` with a value of 4, then `double answer = (int)value` is a valid statement.

The false statement is #2. If `deptNum` is an `int` with a value of 10, and `answer` is a `double` with a value of 4, then `deptNum = answer` is invalid because a `double` cannot be implicitly converted to an `int`.

USING THE char DATA TYPE

You use the **char** data type to hold any single character. You place constant character values within single quotation marks because the computer stores characters and integers differently. For example, the following statements are both legal:

```
char aCharValue = '9';
int aNumValue = 9;
```

However, the following statements are both illegal:

```
char aCharValue = 9;
int aNumValue = '9';
```

A number can be a character, in which case it must be enclosed in single quotation marks and declared as a char type. An alphabetic letter, however, cannot be stored in a numeric type variable. The following code shows how you can store several characters using the char data type:

```
char myInitial = 'J';
char percentSign = '%';
char numThatIsAChar = '9';
```

> **» NOTE** A variable of type char can hold only one character. To store a string of characters, such as a person's name, you must use a string. You will learn about strings later in this chapter.

You can store any character—including nonprinting characters such as a backspace or a tab—in a char variable. To store these characters, you use two symbols in an **escape sequence**, which always begins with a backslash. The pair of symbols represents a single character. For example, the following code stores a backspace character and a tab character in the char variables aBackspaceChar and aTabChar, respectively:

```
char aBackspaceChar = '\b';
char aTabChar = '\t';
```

In the preceding code, the escape sequence indicates a unique value for each character—a backspace or tab instead of the letter *b* or *t*. Table 2-5 describes some common escape sequences that are used in C#.

The characters used in C# are represented in **Unicode**, which is a 16-bit coding scheme for characters. For example, the letter *A* actually is stored in computer memory as a set of 16 zeros and ones—namely, 0000 0000 0100 0001. (The spaces are inserted here after every set of four digits for readability.) Because 16-bit numbers are difficult to read, programmers often use a shorthand notation called **hexadecimal**, or **base 16**. In hexadecimal shorthand, 0000 becomes 0, 0100 becomes 4, and 0001 becomes 1. Thus, the letter *A* is represented in hexadecimal as 0041. You tell the compiler to treat the four-digit hexadecimal 0041 as a single

Escape Sequence	Character Name
\'	Single quotation mark
\"	Double quotation mark
\\	Backslash
\0	Null
\a	Alert
\b	Backspace
\f	Form feed
\n	Newline
\r	Carriage return
\t	Horizontal tab
\v	Vertical tab

Table 2-5 Common escape sequences

character by preceding it with the \u escape sequence. Therefore, there are two ways to store the character *A*:

```
char letter = 'A';
char letter = '\u0041';
```

» NOTE
For more information about Unicode, go to *www.unicode.org*.

The second option, using hexadecimal, obviously is more difficult and confusing than the first option, so it is not recommended that you store letters of the alphabet using the hexadecimal method. However, you can produce some interesting values using the Unicode format, and so you should know how to use it. For example, letters from foreign alphabets that use characters instead of letters (Greek, Hebrew, Chinese, and so on) and other special symbols (foreign currency symbols, mathematical symbols, geometric shapes, and so on) are not available on a standard keyboard, but they are available in Unicode.

»TWO TRUTHS AND A LIE: USING THE char DATA TYPE

1. The following statement is legal in C#:
   ```
   char department = '5';
   ```
2. The following statement is legal in C#:
   ```
   char department = '\f';
   ```
3. The following statement is legal in C#:
   ```
   char department = '32';
   ```

The false statement is #3. Only a single character can appear between single quotes, with the exception of escape sequence characters such as '\f' and '\f'. In these cases, a single character is created using two symbols.

USING THE `string` DATA TYPE

In C#, you use the **string** data type to hold a series of characters. The value of a `string` is always expressed within double quotation marks. For example, the following statement declares a `string` named `firstName` and assigns "Jane" to it:

```
string firstName = "Jane";
```

When you assign a literal (such as "Jane") to a `string`, you can compare the `string` to another `string` using the == and != operators in the same ways that you compare numeric or character variables. For example, the program in Figure 2-11 declares three `string` variables. Figure 2-12 shows the results: `strings` that contain "Amy" and "Amy" are considered equal, but `strings` that contain "Amy" and "Matthew" are not.

```csharp
using System;
public class CompareNames1
{
    public static void Main()
    {
        string name1 = "Amy";
        string name2 = "Amy";
        string name3 = "Matthew";
        Console.WriteLine("compare {0} to {1}: {2}",
            name1, name2, name1 == name2);
        Console.WriteLine("compare {0} to {1}: {2}",
            name1, name3, name1 == name3);
    }
}
```

Figure 2-11 Program that compares two strings using == operator (not recommended)

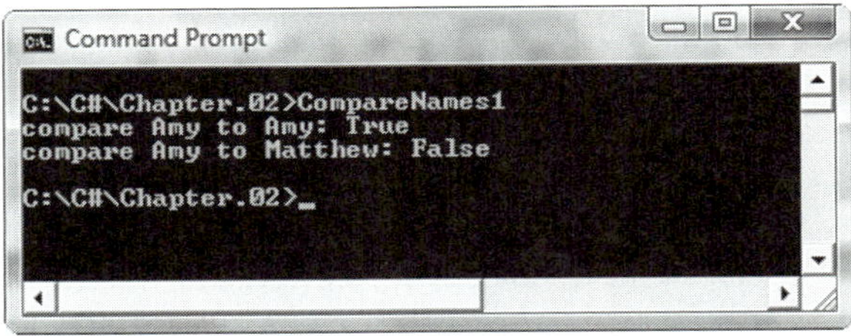

Figure 2-12 Output of `CompareNames1` program

Later in this chapter, you learn how to allow a user to enter data into a program from the keyboard.

Besides the == comparison operator, you can use several prewritten methods to compare `strings`. The advantage to using these other methods is that other classes you eventually will create use methods with the same names to compare their objects.

You can compare `strings` with any of the following methods: `Equals()`, `Compare()`, and `CompareTo()`.

The `String` class **Equals()** method requires two `string` arguments that you place within its parentheses, separated by a comma. As when you use the `==` operator, the `Equals()` method returns true or false.

The **Compare()** method also requires two `string` arguments, but it returns an integer. When it returns 0, the two `strings` are equivalent; when it returns a positive number, the first `string` is greater than the second; and when it returns a negative value, the first `string` is less than the second. A `string` is considered equal to, greater than, or less than another string **lexically**, which in the case of letter values means alphabetically. That is, when you compare two `strings`, you compare each character in turn from left to right. If each Unicode value is the same, then the strings are equivalent. If any corresponding character values are different, the `string` that has the greater Unicode value earlier in the string is considered greater.

The **CompareTo()** method uses a `string`, a dot, and the method name. The `string` to compare to is placed within parentheses. Like the `Compare()` method, it returns a 0 when the compared `strings` are equal, a negative number if the first `string` is less, and a positive number if the second `string` (the one in parentheses) is less. Figure 2-13 shows a program

```
using System;
public class CompareTwoNames
{
    public static void Main()
    {
        string name1 = "Amy";
        string name2 = "Amy";
        string name3 = "Matthew";
        Console.WriteLine("Using Equals() method");
        Console.WriteLine("   compare {0} to {1}: {2}",
            name1, name2, String.Equals(name1, name2));
        Console.WriteLine("   compare {0} to {1}: {2}",
            name1, name3, String.Equals(name1, name3));
        Console.WriteLine("Using Compare() method");
        Console.WriteLine("   compare {0} to {1}: {2}",
            name1, name2, String.Compare(name1, name2));
        Console.WriteLine("   compare {0} to {1}: {2}",
            name1, name3, String.CompareTo(name1, name3));
        Console.WriteLine("Using CompareTo() method");
        Console.WriteLine("   compare {0} to {1}: {2}",
            name1, name2, name1.CompareTo(name2));
        Console.WriteLine("   compare {0} to {1}: {2}",
            name1, name3, name1.CompareTo(name3));
    }
}
```

Figure 2-13 Program that compares two strings using three methods

that makes several comparisons using the three methods; in each case the method name is shaded. Figure 2-14 shows the program's output.

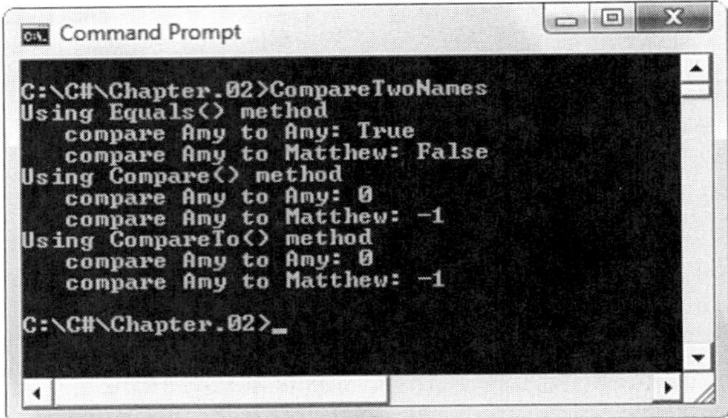

Figure 2-14 Output of `CompareTwoNames` program

>> **NOTE** The `Equals()`, `Compare()`, and `CompareTo()` methods are case sensitive. In other words, "Amy" does not equal "amy". In Unicode, the decimal value of each uppercase letter is exactly 32 less than its lowercase equivalent. For example, the decimal value of a Unicode 'a' is 97 and the value of 'A' is 65.

>> **NOTE** In C#, a string is **immutable**. That is, a string's value is not actually modified when you assign a new value to it. For example, when you write `name = "Amy";` followed by `name = "Donald";`, the first literal string of characters "Amy" still exists in computer memory, but the `name` variable no longer refers to the string's memory address. The situation is different than with numbers; when you assign a new value to a numeric variable, the value at the named memory address actually changes.

>> **NOTE** In Chapter 7, you will learn how to write your own `CompareTo()` methods for classes you create.

>> **NOTE** Another useful string method is **`StartsWith()`**. In the `CompareTwoNames` program, the expression `name3.StartsWith("Ma")` would be true.

>>TWO TRUTHS AND A LIE: USING THE string DATA TYPE

1. If `creature1 = "dog"` and `creature2 = "cat"`, then the value of `String.Equals(creature1, creature2)` is false.

2. If `creature1 = "dog"` and `creature2 = "cat"`, then the value of `String.Compare(creature1, creature2)` is false.

3. If `creature1 = "dog"` and `creature2 = "cat"`, then the value of `creature1.CompareTo(creature2)` is a positive number.

The false statement is #2. If `creature1 = "dog"` and `creature2 = "cat"`, then the value of `String.Compare(creature1, creature2)` is a positive number.

DEFINING NAMED CONSTANTS

By definition, a variable's value can vary, or change. Sometimes you want to create a **named constant** (often called simply a constant), an identifier for a memory location whose contents cannot change. You create a named constant similarly to the way you create a named variable, but by using the keyword `const`. Although there is no requirement to do so, programmers usually name constants using all uppercase letters, inserting underscores for readability. This convention makes constant names stand out so that the reader is less likely to confuse them with changeable variable names. For example, the following declares a constant named `TAX_RATE` that is assigned a value of 0.06:

```
const double TAX_RATE = 0.06;
```

You must assign a value to a constant when you create it. You can use a constant just as you would use a variable of the same type—for example, display it or use it in a mathematical equation—but you cannot assign any new value to it. Figure 2-15 shows a program that uses a `TAX_RATE` constant to calculate the tax on two different-priced items. Figure 2-16 shows the output.

```
using System;
public class SalesTax
{
   public static void Main()
   {
      const double TAX_RATE = .06;
      double itemPrice = 3.99;
      double tax;
      tax = itemPrice * TAX_RATE;
      Console.WriteLine("With {0} tax, a {1} item costs {2} more",
         TAX_RATE, itemPrice.ToString("C"), tax.ToString("C"));
      itemPrice = 145.65;
      tax = itemPrice * TAX_RATE;
      Console.WriteLine("With {0} tax, a {1} item costs {2} more",
         TAX_RATE, itemPrice.ToString("C"), tax.ToString("C"));
   }
}
```

Figure 2-15 `SalesTax` program

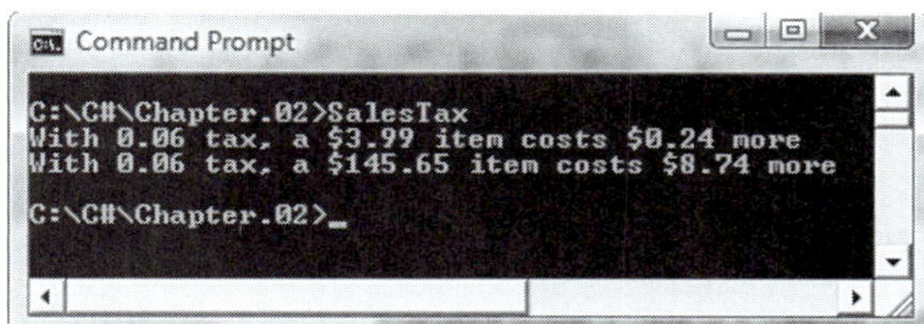

Figure 2-16 Output of `SalesTax` program

It's good programming practice to declare constants for any value that should never change; doing so makes your programs clearer. For example, when you declare a constant `const int INCHES_IN_A_FOOT = 12;` within a program, then you can use a statement such as the following:

```
lengthInInches = lengthInFeet * INCHES_IN_A_FOOT;
```

This statement is **self-documenting**; that is, even without a program comment, it is easy for someone reading your program to tell why you performed the calculation in the way you did.

»TWO TRUTHS AND A LIE: DEFINING NAMED CONSTANTS

1. The following is a valid C# constant:

    ```
    const string FIRST_HEADING = "Progress Report";
    ```
2. The following is a valid C# constant:

    ```
    const int maximumDays = 7;
    ```
3. The following is a valid C# constant:

    ```
    const double COMMISSION_RATE;
    ```

The false answer is #3. A constant must be assigned a value when it is declared. Answer #2 is legal, but not conventional because constants generally are declared using all uppercase characters.

ACCEPTING CONSOLE INPUT

When you write a program in which you assign values to variables and then manipulate those values, the output of the program is always the same. For example, no matter how many times you execute the `SalesTax` program in Figure 2-15, the two tax values are always calculated as $0.24 and $8.74. A more useful program would allow a user to input any price for which the tax could be calculated. A program that allows user input is an **interactive program**.

You can use the **`Console.ReadLine()`** method to accept user input from the keyboard. This method accepts all of the characters entered by a user until the user presses Enter. The characters can be assigned to a `string`. For example, the following statement accepts a user's input and stores it in the variable `myString`:

```
myString = Console.ReadLine();
```

If you want to use the data as a `string`—for example, if the input is a word or a name—then you simply use the variable to which you assigned the value. If you want to use the data as a number, then you must use a `Convert()` method to convert the input `string` to the proper type.

> **»NOTE** The `Console.Read()` method is similar to the `Console.ReadLine()` method. `Console.Read()` reads just one character from the input stream, whereas `Console.ReadLine()` reads every character in the input stream until the user presses the Enter key.

Figure 2-17 shows an interactive program that prompts the user for a price and calculates a 6 percent sales tax. The program displays "Enter the price of an item" on the screen. Such an instruction to the user to enter data is called a **prompt**. After the prompt appears, the `Console.ReadLine()` statement accepts a string of characters and assigns them to the variable `itemPriceAsString`. Before the tax can be calculated, this value must be converted to a number. This conversion is accomplished in the shaded statement. Figure 2-18 shows a typical execution of the program in which the user typed 28.77 as the input value.

```
using System;
public class InteractiveSalesTax
{
    public static void Main()
    {
        const double TAX_RATE = 0.06;
        string itemPriceAsString;
        double itemPrice;
        double total;
        Console.WriteLine("Enter the price of an item");
        itemPriceAsString = Console.ReadLine();
        itemPrice = Convert.ToDouble(itemPriceAsString);
        total = itemPrice * TAX_RATE;
        Console.WriteLine("With a tax rate of {0}, a {1} item " +
            "costs {2} more.", TAX_RATE, itemPrice.ToString("C"),
            total.ToString("C"));
    }
}
```

Figure 2-17 `InteractiveSalesTax` program

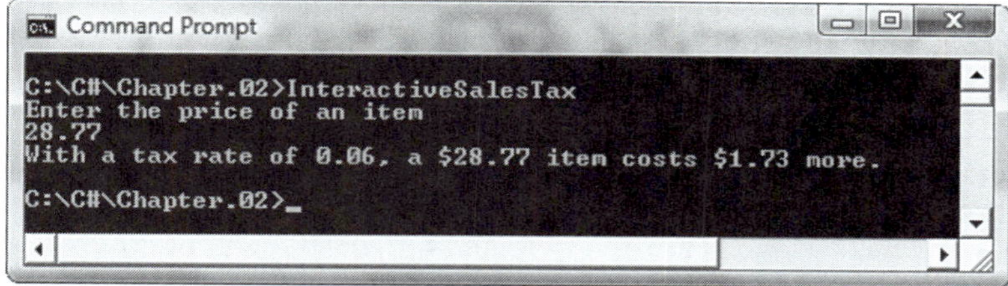

Figure 2-18 Typical execution of `InteractiveSalesTax` program

As a shortcut, you can avoid declaring and using the `string itemPriceAsString` in the program in Figure 2-17. Instead, you can accept and convert the input string in one step, as in the following:

```
itemPrice = Convert.ToDouble(Console.ReadLine());
```

Table 2-6 shows `Convert` class methods you can use to change `strings` into more useful data types. The methods use the class types (also called run-time types) in their names. For example, recall from Table 2-1 that the "formal" name for an `int` is `Int32`, so the method you use to convert a `string` to an `int` is named `Convert.ToInt32()`.

Method	Description
`ToBoolean()`	Converts a specified value to an equivalent Boolean value
`ToByte()`	Converts a specified value to an 8-bit unsigned integer
`ToChar()`	Converts a specified value to a Unicode character
`ToDecimal()`	Converts a specified value to a decimal number
`ToDouble()`	Converts a specified value to a double-precision floating-point number
`ToInt16()`	Converts a specified value to a 16-bit signed integer
`ToInt32()`	Converts a specified value to a 32-bit signed integer
`ToInt64()`	Converts a specified value to a 64-bit signed integer
`ToSByte()`	Converts a specified value to an 8-bit signed integer
`ToSingle()`	Converts a specified value to a single-precision floating-point number
`ToString()`	Converts the specified value to its equivalent `String` representation
`ToUInt16()`	Converts a specified value to a 16-bit unsigned integer
`ToUInt32()`	Converts a specified value to a 32-bit unsigned integer
`ToUInt64()`	Converts a specified value to a 64-bit unsigned integer

Table 2-6 Selected `Convert` class methods

»TWO TRUTHS AND A LIE: ACCEPTING CONSOLE INPUT

1. The following is valid:

```
int age = Convert.ToInt(Console.ReadLine());
```

2. The following is valid:

```
double payRate = Convert.ToDouble(Console.ReadLine());
```

3. The following is valid:

```
char middleInitial = Convert.ToChar(Console.ReadLine());
```

The false statement is #1. The method to convert a string to an integer is `ToInt32()`, not `ToInt()`.

YOU DO IT
DECLARING AND USING VARIABLES

In the following steps, you will write a program that declares several integral variables, assigns values to them, and displays the results.

To write a program with integral variables:

1. Open a new file in the text editor you are using to write your C# programs. Create the beginning of a program that will demonstrate variable use. Use the `System` namespace, name the class **DemoVariables**, and type the class-opening curly brace.

```
using System;
public class DemoVariables
{
```

2. In the `Main()` method, declare two variables (an integer and an unsigned integer) and assign values to them.

```
public static void Main()
{
    int anInt = -123;
    uint anUnsignedInt = 567;
```

3. Add a statement to display the two values.

```
Console.WriteLine("The int is {0} and the unsigned int
    is {1}.", anInt, anUnsignedInt);
```

4. Add two closing curly braces—one that closes the `Main()` method, and one that closes the `DemoVariables` class. Align each closing curly brace vertically with the opening brace that is its partner. In other words, the first closing brace aligns with the brace that opens `Main()`, and the second aligns with the brace that opens `DemoVariables`.

5. Save the program as **DemoVariables.cs** and compile it. If you receive any error messages, correct the errors and compile the program again. When the file is error-free, execute the program. The output should look like Figure 2-19.

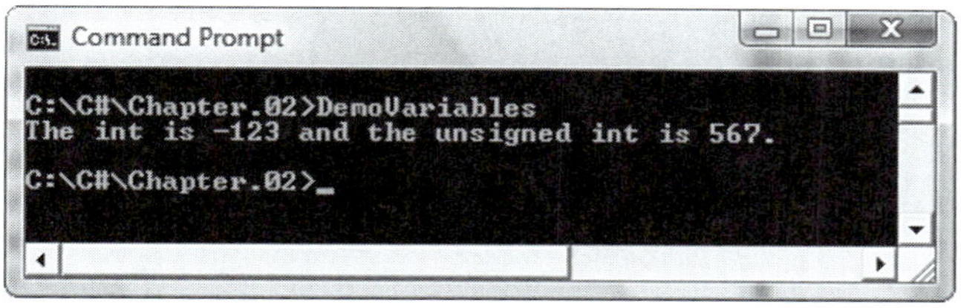

》NOTE

Recall from Chapter 1 that you can write C# programs in any editor with which you are comfortable.

Figure 2-19 Output of `DemoVariables` program

6. Experiment with the program by introducing invalid values for the named variables. For example, change the value of `anUnsignedInt` to **–567** by typing a minus sign in front of the constant value. Compile the program. You receive the following error message:

   Constant value '-567' cannot be converted to a 'uint'.

7. Correct the error either by removing the minus sign or by changing the data type of the variable to **int**, and compile the program again. You should not receive any error messages. Remember to save your program file after you make each change and before you compile.

8. Change the value of `anInt` from –123 to **–123456789000**. When you compile the program, the following error message appears:

   Cannot implicitly convert type 'long' to 'int'.

   The value is a `long` because it is greater than the highest allowed `int` value. Correct the error either by using a lower value or by changing the variable type to **long**, and compile the program again. You should not receive any error messages.

9. Experiment with other changes to the variables. Include some variables of type `short`, `ushort`, `byte`, and `sbyte`, and experiment with their values.

PERFORMING ARITHMETIC

In the following steps, you will add some arithmetic statements to a program.

To use arithmetic statements in a program:

1. Open a new C# program file and enter the following statements to start a program that demonstrates arithmetic operations:

```
using System;
public class DemoVariables2
{
    public static void Main()
    {
```

2. Write a statement that will declare seven integer variables. You will assign initial values to two of the variables; the values for the other five variables will be calculated. Because all of these variables are the same type, you can use a single statement to declare all seven integers. Recall that to do this, you insert commas between variable names and place a single semicolon at the end. You can place line breaks wherever you want for readability. (Alternatively, you could use as many as seven separate declarations.)

```
int value1 = 43, value2 = 10,
        sum, diff, product, quotient, remainder;
```

3. Write the arithmetic statements that calculate the sum of, difference between, product of, quotient of, and remainder of the two assigned variables.

```
sum = value1 + value2;
diff = value1 - value2;
product = value1 * value2;
quotient = value1 / value2;
remainder = value1 % value2;
```

> **NOTE** Instead of declaring the variables `sum`, `diff`, `product`, `quotient`, and `remainder` and assigning values later, you could declare and assign all of them at once, as in `int sum = value1 + value2;`. The only requirement is that `value1` and `value2` must be assigned values before you can use them in a calculation.

4. Include five `WriteLine()` statements to display the results.

```
Console.WriteLine("The sum of {0} and {1} is {2}",
    value1, value2, sum);
Console.WriteLine("The difference between {0} and {1}" +
    " is {2}", value1, value2, diff);
Console.WriteLine("The product of {0} and {1} is {2}",
    value1, value2, product);
Console.WriteLine("{0} divided by {1} is {2}", value1,
    value2, quotient);
Console.WriteLine("and the remainder is {0}", remainder);
```

5. Add two closing curly braces—one for the `Main()` method and the other for the `DemoVariables2` class.

6. Save the file as **DemoVariables2.cs**. Compile and execute the program. The output should look like Figure 2-20.

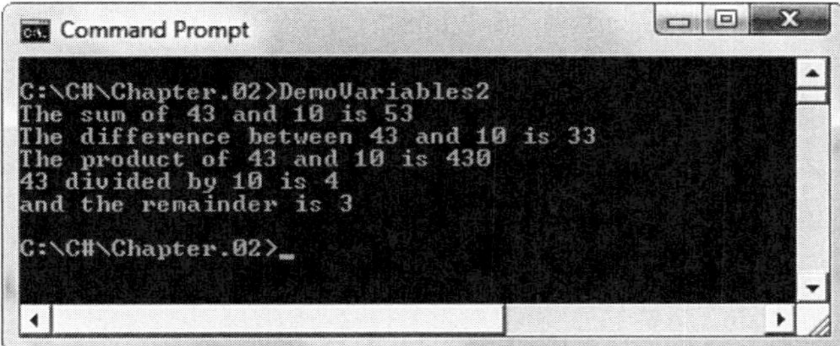

Figure 2-20 Output of `DemoVariables2` program

7. Change the values of the `value1` and `value2` variables, save the program, and compile and run it again. Repeat this process several times. After each execution, analyze the output to make sure you understand the results of the arithmetic operations.

WORKING WITH BOOLEAN VARIABLES

Next, you will write a program that demonstrates how Boolean variables operate.

To write a program that uses Boolean variables:

1. Open a new file in your editor and enter the following code. In the `Main()` method, you declare an integer value, then assign different values to a Boolean variable. Notice that when you declare `value` and `isSixMore`, you assign types. When you reassign values to

these variables later in the program, you do not redeclare them by using a type name. Instead, you simply assign new values to the already declared variables.

```csharp
using System;
public class DemoVariables3
{
    public static void Main()
    {
        int value = 4;
        bool isSixMore = 6 > value;
        Console.WriteLine("When value is {0} isSixMore is {1}",
            value, isSixMore);
        value = 35;
        isSixMore = 6 > value;
        Console.WriteLine("When value is {0} isSixMore is {1}",
            value, isSixMore);
    }
}
```

2. Save the program as **DemoVariables3.cs**. Compile and run the program. The output looks like Figure 2-21.

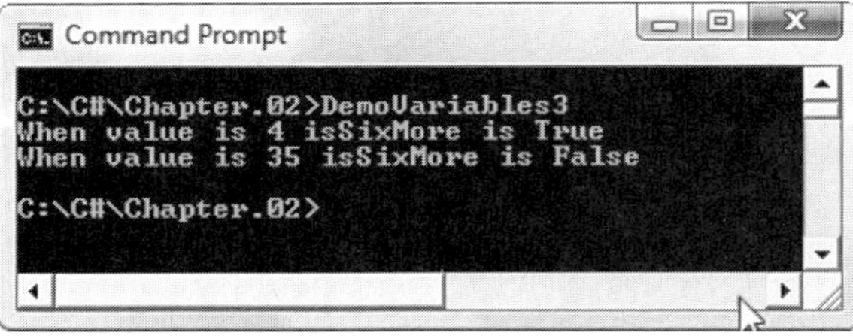

Figure 2-21 Output of `DemoVariables3` program

3. Change the value of the variable named `value` and try to predict the outcome. Run the program to confirm your prediction.

USING ESCAPE SEQUENCES

Next, you will write a short program to demonstrate the use of escape sequences.

To write a program using escape sequences:

1. Open a new file in your text editor and name it **DemoEscapeSequences**.

2. Enter the following code. The three `WriteLine()` statements demonstrate using escape sequences for tabs, a newline, and alerts.

```csharp
using System;
public class DemoEscapeSequences
{
    public static void Main()
    {
```

```
      Console.WriteLine("This line\tcontains two\ttabs");
      Console.WriteLine("This statement\ncontains a new line");
      Console.WriteLine("This statement sounds " +
         "three alerts\a\a\a");
   }
}
```

3. Save the program as **DemoEscapeSequences.cs**. Compile and test the program. Your output should look like Figure 2-22. Additionally, if your system has speakers and they are on, you should hear three "beep" sounds caused by the three alert characters: '\a'.

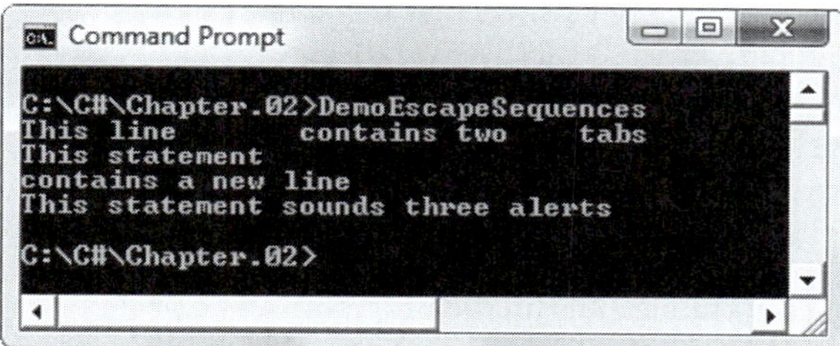

Figure 2-22 Output of DemoEscapeSequences program

WRITING A PROGRAM THAT ACCEPTS USER INPUT

In the next steps, you will write an interactive program that allows the user to enter two integer values. The program then calculates and displays their sum.

To write the interactive addition program:

1. Open a new file in your editor. Type the first few lines needed for the Main() method of an InteractiveAddition class.

```
using System;
public class InteractiveAddition
{
   public static void Main()
   {
```

2. Add variable declarations for two strings that will accept the user's input values. Also, declare three integers for the numeric equivalents of the string input values and their sum.

```
string name, firstString, secondString;
int first, second, sum;
```

3. Prompt the user for his or her name, accept it into the name string, and then display a personalized greeting to the user, along with the prompt for the first integer value.

```
Console.WriteLine("Enter your name");
name = Console.ReadLine();
Console.WriteLine("Hello {0}! Enter the first integer", name);
```

4. Accept the user's input as a `string`, and then convert the input `string` to an integer.

```
firstString = Console.ReadLine();
first = Convert.ToInt32(firstString);
```

5. Add statements that prompt for and accept the second `string` and convert it to an integer.

```
Console.WriteLine("Enter the second integer");
secondString = Console.ReadLine();
second = Convert.ToInt32(secondString);
```

6. Assign the sum of the two integers to the `sum` variable and display all of the values. Add the closing curly brace for the `Main()` method and the closing curly brace for the class.

```
        sum = first + second;
        Console.WriteLine("{0}, the sum of {1} and {2} is {3}",
            name, first, second, sum);
    }
}
```

7. Save the file as **InteractiveAddition.cs**. Compile and run the program. When prompted, supply your name and any integers you want, and confirm that the result appears correctly. Figure 2-23 shows a typical run of the program.

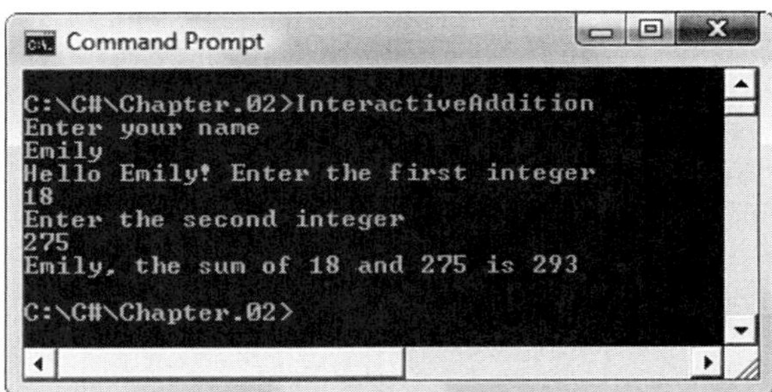

Figure 2-23 Typical execution of `InteractiveAddition` program

CHAPTER SUMMARY

» Data is constant when it cannot be changed after a program is compiled; data is variable when it might change. C# provides for 14 basic built-in types of data. A variable declaration includes a data type, an identifier, an optional assigned value, and a semicolon.

» You can display variable values by using the variable name within a `WriteLine()` or `Write()` method call. To make producing output easier, you can combine strings and variable values into a single `Write()` or `WriteLine()` statement by using a format string.

» In C#, nine data types are considered integral data types—`byte`, `sbyte`, `short`, `ushort`, `int`, `uint`, `long`, `ulong`, and `char`.

» C# supports three floating-point data types: float, double, and decimal. You can perform the mathematical operations of addition, subtraction, multiplication, and division with floating-point data, but not modulus. You can use format and precision specifiers to display floating-point data to a specified number of decimal places.

» You use the binary arithmetic operators +, -, *, /, and % to manipulate values in your programs. When you combine mathematical operations in a single statement, you must understand operator precedence, or the order in which parts of a mathematical expression are evaluated. Multiplication, division, and remainder always take place prior to addition or subtraction in an expression, unless you use parentheses to override the normal precedence.

» Because altering the value of a variable is a common task, C# provides you with several shortcut arithmetic operators. They include the binary operators +=, -=, *=, /=, and the unary prefix and postfix increment (++) and decrement (--) operators.

» A bool variable can hold only one of two values—true or false. C# supports six comparison operators: >, <, >=, <=, ==, and !=. An expression containing a comparison operator has a Boolean value.

» When you perform arithmetic with variables or constants of the same type, the result of the arithmetic retains the same type. When you perform arithmetic operations with operands of different types, C# chooses a unifying type for the result and implicitly converts nonconforming operands to the unifying type. You may explicitly override the unifying type imposed by C# by performing a cast.

» You use the char data type to hold any single character. You place constant character values within single quotation marks. You can store any character—including nonprinting characters such as a backspace or a tab—in a char variable. To store these characters, you must use an escape sequence, which always begins with a backslash.

» In C#, you use the string data type to hold a series of characters. The value of a string is always expressed within double quotation marks. Although the == and != comparison operators can be used with strings that are assigned literal values, you also can use the Equals(), Compare(), and CompareTo() methods that belong to the String class.

» Named constants are program identifiers you cannot change.

» You can use the Console.ReadLine() method to accept user input. Often you must use a Convert class method to change the input string into a usable data type.

KEY TERMS

A data item is **constant** when it cannot be changed after a program is compiled—in other words, when it cannot vary.

A **literal constant** is a value that is taken literally at each use.

A **variable** is a named location in computer memory that can hold different values at different points in time.

A **data type** describes the format and size of a data item.

Intrinsic types of data are basic types; C# provides 14 intrinsic types.

An **alias** is another name for something.

A **variable declaration** is the statement that names a variable; it includes the data type that the variable will store, an identifier that is the variable's name, an optional assignment operator and assigned value when you want a variable to contain an initial value, and an ending semicolon.

The **assignment operator** is the equal sign (=); any value to the right of the assignment operator is assigned to, or taken on by, the variable to the left.

An **initialization** is an assignment made when a variable is declared.

An **assignment** is a statement that provides a variable with a value.

A **format string** is a string of characters that contains one or more placeholders for variable values.

A **placeholder** in a format string consists of a pair of curly braces containing a number that indicates the desired variable's position in a list that follows the string.

To **concatenate** strings is to join them together in a chain.

Integral data types are those that store whole numbers.

The nine integral types are `byte`, `sbyte`, `short`, `ushort`, `int`, `uint`, `long`, `ulong`, and `char`. The first eight always represent whole numbers, and the ninth type, `char`, is used for characters like 'A' or 'a'.

Integers are whole numbers.

A **floating-point** number is one that contains decimal positions.

A `float` data type can hold a floating-point number with as many as seven significant digits of accuracy.

A `double` data type can hold a floating-point number with 15 or 16 significant digits of accuracy.

A value's number of **significant digits** specifies the mathematical accuracy of the value.

The `decimal` data type is a floating-point type that has a greater precision and a smaller range than a `float` or `double`, which makes it suitable for financial and monetary calculations.

Values expressed in **scientific notation** include an *E* (for exponent).

Standard numeric format strings are strings of characters expressed within double quotation marks that indicate a format for output.

The **format specifier** in a format string can be one of nine built-in format characters that define the most commonly used numeric format types.

The **precision specifier** in a format string controls the number of significant digits or zeros to the right of the decimal point.

A **culture** is a set of rules that determines how culturally dependent values such as money and dates are formatted.

Binary operators use two arguments—one value to the left of the operator and another value to the right of it.

Operands are the values that operators use in expressions.

Operator precedence determines the order in which parts of a mathematical expression are evaluated.

Operator precedence is also called **order of operation**.

Associativity specifies the order in which a sequence of operations with the same precedence are evaluated.

The **add and assign operator** (+=) adds the operand on the right to the operand on the left and assigns it to the operand on the left in one step.

The **prefix increment operator** (++ before a variable) increases the variable's value by 1 and then evaluates it.

The **postfix increment operator** (++ after a variable) evaluates a variable and then adds 1 to it.

Unary operators are operators used with one operand.

The **decrement operator** (--) reduces a variable's value by 1. There is a prefix and a postfix version.

A **Boolean variable** can hold only one of two values—true or false.

The `bool` data type holds a Boolean value.

A **comparison operator** compares two items; an expression containing a comparison operator has a Boolean value.

A **unifying type** is the type chosen for an arithmetic result when operands are of dissimilar types.

Implicitly means automatically.

Type precedence is a hierarchy of data types used to determine the unifying type in arithmetic expressions containing dissimilar data types.

An **implicit cast** is the automatic transformation that occurs when a value is assigned to a type with higher precedence.

Explicitly means purposefully.

An **explicit cast** purposefully assigns a value to a different data type; it involves placing the desired result type in parentheses followed by the variable or constant to be cast.

The `char` data type can hold any single character.

An **escape sequence** is two symbols beginning with a backslash that represent a nonprinting character such as a tab.

Unicode is a 16-bit coding scheme for characters.

Hexadecimal, or **base 16**, is a mathematical system that uses 16 symbols to represent numbers.

The **string** data type is used to hold a series of characters.

The String class **Equals()** method determines if two strings have the same value; it requires two string arguments that you place within its parentheses, separated by a comma.

The **Compare()** method requires two string arguments. When it returns 0, the two strings are equivalent; when it returns a positive number, the first string is greater than the second; and when it returns a negative value, the first string is less than the second.

Lexically means alphabetically.

The **CompareTo()** method uses a string, a dot, and the method name. When it returns 0, the two strings are equivalent; when it returns a positive number, the first string is greater than the second; and when it returns a negative value, the first string is less than the second.

In C#, a string is **immutable**, or unchangeable. That is, a string's value is not actually modified when you assign a new value to it; instead, the string refers to a new memory location.

The **StartsWith()** method is used with a string and a dot, and its parentheses contain another string. It returns true if the first string starts with the characters contained in the second string.

A **named constant** (often called simply a constant) is an identifier whose contents cannot change.

A **self-documenting** program element is one that is self-explanatory.

An **interactive program** is one that allows user input.

The **Console.ReadLine()** method accepts user input from the keyboard.

A **prompt** is an instruction to the user to enter data.

REVIEW QUESTIONS

1. When you use a number such as 45 in a C# program, the number is a _________ .

   a. literal constant   c. literal variable

   b. figurative constant   d. figurative variable

2. A variable declaration must contain all of the following *except* a(n) _________ .

   a. data type   c. assigned value

   b. identifier   d. ending semicolon

3. Which of the following is true of variable declarations?

   a. Two variables of the same type can be declared in the same statement.

   b. Two variables of different types can be declared in the same statement.

   c. Two variables of the same type must be declared in the same statement.

   d. Two variables of the same type cannot coexist in a program.

4. Assume you have two variables declared as `int var1 = 3;` and `int var2 = 8;`. Which of the following would display *838*?

   a. `Console.WriteLine("{0}{1}{2}", var1, var2);`

   b. `Console.WriteLine("{0}{1}{0}", var1, var2);`

   c. `Console.WriteLine("{0}{1}{2}", var2, var1);`

   d. `Console.WriteLine("{0}{1}{0}", var2, var1);`

5. Assume you have a variable declared as `int var1 = 3;`. Which of the following would display *X 3X*?

   a. `Console.WriteLine("X{0}X", var1);`

   b. `Console.WriteLine("X{0,2}X", var1);`

   c. `Console.WriteLine("X{2,0}X", var1);`

   d. `Console.WriteLine("X{0}{2}", var1);`

6. Assume you have a variable declared as `int var1 = 3;`. What is the value of `22 % var1`?

   a. 0

   b. 1

   c. 7

   d. 21

7. Assume you have a variable declared as `int var1 = 3;`. What is the value of `22 / var1`?

   a. 1

   b. 7

   c. 7.333

   d. 21

8. What is the value of the expression `4 + 2 * 3`?

   a. 0

   b. 10

   c. 18

   d. 36

9. Assume you have a variable declared as `int var1 = 3;`. If `var2 = ++var1`, what is the value of `var2`?

   a. 2

   b. 3

   c. 4

   d. 5

10. Assume you have a variable declared as `int var1 = 3;`. If `var2 = var1++`, what is the value of `var2`?

    a. 2

    b. 3

    c. 4

    d. 5

11. A variable that can hold the two values `true` and `false` is of type ________ .

    a. `int`

    b. `bool`

    c. `char`

    d. `double`

12. Which of the following is *not* a C# comparison operator?

    a. `=>`

    b. `!=`

    c. `==`

    d. `<`

13. What is the value of the expression `6 >= 7`?

    a. 0

    b. 1

    c. true

    d. false

14. Which of the following C# types *cannot* contain floating-point numbers?

    a. `float`

    b. `double`

    c. `decimal`

    d. `int`

15. Assume you have declared a variable as `double hourly = 13.00;`. What will the statement `Console.WriteLine(hourly);` display?

    a. 13

    b. 13.0

    c. 13.00

    d. 13.000000

16. Assume you have declared a variable as `double salary = 45000.00;`. Which of the following will display *$45,000*?

    a. `Console.WriteLine(salary.toString("f"));`

    b. `Console.WriteLine(salary.toString("c"));`

    c. `Console.WriteLine(salary);`

    d. two of these

17. When you perform arithmetic operations with operands of different types, such as adding an `int` and a `float`, ________ .

    a. C# chooses a unifying type for the result

    b. you must choose a unifying type for the result

    c. you must provide a cast

    d. you receive an error message

18. Unicode is ________ .

    a. an object-oriented language

    b. a subset of the C# language

    c. a 16-bit coding scheme

    d. another term for hexadecimal

19. Which of the following declares a variable that can hold the word *computer*?

    a. `string device = 'computer';`

    b. `string device = "computer";`

    c. `char device = 'computer';`

    d. `char device = "computer";`

20. Which of the following compares two string variables named `string1` and `string2` to determine if their contents are equal?

    a. `string1 = string2`

    b. `string1 == string2`

    c. `Equals.String(string1,string2)`

    d. Two of the above

EXERCISES

1. What is the numeric value of each of the following expressions, as evaluated by the C# programming language?

    a. 4 + 2 * 3

    b. 6 / 4 * 7

    c. 16 / 2 + 14 / 2

    d. 18 / 2

    e. 17 / 2

    f. 32 / 5

    g. 14 % 2

    h. 15 % 2

    i. 28 % 5

    j. 28 % 4 * 3 + 1

    k. (2 + 6) * 4

    l. 20 / (4 + 1)

2. What is the value of each of the following Boolean expressions?

    a. 5 > 2

    b. 6 <= 18

    c. 49 >= 49

    d. 2 == 3

    e. 2 + 6 == 7

    f. 3 + 7 <= 10

    g. 3 != 9

    h. 12 != 12

    i. –2 != 2

    j. 2 + 5 * 3 ==21

3. Are any of the following expressions illegal? For the legal expressions, what is the numeric value of each statement, as evaluated by the C# programming language?

    a. 2.2 * 1.4

    b. 6.78 – 2

    c. 24.0 / 6.0

    d. 7.0 % 3.0

    e. 9 % 2.0

4. Choose the best data type for each of the following, so that no memory storage is wasted. Give an example of a typical value that would be held by the variable and explain why you chose the type you did.

    a. your age

    b. the U.S. national debt

    c. your shoe size

    d. your middle initial

5. In this chapter you learned that although a `double` and a `decimal` both hold floating-point numbers, a `double` can hold a larger value. Write a C# program that declares two variables—a `double` and a `decimal`. Experiment by assigning the same constant value to

each variable so that the assignment to the `double` is legal but the assignment to the `decimal` is not. In other words, when you leave the `decimal` assignment statement in the program, an error message should be generated that indicates the value is outside the range of the type `decimal`, but when you comment out the `decimal` assignment, the program should compile correctly. Save the program as **DoubleDecimalTest.cs**.

6. Write a C# program that declares variables to represent the length and width of a room in feet. Assign appropriate values to the variables, such as `length = 15` and `width = 25`. Compute and display the floor space of the room in square feet (area = length * width). As output, do not display only a value; instead, display explanatory text with the value, such as *The floor space is 375 square feet*. Save the program as **Room.cs**.

7. Write a C# program that declares variables to represent the length and width of a room in feet and the price of carpeting *per square foot* in dollars and cents. Assign appropriate values to the variables. Compute and display, with explanatory text, the cost of carpeting the room. Save the program as **Carpet.cs**.

8. Write a program that declares variables to represent the length and width of a room in feet and the price of carpeting *per square yard* in dollars and cents. Assign the value 25 to the `length` variable and the value 42 to the `width` variable. Compute and display the cost of carpeting the room. (*Hint:* There are nine square feet in one square yard.) Save the program as **Yards.cs**.

9. Write a program that declares a `minutes` variable to represent minutes worked on a job, and assign a value to it. Display the value in hours and minutes. For example, 197 minutes becomes 3 hours and 17 minutes. Save the program as **HoursAndMinutes.cs**.

10. Write a program that declares four variables to hold the number of eggs produced in a month by each of four chickens, and assign a value to each variable. Sum the eggs, then display the total in dozens and eggs. For example, a total of 127 eggs is 10 dozen and 7 eggs. Save the program as **Eggs.cs**.

11. Modify the `Eggs` program in Exercise 10 so it prompts the user for and accepts a number of eggs for each chicken. Save the program as **EggsInteractive.cs**.

12. Write a program that declares five variables to hold scores for five tests you have taken, and assign a value to each variable. Display the average of the test scores to two decimal places. Save the program as **Tests.cs**.

13. Modify the `Tests` program in Exercise 12 so it accepts five test scores from a user. Save the program as **TestsInteractive.cs**.

14. Write a program that declares two variables to hold the names of two of your friends, and assign a value to each variable. Display the result of using the `String.Compare()` method with your friends' names. Save the program as **TwoFriends.cs**.

15. Modify the `TwoFriends` program in Exercise 14 so it accepts your friends' names from the keyboard. Save the program as **TwoFriendsInteractive.cs**.

16. Write a program that prompts the user for a name, Social Security number, hourly pay rate, and number of hours worked. In an attractive format (similar to Figure 2-24), display all the input data as well as the following:

    » Gross pay, defined as hourly pay rate times hours worked

    » Federal withholding tax, defined as 15% of the gross pay

    » State withholding tax, defined as 5% of the gross pay

    » Net pay, defined as gross pay minus taxes

    Save the program as **Payroll.cs**.

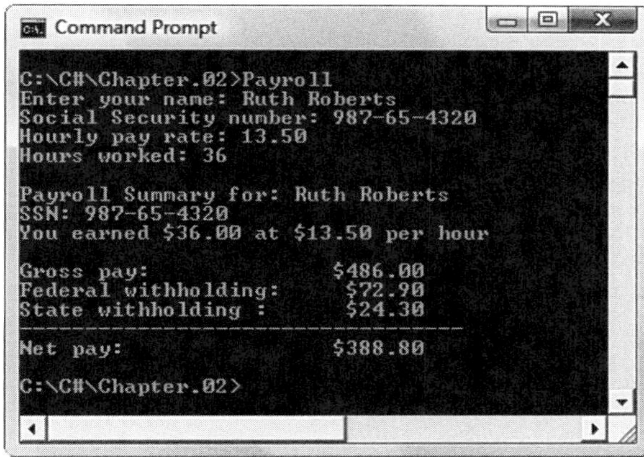

Figure 2-24 Typical execution of `Payroll` program

17. Write a program for the Magic Blender Company. The program prompts the user for a name, street address, city, state, zip code, and quantity of blenders ordered at $39.95 each. In an attractive format (similar to Figure 2-25), display all the input data as well as the following:

    » Amount due before tax, defined as number ordered times price each

    » Sales tax, defined as 7% of the amount due

    » Net due, defined as amount due before tax, plus tax

    Save the program as **OrderReceipt.cs**.

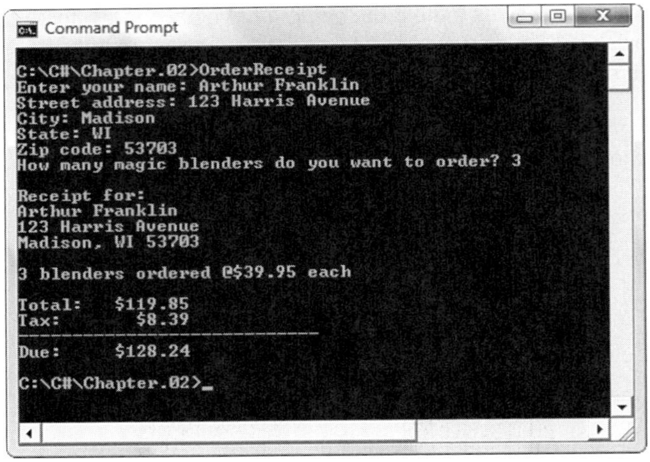

Figure 2-25 Typical execution of OrderReceipt program

DEBUGGING EXERCISES

Each of the following files in the Chapter.02 folder on your Student Disk has syntax and/or logical errors. In each case, determine the problem and fix the program. After you correct the errors, save each file using the same filename preceded with "Fixed". For example, DebugTwo1.cs will become FixedDebugTwo1.cs.

a. DebugTwo1.cs

b. DebugTwo2.cs

c. DebugTwo3.cs

d. DebugTwo4.cs

UP FOR DISCUSSION

1. What advantages are there to requiring variables to have a data type?

2. Some programmers use a system called Hungarian notation when naming their variables. What is Hungarian notation, and why do many object-oriented programmers feel it is not a valuable style to use?

3. Computers can perform millions of arithmetic calculations in an hour. How can we possibly know the results are correct?

3

MAKING DECISIONS

In this chapter you will:

Understand logic-planning tools and decision making
Learn how to make decisions using the `if` statement
Learn how to make decisions using the `if-else` statement
Use compound expressions in `if` statements
Make decisions using the `switch` statement
Use the conditional operator
Use the NOT operator
Learn to avoid common errors when making decisions

A major reason that computer programs seem so powerful is their ability to make decisions. Programs that decide which travel route will afford the best weather conditions, which Web site will provide the closest match to search criteria, or which recommended medical treatment has the highest probability of success all rely on a program's decision making. In this chapter you will learn to make decisions in C# programs.

UNDERSTANDING LOGIC-PLANNING TOOLS AND DECISION MAKING

When computer programmers write programs, they rarely just sit down at a keyboard and begin typing. Programmers must plan the complex portions of programs using paper and pencil. Programmers often use **pseudocode**, a tool that helps them plan a program's logic by writing plain English statements. Using pseudocode requires that you write down the steps needed to accomplish a given task. You write pseudocode in everyday language, not the syntax used in a programming language. In fact, a task you write in pseudocode does not have to be computer-related. If you have ever written a list of directions to your house—for example, (1) go west on Algonquin Road, (2) turn left on Roselle Road, (3) enter expressway heading east, and so on—you have written pseudocode. A **flowchart** is similar to pseudocode, but you write the steps in diagram form, as a series of shapes connected by arrows.

Some programmers use a variety of shapes to represent different tasks in their flowcharts, but you can draw simple flowcharts that express very complex situations using just rectangles and diamonds. You use a rectangle to represent any unconditional step and a diamond to represent any decision. For example, Figure 3-1 shows a flowchart and pseudocode describing

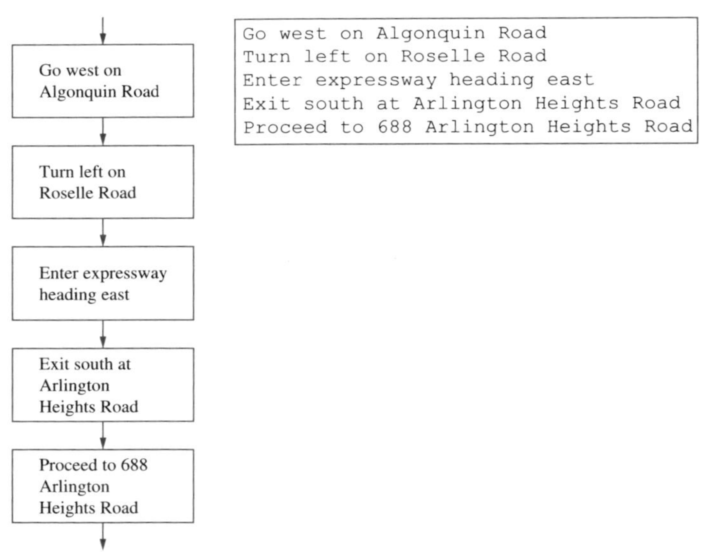

Figure 3-1 Flowchart and pseudocode of a series of sequential steps

driving directions to a friend's house. Notice how the actions illustrated in the flowchart and the pseudocode statements correspond. The logic in Figure 3-1 is an example of a logical structure called a **sequence structure**—one step follows another unconditionally. A sequence structure might contain any number of steps, but when one task follows another with no chance to branch away or skip a step, you are using a sequence.

Sometimes, logical steps do not follow in an unconditional sequence—some tasks might or might not occur based on decisions you make. Flowchart creators use diamond shapes to indicate alternative courses of action, which are drawn starting from the sides of the diamonds. Figure 3-2 shows a flowchart describing directions in which the execution of some steps depends on decisions.

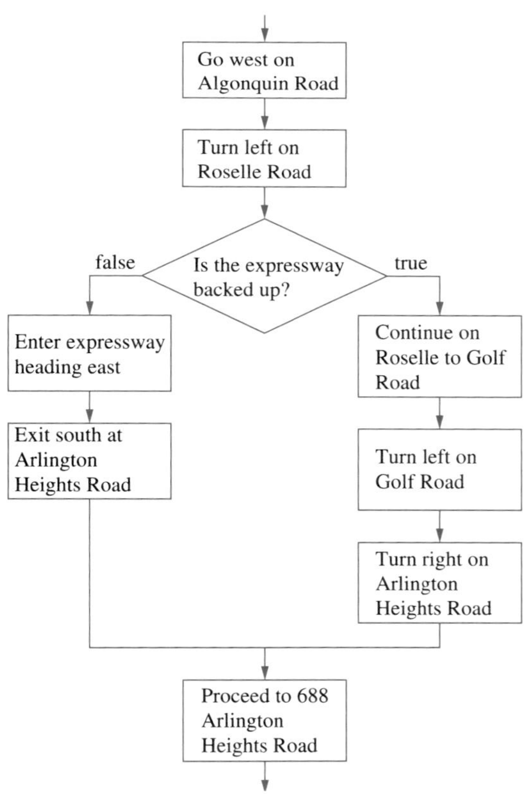

Figure 3-2 Flowchart including a decision

Figure 3-2 shows a **decision structure**—one that involves choosing between alternative courses of action based on some value within a program. For example, the program that produces your paycheck can make decisions about the proper amount to withhold for taxes, the program that guides a missile can alter its course, and a program that monitors your blood pressure during surgery can determine when to sound an alarm. Making decisions is what makes computer programs seem "smart."

When reduced to their most basic form, all computer decisions are yes-or-no decisions. That is, the answer to every computer question is "yes" or "no" (or "true" or "false," or "on" or "off"). This is because computer circuitry consists of millions of tiny switches that are either "on" or "off," and the result of every decision sets one of these switches in memory. The values `true` and `false` are Boolean values; every computer decision results in a Boolean value. Thus, internally, a program you write never asks, for example, "What number did the user enter?" Instead, the decisions might be "Did the user enter a 1?" "If not, did the user enter a 2?" "If not, did the user enter a 3?"

»TWO TRUTHS AND A LIE: UNDERSTANDING DECISION MAKING

1. A sequence structure has three or more alternative logical paths.
2. A decision structure involves choosing between alternative courses of action based on some value within a program.
3. When reduced to their most basic form, all computer decisions are yes-or-no decisions.

The false statement is #1. In a sequence structure, one step follows another unconditionally.

MAKING DECISIONS USING THE `if` STATEMENT

The `if` and `if-else` statements are the two most commonly used decision-making statements in C#. You use an **if statement** to make a single-alternative decision. In other words, you use an `if` statement to determine whether an action will occur. The `if` statement takes the following form:

```
if(expression)
    statement;
```

where *expression* represents any C# expression that can be evaluated as `true` or `false` and *statement* represents the action that will take place if the expression evaluates as `true`. You must place the `if` statement's evaluated expression between parentheses.

Usable expressions in an `if` statement include Boolean expressions such as `amount > 5` and `month == "May"` as well as the value of `bool` variables such as `isValidIDNumber`. If the expression evaluates as `true`, then the statement executes. Whether the expression evaluates as `true` or `false`, the program continues with the next statement following the complete `if` statement.

For example, the code segment written and diagrammed in Figure 3-3 displays "A" and "B" when `number` holds a value less than 5. The expression `number < 5` evaluates as `true`, so the statement that displays "A" executes. Then the independent statement that displays "B" executes.

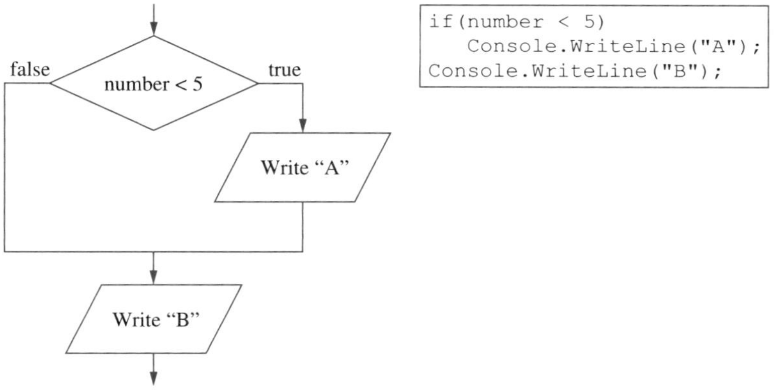


```
if(number < 5)
    Console.WriteLine("A");
Console.WriteLine("B");
```

NOTE
You can leave a space between the keyword `if` and the opening parenthesis if you think that format is easier to read.

Figure 3-3 Flowchart and code including a typical `if` statement followed by a separate statement

When an evaluated expression is `false`, the rest of the statement does not execute. For example, when `number` is 5 or greater in Figure 3-3, only "B" is displayed. Because the expression `number < 5` is `false`, the statement that displays "A" never executes.

In Figure 3-3, notice there is no semicolon at the end of the line that contains `if(number < 5)`. The statement does not end at that point; it ends after `Console.WriteLine("A");`. If you incorrectly insert a semicolon at the end of `if(number < 5)`, then the statement says,

"If `number` is less than 5, do nothing; then, no matter what the value of `number` is, print 'A'".
Figure 3-4 shows the flowchart logic that matches the code when a semicolon is placed at the
end of the `if` expression.

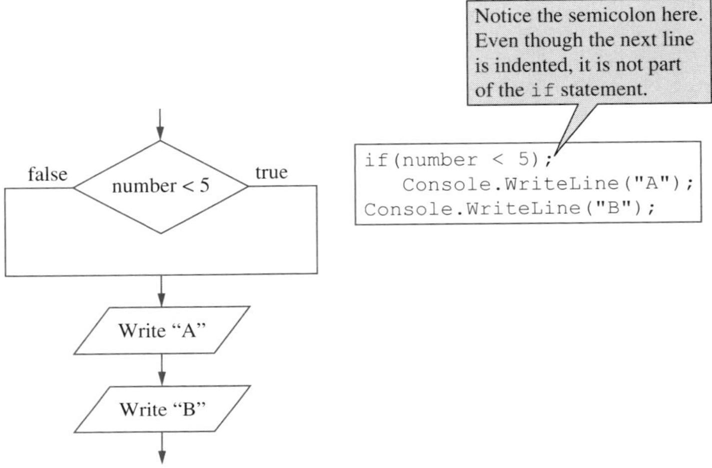

Figure 3-4 Flowchart and code including an `if` statement with a semicolon following
the `if` expression

Although it is customary, and good style, to indent any statement that executes when an `if`
Boolean expression evaluates as `true`, the C# compiler does not pay any attention to the
indentation. Each of the following `if` statements displays "A" when `number` is less than 5.
The first shows an `if` written on a single line; the second shows an `if` on two lines but with
no indentation. The third uses conventional indentation.

```
if(number < 5) Console.WriteLine("A");


if(number < 5)
Console.WriteLine("A");


if(number < 5)
    Console.WriteLine("A");
```

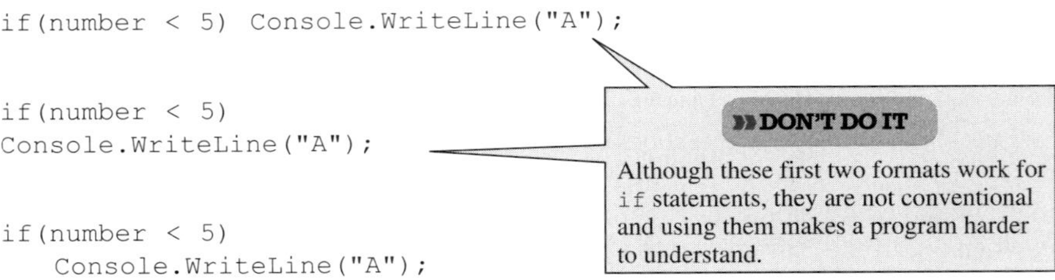

When you want to execute two or more statements conditionally, you must place the statements
within a block. A **block** is a collection of one or more statements contained within a pair of

curly braces. For example, the code segment written and diagrammed in Figure 3-5 displays both "C" and "D" when number is less than 5, and it displays neither when number is not less than 5.

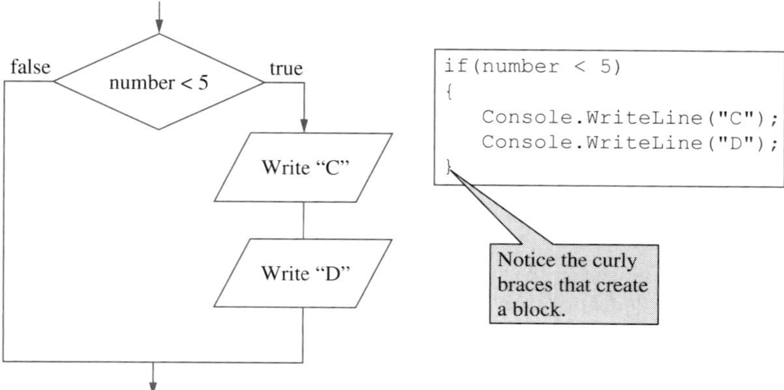

Figure 3-5 Flowchart and code including a typical if statement containing a block

Indenting alone does not cause multiple statements to depend on the evaluation of a Boolean expression in an if. For multiple statements to depend on an if, they must be blocked with braces. For example, Figure 3-6 shows two statements that are indented below an if expression. When you glance at the code, it might first appear that both statements depend on the if; in fact, however, only the first one does, as shown in the flowchart, because the statements are not blocked.

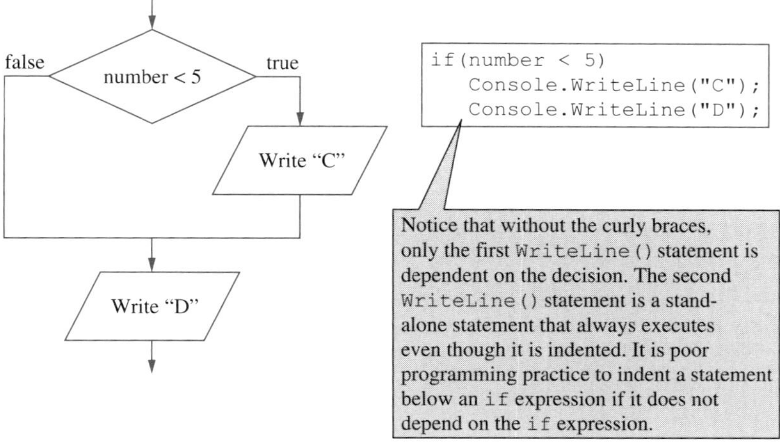

Figure 3-6 Flowchart and code including an if statement that is missing curly braces or that has inappropriate indenting

> **NOTE** When you create a block using curly braces, you do not have to place multiple statements within it. It is perfectly legal to block a single statement. Blocking a single statement can be a useful technique to help prevent future errors. When a program later is modified to include multiple statements that depend on the `if`, it is easy to forget to add curly braces. You will naturally place the additional statements within the block if the braces are already in place.

> **NOTE** It also is legal to create a block that contains no statements. You usually do so only when starting to write a program, as a reminder to yourself to add statements later.

You can place any number of statements within the block contained by the curly braces, including another `if` statement. Of course, if the second `if` statement is the only statement that depends on the `if`, then no braces are required. Figure 3-7 shows the logic for a **nested if** statement—one in which one decision structure is contained within another. With a nested `if` statement, a second `if`'s Boolean expression is tested only when the first `if`'s Boolean expression evaluates as `true`.

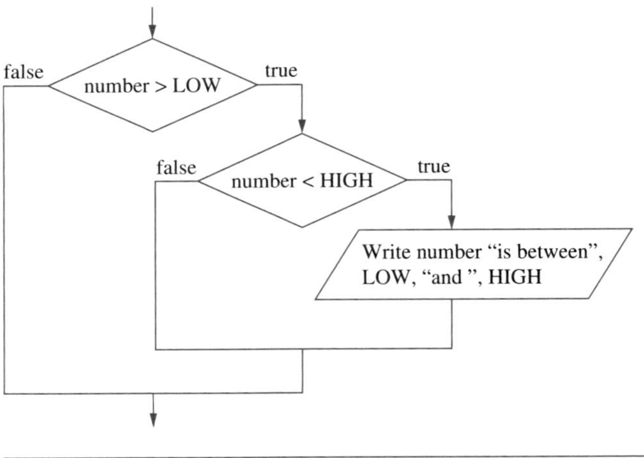


```
if(number > LOW)
   if(number < HIGH)
      Console.WriteLine("{0} is between {1} and {2}",
         number, LOW, HIGH);
```

Figure 3-7 Flowchart and code showing the logic of a nested `if`

Figure 3-8 shows a program that contains the logic. When a user enters a number greater than 5 in the program in Figure 3-8, the first `if` expression evaluates as `true` and the `if`

```
using System;
public class NestedDecision
{
   public static void Main()
   {
      const int HIGH = 10, LOW = 5;
      string numberString;
      int number;
      Console.Write("Enter an integer ");
      numberString = Console.ReadLine();
      number = Convert.ToInt32(numberString);
       if(number > LOW)
          if(number < HIGH)
             Console.WriteLine("{0} is between {1} and {2}",
                   number, LOW, HIGH);
   }
}
```

Figure 3-8 Program using nested `if`

statement that tests whether the number is less than 10 executes. When the second `if` evaluates as `true`, the `Console.WriteLine()` statement executes. However, if the second `if` is `false`, no output occurs. When the user enters a number less than or equal to 5, the first `if` expression is `false` and the second `if` expression is never tested, and again no output occurs. Figure 3-9 shows the output after the program is executed three times using three different input values. Notice that when the value input by the user is not between 5 and 10, no output message appears; the message is displayed only when both `if` expressions are `true`.

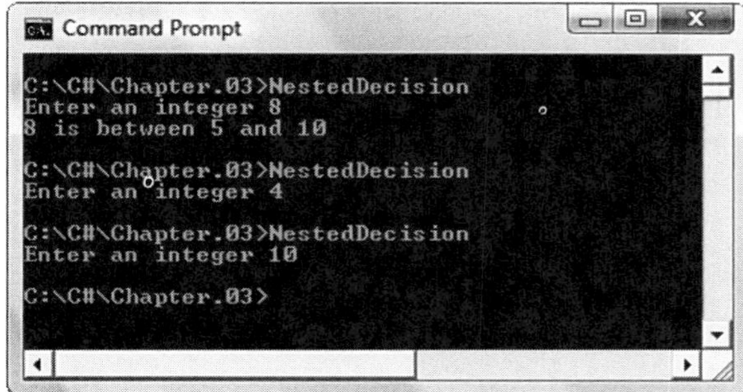

Figure 3-9 Output of three executions of the `NestedDecision` program

»TWO TRUTHS AND A LIE: MAKING DECISIONS USING THE if STATEMENT

1. In C#, you must place an if statement's evaluated expression between parentheses.
2. In C#, for multiple statements to depend on an if, they must be indented.
3. In C#, you can place one if statement within a block that depends on another if statement.

The false statement is #2. Indenting alone does not cause multiple statements to depend on the evaluation of a Boolean expression in an if. For multiple statements to depend on an if, they must be blocked with braces.

MAKING DECISIONS USING THE if-else STATEMENT

Some decisions you make are **dual-alternative decisions**; they have two possible resulting actions. If you want to perform one action when a Boolean expression evaluates as true and an alternate action when it evaluates as false, you can use an **if-else statement**. The if-else statement takes the following form:

```
if(expression)
    statement1;
else
    statement2;
```

For example, Figure 3-10 shows the logic for an if-else statement, and Figure 3-11 shows a program that contains the statement. With every execution of the program,

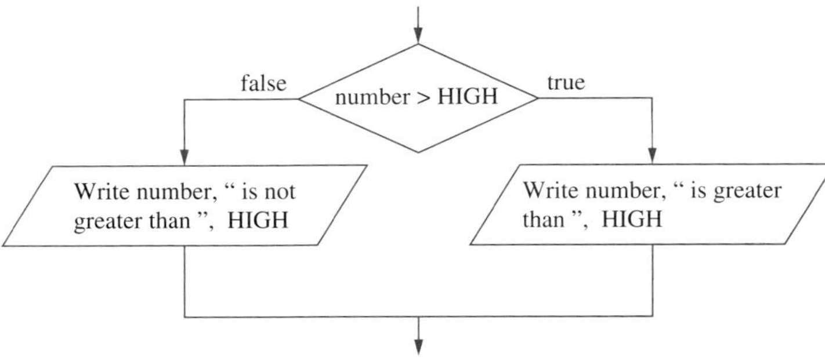


```
if(number > HIGH)
   Console.WriteLine("{0} is greater than {1}",
      number, HIGH);
else
   Console.WriteLine("{0} is not greater than {1}",
      number, HIGH);
```

Figure 3-10 Flowchart and code showing the logic of a dual-alternative if-else statement

```csharp
using System;
public class IfElseDecision
{
    public static void Main()
    {
        const int HIGH = 10;
        string numberString;
        int number;
        Console.Write("Enter an integer ");
        numberString = Console.ReadLine();
        number = Convert.ToInt32(numberString);
        if(number > HIGH)
            Console.WriteLine("{0} is greater than {1}",
                number, HIGH);
        else
            Console.WriteLine("{0} is not greater than {1}",
                number, HIGH);
    }
}
```

Figure 3-11 Program with a dual-alternative `if-else` statement

one or the other of the two `WriteLine()` statements executes. Figure 3-12 shows two executions of the program.

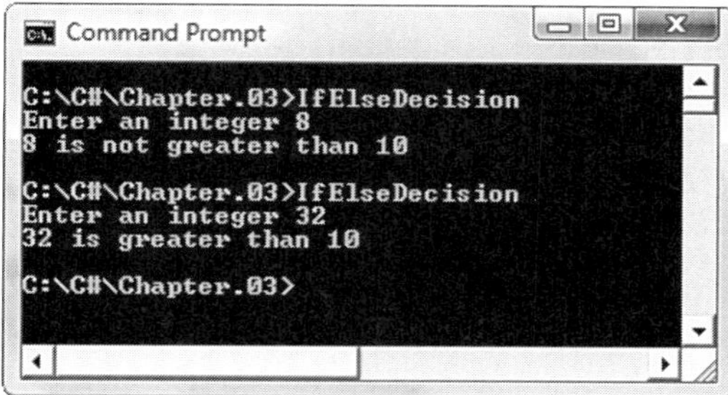

Figure 3-12 Output of two executions of the `IfElseDecision` program

▶▶NOTE The indentation shown in the `if-else` example in Figure 3-11 is not required, but is standard. You vertically align the keyword `if` with the keyword `else`, and then indent the action statements that depend on the evaluation.

▶▶NOTE Just as you can block several statements so they all execute when an expression within an `if` is `true`, you can block multiple statements after an `else` so that they will all execute when the evaluated expression is `false`.

When `if-else` statements are nested, each `else` always is paired with the most recent unpaired `if`. For example, in the following code, the `else` is paired with the second `if`.

```
if(saleAmount > 1000)
    if(saleAmount < 2000)
        bonus = 100;
    else
        bonus = 50;
```

In this example, the following bonuses are assigned:

» If `saleAmount` is between $1000 and $2000, `bonus` is $100 because both evaluated expressions are `true`.

» If `saleAmount` is $2000 or more, `bonus` is $50 because the first evaluated expression is `true` and the second one is `false`.

» If `saleAmount` is $1000 or less, `bonus` is unassigned because the first evaluated expression is `false` and there is no corresponding `else`.

»TWO TRUTHS AND A LIE: MAKING DECISIONS USING THE `if-else` STATEMENT

1. Dual-alternative decisions have two possible outcomes.
2. In an `if-else` statement, a semicolon is always the last character typed before the `else`.
3. When `if-else` statements are nested, the first `if` always is paired with the first `else`.

The false statement is #3. When `if-else` statements are nested, each `else` always is paired with the most recent unpaired `if`.

USING COMPOUND EXPRESSIONS IN `if` STATEMENTS

In many programming situations you encounter, you need to make multiple decisions. For example, suppose a specific college scholarship is available:

» If your high school class rank is higher than 75 percent
» And if your grade-point average is higher than 3.0
» And if you are a state resident
» Or if you are a resident of a cooperating state
» Or if one of your parents went to the college

No matter how many decisions must be made, you can decide on the scholarship eligibility for any student by using a series of `if` statements to test the appropriate variables. For convenience and clarity, however, you can combine multiple decisions into a single `if` statement using a combination of AND and OR operators.

USING THE CONDITIONAL AND OPERATOR

As an alternative to nested `if` statements, you can use the **conditional AND operator** (or simply the **AND operator**) within a Boolean expression to determine whether two expressions are both `true`. The AND operator is written as two ampersands (`&&`). For example, the two code samples shown in Figure 3-13 work exactly the same way. The `age` variable is tested, and if it is greater than or equal to 0 and less than 120, a message prints to explain that the value is valid.

```
// using &&
 if(age >= 0 && age < 120)
    Console.WriteLine("Age is valid");
// using nested ifs
 if(age >= 0)
    if(age < 120)
       Console.WriteLine("Age is valid");
```

Figure 3-13 Comparing using the AND operator and nested `if` statements

You are never required to use the AND operator, because nested `if` statements achieve the same result, but using the AND operator often makes your code more concise, less error-prone, and easier to understand.

It is important to note that when you use the AND operator, you must include a complete Boolean expression on each side of the `&&` operator. If you want to set a bonus to $400 when a `saleAmount` is both over $1000 and under $5000, the correct statement is as follows:

```
if(saleAmount > 1000 && saleAmount < 5000)
   bonus = 400;
```

The following statement is incorrect and will not compile:

```
if(saleAmount > 1000 && < 5000)
   bonus = 400;
```


The statement is invalid because the numeric expression `< 5000` is used on the right side of the AND expression, and `< 5000` is not a complete Boolean expression.

The expressions in each part of an AND expression are evaluated only as much as necessary to determine whether the entire expression is `true` or `false`. This feature is called **short-circuit evaluation**. With the AND operator, both Boolean expressions must be `true` before the action in the statement can occur. If the first expression is `false`, the second expression is never evaluated, because its value does not matter. For example, if `a` is not greater than `LIMIT` in the following `if` statement, then the evaluation is complete because there is no need to evaluate whether `b` is greater than `LIMIT`.

```
if(a > LIMIT && b > LIMIT)
    Console.WriteLine("Both are greater than LIMIT");
```

USING THE CONDITIONAL OR OPERATOR

You can use the **conditional OR operator** (or simply the **OR operator**) when you want some action to occur even if only one of two conditions is `true`. The OR operator is written as `||`. For example, if you want to print a message indicating an invalid age when the variable is less than 0 or is 120 or greater, you can use either code sample in Figure 3-14.


```
// using ||
 if(age < 0 || age >= 120)
    Console.WriteLine("Age is not valid");
// using nested ifs
 if(age < 0)
    Console.WriteLine("Age is not valid");
 else
    if(age >= 120)
        Console.WriteLine("Age is not valid");
```

Figure 3-14 Using the OR operator or nested `if` statements

When the OR operator is used in an `if` statement, only one of the two Boolean expressions in the tested expression needs to be `true` for the resulting action to occur. As with the AND operator, this feature is called short-circuit evaluation. When you use the OR operator and the first Boolean expression is `true`, the second expression is never evaluated, because it doesn't matter whether it is `true` or `false`.

USING THE LOGICAL AND AND OR OPERATORS

The **Boolean logical AND** (&) and **Boolean logical inclusive OR** (|) operators work just like their && and || (*conditional* AND and OR) counterparts, except they do not support short-circuit evaluation. That is, they always evaluate both sides of the expression, no matter what the first evaluation is. This can lead to a **side effect**, or unintended consequence. For example, in the following statement that uses &&, if `salesAmountForYear` is not at least $10000, the first half of the expression is `false`, so the second half of the Boolean expression is never evaluated and `yearsOfService` is not increased.

```
if(salesAmountForYear >= 10000 && ++yearsOfService > 10)
   bonus = 200;
```

On the other hand, when a single & is used and `salesAmountForYear` is not at least 10000, then even though the first half of the expression is `false`, the second half is still evaluated, and `yearsOfService` is increased:

```
if(salesAmountForYear >= 10000 & ++yearsOfService > 10)
   bonus = 200;
```

Because the first half of the expression is `false`, the entire evaluation is `false`, and, as with &&, bonus is still not set to 200. However, a side effect has occurred: `yearsOfService` is incremented.

In general, you should avoid writing expressions that contain side effects. If you want `yearsOfService` to increase no matter what the `salesAmountForYear` is, then you should increase it in a stand-alone statement.

COMBINING AND AND OR OPERATORS

You can combine as many AND and OR operators in an expression as you need. For example, when three conditions must be `true` before performing an action, you can use an expression such as `if(a && b && c)`. When you combine AND and OR operators within the same Boolean expression, the AND operators take precedence, meaning their Boolean values are evaluated first.

For example, consider a program that determines whether a movie theater patron can purchase a discounted ticket. Assume discounts are allowed for children (age 12 and younger) and for senior citizens (age 65 and older) who attend G-rated movies. The following code looks reasonable, but it produces incorrect results because the && evaluates before the ||.

```
if(age <= 12 || age >= 65 && rating == 'G')
   Console.WriteLine("Discount applies");
```

For example, assume a movie patron is 10 years old and the movie rating is 'R'. The patron should not receive a discount (or be allowed to see the movie!). However, within the `if` statement above, the expression `age >= 65 && rating == 'G'` evaluates first. It is `false`, so the `if` becomes the equivalent of `if(age <= 12 || false)`. Because `age <= 12` is `true`, the `if` becomes the equivalent of `if(true || false)`, which evaluates as `true`, and the statement "Discount applies" incorrectly displays.

You can use parentheses to correct the logic and force the expression `age <= 12 || age >= 65` to evaluate first, as shown in the following code.

```
if((age <= 12 || age >= 65) && rating == 'G')
    Console.WriteLine("Discount applies");
```

With the added parentheses, if `age` is 12 or less OR 65 or greater, the expression is evaluated as `if(true && rating == 'G')`. When the `age` value qualifies a patron for a discount, then the `rating` value must also be acceptable. Figure 3-15 shows the `if` within a complete program; note that the discount age limits now are represented as named constants. Figure 3-16 shows the execution before the parentheses

```
using System;
public class MovieDiscount
{
    public static void Main()
    {
        int age = 10;
        char rating = 'R';
        const int CHILD_AGE = 12;
        const int SENIOR_AGE = 65;
        Console.WriteLine("When age is {0} and rating is {1}",
            age, rating);
        if((age <= CHILD_AGE || age >= SENIOR_AGE) && rating == 'G')
            Console.WriteLine("Discount applies");
        else
            Console.WriteLine("Full price");
    }
}
```

Figure 3-15 Movie ticket discount program using parentheses to alter precedence of Boolean evaluations

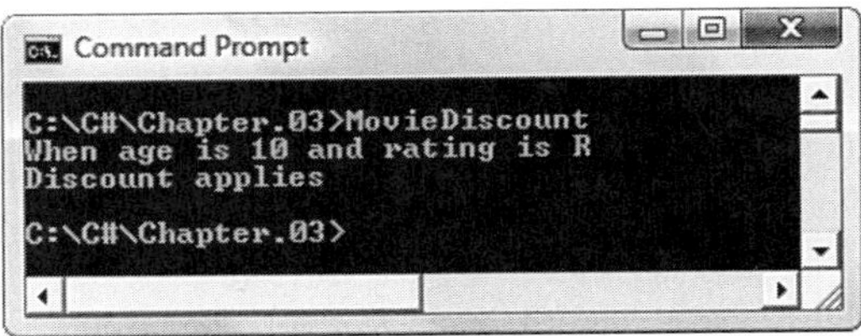

Figure 3-16 Incorrect results when `MovieDiscount` program is executed without added parentheses

were added to the `if` statement, and Figure 3-17 shows the output after the inclusion of the parentheses.

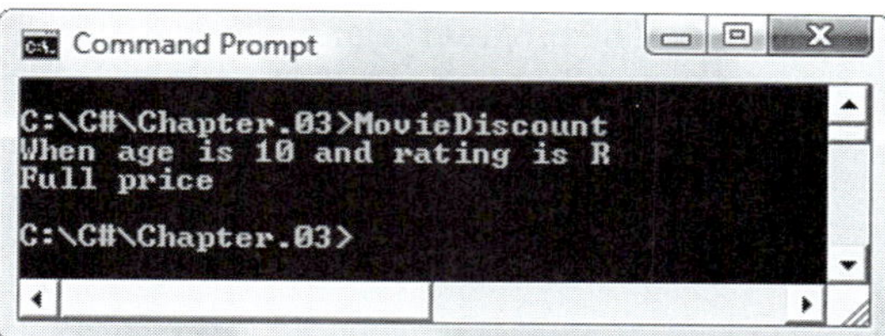

Figure 3-17 Correct results when parentheses are added to `MovieDiscount` program

> **» NOTE** You can use parentheses for clarity even when they are not required. For example, the following expressions both evaluate `a && b` first:
>
> ```
> a && b || c
> (a && b) || c
> ```
>
> If the version with parentheses makes your intentions clearer, you should use it.

> **» NOTE** In Chapter 2, you controlled arithmetic operator precedence by using parentheses. Appendix A describes the precedence of every C# operator. For example, in Appendix A you can see that the comparison operators <= and >= have higher precedence than both `&&` and `||`.

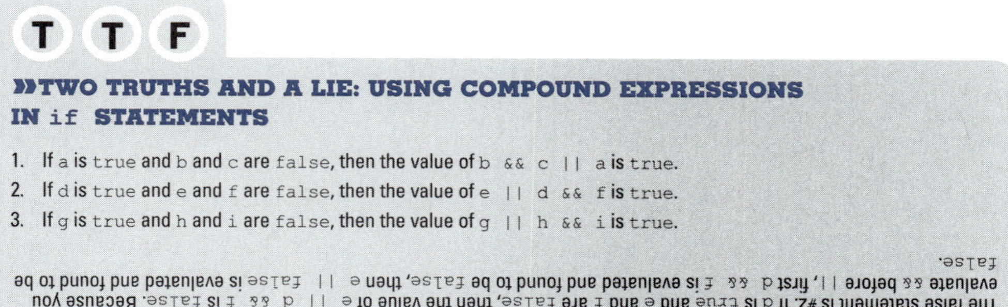

»TWO TRUTHS AND A LIE: USING COMPOUND EXPRESSIONS IN `if` STATEMENTS

1. If `a` is `true` and `b` and `c` are `false`, then the value of `b && c || a` is `true`.
2. If `d` is `true` and `e` and `f` are `false`, then the value of `e || d && f` is `true`.
3. If `g` is `true` and `h` and `i` are `false`, then the value of `g || h && i` is `true`.

The false statement is #2. If `d` is `true` and `e` and `f` are `false`, then the value of `e || d && f` is `false`. Because you evaluate `&&` before `||`, first `d && f` is evaluated and found to be `false`, then `e || false` is evaluated and found to be `false`.

MAKING DECISIONS USING THE `switch` STATEMENT

By nesting a series of `if` and `else` statements, you can choose from any number of alternatives. For example, suppose you want to print different strings based on a student's class year. Figure 3-18 shows the logic using nested `if` statements. The program segment tests the `year` variable four times and executes one of four statements, or displays an error message.

```
if(year == 1)
   Console.WriteLine("Freshman");
else
   if(year == 2)
      Console.WriteLine("Sophomore");
   else
      if(year == 3)
         Console.WriteLine("Junior");
      else
         if(year == 4)
            Console.WriteLine("Senior");
         else
            Console.WriteLine("Invalid year");
```

Figure 3-18 Executing multiple alternatives using a series of `if` statements

An alternative to the series of nested `if` statements in Figure 3-18 is to use the `switch` structure (see Figure 3-19). The **switch structure** tests a single variable against a series of exact

```
switch(year)
{
   case 1:
      Console.WriteLine("Freshman");
      break;
   case 2:
      Console.WriteLine("Sophomore");
      break;
   case 3:
      Console.WriteLine("Junior");
      break;
   case 4:
      Console.WriteLine("Senior");
      break;
   default:
      Console.WriteLine("Invalid year");
      break;
}
```

Figure 3-19 Executing multiple alternatives using a `switch` statement

matches. The switch structure in Figure 3-19 is easier to read and interpret than the series of nested if statements in Figure 3-18. The if statements would become harder to read if additional choices were required and if multiple statements had to execute in each case. These additional choices and statements might also make it easier to make mistakes.

The switch structure uses four new keywords:

» The keyword **switch** starts the structure and is followed immediately by a test expression (called the **switch expression**) enclosed in parentheses.

» The keyword **case** is followed by one of the possible values that might equal the switch expression. A colon follows the value. The entire expression—for example, case 1:—is a case label. A **case label** identifies a course of action in a switch structure. Most switch structures contain several case labels.

» The keyword **break** usually terminates a switch structure at the end of each case. Although other statements can end a case, break is the most commonly used.

» The keyword **default** optionally is used prior to any action that should occur if the test expression does not match any case.

>> **NOTE**
The switch statement is not as flexible as the if because you can test only one variable, and it must be tested for equality.

>> **NOTE** Besides break, you can use a return statement or a throw statement to end a case. You learn about return statements in Chapter 6 and throw statements in Chapter 9.

>> **NOTE** You are not required to list the case label values in ascending order, as shown in Figure 3-19. It is most efficient to list the most common case first, instead of the case with the lowest value. Often, the default case is the most common.

The switch structure shown in Figure 3-19 begins by evaluating the year variable shown in the switch statement. If year is equal to the first case label value, which is 1, then the statement that displays "Freshman" will execute. The break statement causes a bypass of the rest of the switch structure, and execution continues with any statement after the closing curly brace of the switch structure.

If the year variable is not equivalent to the first case label value of 1, then the next case label value is compared, and so on. If the year variable does not contain the same value as any of the case label expressions, then the default statement or statements execute.

In C#, an error occurs if you reach the end point of the statement list of a switch section. For example, the following code is not allowed, because when the year value is 1, "Freshman" is displayed, and the code reaches the end of the case.

```
switch(year)
{
    case 1:
        Console.WriteLine("Freshman");
    case 2:
        Console.WriteLine("Sophomore");
        break;
}
```

>> **DON'T DO IT**
This code is invalid because the end of the case is reached after "Freshman" is displayed.

Not allowing code to reach the end of a `case` is known as the "no fall through rule" because in other programming languages, such as Java and C++, this syntax would be allowed; when `year` equals 1, both `"Freshman"` and `"Sophomore"` would be displayed. Falling through to the next `case` is not allowed in C#; the most common way to avoid this error is to use a `break` statement at the end of each `case`.

> **» NOTE** The **governing type** of a `switch` statement is established by the `switch` expression. The governing type can be `sbyte`, `byte`, `short`, `ushort`, `int`, `uint`, `long`, `ulong`, `char`, `string`, or an `enum` type. An **enum** is an enumeration—a programmer-defined type that declares a set of constants. You will use enumerations in Chapter 11.

A `switch` does not need to contain a `default` case. If the test expression in a `switch` does not match any of the `case` label values, and there is no `default` value, then the program simply continues with the next executable statement. However, it is good programming practice to include a `default` label in a `switch` structure; that way, you provide for actions when your data does not match any case. The `default` label does not have to appear last, although usually it does.

You can use multiple labels to govern a list of statements. For example, in the code in Figure 3-20, `"Upperclass"` is displayed whether the `year` value is 3 or 4.

> **» NOTE**
> You receive a compiler error if two or more `case` label values in a `switch` statement are the same.

```
switch(year)
{
    case 1:
        Console.WriteLine("Freshman");
        break;
    case 2:
        Console.WriteLine("Sophomore");
        break;
    case 3:
    case 4:
        Console.WriteLine("Upperclass");
        break;
    default:
        Console.WriteLine("Invalid year");
        break;
}
```


Figure 3-20 Example `switch` structure using multiple labels to execute a single statement block

You are never required to use a `switch` structure; you can always achieve the same results with nested `if` statements. The `switch` structure is simply a convenience you can use when there are several alternative courses of action depending on a match with a variable. Additionally, it makes sense to use a `switch` only when there are a reasonable number of specific matching values to be tested. For example, if every sale amount from $1 to $500 requires a 5 percent commission, it is not reasonable to test every possible dollar amount using the following code:

```
switch(saleAmount)
{
    case 1:
        commRate = .05;
        break;
    case 2:
        commRate = .05;
        break;
    case 3:
        commRate = .05;
        break;
// ...and so on for several hundred more cases
```

With 500 different dollar values resulting in the same commission, one test—`if(saleAmount <= 500)`—is far more reasonable than listing 500 separate cases.

»TWO TRUTHS AND A LIE: MAKING DECISIONS USING THE `switch` STATEMENT

1. In a `switch` statement, the keyword `case` is followed by one of the possible values that might equal the `switch` expression, and a colon follows the value.
2. The keyword `break` always terminates a `switch` structure at the end of each `case`.
3. A `switch` statement does not need to contain a `default` case.

The false statement is #2. The keyword `break` usually terminates a `switch` structure at the end of each `case`, but other statements can end a case.

USING THE CONDITIONAL OPERATOR

The **conditional operator** is used as an abbreviated version of the `if-else` statement; it requires three expressions separated with a question mark and a colon. Like the `switch` structure, you never are required to use the conditional operator. Rather, it is simply a convenient shortcut, especially when you want to use the result immediately as an expression. The syntax of the conditional operator is:

```
testExpression ? trueResult : falseResult;
```

»NOTE Unary operators use one operand; binary operators use two. The conditional operator ?: is **ternary** because it requires three arguments: a test expression and `true` and `false` result expressions. The conditional operator is the only ternary operator in C#.

The first expression, `testExpression`, is evaluated as `true` or `false`. If it is `true`, then the entire conditional expression takes on the value of the expression following the question mark (`trueResult`). If the value of the `testExpression` is `false`, then the entire expression takes on the value of `falseResult`. For example, consider the following statement:

```
biggerNum = (a > b) ? a : b;
```

This statement evaluates `a > b`. If `a` is greater than `b`, then the entire conditional expression takes the value of `a`, which then is assigned to `biggerNum`. If `a` is not greater than `b`, then the expression assumes the value of `b`, and `b` is assigned to `biggerNum`.

The conditional operator is most often used when you want to use the result as an expression without creating an intermediate variable. For example, suppose an income tax program has declared `doubles` for tax owed when calculated using a standard formula and when calculated using an alternative minimum-tax formula. A taxpayer is required to make a quarterly payment that is one-fourth of the larger of the two values. A usable statement might be as follows:

```
double payment = ((altMinTax > stdTax) ? altMinTax : stdTax) / 4;
```

This code provides the same results as the following:

```
double payment;
if(altMinTax > stdTax)
    payment = altMinTax / 4;
else
    payment = stdTax / 4;
```

As another example, a conditional operator can be used directly in an output statement such as the following:

```
Console.WriteLine((testScore >= 60) ? "Pass" : "Fail");
```

Conditional expressions are frequently more difficult to read than `if-else` statements, but they can be used in places where `if-else` statements cannot.

»TWO TRUTHS AND A LIE: USING THE CONDITIONAL OPERATOR

1. If `j = 2` and `k = 3`, then the value of the following expression is 2:
   ```
   int m = j < k ? j : k;
   ```
2. If `j = 2` and `k = 3`, then the value of the following expression is "yes":
   ```
   string ans = j < k ? "yes" : "no";
   ```
3. If `j = 2` and `k = 3`, then the value of the following expression is 5:
   ```
   int n = j > k? j + k : j * k;
   ```

The false statement is #3. If `j = 2` and `k = 3`, then the value of the expression `int n = j > k? j + k : j * k;` is 6 because `j` is not greater than `k` and the `false` result is `j * k`, which is 2 * 3.

USING THE NOT OPERATOR

You use the **NOT operator**, which is written as an exclamation point (!), to negate the result of any Boolean expression. Any expression that evaluates as `true` becomes `false` when preceded by the NOT operator, and any `false` expression preceded by the NOT operator becomes `true`.

For example, suppose a monthly car insurance premium is $200 if the driver is younger than age 26 and $125 if the driver is age 26 or older. Each of the following `if` statements (which have been placed on single lines for convenience) correctly assigns the premium values.

```
if(age < 26) premium = 200;    else premium = 125;
if(!(age < 26)) premium = 125;    else premium = 200;
if(age >= 26) premium = 125;    else premium = 200;
if(!(age >= 26)) premium = 200;    else premium = 125;
```

The statements with the NOT operator are somewhat more difficult to read, particularly because they require the double set of parentheses, but the result is the same in each case. Using the NOT operator is clearer when the value of a Boolean variable is tested. For example, a variable initialized as `bool oldEnough = (age >= 25);` can become part of the relatively easy-to-read expression `if(!oldEnough)`....

> **NOTE** The NOT operator has higher precedence than the AND and OR operators. For example, suppose you have declared two Boolean variables named `ageOverMinimum` and `ticketsUnderMinimum`. The following expressions are evaluated in the same way:
>
> ```
> ageOverMinimum && !ticketsUnderMinimum
> ageOverMinimum && (!ticketsUnderMinimum)
> ```

> **NOTE** Augustus de Morgan was a 19th-century mathematician who originally observed the following:
>
> ```
> !(a && b) is equivalent to !a || !b
> !(a || b) is equivalent to !(a && b)
> ```

T T F

» TWO TRUTHS AND A LIE: USING THE NOT OPERATOR

1. Assume `p`, `q`, and `r` are all Boolean variables that have been assigned the value `true`. After the following statement executes, the value of `p` is still `true`.

   ```
   p = !q || r;
   ```
2. Assume `p`, `q`, and `r` are all Boolean variables that have been assigned the value `true`. After the following statement executes, the value of `p` is still `true`.

   ```
   p = !(!q && !r);
   ```
3. Assume `p`, `q`, and `r` are all Boolean variables that have been assigned the value `true`. After the following statement executes, the value of `p` is still `true`.

   ```
   p = !(q || !r);
   ```

The false statement is #3. If p, q, and r are all Boolean variables that have been assigned the value true, then after p = !(q || !r); executes, the value of p is false. First q is evaluated as true, so the entire expression within the parentheses is true. The leading NOT operator reverses that result to false and assigns it to p.

AVOIDING COMMON ERRORS WHEN MAKING DECISIONS

New programmers frequently make errors when they first learn to make decisions. As you have seen, the most frequent errors include the following:

» Using the assignment operator instead of the comparison operator when testing for equality

» Inserting a semicolon after the Boolean expression in an `if` statement instead of after the entire statement is completed

» Failing to block a set of statements with curly braces when several statements depend on the `if` or the `else` statement

» Failing to include a complete Boolean expression on each side of an `&&` or `||` operator in an `if` statement

In this section, you will learn to avoid other types of errors with `if` statements. Programmers often make errors at the following times:

» When performing a range check incorrectly or inefficiently

» When using the wrong operator with AND and OR

» Using NOT incorrectly

PERFORMING ACCURATE AND EFFICIENT RANGE CHECKS

When new programmers must make a range check, they often introduce incorrect or inefficient code into their programs. A **range check** is a series of `if` statements that determine whether a value falls within a specified range. Consider a situation in which salespeople can receive one of three possible commission rates based on their sales. For example, a sale totaling $1000 or more earns the salesperson an 8% commission, a sale totaling $500 through $999 earns 6% of the sale amount, and any sale totaling $499 or less earns 5%. Using three separate `if` statements to test single Boolean expressions might result in some incorrect commission assignments. For example, examine the following code:

```
if(saleAmount >= 1000)
   commissionRate = 0.08;
if(saleAmount >= 500)
   commissionRate = 0.06;
if(saleAmount <= 499)
   commissionRate = 0.05;
```

> **» DON'T DO IT**
>
> Although it was not the programmer's intention, both of the first two `if` statements are true for any `saleAmount` greater than or equal to 1000.

> **» NOTE** In this example, `saleAmount` is assumed to be an integer. As long as you are dealing with whole dollar amounts, the expression `if(saleAmount >= 1000)` can be expressed just as well as `if(saleAmount > 999)`. If `saleAmount` was a floating-point variable, the preceding code would fail to assign a commission rate for sales from $499.01 through $499.99.

Using this code, if a `saleAmount` is $5000, the first `if` statement executes. The Boolean expression `(saleAmount >= 1000)` evaluates as `true`, and 0.08 is correctly assigned to `commissionRate`. However, when a `saleAmount` is $5000, the next `if` expression, `(saleAmount >= 500)`, also evaluates as `true`, so the `commissionRate`, which was 8%, is incorrectly reset to 6%.

A partial solution to this problem is to use an `else` statement following the `if(saleAmount >= 1000)` expression:

```
if(saleAmount >= 1000)
    commissionRate = 0.08;
else if(saleAmount >= 500)
    commissionRate = 0.06;
else if(saleAmount <= 499)
    commissionRate = 0.05;
```


> **» NOTE** The last two logical tests in this code are sometimes called `else-if` statements because each `else` and its subsequent `if` are placed on the same line. When the `else-if` format is used to test multiple cases, programmers frequently forego the traditional indentation and align each `else-if` with the others.

With this code, when the `saleAmount` is $5000, the expression `(saleAmount >= 1000)` is `true` and the `commissionRate` becomes 8%; then the entire `if` structure ends. When the `saleAmount` is not greater than or equal to $1000 (for example, $800), the first `if` expression is `false` and the `else` statement executes and correctly sets the `commissionRate` to 6%.

This version of the code works, but it is somewhat inefficient. When the `saleAmount` is any amount that is at least $500, either the first `if` sets `commissionRate` to 8% for amounts of at least $1000, or its `else` sets `commissionRate` to 6% for amounts of at least $500. In either of these two cases, the Boolean value tested in the next statement, `if(saleAmount <= 499)`, is always `false`. After you know that the `saleAmount` is not at least $500, rather than asking `if(saleAmount <= 499)`, it's easier and more efficient to use an `else`. If the `saleAmount` is not at least $1000 and is also not at least $500, it must by default be less than or equal to $499. The improved code is as follows:

```
if(saleAmount >= 1000)
    commissionRate = 0.08;
else if(saleAmount >= 500)
    commissionRate = 0.06;
else commissionRate = 0.05;
```

In other words, because this example uses three commission rates, two boundaries should be checked. If there were four rates, there would be three boundaries, and so on.

Within a nested `if-else`, it is most efficient to ask the most likely question first. In other words, if you know that most `saleAmount` values are over $1000, compare `saleAmount` to that value first. That way, you most frequently avoid asking multiple questions. If, however, you know that most `saleAmount`s are small, you should ask `if(saleAmount < 500)` first.

USING AND AND OR APPROPRIATELY

Beginning programmers often use the AND operator when they mean to use OR, and often use OR when they should use AND. Part of the problem lies in the way we use the English language. For example, your boss might request, "Print an error message when an employee's hourly pay rate is under $5.65 and when an employee's hourly pay rate is over $60." Because your boss used the word "and" in the request, you might be tempted to write a program statement like the following:

```
if(payRate < 5.65 && payRate > 60)
    Console.WriteLine("Error in pay rate");
```

»DON'T DO IT
This expression can never be true.

However, as a single variable, no `payRate` value can ever be both below 5.65 and over 60 at the same time, so the print statement can never execute, no matter what value the `payRate` has. In this case, you must write the following statement to print the error message under the correct circumstances:

```
if(payRate < 5.65 || payRate > 60)
    Console.WriteLine("Error in pay rate");
```

Similarly, your boss might request, "Print the names of those employees in departments 1 and 2." Because the boss used the word "and" in the request, you might be tempted to write the following:

```
if(department == 1 && department == 2)
    Console.WriteLine("Name is: {0}", name);
```

»DON'T DO IT
This expression can never be true.

However, the variable `department` can never contain both a 1 and a 2 at the same time, so no employee name will ever be printed, no matter what department the employee is in.

USING NOT CORRECTLY

Whenever you use negatives, it is easy to make logical mistakes. For example, suppose your boss says, "Make sure if the sales code is not 'A' or 'B', the customer gets a 10% discount. You might be tempted to code the following:

```
if(salesCode != 'A' || salesCode != 'B')
    discount = 0.10;
```

»DON'T DO IT
This expression can never be true.

However, this logic will result in every customer receiving the 10% discount because every `salesCode` is either not 'A' or not 'B'. For example, a `salesCode` of 'A' is not 'B'. The statement above is always `true`. The correct statement is either one of the following:

```
if(salesCode != 'A' && salesCode != 'B')
    discount = 0.10;
if(!(salesCode == 'A' || salesCode == 'B'))
    discount = 0.10;
```

In the first example, if the `salesCode` is not 'A' and it also is not 'B', then the discount is applied correctly. In the second example, if the `salesCode` is 'A' or 'B', the inner Boolean expression is `true`, and the NOT operator (!) changes the evaluation to `false`, not applying the discount for 'A' or 'B' sales. You also could avoid the confusing negative situation by asking questions in a positive way, as in the following:

```
if(salesCode == 'A' || salesCode == 'B')
    discount = 0;
else
    discount = 0.10;
```

»TWO TRUTHS AND A LIE: AVOIDING COMMON ERRORS WHEN MAKING DECISIONS

1. If you want to display "OK" when `userEntry` is 12 and when it is 13, then the following is a usable C# statement:

   ```
   if(userEntry == 12 && userEntry == 13)
       Console.WriteLine("OK");
   ```

2. If you want to display "OK" when `userEntry` is 20 or when `highestScore` is at least 70, then the following is a usable C# statement:

   ```
   if(userEntry == 20 || highestScore >= 70)
       Console.WriteLine("OK");
   ```

3. If you want to display "OK" when `userEntry` is anything other than 99 or 100, then the following is a usable C# statement:

   ```
   if(userEntry != 99 && userEntry != 100)
       Console.WriteLine("OK");
   ```

The false statement is #1. If you want to display "OK" when `userEntry` is 12 and when it is 13, then you want to display it when it is either 12 or 13 because it cannot be both simultaneously. The expression `userEntry == 12 && userEntry == 13` can never be true. The correct Boolean expression is `userEntry == 12 || userEntry == 13`.

YOU DO IT

USING `if-else` STATEMENTS

In the next steps, you will write a program that requires using multiple, nested `if-else` statements to accomplish its goal—determining whether any of the three integers entered by a user are equal.

To create a program that uses nested `if-else` statements:

1. Open a new text file and write the first lines necessary for a `CompareThreeNumbers` class.

   ```
   using System;
   public class CompareThreeNumbers
   {
   ```

2. Begin a `Main()` method by declaring a string for input and three integers that will hold the input values.

```
public static void Main()
{
    string numberString;
    int num1, num2, num3;
```

3. Add the statements that retrieve the three integers from the user and assign them to the appropriate variables.

```
            Console.Write("Enter an integer ");
            numberString = Console.ReadLine();
            num1 = Convert.ToInt32(numberString);
            Console.Write("Enter an integer ");
            numberString = Console.ReadLine();
            num2 = Convert.ToInt32(numberString);
            Console.Write("Enter an integer ");
            numberString = Console.ReadLine();
            num3 = Convert.ToInt32(numberString);
```

> **» NOTE**
> In Chapter 6, you will learn to write methods, avoiding repetitive code like that shown here.

4. If the first number and the second number are equal, there are two possibilities: either the first is also equal to the third, in which case all three numbers are equal, or the first is not equal to the third, in which case only the first two numbers are equal. Insert the following code:

```
if(num1 == num2)
    if(num1 == num3)
        Console.WriteLine("All three numbers are equal");
    else
        Console.WriteLine("First two are equal");
```

5. If the first two numbers are not equal, but the first and third are equal, print an appropriate message. For clarity, the `else` should vertically align under `if(num1 == num2)`.

```
else
    if(num1 == num3)
        Console.WriteLine("First and last are equal");
```

6. When `num1` and `num2` are not equal, and `num1` and `num3` are not equal, but `num2` and `num3` are equal, display an appropriate message. For clarity, the `else` should vertically align under `if(num1 == num3)`.

```
    else
        if(num2 == num3)
            Console.WriteLine("Last two are equal");
```

7. Finally, if none of the pairs (`num1` and `num2`, `num1` and `num3`, or `num2` and `num3`) is equal, display an appropriate message. For clarity, the `else` should vertically align under `if(num2 == num3)`.

```
else
    Console.WriteLine
        ("No two numbers are equal");
```

8. Add a closing curly brace for the `Main()` method and a closing curly brace for the class.

9. Save the file as **CompareThreeNumbers.cs**. Compile the program, then execute it several times, providing different combinations of equal and nonequal integers when prompted. Figure 3-21 shows several executions of the program.

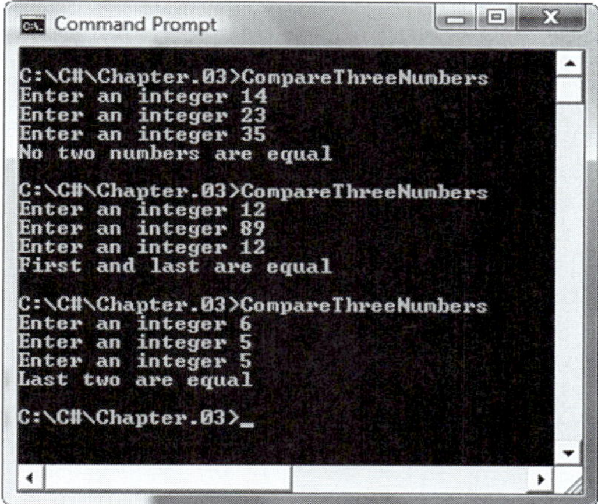

Figure 3-21 Several executions of the `CompareThreeNumbers` program

USING AND AND OR LOGIC

In the next steps, you will create an interactive program that allows you to test AND and OR logic for yourself. The program decides whether a delivery charge applies to a shipment. If the customer lives in Zone 1 or Zone 2, then shipping is free, as long as the order contains fewer than 10 boxes. If the customer lives in another zone or if the order is too large, then a delivery charge applies. First, you will create a program with incorrect logic; then you will fix it to demonstrate correct use of parentheses when combining ANDs and ORs.

To create the delivery charge program:

1. Open a new file in your text editor and enter the first few lines of the program. Define constants for `ZONE1`, `ZONE2`, and the `LOWQUANTITY` limit, as well as variables to hold the customer's input string, which will be converted to the zone and number of boxes in the shipment.

```
using System;
public class DemoORAndANDWrongLogic
{
    public static void Main()
    {
```

```
const int ZONE1 = 1, ZONE2 = 2;
const int LOWQUANTITY = 10;
string inputString;
int quantity;
int deliveryZone;
```

2. Enter statements that describe the delivery charge criteria to the user and accept keyboard values for the customer's delivery zone and shipment size.

```
Console.WriteLine("Delivery is free for zone {0} or {1}",
    ZONE1, ZONE2);
Console.WriteLine("when the number of boxes is less than {0}",
    LOWQUANTITY);
Console.WriteLine("Enter delivery zone ");
inputString = Console.ReadLine();
deliveryZone = Convert.ToInt32(inputString);
Console.WriteLine
    ("Enter the number of boxes in the shipment");
inputString = Console.ReadLine();
quantity = Convert.ToInt32(inputString);
```

3. Write a compound `if` statement that appears to test whether the customer lives in Zone 1 or 2 and has a shipment consisting of fewer than 10 boxes.

```
if(deliveryZone == ZONE1 || deliveryZone == ZONE2    &&
    quantity < LOWQUANTITY)
        Console.WriteLine("Delivery is free");
else
    Console.WriteLine("A delivery charge applies");
```

4. Add closing curly braces for the `Main()` method and for the class, and save the file as **DemoORAndANDWrongLogic.cs**. Compile and execute the program. Enter values for the zone and shipment size. The program appears to run correctly until you enter a shipment for Zone 1 that exceeds nine boxes. Such a shipment should not be free, but the output indicates that it is. Figure 3-22 shows the output.

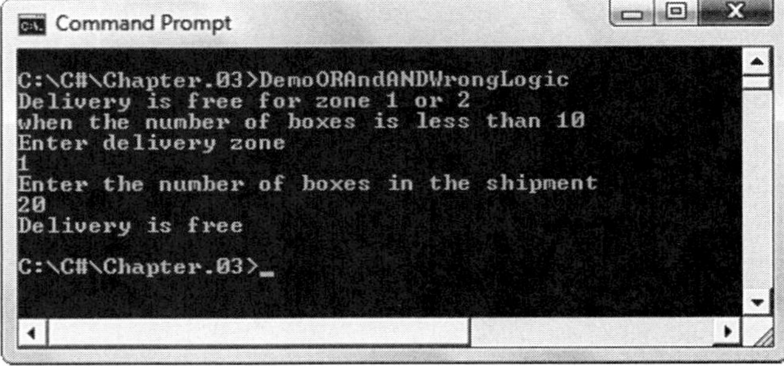

Figure 3-22 Sample execution of `DemoORAndANDWrongLogic` program

5. To remedy the problem, insert parentheses around the expression `deliveryZone ==
   ZONE1 || deliveryZone == ZONE2` within the `if` statement in the `Main()` method.
   Change the class name to `DemoORAndAND` (removing *WrongLogic*). Save the new version of
   the program as **DemoORAndAND.cs**. When you compile and execute this version of the
   program, every combination of zone and quantity values should work correctly. Figure 3-23
   shows the output for a Zone 1 delivery of 20 boxes.

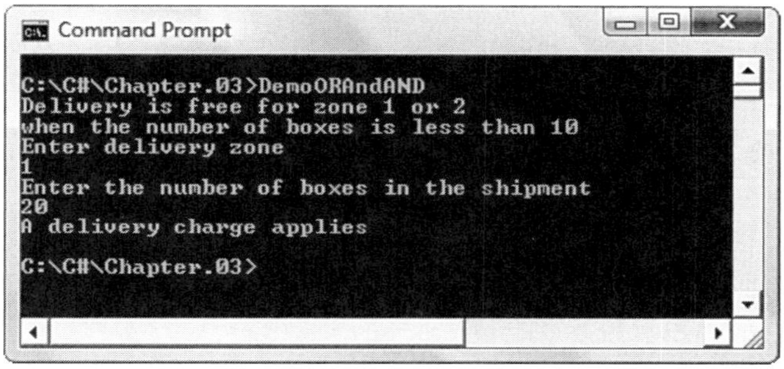

Figure 3-23 Output of `DemoORAndAND` program when user enters 1 and 20

CHAPTER SUMMARY

» A flowchart is a pictorial tool that helps you understand a program's logic. A decision
  structure is one that involves choosing between alternative courses of action based on
  some value within a program.

» You use an `if` statement to make a single-alternative decision. The `if` statement
  takes the form `if(expression) statement;`. When you want to execute multiple
  statements conditionally, you can place the statements within a block defined by curly
  braces.

» When you make a dual-alternative decision, you can use an `if-else` statement. The
  `if-else` statement takes the following form:

```
if(expression) statement1;
else statement2;
```

Just as you can block several statements so they all execute when an expression within
an `if` is `true`, you can block multiple statements after an `else` so they all execute when
the evaluated expression is `false`.

» You can use the conditional AND operator (or simply the AND operator) within a
  Boolean expression to determine whether two expressions are both `true`. The AND
  operator is written as two ampersands (`&&`). When you use the AND operator, you must
  include a complete Boolean expression on each side of the `&&` operator.

» You can use the conditional OR operator (or simply the OR operator) when you want some action to occur when one or both of two conditions are `true`. The OR operator is written as `||`.

» When you combine AND and OR operators within the same Boolean expression without parentheses, the AND operators take precedence, meaning their Boolean values are evaluated first.

» The `switch` statement tests a single variable against a series of exact matches.

» The conditional operator is used as an abbreviated version of the `if-else` statement. It requires three expressions separated with a question mark and a colon.

» You use the NOT operator, which is written as an exclamation point (!), to negate the result of any Boolean expression.

» Common errors when making decisions include using the assignment operator instead of the comparison operator, inserting a semicolon after the Boolean expression in an `if` statement, failing to block a set of statements when they should be blocked, failing to include a complete Boolean expression on each side of an `&&` or `||` operator in an `if` statement, performing a range check incorrectly or inefficiently, using the wrong operator with AND and OR, and using the NOT operator incorrectly.

KEY TERMS

Pseudocode is a tool that helps programmers plan a program's logic by writing plain English statements.

A **flowchart** is a tool that helps programmers plan a program's logic by writing program steps in diagram form, as a series of shapes connected by arrows.

A **sequence structure** is a unit of program logic in which one step follows another unconditionally.

A **decision structure** is a unit of program logic that involves choosing between alternative courses of action based on some value.

An **if statement** is used to make a single-alternative decision.

A **block** is a collection of one or more statements contained within a pair of curly braces.

A **nested if** statement is one in which one decision structure is contained within another.

Dual-alternative decisions have two possible outcomes.

An **if-else statement** performs a dual-alternative decision.

The **conditional AND operator** (or simply the **AND operator**) determines whether two expressions are both `true`; it is written using two ampersands (`&&`).

Short-circuit evaluation is the C# feature in which parts of an AND or OR expression are evaluated only as far as necessary to determine whether the entire expression is `true` or `false`.

The **conditional OR operator** (or simply the **OR operator**) determines whether at least one of two conditions is `true`; it is written using two pipes (`||`).

The **Boolean logical AND** operator determines whether two expressions are both `true`; it is written using a single ampersand (&). Unlike the conditional AND operator, it does not use short-circuit evaluation.

The **Boolean logical inclusive OR** operator determines whether at least one of two conditions is `true`; it is written using a single pipe (|). Unlike the conditional OR operator, it does not use short-circuit evaluation.

A **side effect** is an unintended consequence.

The **switch structure** tests a single variable against a series of exact matches.

The keyword **switch** starts a `switch` structure.

The **switch expression** is a condition in a `switch` statement enclosed in parentheses.

The keyword **case** in a `switch` structure is followed by one of the possible values that might equal the `switch` expression.

A **case label** identifies a course of action in a `switch` structure.

The keyword **break** optionally terminates a `switch` structure at the end of each `case`.

The keyword **default** optionally is used prior to any action that should occur if the test expression in a `case` structure does not match any `case`.

The **governing type** of a `switch` statement is established by the `switch` expression. The governing type can be `sbyte`, `byte`, `short`, `ushort`, `int`, `uint`, `long`, `ulong`, `char`, `string`, or `enum`.

An **enum** is an enumeration—a programmer-defined type that declares a set of constants.

The **conditional operator** is used as an abbreviated version of the `if-else` statement; it requires three expressions separated by a question mark and a colon.

A **ternary** operator requires three arguments.

The **NOT operator** (!) negates the result of any Boolean expression.

A **range check** is a series of `if` statements that determine whether a value falls within a specified range.

REVIEW QUESTIONS

1. What is the output of the following code segment?

```
int a = 3, b = 4;
if(a == b)
    Console.Write("Black ");
    Console.WriteLine("White");
```

a. Black

b. White

c. Black White

d. nothing

2. What is the output of the following code segment?

```
int a = 3, b = 4;
if(a < b)
{
    Console.Write("Black ");
    Console.WriteLine("White");
}
```

a. Black

b. White

c. Black White

d. nothing

3. What is the output of the following code segment?

```
int a = 3, b = 4;
if(a > b)
    Console.Write("Black ");
else
    Console.WriteLine("White");
```

a. Black

b. White

c. Black White

d. nothing

4. If the following code segment compiles correctly, what do you know about the variable x?

```
if(x) Console.WriteLine("OK");
```

a. x is an integer variable

b. x is a Boolean variable

c. x is greater than 0

d. none of these

5. What is the output of the following code segment?

```
int c = 6, d = 12;
if(c > d);
    Console.Write("Green ");
    Console.WriteLine("Yellow");
```

a. Green

b. Yellow

c. Green Yellow

d. nothing

6. What is the output of the following code segment?

```
int c = 6, d = 12;
if(c < d)
    if(c > 8)
        Console.Write("Green");
    else
        Console.Write("Yellow");
else
    Console.Write("Blue");
```

    a. Green   c. Blue

    b. Yellow   d. nothing

7. What is the output of the following code segment?

```
int e = 5, f = 10;
if(e < f && f < 0)
   Console.Write("Red ");
else
   Console.Write("Orange");
```

    a. Red   c. Red Orange

    b. Orange   d. nothing

8. What is the output of the following code segment?

```
int e = 5, f = 10;
if(e < f || f < 0)
   Console.Write("Red ");
else
   Console.Write("Orange");
```

    a. Red   c. Red Orange

    b. Orange   d. nothing

9. Which of the following expressions is equivalent to the following code segment?

```
if(g > h)
   if(g < k)
      Console.Write("Brown");
```

    a. `if(g > h && g < k) Console.Write("Brown");`

    b. `if(g > h && < k) Console.Write("Brown");`

    c. `if(g > h || g < k) Console.Write("Brown");`

    d. two of these

10. Which of the following expressions assigns `true` to a Boolean variable named `isIDValid` when the `idNumber` is greater than 1000, less than or equal to 9999, or equal to 123456?

    a.
```
isIDValid = (idNumber > 1000 && idNumber <= 9999 &&
  idNumber == 123456)
```

    b.
```
isIDValid = (idNumber > 1000 && idNumber <= 9999 ||
  idNumber == 123456)
```

    c.
```
isIDValid = ((idNumber > 1000 && idNumber <= 9999) ||
  idNumber == 123456)
```

    d. two of these

11. Which of the following expressions is equivalent to `a || b && c || d`?

    a. `a && b || c && d`

    b. `(a || b) && (c || d)`

    c. `a || (b && c) || d`

    d. two of these

12. How many `case` labels would a `switch` statement require to be equivalent to the following `if` statement?

    ```
    if(v == 1)
        Console.WriteLine("one");
    else
        Console.WriteLine("two");
    ```

    a. zero

    b. one

    c. two

    d. impossible to tell

13. Falling through a `switch` `case` is most often prevented by using the __________ .

    a. `break` statement

    b. `default` statement

    c. `case` statement

    d. `end` statement

14. If the test expression in a `switch` does not match any of the `case` values, and there is no `default` value, then __________ .

    a. a compiler error occurs

    b. a run-time error occurs

    c. the program continues with the next executable statement

    d. the expression is incremented and the `case` values are tested again

15. Which of the following is equivalent to the statement `if(m == 0) d = 0 ; else d = 1;`?

    a. `? m == 0 : d = 0, d = 1;`

    b. `m? d = 0; d = 1;`

    c. `m == 0 ; d = 0; d = 1?`

    d. `m == 0 ? d = 0 : d = 1;`

16. Which of the following C# expressions is equivalent to `a < b && b < c`?

    a. `c > b > a`

    b. `a < b && c >= b`

    c. `!(b <= a) && b < c`

    d. two of these

17. Which of the following C# expressions means, "If `itemNumber` is not 8 or 9, add TAX to `price`"?

    a. `if(itemNumber != 8 || itemNumber != 9)`
       `price = price + TAX;`

    b. `if(itemNumber != 8 && itemNumber != 9)`
       `price = price + TAX;`

    c. `if(itemNumber != 8 && != 9)`
       `price = price + TAX;`

    d. two of these

18. Which of the following C# expressions means, "If `itemNumber` is 1 or 2 and `quantity` is 12 or more, add TAX to `price`"?

    a. `if(itemNumber = 1 || itemNumber = 2 && quantity >= 12)`
       `price = price + TAX;`

    b. `if(itemNumber == 1 || itemNumber == 2 || quantity >= 12)`
       `price = price + TAX;`

    c. `if(itemNumber == 1 && itemNumber == 2 && quantity >= 12)`
       `price = price + TAX;`

    d. none of these

19. Which of the following C# expressions means, "If `itemNumber` is 5 and `zone` is 1 or 3, add TAX to `price`"?

    a. `if(itemNumber == 5 && zone == 1 || zone == 3)`
       `price = price + TAX;`

    b. `if(itemNumber == 5 && (zone == 1 || zone == 3))`
       `price = price + TAX;`

    c. `if(itemNumber == 5 && (zone == 1 || 3))`
       `price = price + TAX;`

    d. two of these

20. Which of the following C# expressions means, "If `itemNumber` is not 100, add TAX to `price`"?

    a. `if(itemNumber != 100)`
       `price = price + TAX;`

    b. `if(!(itemNumber == 100)`
       `price = price + TAX;`

    c. `if(!(itemNumber <100) && !(itemNumber > 100)`
       `price = price + TAX;`

    d. all of these

EXERCISES

1. Write a program that prompts the user for an hourly pay rate. If the value entered is less than $5.65, display an error message. Save the program as **CheckLowRate.cs**.

2. Write a program that prompts a user for an hourly pay rate. If the value entered is less than $5.65 or greater than $49.99, display an error message. Save the program as **CheckLowAndHighRate.cs**.

3. Write a program that prompts a user for an hourly pay rate. If the user enters values less than $5.65 or greater than $49.99, prompt the user again. If the user enters an invalid value again, display an appropriate error message. If the user enters a valid value on either the first or second attempt, display the pay rate as well as the weekly rate, which is calculated as 40 times the hourly rate. Save the program as **EnsureValidPayRate.cs**.

4. Write a program for a furniture company. Ask the user to choose *P* for pine, *O* for oak, or *M* for mahogany. Show the price of a table manufactured with the chosen wood. Pine tables cost $100, oak tables cost $225, and mahogany tables cost $310. (If the user enters something other than *P*, *O*, or *M*, set the price to 0.) Save the program as **Furniture.cs**.

5. Write a program for a college's admissions office. The user enters a numeric high school grade point average (for example, 3.2) and an admission test score. Print the message "Accept" if the student meets either of the following requirements:

    » A grade point average of 3.0 or higher and an admission test score of at least 60
    » A grade point average of less than 3.0 and an admission test score of at least 80

    If the student does not meet either of the qualification criteria, print "Reject". Save the program as **Admission.cs**.

6. Write a program that prompts the user for an hourly pay rate and hours worked. Compute gross pay (hours times pay rate), withholding tax, and net pay (gross pay minus withholding tax). Withholding tax is computed as a percentage of gross pay based on the following:

Gross Pay	**Withholding Percentage**
Up to and including 300.00	10%
300.01 and up	12%

    Save the program as **Payroll.cs**.

7. Write a program that allows the user to enter two integers and a character. If the character is *A*, add the two integers. If it is *S*, subtract the second integer from the first. If it is *M*, multiply the integers. Display the results of the arithmetic. Save the file as **Calculate.cs**.

8. a. Write an application for a lawn-mowing service. The lawn-mowing season lasts 20 weeks. The weekly fee for mowing a lot under 400 square feet is $25. The fee for a lot that is 400 square feet or more, but under 600 square feet, is $35 per week. The fee for a lot that is 600 square feet or over is $50 per week. Prompt the user for the length and width of a lawn, and then print the weekly mowing fee, as well as the total fee for the 20-week season. Save the file as **Lawn.cs**.

   b. To the Lawn application you created in Exercise 8a, add a prompt that asks the user whether the customer wants to pay (1) once, (2) twice, or (3) 20 times per year. If the user enters 1 for once, the fee for the season is simply the seasonal total. If the customer requests two payments, each payment is half the seasonal fee plus a $5 service charge. If the user requests 20 separate payments, add a $3 service charge per week. Display the number of payments the customer must make, each payment amount, and the total for the season. Save the file as **Lawn2.cs**.

9. Write an application that asks a user to enter an IQ score. If the score is a number less than 0 or greater than 200, issue an error message; otherwise, issue an "above average", "average", or "below average" message for scores over, at, or under 100, respectively. Save the file as **IQ.cs**.

DEBUGGING EXERCISES

Each of the following files in the Chapter.03 folder on your Student Disk has syntax and/or logical errors. In each case, determine the problem and fix the program. After you correct the errors, save each file using the same filename preceded with *Fixed*. For example, save DebugThree1.cs as **FixedDebugThree1.cs**.

   a. DebugThree1.cs

   b. DebugThree2.cs

   c. DebugThree3.cs

   d. DebugThree4.cs

UP FOR DISCUSSION

1. In this chapter, you learned how computer programs make decisions. Insurance companies use programs to make decisions about your insurability as well as the rates you will be charged for health and life insurance policies. For example, certain preexisting conditions may raise your insurance premiums considerably. Is it ethical for insurance companies to access your health records and then make insurance decisions about you?

2. Job applications are sometimes screened by software that makes decisions about a candidate's suitability based on keywords in the applications. For example, when a help-wanted ad lists "management experience," the presence of those exact words might determine which résumés are chosen for further scrutiny. Is such screening fair to applicants?

3. Medical facilities often have more patients waiting for organ transplants than there are available organs. Suppose you have been asked to write a computer program that selects which of several candidates should receive an available organ. What data would you want on file to use in your program, and what decisions would you make based on the data? What data do you think others might use that you would not use?

4

LOOPING

In thɪs chapter you wɪll:

Learn about the loop structure
Learn how to create loops using the `while` statement
Learn how to create loops using the `for` statement
Learn how to create loops using the `do` statement
Use nested loops
Accumulate totals
Understand how to improve loop performance

In Chapter 3, you learned how computers make decisions. Looping allows a program to repeat tasks based on a decision. For example, programs that produce thousands of paychecks or invoices rely on the ability to loop to repeat instructions. Likewise, programs that repeatedly prompt you for a valid credit card number or for the correct answer to a tutorial question require the ability to loop to do their jobs efficiently. In this chapter, you will learn to create loops in C# programs.

LEARNING ABOUT THE LOOP STRUCTURE

>> **NOTE**
One execution of any loop is called an **iteration**.

If making decisions is what makes programs seem smart, looping is what makes programs seem powerful. A **loop** is a structure that allows repeated execution of a block of statements. Within a looping structure, a Boolean expression is evaluated. If it is `true`, a block of statements called the **loop body** executes, and the Boolean expression is evaluated again. As long as the expression is `true`, the statements in the loop body continue to execute. When the Boolean evaluation is `false`, the loop ends. Figure 4-1 shows a diagram of the logic of a loop.

>> **NOTE**
Recall from Chapter 3 that a block of statements might be a single statement with or without curly braces, or it might be multiple statements with curly braces.

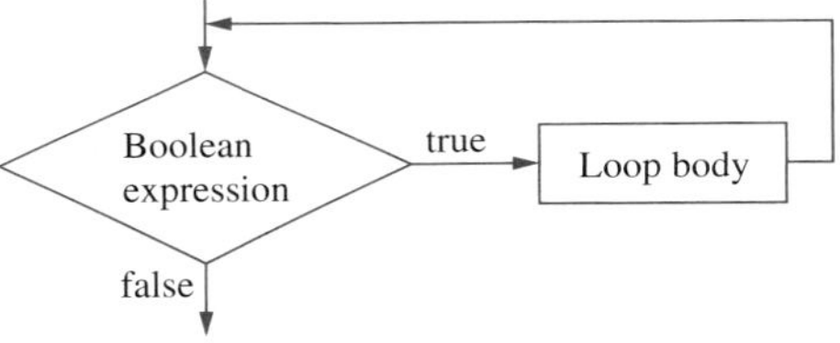

Figure 4-1 Flowchart of a loop structure

In C#, you can use several mechanisms to create loops. In this chapter, you will learn to use three types of loops:

» A `while` loop, in which the loop-controlling Boolean expression is the first statement in the loop

» A `for` loop, which is usually used as a concise format in which to execute loops

» A `do` loop (or `do-while` loop), in which the loop-controlling Boolean expression is the last statement in the loop

»TWO TRUTHS AND A LIE: LEARNING ABOUT THE LOOP STRUCTURE

1. A loop is a structure that allows repeated execution of a block of statements.
2. In a loop, when a tested expression is `true`, the loop ends.
3. In a `while` loop, a loop-controlling Boolean expression is the first statement.

The false statement is #2. A loop continues while a tested expression is `true` and ends when it is `false`.

USING THE while LOOP

You can use a **while loop** to execute a body of statements continuously as long as some condition continues to be true. A while loop consists of the keyword while, followed by a Boolean expression within parentheses, followed by the body of the loop. The body can be a single statement or a block of statements surrounded by curly braces.

For example, the following code shows an integer declaration followed by a loop that causes the message "Hello" to display (theoretically) forever because there is no code to end the loop. A loop that never ends is called an **infinite loop**.

```
int number = 1;
while (number > 0)
    Console.WriteLine("Hello");
```

In this loop, the expression number > 0 evaluates as true, and "Hello" is displayed. The expression number > 0 evaluates as true again and "Hello" is displayed again. Because nothing ever alters the value of number, the loop runs forever, evaluating the same Boolean expression and repeatedly printing "Hello" (as long as computer memory and hardware allow).

> **»NOTE** It is always a bad idea to write an infinite loop, although even experienced programmers write them by accident. If you ever find yourself in the midst of executing an infinite loop, you can break out by holding down the Ctrl key and pressing the C key or the Break (Pause) key.

To make a while loop end correctly, three separate actions should occur:

» A variable, the **loop control variable**, is initialized (before entering the loop).

» The loop control variable is tested in the while expression.

» The body of the while statement must take some action that alters the value of the loop control variable (so that the while expression eventually evaluates as false).

For example, Figure 4-2 shows the logic for a loop that displays "Hello" four times. The variable number is initialized to 1 and a constant, LIMIT, is initialized to 5. The variable is less

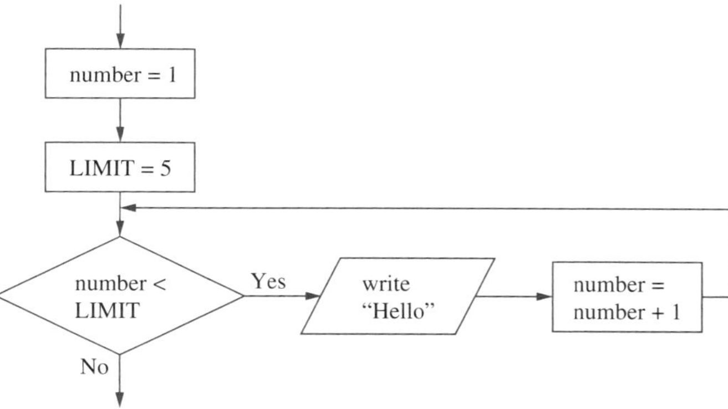

Figure 4-2 Flowchart for the logic of a while loop whose body executes four times

than `LIMIT`, and so the loop body executes. The loop body shown in Figure 4-2 contains two statements. The first prints "Hello" and the second adds 1 to `number`. The next time `number` is evaluated, its value is 2, which is still less than `LIMIT`, so the loop body executes again. "Hello" prints a third time and the `number` becomes 4, then "Hello" prints a fourth time and the `number` becomes 5. Now when the expression `number < LIMIT` evaluates, it is `false`, so the loop ends. If there were any subsequent statements following the `while` loop's closing curly brace, they would execute after the loop was finished.

Figure 4-3 shows a C# program that uses the same logic as diagrammed in Figure 4-2. After the declarations, the shaded `while` expression compares `number` to `LIMIT`. The two statements that execute each time the Boolean expression is `true` are blocked using a pair of curly braces. Figure 4-4 shows the output.

```csharp
using System;
public class FourHellos
{
    public static void Main()
    {
        int number = 1;
        const int LIMIT = 5;
        while(number < LIMIT)
        {
            Console.WriteLine("Hello");
            number = number + 1;
        }
    }
}
```

Figure 4-3 A program that contains a `while` loop whose body executes four times

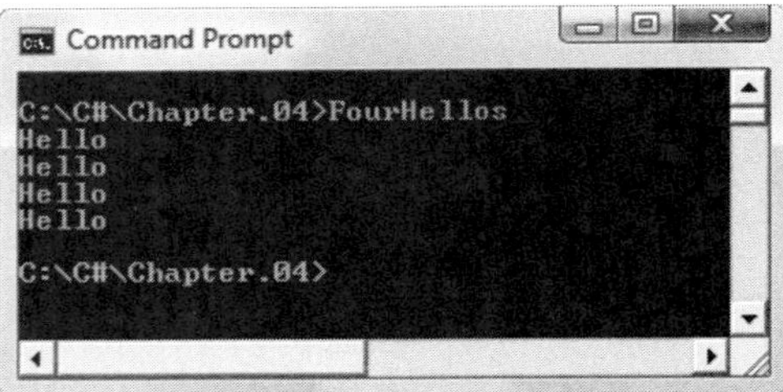

Figure 4-4 Output of `FourHellos` program

▶▶ NOTE To an algebra student, a statement such as `number = number + 1;` looks wrong—a value can never be one more than itself. In C# (and many other programming languages), however, the expression `number = number + 1;` isn't a mathematical equation; rather, it is a programming language statement that takes the value of `number`, adds 1 to it, and assigns the new value back into `number`. Recall from Chapter 2 that you also can use a shortcut operator to increase the value of a variable by 1. Instead of `number = number + 1`, you could achieve the same final result by writing `number++`, `++number`, or `number += 1`.

The curly braces surrounding the body of the `while` loop in Figure 4-3 are important. If they are omitted, the `while` loop ends at the end of the "Hello" statement. Adding 1 to `number` would no longer be part of the loop body, so an infinite loop would be created. Even if the statement `number = number + 1;` was indented under the `while` statement, it would not be part of the loop without the surrounding curly braces. Figure 4-5 shows the incorrect logic that would result from omitting the curly braces.

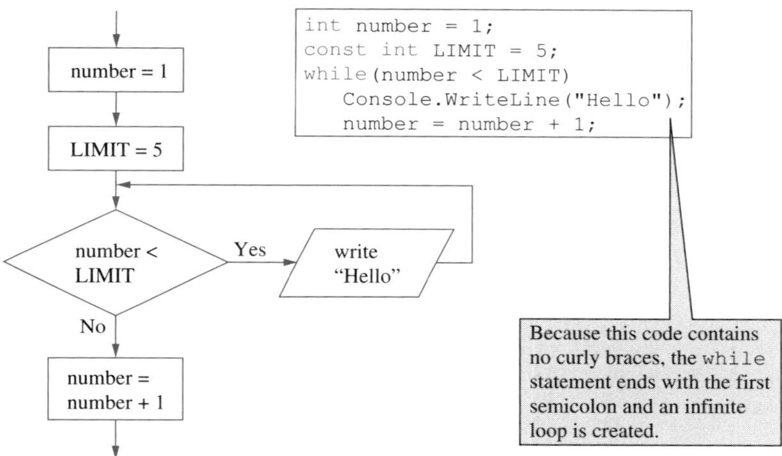


```
int number = 1;
const int LIMIT = 5;
while (number < LIMIT)
    Console.WriteLine("Hello");
    number = number + 1;
```

Figure 4-5 Incorrect logic when curly braces are omitted from the loop in the `FourHellos` program

Also, if a semicolon is mistakenly placed at the end of the partial statement, as in Figure 4-6, then the loop is also infinite. This loop has an **empty body**, or a body with no statements in it. In this case, `number` is initialized to 1, the Boolean expression `number < LIMIT` evaluates, and because it is `true`, the loop body is entered. Because the loop body is empty, ending at the semicolon, no action takes place, and the Boolean expression evaluates again. It is still `true` (nothing has changed), so the empty body is entered again, and the infinite loop continues. The program can never progress to either the statement that displays "Hello" or the statement that increases the value of `number`. The fact that these two statements are blocked using curly braces has no effect because of the incorrectly placed semicolon.

Within a correctly functioning loop's body, you can change the value of the loop control variable in a number of ways. Many loop control variable values are altered by **incrementing**, or adding to them, as in Figures 4-2 and 4-3. Other loops are controlled by reducing, or **decrementing**, a variable and testing whether the value remains greater than some benchmark value. A loop for which the number of iterations is predetermined is called a **definite loop** or **counted loop**. Often, the value of a loop control variable is not altered by arithmetic, but instead is altered by user input. For example, perhaps you want to continue performing some task while the user indicates a desire to continue. In that case, you do not know when you write the program whether the loop will be executed two times, 200 times, or not at all. This type of loop is an **indefinite loop**.

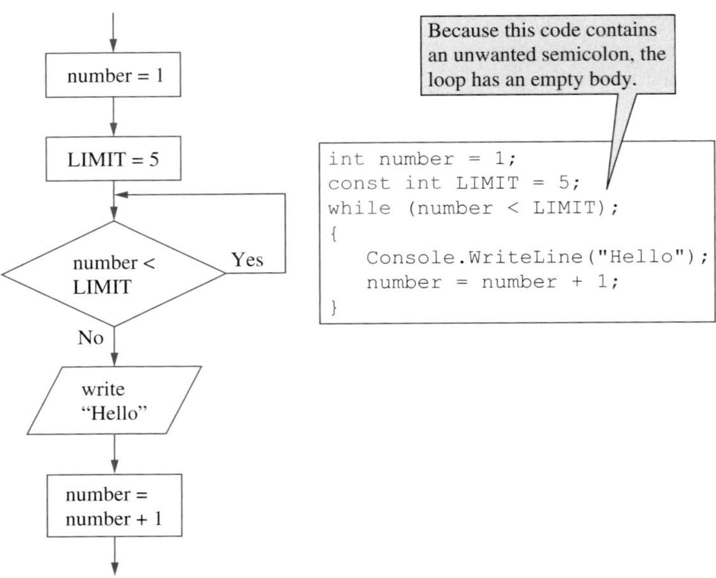


```
int number = 1;
const int LIMIT = 5;
while (number < LIMIT);
{
    Console.WriteLine("Hello");
    number = number + 1;
}
```

Figure 4-6 Incorrect logic when an unwanted semicolon is mistakenly added to the loop in the `FourHellos` program

Consider a program that displays a bank balance and asks if the user wants to see what the balance will be after one year of interest has accumulated. Each time the user indicates she wants to continue, an increased balance appears. When the user finally indicates she has had enough, the program ends. The program appears in Figure 4-7, and a typical execution appears in Figure 4-8.

> **» NOTE** The program shown in Figure 4-7 continues to display bank balances while the response is *Y*. It could also be written to display while the response is not *N*, as in `while (response != 'N')`. . . . A value such as `'Y'` or `'N'` that a user must supply to stop a loop is called a **sentinel value**.

The program shown in Figure 4-7 contains two variables and a constant that are involved in the looping process: a bank balance, an interest rate, and a response. The `response` is the loop control variable. It is initialized when the program asks the user, "Do you want to see your balance?" and reads the response. The loop control variable is tested with `while(response == 'Y')`. If the user types any response other than *Y*, then the loop body never executes; instead, the next statement to execute is the display of "Have a nice day!". However, if the user enters *Y*, then all five statements within the loop body execute. The current balance is displayed, and the program increases the balance by the interest rate value; this value will not be displayed unless the user requests another loop repetition. Within the loop, the program prompts the user and reads in a new value for `response`. This is the statement that potentially alters the loop control variable. The loop ends with

```
using System;
public class LoopingBankBal
{
    public static void Main()
    {
        double bankBal = 1000;
        const double INT_RATE = 0.04;
        string inputString;
        char response;
        Console.Write("Do you want to see your balance? Y or N ...");
        inputString = Console.ReadLine();
        response = Convert.ToChar(inputString);
        while(response == 'Y')
        {
            Console.WriteLine("Bank balance is {0}", bankBal.ToString("C"));
            bankBal = bankBal + bankBal * INT_RATE;
            Console.Write("Do you want to see next year's balance? Y or N ...");
            inputString = Console.ReadLine();
            response = Convert.ToChar(inputString);
        }
        Console.WriteLine("Have a nice day!");
    }
}
```

Figure 4-7 LoopingBankBal program

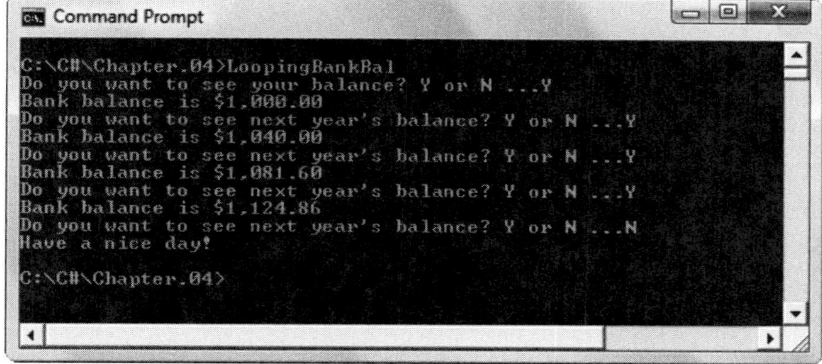

Figure 4-8 Typical execution of the LoopingBankBal program

a closing curly brace, and program control returns to the top of the loop, where the Boolean expression in the while loop is tested again. If the user typed Y at the last prompt, then the loop is entered and the increased bankBal value that was calculated during the last loop cycle is finally displayed.

> **» NOTE** In C#, character data is case sensitive. If a program tests `response == 'Y'`, a user response of *y* will result in a `false` evaluation. Beware of the pitfall of writing a loop similar to `while(response != 'Y' || response != 'y')...` to test both for uppercase and lowercase versions of the response. Every character is either not 'Y' or not 'y', even 'Y' and 'y'. The correct loop begins with `while(response != 'Y' && response != 'y')....`

» TWO TRUTHS AND A LIE: USING THE `while` LOOP

1. To make a `while` loop that executes correctly, a loop control variable is initialized before entering the loop.
2. To make a `while` loop that executes correctly, the loop control variable is tested in the `while` expression.
3. To make a `while` loop that executes correctly, the body of the `while` statement must never alter the value of the loop control variable.

The false statement is #3. To make a `while` loop that executes correctly, the body of the `while` statement must take some action that alters the value of the loop control variable.

USING THE `for` LOOP

Each time the `LoopingBankBal` program in Figure 4-7 executes, the user might continue the loop a different number of times, which makes it an indefinite loop. You can use a `while` loop for either definite or indefinite loops. To write either type of `while` loop, you initialize a loop control variable, and as long as its test expression is `true`, you continue to execute the body of the `while` loop. To avoid an infinite loop, the body of the `while` loop must contain a statement that alters the loop control variable.

Because you need definite loops so frequently when you write programs, C# provides a shorthand way to create such a loop. This shorthand structure is called a **for loop**. With a `for` loop, you can indicate the starting value for the loop control variable, the test condition that controls loop entry, and the expression that alters the loop control variable, all in one convenient place.

You begin a `for` statement with the keyword `for` followed by a set of parentheses. Within the parentheses are three sections separated by exactly two semicolons. The three sections are usually used for:

» Initializing the loop control variable
» Testing the loop control variable
» Updating the loop control variable

> **» NOTE**
> The amount by which a loop control variable increases or decreases on each cycle through the loop is often called the **step value**. That's because in the BASIC programming language, the keyword `STEP` was actually used in `for` loops.

The body of the `for` statement follows the parentheses. As with an `if` or a `while` statement, you can use a single statement as the body of a `for` loop, or you can use a block of statements enclosed in curly braces. The `while` and `for` statements shown in Figure 4-9 produce the same output—the integers 1 through 10.

Within the parentheses of the `for` statement shown in Figure 4-9, the initialization section prior to the first semicolon sets a variable named `x` to 1. The program will execute this statement once, no matter how many times the body of the `for` loop eventually executes.

```
// Declare loop control variable and limit
int x;
const int LIMIT = 10

// Using a while loop to display 1 through 10
x = 1;
while(x <= LIMIT)
{
    Console.WriteLine(x);
    ++x;
}

// Using a for loop to display 1 through 10
for(x = 1; x <= LIMIT; ++x)
    Console.WriteLine(x);
```

Figure 4-9 Printing integers 1 through 10 with `while` and `for` loops

After the initialization expression executes, program control passes to the middle, or test, section of the `for` statement. If the Boolean expression found there evaluates to `true`, then the body of the `for` loop is entered. In the program segment shown in Figure 4-9, x is initialized to 1, so when x <= LIMIT is tested, it evaluates to `true` and the loop body prints the value of x.

After the loop body executes, the final one-third of the `for` expression (the update section) executes, and x increases to 2. Following the third section, program control returns to the second (test) section, where x is compared to LIMIT a second time. Because the value of x is 2, it is still less than or equal to LIMIT, so the body of the `for` loop executes. The value of x is displayed. Then the third, altering portion of the `for` statement executes again. The variable x increases to 3, and the `for` loop continues.

Eventually, when x is *not* less than or equal to LIMIT (after 1 through 10 have printed), the `for` loop ends, and the program continues with any statements that follow the `for` loop.

Although the three sections of the `for` loop are most commonly used for initializing, testing, and incrementing, you can also perform other tasks:

» You can initialize more than one variable by placing commas between the separate statements, as in the following:

```
for(g = 0, h = 1; g < 6; ++g)
```

» You can declare a new variable, as in the following:

```
for(int k = 0; k < 5; ++k)
```

» In this example, k is declared to be an `int` and is initialized to 0. This technique is used frequently when the variable exists only to control the loop and for no other purpose. When a variable is declared inside a loop, as k is in this example, it can be referenced only for the duration of the loop body; then it is **out of scope**, which means it is not usable because it has ceased to exist.

» You can perform more than one test by evaluating compound conditions, as in the following:

```
for(g = 0; g < 3 && h > 1; ++g)
```

» You can decrement or perform some other task at the end of the loop's execution, as in:

```
for(g = 5; g >= 1; --g)
```

» You can perform multiple tasks at the end of the loop's execution, as in:

```
for(g = 0; g < 5; ++g, ++h)
```

» You can leave one or more portions of the `for` expression empty, although the two semicolons are still required as placeholders to separate the three sections.

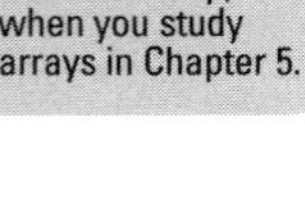

You will learn about a similar loop, the `foreach` loop, when you study arrays in Chapter 5.

Generally, you should use the `for` loop for its intended purpose, which is a shorthand way of programming a definite loop.

Just as with a decision or a `while` loop, statements in a `for` loop can be blocked. For example, the following loop displays "Hello" and "Goodbye" four times each:

```
const int TIMES = 4;
for(int var = 0; var < TIMES; ++var)
{
    Console.WriteLine("Hello");
    Console.WriteLine("Goodbye");
}
```

Without the curly braces in this code, "Hello" would be displayed four times, but "Goodbye" would be displayed only once.

» TWO TRUTHS AND A LIE: USING THE `for` LOOP

1. The following statement displays the numbers 3 through 6:

```
for(int x = 3; x <= 6; ++x)
    Console.WriteLine(x);
```

2. The following statement displays the numbers 4 through 9:

```
for(int x = 3; x < 9; ++x)
    Console.WriteLine(x + 1);
```

3. The following statement displays the numbers 5 through 12:

```
for(int x = 5; x < 12; ++x)
    Console.WriteLine(x);
```

The false statement is #3. That loop only displays the numbers 5 through 11, because when x is 12, the loop body is not entered.

USING THE do LOOP

With each of the loops you have learned about so far, the loop body might execute many times, but it is also possible that the loop will not execute at all. For example, recall the bank balance program that displays compound interest, part of which is shown in Figure 4-10. The loop begins by testing the value of response. If the user has not entered *Y*, the loop body never executes. The while loop checks a value at the "top" of the loop before the body has a chance to execute.

```
Console.Write("Do you want to see your balance? Y or N ...");
inputString = Console.ReadLine();
response = Convert.ToChar(inputString);
while(response == 'Y')
{
    Console.WriteLine("Bank balance is {0}", bankBal.ToString("C"));
    bankBal = bankBal + bankBal * INT_RATE;
    Console.Write("Do you want to see next year's balance? Y or N ...");
    inputString = Console.ReadLine();
    response = Convert.ToChar(inputString);
}
```

Figure 4-10 Part of the bank balance program using a while loop

Sometimes you might need a loop body to execute at least one time. If so, you want to write a loop that checks at the "bottom" of the loop after the first iteration. The **do loop** checks the bottom of the loop after one repetition has occurred. Figure 4-11 shows a diagram of the structure of a do loop.

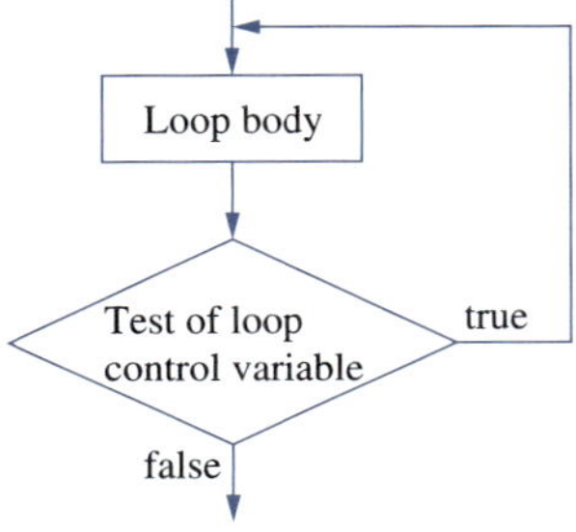

Figure 4-11 Flowchart of a do loop

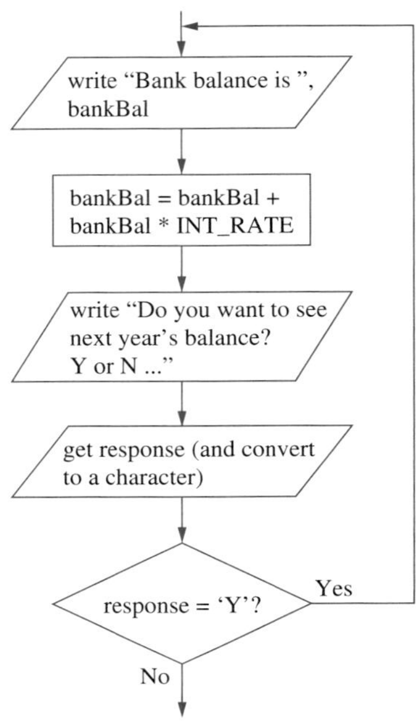


```
do
{
    Console.WriteLine("Bank balance is {0}", bankBal.ToString("C"));
    bankBal = bankBal + bankBal * INT_RATE;
    Console.Write("Do you want to see next year's balance? Y or N ...");
    inputString = Console.ReadLineGetChar();
    response = Convert.ToChar(inputString);
}   while(response == 'Y');
```


Figure 4-12 Part of the bank balance program using a do loop

Figure 4-12 shows the logic for a do loop in a bank balance program, along with the C# code. The loop starts with the keyword do. The body of the loop follows and is contained within curly braces. Within the loop, the next balance is calculated and the user is prompted for a response. The Boolean expression that controls loop execution is written using a while statement, placed after the loop body. The bankBal variable is output the first time before the user has any option of responding. At the end of the loop, the user is prompted, "Do you want to see next year's balance? Y or N ...". Now the user has the option of seeing more balances, but the first view of the balance was unavoidable. The user's response is checked at the bottom of the loop. If it is *Y*, then the loop repeats.

In any situation where you want to loop, you never are required to use a do loop. Within the bank balance example, you could unconditionally display the bank balance once, prompt the user, and then start a `while` loop that might not be entered. However, when you know you want to perform some task at least one time, the do loop is convenient.

» TWO TRUTHS AND A LIE: USING THE do LOOP

1. The do loop checks the bottom of the loop after one repetition has occurred.
2. The Boolean expression that controls do loop execution is written using a do statement, placed after the loop body.
3. You never are required to use a do loop; you can always substitute one execution of the body statements followed by a `while` loop.

The false statement is #2. The Boolean expression that controls do loop execution is written using a `while` statement, placed after the loop body.

USING NESTED LOOPS

Just as `if` statements can be nested, so can loop statements. You can place a `while` loop within a `while` loop, a `for` loop within a `for` loop, a `while` loop within a `for` loop, or any other combination. When loops are nested, each pair contains an **inner loop** and an **outer loop**. The inner loop must be entirely contained within the outer loop; loops can never overlap. Figure 4-13 shows a diagram in which the shaded loop is nested within another loop; the shaded area is the inner loop as well as the body of the outer loop.

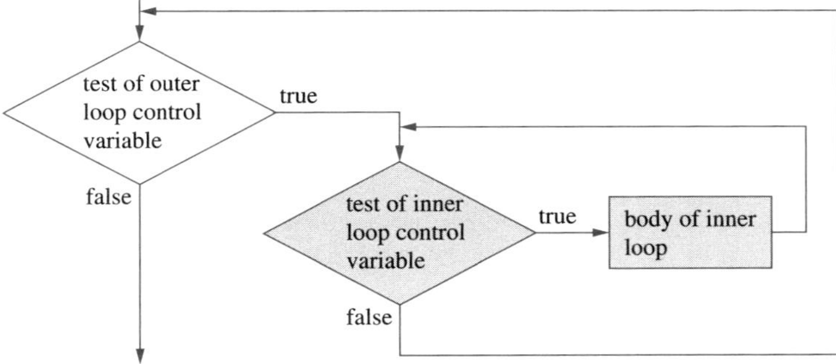

Figure 4-13 Nested loops

Suppose you want to display future bank balances for different years at a variety of interest rates. Figure 4-14 shows an application that contains an outer loop controlled by interest rates (starting with the first shaded statement in the figure) and an inner loop controlled by years (starting with the second shaded statement). The application displays annually compounded interest on $1000 at 4%, 6%, and 8% interest rates for 1 through 5 years. Figure 4-15 shows the output.

When you use a loop within a loop, you should always think of the outer loop as the all-encompassing loop. When you describe the task at hand, you often use the word "each" to refer to the inner loop. For example, if you wanted to print balances for different

```
using System;
public class LoopingBankBal2
{
   public static void Main()
   {
      double bankBal;
      double rate;
      int year;
      const double START_BAL = 1000;
      const double START_INT = 0.04;
      const double INT_INCREASE = 0.02;
      const double LAST_INT = 0.08;
      const int END_YEAR = 5;
      for(rate = START_INT; rate <= LAST_INT; rate += INT_INCREASE)
      {
         bankBal = START_BAL;
         Console.WriteLine("Starting bank balance is {0}",
            bankBal.ToString("C"));
         Console.WriteLine("  Interest Rate: {0}",
            rate.ToString("P"));
         for(year = 1; year <= END_YEAR; ++year)
         {
            bankBal = bankBal + bankBal * rate;
            Console.WriteLine("   After year {0}, bank balance is {1}",
               year, bankBal.ToString("C"));
         }
      }
   }
}
```

Figure 4-14 The `LoopingBankBal2` program

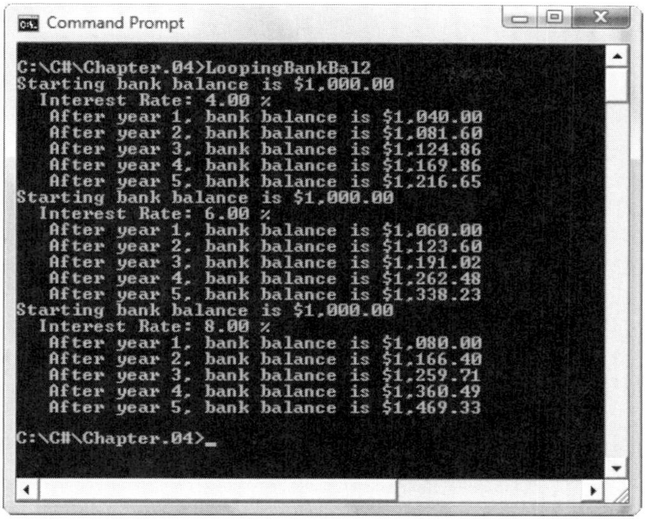

Figure 4-15 Output of the `LoopingBankBal2` program

interest rates each year for 10 years, you could appropriately initialize some constants
as follows:

```
const double RATE1 = 0.03;
const double RATE2= 0.07
const double RATE_INCREASE = 0.01
const int END_YEAR = 10;
```

Then you could use the following nested `for` loops:

```
for(rate = RATE1; rate <= RATE2; rate += RATE_INCREASE)
   for(year = 1; year <= END_YEAR; ++year)
      Console.WriteLine(bankBal + bankBal * rate);
```

However, if you wanted to print balances for years 1 through 10 for each possible interest rate,
you would use the following:

```
for(year = 1; year <= END_YEAR; ++year)
   for(rate = RATE1; rate <= RATE2; rate += RATE_INCREASE)
      Console.WriteLine(bankBal + bankBal * rate);
```

In both of these examples, the same 50 values would be displayed—five different interest rates
for 10 years. However, in the first example, balances for years 1 through 10 would display
"within" each interest rate, and in the second example, each balance for each interest rate
would display "within" each year, 1 through 10. In other words, in the first example, the first 10
amounts to display would be annual values using a rate of 0.03, and in the second example, the
first five amounts to display would be based on different interest values in the first year.

»TWO TRUTHS AND A LIE: USING NESTED LOOPS

1. The body of the following loop executes six times:

```
for(a = 1; a < 4; ++a)
    for(b = 2; b < 3; ++b)
```

2. The body of the following loop executes four times:

```
for(c = 1; c < 3; ++c)
    for(d = 1; d < 3; ++d)
```

3. The body of the following loop executes 15 times:

```
for(e = 1; e <= 5; ++e)
    for(f = 2; f <= 4; ++f)
```

The false statement is #1. That loop executes only three times. First, a = 1, and it is less than 4, so the inner loop executes. In the inner loop, b is 2 and it is less than 3, so the loop body executes a second time. Then a becomes 3, and it is still less than 4, so the inner loop executes a third time. Then a becomes 4, and it is no longer less than 4, so the outer loop is done.

ACCUMULATING TOTALS

Many computer programs display totals. When you receive a credit card or telephone service bill, you are usually provided with individual transaction details, but you are most interested in the total bill. Similarly, some programs total the number of credit hours generated by college students, the gross payroll for all employees of a company, or the total accounts receivable value for an organization. These totals are **accumulated**—that is, gathered together and added into a final sum by processing individual records one at a time in a loop.

Figure 4-16 shows an example of an interactive program that accumulates the user's total purchases. The program prompts the user to enter a purchase price or 0 to quit. While the user continues to enter nonzero values, the amounts are added to a total. With each pass through the loop, the total is calculated to be its current amount plus the new purchase amount. After the user enters the loop-terminating 0, the accumulated total can be displayed. Figure 4-17 shows a typical program execution.

In the application in Figure 4-16, it is very important that the `total` variable used for accumulation is initialized to 0. When it is not, the program will not compile. When `total` is not initialized, it might hold any value. The value could be 0 by chance, but it also could be any other value that happens to be located at the memory address of `total`. (For example, by chance, it could hold 1000 and your total would end up $1000 too high.) An unknown value like this is known as **garbage**. The C# compiler prevents you from seeing an incorrect total by requiring you to provide a starting value; C# will not use the garbage value that happens to be stored at an uninitialized memory location.

```
using System;
public class TotalPurchase
{
   public static void Main()
   {
      double purchase;
      double total = 0;
      string inputString;
      const double QUIT = 0;
      Console.WriteLine("Enter purchase amount ");
      inputString = Console.ReadLine();
      purchase = Convert.ToDouble(inputString);
      while(purchase != QUIT)
      {
         total += purchase;
         Console.WriteLine("Enter next purchase amount, or " +
            QUIT + " to quit ");
         inputString = Console.ReadLine();
         purchase = Convert.ToDouble(inputString);
      }
      Console.WriteLine("Your total is {0}", total.ToString("C"));
   }
}
```

Figure 4-16 An application that accumulates total purchases entered by the user

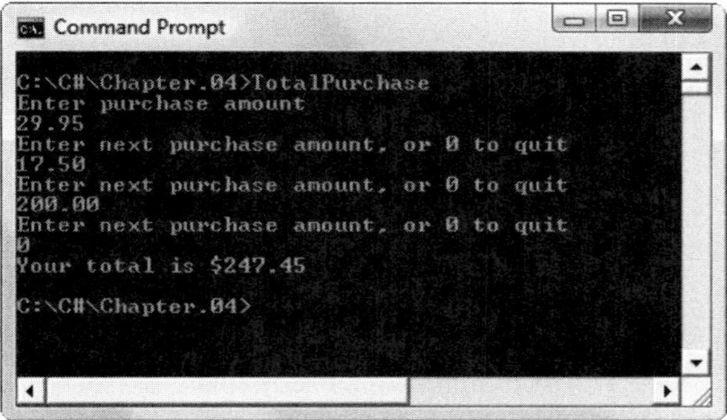

Figure 4-17 Typical execution of the TotalPurchase program

>> **NOTE** In the application in Figure 4-16, the total variable must be initialized to 0, but the purchase variable is uninitialized. Many programmers would say it makes no sense to initialize this variable because no matter what starting value you provide, the value can be changed by the first input statement before the variable is ever used. As a matter of style, this book will not initialize a variable if the initialization value is never used; doing so might mislead you into thinking the starting value had some purpose.

»TWO TRUTHS AND A LIE: ACCUMULATING TOTALS

1. When totals are accumulated, 1 is added to a variable that represents the total.
2. A variable used to hold a total must be set to 0 before it is used to accumulate a total.
3. The C# compiler will not allow you to accumulate totals in an uninitialized variable.

The false answer is #1. When totals are accumulated, any value might be added to a variable that represents the total. For example, if you total 10 test scores, then each score is added. If you add only 1 to a total variable on each cycle through a loop, then you are counting rather than accumulating a total.

IMPROVING LOOP PERFORMANCE

Whether you decide to use a `while`, `for`, or `do-while` loop in an application, you can improve loop performance by making sure the loop does not include unnecessary operations or statements. For example, suppose a loop should execute while `x` is less than the sum of two integers, `a` and `b`. The loop could be written as:

```
while (x < a + b)
    // loop body
```

If this loop executes 1000 times, then the expression `a + b` is calculated 1000 times. Instead, if you use the following code, the results are the same, but the arithmetic is performed only once:

```
int sum = a + b;
while(x < sum)
    // loop body
```

Of course, if `a` or `b` is altered in the loop body, then a new sum must be calculated with every loop iteration. However, if the sum of `a` and `b` is fixed prior to the start of the loop, then writing the code the second way is far more efficient.

As another example, suppose you need a temporary variable within a loop to use for some calculation. The loop could be written as follows:

```
while x < LIMIT)
{
    int tempTotal = a + b;
    // more statements here
}
```

When you declare a variable like `tempTotal` within a loop, it exists only for the duration of the loop; that is, it exists only until the loop's closing brace. Each time the loop executes, the variable is recreated. A more efficient solution is to declare the variable outside of the loop, as follows:

```
int tempTotal;
while x < LIMIT)
{
    tempTotal = a + b;
    // more statements here
}
```

> It is more efficient to declare this variable outside the loop than to redeclare it on every loop iteration.

As you continue to study programming, you will discover many situations in which you can make your programs more efficient. You should always be on the lookout for ways to improve program performance.

»TWO TRUTHS AND A LIE: IMPROVING LOOP PERFORMANCE

1. You can improve loop performance by making sure the loop does not include unnecessary operations or statements.
2. You can improve loop performance by declaring temporary variables outside of a loop instead of continuously redeclaring them.
3. You can improve loop performance by omitting the initialization of the loop control variable.

The false answer is #3. A loop control variable must be initialized for every loop.

YOU DO IT

USING A `while` LOOP

In the next steps, you will write a program that continuously prompts the user for a valid ID number until the user enters an ID that is acceptable. For this application, assume that a valid ID number must be between 1000 and 9999 inclusive.

To create an application that verifies an ID number:

1. Open a new file in your text editor and enter the beginning of the program. It begins by declaring variables for an ID number, the user's input, and constant values for the highest and lowest acceptable ID numbers.

```
using System;
public class ValidID
{
    public static void Main()
    {
        int idNum;
        string input;
        const int LOW = 1000;
        const int HIGH = 9999;
```

2. Add code to prompt the user for an ID number and to then convert it to an integer.

```
Console.Write("Enter an ID number: ");
input = Console.ReadLine();
idNum = Convert.ToInt32(input);
```

3. Create a loop that continues while the entered ID number is out of range. While the number is invalid, explain valid ID parameters and reprompt the user, converting the input to an integer.

```
while(idNum < LOW || idNum > HIGH)
{
    Console.WriteLine("{0} is an invalid ID number", idNum);
    Console.Write("ID numbers must be ");
    Console.WriteLine("between {0} and {1} inclusive",
        LOW, HIGH);
    Console.Write("Enter an ID number: ");
    input = Console.ReadLine();
    idNum = Convert.ToInt32(input);
}
```

4. When the user eventually enters a valid ID number, the loop ends. Display a message and add closing curly braces for the `Main()` method and for the class.

```
        Console.WriteLine("ID number {0} is valid", idNum);
    }
}
```

5. Save the file as **ValidID.cs**. Compile and execute the program. A typical execution during which the user makes several invalid entries is shown in Figure 4-18.

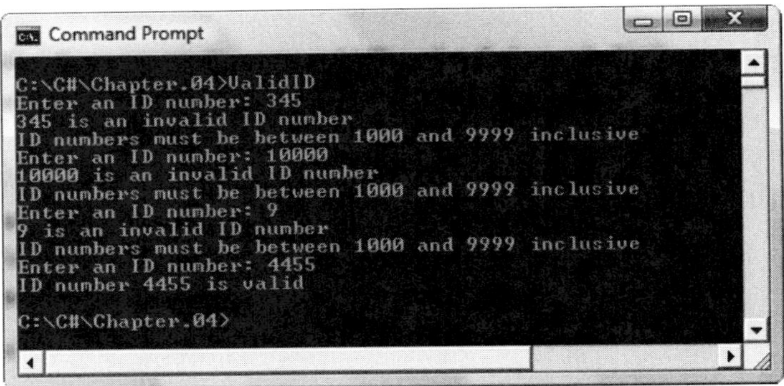

Figure 4-18 Typical execution of `ValidID` program

USING for LOOPS

In the next steps, you will write a program that creates a tipping table. Restaurant patrons can use this table to approximate the correct tip for meal prices from $10 to $100, at tipping percentage rates from 10 percent to 25 percent. The program uses several loops.

To create the tipping table:

1. Open a new file in your text editor and enter the beginning of the program. It begins by declaring variables to use for the price of a dinner, a tip percentage rate, and the amount of the tip.

```
using System;
public class TippingTable
{
   public static void Main()
   {
      double dinnerPrice = 10.00;
      double tipRate;
      double tip;
```

2. Next, create some constants. Every tip from 10% through 25% will be computed in 5% intervals, so declare those values as LOWRATE, MAXRATE, and TIPSTEP. Tips will be calculated on dinner prices up to $100.00 in $10.00 intervals, so declare those constants too.

```
      const double LOWRATE = 0.10;
      const double MAXRATE = 0.25;
      const double TIPSTEP = 0.05;
      const double MAXDINNER = 100.00;
      const double DINNERSTEP = 10.00;
```

3. To create a heading for the table, display "Price". (For alignment, insert three spaces after the quotes and before the *P* in *Price*.) On the same line, use a loop that displays every tip rate from LOWRATE through MAXRATE in increments of TIPSTEP. In other words, the tip rates are 0.10, 0.15, 0.20, and 0.25. Complete the heading for the table using a WriteLine() statement that advances the cursor to the next line of output and a WriteLine() statement that displays a dashed line.

```
Console.Write("   Price");
for(tipRate = LOWRATE; tipRate <= MAXRATE; tipRate += TIPSTEP)
   Console.Write("{0, 8}",tipRate.ToString("F"));
Console.WriteLine();
Console.WriteLine
("----------------------------------------");
const int NUM_DASHES = 40;
for(int x = 0; x < NUM_DASHES; ++x)
   Console.Write("-");
Console.WriteLine();
```

>> **NOTE** Recall that within a `for` loop, the expression before the first semicolon executes once, the middle expression is tested, the loop body executes, and then the expression to the right of the second semicolon executes. In other words, TIPSTEP is not added to `tipRate` until after the `tipRate` displays on each cycle through the loop.

>> **NOTE** As an alternative to typing 40 dashes in the `WriteLine()` statement, you could use the following loop to display a single dash 40 times. When the 40 dashes are completed, use `WriteLine()` to advance the cursor to a new line.

4. Reset `tipRate` to 0.10. You must reset the rate because after the last loop, the rate will have been increased to greater than 0.25.

```
tipRate = LOWRATE;
```

5. Create a nested loop that continues while the `dinnerPrice` remains 100.00 (`MAXDINNER`) or less. Each iteration of this loop displays one row of the tip table. Within this loop, display the `dinnerPrice`, then loop to display four tips while the `tipRate` varies from 0.10 through 0.25. At the end of the loop, increase the `dinnerPrice` by 10.00, reset the `tipRate` to 0.10 so it is ready for the next row, and write a new line to advance the cursor.

```
while(dinnerPrice <= MAXDINNER)
{
    Console.Write("{0, 8}", dinnerPrice.ToString("C"));
    while(tipRate <= MAXRATE)
    {
        tip = dinnerPrice * tipRate;
        Console.Write("{0, 8}",tip.ToString("F"));
        tipRate += 0.05;
    }
    dinnerPrice += DINNERSTEP;
    tipRate = LOWRATE;
    Console.WriteLine();
}
```

> **NOTE** Recall that the {0, 8} format string in the `Write()` statements displays the first argument in fields that are eight characters wide. You learned about format strings in Chapter 2.

6. Add two closing curly braces—one for the `Main()` method and one for the class.

7. Save the file as **TippingTable.cs**. Compile and execute the program. The output looks like Figure 4-19.

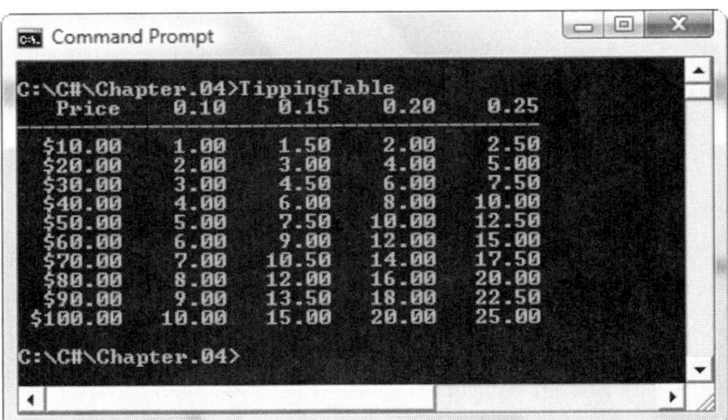

Figure 4-19 Output of `TippingTable` program

> **» NOTE** In the exercises at the end of this chapter, you will be instructed to make an interactive version of the `TippingTable` program in which many of the values are input by the user instead of being coded into the program as unnamed constants.

CHAPTER SUMMARY

» A loop is a structure that allows repeated execution of a block of statements. Within a looping structure, a Boolean expression is evaluated. As long as it is `true`, a block of statements called the loop body executes and the Boolean expression is evaluated again.

» You can use a `while` loop to execute a body of statements continuously while some condition continues to be `true`. A `while` loop consists of the keyword `while`, followed by a Boolean expression within parentheses, followed by the body of the loop, which can be a single statement or a block of statements surrounded by curly braces.

» When you use a `for` statement, you can indicate the starting value for the loop control variable, the test condition that controls loop entry, and the expression that alters the loop control variable, all in one convenient place. You begin a `for` statement with the keyword `for`, followed by a set of parentheses. Within the parentheses are three sections that are separated by exactly two semicolons. The three sections are typically used to initialize, test, and update the loop control variable.

» The `do` loop checks the bottom of the loop after one repetition has occurred.

» You can nest any combination of loops to achieve desired results.

» In computer programs, totals frequently are accumulated—that is, gathered together and added into a final sum by processing individual records one at a time in a loop.

» You can improve loop performance by making sure the loop does not include unnecessary operations or statements.

KEY TERMS

A **loop** is a structure that allows repeated execution of a block of statements.

A **loop body** is the block of statements executed in a loop.

An **iteration** is one execution of any loop.

A **while loop** executes a body of statements continuously while some condition continues to be `true`; it uses the keyword `while`.

An **infinite loop** is one that (theoretically) never ends.

A **loop control variable** determines whether loop execution will continue.

An **empty body** has no statements in it.

Incrementing a variable means adding a value to it. (Specifically, the term often means to add 1 to a variable.)

Decrementing a variable means subtracting a value from it. (Specifically, the term often means to subtract 1 from a variable.)

In a **definite loop**, the number of iterations is predetermined.

A **counted loop** is a definite loop.

In an **indefinite loop**, the number of iterations is not predetermined.

A **sentinel value** is one that a user must supply to stop a loop.

A **`for` loop** contains the starting value for the loop control variable, the test condition that controls loop entry, and the expression that alters the loop control variable, all in one statement.

A **step value** is the amount by which a loop control variable is altered, especially in a `for` loop.

When a variable is **out of scope**, it is not usable because it has ceased to exist.

The **do loop** checks the bottom of the loop after one repetition has occurred.

In a **pretest loop**, the loop control variable is tested before the loop body executes.

In a **posttest loop**, the loop control variable is tested after the loop body executes.

An **inner loop** is the loop in a pair of nested loops that is entirely contained within another loop.

An **outer loop** is the loop in a pair of nested loops that contains another loop.

Accumulated totals are added into a final sum by processing individual records one at a time in a loop.

An unknown memory value is known as **garbage**.

REVIEW QUESTIONS

1. A structure that allows repeated execution of a block of statements is a(n) _________ .

   a. selection

   b. loop

   c. sequence

   d. array

2. The body of a `while` loop can consist of _________ .

   a. a single statement

   b. a block of statements within curly braces

   c. either a or b

   d. neither a nor b

3. A loop that never ends is called a(n) _________ loop.

   a. `while`

   b. `for`

   c. counted

   d. infinite

4. Which of the following is not required of a loop control variable in a correctly working loop?

    a. It is initialized before the loop starts.

    b. It is tested.

    c. It is reset to its initial value before the loop ends.

    d. It is altered in the loop body.

5. A `while` loop with an empty body contains no _________ .

    a. loop control variable

    b. statements

    c. curly braces

    d. test within the parentheses of the `while` statement

6. A loop for which you do not know the number of iterations is a(n) _________ .

    a. definite loop

    b. indefinite loop

    c. counted loop

    d. `for` loop

7. What is the major advantage of using a `for` loop instead of a `while` loop?

    a. With a `for` loop, it is impossible to create an infinite loop.

    b. It is the only way to achieve an indefinite loop.

    c. Unlike with a `while` loop, the execution of multiple statements can depend on the test condition.

    d. The loop control variable is initialized, tested, and altered all in one place.

8. A `for` loop statement must contain _________ .

    a. two semicolons

    b. three commas

    c. four dots

    d. five pipes

9. In a `for` statement, the section before the first semicolon executes _________ .

    a. once

    b. once prior to each loop iteration

    c. once after each loop iteration

    d. one less time than the initial loop control variable value

10. The three sections of the `for` loop are most commonly used for _________ the loop control variable.

    a. testing, printing, and incrementing

    b. initializing, testing, and incrementing

    c. incrementing, selecting, and testing

    d. initializing, converting, and displaying

11. Which loop is most convenient to use if the loop body must always execute at least once?

    a. a `do` loop

    b. a `while` loop

    c. a `for` loop

    d. an `if` loop

12. The loop control variable is checked at the bottom of which kind of loop?

    a. a `while` loop

    b. a `do` loop

    c. a `for` loop

    d. all of the above

13. A `for` loop is an example of a(n) _________ loop.

    a. untested

    b. pretest

    c. posttest

    d. infinite

14. A `while` loop is an example of a(n) _________ loop.

    a. untested

    b. pretest

    c. posttest

    d. infinite

15. When a loop is placed within another loop, the loops are said to be _________.

    a. infinite

    b. bubbled

    c. nested

    d. overlapping

16. What does the following code segment display?

```
a = 1;
while (a < 5);
{
    Console.Write("{0} ", a);
    ++a;
}
```

    a. 1 2 3 4

    b. 1

    c. 4

    d. nothing

17. What is the output of the following code segment?

```
s = 1;
while (s < 4)
    ++s;
    Console.Write(" {0}", s);
```

    a. 1

    b. 4

    c. 1 2 3 4

    d. 2 3 4

18. What is the output of the following code segment?

```
j = 5;
while(j > 0)
{
    Console.Write("{0} ", j);
    j--;
}
```

a. 0

b. 5

c. 5 4 3 2 1

d. 5 4 3 2 1 0

19. What does the following code segment display?

```
for(f = 0; f < 3; ++f);
    Console.Write("{0} ", f);
```

a. 0

b. 0 1 2

c. 3

d. nothing

20. What does the following code segment display?

```
for(t = 0; t < 3; ++t)
    Console.Write("{0} ", t);
```

a. 0

b. 0 1

c. 0 1 2

d. 0 1 2 3

EXERCISES

1. Write a program that allows the user to enter any number of integer values continuously (in any order) until the user enters 999. Display the sum of the values entered, not including 999. Save the file as **Sum.cs**.

2. Write a program that asks the user to type a vowel from the keyboard. If the character entered is a vowel, display "OK"; if it is not a vowel, display an error message. Be sure to allow both uppercase and lowercase vowels. The program continues until the user types '!'. Save the file as **GetVowel.cs**.

3. Write a program that prompts a user for an hourly pay rate. While the user enters values less than $5.65 or greater than $49.99, continue to prompt the user. Save the program as **EnsureValidPayRateLoop.cs**.

4. Three salespeople work at Sunshine Hot Tubs—Andrea, Brittany, and Eric. Write a program that prompts the user for a salesperson's initial ('A', 'B', or 'E'). While the user does not type 'Z', continue by prompting for the amount of a sale the salesperson

made. Calculate the salesperson's commission as 10 percent of the sale amount, and add the commission to a running total for that salesperson. After the user types 'Z' for an initial, display each salesperson's total commission earned. Save the file as **TubSales.cs**.

5. Display a multiplication table that shows the product of every integer from 1 through 10 multiplied by every integer from 1 through 10. Save the file as **MultiplicationTable.cs**.

6. Write a program that prints all even numbers from 2 to 100, inclusive. Save the file as **EvenNums.cs**.

7. Write a program that prints every integer value from 1 to 20, along with its squared value. Save the file as **TableOfSquares.cs**.

8. Write a program that sums the integers from 1 to 50. Save the file as **Sum50.cs**.

9. Write a program that prints every perfect number from 1 through 1000. A number is perfect if it equals the sum of all the smaller positive integers that divide evenly into it. For example, 6 is perfect because 1, 2, and 3 divide evenly into it and their sum is 6. Save the file as **Perfect.cs**.

10. In the "You Do It" section of this chapter, you created a tipping table for patrons to use when analyzing their restaurant bills. Modify the program so that each of the following values is obtained from user input:
    » The lowest tipping percentage
    » The highest tipping percentage
    » The lowest possible restaurant bill
    » The highest restaurant bill

    Save the file as **TippingTable2.cs**.

DEBUGGING EXERCISES

Each of the following files in the Chapter.04 folder on your Student Disk has syntax and/or logical errors. In each case, determine the problem and fix the program. After you correct the errors, save each file using the same filename preceded with *Fixed*. For example, save DebugFour1.cs as **FixedDebugFour1.cs**.

   a. DebugFour1.cs

   b. DebugFour2.cs

   c. DebugFour3.cs

   d. DebugFour4.cs

UP FOR DISCUSSION

1. Suppose you wrote a program that you suspect is in an infinite loop because it keeps running for several minutes with no output and without ending. What would you add to your program to help you discover the origin of the problem?

2. Suppose that every employee in your organization has a seven-digit logon ID number for retrieving personal information, some of which might be sensitive in nature. For example, each employee has access to his own salary data and insurance claim information, but not to the information of others. Writing a loop would be useful to guess every combination of seven digits in an ID. Are there any circumstances in which you should try to guess another employee's ID number?

5

USING ARRAYS

In this chapter you will:

Declare an array and assign values to array elements
Initialize an array
Use subscripts to access array elements
Use the `Length` property
Use `foreach` to control array access
Search an array to find an exact match
Search an array to find a range match
Use the `BinarySearch()` method
Use the `Sort()` and `Reverse()` methods
Use multidimensional arrays

Storing values in variables provides programs with flexibility—a program that uses variables to replace constants can manipulate different values each time the program executes. When you add loops to your programs, the same variable can hold different values during successive cycles through the loop within the same program execution. This ability makes the program even more flexible. Learning to use the data structure known as an array provides you with further flexibility—you can store multiple values in adjacent memory locations and access them by varying a value that indicates which of the stored values you want to use. In this chapter, you will learn to create and manage C# arrays.

DECLARING AN ARRAY AND ASSIGNING VALUES TO ARRAY ELEMENTS

Sometimes, storing just one value in memory at a time isn't adequate. For example, a sales manager who supervises 20 employees might want to determine whether each employee has produced sales above or below the average amount. When you enter the first employee's sales figure into a program, you can't determine whether it is above or below average, because you won't know the average until you have entered all 20 figures. You might plan to assign 20 sales figures to 20 separate variables, each with a unique name, then sum and average them. That process is awkward and unwieldy, however—you need 20 prompts, 20 read statements using 20 separate storage locations (in other words, 20 separate variable names), and 20 addition statements. This method might work for 20 salespeople, but what if you have 30, 40, or 10,000 salespeople?

A superior approach is to assign the sales value to the same variable in 20 successive iterations through a loop that contains one prompt, one read statement, and one addition statement. Unfortunately, when you read in the sales value for the second employee, that data item replaces the figure for the first employee, and the first employee's value is no longer available to compare to the average of all 20 values. When the data-entry loop finishes, the only sales value left in memory is the last one entered.

The best solution to this problem is to create an array. An **array** is a list of data items that all have the same data type and the same name. (As you will learn shortly, each item in the list is distinguished from the others by an index.) You declare an array variable in the same way as you declare any other variable, but you insert a pair of square brackets after the type. For example, to declare an array of `double` values to hold sales figures for salespeople, you write the following:

```
double[] sales;
```

After you create an array variable, you still need to create the actual array. Declaring an array and actually reserving memory space for it are two distinct processes. To reserve memory locations for 20 `sales` objects, you declare the array variable with the following two statements:

```
double[] sales;
sales = new double[20];
```

The keyword **new** is also known as the **new operator**; it is used to create objects. In this case, it creates 20 separate `sales`. You also can declare and create an array in one statement, such as the following:

```
double[] sales = new double[20];
```

> **NOTE** You can change the size of an array associated with an identifier, if necessary. For example, if you declare `int[] array;`, you can assign five elements later with `array = new int[5];`; later in the program, you might alter the array size to 100 with `array = new int[100];`. Still later, you could alter it again to be either larger or smaller. Most other programming languages do not provide this capability. If you resize an array in this manner, the same identifier refers to a new array in memory and all the values are set to 0.

The statement `double[] sales = new double[20];` reserves 20 memory locations for 20 `sales` objects. Each object in an array is an **array element**. You can distinguish each element from the others in an array with a subscript. A **subscript** (also called an **index**) is an integer contained within square brackets that indicates the position of one of an array's elements. In C#, an array's elements are numbered beginning with 0, so you can legally use any subscript from 0 through 19 when working with an array that has 20 elements. In other words, the first `sales` array element is `sales[0]` and the last `sales` element is `sales[19]`. Figure 5-1 shows how the array of 20 sales figures appears in computer memory. The figure assumes that the array begins at memory address 20000. Because a `double` takes eight bytes of storage, each element of the array is stored in succession at an address that is eight bytes higher than the previous one.

> **NOTE** You will learn about creating other objects using the `new` operator in Chapter 6.

> **NOTE** In C#, an array subscript must be an integer. For example, no array contains an element with a subscript of 1.5.

> **NOTE** The first element in an array is sometimes called the "zeroth element."

Figure 5-1 An array of 20 `sales` items in memory

>> **NOTE** When you instantiate an array, you cannot choose its location in memory any more than you can choose the location of any other variable. However, you do know that after the first array element, the subsequent elements will follow immediately.

>> **NOTE** Some other languages, such as COBOL, BASIC, and Visual Basic, use parentheses rather than square brackets to refer to individual array elements. By using brackets, the creators of C# made it easier for you to distinguish arrays from methods. Like C#, C++ and Java also use brackets surrounding array subscripts.

A common mistake is to forget that the first element in an array is element 0, especially if you know another programming language in which the first array element is element 1. Making this mistake means you will be "off by one" in your use of any array.

>> **NOTE** If you are "off by one" but still using a valid subscript when accessing an array element, your program will produce incorrect output. If you are "off by one" so that your subscript becomes larger than the highest value allowed, you will cause a program error.

>> **NOTE** To remember that array elements begin with element 0, it might be helpful to think of the first array element as being "zero elements away from" the beginning of the array, the second element as being "one element away from" the beginning of the array, and so on.

>> **NOTE**
An array subscript can be an expression, as long as the expression evaluates to an integer. For example, if `x` and `y` are integers and their sum is at least 0 but less than the size of an array named `array`, then it is legal to refer to `array[x + y]`.

When you work with any individual array element, you treat it no differently than you treat a single variable of the same type. For example, to assign a value to the first `sales` in an array, you use a simple assignment statement, such as the following:

```
sales[0] = 2100.00;
```

To print the value of the last `sales` in a 20-element array, you write:

```
Console.WriteLine(sales[19]);
```

T T F

»TWO TRUTHS AND A LIE: DECLARING AN ARRAY AND ASSIGNING VALUES TO ARRAY ELEMENTS

1. To reserve memory locations for 10 `testScore` objects, you can use the following statement:
   ```
   int[] testScore = new int[9];
   ```
2. To assign 90 to the third element in a 10-element array named `testScore`, you can use the following statement:
   ```
   testScore[2] = 90;
   ```
3. To assign 60 to the last element in a 10-element array named `testScore`, you can use the following statement:
   ```
   testScore[9] = 60;
   ```

The false statement is #1. To reserve memory locations for 10 `testScore` objects, you must use 10 within the second set of square braces. The 10 elements will use the subscripts 0 through 9.

INITIALIZING AN ARRAY

In C#, arrays are objects. When you instantiate an array, you are creating a specific instance of a class named `System.Array`. When you declare objects, their numeric fields initialize to 0, character fields are set to '\u0000' or `null`, and `bool` fields are set to `false`. For example, when you initialize an array with a statement such as the following, each of the five elements of `someNums` has a value of 0 because `someNums` is a numeric array object:

```
int[] someNums = new int[5];
```

You already know how to assign a different value to a single element of an array, as in `someNums[0] = 46;`. You also can assign nondefault values to array elements upon creation. To initialize an array to nondefault values, you use a list of values that are separated by commas and enclosed within curly braces. For example, if you want to create an array named `myScores` and store five test scores within the array, you can use any of the following declarations:

```
int[] myScores = new int[5] {100, 76, 88, 100, 90};
int[] myScores = new int[] {100, 76, 88, 100, 90};
int[] myScores = {100, 76, 88, 100, 90};
```

> **»NOTE** You first learned the term *instance* in Chapter 1. You will understand classes and their instances more thoroughly after you complete Chapter 7.

The list of values provided for an array is an **initializer list**. When you initialize an array by providing a size and an initializer list, as in the first example, the stated size and number of list elements must match. However, when you initialize an array by giving it values upon creation, you are not required to give the array a size, as shown in the second example; in that case, the size is assigned based on the number of values in the initializing list. The third example shows that when you initialize an array, you do not need to use the keyword `new` and repeat the type; instead, new memory is assigned based on the stated array type and the length of the list of provided values. Use the form of array initialization that is clearest to you.

> **»NOTE** When you use curly braces at the end of a block of code, you do not follow the closing curly brace with a semicolon. Conversely, when you use curly braces to enclose a list of array values, you must complete the statement with a semicolon.

> **»NOTE** Programmers who have used other languages such as C++ and Java might expect that when an initialization list is shorter than the number of declared array elements, the "extra" elements will be set to default values. This is not the case in C#; if you declare a size, then you must list a value for each element.

> **»NOTE**
> You learned about the notation '\u0000' in Chapter 2.

»TWO TRUTHS AND A LIE: INITIALIZING AN ARRAY

1. The following statement creates an array named purchases and stores four values within the array:

```
double[] purchases = new [4] {23.55, 99.20, 4.67, 9.99};
```

2. The following statement creates an array named purchases and stores four values within the array:

```
double[] purchases = new double[] {23.55, 99.20, 4.67, 9.99};
```

3. The following statement creates an array named purchases and stores four values within the array:

```
double[] purchases = {23.55, 99.20, 4.67, 9.99};
```

The false statement is #1. If you chose to use the keyword new after the assignment operator when initializing an array, then you must include the data type, as in the following:

```
double[] purchases = new double[4] {23.55, 99.20, 4.67, 9.99};
```

Inserting the size within the brackets that follow new and the data type, as in #2, is optional. C# counts the number of initializers for you and uses that value.

USING SUBSCRIPTS TO ACCESS ARRAY ELEMENTS

If you treat each array element as an individual entity, there isn't much of an advantage to declaring an array over declaring individual variables. The power of arrays becomes apparent when you use subscripts that are variables rather than constant values.

For example, when you declare an array of five integers, such as the following, you often want to perform the same operation on each array element:

```
int[] myScores = {100, 76, 88, 100, 90};
```

To increase each array element by 3, for example, you can write the following five statements:

```
myScores[0] += 3;
myScores[1] += 3;
myScores[2] += 3;
myScores[3] += 3;
myScores[4] += 3;
```

With five array elements, this task is manageable. However, you can shorten the task by using a variable as the subscript. Then you can use a loop to perform arithmetic on each element in the array. For example:

```
for(int sub = 0; sub < 5; ++sub)
   myScores[sub] += 3;
```

The variable sub is declared and initialized to 0, then compared to 5. Because it is less than 5, the loop executes and myScores[0] increases by 3. The variable sub is incremented and becomes 1, which is still less than 5, so when the loop executes again, myScores[1] increases by 3, and so on. A process that took five statements now takes only one. Additionally, if the array had 100 elements, the first method of individually increasing the array values by 3 would require 95 additional statements. The only change required using the `for` loop would be to compare `sub` to 100 instead of 5.

> **NOTE** New array users sometimes think there is a permanent connection between a variable used as a subscript and the array with which it is used, but that is not the case. For example, if you vary `sub` from 0 to 10 to fill an array, you do not need to use `sub` later when displaying the array elements—either the same variable or a different variable can be used as a subscript elsewhere in the program.

»TWO TRUTHS AND A LIE: USING SUBSCRIPTS TO ACCESS ARRAY ELEMENTS

1. Assume you have declared an array of six `double`s named `balances`. The following statement displays all the elements:

```
for(int index = 0; index < 6; ++index)
   Console.WriteLine(balances[index]);
```

2. Assume you have declared an array of eight `double`s named `prices`. The following statement subtracts 2 from each element:

```
for(double pr = 0; pr < 8; ++pr)
   prices[pr] -= 2;
```

3. Assume you have declared an array of four `string`s named `titles`. The following statement displays each element in reverse order:

```
for(int whichOne = 3; whichOne >= 0; --whichOne)
   Console.WriteLine(titles[whichOne]);
```

The false statement is #2. You can only use an `int` as the subscript to an array, and this example attempts to use a `double`.

USING THE `Length` PROPERTY

When you work with array elements, you must ensure that the subscript you use remains in the range of 0 through one less than the array's length. If you declare an array with five elements and use a subscript that is negative or more than 4, you will receive the error message "IndexOutOfRangeException" when you run the program. This message means the index, or subscript, does not hold a value that legally can access an array element. When you declare an array of five integers, as in the following example, you can access all five elements by coding the number 5 explicitly within the middle expression in the `for` statement. The example displays all five scores, each separated by a space.

```
int[] myScores = {100, 75, 88, 100, 90};
for(int sub = 0; sub < 5; ++sub)
   Console.WriteLine("{0} ", myScores[sub]);
```

> **»NOTE** You will learn about the term `Exception` in `IndexOutOfRangeException` in Chapter 9.

If you use this code and then modify your program to hold more or fewer array elements, you must remember to change the comparison in the display loop as well as every other reference to the array size within the program. Many text editors have a "find and replace" feature that lets you change (for example) all of the 5s either simultaneously or one by one. However, you must be careful not to change 5s that have nothing to do with the array; for example, do not change the 5 in 75 inadvertently—it is the second listed value in the `myScores` array and has nothing to do with the array size. As another example, the program might also have a stored interest rate variable holding 5 percent, and you would not want to alter that value. A better technique is to use a named constant that holds the array size and use it to control any loops, as in the following:

```
int[] myScores = {100, 75, 88, 100, 90};
const int MY_ARRAYS_LENGTH = 5;
for(sub = 0; sub < MY_ARRAYS_LENGTH; ++sub)
    Console.WriteLine("{0} ", myScores[sub]);
```


That way, if you change the size of the array and the value of the MY_ARRAYS_LENGTH constant, the loop always will use the correct maximum length. However, even this approach has a drawback, because when you change the number of elements in the array declaration, you also must remember to change the value of the named constant.

The superior approach is to use a value that is automatically altered when you change the number of elements in an array declaration. Because every array automatically is a member of the class **System.Array**, you can use the fields and methods that are part of the System.Array class with any array you create. The **Length property** is a member of the System.Array class and automatically holds an array's length. Instead of creating your own variable or constant, it is most efficient to use this property, which always updates to reflect any changes you make to your array's size. The following segment of code displays "Array size is 5" and subsequently displays the array's contents:


```
int[] myScores = {100, 76, 88, 100, 90};
Console.WriteLine("Array size is {0}", myScores.Length);
for(int x = 0; x < myScores.Length; ++x)
    Console.WriteLine(myScores[x]);
```

▶▶TWO TRUTHS AND A LIE: USING THE Length PROPERTY

1. The following code displays 3:

```
int[] array = {1, 2, 3};
Console.WriteLine(array.Length);
```

2. The following code displays 3:

```
int[] array = {1, 2, 3};
Console.WriteLine(array[array.Length - 1]);
```

3. The following code displays 3:

```
int[] array = {1, 2, 3};
Console.WriteLine(array[array.Length] - 1);
```

The false statement is #3. When you declare an array with three elements, then the value of the array's Length property is 3. It is illegal to access element 3 of the array because the legitimate subscripts are only 0, 1, and 2.

USING `foreach` TO CONTROL ARRAY ACCESS

You can easily navigate through arrays using a `for` or `while` loop that varies a subscript from 0 to `Array.Length` – 1. C# also supports a **foreach statement** that you can use to cycle through every array element without using a subscript. With the `foreach` statement, you provide a temporary **iteration variable** that automatically holds each array value in turn.

For example, the following code prints each element in the `payRate` array in sequence:

```
double[] payRate = {6.00, 7.35, 8.12, 12.45, 22.22};
foreach(double money in payRate)
    Console.WriteLine("{0}", money.ToString("C"));
```

The variable `money` is declared as a `double` within the `foreach` statement. During the execution of the loop, `money` holds each `payRate` value in turn—first, `payRate[0]`, then `payRate[1]`, and so on. As a simple variable, `money` does not require a subscript, making it easier to work with.

The `foreach` statement is used only under certain circumstances:

» You typically use `foreach` only when you want to access every array element; to access only selected array elements, you must manipulate subscripts using some other technique—for example, using a `for` loop or `while` loop.

» The `foreach` iteration variable is read-only—that is, you cannot assign a value to it. If you want to assign a value to array elements, you must use a different type of loop.

»TWO TRUTHS AND A LIE: USING `foreach` TO CONTROL ARRAY ACCESS

1. The `foreach` statement is used to cycle through every element in an array without using a subscript.
2. With the `foreach` statement, you declare a temporary iteration variable that automatically holds each array subscript in turn.
3. You cannot assign a value to the `foreach` iteration variable.

The false statement is #2. With the `foreach` statement, you declare a temporary iteration variable that automatically holds each array value in turn, not each subscript.

SEARCHING AN ARRAY FOR AN EXACT MATCH

When you want to determine whether some variable holds one of many possible valid values, one option is to use a series of `if` statements to compare the variable to a series of valid values. For example, suppose that a company manufactures 10 items. When a customer places an order for an item, you need to determine whether the item number is valid. If valid item numbers are sequential, say 101 through 110, then the following simple `if` statement that uses a logical AND operator can verify the order number and set a Boolean field to `true`:

```
if(itemOrdered >= 101 && itemOrdered <= 110)
    isValidItem = true;
```

If the valid item numbers are nonsequential, however—for example, 101, 108, 201, 213, 266, 304, and so on—you must code the following deeply nested `if` statement or a lengthy OR comparison to determine the validity of an item number:

```
if(itemOrdered == 101)
    isValidItem = true;
else if(itemOrdered == 108)
    isValidItem = true;
else if(itemOrdered == 201)
    isValidItem = true;
// and so on
```

USING A `for` LOOP TO SEARCH AN ARRAY

Instead of creating a long series of `if` statements, a more elegant solution is to compare the `itemOrdered` variable to a list of values in an array. You can initialize the array with the valid values by using the following statement:

```
int[] validValues = {101, 108, 201, 213, 266, 304, 311,
        409, 411, 412};
```

> **» NOTE** You might prefer to declare the `validValues` array as a constant because presumably, the valid item numbers should not change during program execution. In C# you must use the keywords `static` and `readonly` prior to the constant declaration. To keep these examples simple, all arrays in this chapter are declared as variable arrays.

Next, you can use a `for` statement to loop through the array and set a Boolean variable to `true` when a match is found:

```
for(int x = 0; x < validValues.Length; ++x)
    if(itemOrdered == validValues[x])
        isValidItem = true;
```

> **» NOTE**
> In place of the `for` loop, you could use a `foreach` loop.

This simple `for` loop replaces the long series of `if` statements. What's more, if a company carries 1000 items instead of 10, then the list of valid items in the array must be altered, but the `for` statement does not change at all. As an added bonus, if you set up another array as a **parallel array** with the same number of elements and corresponding data, you can use the same subscript to access additional information. For example, if the 10 items your company carries have 10 different prices, then you can set up any array to hold those prices as follows:

```
double[] prices = {0.89, 1.23, 3.50, 0.69...}; // and so on
```

The prices must appear in the same order as their corresponding item numbers in the `validValues` array. Now the same `for` loop that finds the valid item number also finds the price, as shown in the program in Figure 5-2. In other words, if the item number is found in the second position in the `validValues` array, then you can find the correct price in the

```csharp
using System;
public class FindPriceWithForLoop
{
   public static void Main()
   {
    int[] validValues = {101,  108,   201,  213,  266,
        304,   311,  409,  411,  412};
    double[] prices =    {0.89, 1.23, 3.50, 0.69, 5.79,
        3.19, 0.99, 0.89, 1.26, 8.00};
    int itemOrdered;
    double itemPrice = 0;
    bool isValidItem = false;
    Console.Write("Please enter an item ");
    itemOrdered = Convert.ToInt32(Console.ReadLine());
    for(int x = 0; x < validValues.Length; ++x)
    {
        if(itemOrdered == validValues[x])
        {
            isValidItem = true;
            itemPrice = prices[x];
        }
    }
    if(isValidItem)
        Console.WriteLine("Price is {0}", itemPrice);
    else
        Console.WriteLine("Sorry - item not found");
   }
}
```

Figure 5-2 The `FindPriceWithForLoop` program

second position in the `prices` array. In the program in Figure 5-2, the variable used as a subscript, x, is set to 0 and the Boolean variable `isValidItem` is `false`. In the shaded portion of the figure, while the subscript remains smaller than the length of the array of valid item numbers, the subscript is continuously increased so that subsequent array values can be tested. When a match between the user's item and an item in the array is found, `isValidItem` is set to `true` and the price of the item is stored in `itemPrice`.

Figure 5-3 shows two typical program executions.

Within the code shown in Figure 5-2, you compare every `itemOrdered` with each of the 10 `validValues`. Even when an `itemOrdered` is equivalent to the first value in the `validValues`

> **» NOTE**
> If you initialize parallel arrays, it is convenient to use spacing so that the corresponding values visually align on the screen or printed page.

> **» NOTE** In the fourth statement of the `Main()` method in Figure 5-2, `itemPrice` is set to 0. Setting this variable is required, because its value is later altered only if an item number match is found in the `validValues` array. When C# determines that a variable's value is only set depending on an `if` statement, C# will not allow you to display the variable, because the compiler assumes the variable might not have been set to a valid value.

Figure 5-3 Two typical executions of the `FindPriceWithForLoop` program

> **NOTE**
> In an array with many possible matches, it is most efficient to place the most common items first, so they are matched right away. For example, if item 311 is ordered most often, place 311 first in the `validValues` array and its price ($0.99) first in the `prices` array.

array (101), you always make nine additional cycles through the array. On each of these nine additional iterations, the comparison between `itemOrdered` and `validValues[x]` is always `false`. As soon as a match for an `itemOrdered` is found, it is most efficient to break out of the `for` loop early. An easy way to accomplish this task is to set `x` to a high value within the block of statements executed when a match is found. Then, after a match, the `for` loop will not execute again because the limiting comparison (`x < validValues.Length`) will have been surpassed. The following code shows this approach:

```
for(int x = 0; x < validValues.Length; ++x)
{
    if(itemOrdered == validValues[x])
    {
        isValidItem = true;
        itemPrice = prices[x];
        x = validValues.Length;
            // break out of loop when you find a match
    }
}
```

Instead of the statement that sets `x` to `validValues.Length` when a match is found, you could remove that statement and change the comparison in the middle section of the `for` statement to a compound statement, as follows:

```
for(int x = 0; x < validValues.Length && !isValidItem; ++x)...
```

As another alternative, you could remove the statement that sets `x` to `validValues.Length` and place a `break` statement within the loop in its place. Some programmers disapprove of exiting a `for` loop early, whether by setting a variable's value or by using a `break` statement. They argue that programs are easier to debug and maintain if each program segment has only one entry and one exit point. If you (or your instructor) agree with this philosophy, then you can select an approach that uses a `while` statement, as described next.

> **NOTE** Although parallel arrays can be very useful, they also can increase the likelihood of mistakes. Any time you make a change to one array, you must remember to make the corresponding change in its parallel array. As you continue to study C#, you will learn superior ways to correlate data items. For example, Chapter 7 explains how you can encapsulate corresponding data items in objects and create arrays of objects.

USING A while LOOP TO SEARCH AN ARRAY

As an alternative to using a for or foreach loop to search an array, you can use a while loop to search for a match. Using this approach, you set a subscript to 0 and, while the itemOrdered is not equal to a value in the array, increase the subscript and keep looking. You search only while the subscript remains lower than the number of elements in the array. If the subscript increases to match validValues.Length, then you never found a match in the 10-element array. If the loop ends before the subscript reaches validValues.Length, then you found a match and the correct price can be assigned to the itemPrice variable. Figure 5-4 shows a program that uses this approach.

```
using System;
public class FindPriceWithWhileLoop
{
    public static void Main()
    {
        int x;
        string inputString;
        int itemOrdered;
        double itemPrice = 0;
        bool isValidItem = false;
        int[] validValues = {101,   108,   201,  213,  266,
            304,   311,  409,  411,  412};
        double[] prices =   {0.89, 1.23, 3.50, 0.69, 5.79,
            3.19,  0.99, 0.89, 1.26, 8.00};
        Console.Write("Enter item number ");
        inputString = Console.ReadLine();
        itemOrdered = Convert.ToInt32(inputString);
        x = 0;
        while(x < validValues.Length &&
            itemOrdered != validValues[x])
                ++x;
        if(x != validValues.Length)
        {
            isValidItem = true;
            itemPrice = prices[x];
        }
        if(isValidItem)
            Console.WriteLine("Item {0} sells for {1}",
                itemOrdered, itemPrice.ToString("C"));
        else
            Console.WriteLine("No such item as {0}",
                itemOrdered);
    }
}
```

Figure 5-4 The FindPriceWithWhileLoop program that searches with a while loop

In the application in Figure 5-4, the variable used as a subscript, x, is set to 0 and the Boolean variable isValidItem is false. In the shaded portion of the figure, while the subscript remains smaller than the length of the array of valid item numbers, and while the user's requested item does not match a valid item, the subscript is increased so that subsequent array values can be tested. The while loop ends when a match is found or the array tests have been exhausted, whichever comes first. When the loop ends, if x is not equal to the size of the array, then a valid item has been found and its price can be retrieved from the prices array. Figure 5-5 shows two executions of the program. In the first execution, a match is found; in the second, an invalid item number is entered, so no match is found.

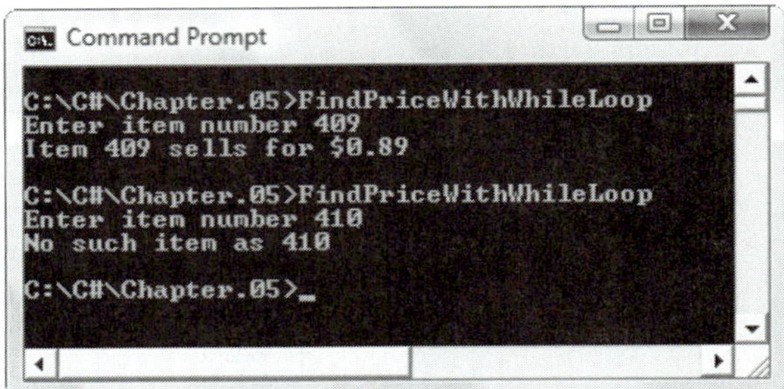

Figure 5-5 Two executions of the FindPriceWithWhileLoop application

T T F

»TWO TRUTHS AND A LIE: SEARCHING AN ARRAY FOR AN EXACT MATCH

1. You can use a for, foreach, or while loop to search through an array for an exact match.
2. A parallel array has the same number of elements as another array, and corresponding data.
3. When you search an array for an exact match in a parallel array, you must perform a loop as many times as there are elements in the arrays.

The false statement is #3. When you search an array for an exact match in a parallel array, you can perform a loop as many times as there are elements in the arrays, but once a match is found, the additional loop iterations are unnecessary. It is most efficient to terminate the loop cycles as soon as a match is found.

SEARCHING AN ARRAY
FOR A RANGE MATCH

Searching an array for an exact match is not always practical. For example, suppose your mail-order company gives customer discounts based on the quantity of items ordered. Perhaps no discount is given for any order of fewer than a dozen items, but increasing discounts are available for orders of increasing quantities, as shown in Figure 5-6.

Total Quantity Ordered	Discount (%)
1 to 12	None
13 to 49	10
50 to 99	14
100 to 199	18
200 or more	20

Figure 5-6 Discount table for a mail-order company

One awkward, impractical option is to create a single array to store the discount rates. You could use a variable named `numOfItems` as a subscript to the array, but the array would need hundreds of entries, such as the following:

```
double[] discount = {0, 0, 0, 0, 0, 0, 0, 0, 0, 0,
     0, 0, 0, 0.10, 0.10, 0.10 ...}; // and so on
```

When `numOfItems` is 3, for example, then `discount[numOfItems]` or `discount[3]` is 0. When `numOfItems` is 14, then `discount[numOfItems]` or `discount[14]` is 0.10. Because a customer might order thousands of items, the array would need to be ridiculously large.

A better option is to create parallel arrays. One array will hold the five discount rates, and the other array will hold five discount range limits. Then you can perform a **range match** by determining the pair of limiting values between which a customer's order falls. The Total Quantity Ordered column in Figure 5-6 shows five ranges. If you use only the first figure in each range, then you can create an array that holds five low limits:

```
int[] discountRangeLowLimit = {1, 13, 50, 100, 200};
```

A parallel array will hold the five discount rates:

```
double[] discount = {0, 0.10, 0.14, 0.18, 0.20};
```

Then, starting at the last `discountRangeLowLimit` array element, for any `numOfItems` greater than or equal to `discountRangeLowLimit[4]`, the appropriate discount is `discount[4]`. In other words, for any `numOfItems` less than `discountRangeLowLimit[4]`, you should decrement the subscript and look in a lower range. Figure 5-7 shows the code.

> **» NOTE**
> Notice that 13 zeroes are listed in the discount array in this example. The first array element has a 0 subscript (and a 0 discount for 0 items). The next 12 discounts (1 through 12 items) also have 0 discounts.

```
// assume numOfItems is a declared integer for which a user
// has input a value
int[] discountRangeLowLimit = {1,    13,    50,   100,    200};
double[] discount =           {0, 0.10, 0.14, 0.18, 0.20};
double customerDiscount;
int sub = discountRangeLowLimit.Length - 1;
while(sub >= 0 && numOfItems < discountRangeLowLimit[sub])
    --sub;
customerDiscount = discount[sub];
```

Figure 5-7 Searching an array of ranges

As an alternate approach to the range-checking logic in Figure 5-7, you can choose to create an array that contains the upper limit of each range, such as the following:

```
int[] discountRangeUpperLimit = {12, 49, 99, 199, 9999999};
```

Then the logic can be written to compare `numOfItems` to each range limit until the correct range is located, as follows:

```
int sub = 0;
while(sub < discountRangeUpperLimit.Length && numOfItems >
    discountRangeUpperLimit[sub])
        ++sub;
customerDiscount = discount[sub];
```

In this example, `sub` is initialized to 0. While it remains within array bounds, and while `numOfItems` is more than each upper-range limit, `sub` is increased. In other words, if `numOfItems` is 3, the `while` expression is false on the first loop iteration, the loop ends, `sub` remains 0, and the customer discount is the first discount. However, if `numOfItems` is 30, then the `while` expression is true on the first loop iteration, `sub` becomes 1, the `while` expression is false on the second iteration, and the second discount is used. In this example, the last `discountRangeUpperLimit` array value is 9999999. This very high value was used with the assumption that no `numOfItems` would ever exceed it. As with many issues in programming, multiple correct approaches frequently exist for the same problem.

» TWO TRUTHS AND A LIE: SEARCHING AN ARRAY FOR A RANGE MATCH

1. A practical solution to creating an array with which to perform a range check is to design the array to hold the lowest value in each range.
2. A practical solution to creating an array with which to perform a range check is to design the array to hold the highest value in each range.
3. A practical solution to creating an array with which to perform a range check is to design the array to hold the average value in each range.

The false statement is #3. It would be impractical to design an array with average range values to use in a program that should check ranges.

USING THE `BinarySearch()` METHOD

You have already learned that because every array in C# automatically is a member of the `System.Array` class, you can use the `Length` property. Additionally, the `System.Array` class contains a variety of useful, built-in methods.

The **BinarySearch() method** finds a requested value in a sorted array. Instead of employing the logic you used to find a match in the last section, you can take advantage of this built-in method to locate a value within an array, as long as the array items are organized in ascending order.

>> NOTE A binary search is one in which a sorted list of objects is split in half repeatedly as the search gets closer and closer to a match. Perhaps you have played a guessing game, trying to guess a number from 1 to 100. If you asked, "Is it less than 50?," then continued to narrow your guesses upon hearing each subsequent answer, then you have performed a binary search.

Figure 5-8 shows a program that declares an array of integer `idNumbers` arranged in ascending order. The program prompts a user for a value, converts it to an integer, and, rather than using a loop to examine each array element and compare it to the entered value, simply passes the array and the entered value to the `BinarySearch()` method in the shaded statement. The method returns –1 if the value is not found in the array; otherwise, it returns the array position of the sought value. Figure 5-9 shows two executions of this program.

>> NOTE The `BinarySearch()` method takes two arguments—the array name and the value for which to search. In Chapter 1 you learned that arguments represent information that a method needs to perform its task. When methods require multiple arguments, they are separated by commas. For example, when you have used the `Console.WriteLine()` method, you have passed a format string and values to be displayed, all separated by commas.

```
using System;
public class BinarySearchDemo
{
    public static void Main()
    {
        int[] idNumbers = {122, 167, 204, 219, 345};
        int x;
        string entryString;
        int entryId;
        Console.Write("Enter an Employee ID ");
        entryString = Console.ReadLine();
        entryId = Convert.ToInt32(entryString);
        x = Array.BinarySearch(idNumbers, entryId);
        if(x < 0)
            Console.WriteLine("ID {0} not found", entryId);
        else
            Console.WriteLine("ID {0} found at position {1} ",
                entryId, x);
    }
}
```

Figure 5-8 `BinarySearchDemo` program

When you use the following statement, you send a string to the `Write()` method:

```
Console.Write("Enter an Employee ID ");
```

When you use the following statement, you get a value back from the `ReadLine()` method:

```
entryString = Console.ReadLine();
```

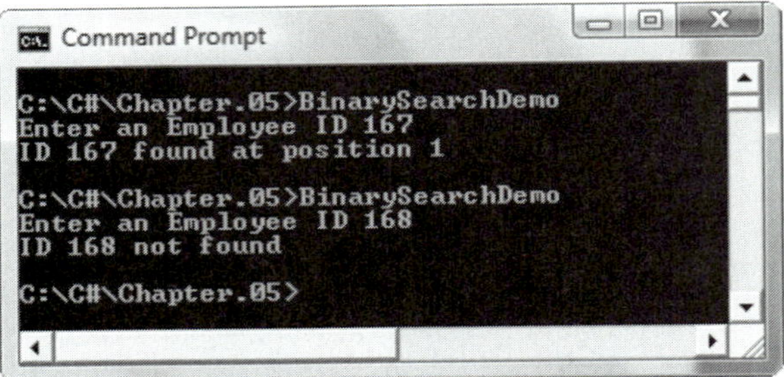

Figure 5-9 Two executions of the `BinarySearchDemo` program

In Figure 5-8, the following single statement both sends a value to a method and gets a value back:

```
x = Array.BinarySearch(idNumbers, entryId);
```

The statement calls the method that performs the search, returning a –1 or the position where `entryId` was found; that value is then stored in `x`. This single line of code is easier to write, less prone to error, and easier to understand than writing a loop to cycle through the `idNumbers` array looking for a match. Still, it is worthwhile to understand how to perform the search without the `BinarySearch()` method, as you learned while studying parallel arrays. You will need to use that technique under the following conditions, when the `BinarySearch()` method proves inadequate:

» If your array items are not arranged in ascending order, the `BinarySearch()` method does not work correctly.

» If your array holds duplicate values and you want to find all of them, the `BinarySearch()` method doesn't work—it can return only one value, so it returns the position of the first matching value it finds (which is not necessarily the first instance of the value in the array).

» If you want to find a range match rather than an exact match, the `BinarySearch()` method does not work.

»TWO TRUTHS AND A LIE: USING THE `BinarySearch()` METHOD

1. When you use the `BinarySearch()` method with an array, the array items must first be organized in ascending order.

2. The `BinarySearch()` method requires three arguments—the name of an array, a value for which you want to search, and a code that indicates whether the array has been presorted.

3. The `BinarySearch()` method returns –1 if the search value is not found in the array; otherwise, it returns the array position of the sought value.

The false statement is #2. The `BinarySearch()` method requires two arguments—the name of an array and a value for which you want to search. The array items must be sorted in ascending order for the method to work correctly.

USING THE `Sort()` AND `Reverse()` METHODS

The `System.Array` class contains other useful methods you can use to manipulate your arrays. As with the `BinarySearch()` method, you could write all of these methods yourself. C# provides them as a convenience, however.

The **`Sort()` method** arranges array items in ascending order. Ascending order is lowest to highest; it works numerically for number types and alphabetically for characters and strings. To use the method, you pass the array name to `Array.Sort()`, and the element positions within the array are rearranged appropriately. Figure 5-10 shows a program that sorts an array of strings; Figure 5-11 shows its execution.

```
using System;
public class SortArray
{
    public static void Main()
    {
        string[] names = {"Olive", "Patty",
            "Richard", "Ned", "Mindy"};
        int x;
        Array.Sort(names);
        for(x = 0; x < names.Length; ++x)
            Console.WriteLine(names[x]);
    }
}
```

Figure 5-10 `SortArray` program

Figure 5-11 Execution of `SortArray` program

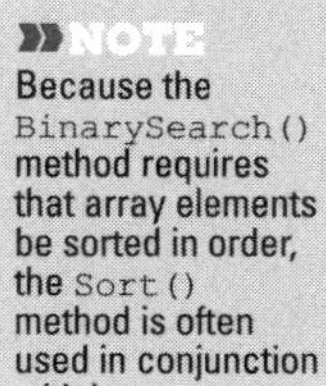

NOTE
Because the `BinarySearch()` method requires that array elements be sorted in order, the `Sort()` method is often used in conjunction with it.

NOTE
When you `Reverse()` an array that contains an odd number of elements, the middle element will remain in its original location.

The **`Reverse()` method** reverses the order of items in an array. In other words, for any array, the element that starts in position 0 is relocated to position `Length – 1`, the element that starts in position 1 is relocated to position `Length – 2`, and so on until the element that starts in position `Length – 1` is relocated to position 0. You call the `Reverse()` method the same

> **»NOTE**
> The Reverse() method does not sort array elements; it only rearranges their positions to the opposite order.

way you call the Sort() method—you simply pass the array name to the method. Figure 5-12 shows a program that uses Reverse() with an array of strings, and Figure 5-13 shows its execution.

```
using System;
public class ReverseArray
{
    public static void Main()
    {
        string[] names = {"Zach", "Rose", "Wendy", "Marcia"};
        int x;
        Array.Reverse(names);
        for(x = 0; x < names.Length; ++x)
            Console.WriteLine(names[x]);
    }
}
```

Figure 5-12 ReverseArray program

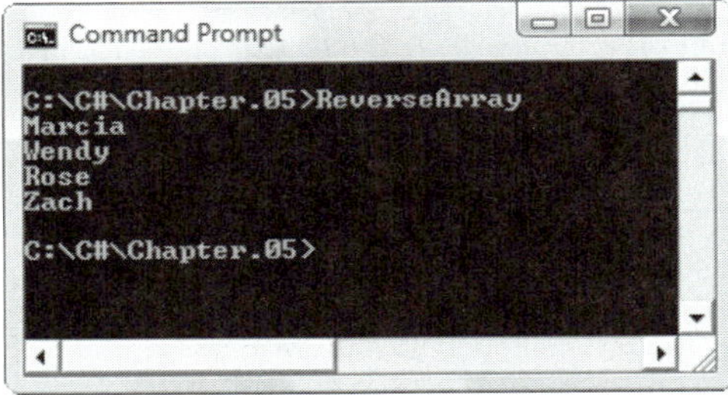

Figure 5-13 Execution of ReverseArray program

»TWO TRUTHS AND A LIE: USING THE Sort() AND Reverse() METHODS

1. The Array.Sort() and Array.Reverse() methods are similar in that both belong to the Array class.
2. The Array.Sort() and Array.Reverse() methods are similar in that both require a single argument.
3. The Array.Sort() and Array.Reverse() methods are different in that one places items in ascending order and the other places them in descending order.

The false statement is #3. The Array.Sort() method places items in ascending order, but the Array.Reverse() method simply reverses the existing order of any array whether it was presorted or not.

USING MULTIDIMENSIONAL ARRAYS

When you declare an array such as `double[] sales = new double[20];`, you can envision the declared integers as a column of numbers in memory, as shown at the beginning of this chapter in Figure 5-1. In other words, you can picture the 20 declared numbers stacked one on top of the next. An array that you can picture as a column of values, and whose elements you can access using a single subscript, is a **one-dimensional** or **single-dimensional array**.

C# also supports **multidimensional arrays**—those that require multiple subscripts to access the array elements. The most commonly used multidimensional arrays are two-dimensional arrays that are rectangular. **Two-dimensional arrays** have two or more columns of values for each row, as shown in Figure 5-14. In a **rectangular array**, each row has the same number of columns. You must use two subscripts when you access an element in a two-dimensional array. When mathematicians use a two-dimensional array, they often call it a **matrix** or a **table**; you might have used a two-dimensional array called a spreadsheet.

> **» NOTE**
> You can think of the single dimension of a single-dimensional array as the height of the array.

sales[0, 0]	sales[0, 1]	sales[0, 2]	sales[0, 3]
sales[1, 0]	sales[1, 1]	sales[1, 2]	sales[1, 3]
sales[2, 0]	sales[2, 1]	sales[2, 2]	sales[2, 3]

Figure 5-14 View of a rectangular, two-dimensional array in memory

> **» NOTE**
> You can think of the two dimensions of a two-dimensional array as height and width.

> **» NOTE** You might want to create a `sales` array with two dimensions as shown in Figure 5-14 if, for example, each row represented a category of items sold, and each column represented a salesperson who sold them.

When you declare a one-dimensional array, you type a single, empty set of square brackets after the array type, and you use a single subscript in a set of square brackets when reserving memory. To declare a two-dimensional array, you type a comma in the square brackets after the array type, and you use two subscripts, separated by a comma in brackets, when reserving memory. For example, the array in Figure 5-14 can be declared as the following, creating an array named `saleFigures` that holds three rows and four columns:

> **» NOTE**
> When you declare a two-dimensional array, spaces surrounding the comma within the square brackets are optional.

```
double[ , ]sales = new double[3, 4];
```

Just as with a one-dimensional array, if you do not provide values for the elements in a two-dimensional numerical array, the values are set to the default value for the data type (zero for numeric data). You can assign other values to the array elements later. For example, the following statement assigns the value 14.00 to the element of the `sales` array that is in the first column of the first row:

```
sales[0, 0] = 14.00;
```

Alternatively, you can initialize a two-dimensional array with values when it is created. For example, the following code assigns values to `sales` when it is created:

```
double[ , ] sales = {{14.00, 15.00, 16.00, 17.00},
                     {21.99, 34.55, 67.88, 31.99},
                     {12.03, 55.55, 32.89,  1.17}};
```


The `sales` array contains three rows and four columns. You contain the entire set of values within a pair of curly braces. The first row of the array holds the four `doubles` 14.00, 15.00, 16.00, and 17.00. Notice that these four values are placed within their own inner set of curly braces to indicate that they constitute one row, or the first row, which is row 0. Similarly, the next four values make up the second row (row 1), which you reference with the subscript 1. The value of `sales[0, 0]` is 14.00. The value of `sales[0, 1]` is 15.00. The value of `sales[2, 3]` is 1.17. The first value within the brackets following the array name always refers to the row; the second value, after the comma, refers to the column.

As an example of how useful two-dimensional arrays can be, assume you own an apartment building with four floors—a basement, which you refer to as floor zero, and three other floors numbered one, two, and three. In addition, each of the floors has studio (with no bedroom), one-, and two-bedroom apartments. The monthly rent for each type of apartment is different, and the rent is higher for apartments with more bedrooms. Table 5-1 shows the rental amounts.

Floor	Zero Bedrooms	One Bedroom	Two Bedrooms
0	400	450	510
1	500	560	630
2	625	676	740
3	1000	1250	1600

Table 5-1 Rents charged (in dollars)

To determine a tenant's rent, you need to know two pieces of information: the floor on which the tenant rents an apartment and the number of bedrooms in the apartment. Within a C# program, you can declare an array of rents using the following code:

```
int[ , ] rents = { {400, 450, 510},
                   {500, 560, 630},
                   {625, 676, 740},
                   {1000, 1250, 1600} };
```

Assume you declare two integers to hold the floor number and bedroom count, as in the following statement:

```
int floor, bedrooms;
```

Then any tenant's rent can be referred to as `rents[floor, bedrooms]`.

Figure 5-15 shows a complete program that uses a rectangular, two-dimensional array to hold rent values. Figure 5-16 shows a typical execution.

```
using System;
public class Rents
{
    public static void Main()
    {
        int[ , ] rents = {  {400,  450,  510},
                            {500,  560,  630},
                            {625,  676,  740},
                            {1000,  1250,  1600} };
        int floor;
        int bedrooms;
        string inputString;
        Console.Write("Enter the floor on which you want to live ");
        inputString = Console.ReadLine();
        floor = Convert.ToInt32(inputString);
        Console.Write("Enter the number of bedrooms you need ");
        inputString = Console.ReadLine();
        bedrooms = Convert.ToInt32(inputString);
        Console.WriteLine("The rent is {0}",
            rents[floor, bedrooms]);
    }
}
```

Figure 5-15 The `Rents` program

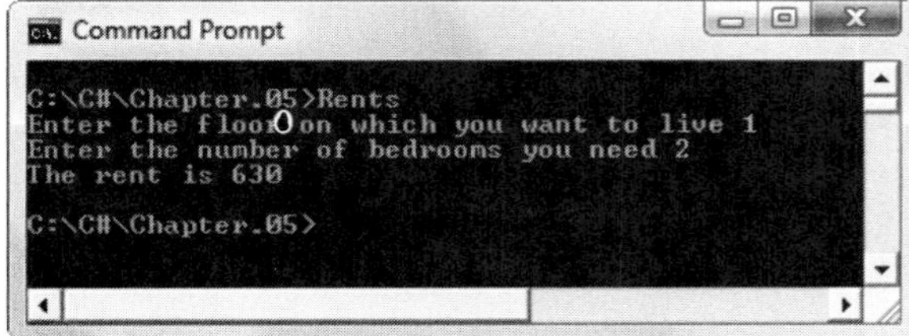

Figure 5-16 Typical execution of the `Rents` program

C# supports arrays with more than two dimensions. For example, if you own a multistory apartment building with different numbers of bedrooms available in apartments on each floor, you can use a two-dimensional array to store the rental fees. If you own several apartment buildings, you might want to employ a third dimension to store the building number. Suppose you want to store rents for four buildings that have three floors each and that each hold two types of apartments. Figure 5-17 shows how you might define such an array.

```
int[ , , ] rents = {  { {400,  500}, {450,  550}, {500,  550}},
                      { {510,  610}, {710,  810}, {910,  1010}},
                      { {525,  625}, {725,  825}, {925,  1025}},
                      { {850,  950}, {1050,  1150}, {1250,  1350}}};
```

Figure 5-17 A three-dimensional array definition

The empty brackets that follow the data type contain two commas, showing that the array supports three dimensions. A set of curly braces surrounds all the data. Four inner sets of braces surround the data for each floor. In this example, each row of values represents a building (0 through 3). Then 12 sets of innermost brackets surround the values for each floor—first a zero-bedroom apartment and then a one-bedroom apartment.

Using the three-dimensional array in Figure 5-17, an expression such as `rents[building, floor, bedrooms]` refers to a specific rent figure for a building whose number is stored in the `building` variable and whose floor and bedroom numbers are stored in the `floor` and `bedrooms` variables. Specifically, `rents[3, 1, 0]` refers to a studio (zero-bedroom) apartment on the first floor of building 3 ($1050 in Figure 5-17). When you are programming in C#, you can use four, five, or more dimensions in an array. As long as you can keep track of the order of the variables needed as subscripts, and as long as you don't exhaust your computer's memory, C# lets you create arrays of any size.

C# also supports jagged arrays. A **jagged array** is a one-dimensional array in which each element is another array. The major difference between jagged and rectangular arrays is that in jagged arrays, each row can be a different length.

For example, consider an application in which you want to store train ticket prices for each stop along five different routes. Suppose some of the routes have as many as 10 stops and others have as few as two. Each of the five routes could be represented by a row in a multidimensional array. Then you would have two logical choices for the columns:

» You could create a rectangular, two-dimensional array, allowing 10 columns for each row. In some of the rows, as many as eight of the columns would be empty, because some routes have only two stops.

» You could create a jagged two-dimensional array, allowing a different number of columns for each row. Figure 5-18 shows how you could implement this option.

```
double [][] tickets = {
   new double[] {5.50, 6.75, 7.95, 9.00, 12.00,
      13.00, 14.50, 17.00, 19.00, 20.25},
   new double[] {5.00, 6.00},
   new double[] {7.50, 9.00, 9.95, 12.00, 13.00, 14.00},
   new double[] {3.50, 6.45, 9.95, 10.00, 12.75},
   new double[] {15.00, 16.00} };
```

Figure 5-18 A jagged, two-dimensional array

The array in Figure 5-18 contains five separate one-dimensional arrays. Two square brackets are used following the data type. Then, within the array, each row needs its own `new` operator and data type. To refer to a jagged array element, you use two sets of brackets after the array name—for example, `tickets[route][stop]`. In Figure 5-18, the value of `tickets[0][0]` is 5.50, the value of `tickets[0][1]` is 6.75, and the value of `tickets[0][2]` is 7.95. The value of `tickets[1][0]` is 5.00, and the value of `tickets[1][1]` is 6.00. Referring to `tickets[1][2]` is invalid because there is no column 2 in the second row (that is, there are only two stops, not three, on the second train route).

»TWO TRUTHS AND A LIE: USING MULTIDIMENSIONAL ARRAYS

1. A rectangular array has the same number of columns as rows.

2. The following array contains two rows and three columns:

```
int[ , ] departments = {{12, 54, 16},
                        {22, 44, 47}};
```

3. A jagged array is a one-dimensional array in which each element is another array.

The false statement is #1. In a rectangular array, each row has the same number of columns, but there is no requirement that the numbers of rows and columns be the same.

YOU DO IT

CREATING AND USING AN ARRAY

In the next steps, you will create a small array to see how arrays are used. The array will hold salaries for four categories of employees.

To create a program that uses an array:

1. Open a new text file in your text editor.

2. Begin the class that will demonstrate array use by typing the following:

```
using System;
public class ArrayDemo1
{
    public static void Main()
    {
```

3. Declare and create an array that can hold four `double` values by typing:

```
double[] payRate;
payRate = new double[4];
```

4. One by one, assign four values to the four pay rate array elements by typing:

```
payRate[0] = 6.00;
payRate[1] = 7.35;
payRate[2] = 8.12;
payRate[3] = 12.45;
```

5. To confirm that the four values have been assigned, print the pay rates, one by one, using the following code:

```
Console.WriteLine("Pay rate {0} is {1}",
    0, payRate[0].ToString("C"));
Console.WriteLine("Pay rate {0} is {1}",
    1, payRate[1].ToString("C"));
Console.WriteLine("Pay rate {0} is {1}",
    2, payRate[2].ToString("C"));
Console.WriteLine("Pay rate {0} is {1}",
    3, payRate[3].ToString("C"));
```

6. Add the two closing curly brackets that end the `Main()` method and the `ArrayDemo1` class.

7. Save the program as **ArrayDemo1.cs**.

8. Compile and run the program. The program's output appears in Figure 5-19.

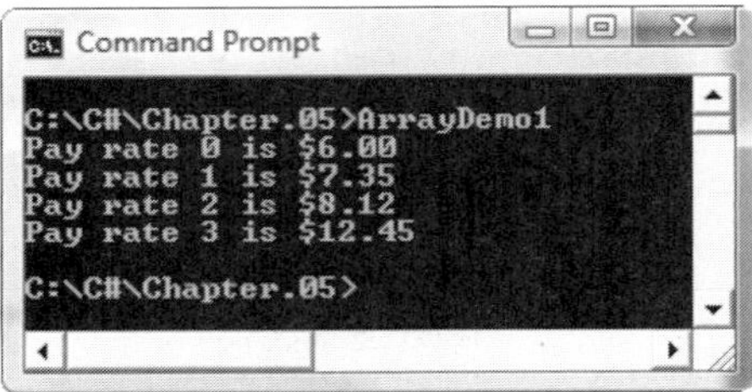

Figure 5-19 Output of `ArrayDemo1` program

INITIALIZING AN ARRAY

Next, you will alter your `ArrayDemo1` program to initialize the array of `doubles`, rather than declaring the array in one step and assigning values later.

To initialize an array of `doubles`:

1. Open the **ArrayDemo1.cs** file in your text editor and immediately save it as **ArrayDemo2.cs**. Change the class name from `ArrayDemo1` to **ArrayDemo2**.

2. Delete the first six statements within the `Main()` method; these statements declare the array, instantiate it, and assign four values. Replace them with a single statement that accomplishes the same tasks:

```
double[] payRate = {6.00, 7.35, 8.12, 12.45};
```

3. Save, compile, and execute the program. The output looks the same as in Figure 5-19.

USING A `for` LOOP WITH AN ARRAY

Next, you will modify the `ArrayDemo2` program to use a `for` loop with the array.

To use a `for` loop with an array:

1. Open the **ArrayDemo2.cs** file in your text editor and immediately save it as **ArrayDemo3.cs**. Change the class name to **ArrayDemo3**.

2. Delete the four `WriteLine()` statements that print the four array values and replace them with the following `for` loop:

```
for(int x = 0; x < 4; ++x)
   Console.WriteLine("Pay rate {0} is {1}",
        x, payRate[x].ToString("C"));
```

In this version of the statement, as x varies from 0 through 3, the value of x and the value of `payRate[x]` are both displayed.

3. Save, compile, and run the program. Again, the output is the same as in Figure 5-19.

USING THE Length PROPERTY WITH AN ARRAY

Next, you will modify the `ArrayDemo3` program to use the `Length` property. By doing so, no changes will be necessary to the `for` loop if you change the array size later—the `Length` field will automatically be updated to hold the current size of the array.

To use the Length property:

1. Open the **ArrayDemo3.cs** file in your text editor and immediately save it as **ArrayDemo4.cs**. Change the class name to **ArrayDemo4**.

2. Within the `for` statement that prints the array elements, change the 4 to **payRate.Length**.

3. Save, compile, and execute the program. The output is the same as in Figure 5-19.

4. At the end of the list of pay rates, insert a comma and a new, fifth rate of **22.22**.

5. Save the program, then compile and execute it again. The output looks like Figure 5-20. Even though you only added a new pay rate without making any other adjustments to the program, all five pay rates print correctly because C# adjusted the `Length` property.

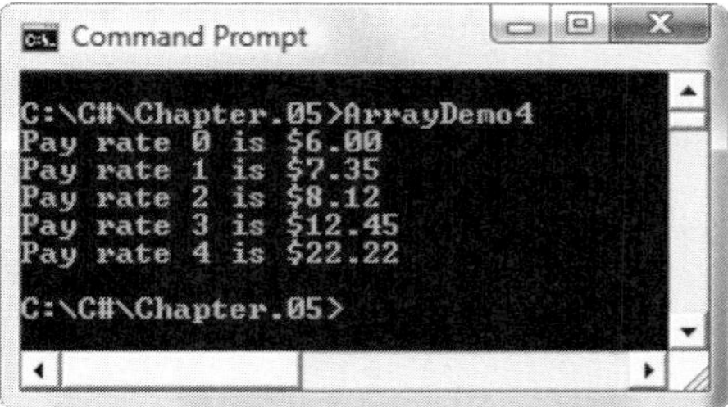

Figure 5-20 Output of `ArrayDemo4` program

USING THE Sort() AND Reverse() METHODS

In the next steps you will create an array of integers and use the `Sort()` and `Reverse()` methods to manipulate it.

To use the `Sort()` and `Reverse()` methods:

1. Open a new file in your text editor.

2. Type the beginning of a class named `MyTestScores` that includes an array of eight integer test scores, an integer you will use as a subscript, and a string that will hold user-entered data.

```
using System;
public class MyTestScores
{
    public static void Main()
    {
        int[] scores = new int[8];
        int x;
        string inputString;
```

> **NOTE**
> The program displays `x + 1` with each `score[x]` because, although array elements are numbered starting with 0, people usually count items starting with 1.

3. Add a loop that prompts the user, accepts a test score, converts the score to an integer, and stores it as the appropriate element of the `scores` array.

```
for(x = 0; x < scores.Length; ++x)
{
    Console.Write("Enter your score on test {0} ", x + 1);
    inputString = Console.ReadLine();
    scores[x] = Convert.ToInt32(inputString);
}
```

> **NOTE**
> You learned to set display field sizes when you learned about format strings in Chapter 2.

4. Add a statement that creates a dashed line to visually separate the input from the output. Display "Scores in original order:", then use a loop to display each score in a field that is six characters wide.

```
Console.WriteLine("\n------------------------------");
Console.WriteLine("Scores in original order:");
for(x = 0; x < scores.Length; ++x)
    Console.Write("{0, 6}", scores[x]);
```

5. Add another dashed line for visual separation, then pass the `scores` array to the `Array.Sort()` method. Print "Scores in sorted order:", then use a loop to display each of the newly sorted scores.

```
Console.WriteLine("\n------------------------------");
Array.Sort(scores);
Console.WriteLine("Scores in sorted order:");
for(x = 0; x < scores.Length; ++x)
    Console.Write("{0, 6}", scores[x]);
```

6. Add one more dashed line, reverse the array elements by passing `scores` to the `Array.Reverse()` method, display "Scores in reverse order:", and show the rearranged scores.

```
Console.WriteLine("\n------------------------------");
Array.Reverse(scores);
Console.WriteLine("Scores in reverse order:");
for(x = 0; x < scores.Length; ++x)
    Console.Write("{0, 6}", scores[x]);
```

7. Add two closing curly braces—one for the `Main()` method and one for the class. Save the file as **MyTestScores.cs**. Compile and execute the program. Figure 5-21 shows a typical execution of the program. The user-entered scores are not in order, but after the call to the `Sort()` method, they appear in ascending order. After the call to the `Reverse()` method, they appear in descending order.

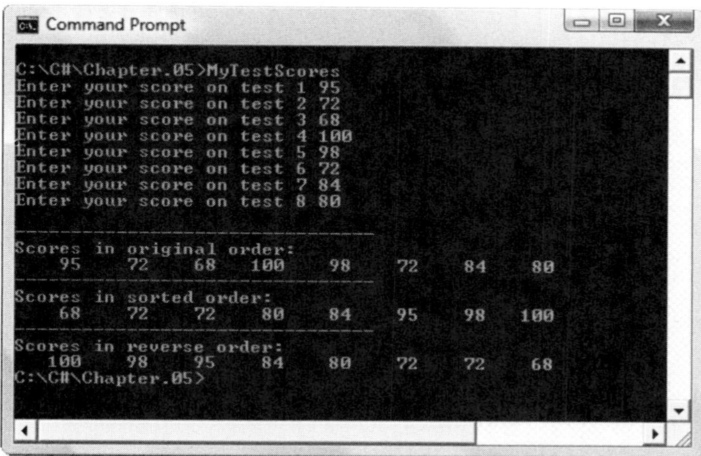

Figure 5-21 Typical execution of `MyTestScores` program

USING A CONSTANT FORMAT STRING

In the `MyTestScores` application, you repeatedly use the format string `"{0, 6}"` in the `Write()` statements to display each score in a field of size 6. Throughout this book, when a constant value has been used repeatedly, you have seen examples that employ a named constant. The advantage of creating a named constant to represent the format string in this program is that you can reformat the output's appearance in the future just by changing one line of code. Next, you will modify the `MyTestScores` class so the format string used for output can be easily modified.

To modify `MyTestScores` to use a constant format string for output:

1. Open the `MyTestScores` application in your text editor. Change the class name to **MyTestScoresWithConstantFormat** and immediately save the file as **MyTestScoresWithConstantFormat.cs**.

2. At the end of the existing list of declared variables, add a constant declaration as follows:

```
const string FORMAT = "{0, 6}";
```

3. Replace each occurrence of `"{0, 6}"` in the program with **FORMAT**. (With the addition of the constant format string in Step 2, these occurrences should be at lines 18, 23, and 28.) Make sure you replace all eight characters, including the existing quotation marks.

4. Save the file and execute the program. The output is identical to the output in Figure 5-21.

5. Modify the declaration of the FORMAT constant to the following:

```
const string FORMAT = "{0, 9}";
```

6. Save and execute the program. The output looks like Figure 5-22. By changing one character, you have consistently altered the output throughout the program. Whenever possible, you should consider how constants might help expedite future program modifications.

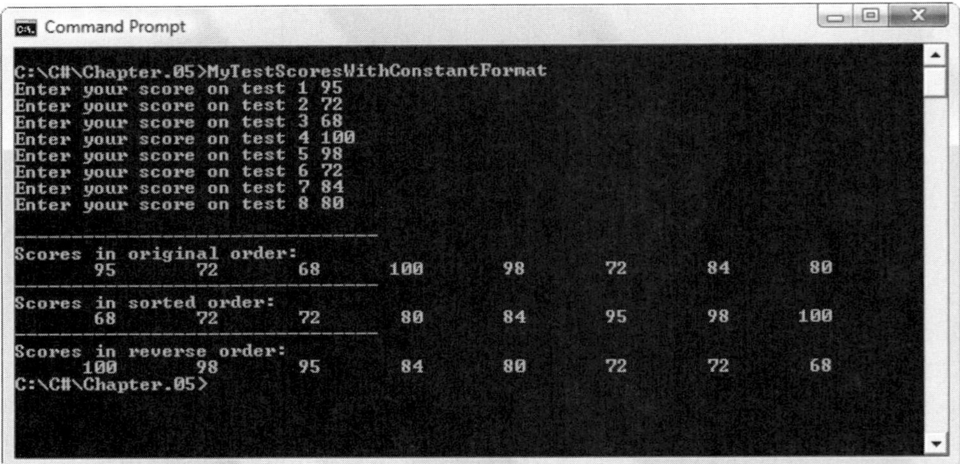

Figure 5-22 Typical execution of `MyTestScoresWithConstantFormat` program

> **NOTE** If it makes more sense to your application, you could define a constant integer such as `const int SIZE = 6;`, and then create a format string with a statement such as `string format = "{0, " + SIZE + "}";`. In this case, `SIZE` would be constant, but `format` would be required to be a variable.

CHAPTER SUMMARY

» An array is a list of data items, all of which have the same type and the same name, but are distinguished from each other using a subscript or index. You declare an array variable by inserting a pair of square brackets after the type. You reserve memory for an array by using the keyword `new`. A subscript (also called an index) is an integer contained within square brackets that indicates one of an array's variables, or elements. Any array's elements are numbered 0 through one less than the array's length.

» In C#, arrays are objects of a class named `System.Array`. An array's fields are initialized to default values. To initialize an array to nondefault values, you use a list of values that are separated by commas and enclosed within curly braces.

» The power of arrays becomes apparent when you begin to use subscripts that are variables rather than constant values, and when you use loops to process array elements.

» When you work with array elements, you must ensure that the subscript you use remains in the range of 0 through `length - 1`. You can use the `Length` property, which is a member of the `System.Array` class, to automatically hold an array's length.

» You can use the `foreach` statement to cycle through every array element without using subscripts. With the `foreach` statement, you provide a temporary variable that automatically holds each array value in turn.

» When you want to determine whether some variable holds one of many possible valid values, you can compare the variable to a list of values in an array. If you set up a parallel array with the same number of elements and corresponding data, you can use the same subscript to access additional information.

» You can create parallel arrays to more easily perform a range match.

» The `BinarySearch()` method finds a requested value in a sorted array. The method returns –1 if the value is not found in the array; otherwise, it returns the array position of the sought value. You cannot use the `BinarySearch()` method if your array items are not arranged in ascending order, if the array holds duplicate values and you want to find all of them, or if you want to find a range match rather than an exact match.

» The `Sort()` method arranges array items in ascending order. The `Reverse()` method reverses the order of items in an array.

» C# supports multidimensional arrays—those that require multiple subscripts to access the array elements. The most commonly used multidimensional arrays are two-dimensional arrays that are rectangular. Two-dimensional arrays have two or more columns of values for each row. In a rectangular array, each row has the same number of columns. C# also supports jagged arrays, which are arrays of arrays.

KEY TERMS

An **array** is a list of data items that all have the same data type and the same name, but are distinguished from each other by a subscript or index.

The keyword **new** is also known as the **new operator**; it is used to create objects.

Each object in an array is an **array element**.

A **subscript** (also called an **index**) is an integer contained within square brackets that indicates the position of one of an array's elements.

An **initializer list** is the list of values provided for an array.

The class **System.Array** defines fields and methods that belong to every array.

The **Length property** is a member of the `System.Array` class that automatically holds an array's length.

The **foreach statement** is used to cycle through every array element without using a subscript.

A temporary **iteration variable** holds each array value in turn in a `foreach` statement.

A **parallel array** has the same number of elements as another array and corresponding data.

A **range match** determines the pair of limiting values between which a value falls.

The **BinarySearch() method** finds a requested value in a sorted array.

The **Sort() method** arranges array items in ascending order.

The **Reverse() method** reverses the order of items in an array.

A **one-dimensional** or **single-dimensional array** is an array whose elements you can access using a single subscript.

Multidimensional arrays require multiple subscripts to access the array elements.

Two-dimensional arrays have two or more columns of values for each row.

In a **rectangular array**, each row has the same number of columns.

When mathematicians use a two-dimensional array, they often call it a **matrix** or a **table**.

A **jagged array** is a one-dimensional array in which each element is another array.

REVIEW QUESTIONS

1. In an array, every element has the same __________ .

   a. subscript

   b. data type

   c. memory location

   d. all of the above

2. The operator used to create objects is __________ .

   a. `=`

   b. `+=`

   c. `new`

   d. `create`

3. Which of the following correctly declares an array of four integers?

   a. `int array[4];`

   b. `int[] array = 4;`

   c. `int[4] array;`

   d. `int[] array = new int[4];`

4. The value placed within square brackets after an array name is __________ .

   a. a subscript

   b. an index

   c. always an integer

   d. all of these

5. If you define an array to contain seven elements, then the highest array subscript you can use is __________ .

   a. 5

   b. 6

   c. 7

   d. 8

6. Initializing an array is __________ in C#.

   a. required

   b. optional

   c. difficult

   d. prohibited

7. When you declare an array of six `double` elements but provide no initialization values, the value of the first element is __________ .

   a. 0.0

   b. 1.0

   c. 5.0

   d. unknown

8. Which of the following correctly declares an array of four integers?

   a. `int[] ages = new int[4] {20, 30, 40, 50};`

   b. `int[] ages = new int[] {20, 30, 40, 50};`

   c. `int[] ages = {20, 30, 40, 50};`

   d. all of these

9. When an `ages` array is correctly initialized using the values `{20, 30, 40, 50}`, as in Question 8, then the value of `ages[1]` is __________ .

   a. 0

   b. 20

   c. 30

   d. undefined

10. When an `ages` array is correctly initialized using the values `{20, 30, 40, 50}`, as in Question 8, then the value of `ages[4]` is __________ .

    a. 0

    b. 4

    c. 50

    d. undefined

11. When you declare an array as `int[] temperature = {0, 32, 50, 90, 212, 451};`, the value of `temperature.Length` is __________ .

    a. 5

    b. 6

    c. 7

    d. unknown

12. Which of the following doubles every value in a 10-element integer array named `amount`?

    a. `for(int x = 9; x >= 0; --x)   amount[x] *= 2;`

    b. `foreach(int number in amount) number *= 2;`

    c. both of these

    d. neither of these

13. Which of the following adds 10 to every value in a 15-element integer array named `points`?

    a. `for(int sub = 0; sub > 15; ++sub)   points[sub] += 10;`

    b. `foreach(int sub in points) points += 10;`

    c. both of these

    d. neither of these

14. Two arrays that store related information in corresponding element positions
    are __________ .

    a. analogous arrays

    b. polymorphic arrays

    c. relative arrays

    d. parallel arrays

15. Assume an array is defined as `int[] nums = {2, 3, 4, 5};`. Which of the
    following would display the values in the array in reverse?

    a. `for(int x = 4; x > 0; --x) Console.Write(nums[x]);`

    b. `for(int x = 3; x >= 0; --x) Console.Write(nums[x]);`

    c. `for(int x = 3; x > 0; --x) Console.Write(nums[x]);`

    d. `for(int x = 4; x >= 0; --x) Console.Write(nums[x]);`

16. Assume an array is defined as `int[] nums = {7, 15, 23, 5};`. Which of the
    following would place the values in the array in descending numeric order?

    a. `Array.Sort(nums);`

    b. `Array.Reverse(nums);`

    c. `Array.Sort(nums); Array.Reverse(nums);`

    d. `Array.Reverse(nums); Array.Sort(nums);`

17. Which of the following traits do the `BinarySearch()` and `Sort()` methods have
    in common?

    a. Both methods take a single argument that must be an array.

    b. Both methods belong to the `System.Array` class.

    c. The array that each method uses must be in ascending order.

    d. They both operate on arrays made up of simple data types but not class objects.

18. If you use the `BinarySearch()` method and the object you seek is not found in the
    array, __________ .

    a. an error message is displayed

    b. a zero is returned

    c. the value `false` is returned

    d. a negative value is returned

19. The `BinarySearch()` method is inadequate when __________ .

    a. array items are in ascending order

    b. the array holds duplicate values and you want to find them all

    c. you want to find an exact match for a value

    d. array items are not numeric

20. Which of the following declares an integer array that contains eight rows and five columns?

```
a. int[8, 5] num = new int[ , ];

b. int [8][5] num = new int[];

c. int [ , ] num = new int[5, 8];

d. int [ , ] num = new int[8, 5];
```

EXERCISES

1. Write a program containing an array that holds five integers. Assign values to the integers. Display the integers from first to last, and then display them from last to first. Save the program as **IntegerList.cs**.

2. Write a program for a package delivery service. The program contains an array that holds the 10 zip codes to which the company delivers packages. Prompt a user to enter a zip code and display a message indicating whether the zip code is one to which the company delivers. Save the program as **CheckZips.cs**.

3. Write another program for the package delivery service in Exercise 2. The program should again use an array that holds the 10 zip codes to which the company delivers packages. Create a parallel array containing 10 delivery charges that differ for each zip code. Prompt a user to enter a zip code and then display either a message indicating the price of delivery to that zip code or a message indicating that the company does not deliver to the requested zip code. Save the program as **DeliveryCharges.cs**.

4. The Chat-A-While phone company provides service to six area codes and charges the following per-minute rates for phone calls:

Area Code	Per-Minute Rate ($)
262	0.07
414	0.10
608	0.05
715	0.16
815	0.24
920	0.14

Write a program that allows a user to enter an area code and the length of time for a call in minutes, then display the total cost of the call. Save the program as **ChatAWhile.cs**.

5. The Whippet Bus Company charges prices for tickets based on distance traveled, as follows:

Distance (miles)	Ticket Price ($)
0–99	25.00
100–299	40.00
300–499	55.00
500 and farther	70.00

Write a program that allows a user to enter a trip distance. The output is the ticket price. Save the program as **WhippetBus.cs**.

6. a. Write a program that prompts the user to make a choice for a pizza size—*S*, *M*, *L*, or *X*—and then displays the price as $6.99, $8.99, $12.50, or $15.00, respectively. Save the program as **PizzaPrices.cs**.

   b. Modify the `PizzaPrices` program so that the following discounts apply: no discount for one pizza, 10% for two pizzas, 15% for three or four pizzas, and 20% for five or more pizzas. Display a full accounting of the transaction, similar to that shown in Figure 5-23. Save the program as **PizzaPrices2.cs**.

Figure 5-23 Typical execution of `PizzaPrices2` program

7. Write a program that computes commissions for automobile salespeople based on the value of the car. Salespeople receive 5 percent of the sale price for any car sold for up to and including $15,000; 7 percent for any car over $15,000 up to and including $24,000; and 10 percent of the sale price of any car over $24,000. Write a program that allows a user to enter a car price. The output is the salesperson's commission. Save the program as **Commission.cs**.

8. Create an array that stores 20 prices. Prompt a user to enter 20 values, then display the sum of the values. Next, display all values of less than $5.00. Finally, calculate the average of the prices, and display all values that are higher than the calculated average. Save the program as **Prices.cs**.

9. The Tiny Tots Tee-Ball league has 12 players who have jersey numbers 0 through 11. The coach wants a program into which he can type a player's number and the number of bases the player got in a turn at bat (a number 0 through 4). Write a program that allows the coach to continually enter the values until 999 is entered. Store the statistics in a two-dimensional array. At the end of a data-entry session, display each player's number and the number of 0-base, 1-base, 2-base, 3-base, and 4-base turns the player had. Display a separate count of the number of data-entry errors the coach makes (a player number greater than 11 or a number of bases greater than 4). The output should look similar to Figure 5-24. Save the program as **TeeBall.cs**.

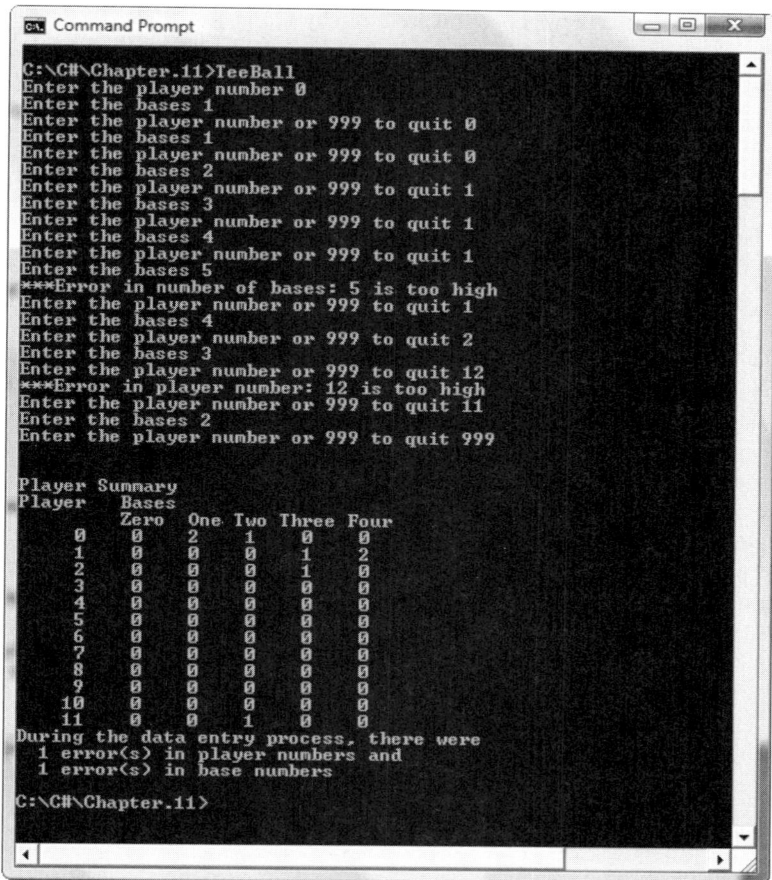

Figure 5-24 Typical execution of TeeBall program

DEBUGGING EXERCISES

Each of the following files in the Chapter.05 folder on your Student Disk has syntax and/or logical errors. In each case, determine the problem and fix the program. After you correct the errors, save each file using the same filename preceded with *Fixed*. For example, DebugFive01.cs will become FixedDebugFive01.cs.

a. DebugFive01.cs

b. DebugFive02.cs

c. DebugFive03.cs

d. DebugFive04.cs

UP FOR DISCUSSION

1. A train schedule is an everyday, real-life example of an array. Think of at least four more.

2. This chapter discusses sorting data. Suppose you are hired by a large hospital to write a program that displays lists of potential organ recipients. The hospital's doctors will consult this list if they have an organ that can be transplanted. You are instructed to sort potential recipients by last name and display them sequentially in alphabetical order. If more than 10 patients are waiting for a particular organ, the first 10 patients are displayed; the user can either select one of these or move on to view the next set of 10 patients. You worry that this system gives an unfair advantage to patients with last names that start with A, B, C, and D. Should you write and install the program? If you do not, many transplant opportunities will be missed while the hospital searches for another programmer to write the program.

3. This chapter discusses sorting data. Suppose your supervisor asks you to create a report that lists all employees sorted by salary. Suppose you also know that your employer will use this report to lay off the highest-paid employee in each department. Would you agree to write the program? Instead, what if the report's purpose was to list the worst performer in each department in terms of sales? What if the report grouped employees by gender? What if the report grouped employees by race? Suppose your supervisor asks you to sort employees by the dollar value of medical insurance claims they have in a year, and you fear the employer will use the report to eliminate workers who are driving up the organization's medical insurance costs. Do you agree to write the program even if you know that the purpose of the report is to eliminate workers?

6

USING METHODS

In this chapter you will:

Learn about methods
Write methods with no parameters and no return value
Learn about implementation hiding
Write methods that require a single argument
Write methods that require multiple arguments
Write a method that returns a value
Pass an array to a method
Use reference parameters, output parameters, and
    parameter arrays with methods
Overload methods
Learn how to avoid ambiguous methods

In the first five chapters of this book, you learned to create C# programs containing `Main()` methods that declare variables, accept input, perform arithmetic, and produce output. You learned to add decisions, loops, and arrays to your programs. As your programs grow in complexity, their `Main()` methods will contain many additional statements. Rather than creating increasingly long `Main()` methods, most programmers prefer to modularize their programs, placing instructions in smaller "packages" called methods. In this chapter, you learn to create many types of C# methods. You will gain the ability to send data to these methods and to receive information back from them.

UNDERSTANDING METHODS

A **method** is an encapsulated series of statements that carry out a task. Any class can contain an unlimited number of methods. So far, you have written classes that contain a `Main()` method, but no others. Your `Main()` methods have **invoked**, or **called**, other methods; that is, your program used a method's name and the method performed a job for the class. For example, you have created many programs that call the `WriteLine()` and `ReadLine()` methods. When you used arrays in Chapter 5, you learned how to use the `BinarySearch()`, `Sort()`, and `Reverse()` methods. The methods you have used were written for you; you only had to call them to have them work.

For example, consider the simple `HelloClass` program shown in Figure 6-1. The `Main()` method contains a statement that calls the `Console.WriteLine()` method. You can identify method names because they always are followed by a set of parentheses. Depending on the method, there might be an argument within the parentheses. The call to the `WriteLine()` method within the `HelloClass` program in Figure 6-1 contains the string argument "Hello". The simplest methods you can invoke don't require any arguments.

> **» NOTE**
> You first learned the term "argument" in Chapter 1.

> **» NOTE**
> Methods are similar to the procedures, functions, and subroutines used in other programming languages.

```
using System;
public class HelloClass
{
    public static void Main()
    {
        Console.WriteLine("Hello");
    }
}
```

Figure 6-1 The `HelloClass` program

> **» NOTE**
> In the `HelloClass` program in Figure 6-1, `Main()` is a **calling method**—one that calls another. The `WriteLine()` method is a **called method**.

When you call the `WriteLine()` method within the `HelloClass` program in Figure 6-1, you use a method that has already been created for you. Because the creators of C# knew you would often want to write a message to the output screen, they created a method you could call to accomplish that task. This method takes care of all the hardware details of producing a message on the output device; you simply call the method and pass the desired message to it. The creators of C# were able to anticipate many of the methods you would need for your programs; you will continue to use many of these methods throughout this book. However, your programs often will require custom methods that the creators of C# could not have expected. In this chapter, you will learn to write your own custom methods.

»TWO TRUTHS AND A LIE: UNDERSTANDING METHODS

1. A method is an encapsulated series of statements that carry out a task.
2. Any class can contain an unlimited number of methods.
3. All the methods your programs will use have been written for you and stored in files.

The false statement is #3. As you write programs, you will want to write many of your own custom methods.

WRITING METHODS WITH NO PARAMETERS AND NO RETURN VALUE

The output of the program in Figure 6-1 is simply the word "Hello". Suppose you want to add three more lines of output to display a standard welcoming message when users execute your program. Of course, you can add three new `WriteLine()` statements to the existing program, but you also can create a method to display the three new lines.

There are two major reasons to create a method instead of adding three lines to the existing program:

» If you add a method call instead of three new lines, the `Main()` method will remain short and easy to follow. The `Main()` method will contain just one new statement that calls a method rather than three separate `WriteLine()` statements.

» More importantly, a method is easily *reusable*. After you create the welcoming method, you can use it in any program. In other words, you do the work once, and then you can use the method many times.

» NOTE When you place code in a callable method instead of repeating the same code at several points in a program, you are avoiding **code bloat**—a colorful term that describes unnecessarily long or repetitive statements.

In C#, a method must include:

» A **method declaration**, which is also known as a **method header** or **method definition**
» An opening curly brace
» A **method body**, which is a block of statements that carry out the method's work
» A closing curly brace

The method declaration defines the rules for using the method; it contains:

» Optional declared accessibility
» An optional `static` modifier
» The return type for the method
» The method name, or identifier
» An opening parenthesis
» An optional list of method parameters (you separate the parameters with commas if there is more than one)
» A closing parenthesis

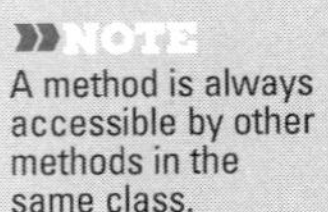

A method is always accessible by other methods in the same class.

The optional declared **accessibility** for a method sets limits as to how other methods can use your method; it can be any of the following:

» **Public access**, which you select by including a `public` modifier in the member declaration. This modifier allows unlimited access to a method.
» **Protected internal access**, which you select by including both a `protected` and an `internal` modifier in the member declaration. This modifier limits method access to the containing program, the containing class, or types derived from the containing class.
» **Protected access**, which you select by including a `protected` modifier in the member declaration. This modifier limits method access to the containing class or types derived from the containing class.
» **Internal access**, which you select by including an `internal` modifier in the member declaration. This modifier limits method access to the containing class or program.
» **Private access**, which you select by including a `private` modifier in the member declaration. This modifier limits method access to the containing class.

»NOTE
You will learn about protected access and what it means to derive types in Chapter 8.

Table 6-1 summarizes where a method is accessible, depending on its accessibility modifier. If you do not provide an accessibility modifier for a method, it is `private` by default. As you study C#, deciding which access modifier to choose will become clearer. For example, when you begin to create your own class objects, you usually will provide them with `public` methods, but sometimes you will make methods `private`. For now, all the methods you create will be `public`.

Declared accessibility	Containing classes	Derived classes	Containing programs	All classes
`public`	Yes	Yes	Yes	Yes
`protected internal`	Yes	Yes	Yes	No
`protected`	Yes	Yes	No	No
`internal`	Yes	No	Yes	No
`private`	Yes	No	No	No

Table 6-1 Summary of method accessibility

Additionally, you can declare a method to be **static** or **nonstatic**. If you use the keyword modifier `static`, you indicate that a method can be called without referring to an object. Instead, you refer to the class. If you do not indicate that a method is `static`, it is nonstatic by default and can only be used in conjunction with an object. When you begin to create your own class objects in Chapter 7, you will write many nonstatic methods and your understanding of the use of these terms will become clearer. For now, all methods you create will be `static`.

Every method has a **return type**, indicating what kind of value the method will return to any other method that calls it. If a method does not return a value, its return type is `void`. A method's return type is known more succinctly as a **method's type**. Later in this chapter, you will create methods that return values; for now, the methods will be `void` methods.

> **》》 NOTE**
> When a method's return type is `void`, most C# programmers do not end the method with a `return` statement. However, you can end a `void` method with the following statement that indicates nothing is returned:
>
> `return;`

> **》》 NOTE** You have used a return value from the `ReadLine()` method when you have written a statement such as `inputString = Console.ReadLine();`.

Every method has a name that must be a legal C# identifier; that is, it must not contain spaces and must begin with a letter of the alphabet or an underscore.

Every method name is followed by a set of parentheses. Sometimes these parentheses contain parameters, but in the simplest methods, the parentheses are empty.

In summary, the first methods you write will be `public`, `static`, and `void` and will have empty parameter lists. Therefore, you can write the `WelcomeMessage()` method as it is shown in Figure 6-2. According to its declaration, it is `public` and `static`. It returns nothing, so its return type is `void`. Its identifier is `WelcomeMessage`, and it receives nothing, so its parentheses are empty. Its body, consisting of three `WriteLine()` statements, appears within curly braces.

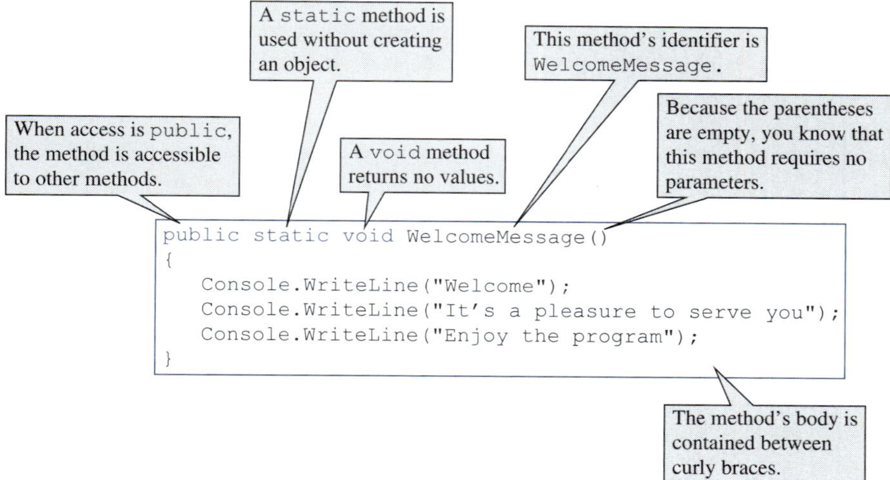


```
public static void WelcomeMessage()
{
    Console.WriteLine("Welcome");
    Console.WriteLine("It's a pleasure to serve you");
    Console.WriteLine("Enjoy the program");
}
```

Figure 6-2 The `WelcomeMessage()` method

You can place any statements you want within a method body, and you can declare variables within a method. When a variable is declared within a method, it is known only from that point to the end of the method. The area in which a variable is known is its **scope**.

You can place a method in its own file, as you will learn in the next section. You also can place a method within the file of a program that will use it, but you cannot place a method within any other method. Figure 6-3 shows the two locations where you can place the `WelcomeMessage()` method within the `HelloClass` program file—before the `Main()` method header or after the `Main()` method's closing brace.


```
using System;
public class HelloClass
{
    // The WelcomeMessage() method could go here
    public static void Main()
    {
        Console.WriteLine("Hello");
    }
    // Alternatively, the WelcomeMessage() method could go here
    // But it cannot go in both places
}
```

Figure 6-3 Placement of methods

If a `Main()` method calls the `WelcomeMessage()` method, then you simply use the `WelcomeMessage()` method's name as a statement within the body of the `Main()` method. Figure 6-4 shows the complete program with the method call shaded, and Figure 6-5 shows the output.

```
using System;
public class HelloClass
{
    public static void Main()
    {
        WelcomeMessage();
        Console.WriteLine("Hello");
    }
    public static void WelcomeMessage()
    {
        Console.WriteLine("Welcome");
        Console.WriteLine("It's a pleasure to serve you");
        Console.WriteLine("Enjoy the program");
    }
}
```

Figure 6-4 `HelloClass` program with `Main()` method calling the `WelcomeMessage()` method

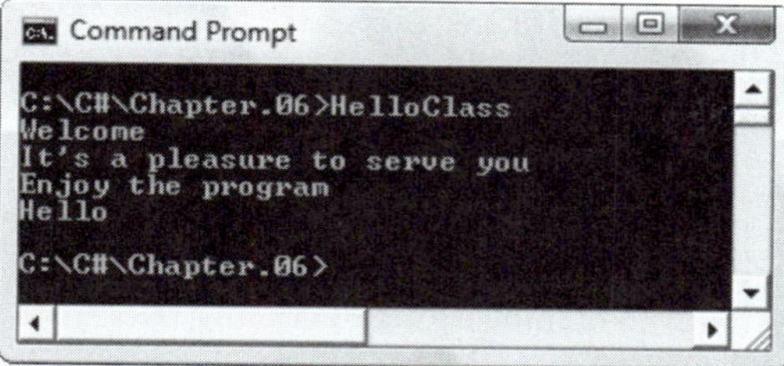

Figure 6-5 Output of `HelloClass` program

When the `Main()` method executes, it calls the `WelcomeMessage()` method, then it prints "Hello". Because the `Main()` method calls the `WelcomeMessage()` method before it prints "Hello", the three lines that make up the welcome message appear first in the output.

> **»NOTE** Each of two different classes can have its own method named `WelcomeMessage()`. Such a method in the second class would be entirely distinct from the identically named method in the first class.

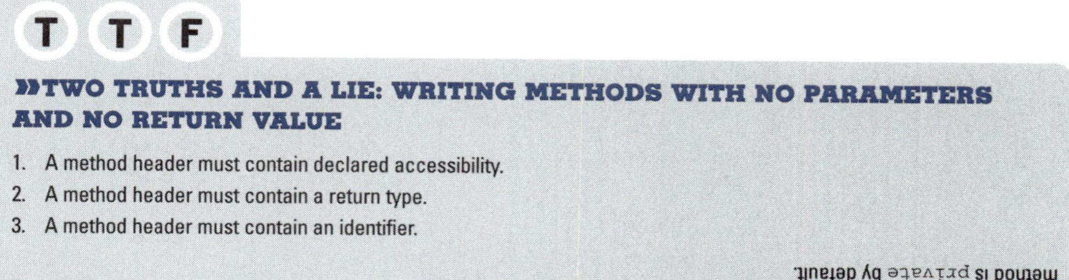

»TWO TRUTHS AND A LIE: WRITING METHODS WITH NO PARAMETERS AND NO RETURN VALUE

1. A method header must contain declared accessibility.
2. A method header must contain a return type.
3. A method header must contain an identifier.

The false statement is #1. Declaring accessibility in a method header is optional. If you do not use an access modifier, the method is `private` by default.

HIDING IMPLEMENTATION

An important principle of object-oriented programming is the notion of **implementation hiding**—keeping the details of a method's operations hidden. When you make a request to a method, you don't need to know the details of how the method is implemented. For example, when you make a dental appointment, you do not need to know how the appointment is actually recorded at the dental office—perhaps it is written in a book, marked on a large chalkboard, or entered into a computerized database. The implementation details are of no concern to you as a client, and if the dental office changes its methods from one year to the next, the change does not affect your use of the appointment method. Your only concern is the way you **interface** or interact with the dental office, not how the office records appointments. Similarly, if you use a thermostat to raise the temperature in your apartment or house, you do not need to know whether the heat is generated by natural gas, electricity, solar energy, or a hamster on a wheel. As long as you receive heat, the implementation details can remain hidden.

The same is true with well-written program methods; the invoking program or method must know the name of the method it is using (and what type of information to send it), but the program does not need to know how the method works. Later, you can substitute a new, improved method for the old one, and if the interface to the method does not change, you won't need to make any changes in programs that invoke the method.

For example, suppose you rewrite the `WelcomeMessage()` method as shown in Figure 6-6. The method is constructed differently from the one with the identical name shown in Figure 6-2—the new method uses two statements instead of three, uses a `Write()` method for a portion of its output instead of all `WriteLine()` methods, and uses two newline escape sequences ('\n'). Nevertheless, if you substitute the new version for the old one, any program that uses the method does not need to be altered, and the output is identical.

```
public static void WelcomeMessage()
{
    Console.Write("Welcome\nIt's a pleasure ");
    Console.WriteLine("to serve you\nEnjoy the program");
}
```

Figure 6-6 Alternate `WelcomeMessage()` method

You should not alter the `WelcomeMessage()` method arbitrarily. However, as you learn to program, you will encounter many opportunities to substitute an improved method for an older, less efficient one. Also, you often will use methods written by others or that you "borrow" from other applications you have written. To more easily incorporate methods into a program, it is common practice to store methods (or groups of associated methods) in their own classes and files. Then you can add them into any application that uses them. The resulting compound program is called a **multifile assembly**. As you learn more about C#, you might prefer to take this approach with your own programs. For now, for simplicity, methods will be contained in the same file as any other methods that use them.

»TWO TRUTHS AND A LIE: HIDING IMPLEMENTATION

1. When you call a method, you must know the method's identifier.
2. When you call a method, you must know what type of information to send it.
3. When you call a method, you must know how the method works.

The false statement is #3. You do not need to know how a method is implemented in order to use it.

WRITING METHODS THAT REQUIRE A SINGLE ARGUMENT

Some methods require additional information. If a method could not receive arguments, then you would have to write an infinite number of methods to cover every possible situation. For example, when you make a dental appointment, you do not need to employ a different method for every date of the year at every possible time of day. Rather, you can supply the date and time as information to the method, and no matter what date and time you supply, the method is carried out in the same manner. If you design a method to triple numeric values, it makes sense that you can supply the `Triple()` method with an argument representing the value to be tripled, rather than having to develop a `Triple1()` method, a `Triple2()` method, and so on.

> **» NOTE**
> In Chapter 1, you learned that arguments are passed into methods in the method call. A data item accepted by a method in its header is a parameter.

> **» NOTE** You already have used a method to which you supplied a wide variety of parameters. At any call, the `System.WriteLine()` method can receive any one of an infinite number of strings as a parameter—"Hello", "Goodbye", and so on. No matter what message you send to the `WriteLine()` method, the message will be displayed correctly.

When you write the declaration for a method that can receive a parameter, you need to include the following items within the method declaration parentheses:

» The type of the parameter
» A local identifier (name) for the parameter

For example, consider a `public` method named `DisplaySalesTax()`, which displays the result of multiplying a value that represents a selling price by 7%. The method header for a usable `DisplaySalesTax()` method could be the following:

```
public static void DisplaySalesTax(double saleAmount)
```

You can think of the parentheses in a method declaration as a funnel into the method—data parameters listed there are "dropping in" to the method.

The parameter `double saleAmount` within the parentheses indicates that the `DisplaySalesTax()` method will receive a value of type `double`. Within the method, the value will be known as `saleAmount`. Figure 6-7 shows a complete method.

```
public static void DisplaySalesTax(double saleAmount)
{
    double tax;
    const double RATE = 0.07;
    tax = saleAmount * RATE;
    Console.WriteLine("The tax on {0} is {1}",
        saleAmount, tax.ToString("C"));
}
```

Figure 6-7 The `DisplaySalesTax()` method

You create the `DisplaySalesTax()` method as a `void` method (it has a `void` return type) because you do not need it to return any value to any method that uses it—its only function is to receive the `saleAmount` value, multiply it by 0.07, and then display the result. You create it as a `static` method because you do not want to create an object with which to use it.

Within a program, you can call the `DisplaySalesTax()` method by using the method's name, and, within parentheses, an argument that is either a constant value or a variable. Thus, both of the following calls to the `DisplaySalesTax()` method invoke it correctly:

```
double myPurchase = 12.99;
DisplaySalesTax(12.99);
DisplaySalesTax(myPurchase);
```


You can call the `DisplaySalesTax()` method any number of times, with a different constant or variable argument each time. The value of each of these arguments becomes known as `saleAmount` within the method. The identifier `saleAmount` holds any `double` value passed into the method. Interestingly, if the argument in the method call is a variable, it might possess the same identifier as `saleAmount` or a different one, such as `myPurchase`. The identifier `saleAmount` is simply the name the value "goes by" while being used within the method, no matter what name it goes by in the calling program. That is, the variable `saleAmount` is a **local variable** to the `DisplaySalesTax()` method. The variable `saleAmount` is also an example of a **formal parameter**, a parameter within a method header that accepts a value. In contrast, arguments within a method *call* often are referred to as **actual parameters**.

If a programmer changes the way in which the tax value is calculated—for example, by coding one of the following—programs that use the `DisplaySalesTax()` method will not be affected and will not need to be modified:

```
tax = saleAmount * 7 / 100;
tax = 0.07 * saleAmount;
tax = RATE * saleAmount;
```

Each of these statements computes `tax` as 7% of `saleAmount`. No matter how the tax is calculated, a calling program passes a value into the `DisplaySalesTax()` method, and a calculated result appears on the screen.

Figure 6-8 shows a complete program called `UseTaxMethod`. It uses the `DisplaySalesTax()` method twice, first with a variable argument, and then with a constant argument. The program's output appears in Figure 6-9.

```
using System;
public class UseTaxMethod
{
    public static void Main()
    {
        double myPurchase = 12.99;
        DisplaySalesTax(myPurchase);
        DisplaySalesTax(35.67);
    }
    public static void DisplaySalesTax(double saleAmount)
    {
        double tax;
        const double RATE = 0.07;
        tax = saleAmount * RATE;
        Console.WriteLine("The tax on {0} is {1}",
            saleAmount.ToString("C"), tax.ToString("C"));
    }
}
```

Figure 6-8 Complete program using the `DisplaySalesTax()` method two times

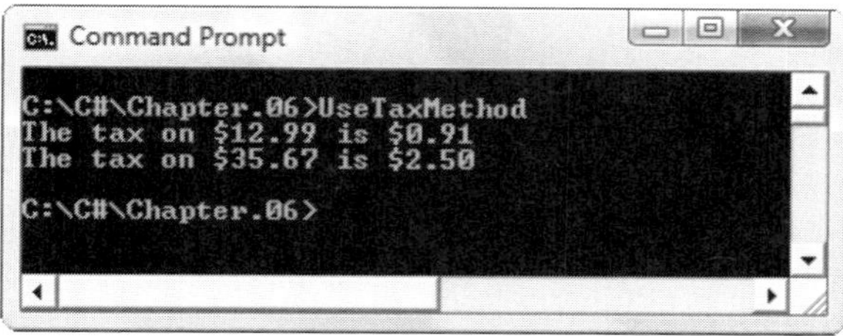

Figure 6-9 Output of the `UseTaxMethod` program

» NOTE Now that you have seen how to write methods that accept an argument, you might guess that when you write `Console.WriteLine("Hello");`, the header for the called method is similar to `public void WriteLine(string s)`. You might not know the parameter name the creators of C# have chosen, but you do know the method's return type, name, and parameter type. (If you use the IntelliSense feature of Visual Studio, you can discover the parameter name. See Appendix C for more details.)

»TWO TRUTHS AND A LIE: WRITING METHODS THAT REQUIRE A SINGLE ARGUMENT

1. When you write the declaration for a method that can receive a parameter, you need to include the parameter's data type within the method header.

2. When you write the declaration for a method that can receive a parameter, you need to include the identifier of the argument that will be sent to the method within the method header.

3. When you write the declaration for a method that can receive a parameter, you need to include a local identifier for the parameter within the method header.

The false statement is #2. When you write the definition for a method, you include the data type and a local parameter name within the parentheses of the method header, but you do not include the name of any argument that will be sent from a calling method. After all, the method might be invoked any number of times with any number of different arguments.

WRITING METHODS THAT REQUIRE MULTIPLE ARGUMENTS

A method can require more than one argument. You can pass multiple arguments to a method by listing the arguments within the call to the method and separating them with commas. For example, rather than creating a `DisplaySalesTax()` method that multiplies an amount by 0.07, you might prefer to create a more flexible method to which you can pass two values—the value on which the tax is calculated and the tax percentage by which it should be multiplied. Figure 6-10 shows a method that uses two such arguments.

```
public static void DisplaySalesTax(double saleAmount, double taxRate)
{
   double tax;
   tax = saleAmount * taxRate;
   Console.WriteLine("The tax on {0} at {1} is {2}",
      saleAmount.ToString("C"),
      taxRate.ToString("P"), tax.ToString("C"));
}
```

Figure 6-10 The `DisplaySalesTax()` method that takes two arguments

In Figure 6-10, two parameters (`double saleAmount` and `double taxRate`) appear within the parentheses in the method header. A comma separates the parameters, and each parameter requires its own named type (in this case, both parameters are of type `double`) and an identifier. When you pass values to the method in a statement such as `DisplaySalesTax(myPurchase, localRate);`, the first value passed will be referenced as `saleAmount` within the method, and the second value passed will be referenced as `taxRate`. Therefore, it is very important that arguments be passed to a method in the correct order. The following call results in output stating that "The tax on $200.00 is $20.00":

```
DisplaySalesTax(200.00, 0.10);
```

However, the following call results in output stating that "The tax on $0.10 is $20.00", which is clearly incorrect.

```
DisplaySalesTax(0.10, 200.00);
```

> **NOTE** If two method parameters are of the same type—for example, two `doubles`—passing arguments to a method in the wrong order results in a logical error. If a method expects parameters of diverse types, then passing arguments in reverse order constitutes a syntax error.

> **NOTE** A declaration for a method that receives two or more arguments must list the type for each parameter separately, even if the parameters have the *same* type.

Figure 6-11 shows a complete program that calls the `DisplaySalesTax()` method two times. Figure 6-12 shows the output.

```
using System;
public class UseTaxMethod2
{
    public static void Main()
    {
        double myPurchase = 239.11;
        double myRate = 0.10;
        DisplaySalesTax(myPurchase, myRate);
        DisplaySalesTax(16.55, 0.02);
    }
    public static void DisplaySalesTax(double saleAmount,
        double taxRate)
    {
        double tax;
        tax = saleAmount * taxRate;
        Console.WriteLine("The tax on {0} at {1} is {2}",
            saleAmount.ToString("C"),
            taxRate.ToString("P"), tax.ToString("C"));
    }
}
```

Figure 6-11 The `UseTaxMethod2` program

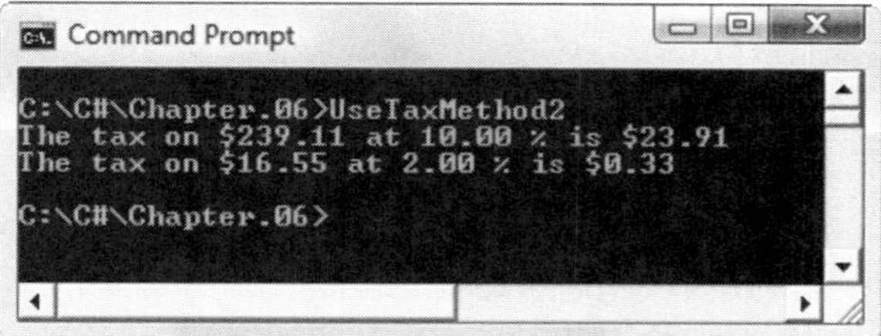

Figure 6-12 Output of the `UseTaxMethod2` program

You can write a method to take any number of parameters in any order. When you call the method, however, the arguments you send to it must match (in both number and type) the parameters listed in the method declaration. Thus, a method to compute an automobile salesperson's commission might require arguments such as an integer value of a sold car, a `double` percentage commission rate, and a character code for the vehicle type. The correct method will execute only when three arguments of the correct types are sent in the correct order.

»TWO TRUTHS AND A LIE: WRITING METHODS THAT REQUIRE MULTIPLE ARGUMENTS

1. The following is a usable C# method header:

   ```
   public static void MyMethod(double amt, sum)
   ```

2. The following is a usable C# method header:

   ```
   private void MyMethod2(int x, double y)
   ```

3. The following is a usable C# method header:

   ```
   static void MyMethod3(int id, string name, double rate)
   ```

The false statement is #1. In a method header, each parameter must have a data type, even if the data types for all the parameters are the same. The header in #2 does not contain the keyword `static`, but that is optional. Likewise, the header in #3 does not contain an accessibility indicator, but that is optional also.

WRITING A METHOD
THAT RETURNS A VALUE

A method can return, at most, one value to a method that calls it. The return type for a method can be any type used in the C# programming language, which includes the basic built-in types `int`, `double`, `char`, and so on, as well as class types (including class types you create). Of course, a method also can return nothing, in which case the return type is `void`.

»NOTE In addition to the primitive types, a method can return a class type. If a class named `BankLoan` exists, a method might return an instance of a `BankLoan` as in `public BankLoan ApprovalProcess()`. In other words, a method can return anything from a simple `int` to a complicated `BankLoan` object that contains 20 data fields. You will create classes like `BankLoan` in Chapter 7.

For example, the declaration for the `WelcomeMessage()` method shown in Figure 6-2 is:

```
public static void WelcomeMessage()
```

This method is `public` and returns no value, so it is of type `void`. A method that returns `true` or `false` depending on whether an employee worked overtime hours might be defined as:

```
public bool IsOvertimeEarned()
```

This method is `public` and returns a `bool` value, so it is of type `bool`.

Suppose you want to create a method to accept the hours an employee worked and the hourly pay rate, and to return a calculated gross pay value. The header for this method could be:

```
public static double CalcPay(double hours, double rate)
```

Figure 6-13 shows this method.

```
public static double CalcPay(double hours, double rate)
{
    double gross;
    gross = hours * rate;
    return gross;
}
```

Figure 6-13 The `CalcPay()` method

Notice the return type `double` in the method header. Also notice the `return` statement, which is the last statement within the method. A **return statement** causes a value to be sent back to the calling method; in the `CalcPay()` method, the value stored in `gross` is sent back to any method that calls the `CalcPay()` method. The data type used in a method's `return` statement must be the same as the return type declared in the method's header.

If a method returns a value and you call the method, you typically will want to use the returned value, although you are not required to use it. For example, when you invoke the `CalcPay()` method, you might want to assign the value to a `double` variable named `grossPay`, as in the following statement:

```
grossPay = CalcPay(myHours, myRate);
```

The `CalcPay()` method returns a `double`, so it is appropriate to assign the returned value to a `double` variable. Figure 6-14 shows a program that uses the `CalcPay()` method in the shaded statement, and Figure 6-15 shows the output.

Instead of storing a method's returned value in a variable, you can use it directly, as in either of the following statements:

```
Console.WriteLine("My gross pay is {0}",
    CalcPay(myHours, myRate).ToString("C"));
double tax = CalcPay(myHours, myRate) * TAX_RATE;
```

In the first statement, the call to the `CalcPay()` method is made from within the `WriteLine()` method call. In the second, `CalcPay()`'s returned value is used in an arithmetic statement. Because `CalcPay()` returns a `double`, you can use the method call `CalcPay()` in the same way you would use any `double` value. The method call `CalcPay()` has a `double` value in the same way a `double` variable has a `double` value.

```csharp
using System;
public class UseCalcPay
{
    public static void Main()
    {
        double myHours = 37.5;
        double myRate = 12.75;
        double grossPay;
        grossPay = CalcPay(myHours, myRate);
        Console.WriteLine("I worked {0} hours at {1} per hour",
            myHours, myRate);
        Console.WriteLine("My gross pay is {0}",
            grossPay.ToString("C"));
    }
    public static double CalcPay(double hours, double rate)
    {
        double gross;
        gross = hours * rate;
        return gross;
    }
}
```

Figure 6-14 Program using the `CalcPay()` method

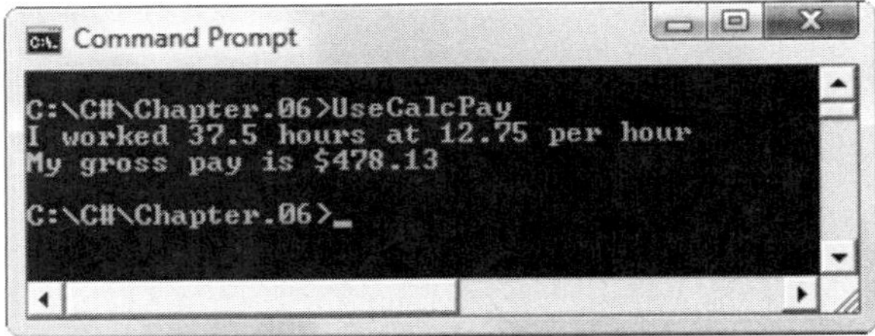

Figure 6-15 Output of `UseCalcPay` program

As an additional example, suppose you have a method named `GetPrice()` whose header is as follows:

```csharp
double GetPrice(int itemNumber)
```

The method accepts an integer item number and returns its price. Further suppose that you want to ask the user to enter an item number from the keyboard so you can pass it to the `GetPrice()` method. You can get the value from the user, store it in a string, convert the string to an integer, pass the integer to the `GetPrice()` method, and store the returned value in a variable named `price` in four or five separate statements, or you can write the following:

```
price = GetPrice(Convert.ToInt32(Console.ReadLine));
```

This statement contains a method call to `ReadLine()` within a method call to `Convert.ToInt32()`, within a method call to `GetPrice()`. When method calls are placed inside other method calls, the calls are **nested method calls**. When you write a statement with three nested method calls like the previous statement, the innermost method executes first. Its return value is then used as an argument to the intermediate method, and its return value is used as an argument to the outer method. There is no limit to how "deep" you can go with nested method calls.

> **» NOTE**   Now that you have seen how to write methods that accept arguments, you might guess that the method header for the `Console.ReadLine()` method is `public static string ReadLine()`. You know the method returns a `string`, and you know it takes no parameters.

» TWO TRUTHS AND A LIE: WRITING A METHOD THAT RETURNS A VALUE

1. A method can return, at most, one value to a method that calls it.
2. The data type used in a method's `return` statement must be the same as the return type declared in the method's header.
3. If a method returns a value and you call the method, you must store the value in a variable that has the same data type as the method's parameter.

The false statement is #3. If a method returns a value and you call the method, you typically will want to use the returned value, but you are not required to use it. Furthermore, if you do store the returned value in a variable, that variable must be the same data type as the method's return value, not its parameter's value.

PASSING AN ARRAY TO A METHOD

In Chapter 5, you learned that you can declare an array to create a list of elements, and that you can use any individual array element in the same manner as you would use any single variable of the same type. That is, suppose you declare an integer array as follows:

```
int[] someNums = new int[12];
```

You can subsequently print `someNums[0]` or add one to `someNums[1]`, just as you would for any integer. Similarly, you can pass a single array element to a method in exactly the same manner as you would pass a variable.

```csharp
using System;
public class PassArrayElement
{
    public static void Main()
    {
        int[] someNums = {10, 12, 22, 35};
        int x;
        Console.Write("\nAt beginning of Main() method...");
        for(x = 0; x < someNums.Length; ++x)
            Console.Write("{0, 6}", someNums[x]);
        Console.WriteLine();
        for(x = 0; x < someNums.Length; ++x)
            MethodGetsOneInt(someNums[x]);
        Console.Write("At end of Main() method..........");
        for(x = 0; x < someNums.Length; ++x)
            Console.Write("{0, 6}", someNums[x]);
    }
    public static void MethodGetsOneInt(int oneVal)
    {
        Console.Write("In MethodGetsOneInt() {0}", oneVal);
        oneVal = 999;
        Console.WriteLine("      After change {0}", oneVal);
    }
}
```

Figure 6-16 PassArrayElement program

Consider the program shown in Figure 6-16. This program creates an array of four integers and prints them. Next, the program calls a method named MethodGetsOneInt() four times, passing each of the array elements in turn. The method prints the passed value, changes the number to 999, and then prints the number again. Finally, back in the Main() method, the four numbers print again. Figure 6-17 shows the output.

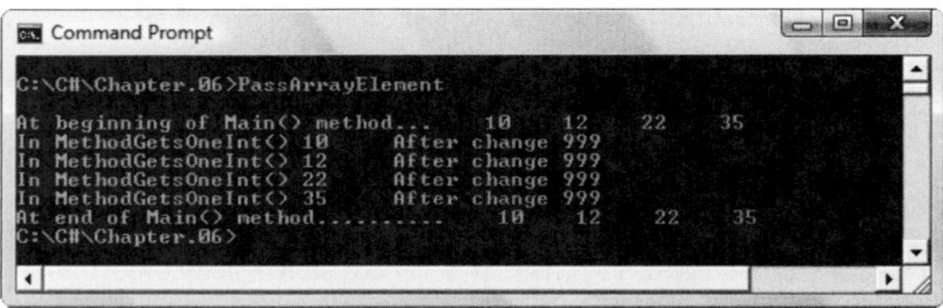

Figure 6-17 Output of PassArrayElement program

As you can see in Figure 6-17, the program displays the four original values, then passes each to the `MethodGetsOneInt()` method, where it is displayed and then changed to 999. After the method executes four times, the `Main()` method displays the four values again, showing that they are unchanged by the assignments within `MethodGetsOneInt()`. The `oneVal` variable is local to the `MethodGetsOneInt()` method; therefore, any changes to variables passed into the method are not permanent and are not reflected in the array declared in the `Main()` program. Each `oneVal` variable in the `MethodGetsOneInt()` method holds only a copy of the array element passed into the method, and the `oneVal` variable holding the assigned value of 999 exists only while the `MethodGetsOneInt()` method is executing.

Instead of passing a single array element to a method, you can pass an entire array as a parameter. You indicate that a method parameter must be an array by placing square brackets after the data type in the method's parameter list. When you pass an array to a method, changes you make to array elements within the method are permanent; that is, they are reflected in the original array that was sent to the method. Arrays, like all objects but unlike built-in types, are **passed by reference**; that is, the method receives the actual memory address of the array and has access to the actual values in the array elements.

> **NOTE**
> You already have seen that methods can alter arrays passed to them. When you use the `Sort()` and `Reverse()` methods, the methods change the array contents.

> **NOTE** You can create and pass an unnamed array to a method in a single step. For example, you can write the following:
> ```
> MethodThatAcceptsArray(new int[] {45, 67, 89});
> ```

The program shown in Figure 6-18 creates an array of four integers. After the integers are printed, the entire array is passed to a method named `MethodGetsArray()` in the shaded statement. Within the method header, the parameter is declared as an array by using square brackets after the parameter type. Within the method, the numbers are printed, which shows that they retain their values from `Main()` upon entering the method, but then the value 888 is assigned to each number. Even though `MethodGetsArray()` is a `void` method (meaning that nothing is returned to the `Main()` method), when the program prints the array for the second time within the `Main()` method, all of the values have been changed to 888, as you can see in Figure 6-19. Because arrays are passed by reference, the `MethodGetsArray()` method "knows" the address of the array declared in `Main()` and makes its changes directly to the original array that was declared in the `Main()` method.

You can pass a multidimensional array to a method by indicating the appropriate number of dimensions after the data type in the method header. For example, the following method headers accept two-dimensional arrays of `int`s and `double`s, respectively:

> **NOTE**
> Recall that in Chapter 5 you learned how two-dimensional arrays are stored in computer memory.

```
public static void displayScores(int[,]scoresArray)
public static boolean areAllPricesHigh(double[,] prices)
```

With jagged arrays, you can insert the appropriate number of square brackets after the data type in the method header. For example, the following method headers accept jagged arrays of `int`s and `double`s, respectively:

```
public static void displayIDs(int[][] idArray)
public static double computeTotal(double[][] prices)
```

```csharp
using System;
public class PassEntireArray
{
   public static void Main()
   {
      int[] someNums = {10, 12, 22, 35};
      int x;
      Console.Write("\nAt beginning of Main() method...");
      for(x = 0; x < someNums.Length; ++x)
         Console.Write("{0, 6}", someNums[x]);
      Console.WriteLine();
      MethodGetsArray(someNums);
      Console.Write("At end of Main() method..........");
      for(x = 0; x < someNums.Length; ++x)
         Console.Write("{0, 6}", someNums[x]);
   }
   public static void MethodGetsArray(int[] vals)
   {
      int x;
      Console.Write("In MethodGetsArray() ");
      for(x = 0; x < vals.Length; ++x)
         Console.Write(" {0}", vals[x]);
      Console.WriteLine();
      for(x = 0; x < vals.Length; ++x)
         vals[x] = 888;
      Console.Write("After change");
      for(x = 0; x < vals.Length; ++x)
         Console.Write(" {0}", vals[x]);
      Console.WriteLine();
   }
}
```

Figure 6-18 `PassEntireArray` program

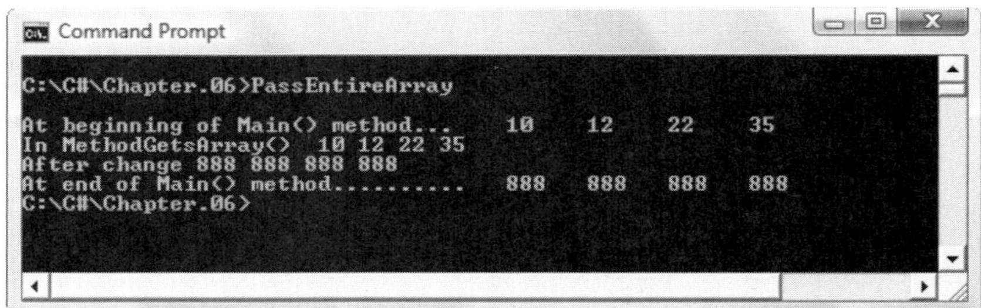

Figure 6-19 Output of the `PassEntireArray` program

In each case, notice that the brackets that define the array in the method header are empty. There is no need to insert numbers into the brackets because each passed array name is a starting memory address. The way you manipulate subscripts within the method determines how rows and columns are accessed.

> **» NOTE** The size of each dimension of a multidimensional array can be accessed using the `GetLength()` method. For example, `scoresArray.GetLength(0)` returns the value of the first dimension of `scoresArray`.

» TWO TRUTHS AND A LIE: PASSING AN ARRAY TO A METHOD

1. You indicate that a method parameter can be an array element by placing a data type and identifier in the method's parameter list.

2. You indicate that a method parameter must be an array by placing parentheses after the data type in the method's parameter list.

3. Arrays are passed by reference; that is, the method receives the actual memory address of the array and has access to the actual values in the array elements.

The false statement is #2. You indicate that a method parameter must be an array by placing square brackets after the data type in the method's parameter list.

USING ref, out, AND params PARAMETERS WITHIN METHODS

In C#, you can write methods with four kinds of formal parameters listed within the parentheses in the method header. These four types are:

» Value parameters, which are declared without any modifiers

» Reference parameters, which are declared with the `ref` modifier

» Output parameters, which are declared with the `out` modifier

» Parameter arrays, which are declared with the `params` modifier

USING VALUE PARAMETERS

So far, all of the method parameters you have created (except arrays) have been value parameters. When you use a **value parameter** in a method header, you indicate the parameter's type and name, and the method receives a copy of the value passed to it. This copy—the formal parameter—is stored at a different memory address than the variable that was used as the parameter in the method call—the actual parameter. In other words, the actual parameter and the formal parameter refer to two separate memory locations, and any change to the formal parameter value within the method has no effect on the actual parameter value back in the calling method. Changes to value parameters never affect the original argument in the calling method.

NOTE Using a real-world analogy, you know that people with the same name living in different places are not the same person. Changes in the life of Jane Doe in Maine, such as a raise or a department transfer, have no effect on Jane Doe in Vermont. The same is true of like-named variables located in different methods.

Figure 6-20 shows a program that declares a variable named `var`, assigns 4 to it, prints it, and passes it to a method that accepts a value parameter. The method assigns a new value, 777, to the formal, passed parameter and prints it. When control returns to the `Main()` method, the value of `var` remains 4. Changing the value of `var` within the `MethodWithValueParam()` method has no effect on `var` in `Main()`. Even though both methods contain a variable named `var`, they represent two separate variables, each with its own memory location. Figure 6-21 shows the output.

```
using System;
public class ParameterDemo1
{
   public static void Main()
   {
      int var = 4;
      Console.WriteLine("In Main var is {0}", var);
      MethodWithValueParam(var);
      Console.WriteLine("In Main var is {0}", var);
   }
   public static void MethodWithValueParam(int var)
   {
      var = 777;
      Console.WriteLine("In MethodWithValueParam, param is {0}", var);
   }
}
```

Figure 6-20 Program calling method with a value parameter

NOTE A variable that is used as an argument to a method with a value parameter must have a value assigned to it. If it does not, the program will not compile.

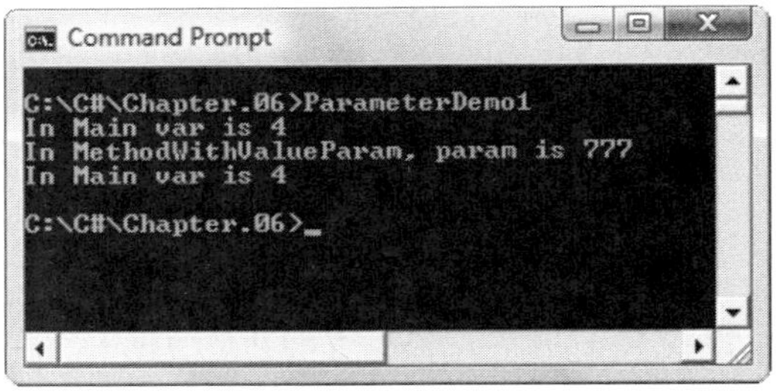

Figure 6-21 Output of `ParameterDemo1` program

NOTE Programmers say that a value parameter is used for "in" parameter passing—that is, values for these parameters go into a method, but modifications to them do not come "out."

In the `MethodWithValueParam()` method, it makes no difference whether you use the name `var` as the `Main()` method's actual parameter or use some other name. In either case, the passed and received variables occupy separate memory locations.

USING REFERENCE AND OUTPUT PARAMETERS

On occasion, you might want a method to be able to alter a value you pass to it. In that case, you can use a reference parameter or an output parameter. Both **reference** and **output parameters** have memory addresses that are passed to a method, allowing it to alter the original variables. Reference and output parameters differ as follows:

» When you declare a reference parameter in a method header, the parameter must have been assigned a value; in other words, in the calling method, any argument must be a constant or a variable with an assigned value.

» When you use an output parameter, it need not contain an original value. However, an output parameter must receive a value before the method ends.

Neither reference nor output parameters occupy their own memory locations. Rather, both reference and output parameters act as **aliases**, or pseudonyms (other names), for the same memory location occupied by the original passed variable. You use the keyword `ref` as a modifier to indicate a reference parameter and the keyword `out` as a modifier to indicate an output parameter.

Figure 6-22 shows a `Main()` program that calls a `MethodWithRefParam()` method. The `Main()` method declares a variable, displays its value, and then passes the variable to the `MethodWithRefParam()` method in the shaded statement. The modifier `ref` precedes the variable name `var` in both the method call and the method header. The method's parameter `myParam` holds the memory address of `var`, making `myParam` an alias for `var`. When the


```
using System;
public class ParameterDemo2
{
   public static void Main()
   {
      int var = 4;
      Console.WriteLine("In Main var is {0}", var);
      MethodWithRefParam(ref var);   // notice use of ref
      Console.WriteLine("In Main var is {0}", var);
   }
   public static void MethodWithRefParam(ref int myParam)
      // notice use of ref
   {
      myParam = 888;
      Console.WriteLine("In MethodWithRefParam, myParam is {0}",
         myParam);
   }
}
```

Figure 6-22 Program calling method with a reference parameter

method changes the value of `myParam`, the change persists in the `var` variable within `Main()`. Figure 6-23 shows the output of the program.

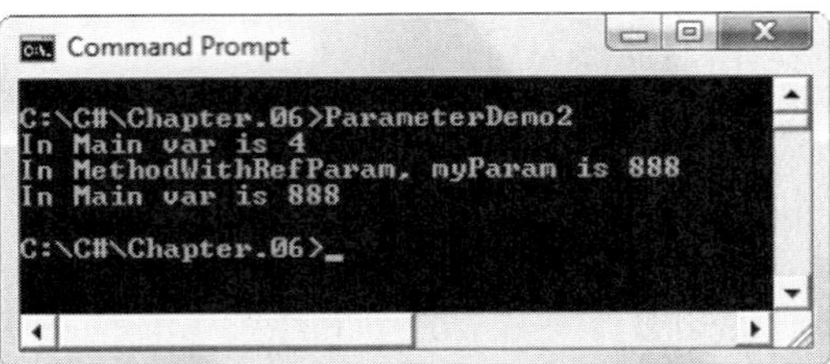

Figure 6-23 Output of `ParameterDemo2` program

In the header for the `MethodWithRefParam()` method, it makes no difference whether you use the same name as the `Main()` method's passed variable (`var`) or some other name, such as `myParam`. In either case, the passed and received variables occupy the same memory location—the address of one is the address of the other.

When you use a reference parameter, the passed variable must have an assigned value. Using an output parameter is convenient when the passed variable doesn't have a value yet. For example, the program in Figure 6-24 uses `InputMethod()` to obtain values for two parameters. The

```csharp
using System;
public class InputMethodDemo
{
    public static void Main()
    {
        int first, second;
        InputMethod(out first, out second); // notice use of out
        Console.WriteLine("After InputMethod first is {0}", first);
        Console.WriteLine("and second is {0}", second);
    }
    public static void InputMethod(out int one, out int two)
        // notice use of out
    {
        string s1, s2;
        Console.Write("Enter first integer ");
        s1 = Console.ReadLine();
        Console.Write("Enter second integer ");
        s2 = Console.ReadLine();
        one = Convert.ToInt32(s1);
        two = Convert.ToInt32(s2);
    }
}
```

Figure 6-24 `InputMethodDemo` program

parameters that are sent in the shaded statement get their values from the method, so it makes sense to provide them with no values going in. Instead, they acquire values in the method and retain the values coming out. Figure 6-25 shows a typical execution of the program.

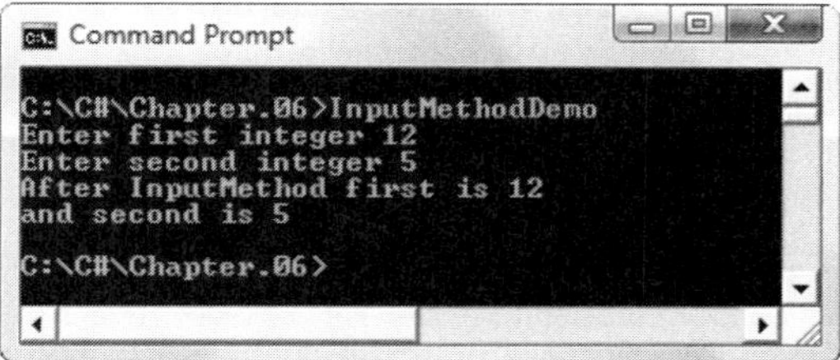

Figure 6-25 Output of `InputMethodDemo` program

In summary, when you need a method to alter a single value, you have two options:

» You can send a value parameter to a method, alter the local version of the variable within the method, return the altered value, and assign the return value to the original variable back in the calling method.

» You can send a reference or output parameter and alter the original value from within the method.

A major advantage to using reference or output parameters exists when you want a method to change multiple variables. A method can have only a single return type and can return at most only one value. By using reference or output parameters to a method, you can change multiple values.

> **»NOTE** As with simple parameters, you can use `out` or `ref` when passing an array to a method. You do so when you want the method to create a new array by using the location of the named array in the calling method. For example, assume a `Main()` method declares an array without assigning any values or using the `new` operator to assign memory, as in:
>
> ```
> double[] payRate;
> ```
>
> Then you can pass the array to a method with the header:
>
> ```
> AssignValues(out double[] money);
> ```
>
> You do so by using the statement:
>
> ```
> AssignValues(out payRate);
> ```
>
> Within the `AssignValues()` method, you can initialize the array as `money = new double[6];`, thereby creating a new array.

USING PARAMETER ARRAYS

When you don't know how many arguments you might eventually send to a method, you can declare a **parameter array**—a local array declared within the method header by using the keyword **params**. Such a method accepts any number of arguments.

For example, a method with the following header accepts an array of strings:

```
public static void DisplayStrings(params string[] people)
```

In the call to this method, you can use one, two, or any other number of strings as actual parameters; within the method, they will be treated as an array. Figure 6-26 shows a program that calls `DisplayStrings()` three times—once with one string argument, once with three string arguments, and once with an array of strings. In each case, the method works correctly, treating the passed strings as an array and displaying them appropriately. Figure 6-27 shows the output.

```
using System;
public class ParamsDemo
{
   public static void Main()
   {
      string[] names = {"Mark", "Paulette", "Carol", "James"};
      DisplayStrings("Ginger");
      DisplayStrings("George", "Maria", "Thomas");
      DisplayStrings(names);
   }
   public static void DisplayStrings(params string[] people)
   {
      foreach(string person in people)
         Console.Write("{0} ", person);
      Console.WriteLine("\n----------------");
   }
}
```

Figure 6-26 `ParamsDemo` program

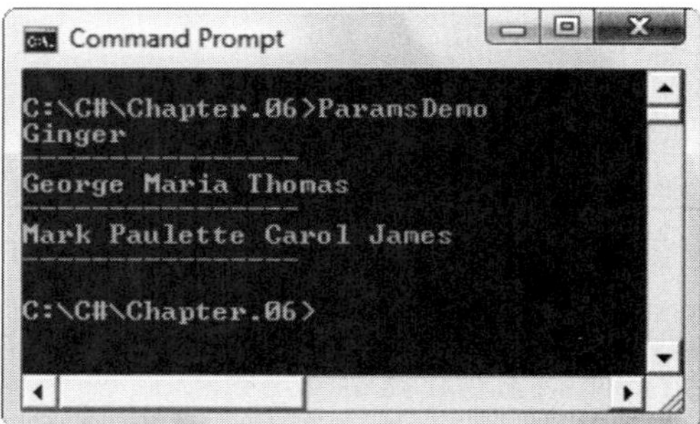

Figure 6-27 Output of `ParamsDemo` program

>> **NOTE** You could create an even more flexible method by using a method header such as `Display(params Object[] things)`. Then the passed parameters could be any type—strings, integers, other classes, and so on. The method could be implemented as follows:

```
public static void Display(params Object[] things)
{
    foreach(Object obj in things)
        Console.Write("{0} ", obj);
    Console.WriteLine("\n--------------")
}
```

All data types are `Object`s; you will learn more about the `Object` class in Chapter 7.

>> **NOTE** No additional parameters are permitted after the `params` keyword in a method declaration, and only one `params` keyword is permitted in a method declaration.

>> **TWO TRUTHS AND A LIE: USING `ref`, `out`, AND `params` PARAMETERS WITHIN METHODS**

1. A value parameter is declared without a modifier and receives a copy of the argument passed in; the argument must have been assigned a value.

2. A reference parameter is declared with the `ref` modifier, receives a memory address, and the argument passed in must have been assigned a value.

3. An output parameter is declared with the `out` modifier, receives a memory address, and the argument passed in must not have been assigned a value.

The false statement is #3. When you use an output parameter, it need not contain an original value, but it can have one. However, an output parameter must receive a value before the method ends.

OVERLOADING METHODS

Overloading involves using one term to indicate diverse meanings. When you use the English language, you frequently overload words. When you say "open the door," "open your eyes," and "open a computer file," you describe three very different actions that use different methods and produce different results. However, anyone who speaks English fluently has no trouble comprehending your meaning because the verb "open" is understood in the context of the noun that follows it.

>> **NOTE** Overloading a method is an example of polymorphism—the ability of a method to act appropriately depending on the context. You first learned the term *polymorphism* in Chapter 1.

>> **NOTE** Some C# operators are overloaded. For example, a + between two values indicates addition, but a single + to the left of a value means the value is positive. The + sign has different meanings based on the arguments used with it. In Chapter 7, you will learn how to overload operators to make them mean what you want with your own classes.

When you overload a C# method, you write multiple methods with a shared name. The compiler understands your meaning based on the arguments you use with the method. For example, suppose you create a method to display a string surrounded by a border. The method receives a string and uses the string Length property to determine how many asterisks to use to construct a border around the string. Figure 6-28 shows the method.


```csharp
public static void DisplayWithBorder(string word)
{
    const int EXTRA_STARS = 4;
    const string SYMBOL = "*";
    int size = word.Length + EXTRA_STARS;
    int x;
    for(x = 0; x < size; ++x)
        Console.Write(SYMBOL);
    Console.WriteLine();
    Console.WriteLine(SYMBOL + " " + word + " " + SYMBOL);
    for(x = 0; x < size; ++x)
        Console.Write(SYMBOL);
    Console.WriteLine("\n\n");
}
```

Figure 6-28 The DisplayWithBorder() method with a string parameter

When a program calls the DisplayWithBorder() method and passes a string value, as in DisplayWithBorder("Ed"), the method calculates a size as the length of the string plus 4, and then draws that many symbols on a single line. The method then displays a symbol, a space, the string, another space, and another symbol on the next line. The method ends by again displaying a row of symbols and some blank lines. Figure 6-29 shows a sample program that uses the method, and Figure 6-30 shows the output.

Suppose you are so pleased with the output of the DisplayWithBorder() method that you want to use something similar to display your company's weekly sales goal figure. The problem is that the weekly sales goal amount is stored as an integer, and so it cannot be passed to the existing method. You can take one of several approaches:

» You can convert the integer sales goal to a string and use the existing method. This is an acceptable approach, but it requires that you remember to write an extra step in any program in which you display an integer using the border.

» You can create a new method with a unique name such as DisplayWithBorderUsingInt() and use it to accept an integer parameter. The drawback to this approach is that you must remember different method names when you use different data types.

```
using System;
public class BorderDemo1
{
   public static void Main()
   {
      DisplayWithBorder("Ed");
      DisplayWithBorder("Theodore");
      DisplayWithBorder("Jennifer Ann");
   }
   public static void DisplayWithBorder(string word)
   {
      const int EXTRA_STARS = 4;
      const string SYMBOL = "*";
      int size = word.Length + EXTRA_STARS;
      int x;
      for(x = 0; x < size; ++x)
         Console.Write(SYMBOL);
      Console.WriteLine();
      Console.WriteLine(SYMBOL + " " + word + " " + SYMBOL);
      for(x = 0; x < size; ++x)
         Console.Write(SYMBOL);
      Console.WriteLine("\n\n");
   }
}
```

Figure 6-29 The `BorderDemo1` program

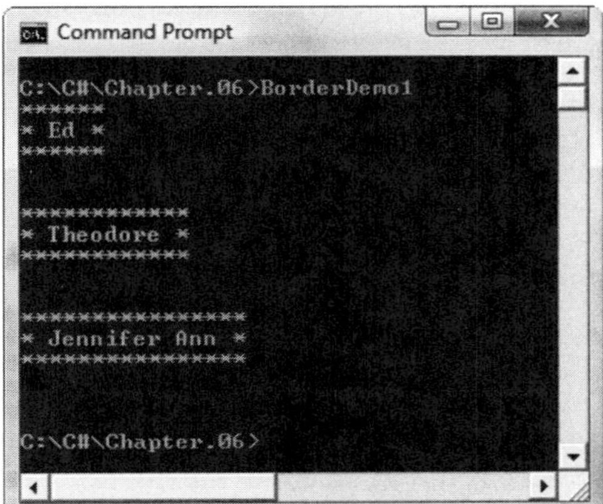

Figure 6-30 Output of the `BorderDemo1` program

» You can overload the `DisplayWithBorder()` method. Overloading methods involves writing multiple methods with the same name, but with different parameter types. For example, in addition to the `DisplayWithBorder()` method shown in Figure 6-28, you could use the method shown in Figure 6-31.

```
public static void DisplayWithBorder(int number)
{
    const int EXTRA_STARS = 4;
    const string SYMBOL = "*";
    int size = EXTRA_STARS + 1;
    int leftOver = number;
    int x;
    while(leftOver >= 10)
    {
        leftOver = leftOver / 10;
        ++size;
    }
    for(x = 0; x < size; ++x)
        Console.Write(SYMBOL);
    Console.WriteLine();
    Console.WriteLine(SYMBOL + " " + number + " " + SYMBOL);
    for(x = 0; x < size; ++x)
        Console.Write(SYMBOL);
    Console.WriteLine("\n\n");
}
```

Figure 6-31 The `DisplayWithBorder()` method with an integer parameter

In the version of the `DisplayWithBorder()` method in Figure 6-31, the parameter is an `int`. The method used to determine how many asterisks to display is to discover the number of digits in the parameter by repeatedly dividing by 10. For example, when the argument to the method is 456, `leftOver` is initialized to 456. Because it is at least 10, it is divided by 10, giving 45, and `size` is increased to 2. Then 45 is divided by 10, giving 4, and `size` is increased to 3. Because 4 is not at least 10, the loop ends, and the program has determined that the parameter contains three digits. The rest of the method executes like the original version that accepts a `string` parameter.

» **NOTE** The `DisplayWithBorder()` method does not work correctly if a negative integer is passed to it because the negative sign occupies an additional display space. To rectify the problem, you could modify the method to add an extra symbol to the border when a negative argument is passed in, or you could force all negative numbers to be their positive equivalent.

If both versions of `DisplayWithBorder()` are included in a program and you call the method using a `string`, as in `DisplayWithBorder("Ed")`, the first version of the method shown in Figure 6-28 executes. If you use an integer as the argument in the call to `DisplayWithBorder()`, as in `DisplayWithBorder(456)`, then the method shown in Figure 6-31 executes. Figure 6-32 shows a program that demonstrates several method calls, and Figure 6-33 shows the output.

```csharp
using System;
public class BorderDemo2
{
    public static void Main()
    {
        DisplayWithBorder("Ed");
        DisplayWithBorder(3);
        DisplayWithBorder(456);
        DisplayWithBorder(897654);
        DisplayWithBorder("Veronica");
    }
    public static void DisplayWithBorder(string word)
    {
        const int EXTRA_STARS = 4;
        const string SYMBOL = "*";
        int size = word.Length + EXTRA_STARS;
        int x;
        for(x = 0; x < size; ++x)
            Console.Write(SYMBOL);
        Console.WriteLine();
        Console.WriteLine(SYMBOL + " " + word + " " + SYMBOL);
        for(x = 0; x < size; ++x)
            Console.Write(SYMBOL);
        Console.WriteLine("\n\n");
    }
    public static void DisplayWithBorder(int number)
    {
        const int EXTRA_STARS = 4;
        const string SYMBOL = "*";
        int size = EXTRA_STARS + 1;
        int leftOver = number;
        int x;
        while(leftOver >= 10)
        {
            leftOver = leftOver / 10;
            ++size;
        }
        for(x = 0; x < size; ++x)
            Console.Write(SYMBOL);
        Console.WriteLine();
        Console.WriteLine(SYMBOL + " " + number + " " + SYMBOL);
        for(x = 0; x < size; ++x)
            Console.Write(SYMBOL);
        Console.WriteLine("\n\n");
    }
}
```

Figure 6-32 The `BorderDemo2` program

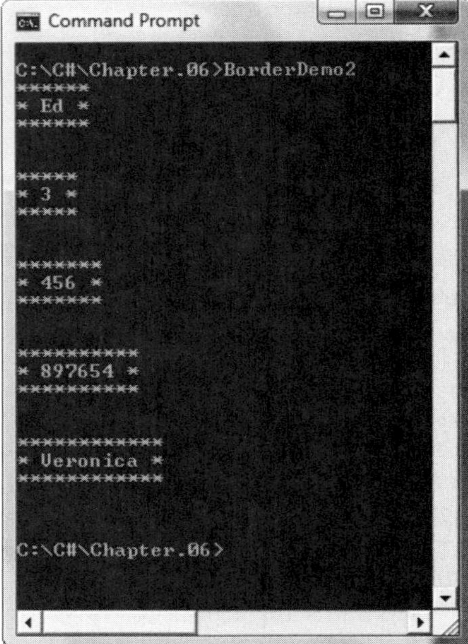

Figure 6-33 Output of the `BorderDemo2` program

Methods are overloaded correctly when they have the same identifier but their parameter types are different. For example, you could write several methods with the same identifier and one could accept an `int`, another two `int`s, and another three `int`s. A fourth version could accept an `int` followed by a `double` and another could accept a `double` followed by an `int`. Yet another version could accept no parameters. The parameter identifiers in overloaded methods do not matter; it is only the method identifier and parameter list types that cause a method to be overloaded.

Instead of overloading methods, you can choose to use methods with different names to accept the diverse data types, and you can place a decision within your program to determine which version of the method to call. However, it is more convenient to use one method name and then let the compiler determine which method to use. Overloading a method also makes it more convenient for other programmers to use your method in the future. Frequently, you create overloaded methods in your classes not because you need them immediately, but because you know client programs might need multiple versions in the future, and it is easier for programmers to remember one reasonable name for tasks that are functionally identical except for parameter types.

TWO TRUTHS AND A LIE: OVERLOADING METHODS

1. The following methods are overloaded:

   ```
   public static void MethodA(int a)
   public static void MethodA(double b)
   ```

2. The following methods are overloaded:

   ```
   public static void MethodC(int c)
   public static void MethodD(int c)
   ```

3. The following methods are overloaded:

   ```
   public static void MethodE(int e)
   public static void MethodE(int e, int f)
   ```

The false answer is #2. Overloaded methods must have the same name, but different parameter lists.

AVOIDING AMBIGUOUS METHODS

When you overload a method, you run the risk of creating **ambiguous** methods—a situation in which the compiler cannot determine which method to use. Every time you call a method, the compiler decides whether a suitable method exists; if so, the method executes, and if not, you receive an error message.

For example, suppose you write two versions of a simple method, as in the program in Figure 6-34. The class contains two versions of a method named SimpleMethod()—one that takes a double and int, and one that takes an int and a double.

```
using System;
public class AmbiguousMethods
{
   public static void Main()
   {
      int iNum = 20;
      double dNum = 4.5;
      SimpleMethod(iNum, dNum);   // calls first version
      SimpleMethod(dNum, iNum);   // calls second version
      SimpleMethod(iNum, iNum);   // error! Call is ambiguous.
   }
   public static void SimpleMethod(int i, double d)
   {
      Console.WriteLine("Method receives int and double");
   }
   public static void SimpleMethod(double d, int i)
   {
      Console.WriteLine("Method receives double and int");
   }
}
```

Figure 6-34 Program containing ambiguous method call

»NOTE In Chapter 2 you learned that when an `int` is promoted to a `double`, the process is called an *implicit conversion.*

In the `Main()` method in Figure 6-34, a call to `SimpleMethod()` with an integer argument first and a `double` argument second executes the first version of the method, and a call to `SimpleMethod()` with a `double` argument first and an integer argument second executes the second version of the method. With each of these calls, the compiler can find an exact match for the arguments you send. However, if you call `SimpleMethod()` using two integer arguments, as in the shaded statement, an ambiguous situation arises because there is no exact match for the method call. Because the first integer could be promoted to a `double` (matching the second version of the overloaded method), or the second integer could be promoted to a `double` (matching the first version), the compiler does not know which version of `SimpleMethod()` to use, and the program will not compile or execute. Figure 6-35 shows the error message that is generated.

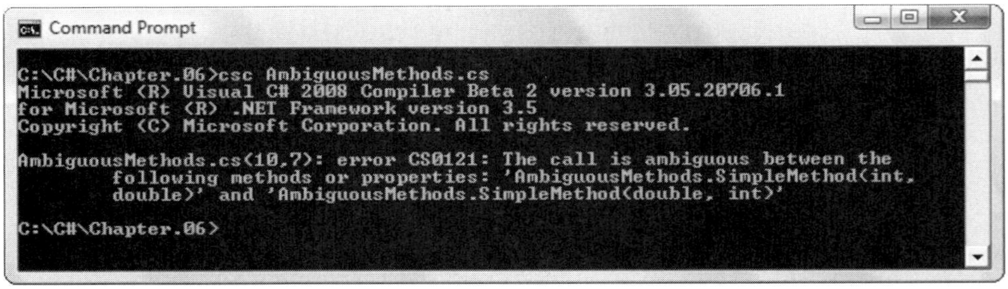

Figure 6-35 Error message generated by ambiguous method call

»NOTE An overloaded method is not ambiguous on its own—it becomes ambiguous only if you create an ambiguous situation. A program with potentially ambiguous methods will run without problems if you make no ambiguous method calls. For example, if you remove the `SimpleMethod()` call that contains two integers from the program in Figure 6-34, the program runs as expected.

»NOTE If you remove one of the versions of `SimpleMethod()` from the program in Figure 6-34, then the method call that uses two integer arguments would work, because one of the integers could be promoted to a `double`.

Methods can be overloaded correctly by providing different parameter lists for methods with the same name. Methods with identical names that have identical parameter lists but different return types are not overloaded—they are illegal. For example, the following two methods cannot coexist within a program:

```
public static int AMethod(int x)
public static void AMethod(int x)
```

The compiler determines which of several versions of a method to call based on parameter lists. When the method call `AMethod(17);` is made, the compiler will not know which method to execute because both possibilities take an integer argument. Similarly, the following method could not coexist with either of the previous versions:

```
public static void AMethod(int someNumber)
```

Even though this method uses a different local identifier for the passed value, its parameter list is still the same to the compiler—a single integer.

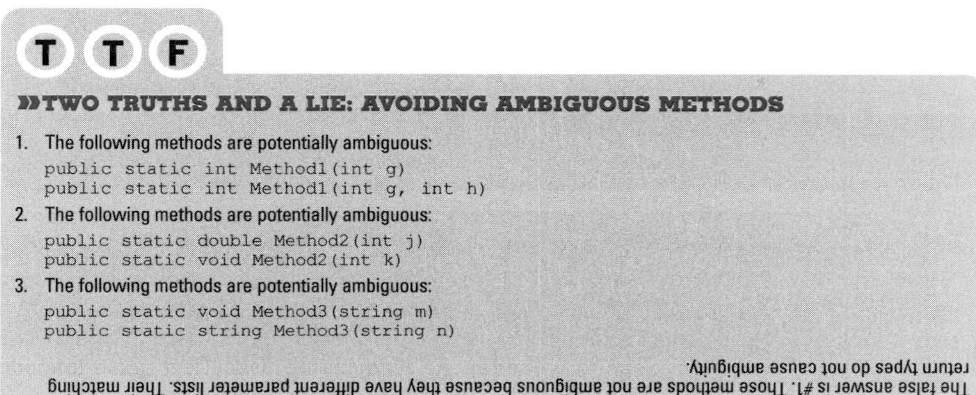

T T F

»TWO TRUTHS AND A LIE: AVOIDING AMBIGUOUS METHODS

1. The following methods are potentially ambiguous:
```
public static int Method1(int g)
public static int Method1(int g, int h)
```
2. The following methods are potentially ambiguous:
```
public static double Method2(int j)
public static void Method2(int k)
```
3. The following methods are potentially ambiguous:
```
public static void Method3(string m)
public static string Method3(string n)
```

The false answer is #1. Those methods are not ambiguous because they have different parameter lists. Their matching return types do not cause ambiguity.

YOU DO IT
CALLING A METHOD

To write a program in which a `Main()` method calls another method that displays a company's logo:

1. Open a new file in your text editor. Enter the statement that uses the `System` namespace, then type the class header for the `DemoLogo` class and type the class-opening curly brace.

```
using System;
public class DemoLogo
{
```

2. Type the `Main()` method for the `DemoLogo` class. This method prints a line, then calls the `PrintCompanyLogo()` method.

```
public static void Main()
{
   Console.Write("Our company is ");
   PrintCompanyLogo();
}
```

3. Add a method that prints a two-line logo for a company.

```
public static void PrintCompanyLogo()
{
   Console.WriteLine("See Sharp Optical");
   Console.WriteLine("We prize your eyes");
}
```

4. Add the closing curly brace for the class (}), then save the file as **DemoLogo.cs**.

5. Compile and execute the program. The output should look like Figure 6-36.

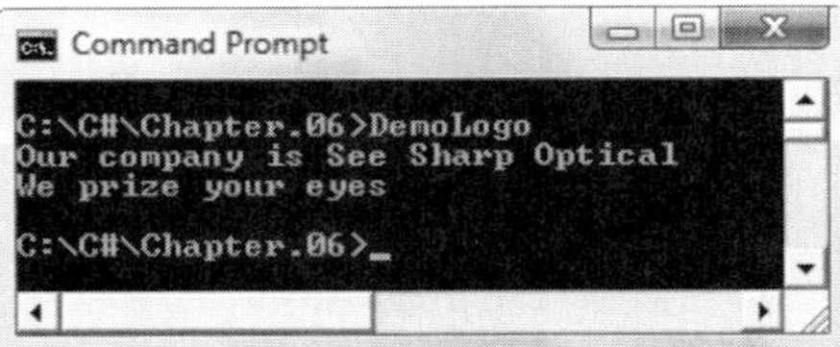

Figure 6-36 Output of DemoLogo program

WRITING A METHOD THAT RECEIVES PARAMETERS AND RETURNS A VALUE

Next, you will write a method named CalcPhoneCallPrice() that both receives parameters and returns a value. The purpose of the method is to take the length of a phone call in minutes and the rate charged per minute, and to then calculate the price of a call, assuming each call includes a 25-cent connection charge in addition to the per-minute charge. After writing the CalcPhoneCallPrice() method, you will write a Main() method that calls the CalcPhoneCallPrice() method using four different sets of data as arguments.

To create a class containing a method that receives two parameters and returns a value:

1. Open your text editor and type the **using System;** statement.

2. Add the class header for **public class PhoneCall** and an opening curly brace.

3. Type the following CalcPhoneCallPrice() method. It receives an integer and a double as parameters. The fee for a call is calculated as 0.25 plus the minutes times the rate per minute. The method returns the phone call fee to the calling method.

```
public static double CalcPhoneCallPrice(int minutes,
   double rate)
{
   const double BASE_FEE = 0.25;
   double callFee;
   callFee = BASE_FEE + minutes * rate;
   return callFee;
}
```

4. Add the Main() method header for the PhoneCall class. Begin the method by declaring two arrays; one contains two call lengths and the other contains two rates. You will use all the possible combinations of call lengths and rates to test the CalcPhoneCallPrice() method. Also, declare a double named priceOfCall that will hold the result of a calculated call price.

```
public static void Main()
{
   int[] callLength = {2, 5};
   double[] rate = {0.03, 0.12};
   double priceOfCall;
```

5. Add a statement that prints column headings under which you can list combinations of call lengths, rates, and prices. The three column headings are right-aligned, each in a field 10 characters wide.

```
Console.WriteLine("{0, 10}{1, 10}{2, 10}",
   "Minutes", "Rate", "Price");
```

6. Add a pair of nested loops that, in turn, passes each `callLength` and each `rate` to the `CalcPhoneCallPrice()` method. As each pair is passed, the result is stored in the `priceOfCall` variable, and the details are displayed. Using the nested loops allows you to pass each combination of call time and rate so that multiple possibilities for the values can be tested conveniently.

```
for(int x = 0; x < callLength.Length; ++x)
   for(int y = 0; y < rate.Length; ++y)
   {
       priceOfCall = CalcPhoneCallPrice(callLength[x],
           rate[y]);
       Console.WriteLine("{0, 10}{1, 10}{2, 10}",
           callLength[x], rate[y],
           priceOfCall.ToString("C"));
   }
```

7. Add a closing curly brace for the `Main()` method and another for the `PhoneCall` class.

8. Save the file as **PhoneCall.cs**. Compile and run the program. The output looks like Figure 6-37. It shows how a single method can produce a variety of results when you use different values for the arguments.

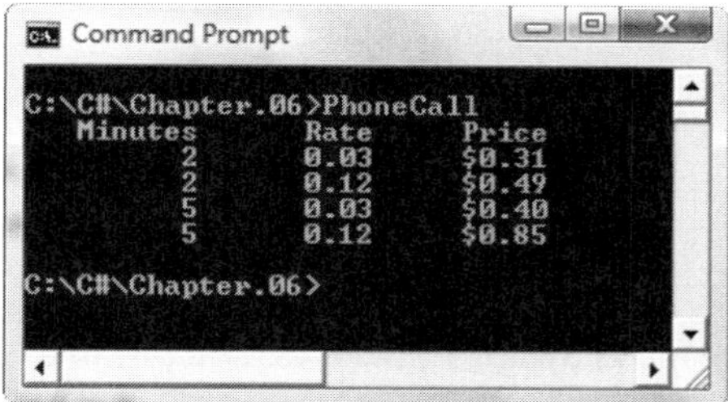

Figure 6-37 Output of the `PhoneCall` program

USING REFERENCE PARAMETERS

You use reference parameters when you want a method to have access to the memory address of arguments in a calling method. For example, suppose you have two values and you want to exchange them (or swap them), making each equal to the value of the other. Because you want to change two values, a method that accepts copies of arguments will not work—a method can return, at most, one value. Therefore, you can use reference parameters to provide your method with the actual addresses of the values you want to change.

To write a program that uses a method to swap two values:

1. Open your editor and begin the `SwapProgram` as follows:

```
using System;
public class SwapProgram
{
    public static void Main()
    {
```

2. Declare two integers and display their values. Call the `Swap()` method and pass in the addresses of the two variables to swap. Because the parameters already have assigned values, and because you want to alter those values in `Main()`, you can use reference parameters. After the method call, display the two values again. Add the closing curly brace for the `Main()` method.

```
    int first = 34, second = 712;
    Console.Write("Before swap first is {0}", first);
    Console.WriteLine(" and second is {0}", second);
    Swap(ref first, ref second);
    Console.Write("After swap first is {0}", first);
    Console.WriteLine(" and second is {0}", second);
}
```

3. Create the `Swap()` method as shown. You can swap two values by storing the first value in a temporary variable, then assigning the second value to the first variable. At this point, both variables hold the value originally held by the second variable. When you assign the temporary variable's value to the second variable, the two values are reversed.

```
public static void Swap(ref int one, ref int two)
{
    int temp;
    temp = one;
    one = two;
    two = temp;
}
```

4. Add the closing curly brace for the class. Save the file as **SwapProgram.cs**. Compile and execute the program. Figure 6-38 shows the output.

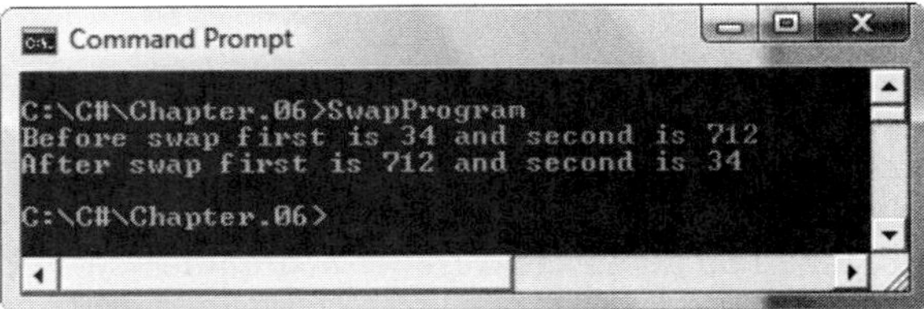

Figure 6-38 Output of `SwapProgram` program

OVERLOADING METHODS

In the next steps you will overload a method that correctly triples an integer or a string, depending on how you call the method.

1. Open a new file in your text editor. Create a method that triples and displays an integer parameter as follows:

```
public static void Triple(int num)
{
    const int THREE = 3;
    Console.WriteLine("{0} times {1} is {2}\n",
        num, THREE, num * THREE);
}
```

2. Create a second method with the same name that takes a string parameter. Assume you want to define tripling a message as printing it three times, separated by tabs.

```
public static void Triple(string message)
{
    Console.WriteLine("{0}\t{0}\t{0}\n", message);
}
```

3. Position your cursor at the top of the file and add a `using` statement, class header, and opening curly brace so the overloaded `Triple()` methods will be contained in a class named `OverloadedTriples`.

```
using System;
public class OverloadedTriples
{
```

4. Position your cursor at the bottom of the file and add the closing curly brace for the `OverloadedTriples` class.

5. Position your cursor after the opening curly brace for the class. On a new line, insert a `Main()` method that declares an integer and a string and, in turn, passes each to the appropriate `Triple()` method.

```
public static void Main()
{
    int num = 20;
    string message = "Go team!";
    Triple(num);
    Triple(message);
}
```

6. Save the file as **OverloadedTriples.cs**. Compile and execute the program. Figure 6-39 shows the output. Even though the same method name is used in the two method calls, the appropriate overloaded method executes each time.

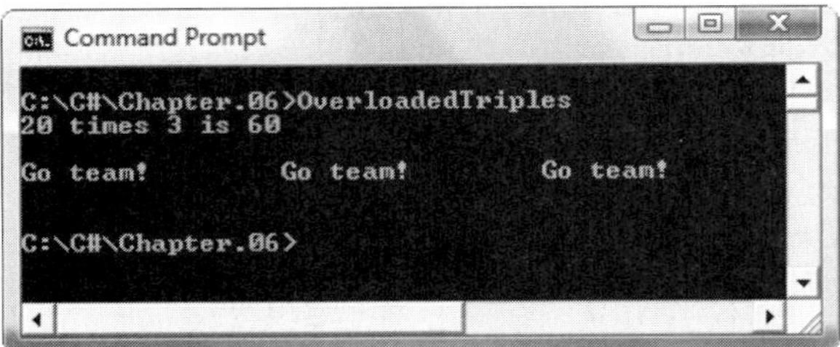

Figure 6-39 Output of `OverloadedTriples` program

CHAPTER SUMMARY

» A method is a series of statements that carry out a task. Any class can contain an unlimited number of methods.

» You write methods to make programs easier to understand and so that you can easily reuse them. In C#, a method must include a method declaration, an opening curly brace, a method body, and a closing curly brace. The method declaration defines the rules for using the method; it contains an optional declared accessibility, an optional `static` modifier, a return type for the method, an identifier, and an optional list of method parameters between parentheses.

» Object-oriented programs hide their methods' implementation. A client method uses an interface to work with the method. To more easily incorporate methods into a program, it is common practice to store methods (or groups of associated methods) in their own classes and files, but methods can also be contained in the same file as the methods that use them.

» Some methods require passed-in information called arguments or parameters. When you write the declaration for a method that can receive a parameter, you need to include the type of parameter and a local identifier for it within the method declaration parentheses. A variable declared in a method header is a formal parameter, and an argument within a method call is an actual parameter.

» You can pass multiple arguments to a method by listing the arguments within the parentheses in the call to the method and separating them with commas. You can write a method to take any number of parameters in any order. When you call the method, however, the arguments you send to it must match in both number and type with the parameters listed in the method declaration.

» The return type for a method can be any type used in the C# programming language, which includes the basic built-in types `int`, `double`, `char`, and so on, as well as class types (including class types you create). A method also can return nothing, in which case the return type is `void`. A method's return type is known more succinctly as a method's type. When a `return` statement includes a value, the value is sent back to the calling method.

» You can pass an array as a parameter to a method. You indicate that a method parameter is an array by placing square brackets after the data type in the method's parameter list. When you pass an array to a method, changes you make to array elements within the method are permanent; that is, they are reflected in the original array that was sent to the method. Arrays, like all objects but unlike built-in types, are passed by reference; that is, the method receives the actual memory address of the array and has access to the actual values in the array elements.

» In C#, you can write methods with four kinds of formal parameters listed within the parentheses in the method header: value parameters, which are declared without any modifiers; reference parameters, which are declared with the `ref` modifier; output parameters, which are declared with the `out` modifier; and parameter arrays, which are declared with the `params` modifier. A major advantage to using reference or output parameters exists when you want a method to change multiple variables. When you don't know how many arguments you might eventually send to a method, you can declare a local array within the method header by using the keyword `params`. Such a method accepts any number of arguments.

» When you overload a C# method, you write multiple methods with a shared name but different argument lists. The compiler understands your meaning based on the combination of arguments you use with the method.

» When you overload a method, you run the risk of creating an ambiguous situation—one in which the compiler cannot determine which method to use. Methods can be overloaded correctly by providing different parameter lists for methods with the same name.

KEY TERMS

A **method** is an encapsulated series of statements that carry out a task.

Methods are **invoked**, or **called**, by other methods.

A **calling method** calls another method.

A method invoked by another is a **called method**.

Code bloat is a term that describes unnecessarily long or repetitive program statements.

A **method declaration** is a **method header** or **method definition**.

A **method body** is a block of statements that carry out a method's work.

The optional declared **accessibility** for a method sets limits as to whether and how other methods can use your method.

Public access is a level of method accessibility that allows unlimited access to a method.

Protected internal access is a level of method accessibility that limits method access to the containing program, containing class, or types derived from the containing class.

Protected access is a level of method accessibility that limits method access to the containing class or types derived from the containing class.

Internal access is a level of method accessibility that limits method access to the containing class or program.

Private access is a level of method accessibility that limits method access to the containing class.

A **static** method can be called without referring to an object.

A **nonstatic** method requires an object reference.

A **return type** indicates what kind of value a method will return to any other method that calls it.

A **method's type** is its return type.

A variable's **scope** is the area where it is known and can be used.

Implementation hiding means keeping the details of a method's operations hidden.

To **interface** with a system is to interact with it.

A **black box** is any device you can use without knowing how it works internally.

A **client** of a method is a method that uses it.

A **multifile assembly** is a group of files containing methods that work together to create an application.

A **local variable** is one that is declared in the current method.

A **formal parameter** is a parameter within a method header that accepts a value.

Actual parameters are arguments within a method call.

A `return statement` causes a value to be sent back from a method to its calling method.

Nested method calls are method calls placed inside other method calls.

When data is **passed by reference** to a method, the method receives the memory address of the argument passed to it.

When you use a **value parameter** in a method header, you indicate the parameter's type and name, and the method receives a copy of the value passed to it.

When you use a **reference parameter** to a method, the parameter must have been assigned a value before you use it in the method call, and the method receives the parameter's address.

When you use an **output parameter**, it need not contain an original value, and the method receives the parameter's address.

Aliases are alternate names or pseudonyms.

A **parameter array** is a local array declared within a method header.

The keyword `params` is used to declare a local array in a method so the method can receive any number of arguments.

Overloading involves using one term to indicate diverse meanings. When you overload a C# method, you write multiple methods with the same name but different parameter lists.

A method's **signature** is composed of its name and parameter list.

Ambiguous methods are overloaded methods for which the compiler cannot determine which one to use.

REVIEW QUESTIONS

1. At most, a class can contain __________ method(s).

   a. 0

   b. 1

   c. 2

   d. any number of

2. What is the most important reason for creating methods within a program?

   a. Methods are easily reusable.

   b. Because all methods must be stored in the same class, they are easy to find.

   c. The `Main()` method becomes more detailed.

   d. All of these are true.

3. In C#, a method must include all of the following *except* a __________ .

   a. method declaration

   b. parameter list

   c. body

   d. closing curly brace

4. A method declaration must contain __________ .

   a. a statement of purpose

   b. declared accessibility

   c. the static modifier

   d. a return type

5. If you use the keyword modifier `static` in a method header, you indicate that the method __________ .

   a. can be called without referring to an object

   b. cannot be copied

   c. cannot be overloaded

   d. can be ambiguous

6. When you write the method declaration for a method that can receive a parameter, you need to include all of the following items *except* __________ .

   a. a pair of parentheses

   b. the type of the parameter

   c. a local name for the parameter

   d. an initial value for the parameter

7. Suppose you have declared a variable as `int myAge = 21;`. Which of the following is a legal call to a method with the declaration `public static void AMethod(int num)`?

   a. `AMethod(int 55);`

   b. `AMethod(myAge);`

   c. `AMethod(int myAge);`

   d. `AMethod();`

8. Suppose you have declared a method named `public static void CalculatePay(double rate)`. Which is true of a method that calls the `CalculatePay()` method?

   a. The calling method must contain a declared `double` named `rate`.

   b. The calling method might contain a declared `double` named `rate`.

   c. The calling method cannot contain a declared `double` named `rate`.

   d. The calling method can contain no declared `double` variables.

9. In the method call `PrintTheData(double salary);`, `salary` is the __________ parameter.

   a. formal

   b. actual

   c. proposed

   d. preferred

10. A program contains the method call `PrintTheData(salary);`. In the method definition, the name of the formal parameter must be __________ .

    a. `salary`

    b. any legal identifier other than `salary`

    c. any legal identifier

    d. omitted

11. What is a correct declaration for a method that receives two `double` arguments and calculates the difference between them?

    a. `public static void CalcDifference(double price1,`
       `     price2)`

    b. `public static void CalcDifference(double price1,`
       `     double price2)`

    c. `public static void CalcDifference(double price1,`
       `     double anotherPrice)`

    d. Two of these are correct.

12. A method is declared as `double CalcPay(int hoursWorked)`. Suppose you write a `Main()` method containing `int hours = 35;` and `double pay;`. Which of the following represents a correct way to call the `CalcPay()` method from the `Main()` method?

    a. `hours = CalcPay();`

    b. `hours = CalcPay(pay);`

    c. `pay = CalcPay(hoursWorked);`

    d. `pay = CalcPay(hours);`

13. Which is *not* a type of method parameter in C#?

    a. value

    b. reference

    c. forensic

    d. output

14. Which type of method parameter receives the address of the variable passed in?

    a. a value parameter   c. an output parameter

    b. a reference parameter   d. two of the above

15. Assume you declare a variable as `int x = 100;` and correctly pass it to a method with the declaration `public static void IncreaseValue(ref int x)`. There is a single statement within the `IncreaseValue()` method: `x = x + 25;`. Back in the `Main()` method, after the method call, what is the value of `x`?

    a. 100   c. It is impossible to tell.

    b. 125   d. The program will not run.

16. Assume you declare a variable as `int x = 100;` and correctly pass it to a method with the declaration `public static void IncreaseValue(int x)`. There is a single statement within the `IncreaseValue()` method: `x = x + 25;`. Back in the `Main()` method, after the method call, what is the value of `x`?

    a. 100   c. It is impossible to tell.

    b. 125   d. The program will not run.

17. What is the difference between a reference parameter and an output parameter?

    a. A reference parameter receives a memory address; an output parameter does not.

    b. A reference parameter occupies a unique memory address; an output parameter does not.

    c. A reference parameter must have an initial value; an output parameter need not.

    d. A reference parameter need not have an initial value; an output parameter must.

18. Methods are ambiguous when they __________ .

    a. are overloaded

    b. are written in a confusing manner

    c. are indistinguishable to the compiler

    d. have the same parameter type as their return type

19. Which of the following pairs of method declarations represent correctly overloaded methods?

```
a. public static void MethodA(int a)
   public static void MethodA(int b, double c)

b. public static void MethodB(double d)
   public static void MethodB()

c. public static double MethodC(int e)
   public static double MethodD(int f)
```

    d. Two of these are correctly overloaded methods.

20. Which of the following pairs of method declarations represent correctly overloaded methods?

    a. ```
    public static void Method(int a)
    public static void Method(int b)
    ```

    b. ```
    public static void Method(double d)
    public static int Method()
    ```

    c. ```
    public static double Method(int e)
    public static int Method(int f)
    ```

    d. Two of these are correctly overloaded methods.

# EXERCISES

1. a. Create a class named `Numbers` whose `Main()` method holds two integer variables. Assign values to the variables. Within the class, create two methods, `Sum()` and `Difference()`, that compute the sum of and difference between the values of the two variables, respectively. Each method should perform the computation and display the results. In turn, call each of the two methods from `Main()`, passing the values of the two integer variables. Save the program as **Numbers.cs**.

   b. Add a method named `Product()` to the `Numbers` class. This method should compute the multiplication product of two integers, but not display the answer. Instead, it should return the answer to the calling `Main()` method, which displays the answer. Save the program as **Numbers2.cs**.

2. a. Create a class named `InchesToFeet`. Its `Main()` method holds an integer variable named `inches` to which you will assign a value. Create a method to which you pass `inches`. The method displays `inches` in feet and inches. For example, 67 inches is 5 feet 7 inches. Save the program as **InchesToFeet.cs**.

   b. Add a second method to the `InchesToFeet` class. This method displays a passed argument as yards, feet, and inches. For example, 67 inches is 1 yard, 2 feet, and 7 inches. Add a statement to the `Main()` method so that after it calls the method to convert inches to feet and inches, it passes the same variable to the new method to convert the same value to yards, feet, and inches. Save the program as **InchesToYards.cs**.

3. Create a class named `Monogram`. Its `Main()` method holds six character variables that hold your first, middle, and last initials, and a friend's first, middle, and last initials, respectively. Create a method named `DisplayMonogram()` to which you pass three initials. The method displays the initials surrounded by two asterisks on each side and with periods following each initial, as shown in the following example:

   ```
   ** J. M. F. **
   ```

   Within the `Main()` method, call the `DisplayMonogram()` method twice—once using your initials and once using your friend's initials. Save the program as **Monogram.cs**.
   ```

4. Create a class named `Exponent`. Its `Main()` method prompts the user for an integer value and, in turn, passes the value to a method that squares the number and to a method that cubes the number. The `Main()` method prints the results returned from each of the other methods. Save the program as **Exponent.cs**.

5. Create a class named `Square`. In the `Main()` method, declare an integer and prompt the user for a value. Display the value of the integer, then pass it to a method that accepts the value as a reference parameter and prints its square (the number times itself). In `Main()`, print the value again, proving that the original argument to the method was altered. Save the program as **Square.cs**.

6. a. Create a class named `Reverse3`. Within its `Main()` method, declare three integers named `firstInt`, `middleInt`, and `lastInt`. Assign values to the variables, display them, and then pass them to a method that places the first value in the `lastInt` variable and the last value in the `firstInt` variable. In the `Main()` method, display the three variables again, demonstrating that their positions have been reversed. Save the program as **Reverse3.cs**.

   b. Create a new class named `Reverse4`, which contains a method that reverses the positions of four variables. Write a `Main()` method that demonstrates the method works correctly. Save the program as **Reverse4.cs**.

7. Create a class named `Area`. Include three overloaded methods that compute the area of a rectangle when two dimensions are passed to it. One method takes two integers as parameters, one takes two `double`s, and the third takes an integer and a `double`. Write a `Main()` method that demonstrates each method works correctly. Save the program as **Area.cs**.

8. Create a class named `ComputeWeeklySalary`. Include two overloaded methods—one that accepts an annual salary as an integer and one that accepts an annual salary as a `double`. Each method should calculate and display a weekly salary, assuming 52 weeks in a year. Include a `Main()` method that demonstrates both overloaded methods work correctly. Save the program as **ComputeWeeklySalary.cs**.

9. Create a class named `TaxCalculation`. Include two overloaded methods—one that accepts a price and a tax rate expressed as `double`s (for example, 79.95 and 0.06, where 0.06 represents 6%), and one that accepts a price as a `double` and a tax rate as an integer (for example, 79.95 and 6, where 6 also represents 6%). Include a `Main()` method that demonstrates each method calculates the same tax amount appropriately. Save the program as **TaxCalculation.cs**.

10. Write an application that contains a method that calculates the conversion of any amount of money into the fewest bills; it calculates the number of 20s, 10s, 5s, and 1s needed. Create a `Main()` method that prompts the user for an integer number of dollars, uses the conversion method, and then displays the monetary breakdown. Save the program as **Dollars.cs**.

11. The `InputMethod()` in the `InputMethodDemo` program in Figure 6-24 contains repetitive code that prompts the user and retrieves integer values. Rewrite the program so the `InputMethod()` calls another method to do the work. The rewritten `InputMethod()` will need to contain only two statements:

```
one = DataEntry("first");
two = DataEntry("second");
```

Save the new program as **InputMethodDemo2.cs**.

12. Create a method named `Sum()` that accepts any number of integer parameters and displays their sum. Write a `Main()` method that demonstrates the `Sum()` method works correctly when passed one, three, five, or an array of 10 integers. Save the program as **UsingSum.cs**.

DEBUGGING EXERCISES

Each of the following files in the Chapter.06 folder on your Student Disk has syntax and/or logical errors. In each case, determine the problem and fix the program. After you correct the errors, save each file using the same filename preceded with *Fixed*. For example, DebugSix1.cs will become FixedDebugSix1.cs.

a. DebugSix1.cs

b. DebugSix2.cs

c. DebugSix3.cs

d. DebugSix4.cs

UP FOR DISCUSSION

1. One of the advantages to writing a program that is subdivided into methods is that such a structure allows different programmers to write separate methods, thus dividing the work. Would you prefer to write a large program by yourself, or to work on a team in which each programmer produces one or more modules? Why?

2. In this chapter, you learned that hidden implementations are often said to exist in a black box. What are the advantages to this approach in both programming and real life? Are there any disadvantages?

7

USING CLASSES AND OBJECTS

In this chapter you will:

Learn about class concepts
Create classes from which objects can be instantiated
Create objects
Create properties, including auto-implemented properties
Learn useful techniques for storing and organizing classes
Learn about using `public` fields and `private` methods
Learn about the `this` reference
Write constructors and use them
Pass objects to methods
Use object initializers
Overload operators
Declare an array of objects and use the `Sort()` and
   `BinarySearch()` methods with them
Write destructors

Much of your understanding of the world comes from your ability to categorize objects and events into classes. As a young child, you learned the concept of "animal" long before you knew the word. Your first encounter with an animal might have been with the family dog, a neighbor's cat, or a goat at a petting zoo. As you developed speech, you might have used the same term for all of these creatures, gleefully shouting "Doggie!" as your parents pointed out cows, horses, and sheep in picture books or along the roadside on drives in the country. As you grew more sophisticated, you learned to distinguish dogs from cows; still later, you learned to distinguish breeds. Your understanding of the class "animal" helps you see the similarities between dogs and cows, and your understanding of the class "dog" helps you see the similarities between a Great Dane and a Chihuahua. Understanding classes gives you a framework for categorizing new experiences. You might not know the term "okapi," but when you learn it's an animal, you begin to develop a concept of what an okapi might be like.

Classes are also the basic building blocks of object-oriented programming. You already understand that differences exist among the `Double`, `Int32`, and `Float` classes, yet you also understand that items that are members of these classes possess similarities—they are all data types, you can perform arithmetic with all of them, they all can be converted to strings, and so on. Understanding classes enables you to see similarities in objects and increases your understanding of the programming process. In this chapter, you will discover how C# handles classes, learn to create your own classes, and learn to construct objects that are members of those classes.

UNDERSTANDING CLASS CONCEPTS

When you write programs in C#, you create two distinct types of classes:

» Classes that are only application programs with a `Main()` method. These classes can contain other methods that the `Main()` method calls.

» Classes from which you instantiate objects; these classes can contain a `Main()` method, but it is not required.

All of the classes you have created so far in this book have been applications with a `Main()` method that executes when you run the program in which it resides. Many classes do not contain a `Main()` method; instead, you use these classes to create objects.

When you think in an object-oriented manner, everything is an object, and every object is a member of a class. You can think of any inanimate physical item as an object—your desk, your computer, and your house are all called "objects" in everyday conversation. You can think of living things as objects, too—your houseplant, your pet fish, and your sister are objects. Events also are objects—the stock purchase you made, the mortgage closing you attended, or a graduation party in your honor are all objects.

Everything is an object, and every object is a member of a more general class. Your desk is a member of the class that includes all desks, and your pet fish is a member of the class that contains all fish. An object-oriented programmer would say that your desk is an instance of the `Desk` class and your fish is an instance of the `Fish` class. These statements represent **is-a relationships** because you can say, "My oak desk with the scratch on top *is a* `Desk` and

»NOTE

In C#, an application you write to use other classes is a class itself.

»NOTE

Object-oriented programmers also use the term *is-a* when describing inheritance. You will learn about inheritance in Chapter 8.

my goldfish named Moby *is a* `Fish`." The difference between a class and an object parallels the difference between abstract and concrete. An object is an **instantiation** of a class; an object is one tangible example of a class. Your goldfish, my guppy, and the zoo's shark each constitute one instantiation of the `Fish` class.

The concept of a class is useful because of its reusability. Objects receive their attributes from classes. For example, if you invite me to a graduation party, I automatically know many things about the object (the party). I assume there will be a starting time, a number of guests, some quantity of food, and some nature of gifts. I understand parties because of my previous knowledge of the `Party` class, of which all parties are members. I don't know the number of guests or the date or time of this particular party, but I understand that because all parties have a date and time, then this one must as well. Similarly, even though every stock purchase is unique, each must have a dollar amount and a number of shares. All objects have predictable attributes because they are members of certain classes.

The data components of a class often are called its **instance variables**. Also, object attributes often are called **fields** to help distinguish them from other variables you might use. The set of contents of an object's instance variables also are known as its **state**. For example, the current state of a particular party is 8 p.m. and Friday; the state of a particular stock purchase is $10 and five shares.

In addition to their attributes, objects have methods associated with them, and every object that is an instance of a class possesses the same methods. For example, at some point you might want to issue invitations for a party. You might name the method `IssueInvitations()`, and it might display some text as well as the values of the party's date and time fields. Your graduation party, then, might possess the identifier `myGraduationParty`. As a member of the `Party` class, it might have data members for the date and time, like all parties, and it might have a method to issue invitations. When you use the method, you might want to be able to send an argument to `IssueInvitations()` that indicates how many copies to print. When you think of an object and its methods, it's as though you can send a message to the object to direct it to accomplish some task—you can tell the party object named `myGraduationParty` to print the number of invitations you request. Even though `yourAnniversaryParty` also is a member of the `Party` class, and even though it also has an `IssueInvitations()` method, you will send a different argument value to `yourAnniversaryParty`'s `IssueInvitations()` method than I send to `myGraduationParty`'s corresponding method. Within any object-oriented program, you continuously make requests to objects' methods, often including arguments as part of those requests.

When you program in C#, you frequently create classes from which objects will be instantiated (or other programmers create them for you). You also write applications to use the objects, along with their data and methods. Often, you will write programs that use classes created by others, as you have used the `Console` class; similarly, you might create a class that other programmers will use to instantiate objects within their own programs. A program or class that instantiates objects of another prewritten class is a **class client** or **class user**.

»TWO TRUTHS AND A LIE: UNDERSTANDING CLASS CONCEPTS

1. C# classes always contain a `Main()` method.
2. An object is an instantiation of a class.
3. The data components of a class often are its instance variables.

The false answer is #1. C# applications always contain a `Main()` method, but some classes do not if they are not meant to be run as programs.

CREATING A CLASS FROM WHICH OBJECTS CAN BE INSTANTIATED

When you create a class, you must assign a name to it, and you must determine what data and methods will be part of the class. For example, suppose you decide to create a class named `Employee`. One instance variable of `Employee` might be an employee number, and one necessary method might display a welcome message to new employees. To begin, you create a **class header** or **class definition** that describes the class. It contains three parts:

1. An optional access modifier

2. The keyword `class`

3. Any legal identifier you choose for the name of your class

For example, a header for an `Employee` class is `internal class Employee`. The keyword `internal` is an example of a **class access modifier**. You can declare a class to be one of the following:

- » **public**, meaning access to the class is not limited.
- » **protected**, meaning access to the class is limited to the class and to any classes derived from the class. (You will learn about deriving classes in Chapter 8.)
- » **internal**, meaning access is limited to the assembly (a group of code modules compiled together) to which the class belongs.
- » **private**, meaning access is limited to another class to which the class belongs. In other words, a class can be `private` if it is contained within another class, and only the containing class should have access to the `private` class.

Note that `private` and `protected` classes have limited uses. Furthermore, when you declare a class using a namespace, you only can declare it to be `public` or `internal`. For now, you will use either the `public` or `internal` modifier with your classes. If you do not explicitly include an access specifier, class access is `internal` by default. Because most classes you create will have `internal` access, typing an access specifier is often unnecessary.

In addition to the class header, classes you create must have a class body enclosed between curly braces. Figure 7-1 shows a shell for an `Employee` class.

```
class Employee
{
    // Instance variables and methods go here
}
```

Figure 7-1 Employee class shell

CREATING INSTANCE VARIABLES AND METHODS

When you create a class, you define both its attributes and its methods. You declare the class's instance variables, which are the attributes or fields, within the curly braces using the same syntax you use to declare other variables—you provide a type and an identifier. When you create an instance variable, you create an attribute to hold a value that describes a feature of every object of that class. For example, within the Employee class, you can declare an integer ID number; when you create Employee objects, each will have its own idNumber. You can define the ID number simply as int idNumber;. However, programmers frequently include an access modifier for each of the class fields and declare the idNumber as private int idNumber;. Figure 7-2 shows an Employee class that contains the idNumber field.


```
class Employee
{
    private int idNumber;
}
```

Figure 7-2 Employee class containing idNumber field

The allowable field modifiers are new, public, protected, internal, private, static, readonly, and volatile. Most class fields are private, which provides the highest level of security. Identifying a field as private means that no other class can access the field's values, and only methods of the same class will be allowed to set, get, or otherwise use the field. Using private fields within classes is an example of **information hiding**, a feature found in all object-oriented languages. You see cases of information hiding in real-life objects every day. For instance, you cannot see into your automobile's gas tank to determine how full it is. Instead, you use a gauge on the dashboard to provide you with the necessary information. Similarly, data fields are frequently private in object-oriented programming, but their contents are accessed through public methods. The private data of a class should be changed or manipulated only by its own methods, not by methods that belong to other classes.

In contrast to a class's `private` data fields, most class methods are not usually `private`; they are `public`. The resulting `private` data/`public` method arrangement provides a means to control outside access to your data—only a class's nonprivate methods can be used to access a class's `private` data. The situation is similar to having a "public" receptionist who controls the messages passed in and out of your private office. The way in which the nonprivate methods are written controls how you will use the `private` data.

For example, one method you need for an `Employee` class that contains an `idNumber` is the method to display the employee's welcoming message to company clients. A reasonable name for this method is `WelcomeMessage()`, and its declaration is `public void WelcomeMessage()`, because it will have `public` access and return nothing. Figure 7-3 shows the `Employee` class with the addition of the `WelcomeMessage()` method.

```
class Employee
{
    private int idNumber;
    public void WelcomeMessage()
    {
        Console.WriteLine("Welcome from Employee #{0}", idNumber);
        Console.WriteLine("How can I help you?");
    }
}
```

Figure 7-3 `Employee` class with `idNumber` field and `WelcomeMessage()` method

Notice that the `WelcomeMessage()` method does not employ the `static` modifier, unlike many other methods you have created. The keyword `static` is used for class-wide methods, but not for instance methods that "belong" to objects. If you are creating a program with a `Main()` method that you will execute to perform some task, then many of your methods will be `static`. You can call the `static` methods from within `Main()` without creating an object. However, if you are creating a class from which objects will be instantiated, most methods will probably be nonstatic, as you will be associating the methods with individual objects and their data. Methods used with object instantiations are called **instance methods**. Each time the `WelcomeMessage()` instance method is used in the class in Figure 7-3, it will display an `idNumber` for a specific object. In other words, the method will work appropriately for each object instance.

»TWO TRUTHS AND A LIE: CREATING A CLASS FROM WHICH OBJECTS CAN BE INSTANTIATED

1. A class header always contains the keyword `class`.
2. When you create a class, you define both its attributes and its methods.
3. Most class fields and methods are `private`.

The false statement is #3. Most class fields are `private`, but most class methods are `public`.

CREATING OBJECTS

Declaring a class does not create any actual objects. A class is just an abstract description of what an object will be like if any objects are ever actually instantiated. Just as you might understand all the characteristics of an item you intend to manufacture long before the first item rolls off the assembly line, you can create a class with fields and methods long before you instantiate any objects that are members of that class.

A two-step process creates an object that is an instance of a class. First, you supply a type and an identifier, just as when you declare any variable. Second, you create the object, which includes allocating computer memory for it. For example, you might define an integer as `int someValue;` and you might define an `Employee` as `Employee myAssistant;`, where `myAssistant` could be any legal identifier you choose to represent an `Employee`.

When you declare an integer as `int myInteger;`, you notify the compiler that an integer named `myInteger` will exist, and computer memory automatically is reserved for it at the same time—the exact amount of computer memory depends on the declared data type. When you declare the `myAssistant` instance of the `Employee` class, you are notifying the compiler that you will use the identifier `myAssistant`. However, you are not yet setting aside computer memory in which the `Employee` named `myAssistant` can be stored—that is done only for the built-in, predefined types. To allocate the needed memory and instantiate the object, you must use the `new` operator.

Defining an `Employee` object named `myAssistant` requires two steps—you must declare a reference to the object and then you must use the statement that actually sets aside enough memory to hold `myAssistant`, as in the following:

```
Employee myAssistant;
myAssistant = new Employee();
```

You also can declare and reserve memory for `myAssistant` in one statement, as in the following:

```
Employee myAssistant = new Employee();
```

> **»NOTE**
> You can think of a class declaration as similar to a blueprint for building a new house or a recipe for baking a cake. In other words, it is a plan that exists before any objects are created.

> **»NOTE**
> Every object name is a reference— that is, a computer memory location where the fields for the object reside.

> **»NOTE**
> In Chapter 5, you used the `new` operator when setting aside memory for arrays.

In this statement, `Employee` is the object's type (as well as its class), and `myAssistant` is the name of the object. The equal sign is the assignment operator, so a value is being assigned to `myAssistant`. The `new` operator is allocating a new, unused portion of computer memory for `myAssistant`. The value being assigned to `myAssistant` is a memory address at which it will be located. You need not be concerned with the actual memory address—when you refer to `myAssistant`, the compiler will locate it at the appropriate address for you.

>> **NOTE** Because the identifiers for objects are references to their memory addresses, you can call any class a **reference type**—in other words, a type that refers to a specific memory location. A reference type is a type that holds an address, as opposed to the predefined types such as `int`, `double`, and `char`, which are **value types**.

>> **NOTE** You also can use the `new` operator for simple data types. For example, to declare an integer variable `x`, you can write the following:

```
int x = new int();
```

However, programmers usually use the simpler form:

```
int x;
```

With the first form, `x` is initialized to 0. With the second form, `x` holds no usable starting value.

In the statement `Employee myAssistant = new Employee();`, the last portion of the statement after the `new` operator, `Employee()`, looks suspiciously like a method name with its parentheses. In fact, it is the name of a method that constructs an `Employee` object. `Employee()` is a constructor. You will write your own constructors later in this chapter. For now, note that when you don't write a constructor for a class, C# writes one for you, and the name of the constructor is always the same as the name of the class whose objects it constructs.

After an object has been instantiated, its public members (usually its methods) can be accessed using the object's identifier, a dot, and a method call. For example, if you declare an `Employee` named `myAssistant`, you can access `myAssistant`'s `WelcomeMessage()` method with the following statement:

```
myAssistant.WelcomeMessage();
```

>> **NOTE** The statement `myAssistant.WelcomeMessage()` would be illegal if `WelcomeMessage()` was a `static` method. The method can be used with an `Employee` object only because it is nonstatic.

No class client (for example, a `Main()` method) can access `myAssistant`'s `idNumber` directly; the only way a client can access the `private` data is by sending a message through one of the object's `public` methods. Because the `WelcomeMessage()` method is part of the same class as `idNumber`, and because `WelcomeMessage()` is `public`, a `Main()` method can use the method that displays the `idNumber`. Figure 7-4 shows a class named `CreateEmployee` whose `Main()` method declares an `Employee` and displays the `Employee`'s welcome message. Figure 7-5 shows the execution of the program.

```csharp
using System;
public class CreateEmployee
{
    public static void Main()
    {
        Employee myAssistant = new Employee();
        myAssistant.WelcomeMessage();
    }
}
```

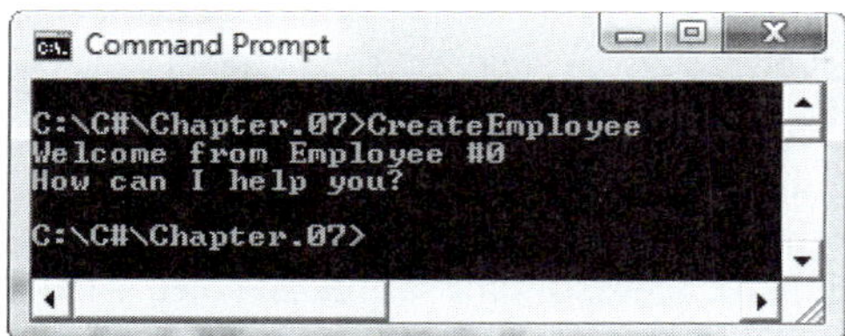

Figure 7-4 The CreateEmployee program

Figure 7-5 Output of the CreateEmployee program

In the output in Figure 7-5, the Employee's ID number is 0. By default, all unassigned numeric fields in an object are initialized to 0. When you compile the program in Figure 7-4, you receive a warning message:

```
Field 'Employee.idNumber' is never assigned to, and will always have
its default value 0.
```

Of course, usually you want to provide a different value for each Employee's idNumber field. To accomplish this, you can create properties.

T T F

»TWO TRUTHS AND A LIE: CREATING OBJECTS

1. Declaring a class creates one object of a new data type.
2. After you declare a class, you must use the new operator to allocate memory for an object of that class and to instantiate it.
3. After an object has been instantiated, its public members can be accessed using the object's identifier, a dot, and a method call.

The false statement is #1. Declaring a class does not create any actual objects; the declaration only describes what an object of that class will be.

CREATING PROPERTIES

Frequently, methods you call with an object are used to alter the states of its fields. For example, you might want to set or change the date or time of a party. If the `Party` class contained a `string` field named `partyDate`, you could write a method such as `SetDate()` to set a party's date, similar to the following method:

```
public void SetDate(string date)
{
    partyDate = date;
}
```

Then, you could call the method with a statement like the following:

```
myGraduationParty.SetDate("May 12");
```

Although this technique would work, and might be used in other programming languages, C# programmers more often create a property to perform this task. A **property** is a member of a class that provides access to a field of a class; properties define how fields will be set and retrieved. Properties have **accessors** that specify the statements that execute when a class's fields are accessed. Specifically, properties contain **set accessors** for setting an object's fields and **get accessors** for retrieving the stored values. When you create properties, the syntax in your client programs becomes more natural and easier to understand.

Figure 7-6 shows an `Employee` class in which a property has been defined in the shaded area. The property is `IdNumber`. A property declaration resembles a variable declaration; it contains an

```
class Employee
{
    private int idNumber;
    public int IdNumber
    {
        get
        {
            return idNumber;
        }
        set
        {
            idNumber = value;
        }
    }
    public void WelcomeMessage()
    {
        Console.WriteLine("Welcome from Employee #{0}", IdNumber);
        Console.WriteLine("How can I help you?");
    }
}
```

Figure 7-6 `Employee` class with defined property

>> NOTE C# programmers refer to properties as "smart fields."

>> NOTE When a property has a `set` accessor, programmers say the property can be "written to." When it has a `get` accessor, programmers say the property can be "read from."

>> NOTE It is important to pay attention to capitalization so you can distinguish a field from a property.

>> NOTE When a property has only a `get` accessor (and not a `set` accessor), it is a **read-only property**.

>> NOTE In C#, the `get` and `set` accessors often are called the **getter** and the **setter**, respectively.

access modifier, a data type, and an identifier. It also resembles a method in that it is followed by curly braces that contain statements. By convention, a property identifier is the same as the field it manipulates, except the first letter is capitalized. Following the property identifier, you define accessors between curly braces. The `IdNumber` property in Figure 7-6 contains both `get` and `set` accessors; a property declaration can contain a `get` accessor, a `set` accessor, or both.

> **» NOTE** In the altered `WelcomeMessage()` method in Figure 7-6, the `IdNumber` property is displayed. Alternately, this method could continue to use the `idNumber` field (as in Figure 7-3) because the method is a member of the same class as the field. Programmers are divided on whether a method of a class should use a field or a property to access its own methods. One popular position is that if `get` and `set` accessors are well-designed, they should be used everywhere, even from within the class. Sometimes, you want a field to be read-only, so you do not create a `set` accessor. In such a case, you can use the field (with the lowercase initial by convention) within class methods.

> **» NOTE** Be careful with capitalization in properties. For example, within a `get` accessor for `IdNumber`, if you return `IdNumber` instead of `idNumber`, you initiate an infinite loop—the property continuously accesses itself.

> **» NOTE** Throughout this book you have seen keywords displayed in blue in the program figures. The words "`get`" and "`set`" are not C# keywords—for example, you could declare a variable named `get` within a C# program. However, within a property, `get` and `set` have special meanings and are not allowed to be declared as identifiers there. In the Visual Studio Integrated Development Environment, the words `get` and `set` appear in blue within properties, but in black elsewhere. The figures in this book follow the same convention.

Each accessor in a property looks like a method, except no parentheses are included in the identifier. A `set` accessor acts like a method that accepts a parameter and assigns it to a variable. However, it is not a method and you do not use parentheses with it. A `get` accessor returns the value of the field associated with the property, but you do not code a `return` type; the `return` type of a `get` accessor is implicitly the type of the property in which it is contained.

> **» NOTE** Identifiers that act like keywords in specific circumstances are **contextual keywords.** C# has six contextual keywords: `get`, `set`, `value`, `partial`, `where`, and `yield`.

When you use `set` and `get` accessors in a method, you do not use the words "set" or "get." Instead, to set a value, you use the assignment operator (=), and to get a value, you simply use the property name. For example, if you declare an `Employee` named `myChef`, you can assign an `IdNumber` as simply as you would a variable, as in the following:

```
Employee myChef = new Employee();
myChef.IdNumber = 2345;
```

In the second statement, the `IdNumber` property is set to 2345. The value to the right of the equal sign is sent to the `set` accessor as an implicit parameter named `value`. (An **implicit parameter** is one that is undeclared and that gets its value automatically.) In the statement `myChef.IdNumber = 2345;`, the constant 2345 is sent to the `set` accessor, where it becomes the value of `value`. Within the `set` accessor, `value` is assigned to the class field `idNumber`. The `idNumber` field could not have been set directly from `Main()` because it is `private`; however, the `IdNumber` property can be set through its `set` accessor because the property is `public`.

Writing a `get` accessor allows you to use a property like you would a simple variable. For example, a declared `Employee`'s ID number can be displayed with the following:

```
Console.WriteLine("ID number is {0}", myChef.IdNumber);
```

The expression `myChef.idNumber` (using the field name that starts with a lowercase *i*) would not be allowed in a client program because `idNumber` is `private`; however, the public `get` accessor of the property allows `myChef.IdNumber` to be displayed. Figure 7-7 shows a complete application that uses the modified class in Figure 7-6. Figure 7-8 shows the output.

```csharp
using System;
public class CreateEmployee2
{
    public static void Main()
    {
        Employee myChef = new Employee();
        myChef.IdNumber = 2345;
        Console.WriteLine("ID number is {0}",
            myChef.IdNumber);
        myChef.WelcomeMessage();
    }
}
```

Figure 7-7 The `CreateEmployee2` application that uses the `Employee` class containing a property

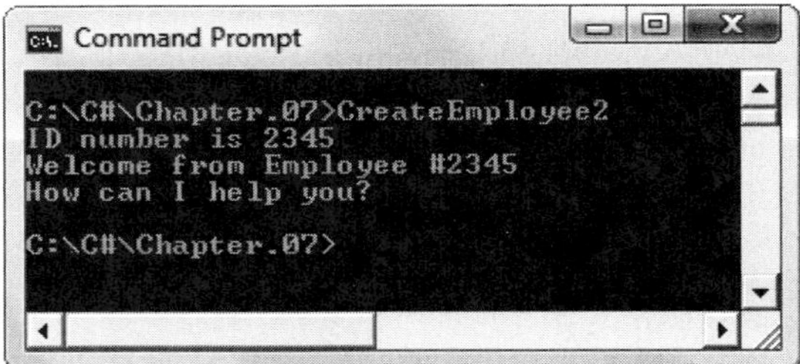

Figure 7-8 Output of the `CreateEmployee2` application

At this point, declaring `get` and `set` accessors that do nothing except retrieve a value from a field or assign a value to one might seem like a lot of work for very little payoff. After all, if a class field was `public` instead of `private`, you would just use it directly and avoid the work of creating the property. However, it is conventional (and consistent with object-oriented principles) to make class fields `private` and allow accessors to manipulate them only as you deem appropriate. Keeping data hidden is an important feature of object-oriented programming, as is controlling how data values are set and used. Additionally, you can customize accessors to suit the restrictions you want to impose on how some class fields are retrieved and accessed. For example, you could write a `set` accessor that restricts ID numbers within the `Employee` class as follows:

```
set
{
    if(value < 500)
        idNumber = value;
    else
        idNumber = 500;
}
```

This `set` accessor would ensure that an `Employee idNumber` would never be greater than 500. If clients had direct access to a `private idNumber` field, you could not control what values could be assigned there, but when you write a custom `set` accessor for your class, you gain full control over the allowed data values.

USING AUTO-IMPLEMENTED PROPERTIES

Although you can include any number of custom statements within the `get` and `set` accessors in a property, the most frequent scenario is that a `set` accessor simply assigns a value to the appropriate class field, and the `get` accessor simply returns the field value. Because the code in `get` and `set` accessors frequently is standard as well as brief, programmers sometimes take one of several shorthand approaches to writing properties.

For example, instead of writing an `IdNumber` property using 11 code lines as in Figure 7-6, a programmer might write the property on five lines, as follows:

```
public int IdNumber
{
    get{return idNumber;}
    set{idNumber = value;}
}
```

This format does not eliminate any of the characters typed in the original version of the property; it only eliminates some of the white space, placing each accessor on a single line.

Other programmers choose an even more condensed form and write the entire property on one line as:

```
public int IdNumber {get{return idNumber;} set{idNumber = value;}}
```

An even more concise format is new to C# 3.0. In this version, you can write a property as follows:

```
public int IdNumber {get; set;}
```

A property written in this format is an **auto-implemented property**—the property's implementation (its set of working statements) is created for you automatically with the assumption that the `set` accessor should simply assign a value to the appropriate field, and the `get` accessor should simply return the field. You cannot use an auto-implemented property if you need to include customized statements within one of your accessors (such as placing restrictions on an assigned value), and you can only declare an auto-implemented property when you use both `get` and `set`.

Conveniently, when you use an auto-implemented property, you do not need to declare the field that corresponds to the property (although you still can do so). For example, Figure 7-9 shows an `Employee` class in which no specialized code is needed for the properties for what would ordinarily be declared as `idNumber` and `salary` fields. In this class, only the properties are declared using auto-implemented properties. The figure also contains a short program that uses the class, and Figure 7-10 shows the output. Auto-implemented properties provide a convenient shortcut when you need both a `get` and `set` but no specialized statements are needed.

```
using System;
public class CreateEmployeeWithAutoImplementedProperty
{
    public static void Main()
    {
        Employee aWorker = new Employee();
        aWorker.IdNumber = 3872;
        aWorker.Salary = 22.11;
        Console.WriteLine("Employee #{0} makes {1}",
            aWorker.IdNumber, aWorker.Salary.ToString("C"));
    }
}
public class Employee
{
    public int IdNumber {get; set;}
    public double Salary {get; set;}
}
```

Figure 7-9 An `Employee` class with no declared fields and auto-implemented properties, and a program that uses them

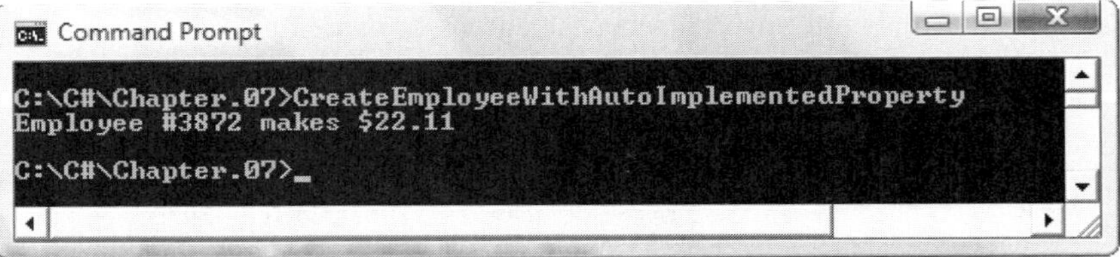

Figure 7-10 Output of the `CreateEmployeeWithAutoImplementedProperty` application

»NOTE If you want to create a read-only property using auto-implemented accessors, you can make the `set` accessor private, as in the following:

```
public int IdNumber {get; private set};
```

Using this technique, the `IdNumber` property cannot be set by any statement in another class. If you use this technique, most likely you want to explicitly declare an `idNumber` field that can be set from within the class, possibly by a constructor.

»TWO TRUTHS AND A LIE: CREATING PROPERTIES

1. A property is a member of a class that defines how fields will be set and retrieved.

2. Properties contain `set` accessors for retrieving an object's fields and `get` accessors for setting the stored values.

3. You can create auto-implemented properties when you want a field's `set` accessor to assign a value to the appropriate class field, and a field's `get` accessor simply to return the field value.

The false statement is #2. Properties contain `set` accessors for setting an object's fields and `get` accessors for retrieving the stored values.

STORING AND ORGANIZING YOUR CLASSES

When you create a class that describes objects to be instantiated, and another class that instantiates those objects, you physically can contain the two classes within a single file or place each class in its own file.

By placing both classes within the same file, you typically reduce development time and simplify the compilation process. When you first develop classes, you are likely to introduce both syntax and logical errors into each file you use. By placing your classes in the same file, you reduce the time needed to navigate through multiple files and to check issues such as consistent spelling of variable and method names and consistent use of data types. Also, when you compile only a single file, the sources of any error messages you receive are easier to locate.

There are also advantages to placing classes in separate files. One advantage is simply organization. Just as you can arrange all your nuts, bolts, and nails in the various drawers of a hardware storage cabinet and then find a quarter-inch bolt when you need it, containing each class in its own file makes the classes more manageable and easier to locate. More importantly, when a class resides within its own file, the class is easier to reuse within additional programs you create in the future.

Most classes you create will have more than a few data fields and property definitions for each field. For example, a typical `Employee` class would contain more than an `idNumber` field—a few of the many possibilities include `firstName`, `lastName`, `address`, `phoneNumber`, `salary`, `departmentNumber`, `hireDate`, `numberOfDependents`, and so on. Although there is no requirement to do so, most programmers place data fields in some logical order at the beginning of a class. For example, the `idNumber` field is most likely used as a unique identifier for each `Employee` (which database users often call a **primary key**), so it makes sense to list the employee ID number first in the class. An employee's last name and first name "go together," so it makes sense to store these two `Employee` components adjacently. Despite these common-sense rules, you have a lot of flexibility in how you position data fields within any class.

»NOTE A unique identifier must have no duplicates within an application. In other words, although an organization might have many employees with the last name "Johnson" or a salary of 400.00, only one employee will have ID number 128. For that reason, if you were designing a professional `Employee` class, you might choose to make the ID number property read-only and to allow assignment only at construction using a formula that provides a unique number, or perhaps accessing a file of available numbers.

Additionally, if you define properties for each data field as well as a few methods, quite a lot of code is required. Finding your way through the list of fields, properties, and methods can become a formidable task. For ease in locating class methods and properties, many programmers prefer to store them in alphabetical order. Another logical organization scheme is to store all properties first, in the same order as their corresponding data fields, followed by other methods. Any of these organizational techniques can produce usable classes and workable programs, but your organization or instructor might have a preference for how to assemble class members.

An additional aid to keeping your classes organized is to use comments liberally. For example, comments can be used to separate functional areas within a class and to describe the purposes of methods.

»NOTE Although good program comments are crucial to creating understandable code, they have been left out of many examples in this book to save space. Your programs should contain many comments that identify your program components and explain the purpose and structure of your methods.

»NOTE Although good comments can help others to understand your programs, they are no substitute for clear, appropriate identifiers.

»TWO TRUTHS AND A LIE: STORING AND ORGANIZING YOUR CLASSES

1. You can contain two classes in the same file.
2. Within a class you must place all properties first.
3. You can store class methods and properties in any order that makes sense for your class.

The false statement is #2. You can place properties first within a class, but there is no requirement to do so. Most programmers place data fields in some logical order at the beginning of a class, followed by properties and methods.

UNUSUAL USE: public FIELDS AND private METHODS

Most of the time, class data fields are private and class methods are public. This technique ensures that data will be used and changed only in the ways provided in your accessors. Novice programmers might make a data field public to avoid having to create a property containing get and set accessors. For example, Figure 7-11 shows a Desk class that contains two public fields. Because the fields are public, no get or set accessors are needed. The program that instantiates a Desk can set and retrieve the values in the fields without "bothering" with the accessors that would be needed if the fields were private. Although it is easy to work with, the Desk class in Figure 7-11 violates a basic principle of object-oriented programming. That is, data should be hidden when at all possible, and access to it should be controlled by well-designed accessors.

```
using System;
class Desk
{
    public string wood;
    public int drawers;
}
public class TestDesk
{
    public static void Main()
    {

        Desk myDesk = new Desk();
        myDesk.wood = "mahogany";   // notice wood and drawers
        myDesk.drawers = 4;         // are accessed directly
        Console.WriteLine("My {0} desk has {1} drawers",
            myDesk.wood, myDesk.drawers);

    }
}
```


Figure 7-11 Poorly designed Desk class with program that instantiates a Desk

Although private fields and public methods and accessors are the norm, occasionally you need to create public fields or private methods. Consider the Carpet class shown in Figure 7-12. Although it contains several private data fields, this class also contains one public data field (shaded). Following the three public property declarations, one private method is defined (also shaded).

```csharp
class Carpet
{
    public const string MOTTO = "Our carpets are quality-made";
    private int length;
    private int width;
    private int area;
    public int Length
    {
        get
        {
            return length;
        }
        set
        {
            length = value;
            CalcArea();
        }
    }
    public int Width
    {
        get
        {
            return width;
        }
        set
        {
            width = value;
            CalcArea();
        }
    }
    public int Area
    {
        get
        {
            return area;
        }
    }
    private void CalcArea()
    {
        area = Length * Width;
    }
}
```

Figure 7-12 The `Carpet` class

>> **NOTE** In the `Carpet` class, the `Area` property does not contain a `set` accessor because no outside program is allowed to set the area. Instead, it is calculated whenever `width` or `length` changes.

For example, you can create a `public` data field when you want all objects of a class to contain the same value. When you create `Carpet` objects from the class in Figure 7-12, each `Carpet` will have its own `length`, `width`, and `area`, but all `Carpet` objects will have the same `MOTTO`. The field `MOTTO` is preceded by the keyword `const`, meaning `MOTTO` is constant. That is, no program can change its value. When you define a named constant within a class, it is always `static`. That is, the field belongs to the entire class, not to any particular instance of the class. When you create a `static` field, only one copy is stored for the entire class, no matter how many objects you instantiate. On the other hand, multiple copies of nonstatic fields exist—one for each object instantiated. When you use a constant field, you use the class name rather than an object name. The class name is followed by a dot and the constant name, as in `Carpet.MOTTO`.

> **》》NOTE**
> Throughout this book, you have been using `static` to describe the `Main()` method of a class. You do not need to create an object of any class that contains a `Main()` method to be able to use `Main()`.

> **》》NOTE** You learned to create named constants in Chapter 2, and learned that identifiers of named constants such as `MOTTO` conventionally are capitalized. Some built-in C# classes contain useful named constants, such as `Math.PI`, which contains the value of pi. You do not create a `Math` object to use `PI`; therefore, you know it is `static`.

Figure 7-13 shows a program that instantiates and uses a `Carpet` object, and Figure 7-14 shows the results when the program executes. Notice that, although the write statements require an object to use `Width`, `Length`, and `Area`, `MOTTO` is referenced using the class name only.

```csharp
using System;
public class TestCarpet
{
    public static void Main()
    {
        Carpet aRug = new Carpet();
        aRug.Width = 12;
        aRug.Length = 14;
        Console.Write("The {0} X {1} carpet ", aRug.Width, aRug.Length);
        Console.WriteLine("has an area of {0}", aRug.Area);
        Console.WriteLine("Our motto is: {0}", Carpet.MOTTO);
    }
}
```

Figure 7-13 The `TestCarpet` class

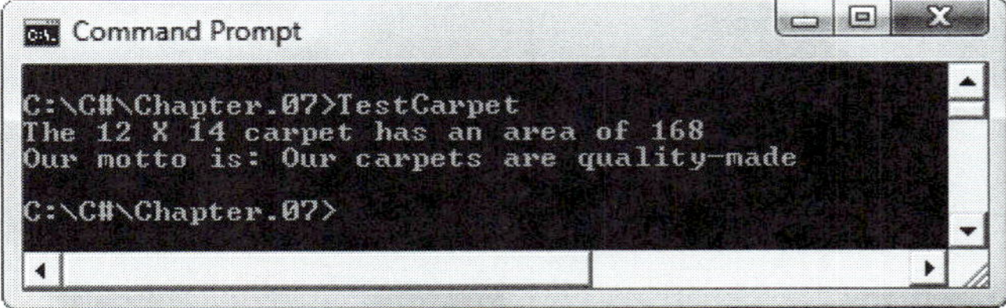

Figure 7-14 Output of the `TestCarpet` program

The `Carpet` class contains one private method named `CalcArea()`. As you examine the code in the `TestCarpet` class in Figure 7-13, notice that `Width` and `Length` are set using an assignment operator, but `Area` is not. The `TestCarpet` class can make assignments to `Width` and `Length` because these properties are `public`. However, you would not want a client program to assign a value to `Area` because the assigned value might not agree with the `Width` and `Length` values. Therefore, the `Area` property is a read-only property—it does not contain a `set` accessor, and no assignments by clients are allowed. Instead, whenever the `Width` or `Length` properties are set, the `private CalcArea()` method is called from the accessor. The `CalcArea()` method is defined as `private` because there is no reason for a client class like `TestCarpet` to call `CalcArea()`. The `Carpet` class's own accessors should call `CalcArea()` only after a valid value has been assigned to the `length` or `width` field. You create a method to be `private` when it should be called only by other methods or accessors within the class and not by outside classes.

> **»NOTE** Programmers probably create `private` methods more frequently than they create `public` data fields. Some programmers feel that the best style is to use `public` methods that are nothing but a list of method calls with descriptive names. Then, the methods that actually do the work are all `private`.

»TWO TRUTHS AND A LIE: UNUSUAL USE: `public` FIELDS AND `private` METHODS

1. Good object-oriented techniques require that data should usually be hidden and access to it should be controlled by well-designed accessors.
2. Although `private` fields, methods, and accessors are the norm, occasionally you need to create `public` versions of them.
3. When you define a named constant within a class, it is always `static`; that is, the field belongs to the entire class, not to any particular instance of the class.

The false statement is #2. Although `private` fields and `public` methods and accessors are the norm, occasionally you need to create `public` fields or `private` methods.

UNDERSTANDING THE `this` REFERENCE

After you create a class, you might eventually create thousands of objects from that class. When you create each object, you provide storage for each of the object's instance variables. For example, Figure 7-15 shows part of a `Book` class that contains only three fields, a property for the title field, and an advertising message method. When you declare several `Book` objects, as in the following statements, each `Book` object requires separate memory locations for its `title`, `numPages`, and `price`:

```
Book myBook = new Book();
Book yourBook = new Book();
```

```csharp
class Book
{
    private string title;
    private int numPages;
    private double price;
    public string Title
    {
      get
      {
          return title;
      }
      set
      {
          title = value;
      }
    }
    public void AdvertisingMessage()
    {
        Console.WriteLine("Buy it now: {0}", Title);
    }
}
```

Figure 7-15 Partially developed `Book` class

Storing a single `Book` object requires allocating storage space for three separate fields; the storage requirements for `Book` objects used by a library or retail bookstore would be far more considerable, but necessary—each `Book` must be able to "hold" its own data, including publisher, date published, author, ISBN, and so on. If each `Book` object also required its own copy of each property and method contained in the class, the storage requirements would multiply. It makes sense that each `Book` needs space to store its unique title and other data, but because every `Book` uses the same methods, storing multiple copies is wasteful and unnecessary.

Fortunately, each `Book` object does not need to store its own copy of each property and method. Whether you make the method call `myBook.AdvertisingMessage()` or `yourBook.AdvertisingMessage()`, you access the same `AdvertisingMessage()` method. However, there must be a difference between the two method calls, because each displays a different title in its message. The difference lies in an implicit, or invisible, reference that is passed to every instance method and property accessor. The implicitly passed reference is the **this reference**. When you call the method `myBook.AdvertisingMessage()`, you automatically pass the `this` reference to the method so the method knows which instance of `Book` to use.

You can explicitly refer to the this reference within an instance method or property, as shown in Figure 7-16. When you refer to Title (or title) within a Book class method or accessor, you are referring to the title field of "this" Book—the Book whose name you used in the method call—perhaps myBook or yourBook. Using the shaded keywords in Figure 7-16 is not required; the version of the methods shown in Figure 7-15 (where this was implied but not written explicitly) works just as well. Figure 7-17 shows an application that uses the Book class, and Figure 7-18 shows the output.

```
class Book
{
    private string title;
    private int numPages;
    private double price;
    public string Title
    {
      get
      {
          return this.title;
      }
      set
      {
          this.title = value;
      }
    }
    public void AdvertisingMessage()
    {
        Console.WriteLine("Buy it now: {0}", this.Title);
    }
}
```

Figure 7-16 Book class with methods explicitly using this references

```
using System;
public class CreateTwoBooks
{
    public static void Main()
    {
        Book myBook = new Book();
        Book yourBook = new Book();
        myBook.Title = "Silas Marner";
        yourBook.Title = "The Time Traveler's Wife";
        myBook.AdvertisingMessage();
        yourBook.AdvertisingMessage();
    }
}
```

Figure 7-17 Program that declares two Book objects

Figure 7-18 Output of `CreateTwoBooks` program

The `Book` class in Figure 7-16 worked without adding the references to `this`. However, you should be aware that the `this` reference is always there, working behind the scenes, even if you do not code it. Sometimes, you may want to include the `this` reference within a method for clarity, so the reader has no doubt when you are referring to a class instance variable.

»TWO TRUTHS AND A LIE: UNDERSTANDING THE `this` REFERENCE

1. An implicit, or invisible, `this` reference is passed to every instance method and property accessor in a class; instance methods and properties are nonstatic.

2. You can explicitly refer to the `this` reference within an instance method or property.

3. Although the `this` reference exists in every instance method, you can never refer to it within a method.

The false statement is #3. Sometimes, you may want to include the `this` reference within a method for clarity, so the reader has no doubt when you are referring to a class instance variable.

UNDERSTANDING CONSTRUCTORS

When you create a class such as `Employee` and instantiate an object with a statement such as `Employee aWorker = new Employee();`, you are actually calling a method named `Employee()` that is provided by C#. A **constructor** is a method that instantiates (creates an instance of) an object. Every class you create is automatically supplied with a `public` constructor with no parameters. A constructor without parameters is a class's **default constructor**. The constructor named `Employee()` establishes one `Employee` with the identifier `aWorker`, and provides the following initial values to the `Employee`'s data fields:

» Numeric fields are set to 0 (zero).

» Character fields are set to '\0'.

» Boolean fields are set to `false`.

» References, such as `string` fields or any other object fields, are set to `null` (or empty).

If you do not want an Employee's fields to hold these default values, or if you want to perform additional tasks when you create an Employee, you can write your own constructor to replace the automatically supplied version. Any constructor you write must have the same name as its class, and constructors cannot have a return type. For example, if you create an Employee class that contains a Salary property, and you want every new Employee object to have a salary of 300.00, you could write the constructor for the Employee class that appears in Figure 7-19. Any instantiated Employee will have a default salary value of 300.00.

```
Employee()
{
    Salary = 300.00;
}
```

Figure 7-19 Employee class constructor that initializes the Salary property

> **NOTE** The constructor in Figure 7-19 assumes a Salary property has been defined with a set accessor. If there is no set accessor, but there is a salary field, then the assignment could be salary = 300;.

You can write any statement in a constructor. Although you usually would have no reason to do so, you could print a message from within a constructor or perform any other task. The most common constructor task is to initialize fields.

PASSING PARAMETERS TO CONSTRUCTORS

You can create a constructor to ensure that all objects of a class are initialized with the same values in their data fields. After construction, you might change the value in an individual object's fields by using the appropriate set accessors in its properties. Alternatively, you might create objects that hold unique field values right from the start by writing constructors to which you pass one or more parameters. You then can use the parameter values to set properties or fields for individual object instantiations. For example, consider an Employee class with two data fields, a constructor, and an auto-implemented property, as shown in Figure 7-20. Its constructor assigns 999 to each potentially instantiated Employee's idNumber. Any time an Employee object is created using a statement such as Employee partTimeWorker = new Employee();, even if no other data-assigning methods are ever used, you are ensured that the Employee's idNumber holds a default value. The partTimeWorker Employee object, like all Employees, will have an initial idNumber of 999.

> **NOTE** Using this technique would cause all employees to have the same ID number, which usually is contrary to the purpose of an ID number.

```
public class Employee
{
    private int idNumber;
    private double salary;
    public Employee()
    {
        IdNumber = 999;
    }
    public int IdNumber {get; set;}
    //  Other class members can go here
}
```

Figure 7-20 `Employee` class with a parameterless constructor

The constructor in Figure 7-20 is a **parameterless constructor**—one that takes no arguments. As an alternative, you might choose to create `Employee`s with initial `idNumber` fields that differ for each `Employee`. To accomplish this task within a constructor, you can pass an employee number to the constructor. Figure 7-21 shows an `Employee` constructor that receives a parameter. With this constructor, an integer is passed in using a statement such as the following:

```
Employee partTimeWorker = new Employee(876);
```

When the constructor executes, the integer used as the actual parameter within the method call is passed to `Employee()` and assigned to the `Employee`'s `idNumber`.


```
public Employee(int empID)
{
    IdNumber = empID;
}
```

Figure 7-21 `Employee` constructor with parameter

≫ NOTE Suppose you want the parameter to the `Employee` class constructor to have the identifier `idNumber`. Further, suppose you want the `Employee` class to contain a read-only property for `idNumber`; that is, there is no `set` accessor for `IdNumber`. Then you would write the constructor as follows:

```
public Employee(int idNumber)
{
    this.idNumber = idNumber);
}
```

≫ NOTE The `idNumber` value on the right of the assignment operator would refer to the constructor parameter, but `this.idNumber` on the left of the assignment statement refers to the current object's `idNumber` field.

OVERLOADING CONSTRUCTORS

NOTE
You learned the meaning of *ambiguity* and how to avoid it in Chapter 6.

NOTE
If you create class constructors but do not create a parameterless version, then the class does not have a default constructor.

If you create a class from which you can instantiate objects, C# automatically provides a default constructor. As soon as you create your own constructor, whether it has parameters or not, you no longer have access to the automatically created version. However, if you want a class to have both parameter and parameterless versions of a constructor, you can create them. Like any other C# methods, constructors can be overloaded. You can write as many constructors for a class as you want, as long as their argument lists do not cause ambiguity. For example, the Employee class in Figure 7-22 contains four constructors. The Main() method within the CreateSomeEmployees class in Figure 7-23 shows how different types of Employees might be instantiated. Notice that one version of the Employee constructor—the one that supports a character parameter—doesn't even use the parameter; sometimes you might create a constructor with a specific parameter type simply to force that constructor to be the version that executes. The output of the CreateSomeEmployees program is shown in Figure 7-24.

```
public class Employee
{
    public int IdNumber {get; set;}
    public double Salary {get; set;}
    public Employee()
    {
        IdNumber = 999;
        Salary = 0;
    }
    public Employee(int empId)
    {
        IdNumber = empId;
        Salary = 0;
    }
    public Employee(int empId, double sal)
    {
        IdNumber = empId;
        Salary = sal;
    }
    public Employee(char code)
    {
        IdNumber = 111;
        Salary = 100000;
    }
}
```


Figure 7-22 Employee class with four constructors

NOTE In Figure 7-22, fields could have been declared for idNumber and salary, but they have been omitted because they are not necessary when auto-implemented properties are declared and the field names are not required by any other methods.

```
using System;
public class CreateSomeEmployees
{
    public static void Main()
    {
        Employee aWorker = new Employee();
        Employee anotherWorker = new Employee(234);
        Employee theBoss = new Employee('A');
        Console.WriteLine("{0,4}{1,14}", aWorker.IdNumber,
            aWorker.Salary.ToString("C"));
        Console.WriteLine("{0,4}{1,14}", anotherWorker.IdNumber,
            anotherWorker.Salary.ToString("C"));
        Console.WriteLine("{0,4}{1,14}", theBoss.IdNumber,
            theBoss.Salary.ToString("C"));
    }
}
```

Figure 7-23 `CreateSomeEmployees` program

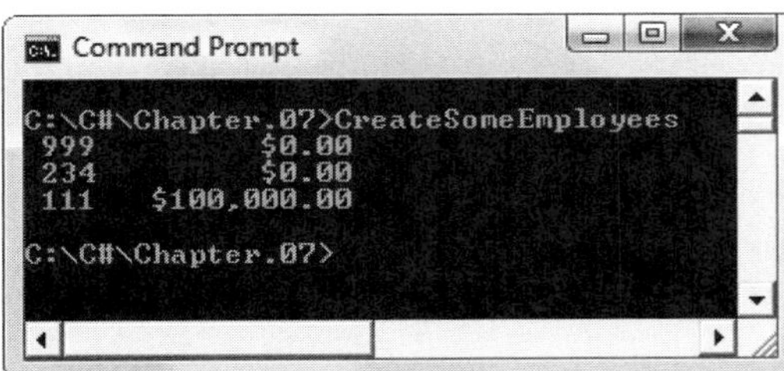

Figure 7-24 Output of `CreateSomeEmployees` program

Most likely, a single application would not use all four constructors of the `Employee` class. More likely, each application that uses the class would use only one or two constructors. You create a class with multiple constructors to provide flexibility for your clients. For example, some clients might choose to construct `Employee` objects with just ID numbers, and others might prefer to construct them with ID numbers and salaries.

USING CONSTRUCTOR INITIALIZERS

The `Employee` class in Figure 7-22 contains four constructors, and each constructor initializes the same two fields. In a fully developed class used by a company, many more fields would be initialized, creating a lot of duplicated code. Besides the original extra work of writing the repetitive statements in these constructors, even more extra work will be required when the class is modified in the future. For example, if your organization institutes a new employee ID number format that requires a specific number of digits, then each constructor will have to be modified. Besides the extra work to modify each constructor, it is possible that one or more of the constructor versions will be overlooked, introducing errors into the programs that are clients of the class.

As an alternative to repeating code in the constructors, you can use a constructor initializer. A **constructor initializer** is a clause that indicates another instance of a class constructor should be executed before any statements in the current constructor body. Figure 7-25 shows a new version of the Employee class using constructor initializers in three of the four overloaded constructor versions.

```
public class Employee
{
    public int IdNumber {get; set;}
    public double Salary {get; set;}
    public Employee() : this(999, 0)
    {
    }
    public Employee(int empId) : this(empId, 0)
    {
    }
    public Employee(int empId, double sal)
    {
        IdNumber = empId;
        Salary = sal;
    }
    public Employee(char code) : this(111, 100000)
    {
    }
}
```

Figure 7-25 Employee class with constructor initializers

In the three shaded clauses in Figure 7-25, the this reference is used to mean "the constructor for this object being constructed." For example, when a client calls the parameterless Employee constructor, 999 and 0 are passed to the two-parameter constructor. There, they become empId and sal, parameters that are assigned to the IdNumber and Salary properties. If there were statements within the parameterless constructor, they would then execute; however, in this class, there is no reason for additional statements. Similarly, if a client uses the constructor version that accepts only an ID number, that parameter and a 0 for salary are passed to the two-parameter constructor. The only time just one version of the constructor executes is when a client uses both an ID number and a salary as constructor arguments. In the future, if additional statements needed to be added to the class (for example, a decision that ensures an ID number was at least five digits at construction), the decision would be added only to the two-parameter version of the constructor, and all the other versions could use it.

»TWO TRUTHS AND A LIE: UNDERSTANDING CONSTRUCTORS

1. Every class you create is automatically supplied with a `public` constructor with no parameters.

2. If you write a constructor for a class, you do not have a default constructor for the class.

3. Any constructor you write must have the same name as its class, and constructors cannot have a return type.

The false statement is #2. If you write a parameterless constructor for a class, it becomes the default constructor, and you lose the automatically supplied version. If you write only constructors that require parameters, then the class no longer contains a default constructor.

PASSING OBJECTS TO METHODS

You can pass objects to methods just as you can simple data types. For example, the `CreateSomeEmployees` application in Figure 7-23 can be rewritten as shown in Figure 7-26. In this version, instead of repeating the details of the `WriteLine()` method, the statement can be placed in its own method, and each `Employee` object can be passed into it, in turn. The output of the program in Figure 7-27 is identical to the output shown in Figure 7-24.

```csharp
using System;
public class CreateSomeEmployees2
{
    public static void Main()
    {
        Employee aWorker = new Employee();
        Employee anotherWorker = new Employee(234);
        Employee theBoss = new Employee('A');
        WriteEmployeeData(aWorker);
        WriteEmployeeData(anotherWorker);
        WriteEmployeeData(theBoss);
    }
    public static void WriteEmployeeData(Employee emp)
    {
        Console.WriteLine("{0,4}{1,14}", emp.IdNumber, emp.Salary.ToString("C"));
    }
}
```

Figure 7-26 `CreateSomeEmployees2` program

Figure 7-27 Output of `CreateSomeEmployees2` program

When you pass an object to a method, you pass a reference. Therefore, any change made to an object parameter in a method also affects the object used as an argument in the calling method.

T T F

»TWO TRUTHS AND A LIE: PASSING OBJECTS TO METHODS

1. You can pass objects to methods just as you can pass simple data types.
2. When you pass an object to a method, you pass a copy of the object used as an argument in the calling statement.
3. Any change made to an object parameter in a method also affects the object used as an argument in the calling method.

The false statement is #2. When you pass an object to a method, you pass a reference. That is, you pass the memory address of the object.

USING OBJECT INITIALIZERS

An **object initializer** allows you to assign values to any accessible members or properties of a class at the time of instantiation without calling a constructor with parameters. For example, assuming an `Employee` class has been created with a public `IdNumber` property and a parameterless constructor, you can write an object initializer as follows:

```
Employee aWorker = new Employee {IdNumber = 101};
```

In this statement, 101 is assigned to the `aWorker` object's `IdNumber` property. The assignment is made within a pair of curly braces; no parentheses are used with the class name. When this statement executes, the parameterless, default constructor for the class is executed first, and then the object initializer assignment is made.

For example, Figure 7-28 shows an `Employee` class that contains properties for `IdNumber` and `Salary` and a default constructor that assigns a value to `Salary`. For demonstration purposes, the constructor displays the current object's ID number and salary. Figure 7-29 shows a program that instantiates one `Employee` object and displays its value, and Figure 7-30 shows the output. When the object is created in the shaded statement in Figure 7-29, the constructor executes,

```
class Employee
{
    public int IdNumber {get; set;}
    public double Salary {get; set;}
    public Employee()
    {
        Salary = 99.99;
        Console.WriteLine("Employee #{0} created. Salary is {1}.",
            IdNumber, Salary);
    }
}
```

Figure 7-28 Employee class with default constructor that assigns Salary and displays data

```
using System;
public class DemoObjectInitializer
{
    public static void Main()
    {
        Employee aWorker = new Employee {IdNumber = 101};
        Console.WriteLine("Employee #{0} exists. Salary is {1}.",
            aWorker.IdNumber, aWorker.Salary);
    }
}
```

Figure 7-29 DemoObjectInitializer program

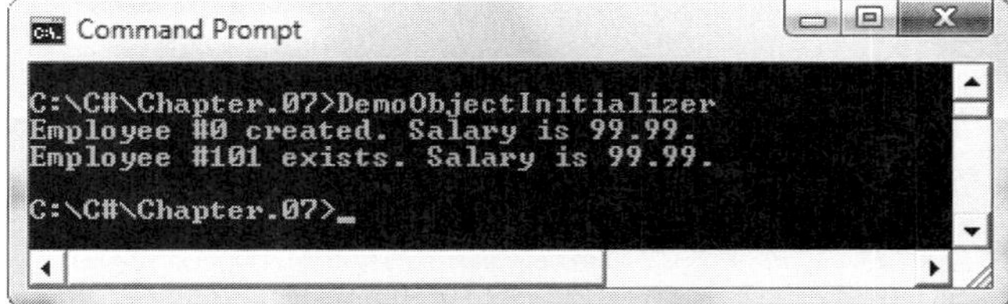

Figure 7-30 Output of DemoObjectInitializer program

assigns 99.99 to Salary, and displays the first line of output in Figure 7-30, showing
IdNumber is still 0. After the object is constructed in the Main() method in Figure 7-29,
the next output line is displayed, showing that the assignment of the ID number occurred
after construction.

For you to use object initializers, a class must have a default constructor. That is, you must not have created any constructors, or you must have created one that requires no parameters.

Multiple assignments can be made with an object initializer by separating them with commas, as in the following:

```
Employee myAssistant = new Employee {IdNumber = 202, Salary = 25.00};
```

This single code line has the same results as the following three statements:

```
Employee myAssistant = new Employee();
myAssistant.IdNumber = 202;
myAssistant.Salary = 25.00;
```

Using object initializers allows you to create multiple objects with different initial assignments without having to provide multiple constructors to cover every possible situation. Additionally, using object initializers allows you to create objects with different starting values for different properties of the same data type. For example, consider a class like the Box class in Figure 7-31 that contains multiple properties of the same type. The constructor sets the Height, Width, and Depth properties to 1. You could write a constructor that accepts an

```
class Box
{
    public int Height {get; set;}
    public int Width {get; set;}
    public int Depth {get; set;}
    public Box()
    {
        Height = 1;
        Width = 1;
        Depth = 1;
    }
}
```

Figure 7-31 The Box class

integer parameter to be assigned to Height (using the default value 1 for the other dimensions), but then you could not write an additional overloaded constructor that accepts an integer parameter to be assigned to Width because the constructors would be ambiguous. However, by using object initializers, you can create objects to which you assign the properties you want. Figure 7-32 shows a program that declares three Box objects, each with a different assigned dimension, and Figure 7-33 shows the output, which demonstrates that each property was assigned appropriately.

```
using System;
public class DemoObjectInitializer2
{
    public static void Main()
    {
      Box box1 = new Box {Height = 3};
      Box box2 = new Box {Width = 15};
      Box box3 = new Box {Depth = 268};
      DisplayDimensions(1, box1);
      DisplayDimensions(2, box2);
      DisplayDimensions(3, box3);
    }
    public static void DisplayDimensions(int num, Box box)
    {
        Console.WriteLine("Box {0}: Height: {1} Width: {2} Depth: {3}",
          num, box.Height, box.Width, box.Depth);
    }
}
```

Figure 7-32 The `DemoObjectInitializer2` program

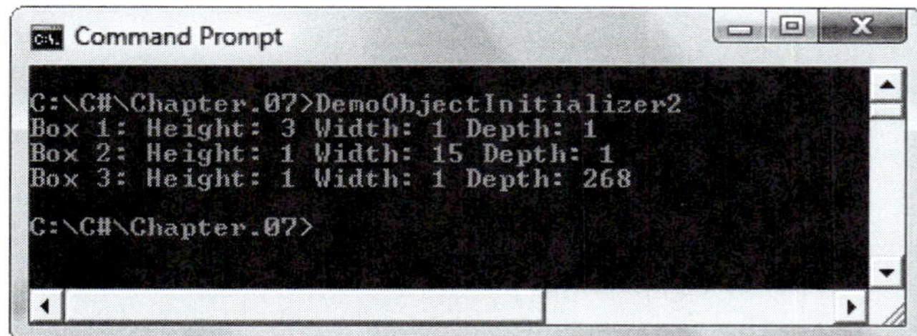

Figure 7-33 Output of the `DemoObjectInitializer2` program

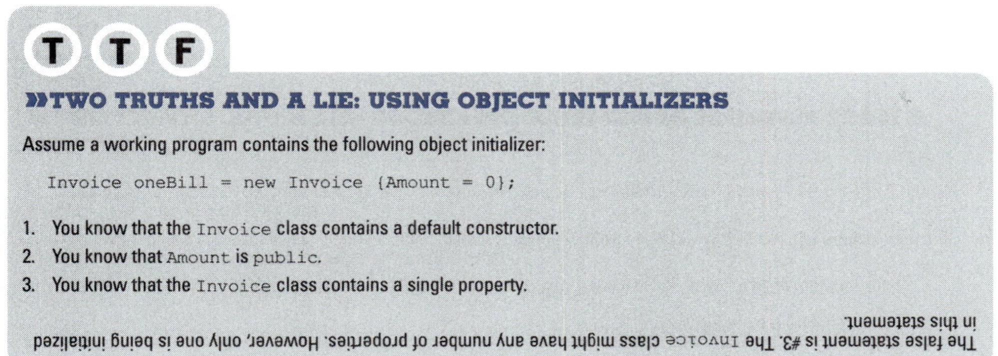

»TWO TRUTHS AND A LIE: USING OBJECT INITIALIZERS

Assume a working program contains the following object initializer:

```
Invoice oneBill = new Invoice {Amount = 0};
```

1. You know that the `Invoice` class contains a default constructor.
2. You know that `Amount` is `public`.
3. You know that the `Invoice` class contains a single property.

The false statement is #3. The `Invoice` class might have any number of properties. However, only one is being initialized in this statement.

OVERLOADING OPERATORS

C# operators are the symbols you use to perform operations on objects. You have used many operators, including arithmetic operators (such as + and –) and logical operators (such as == and <). Separate actions can result from what seems to be the same operation or command. This occurs frequently in all computer programming languages, not just object-oriented languages. For example, in most programming languages and applications such as spreadsheets and databases, the + operator has a variety of meanings. A few of them include:

- » Alone before a value (called unary form), + indicates a positive value, as in the expression +7.
- » Between two integers (called binary form), + indicates integer addition, as in the expression 5 + 9.
- » Between two floating-point numbers (also called binary form), + indicates floating-point addition, as in the expression 6.4 + 2.1.

Expressing a value as positive is a different operation from using the + operator to perform arithmetic, so + is overloaded several times in that it can take one or two arguments and have a different meaning in each case. It also can take different operand types—you use a + to add two `int`s, two `double`s, an `int` and a `double`, and a variety of other combinations. Each use results in different actions behind the scenes.

> **» NOTE** In addition to overloading, compilers often need to perform coercion, or implicit casting, when the + symbol is used with mixed arithmetic. For example, when an integer and floating-point number are added in C#, the integer is coerced into a floating-point number before the appropriate addition code executes. You learned about casting in Chapter 2.

Just as it is convenient to use a + between both integers and `double`s to add them, it also can be convenient to use a + between objects, such as `Employees` or `Books`, to add them. To be able to use arithmetic symbols with your own objects, you must overload the symbols.

C# operators are classified as unary or binary, depending on whether they take one or two arguments, respectively. The rules for overloading are shown in the following list:

- » The overloadable unary operators are:

  ```
  + - ! ~ ++ -- true false
  ```

> **» NOTE** Although `true` and `false` are not used explicitly as operators in expressions, they are considered operators in Boolean expressions and in expressions involving the conditional operator and conditional logical operators.

- » The overloadable binary operators are:

  ```
  + - * / % & | ^ == != > < >= <=
  ```

- » You cannot overload the following operators:

  ```
  = && || ?? ?: checked unchecked new typeof as is
  ```

» You cannot overload an operator for a built-in data type. For example, you cannot change the meaning of + between two `int`s.

» When a binary operator is overloaded and it has a corresponding assignment operator, it is also overloaded. For example, if you overload +, then += is automatically overloaded too.

» Some operators must be overloaded in pairs. For example, when you overload ==, you also must overload !=, and when you overload >, you also must overload <.

> **»NOTE**
> You are already familiar with about half of these operators. You will learn more about the rest as you continue to study C#.

> **»NOTE** When you overload ==, you also receive warnings about methods in the `Object` class. You will learn about this class in Chapter 8; you should not attempt to overload == until you have studied that chapter.

You have used many of the operators listed above. If you want to include these operators in your own classes, you must decide what the operator will mean in your class. When you do, you write statements in a method to carry out your meaning. The method has a return type and arguments just like other methods, but its identifier is required to be followed by the operator being overloaded; for example, `operator+()` or `operator*()`.

> **»NOTE** For an overloaded unary operator, the method has the following format:
> *type* `operator` *overloadable-operator* (*type identifier*)

> **»NOTE** For an overloaded binary operator, the method has the following format:
> *type* `operator` *overloadable-operator* (*type identifier, type operand*)

For example, suppose you create a `Book` class in which each object has a title, number of pages, and a price. Further assume that, as a publisher, you have decided to "add" `Book`s together. That is, you want to take two existing `Book`s and combine them into one. Assume you want the new book to have the following characteristics:

» The new title is a combination of the old titles, joined by the word "and."

» The number of pages in the new book is equal to the sum of the pages in the original `Book`s.

» Instead of charging twice as much for a new `Book`, you have decided to charge the price of the more expensive of the two original `Book`s, plus $10.

A different publisher might have decided that "adding `Book`s" means something different—for example, an added `Book` might have a fixed new price of $29.99. The statements you write in your `operator+()` method depend on how you define adding for your class. You could write an ordinary method to perform these tasks, but you could also overload the + operator to mean "add two `Book`s." Figure 7-34 shows a `Book` class. (This class actually is an expanded version of the `Book` class in Figure 7-15, modified to use auto-implemented properties and to add the `operator+()` method.) This class has properties for each field and a shaded `operator+()` method.

```
class Book
{
    public Book(string title, int pages, double price)
    {
        Title = title;
        NumPages = pages;
        Price = price;
    }
    public static Book operator+(Book first, Book second)
    {
        const double EXTRA = 10.00;
        string newTitle = first.Title + " and " +
            second.Title;
        int newPages = first.NumPages + second.NumPages;
        double newPrice;
        if(first.Price > second.Price)
            newPrice = first.Price + EXTRA;
        else
            newPrice = second.Price + EXTRA;
        return(new Book(newTitle, newPages, newPrice));
    }
    public string Title {get; set;}
    public int NumPages {get; set;}
    public double Price {get; set;}
}
```

Figure 7-34 `Book` class with overloaded + operator

The `operator+()` method in Figure 7-34 is declared to be `public` (so that class clients can use it) and `static`, which is required. The return type is `Book` because the addition of two `Book`s is defined to be a new `Book` with different values from either of the originals. You could overload the + operator so that when two `Book`s are added they return some other type, but it is most common to make the addition of two objects result in an "answer" of the same type.

The two parameters in the `operator+()` method in the `Book` class are both `Book`s. Therefore, when you eventually call this method, the data types on both sides of the + sign will be `Book`s. For example, you could write other methods that add a `Book` and an `Employee`, or a `Book` and a `double`.

Within the `operator+()` method, the statements perform the following tasks:

» A constant is declared to hold the extra price used in creating a new `Book` from two existing ones.

» A new string is created and assigned the first parameter `Book`'s title, plus the `string` " and ", plus the second parameter `Book`'s title.

» A new integer is declared and assigned the sum of the number of pages in each of the parameter `Book`s.

» A new `double` is declared and assigned the value of the more expensive original `Book` plus $10.00.

» Within the `return` statement, a new anonymous `Book` is created (an anonymous object is one without an identifier) using the new title, page number, and price, and returned to the calling method. (Instead of an anonymous `Book`, it would have been perfectly acceptable to use two statements—the first one creating a named `Book` with the same arguments, and the second one returning the named `Book`.)

> **» NOTE** It is possible to rewrite the `operator+()` method in the `Book` class in Figure 7-34 so that all the work is done in the `return` statement. For example:
>
> ```
> public static Book operator+(Book first, Book second)
> {
>    const double EXTRA = 10.00;
>    return(new Book(first.Title + " and " + second.Title,
>       first.NumPages + second.NumPages,
>       first.Price > second.Price ? first.Price + EXTRA :
>          second.Price + EXTRA));
> }
> ```

```
using System;
public class AddBooks
{
   public static void Main()
   {
      Book book1 = new Book("Silas Marner", 350, 15.95);
      Book book2 = new Book("Moby Dick", 250, 16.00);
      Book book3;
      book3 = book1 + book2;
      Console.WriteLine("The new book is \"{0}\"", book3.Title);
      Console.WriteLine("It has {0} pages and costs {1}",
         book3.NumPages, book3.Price.ToString("C"));
   }
}
```

Figure 7-35 The `AddBooks` program

Figure 7-35 shows a client program that can use the + operator in the `Book` class. It first declares three `Book`s; then, in the shaded statement, it adds two `Book`s together and assigns the result to the third. When `book1` and `book2` are added, the `operator+()` method is called automatically because the + sign is used in the code. The returned `Book` is assigned to `book3`, which is then displayed. Figure 7-36 shows the results.

Figure 7-36 Output of the `AddBooks` program

>> **NOTE** Because each addition operation returns a `Book`, it is possible to chain addition in a statement such as `collection = book1 + book2 + book3;` (assuming all the variables have been declared to be `Book` objects). In this example, `book1` and `book2` would be added, returning a temporary `Book`. Then the temporary `Book` and `book3` would be added, returning a different temporary `Book` that would be assigned to `collection`.

In the `Book` class, it took many statements to overload the operator; however, in the client class, just typing a + between objects allows a programmer to use the objects and operator intuitively. You could write any statements you wanted within the operator method. However, for clarity, you should write statements that intuitively have the same meaning as the common use of the operator. For example, although you could overload the `operator*()` method to display a `Book`'s title and price instead of performing multiplication, it would be a bad programming technique.

>> **NOTE** When you overload an operator in a class, at least one argument to the method must be a member of the class. In other words, within the `Book` class, you can overload `operator*()` to multiply a `Book` by an integer, but you cannot overload `operator*()` to multiply a `double` by an integer.

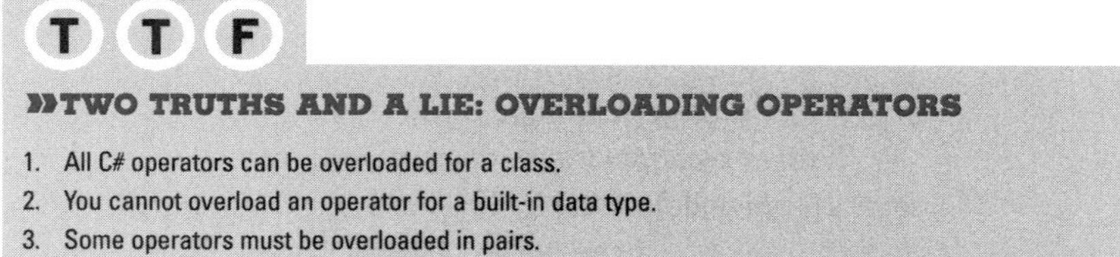

>>TWO TRUTHS AND A LIE: OVERLOADING OPERATORS

1. All C# operators can be overloaded for a class.
2. You cannot overload an operator for a built-in data type.
3. Some operators must be overloaded in pairs.

The false statement is #1. You cannot overload the following operators:
= && || ?? ?: checked unchecked new typeof as is

DECLARING AN ARRAY OF OBJECTS

Just as you can declare arrays of integers or `doubles`, you can declare arrays that hold elements of any type, including objects. For example, Figure 7-37 shows an abbreviated `Employee` class that contains just one property named `IdNumber`, which gets and sets an implied `idNumber` field.

```
class Employee
{
    public int IdNumber {get; set;}
}
```

Figure 7-37 A simple `Employee` class

Of course, you also can create separate `Employee` objects with unique names, such as in the following statement:

```
Employee painter, electrician, plumber;
```

For many programs, however, it is far more convenient to create an array of `Employee` objects. An array named `empArray` that holds seven `Employee` objects is defined by the following:

```
Employee[] empArray = new Employee[7];
```

This statement reserves enough computer memory for the references to seven `Employee` objects named `empArray`[0] through `empArray`[6]. It does not actually construct those `Employees`; instead, you must call the seven individual constructors to do so. Because the `Employee` class in Figure 7-37 contains a default constructor that requires no arguments, the following loop calls the constructor seven times:

```
for(int x = 0; x < empArray.Length; ++x)
    empArray[x] = new Employee();
```

As x varies from 0 through 6, each of the seven `empArray` objects is constructed.

> **NOTE** When you create an array from a value type, such as `int` or `char`, the array holds the actual values. When you create an array from a reference type, such as a class you create, then the array holds the memory addresses of the objects. In other words, the array "refers to" the objects instead of containing the objects.

> **NOTE** You can create an array of objects and provide default values to the elements' constructors in one step. For example, if an `Inventory` class contains a constructor that requires an integer argument, you can declare an array of `Inventory` objects by writing the following:
>
> ```
> Inventory[] items = {new Inventory(123), new
>     Inventory(345), new Inventory(678)};
> ```

To use a method that belongs to an object that is part of an array, you insert the appropriate subscript notation after the array name and before the dot-method. For example, to set all seven `Employee` `IdNumber` properties to 999, you can write the following:

```
for(int x = 0; x < empArray.Length; ++x)
    empArray[x].IdNumber = 999;
```

USING THE `Sort()` AND `BinarySearch()` METHODS WITH ARRAYS OF OBJECTS

In Chapter 6, you learned about using the `System.Array` class's built-in `BinarySearch()` and `Sort()` methods with simple data types such as `int`, `double`, and `string`. The `Sort()` method accepts an array parameter and arranges its elements in descending order. The `BinarySearch()` method accepts a sorted array and a value that it attempts to match in the array.

A complication arises when you consider searching or sorting arrays of objects you create. When you create and sort an array of simple data items, there is only one type of value to consider, and the order is based on the Unicode value of that item. The classes that support simple data items each contain a method named **CompareTo()**, which provides the details of how the basic data types compare to each other. In other words, they define comparisons such as "2 is more than 1" and "B is more than A." The `Sort()` and `BinarySearch()` methods use the `CompareTo()` method for the current type of data being sorted. In other words, `Sort()` uses the `Int32` version of `CompareTo()` when sorting integers and the `Char` version of `CompareTo()` when sorting characters.

> **》》NOTE** You have been using the `String` class (and its `string` alias) throughout this book. The class also contains a `CompareTo()` method that you first used in Chapter 2.

When you create a class that contains many fields, however, you must tell the compiler which field to use when making comparisons. For example, you logically might sort an organization's `Employee` objects by ID number, salary, department number, last name, hire date, or any field contained in the class. To tell C# which field to use for placing `Employee` objects in order, you must create an interface. An **interface** is a collection of abstract methods (and perhaps other members) that can be used by any class, as long as the class provides a definition to override the interface's do-nothing, or abstract, method definitions. When a method **overrides** another, it takes precedence over the method, hiding the original version. In other words, the methods in an interface are empty, and any class that uses them must contain a new version that provides the details. Interfaces define named behaviors that classes must implement, so that all classes can use the same method names but use them appropriately for the class. In this way, interfaces provide for polymorphism—the ability of different objects to use the same method names but act appropriately based on the context.

> **》》NOTE** When a method overrides another, it has the same signature as the method it overrides. When methods are overloaded, they have different signatures. You learned about method signatures in Chapter 6. You will learn more about overriding methods and abstract methods and classes in Chapter 8.

C# contains an **IComparable interface,** which contains the definition for the `CompareTo()` method that compares one object to another and returns an integer. Figure 7-38 shows the definition of `IComparable`. The `CompareTo()` method accepts an `Object`, but does not contain any statements; you must provide an implementation for this method in classes you create if you want the objects to be comparable.

```
interface IComparable
{
    int CompareTo(Object o);
}
```

Figure 7-38 The `IComparable` interface

When you create a class whose members you predict clients will want to compare:

» You must include a single colon and the interface name `IComparable` after the class name.

» You must write a method that contains the following header:

```
int IComparable.CompareTo(Object o)
```

>> **NOTE** `Object` is a class—the most generic of all classes. Every `Employee` object you create is not only an `Employee`, but also an `Object`. (This concept is similar to "every banana is a fruit" or "every collie is a dog.") By using the type `Object` as a parameter, the `CompareTo()` method can accept anything. You will learn more about the `Object` class in Chapter 8.

To work correctly in methods such as `BinarySearch()` and `Sort()`, the `CompareTo()` method you create for your class must return an integer value. Table 7-1 shows the return values that every version of `CompareTo()` should provide.

Return Value	Meaning
Negative	This instance is less than the compared object.
Zero	This instance is equal to the compared object.
Positive	This instance is greater than the compared object.

Table 7-1 Return values of `IComparable.CompareTo()` method

When you create a class that contains an `IComparable.CompareTo()` method, the method is an instance method and receives a `this` reference to the object used to call it. A second object is passed to the method; within the method, you first must convert, or cast, the passed object to the same type as the calling object's class, and then compare the corresponding fields you want from the `this` object and the passed object. For example, Figure 7-39 shows an `Employee` class that contains a shaded `CompareTo()` method and compares `Employee` objects based on the contents of their `idNumber` fields.

>> **NOTE**
You first learned about casting in Chapter 2.

```
class Employee : IComparable
{
    public int IdNumber {get; set;}
    public double Salary {get; set;}
    int IComparable.CompareTo(Object o)
    {
        int returnVal;
        Employee temp = (Employee)o;
        if(this.IdNumber > temp.IdNumber)
            returnVal = 1;
        else
            if(this.IdNumber < temp.IdNumber)
                returnVal = -1;
            else
                returnVal = 0;
        return returnVal;
    }
}
```

Figure 7-39 `Employee` class using `IComparable` interface

The `Employee` class in Figure 7-39 uses a colon and `IComparable` in its class header to indicate an interface. The shaded method is an instance method; that is, it "belongs" to an `Employee` object. When another `Employee` is passed in as `Object o`, it is cast as an `Employee` and stored in the `temp` variable. The `idNumber` values of the `this` Employee and the passed `Employee` are compared, and one of three integer values is returned.

For example, if you declare two `Employee` objects named `worker1` and `worker2`, you can use the following statement:

```
int answer = worker1.CompareTo(worker2);
```


Within the `CompareTo()` method in the `Employee` class, `worker1` would be "`this`" Employee—the controlling `Employee` in the method. The `temp` Employee would be `worker2`. If, for example, `worker1` had a higher ID number than `worker2`, the value of `answer` would be 1.

Figure 7-40 shows a program that uses the `Employee` class. The program declares an array of five `Employee` objects with different ID numbers and salaries; the ID numbers are purposely out of order to demonstrate that the `Sort()` method works correctly. The program also declares a `seekEmp` object with an ID number of 222. The program sorts the array, displays the sorted elements, then finds the array element that matches the `seekEmp` object. Figure 7-41 shows the program execution.

```
using System;
public class ComparableEmployeeArray
{
    public static void Main()
    {
        Employee[] empArray = new Employee[5];
        int x;
        for(x = 0; x < empArray.Length; ++x)
            empArray[x] = new Employee();
        empArray[0].IdNumber = 333;
        empArray[1].IdNumber = 444;
        empArray[2].IdNumber = 555;
        empArray[3].IdNumber = 111;
        empArray[4].IdNumber = 222;
        Employee seekEmp = new Employee();
        seekEmp.IdNumber = 222;
        Array.Sort(empArray);
        Console.WriteLine("Sorted employees:");
        for(x = 0; x < empArray.Length; ++x)
            Console.WriteLine("Employee #{0}: {1} {2}",
                x, empArray[x].IdNumber,
                empArray[x].Salary.ToString("C"));
        x = Array.BinarySearch(empArray, seekEmp);
        Console.WriteLine("Employee #{0} was found at position {1}",
            seekEmp.IdNumber, x);
    }
}
```

Figure 7-40 `ComparableEmployeeArray` program

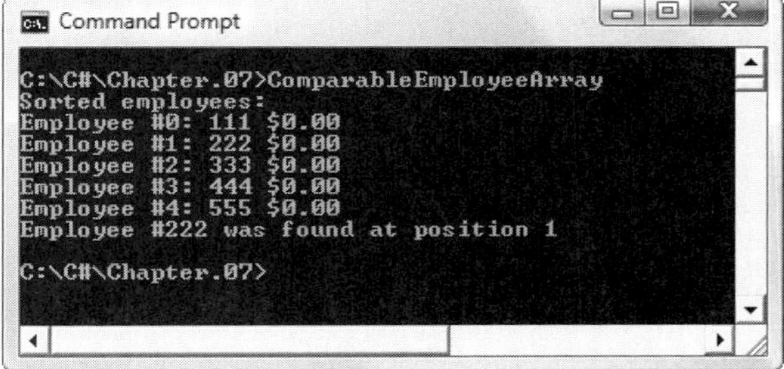

Figure 7-41 Output of `ComparableEmployeeArray` program

Notice that the `seekEmp` object matches the `Employee` in the second array position based on the `idNumber` only—not the salary—because the `CompareTo()` method in the `Employee` class uses only `idNumber` values and not salaries to make comparisons. You *could* have written code that requires both the `idNumber` and `salary` values to match before returning a positive number.

»TWO TRUTHS AND A LIE: DECLARING AN ARRAY OF OBJECTS

Assume a working program contains the following array declaration:

```
BankAccount[] acctArray = new BankAccount[500];
```

1. This statement reserves enough computer memory for 500 `BankAccount` objects.
2. This statement constructs 500 `BankAccount` objects.
3. The valid subscripts for `acctArray` are 0 through 499.

The false statement is #2. This statement declares 500 `BankAccount` objects but does not actually construct those objects; to do so, you must call the 500 individual constructors.

UNDERSTANDING DESTRUCTORS

»NOTE
You learned about an object's scope in Chapter 6.

A **destructor** contains the actions you require when an instance of a class is destroyed. Most often, an instance of a class is destroyed when it goes out of scope. As with constructors, if you do not explicitly create a destructor for a class, C# automatically provides one.

To explicitly declare a destructor, you use an identifier that consists of a tilde (~) followed by the class name. You cannot provide any parameters to a destructor; it must have an empty argument list. As a consequence, destructors cannot be overloaded; a class can have at most one destructor. Like a constructor, a destructor has no return type.

Figure 7-42 shows an `Employee` class that contains only one property (`IdNumber`), a constructor, and a (shaded) destructor. When you execute the `Main()` method in the `DemoEmployeeDestructor` class in Figure 7-43, you instantiate two `Employee` objects, each with its own `idNumber` value. When the `Main()` method ends, the two `Employee` objects go out of scope, and the destructor for each object is called. Figure 7-44 shows the output.

```
class Employee
{
    public int IdNumber {get; set;}
    public Employee(int empID)
    {
        IdNumber = empID;
        Console.WriteLine("Employee object {0} created", IdNumber);
    }
    ~Employee()
    {
        Console.WriteLine("Employee object {0} destroyed!", IdNumber);
    }
}
```

Figure 7-42 `Employee` class with destructor

```
using System;
public class DemoEmployeeDestructor
{
    public static void Main()
    {
        Employee aWorker = new Employee(101);
        Employee anotherWorker = new Employee(202);
    }
}
```

Figure 7-43 `DemoEmployeeDestructor` program

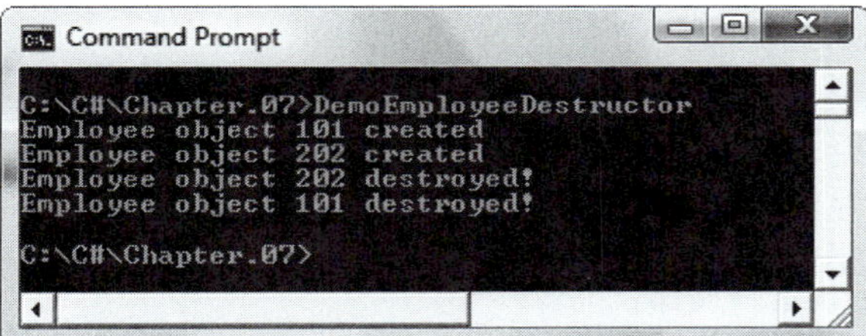

Figure 7-44 Output of `DemoEmployeeDestructor` program

The program in Figure 7-43 never explicitly calls the `Employee` class destructor, yet you can see from the output that the destructor executes twice. Destructors are invoked automatically; you cannot explicitly call one. Interestingly, the last object created is the first object destroyed; the same relationship would hold true no matter how many objects the program instantiated.

For now, you have little reason to create a destructor except to demonstrate how it is called automatically. Later, when you write more sophisticated C# programs that work with files, databases, or large quantities of computer memory, you might want to perform specific clean-up or close-down tasks when an object goes out of scope. Then you will place appropriate instructions within a destructor.

»TWO TRUTHS AND A LIE: UNDERSTANDING DESTRUCTORS

1. To explicitly declare a destructor, you use an identifier that consists of a tilde (~) followed by the class name.
2. You cannot provide any parameters to a destructor; it must have an empty argument list.
3. The return type for a destructor is always `void`.

The false statement is #3. Like a constructor, a destructor has no return type.

YOU DO IT

CREATING A CLASS AND OBJECTS

In this section, you will create a `Student` class and instantiate objects from it. This class contains an ID number, last name, and grade point average for the `Student`. It also contains properties that get and set each of these fields. You will also pass each `Student` object to a method.

To create a `Student` class:

1. Open a new file in your text editor. Begin the `Student` class by declaring the class name, inserting an opening curly brace, and declaring three `private` fields that will hold an ID number, last name, and grade point average, as follows:

```
class Student
{
    private int idNumber;
    private string lastName;
    private double gradePointAverage;
```

2. Add two constants that represent the highest and lowest possible values for a grade point average.

```
public const double HIGHEST_GPA = 4.0;
public const double LOWEST_GPA = 0.0;
```

3. Add two properties that get and set `idNumber` and `lastName`. By convention, properties have an identifier that is the same as the field they service, except they start with a capital letter.

```
public int IdNumber
{
    get
    {
        return idNumber;
    }
    set
    {
        idNumber = value;
    }
}
public string LastName
{
    get
    {
        return lastName;
    }
    set
    {
        lastName = value;
    }
}
```

4. Add the following `set` accessor in the property for the `gradePointAverage` field.
   It sets limits on the value assigned, assigning 0 if the value is out of range.

```
public double GradePointAverage
{
   get
   {
      return gradePointAverage;
   }
   set
   {
      if(value >= LOWEST_GPA && value <= HIGHEST_GPA)
         gradePointAverage = value;
      else
         gradePointAverage = LOWEST_GPA;
   }
}
```

5. Add a closing curly brace for the class. Save the file as **Student.cs**.

6. Open a new file in your text editor and begin a program that creates two `Student`
   objects, assigns some values, and displays the `Student`s.

```
using System;
public class CreateStudents
{
```

7. Add a `Main()` method that declares two `Student`s. Assign field values, including one
   "illegal" value—a grade point average that is too high.

```
public static void Main()
{
   Student first = new Student();
   Student second = new Student();
   first.IdNumber = 123;
   first.LastName = "Anderson";
   first.GradePointAverage = 3.5;
   second.IdNumber = 789;
   second.LastName = "Daniels";
   second.GradePointAverage = 4.1;
```

8. Instead of creating similar `WriteLine()` statements to display the two
   `Student`s, call a method with each `Student`. You will create the method to
   accept a `Student` argument in the next step. Add a closing curly brace for the
   `Main()` method.

```
   Display(first);
   Display(second);
}
```

9. Write the `Display()` method so that the passed-in `Student`'s `IdNumber`, `LastName`, and `GradePointAverage` are displayed and aligned. Add a closing curly brace for the class.

```
public static void Display(Student stu)
{
    Console.WriteLine("{0,5}{1,-10}{2,6}",
        stu.IdNumber, stu.LastName,
        stu.GradePointAverage.ToString("F1"));
}
}
```

10. Save the file as **CreateStudents.cs**.

11. You can choose to create a multifile assembly, as described in Appendix B; or, for convenience, you can combine the two files into one. Either way, compile the files and execute the program. Figure 7-45 shows the output. Each `Student` has unique data values and uses the same `Display()` method. Notice how the second `Student`'s grade point average was forced to 0 by the `set` accessor in the property for the field.

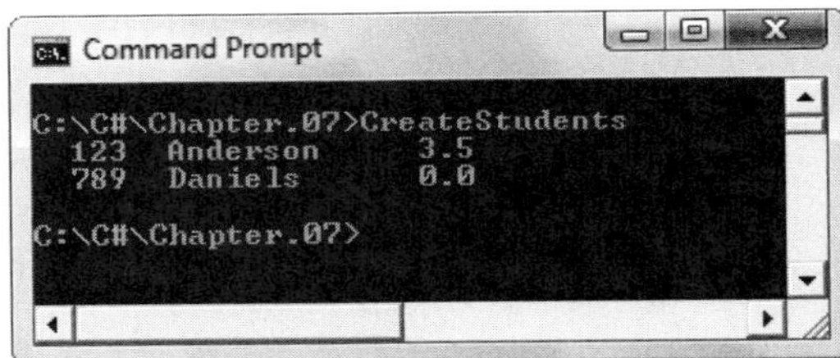

Figure 7-45 Output of `CreateStudents` program

USING AUTO-IMPLEMENTED PROPERTIES

When a property's `get` accessor simply returns the corresponding field's value, and its `set` accessor simply assigns a value to the appropriate field, you can reduce the code in your classes by using auto-implemented properties. In the `Student` class, both `IdNumber` and `LastName` are candidates for this shortcut, so you can replace the full versions of these properties with their auto-implemented versions. The `GradePointAverage` property cannot take advantage of auto-implementation because additional code is required for the property to fulfill its intended function.

To include auto-implemented properties in the `Student` class:

1. Open the file that contains the `Student` class if it is not still open on your screen. Remove the properties for `IdNumber` and `LastName` and replace them with these auto-implemented versions:

```
public int IdNumber {get; set;}
public string LastName {get; set;}
```

2. Save the file and recompile it. Execute the `CreateStudents` program. The output is the same as when the program used the original version of the `Student` class in Figure 7-45.

ADDING OVERLOADED CONSTRUCTORS TO A CLASS

Frequently, you create constructors for a class so that fields will hold initial values when objects are instantiated. You can overload constructors by writing multiple versions with different parameter lists; you often want to do this so that different clients can use your class in the way that suits them best.

To add overloaded constructors to the Student class:

1. Open the file that contains the Student class if it is not still open on your screen. Just before the closing curly brace for the Student class, add the following constructor. It takes three parameters and assigns them to the appropriate fields:

```
public Student(int id, string name, double gpa)
{
    IdNumber = id;
    LastName = name;
    GradePointAverage = gpa;
}
```

2. Add a second parameterless constructor. It calls the first constructor, passing 0 for the ID number, "XXX" for the name, and 0.0 for the grade point average. Its body is empty.

```
public Student() : this(0, "XXX", 0.0)
{
}
```

3. Save the file.

4. Open the **CreateStudents.cs** file and immediately save it as **CreateStudents2.cs**. Change the class name to CreateStudents2. If you previously included a copy of the Student class within this file, replace the Student class with the new version to which you just added constructors.

5. After the existing declarations of the Student objects, add two more declarations. With one, use three arguments, but with the other, do not use any.

```
Student third = new Student(456, "Marco", 2.4);
Student fourth = new Student();
```

6. At the end of the Main() method, just after the two existing calls to the Display() method, add two more calls using the new objects.

```
Display(third);
Display(fourth);
```

7. Save the file, then compile and execute it. The output looks like Figure 7-46. All four objects are displayed. The first two have had values assigned to them after declaration, but the third and fourth ones obtained their values from their constructors.

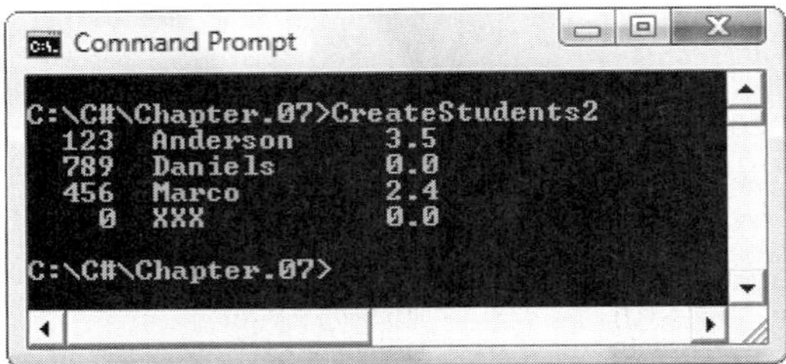

Figure 7-46 Output of CreateStudents2 program

CREATING AN ARRAY OF OBJECTS

Just like variables of the built-in, primitive data types, objects you create can be stored in arrays. In the next steps, you will create an array of Student objects. You will prompt the user for data to fill the array, and you will sort the array by student ID number before displaying all the data.

To create and use an array of objects:

1. Open the **CreateStudents2.cs** file and immediately save it as **CreateStudents3.cs**. Change the class name to **CreateStudents3**.

2. Delete all the existing statements in the Main() method, leaving the opening and closing curly braces. Between the braces, declare an array of eight Student objects. Also declare a variable to use as an array subscript and declare three variables that will temporarily hold a user's input data before Student objects are constructed.

```
Student[] student = new Student[8];
int x;
int id;
string name;
double gpa;
```

3. In a loop, call a GetData() method (which you will write shortly); send it out arguments so that you can retrieve values for variables that will hold an ID number, name, and grade point average. Then, in turn, send these three values to the Student constructor for each of the eight Student objects.

```
for(x = 0; x < student.Length; ++x)
{
    GetData(out id, out name, out gpa);
    student[x] = new Student(id, name, gpa);
}
```

4. Call the Array.Sort() method, sending it the student array. Then, one object at a time in a loop, call the Display() method that you wrote in a previous set of steps.

```
Array.Sort(student);
Console.WriteLine("Sorted List:");
for(x = 0; x < student.Length; ++x)
    Display(student[x]);
```

5. Write the GetData() method. Its parameters are out parameters so that their values will be known to the calling method. The method simply prompts the user for each data item, reads it, and converts it to the appropriate type, if necessary.

```
public static void GetData(out int id, out string name,
   out double gpa)
   {
      string inString;
      Console.Write("Please enter student ID number ");
      inString = Console.ReadLine();
      id = Convert.ToInt32(inString);
      Console.Write("Please enter last name for " +
         "student {0} ", id);
      name = Console.ReadLine();
      Console.Write("Please enter grade point average ");
      inString = Console.ReadLine();
      gpa = Convert.ToDouble(inString);
   }
```

6. Copy the existing Student class to the bottom of the current file, if necessary. After the class header, add a colon and **IComparable** so that objects of the class can be sorted.

```
public class Student : IComparable
```

7. Just before the closing curly brace for the Student class, add the IComparable.CompareTo() method that is required for the objects of the class to be sortable. The method will sort Student objects based on their ID numbers, so it returns 1, –1, or 0 based on IdNumber property comparisons. The method accepts an object that is cast to a Student object. If the IdNumber of the controlling Student object is greater than the argument's IdNumber, then the return value is set to 1. If the IdNumber of the controlling Student object is less than the argument's IdNumber, then the return value is –1. Otherwise, the return value is 0.

```
int IComparable.CompareTo(Object o)
{
   int returnVal;
   Student temp = (Student)o;
   if(this.IdNumber > temp.IdNumber)
      returnVal = 1;
   else
      if(this.IdNumber < temp.IdNumber)
         returnVal = -1;
      else
         returnVal = 0;
   return returnVal;
}
```

8. Save the file (as CreateStudents3.cs) and compile and execute it. When prompted, enter any student IDs, names, and grade point averages you choose. The objects will be sorted and displayed. Figure 7-47 shows a typical execution. After the Student array is sorted, the Student objects appear in idNumber order.

```
C:\C#\Chapter.07>CreateStudents3
Please enter student ID number 546
Please enter last name for student 546 Parker
Please enter grade point average 3.4
Please enter student ID number 312
Please enter last name for student 312 Yoder
Please enter grade point average 2.9
Please enter student ID number 762
Please enter last name for student 762 Kaplan
Please enter grade point average 3.0
Please enter student ID number 455
Please enter last name for student 455 Patel
Please enter grade point average 2.4
Please enter student ID number 810
Please enter last name for student 810 Gonzales
Please enter grade point average 4.0
Please enter student ID number 598
Please enter last name for student 598 Blough
Please enter grade point average 3.1
Please enter student ID number 267
Please enter last name for student 267 Beckmore
Please enter grade point average 3.5
Please enter student ID number 389
Please enter last name for student 389 Walters
Please enter grade point average 2.2
Sorted List:
   267   Beckmore       3.5
   312   Yoder          2.9
   389   Walters        2.2
   455   Patel          2.4
   546   Parker         3.4
   598   Blough         3.1
   762   Kaplan         3.0
   810   Gonzales       4.0

C:\C#\Chapter.07>
```

Figure 7-47 Typical execution of `CreateStudents3` program

CHAPTER SUMMARY

» When you write programs in C#, you create classes that are only programs
with a `Main()` method and classes from which you instantiate objects. The data
components of a class are its instance variables. Object attributes often are called
fields to help distinguish them from other variables you might use. In addition
to their attributes, objects have methods associated with them, and every object
that is an instance of a class is assumed to possess the same methods. A program
or class that instantiates objects of another prewritten class is a class client or
class user.

» When you create a class, you must assign a name to it and determine what data and
methods will be part of the class. A class header or class definition contains an optional
access modifier, the keyword `class`, and any legal identifier you choose for the name of
your class. In addition to the class header, classes you create must have a class body
enclosed between curly braces.

» When you create a class, you define both its attributes and its methods. You usually
declare instance variables to be `private` and instance methods to be `public`.

» When you create an object that is an instance of a class, you supply a type and an identifier, and you allocate computer memory for that object using the `new` operator. After an object has been instantiated, its `public` methods can be accessed using the object's identifier, a dot, and a method call.

» A property is a member of a class that provides access to a field of a class; properties define how fields will be set and retrieved. Properties have `set` accessors for setting an object's fields and `get` accessors for retrieving the stored values. When you create properties, the syntax in your client programs becomes more natural and easier to understand. As a shortcut, you can create an auto-implemented property when a field's `set` accessor should simply assign a value to the appropriate field, and when its `get` accessor should simply return the field.

» When you create a class that describes objects to be instantiated and another class that instantiates those objects, you can contain the two classes within a single file or place each class in its own file. A class can contain many fields and methods. Although there is no requirement to do so, most programmers place data fields in some logical order at the beginning of a class. For ease in locating class methods and properties, many programmers prefer to store them in alphabetical order. Another logical organization scheme is to store all properties first, in the same order as their corresponding data fields, followed by other methods. An additional aid to keeping your classes organized is to use comments liberally.

» Most of the time, class data fields are `private` and class methods are `public`. This technique ensures that data will be used and changed only in the ways provided in your accessors. Occasionally, however, you need to create `public` fields or `private` methods. For example, you can create a `public` data field when you want all objects of a class to contain the same value. You create a method to be `private` when it should be called only by other methods or accessors within the class and not by outside classes.

» Each instantiation of a class accesses the same copy of its methods. This is possible because an implicit reference, the `this` reference, is passed to every instance method and property accessor. You can explicitly refer to the `this` reference within an instance method or property, but usually you are not required to do so.

» A constructor is a method that instantiates (creates an instance of) an object. Every class you create is automatically supplied with a `public` constructor with no parameters. You can write your own constructor to replace the automatically supplied version. Any constructor you write must have the same name as its class, and constructors cannot have a return type.

» You can pass one or more arguments to a constructor. Frequently you do so to initialize fields.

» An object initializer allows you to assign values to any accessible members or properties of a class at the time of instantiation without calling a constructor with parameters. Using object initializers allows you to create multiple objects with different initial assignments without having to provide multiple constructors to cover every possible situation. Additionally, using object initializers allows you to create objects with different starting values for different properties of the same data type.

» Like any other C# methods, constructors can be overloaded. You can write as many constructors for a class as you want, as long as their argument lists do not cause ambiguity.

» A constructor initializer is a clause that indicates another instance of a class constructor should be executed before any statements in the current constructor body.

» You can pass objects to methods just as you can simple data types.

» You can overload operators to use with objects by writing a method to carry out your meaning. The method has a return type and arguments just like other methods, but its identifier is required to be followed by the operator being overloaded—for example, `operator+()` or `operator*()`. When you overload an operator, you should write statements that intuitively have the same meaning as the common use of the operator.

» Just as you can declare arrays of integers or `doubles`, you can declare arrays that hold elements of any type, including objects. After you declare an array of objects, you must call a constructor for each object. To use a method that belongs to an object that is part of an array, you insert the appropriate subscript notation after the array name and before the dot-method.

» When you create a class that contains many fields, you must tell the compiler which field to use when making comparisons by using an interface—a collection of methods (and perhaps other members) that can be used by any class, as long as the class provides a definition to override the interface's do-nothing, or abstract, method definitions. C# contains an interface named `IComparable`, which in turn contains the definition for the `CompareTo()` method that compares one object to another and returns an integer. You must override this definition in classes you create if you want the objects to be comparable.

» A destructor contains the actions you require when an instance of a class is destroyed. If you do not explicitly create a destructor for a class, C# automatically provides one. To explicitly declare a destructor, you use an identifier that consists of a tilde (~) followed by the class name. You cannot provide any parameters to a destructor; a class can have at most one destructor.

KEY TERMS

Is-a relationships describe object-class relationships.

An **instantiation** of a class is a created object.

The **instance variables** of a class are the data components that exist separately for each instantiation.

Fields are instance variables within a class.

An object's **state** is the set of contents of its fields.

A **class client** or **class user** is a program or class that instantiates objects of another prewritten class.

A **class header** or **class definition** describes a class; it contains an optional access modifier, the keyword `class`, and any legal identifier for the name of the class.

A **class access modifier** describes access to a class.

The **public** class access modifier means access to the class is not limited.

The **protected** class access modifier means access to the class is limited to the class and to any classes derived from the class.

The **internal** class access modifier means access is limited to the assembly to which the class belongs.

The **private** class access modifier means access is limited to another class to which the class belongs. In other words, a class can be private if it is contained within another class, and only the containing class should have access to the private class.

Information hiding is a feature found in all object-oriented languages, in which a class's data is private and changed or manipulated only by its own methods.

Instance methods are methods that are used with object instantiations.

Composition is the technique of using an object within another object.

The relationship created using composition is called a **has-a relationship** because one class "has an" instance of another.

A **reference type** is a type that holds a memory address.

Value types hold a value; they are predefined types such as int, double, and char.

A **property** is a member of a class that provides access to a field of a class; properties define how fields will be set and retrieved.

Accessors in properties specify how a class's fields are accessed.

An object's fields are assigned by **set accessors** that allow use of the assignment operator with a property name.

An object's fields are accessed by **get accessors** that allow retrieval of a field value by using a property name.

A **read-only property** has only a get accessor, and not a set accessor.

The **getter** is another term for a class property's get accessor.

The **setter** is another term for a class property's set accessor.

Contextual keywords are identifiers that act like keywords in specific circumstances.

An **implicit parameter** is undeclared and gets its value automatically.

An **auto-implemented property** is one in which the code within the accessors is created automatically. The only action in the set accessor is to assign a value to the associated field, and the only action in the get accessor is to return the associated field value.

A **primary key** is a field that uniquely identifies a record; the term is often used in databases.

The **this reference** is the reference to an object that is implicitly passed to an instance method of its class.

A **constructor** is a method that instantiates (creates an instance of) an object.

A **default constructor** is an automatically supplied parameterless constructor.

The **default value of an object** is the value initialized with a default constructor.

A **parameterless constructor** is one that takes no arguments.

A **constructor initializer** is a clause that indicates another instance of a class constructor should be executed before any statements in the current constructor body.

An **object initializer** allows you to assign values to any accessible members or properties of a class at the time of instantiation without calling a constructor with parameters.

The **CompareTo() method** of the `IComparable` interface compares one object to another and returns an integer.

An **interface** is a collection of abstract methods (and perhaps other members) that can be used by any class, as long as the class provides a definition to override the interface's do-nothing, or abstract, method definitions.

When a method **overrides** another, it takes precedence over the method, hiding the original version.

The **IComparable interface** contains the definition for the `CompareTo()` method.

An instance method's **invoking object** is the object referenced by `this`.

A **destructor** contains the actions you require when an instance of a class is destroyed.

REVIEW QUESTIONS

1. An object is a(n) __________ of a class.

   a. child

   b. institution

   c. instantiation

   d. relative

2. A class header or class definition can contain all of the following *except* __________ .

   a. an optional access modifier

   b. the keyword `class`

   c. an identifier

   d. initial field values

3. Most class fields are created with the __________ modifier.

   a. `public`

   b. `protected`

   c. `new`

   d. `private`

4. Most class methods are created with the __________ modifier.

   a. `public`

   b. `protected`

   c. `new`

   d. `private`

5. Instance methods that belong to individual objects are __________ `static` methods.

   a. always

   b. usually

   c. occasionally

   d. never

6. To allocate memory for an object instantiation, you must use the __________ operator.

   a. `mem`

   b. `alloc`

   c. `new`

   d. `instant`

7. Assume you have created a class named `MyClass`. The header of the `MyClass` constructor can be __________ .

   a. `public void MyClass()`

   b. `public MyClassConstructor()`

   c. Either of these can be the constructor header.

   d. Neither of these can be the constructor header.

8. Assume you have created a class named `MyClass`. The header of the `MyClass` constructor can be __________ .

   a. `public MyClass()`

   b. `public MyClass (double d)`

   c. Either of these can be the constructor header.

   d. Neither of these can be the constructor header.

9. Assume you have created a class named `DemoCar`. Within the `Main()` method of this class, you instantiate a `Car` object named `myCar` and the following statement executes correctly:

   ```
   Console.WriteLine("The Car gets {0} miles per gallon",
       myCar.ComputeMpg());
   ```

   Within the `Car` class, the `ComputeMpg()` method must be __________ .

   a. `public` and `static`

   b. `public` and nonstatic

   c. `private` and `static`

   d. `private` and nonstatic

10. Assume you have created a class named `TermPaper` that contains a character field named `letterGrade`. You also have created a property for the field. Which of the following cannot be true?

    a. The property name is `letterGrade`.

    b. The property is read-only.

    c. The property contains a `set` accessor that does not allow a grade lower than 'C'.

    d. The property does not contain a `get` accessor.

11. A `this` reference is __________ .

    a. implicitly passed to nonstatic methods

    b. implicitly passed to `static` methods

    c. explicitly passed to nonstatic methods

    d. explicitly passed to `static` methods

12. When you use an instance variable within a class's nonstatic methods, you ___________ explicitly refer to the method's `this` reference.

    a. must

    b. can

    c. cannot

    d. should (even though it is not required)

13. A class's default constructor ___________ .

    a. sets numeric fields to 0

    b. is parameterless

    c. both of these

    d. none of these

14. Assume you have created a class named `Chair` with a constructor defined as `Chair(int height)`. Which of the following overloaded constructors could coexist with the `Chair` constructor without ambiguity?

    a. `Chair(int legs)`

    b. `Chair(int height, int legs)`

    c. both of these

    d. none of these

15. Which of the following statements correctly instantiates a `House` object if the `House` class contains a single constructor with the declaration `House(int bedrooms, double price)`?

    a. `House myHouse = new House();`

    b. `House myHouse = new House(3, 125000.00);`

    c. `House myHouse = House(4, 200,000.00);`

    d. two of these

16. You explicitly call a destructor ___________ .

    a. when you are finished using an object

    b. when an object goes out of scope

    c. when a class is destroyed

    d. You cannot explicitly call a destructor.

17. In a program that creates five object instances of a class, the constructor executes ___________ time(s) and the destructor executes ___________ time(s).

    a. one; one

    b. one; five

    c. five; one

    d. five; five

18. Suppose you declare a class named `Furniture` that contains a `string` field named `woodType` and a conventionally named property with a `get` accessor. When you declare an array of 200 `Furniture` objects named `myChairs`, which of the following accesses the last `Furniture` object's wood type?

    a. `Furniture.Get(woodType[199])`

    b. `myChairs[199].WoodType()`

    c. `myChairs.WoodType[199]`

    d. `myChairs[199].WoodType`

19. What is a collection of methods (and perhaps other members) that can be used by any class, as long as the class provides a definition to override the collection's do-nothing, or abstract, definitions?

    a. a superclass

    b. a polymorph

    c. a perimeter

    d. an interface

20. When you create a class whose members clients are likely to want to compare using the `Array.Sort()` or `Array.BinarySearch()` method, you must __________ .

    a. include at least one numeric field within the class

    b. write a `CompareTo()` method for the class

    c. be careful not to override the existing `IComparable.CompareTo()` method

    d. Two of these are true.

EXERCISES

1. Create a class named `Pizza`. Data fields include a string for toppings (such as pepperoni), an integer for diameter in inches (such as 12), and a `double` for price (such as 13.99). Include properties to get and set values for each of these fields. Create a class named `TestPizza` that instantiates one `Pizza` object and demonstrates the use of the `Pizza` set and get accessors. Save this class as **TestPizza.cs**.

2. Create a class named `HousePlant`. A `HousePlant` has fields for a name (for example, "Philodendron"), a price (for example, 29.99), and a value indicating whether the plant has been fed in the last month (for example, `true`). Include properties that contain `get` and `set` accessors for each field. Create a class named `DisplayHousePlants` that instantiates three `HousePlant` objects. Demonstrate the use of each property for each object. Save the file as **DisplayHousePlants.cs**.

3. Create a class named `Circle` with fields named `radius`, `area`, and `diameter`. Include a constructor that sets the radius to 1. Also include `public` properties for each field. The `Radius` property should have `get` and `set` accessors, but `Area` and `Diameter`

should be read-only. The `set` accessor for the radius should also provide values for the `diameter` and `area`. (The diameter of a circle is twice its radius; the area is pi multiplied by the square of the radius. You can use the public `Math` class property `Math.PI` for the value of pi.) Create a class named `TestCircles` whose `Main()` method declares three `Circle` objects. Assign a small radius value to one `Circle` and assign a larger radius value to another `Circle`. Do not assign a value to the radius of the third circle; instead, retain the value assigned at construction. Display the radius, diameter, and area for each `Circle`. (Display the area to two decimal places.) Save the program as **TestCircles.cs**.

4. Create a class named `Square` that contains fields for area and the length of a side and whose constructor requires a parameter for the length of one side of a `Square`. The constructor assigns its parameter to the length of the `Square`'s side field and calls a `private` method that computes the area field. Also include read-only properties to get a `Square`'s side and area. Create a class named `DemoSquares` that instantiates an array of 10 `Square` objects with sides that have values of 1 through 10. Display the values for each `Square`. Save the class as **DemoSquares.cs**.

5. Create a class named `GirlScout` that contains fields for a `GirlScout`'s name, troop number, and dues owed. Include a constant `static` field that contains the last words of the `GirlScout` motto ("to obey the Girl Scout law"). Include overloaded constructors that allow you to set all three nonstatic `GirlScout` fields to default values or to parameter values. Also include properties for each field. Create a class named `DemoScouts` that instantiates two `GirlScout` objects and displays their values. Create one object to use the default constructor and the other to use the constructor that requires arguments. Also display the `GirlScout` motto. Save the class as **DemoScouts.cs**.

6. a. Create a class named `Taxpayer`. Data fields for `Taxpayer` objects include the Social Security number (use a `string` for the type, but do not use dashes within the Social Security number), the yearly gross income, and the tax owed. Include a property with `get` and `set` accessors for the first two data fields, but make the tax owed a read-only property. The tax should be calculated whenever the income is set. Assume the tax is 15% of income for incomes under $30,000 and 28% for incomes that are $30,000 or higher. Write a program that declares an array of 10 `Taxpayer` objects. Prompt the user for data for each object and display the 10 objects. Save the program as **TaxPayerDemo.cs**.

   b. Modify the `Taxpayer` class so its objects are comparable to each other based on tax owed. Modify the `TaxPayerDemo` application so that after the 10 objects are displayed, they are sorted in order by the amount of tax owed; then display the objects again. Save the program as **TaxPayerDemo2.cs**.

7. Create a class named `Car` with fields that hold a vehicle ID number, make, model, color, and value for a `Car` object. Include appropriate properties for each field. Write a `DisplayFleet()` method that accepts any number of `Car` objects, displays their values, and displays the total value of all `Car` objects passed to the method. Write a `Main()` method that declares five `Car` objects and assigns values to each, then calls

`DisplayFleet()` three times—passing three, four, and five `Car` objects in successive calls. Save the program as **CarsDemo.cs**.

8. a. Create a class named `School` that contains fields for the `School` name and number of students enrolled and properties for each field. Also, include an `IComparable.CompareTo()` method so that `School` objects can be sorted by enrollment. Write a program that allows a user to enter information about five `School` objects. Display the `School` objects in order of enrollment size from smallest to largest `School`. Save the program as **SchoolsDemo.cs**.

   b. Modify the program created in Exercise 8a so that after the `School` objects are displayed in order, the program prompts the user to enter a minimum enrollment figure. Display all `School` objects that have an enrollment at least as large as the entered value. Save the program as **SchoolMinEnroll.cs**.

9. a. Create a class named `Friend`. Its fields include a `Friend`'s name, phone number, and three integer fields that together represent the `Friend`'s birthday—month, day, and year. Write a program that declares an array of eight `Friend` objects and prompts the user to enter data about eight friends. Display the `Friend` objects in alphabetical order by first name. Save the program as **FriendList.cs**.

   b. Modify the program created in Exercise 9a so that after the list of `Friend` objects is displayed, the program prompts the user for a specific `Friend`'s name and the program returns the `Friend`'s phone number and birthday. Display an appropriate message if the friend the user requests is not found. Save the program as **FriendBirthday.cs**.

   c. Modify the program in Exercise 9b so that after the requested `Friend`'s birthday displays, the program also displays a list of every `Friend` who has a birthday in the same month. Save the program as **AllFriendsInSameMonth.cs**.

10. a. Design a `Job` class for Harold's Home Services. The class contains four data fields—`Job` description (for example, "wash windows"), time in hours to complete the `Job` (for example, 3.5), per-hour rate charged for the `Job` (for example, $25.00), and total fee for the `Job` (hourly rate times hours). Include properties to get and set each field except the total fee—that field will be read-only, and its value is calculated each time either the hourly fee or the number of hours is set. Overload the + operator so that two `Jobs` can be added. The sum of two `Jobs` is a new `Job` containing the descriptions of both original `Jobs` (joined by "and"), the sum of the time in hours for the original `Jobs`, and the average of the hourly rate for the original `Jobs`. Write a `Main()` function that demonstrates all the methods work correctly. Save the file as **DemoJobs.cs**.

    b. Harold has realized that his method for computing the fee for combined jobs is not fair. For example, consider the following:

    » His fee for painting a house is $100 per hour. If a job takes 10 hours, he earns $1000.

    » His fee for dog walking is $10 per hour. If a job takes 1 hour, he earns $10.

    » If he combines the two jobs and works a total of 11 hours, he earns only the average rate of $55 per hour, or $605.

Devise an improved, weighted method for calculating Harold's fees for combined `Jobs` and include it in the overloaded `operator+()` method. Write a `Main()` function that demonstrates all the methods in the class work correctly. Save the file as **DemoJobs2.cs**.

11. a. Create a `Fraction` class with fields that hold a whole number, a numerator, and a denominator. In addition:

> » Create properties for each field. The `set` accessor for the denominator should not allow a 0 value; the value defaults to 1.

> » Add three constructors. One takes three parameters for a whole number, numerator, and denominator. Another accepts two parameters for the numerator and denominator; when this constructor is used, the whole number value is 0. The last constructor is parameterless; it sets the whole number and numerator to 0 and the denominator to 1. (After construction, `Fractions` do not have to be reduced to proper form. For example, even though 3/9 could be reduced to 1/3, your constructors do not have to perform this task.)

> » Add a `Reduce()` method that reduces a `Fraction` if it is in improper form. For example, 2/4 should be reduced to 1/2.

> » Add an `operator+()` method that adds two `Fractions`. To add two fractions, first eliminate any whole number part of the value. For example, 2 1/4 becomes 9/4 and 1 3/5 becomes 8/5. Find a common denominator and convert the fractions to it. For example, when adding 9/4 and 8/5, you can convert them to 45/20 and 32/20. Then you can add the numerators, giving 77/20. Finally, call the `Reduce()` method to reduce the result, restoring any whole number value so the fractional part of the number is less than 1. For example, 77/20 becomes 3 17/20.

> » Include a function that returns a `string` that contains a `Fraction` in the usual display format—the whole number, a space, the numerator, a slash (/), and a denominator. When the whole number is 0, just the `Fraction` part of the value should be displayed (for example, `1/2` instead of `0 1/2`). If the numerator is 0, just the whole number should display (for example, `2` instead of `2  0/3`).

Write a `Main()` method that instantiates several `Fractions` and demonstrate that all the methods work correctly. Save the program as **FractionDemo.cs**.

b. Add an `operator*()` method to the `Fraction` class created in Exercise 11a so that it correctly multiplies two `Fractions`. The result should be in proper, reduced format. Demonstrate that the method works correctly. Save the program as **FractionDemo2.cs**.

c. Create an array of four `Fractions`. Prompt the user for values for each. Display every possible combination of addition results and every possible combination of multiplication results for each `Fraction` pair (that is, each type will have 16 results). Figure 7-48 shows a sample execution. Save the program as **FractionDemo3.cs**.

```
C:\C#\Chapter.07>FractionDemo3
Enter whole number portion of fraction 1
Enter numerator 2
Enter denominator 3
Enter whole number portion of fraction 4
Enter numerator 1
Enter denominator 2
Enter whole number portion of fraction 0
Enter numerator 1
Enter denominator 4
Enter whole number portion of fraction 3
Enter numerator 4
Enter denominator 5
Addition
1 2/3 + 1 2/3 = 3 1/3
1 2/3 + 4 1/2 = 6 1/6
1 2/3 + 1/4 = 1 11/12
1 2/3 + 3 4/5 = 5 7/15
4 1/2 + 1 2/3 = 6 1/6
4 1/2 + 4 1/2 = 9
4 1/2 + 1/4 = 4 3/4
4 1/2 + 3 4/5 = 8 3/10
1/4 + 1 2/3 = 1 11/12
1/4 + 4 1/2 = 4 3/4
1/4 + 1/4 = 1/2
1/4 + 3 4/5 = 4 1/20
3 4/5 + 1 2/3 = 5 7/15
3 4/5 + 4 1/2 = 8 3/10
3 4/5 + 1/4 = 4 1/20
3 4/5 + 3 4/5 = 7 3/5

Multiplication
1 2/3 * 1 2/3 = 2 7/9
1 2/3 * 4 1/2 = 7 1/2
1 2/3 * 1/4 = 5/12
1 2/3 * 3 4/5 = 6 1/3
4 1/2 * 1 2/3 = 7 1/2
4 1/2 * 4 1/2 = 20 1/4
4 1/2 * 1/4 = 1 1/8
4 1/2 * 3 4/5 = 17 1/10
1/4 * 1 2/3 = 5/12
1/4 * 4 1/2 = 1 1/8
1/4 * 1/4 = 1/16
1/4 * 3 4/5 = 19/20
3 4/5 * 1 2/3 = 6 1/3
3 4/5 * 4 1/2 = 17 1/10
3 4/5 * 1/4 = 19/20
3 4/5 * 3 4/5 = 14 11/25

C:\C#\Chapter.07>
```

Figure 7-48 Sample execution of `FractionDemo3` program

DEBUGGING EXERCISES

Each of the following files saved in the Chapter.07 folder on your Student Disk has syntax and/or logical errors. In each case, determine the problem and fix the program. After you correct the errors, save each file using the same filename preceded with "Fixed." For example, DebugSeven1.cs will become FixedDebugSeven1.cs.

a. DebugSeven1.cs

b. DebugSeven2.cs

c. DebugSeven3.cs

d. DebugSeven4.cs

UP FOR DISCUSSION

1. In this chapter, you learned that instance data and methods belong to objects (which are class members), but that static data and methods belong to a class as a whole. Consider the real-life class named `StateInTheUnitedStates`. Name some real-life attributes of this class that are static attributes and instance attributes. Create another example of a real-life class and discuss what its static and instance members might be.

2. Fifty or 60 years ago, most people's paychecks were produced by hand; now your check is probably printed by a computer, or not printed at all but deposited into an account electronically. Thirty-five years ago, most grocery store checkers keyed item prices into a cash register; now your items are probably scanned. Police officers used to direct traffic at many major urban intersections; now the traffic flow is often computer controlled. Would any other tasks that are currently performed by people be better handled by a computer? Are there any tasks that you hope never become computerized?

3. If you are completing all the programming exercises at the ends of the chapters in this book, you can see how much work goes into a full-blown professional program. How would you feel if someone copied your work without compensating you? Investigate the magnitude of software piracy in our society. What are the penalties for illegally copying software? Are there circumstances under which it is acceptable to copy a program? If a friend asked you to make a copy of a program for him, would you? What do you suggest we do about this problem, if anything?

8

INTRODUCTION TO INHERITANCE

In this chapter you will:

Learn about the concept of inheritance
Learn inheritance terminology
Extend classes
Use the `protected` access specifier
Override base class methods
Access base class methods from a derived class
Understand how a derived class object "is an" instance
  of the base class
Learn about the `Object` class
Work with base class constructors
Create and use abstract classes
Create and use interfaces
Use extension methods
Understand the benefits of inheritance

Understanding classes helps you organize objects in real life. Understanding inheritance helps you organize them more precisely. If you have never heard of a Braford, for example, you would have a hard time forming a picture of one in your mind. When you learn that a Braford is an animal, you gain some understanding of what it must be like. That understanding grows when you learn it is a mammal, and the understanding is almost complete when you learn it is a cow. When you learn that a Braford is a cow, you understand it has many characteristics that are common to all cows. To identify a Braford, you must learn only relatively minor details—its color or markings, for example. Most of a Braford's characteristics, however, derive from its membership in a particular hierarchy of classes: animal, mammal, and cow.

All object-oriented programming languages make use of inheritance for the same reasons—to organize the objects programs use, and to make new objects easier to understand based on your knowledge of their inherited traits. In this chapter, you will learn to make use of inheritance with your C# objects.

UNDERSTANDING THE CONCEPT OF INHERITANCE

Inheritance is the principle that you can apply your knowledge of a general category to more specific objects. You are familiar with the concept of inheritance from all sorts of situations. When you use the term *inheritance,* you might think of genetic inheritance. You know from biology that your blood type and eye color are the products of inherited genes. You can say that many other facts about you (your attributes) are inherited. Similarly, you often can attribute your behaviors to inheritance; for example, the way you handle money might be similar to the way your grandmother handles it, and your gait might be the same as your father's—so your methods are inherited, too.

You also might choose to have plants and animals based on their inherited attributes. You plant impatiens next to your house because they thrive in the shade; you adopt a poodle because you know poodles don't shed. Every plant and pet has slightly different characteristics, but within a species, you can count on many consistent inherited attributes and behaviors. In other words, you can reuse the knowledge you gain about general categories and apply it to more specific categories. Similarly, the classes you create in object-oriented programming languages can inherit data and methods from existing classes. When you create a class by making it inherit from another class, you are provided with data fields and methods automatically; you can reuse fields and methods that are already written and tested.

You already know how to create classes and how to instantiate objects that are members of those classes. For example, consider the `Employee` class in Figure 8-1. The class contains two data fields, `empNum` and `empSal`, as well as properties that contain accessors for each field and a method that creates an `Employee` greeting.

```
public class Employee
{
    private int empNum;
    private double empSal;
    public int EmpNum {get; set;}
    public double EmpSal {get; set;}
    public string GetGreeting()
    {
        string greeting = "Hello. I am employee #" + EmpNum;
        return greeting;
    }
}
```

Figure 8-1 An `Employee` class

>> **NOTE** As you learned in Chapter 7, you are not required to declare `empNum` and `empSal` in the `Employee` class because their declarations are assumed by the property declarations when you use auto-implemented properties. When you use this `Employee` class in a program, you will receive two warnings that these fields are never used. You can safely ignore these warnings.

After you create the `Employee` class, you can create specific `Employee` objects, as in the following:

```
Employee receptionist = new Employee();
Employee deliveryPerson = new Employee();
```

These `Employee` objects can eventually possess different numbers and salaries, but because they are `Employee` objects, you know that each possesses *some* number and salary.

Suppose you hire a new type of `Employee` who earns a commission as well as a salary. You can create a class with a name such as `CommissionEmployee`, and provide this class with three fields (`empNum`, `empSal`, and `commissionRate`), three properties (with accessors to get and set each of the three fields), and a greeting method. However, this work would duplicate much of the work that you already have done for the `Employee` class. The wise and efficient alternative is to create the class `CommissionEmployee` so it inherits all the attributes and methods of `Employee`. Then, you can add just the single field and property with two accessors that are additions within `CommissionEmployee` objects. Figure 8-2 depicts these relationships.

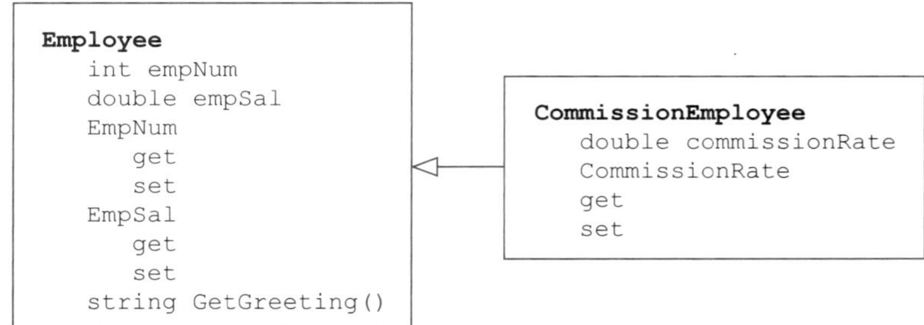

Figure 8-2 `CommissionEmployee` inherits from `Employee`

When you use inheritance to create the `CommissionEmployee` class, you acquire the following benefits:

» You save time, because you need not recreate the `Employee` fields, properties, and methods.

» You reduce the chance of errors, because the `Employee` properties and methods have already been used and tested.

» You make it easier for anyone who has used the `Employee` class to understand the `CommissionEmployee` class because such users can concentrate on the new features only.

The ability to use inheritance makes programs easier to write, easier to understand, and less prone to errors. Imagine that besides `CommissionEmployee`, you want to create several other specific `Employee` classes (perhaps `PartTimeEmployee`, including a field for hours worked, or `DismissedEmployee`, including a reason for dismissal). By using inheritance, you can develop each new class correctly and more quickly.

»TWO TRUTHS AND A LIE: UNDERSTANDING THE CONCEPT OF INHERITANCE

1. When you use inheritance to create a class, you save time because you can copy and paste fields, properties, and methods that have already been created for the original class.

2. When you use inheritance to create a class, you reduce the chance of errors because the original class's properties and methods have already been used and tested.

3. When you use inheritance to create a class, you make it easier for anyone who has used the original class to understand the new class because such users can concentrate on the new features.

The false statement is #1. When you use inheritance to create a class, you save time because you need not recreate fields, properties, and methods that have already been created for the original class. You do not copy these class members; you inherit them.

UNDERSTANDING INHERITANCE TERMINOLOGY

A class that is used as a basis for inheritance, like `Employee`, is called a **base class**. When you create a class that inherits from a base class (such as `CommissionEmployee`), it is a **derived class** or **extended class**. When presented with two classes that have a parent-child relationship, you can tell which class is the base class and which is the derived class by using the two classes in a sentence with the phrase "is a." A derived class always "is a" case or instance of the more general base class. For example, a Tree class may be a base class to an Evergreen class. Every Evergreen "is a" Tree; however, it is not true that every Tree is an Evergreen. Thus, Tree is the base class and Evergreen is the derived class. Similarly, a CommissionEmployee "is an" Employee—not always the other way around—so Employee is the base class and CommissionEmployee is derived.

You can use the terms **superclass** and **subclass** as synonyms for base class and derived class. Thus, Evergreen can be called a subclass of the Tree superclass. You also can use the terms **parent class** and **child class**. A CommissionEmployee is a child to the Employee parent. Use the pair of terms with which you are most comfortable; all of these terms will be used interchangeably in this book.

As an alternative way to discover which of two classes is the base class and which is the derived class, you can try saying the two class names together (although this technique might not work with every superclass-subclass pair). When people say their names together in the English language, they state the more specific name before the all-encompassing family name, such as "Ginny Kroening." Similarly, with classes, the order that "makes more sense" is the child-parent order. Thus, because "Evergreen Tree" makes more sense than "Tree Evergreen," you can deduce that Evergreen is the child class.

>> **NOTE** It also is convenient to think of a derived class as building upon its base class by providing the "adjectives" or additional descriptive terms for the "noun." Frequently, the names of derived classes are formed in this way, as in CommissionEmployee.

Finally, you usually can distinguish base classes from their derived classes by size. Although it is not required, a derived class is generally larger than a base class, in the sense that it usually has additional fields and methods. A subclass description may look small, but any subclass contains all of its superclass's fields and methods as well as its own more specific fields and methods.

>> **NOTE** Do not think of a subclass as a "subset" of another class—in other words, possessing only parts of its superclass. In fact, a derived class usually contains more than its parent.

A derived class can be further extended. In other words, a subclass can have a child of its own. For example, after you create a Tree class and derive Evergreen, you might derive a Spruce class from Evergreen. Similarly, a Poodle class might derive from Dog, Dog from DomesticPet, and DomesticPet from Animal. The entire list of parent classes from which a child class is derived constitutes the **ancestors** of the subclass.

>> **NOTE** After you create the Spruce class, you might be ready to create Spruce objects. For example, you might create theTreeInMyBackYard, or you might create an array of 1000 Spruce objects for a tree farm.

Inheritance is **transitive**, which means a child inherits all the members of all its ancestors. In other words, when you declare a Spruce object, it contains all the attributes and methods of both an Evergreen and a Tree. As you work with C#, you will encounter many examples of such transitive chains of inheritance.

> **»NOTE** When you create your own transitive inheritance chains, you want to place fields and methods at their most general level. In other words, a method named Grow() rightfully belongs in a Tree class, whereas LeavesTurnColor() does not, because the method applies to only some of the Tree child classes. Similarly, a LeavesTurnColor() method would be better located in a Deciduous class than separately within the Oak or Maple child class.

> **»NOTE** In math, a transitive relationship occurs when something that is true for a and b and for b and c is also true for a and c. For example, equality is transitive. If a = b and b = c, then a = c. In inheritance, the term implies that when something is true for the parent, it is also true for the child.

»TWO TRUTHS AND A LIE: UNDERSTANDING INHERITANCE TERMINOLOGY

1. The terms *superclass* and *parent class* both mean the same thing as *base class*.
2. A derived class is generally smaller than a base class.
3. A child class inherits all the members of all its ancestors.

The false statement is #2. A derived class is generally larger than a base class, in the sense that it usually has additional fields and methods.

EXTENDING CLASSES

When you create a class that is an extension or child of another class, you use a single colon between the derived class name and its base class name. For example, the following class header creates a subclass-superclass relationship between CommissionEmployee and Employee.

```
public class CommissionEmployee : Employee
```

Each CommissionEmployee object automatically contains the data fields and methods of the base class; you then can add new fields and methods to the new derived class. Figure 8-3 shows a CommissionEmployee class.

```
public class CommissionEmployee : Employee
{
    private double commissionRate;
    public double CommissionRate {get; set;}
}
```

Figure 8-3 CommissionEmployee class

The CommissionEmployee class in Figure 8-3 contains three fields: empNum and empSal, inherited from Employee, and commissionRate, which is defined within the CommissionEmployee class. Similarly, the CommissionEmployee class contains three properties and a method—two properties and the method are inherited from Employee, and one property is defined within CommissionEmployee itself. When you write a program that instantiates an object using the following statement, then you can use any of the next statements to set field values for the salesperson:

```
CommissionEmployee salesperson = new CommissionEmployee();
salesperson.EmpNum = 234;
salesperson.EmpSal = Convert.ToDouble(Console.ReadLine());
salesperson.CommissionRate = 0.07;
```

The salesperson object has access to all three set accessors (two from its parent and one from its own class) because it is both a CommissionEmployee and an Employee. Similarly, the object has access to three get accessors and the GetGreeting() method. Figure 8-4 shows a Main() method that declares Employee and CommissionEmployee objects and shows all the properties and methods that can be used with each. Figure 8-5 shows the program output.

```
using System;
public class DemoEmployees
{
   public static void Main()
   {
      Employee clerk = new Employee();
      CommissionEmployee salesperson = new CommissionEmployee();
      clerk.EmpNum = 123;
      clerk.EmpSal = 30000.00;
      salesperson.EmpNum = 234;
      salesperson.EmpSal = 20000;
      salesperson.CommissionRate = 0.07;
      Console.WriteLine("\n" + clerk.GetGreeting());
      Console.WriteLine("Clerk #{0} makes {1} per year",
         clerk.EmpNum,
         clerk.EmpSal.ToString("C"));
      Console.WriteLine("\n" + salesperson.GetGreeting());
      Console.WriteLine("Salesperson #{0} makes {1} per year",
         salesperson.EmpNum,
         salesperson.EmpSal.ToString("C"));
      Console.WriteLine("...plus {0} commission on all sales",
         salesperson.CommissionRate.ToString("P"));
   }
}
```

Figure 8-4 DemoEmployees class that declares Employee and CommissionEmployee objects

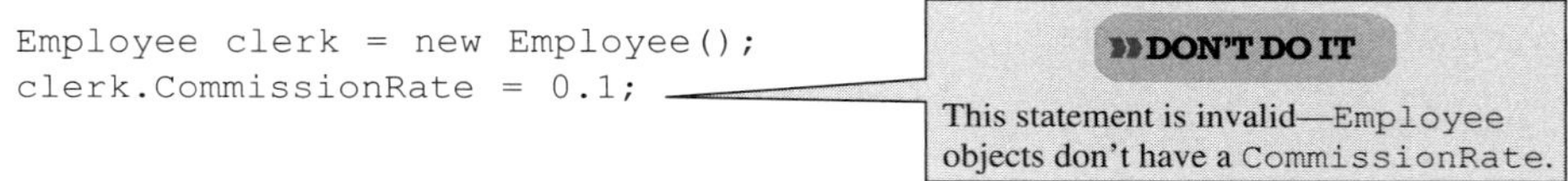

Figure 8-5 Output of the `DemoEmployees` program

Inheritance works only in one direction: A child inherits from a parent—not the other way around. If a program instantiates an `Employee` object as in the following statement, the `Employee` object does *not* have access to the `CommissionEmployee` properties or methods.

```
Employee clerk = new Employee();
clerk.CommissionRate = 0.1;
```

»DON'T DO IT
This statement is invalid—`Employee` objects don't have a `CommissionRate`.

`Employee` is the parent class, and `clerk` is an object of the parent class. It makes sense that a parent class object does not have access to its child's data and methods. When you create the parent class, you do not know how many future child classes might be created, or what their data or methods might look like. In addition, child classes are more specific. A `HeartSurgeon` class and an `Obstetrician` class are children of a `Doctor` class. You do not expect all members of the general parent class `Doctor` to have the `HeartSurgeon`'s `RepairValve()` method or the `Obstetrician`'s `DeliverBaby()` method. However, `HeartSurgeon` and `Obstetrician` objects have access to the more general `Doctor` methods `TakeBloodPressure()` and `BillPatients()`.

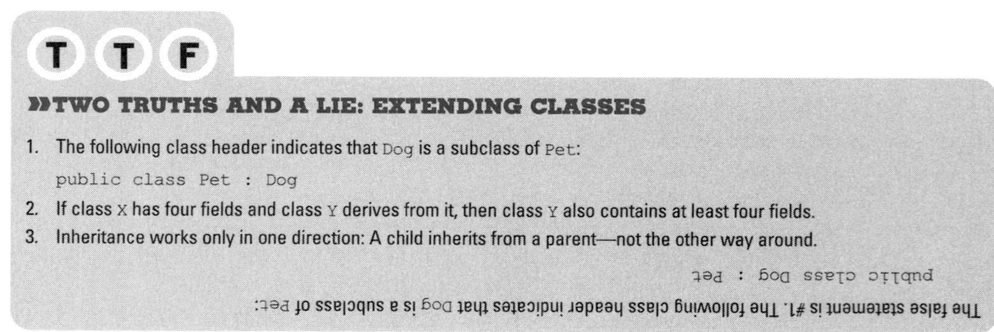

T T F

»TWO TRUTHS AND A LIE: EXTENDING CLASSES

1. The following class header indicates that `Dog` is a subclass of `Pet`:

   `public class Pet : Dog`

2. If class `X` has four fields and class `Y` derives from it, then class `Y` also contains at least four fields.

3. Inheritance works only in one direction: A child inherits from a parent—not the other way around.

The false statement is #1. The following class header indicates that Dog is a subclass of Pet:

public class Dog : Pet

USING THE protected ACCESS SPECIFIER

The `Employee` class in Figure 8-1 is a typical C# class in that its data fields are `private` and its properties and methods are `public`. In Chapter 7, you learned that this scheme provides for information hiding—protecting your `private` data from alteration by methods outside the data's own class. When a program is a client of the `Employee` class (that is, it instantiates an `Employee` object), the client cannot alter the data in any `private` field directly. For example, when you write a `Main()` method that creates an `Employee` named `clerk`, you cannot change the `Employee`'s empNum or empSal directly using a statement such as `clerk.empNum = 2222;`. Instead, you must use the `EmpNum` property to set the empNum field of the `clerk` object.

When you use information hiding, you are assured that your data will be altered only by the properties and methods you choose and only in ways that you can control. If outside classes could alter an `Employee`'s `private` fields, then the fields could be assigned values that the `Employee` class couldn't control. In such a case, the principle of information hiding would be destroyed, causing the behavior of the object to be unpredictable.

Any derived class you create, such as `CommissionEmployee`, inherits all the data and methods of its base class. However, even though a child of `Employee` has empNum and empSal fields, the `CommissionEmployee` methods cannot alter or use those `private` fields directly. If you could use `private` data outside of its class, the principle of information hiding would be destroyed. If you intend the `Employee` class data field empNum to be `private`, then you don't want any outside classes using the field. If a new class could simply extend your `Employee` class and "get to" its data fields without "going through the proper channels," then information hiding would not be operating.

On some occasions, you do want to access parent class data from within a child class. For example, suppose that the `Employee` class `EmpSal` property `set` accessor has been written so that no `Employee`'s salary is ever set to less than 15000, as follows:

```
set
{
    if(value < 15000)
        empSal = 15000;
    else
        empSal = value;
}
```

> **» NOTE**
> In this example, you probably would prefer to use a named constant for the value 15000.

Also assume that a `CommissionEmployee` draws commission only and no regular salary; that is, when you set a `CommissionEmployee`'s commissionRate field, the empSal should become 0. You would write the `CommissionEmployee` class `CommissionRate` property `set` accessor as follows:

```
set
{
    commissionRate = value;
    EmpSal = 0;
}
```

Using this implementation, when you create a `CommissionEmployee` object and set its `CommissionRate`, 0 is sent to the `set` accessor for the `Employee` class `EmpSal` property. There, because the value of the salary is less than 15000, the salary is forced to 15000 even though you want it to be 0.

An alternative is to rewrite the `set` accessor for the `CommissionRate` property in the `CommissionEmployee` class as follows:

```
set
{
    commissionRate = value;
    empSal = 0;
}
```

In this `set` accessor, you bypass the parent class's `EmpSal` set accessor and directly use the `empSal` field. However, when you include this accessor in a program and compile it, you receive an error message: "Employee.empSal is inaccessible due to its protection level". In other words, `Employee.empSal` is `private`, and no other class can access it. So, in summary:

- » Using the `public set` accessor in the parent class does not work because of the minimum salary requirement.
- » Using the `private` field in the parent class does not work because it is inaccessible.
- » Making the parent class field `public` would work, but doing so would violate the principle of information hiding.

Fortunately, there is a fourth option. If you want a derived class property or method to be able to access `empSal`, then it cannot be `private`. However, if you don't want other, nonchild classes to access the field, then it cannot be `public`. The solution is to create the `empSal` field using the modifier `protected`, which provides you with an intermediate level of security between `public` and `private` access. A **protected** data field or method can be used within its own class or in any classes extended from that class, but it cannot be used by "outside" classes. In other words, `protected` members can be used "within the family"—by a class and its descendants.

Figure 8-6 shows how you can declare `empSal` as `protected` within the `Employee` class so that it becomes legal to access it directly within the `CommissionRate set` accessor of the `CommissionEmployee` derived class. Figure 8-7 shows a program that instantiates a `CommissionEmployee` object, and Figure 8-8 shows the output. Notice that the `CommissionEmployee`'s salary initially is set to 20000 in the program, but the salary becomes 0 when the `CommissionRate` is set later.

```csharp
public class Employee
{
    private int empNum;
    protected double empSal;
    public int EmpNum {get; set;}
    public double EmpSal
    {
        get
        {
            return empSal;
        }
        set
        {
            if(value < 15000)
                empSal = 15000;
            else
                empSal = value;
        }
    }
    public string GetGreeting()
    {
        string greeting = "Hello. I am employee #" + EmpNum;
        return greeting;
    }
}
public class CommissionEmployee : Employee
{
    private double commissionRate;
    public double CommissionRate
    {
        get
        {
            return commissionRate;
        }
        set
        {
            commissionRate = value;
            empSal = 0;
        }
    }
}
```

The protected `empSal` field is accessible in the child class.

Figure 8-6 Employee class with a `protected` field and `CommissionEmployee` class

```csharp
using System;
public class DemoSalesperson
{
    public static void Main()
    {
        CommissionEmployee salesperson = new CommissionEmployee();
        salesperson.EmpNum = 345;
        salesperson.EmpSal = 20000;
        salesperson.CommissionRate = 0.07;
        Console.WriteLine("Salesperson #{0} makes {1} per year",
            salesperson.EmpNum,
            salesperson.EmpSal.ToString("C"));
        Console.WriteLine("...plus {0} commission on all sales",
            salesperson.CommissionRate.ToString("P"));
    }
}
```

Figure 8-7 The `DemoSalesperson` program

Figure 8-8 Output of the `DemoSalesperson` program

Using the `protected` access modifier for a field can be convenient, and it also improves program performance a little by using a field directly instead of "going through" property accessors. Also, using the `protected` access modifier is occasionally necessary. However, `protected` data members should be used sparingly. Whenever possible, the principle of information hiding should be observed, and even child classes should have to go through accessors to "get to" their parent's private data. When child classes are allowed direct access to a parent's fields, the likelihood of future errors increases.

»TWO TRUTHS AND A LIE: USING THE `protected` **ACCESS SPECIFIER**

1. A child class does not possess the private members of its parent.
2. A child class cannot use the private members of its parent.
3. A child class can use the protected members of its parent, but outside classes cannot.

The false statement is #1. A child class possesses the private members of its parent, but cannot use them directly.

OVERRIDING BASE CLASS METHODS

When you create a derived class by extending an existing class, the new derived class contains data and methods that were defined in the original base class. Sometimes, the superclass fields, properties, and methods are not entirely appropriate for the subclass objects.

For example, suppose you have created a Student class as shown in Figure 8-9. Students have names, credits for which they are enrolled, and tuition amounts. You can set a Student's name and credits by using the set accessors in the Name and Credits properties, but you cannot set a Student's tuition directly because there is no set accessor for the Tuition property. Instead, tuition is calculated based on a standard RATE (of $55.75) for each credit that the Student takes.

```
class Student
{
    private const double RATE = 55.75;
    private string name;
    protected int credits;
    protected double tuition;
    public string Name {get; set;}
    public int Credits
    {
        get
        {
            return credits;
        }
        set
        {
            credits = value;
            tuition = credits * RATE;
        }
    }
    public double Tuition
    {
        get
        {
            return tuition;
        }
    }
}
```

Figure 8-9 The Student class

> **» NOTE**
> In Figure 8-9, the Student fields that hold credits and tuition are declared as protected because a child class will use them.

Suppose you derive a subclass from Student called ScholarshipStudent. A ScholarshipStudent has a name, credits, and tuition, but the tuition is not calculated in the same way as it is for a Student; instead, tuition for a ScholarshipStudent should be set to 0. You want to use the Credits property to set a ScholarshipStudent's credits, but

> **» NOTE**
> You first learned about polymorphism in Chapter 1.

you want the property to behave differently than the parent class `Student`'s `Credits` property. Using the same method or property name to indicate different implementations is called polymorphism. The word *polymorphism* means "many forms;" it means that many forms of action take place, even though you use the same name to describe the action. In other words, there are many forms of the same method depending on the object associated with the word.

The English language provides many examples of polymorphism:

» A race is *run* differently than a business.

» A chess game is *played* differently than a guitar.

» A door is *opened* differently than a bank account.

You understand each use of these English verbs based on the context in which it is used. In a similar way, C# understands your use of the same method name based on the type of object associated with it. Figure 8-10 shows a `ScholarshipStudent` class. As a child of `Student`, a `ScholarshipStudent` possesses all the attributes, properties, and methods of a `Student`, but its `Credits` property behaves differently.

```
class ScholarshipStudent : Student
{
    new public int Credits
    {
      set
      {
          credits = value;
          tuition = 0;
      }
    }
}
```

Figure 8-10 The `ScholarshipStudent` class

In the child `ScholarshipStudent` class in Figure 8-10, the `Credits` property is declared as `new` (see shading) because it has the same header as a property in its parent class—it overrides and **hides** its counterpart in the parent class. (You could do the same thing with methods.) If you omit `new`, the program will still operate correctly, but you will receive a warning that you are hiding an inherited member with the same name in the base class. Using the keyword `new` eliminates the warning and makes your intentions clear. When you use the `Name` property with a `ScholarshipStudent` object, a program uses the parent class property `Name`; it is not hidden. However, when you use `Credits` to set a value for a `ScholarshipStudent` object, the program uses the new, overriding property from its own class.

Figure 8-11 shows a program that uses `Student` and `ScholarshipStudent` objects. Even though each object assigns the `Credits` property the same number of credit hours (in the two shaded statements), the calculated `tuition` values are different because each object uses a different version of the `Credits` property. Figure 8-12 shows the execution of the program.


```
using System;
class DemoStudents
{
    public static void Main()
    {
        Student payingStudent = new Student();
        ScholarshipStudent freeStudent = new ScholarshipStudent();
        payingStudent.Name = "Megan";
        payingStudent.Credits = 15;
        freeStudent.Name = "Luke";
        freeStudent.Credits = 15;
        Console.WriteLine("{0}'s tuition is {1}",
            payingStudent.Name,
            payingStudent.Tuition.ToString("C"));
        Console.WriteLine("{0}'s tuition is {1}",
            freeStudent.Name,
            freeStudent.Tuition.ToString("C"));
    }
}
```

Figure 8-11 The `DemoStudents` program

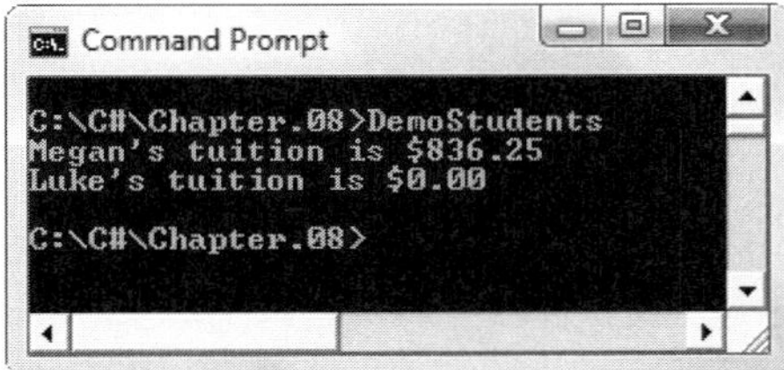

Figure 8-12 Output of the `DemoStudents` program

If a base class and a derived class have methods with the same names but different argument lists, then the derived class method does not override the base class method; instead, it overloads it. For example, if a base class contains a method with the header `public void Display()`, and its child contains a method with the header `public void Display(string s)`, then the child class would have access to both methods.

»TWO TRUTHS AND A LIE: OVERRIDING BASE CLASS METHODS

1. When you override a parent class method in a child class, the methods have the same name.
2. When you override a parent class method in a child class, the methods have the same parameter list.
3. When you override a parent class method in a child class, and you use the child class method, the parent class method executes first, followed by the child class method.

The false statement is #3. When you override a parent class method in a child class and then use the child class method, the child class method executes instead of the parent class version.

ACCESSING BASE CLASS METHODS FROM A DERIVED CLASS

A derived class can contain a method with the same name and arguments as a method in its parent class; when this happens, using the derived class method overrides the parent class method. In some situations, you might want to use the parent class method within a subclass. If so, you can use the keyword `base` to access the parent class method. For example, recall the `GetGreeting()` method that appears in the `Employee` class in Figure 8-6. If its child, `CommissionEmployee`, also contains a `GetGreeting()` method, as shown in Figure 8-13,

```
public class CommissionEmployee : Employee
{
   private double commissionRate;
   public double CommissionRate
   {
      get
      {
         return commissionRate;
      }
      set
      {
         commissionRate = value;
         empSal = 0;
      }
   }
   new public string GetGreeting()
   {
      string greeting = base.GetGreeting();
      greeting += "\nI work on commission.";
      return greeting;
   }
}
```

Figure 8-13 The `CommissionEmployee` class with a `GetGreeting()` method

then within the `CommissionEmployee` class you can call `base.GetGreeting()` to access the base class version of the method. Figure 8-14 shows an application that uses the method with a `CommissionEmployee` object. Figure 8-15 shows the output.

```csharp
using System;
public class DemoSalesperson2
{
   public static void Main()
   {
      CommissionEmployee salesperson = new CommissionEmployee();
      salesperson.EmpNum = 345;
      Console.WriteLine(salesperson.GetGreeting());
   }
}
```

Figure 8-14 The `DemoSalesperson2` program

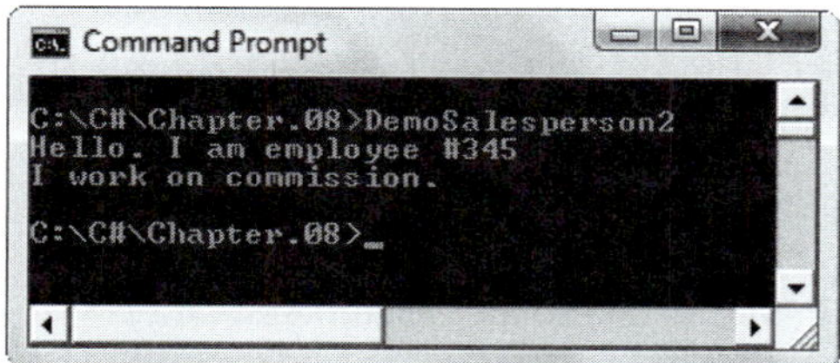

Figure 8-15 Output of the `DemoSalesperson2` program

In Figure 8-13, the child class method uses the keyword `new` to eliminate a compiler warning. Then, within the `GetGreeting()` method, the parent's version is called. The returned string is stored in the `greeting` variable, and then an "I work on commission." statement is added to it before the complete message is returned to the calling program. By overriding the base class method in the child class, the duplicate typing to create the first part of the message was eliminated. Additionally, if the first part of the message is altered in the future, it will be altered in only one place—in the base class.

TWO TRUTHS AND A LIE: ACCESSING BASE CLASS METHODS FROM A DERIVED CLASS

1. If you want to use a parent class method within a subclass, you can just use the method name if the method has not been overridden in the child class.

2. If you want to use a parent class method within a subclass, and the child class has overridden the method, you can use the keyword `base` to access the parent class method.

3. If you have overridden a base class method in a derived class, you can no longer use the base class version.

The false statement is #3. You can use a parent class method that has been overridden in a subclass by using the keyword `base` to access the parent class method.

UNDERSTANDING HOW A DERIVED CLASS OBJECT "IS AN" INSTANCE OF THE BASE CLASS

Every derived class object "is a" specific instance of both the derived class and the base class. In other words, myCar "is a" Car as well as a Vehicle, and myDog "is a" Dog as well as a Mammal. You can assign a derived class object to an object of any of its superclass types. When you do, C# makes an **implicit conversion** from derived class to base class.

>> **NOTE** C# also makes implicit conversions when casting one data type to another. For example, in the statement double money = 10;, the value 10 is implicitly converted (or cast) to a double.

>> **NOTE** When a derived class object is assigned to its ancestor's data type, the conversion can more specifically be called an **implicit reference conversion**. This term is more accurate because it emphasizes the difference between numerical conversions and reference objects. When you assign a derived class object to a base class type, the object is treated as though it had only the characteristics defined in the base class.

For example, when a CommissionEmployee class inherits from Employee, an object of either type can be passed to a method that accepts an Employee parameter. In Figure 8-16, an Employee is passed to DisplayGreeting() in the first shaded statement, and a CommissionEmployee is passed in the second shaded statement. Each is referred to as emp within the method, and each is used correctly, as shown in Figure 8-17.

```csharp
using System;
public class DemoSalesperson3
{
    public static void Main()
    {
        Employee clerk = new Employee();
        CommissionEmployee salesperson = new CommissionEmployee();
        clerk.EmpNum = 234;
        salesperson.EmpNum = 345;
        DisplayGreeting(clerk);
        DisplayGreeting(salesperson);
    }
    public static void DisplayGreeting(Employee emp)
    {
        Console.WriteLine("Hi there from #" + emp.EmpNum);
        Console.WriteLine(emp.GetGreeting());
    }
}
```

Figure 8-16 The DemoSalesperson3 program

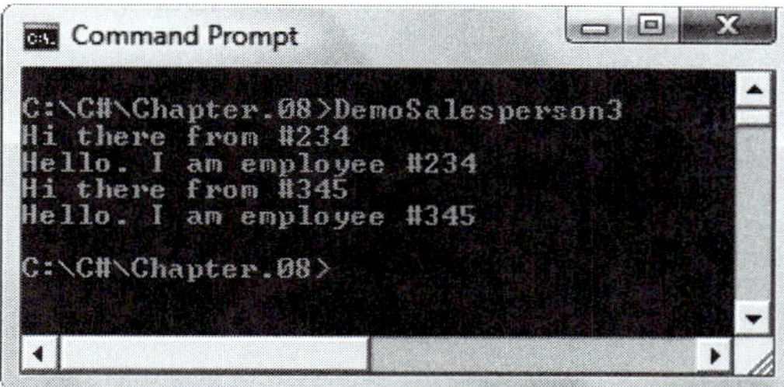

Figure 8-17 Output of the `DemoSalesperson3` program

>>**NOTE** In C#, you can use either `new` or `override` when defining a derived class member that has the same name as a base class member. When you write a statement such as `ScholarshipStudent s1 = new ScholarshipStudent();`, you won't notice the difference. However, if you use `new` when defining the derived class `Credits` property and write a statement such as `Student s2 = new ScholarshipStudent();`, then `s2.Credits` accesses the base class property. On the other hand, if you use `override` when defining `Credits` in the derived class, then `s2.Credits` uses the derived class property.

>>**NOTE** You cannot use both `new` and `override` on the same member because they have mutually exclusive meanings. Using `new` creates a `new` member with the same name and causes the original member to become hidden. Using `override` extends the implementation for an inherited member.

>>**TWO TRUTHS AND A LIE: UNDERSTANDING HOW A DERIVED CLASS OBJECT "IS AN" INSTANCE OF THE BASE CLASS**

1. You can assign a derived class object to an object of any of its superclass types.
2. You can assign a base class object to an object of any of its derived types.
3. An implicit conversion from one type to another is an automatic conversion.

The false statement is #2. You can assign a derived class object to an object of any of its superclass types, but not the other way around.

USING THE `Object` CLASS

Every class you create in C# derives from a single class named `System.Object`. In other words, the **object** (or `Object`) class type in the `System` namespace is the ultimate base class for all other types. The keyword `object` is an alias for the `System.Object` class. You can use the lowercase and uppercase versions of the class interchangeably.

>>**NOTE** When you create a class such as `Employee`, you usually use the header `class Employee`, which implicitly, or automatically, descends from the `Object` class. Alternatively, you could use the header `class Employee : Object` to explicitly show the name of the base class, but you have not seen this format in this book, and it would be extremely unusual to see such a format in a C# program.

Because every class descends from `Object`, every object "is an" `Object`. As proof, you can write a method that accepts an argument of type `Object`; it will accept arguments of any type. Figure 8-18 shows a program that declares three objects—a `Student`, a `ScholarshipStudent`, and an `Employee`. Even though these types possess different attributes and methods (and one type, `Employee`, has nothing in common with the other two), each type can serve as an argument to the `DisplayObjectMessage()` because each type "is an" `Object`. Figure 8-19 shows the execution of the program.

```
using System;
class DiverseObjects
{
    public static void Main()
    {
        Student payingStudent = new Student();
        ScholarshipStudent freeStudent = new ScholarshipStudent();
        Employee clerk = new Employee();
        Console.Write("Using Student: ");
        DisplayObjectMessage(payingStudent);
        Console.Write("Using ScholarshipStudent: ");
        DisplayObjectMessage(freeStudent);
        Console.Write("Using Employee: ");
        DisplayObjectMessage(clerk);
    }
    public static void DisplayObjectMessage(Object o)
    {
        Console.WriteLine("Method successfully called");
    }
}
```

Figure 8-18 `DiverseObjects` program

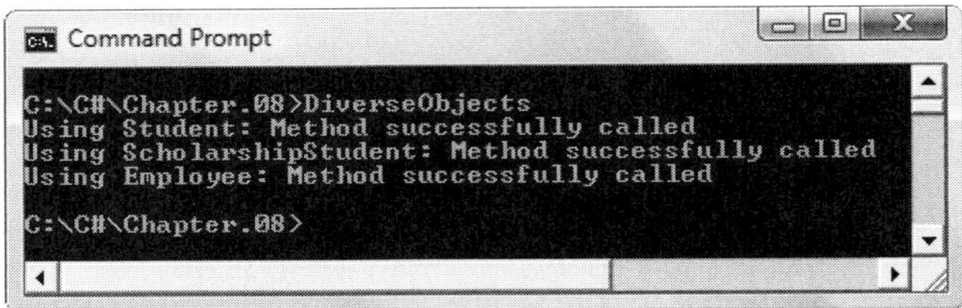

Figure 8-19 Output of the `DiverseObjects` program

When you create any child class, it inherits all the methods of its parent. Because all classes inherit from the `Object` class, all classes inherit the `Object` class methods. The

Object class contains a constructor, a destructor, and four `public` instance methods, as summarized in Table 8-1.

Method	Explanation
Equals()	Determines whether two Object instances are equal
GetHashCode()	Gets a unique code for each object; useful in certain sorting and data management tasks
GetType()	Returns the type, or class, of an object
ToString()	Returns a String that represents the object

Table 8-1 The four `public` instance methods of the Object class

> **NOTE** The Object class contains other nonpublic and noninstance (static) methods in addition to the four methods listed in Table 8-1. The C# documentation provides more details on these methods.

USING THE Object CLASS'S GetType() METHOD

The `GetType()` method returns an object's type, or class. For example, if you have created an `Employee` object named `someWorker`, then the following statement displays `Employee`:

```
Console.WriteLine(someWorker.GetType());
```

> **NOTE**
> If an object's class is defined in a namespace, then `GetType()` returns a string composed of the namespace, a dot, and the class name.

USING THE Object CLASS'S ToString() METHOD

The `Object` class methods are not very useful as they stand. For example, when you use the `Object` class's `ToString()` method with an object you create, it simply returns a string that holds the name of the class, just as `GetType()` does. That is, if `someWorker` is an `Employee`, then the following statement displays `Employee`:

```
Console.WriteLine(someWorker.ToString());
```

When you create a class such as `Employee`, you should override the `Object` class's `ToString()` method with your own, more useful version—perhaps one that returns an `Employee`'s ID number, name, or combination of the two. Of course, you could create a differently named method to do the same thing—perhaps `GetEmployeeIdentification()` or `ConvertEmployeeToString()`. However, by naming your class method `ToString()`, you make the class easier for others to understand and use. Programmers know the `ToString()` method works with every object; when they use it with your objects, you can provide a useful set of information. Additionally, many C# built-in classes use the `ToString()` method; if you have named your method conventionally, those classes will use your version because it is more helpful than the generic one.

For example, you might create an `Employee` class `ToString()` method, as shown in Figure 8-20. This method assumes that `EmpNum` and `Name` are `Employee` properties with `get` accessors. The returned `string` will have a value such as "Employee: 234 Johnson".


```
public override string ToString()
{
    return(getType() + ": " + EmpNum + " " + Name);
}
```

Figure 8-20 An `Employee` class `ToString()` method

USING THE `Object` CLASS'S `Equals()` METHOD AND `GetHashCode()` METHOD

The `Object` class's `Equals()` method returns `true` if two `Object`s have the same memory address—that is, if one object is a reference to the other and both are literally the same object. For example, you might write the following:

```
if oneObject.Equals(anotherObject)...
```


Like the `ToString()` method, this method might not be useful to you in its original form. For example, you might prefer to think of two `Employee` objects as equal if their ID numbers or names are equal. You might want to override the `Equals()` method for any class you create if you anticipate that class clients will want to compare objects based on any of their field values.

If you overload the `Equals()` method, it should meet the following requirements by convention:

» Its header should be as follows (you can use any identifier for the `Object` parameter):
```
public override bool Equals(Object o)
```

» It should return `false` if the argument is `null`.

» It should return `true` if an object is compared to itself.

» It should return `true` only if both of the following are true:
```
oneObject.Equals(anotherObject)
anotherObject.Equals(oneObject)
```

» If `oneObject.Equals(anotherObject)` returns `true` and `oneObject.Equals(aThirdObject)` returns `true`, then `anotherObject.Equals(aThirdObject)` should also be `true`.

When you override the `Equals()` method, you should also override the `GetHashCode()` method, because `Equals()` uses `GetHashCode()` and two objects that are considered equal should have the same hash code. A **hash code** is a number that should uniquely identify an object; you might use hash codes in some advanced C# applications. For example,

Figure 8-21 shows an application that declares two `Employee`s from a class in which the `GetHashCode()` method has not been overridden. The output in Figure 8-22 shows a unique number for each object. (The number, however, is meaningless to you.) If you choose to override the `GetHashCode()` method, you should write this method so it returns a unique integer for every object—an `Employee` number, for example.

> **NOTE** A hash code is sometimes called a "fingerprint" for an object because it uniquely identifies the object. In C#, the default implementation of the `GetHashCode()` method does not guarantee unique return values for different objects. However, if `GetHashCode()` is explicitly implemented in a derived class, it must return a unique hash code.

> **NOTE** In cooking, hash is a dish that is created by combining ingredients. The term *hash code* derives from the fact that the code is sometimes created by mixing some of an object's data.

```csharp
using System;
public class TestHashCode
{
    public static void Main()
    {
        Employee first = new Employee();
        Employee second = new Employee();
        Console.WriteLine(first.GetHashCode());
        Console.WriteLine(second.GetHashCode());
    }
}
```

Figure 8-21 `TestHashCode` program

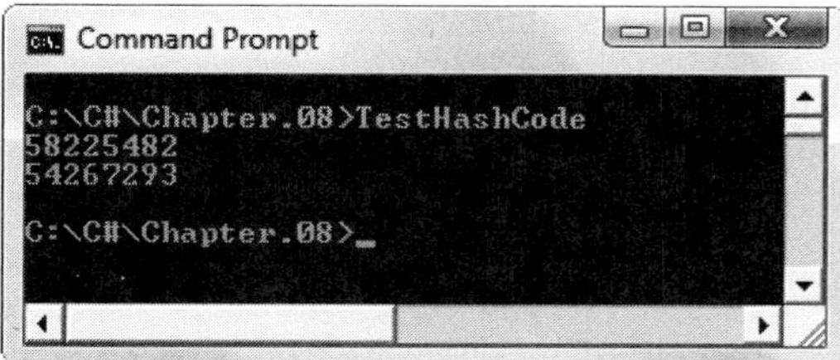

Figure 8-22 Output of the `TestHashCode` program

> **NOTE** You first used the `Equals()` method to compare `String` objects in Chapter 2. When you use `Equals()` with `String`s, you use the `String` class's `Equals()` method that compares `String` contents as opposed to `String` addresses. In other words, the `Object` class's `Equals()` method has already been overridden in the `String` class.

> **NOTE** In Chapter 7, you learned to overload operators. If you overload == or != for a class, you will receive warning messages if you do not also override both the `Equals()` and `GetHashCode()` methods.

> **NOTE** Although you can write an `Equals()` method for a class without overriding `GetHashCode()`, you receive a warning message. See the C# documentation for information on the `HashTable` class.

When you create an `Equals()` method to override the one in the `Object` class, the parameter must be an `Object`. For example, if you consider `Employee` objects equal when the `EmpNum` properties are equal, then an `Employee` class `Equals()` method might be created as follows:

```csharp
public override bool Equals(Object e)
{
    bool equal;
    Employee temp = (Employee)e;
    if(EmpNum == temp.EmpNum)
      equal = true;
    else
      equal = false;
    return equal;
}
```

In the shaded second statement in the method, the `Object` argument is cast to an `Employee` so the `Employee`'s `EmpNum` can be compared. If you did not perform the cast, and tried to make the comparison with `o.EmpNum`, the method would not compile because an `Object` does not have an `EmpNum`.

An even better alternative is to ensure that compared objects are the same type before making any other decisions. For example, the `Equals()` method in Figure 8-23 uses the `GetType()` method with both the `this` object and the parameter before proceeding. If compared objects are not the same type, then the `Equals()` method should return `false`.

```csharp
public override bool Equals(Object e)
{
    bool equal;
    if(this.GetType() != e.GetType())
       equal = false;
    else
    {
       Employee temp = (Employee)e;
       if(EmpNum == temp.EmpNum)
          equal = true;
       else
          equal = false;
    }
    return equal;
}
```

Figure 8-23 An `Equals()` method for the `Employee` class

»TWO TRUTHS AND A LIE: USING THE Object **CLASS**

1. The Object class contains a method named GetType() that returns an object's type, or class.
2. If you do not override the ToString() method for a class, it returns the value of all the strings within the class.
3. The Object class's Equals() method returns true if two Objects have the same memory address—that is, if one object is a reference to the other and both are literally the same object.

The false statement is #2. If you do not override the ToString() method for a class, it returns a string that holds the name of the class.

WORKING WITH BASE CLASS CONSTRUCTORS

When you create any object, you are calling a class constructor method that has the same name as the class itself; for example:

```
SomeClass anObject = new SomeClass();
```

When you instantiate an object that is a member of a derived class, you call both the constructor for the base class and the constructor for the extended, derived class. When you create any derived class object, the base class constructor must execute first; only then does the derived class constructor execute.

»NOTE When you create any object, you call its constructor and the Object constructor because all classes are derived from Object. So, when you create a base class and a derived class, and instantiate a derived class object, you call three constructors: one from the Object class, one from the base class, and one from the derived class.

In the examples of inheritance you have seen so far in this chapter, each class contained default constructors, so their execution was transparent. However, you should realize that when you create a subclass, both the base and derived constructors execute. For example, consider the abbreviated Employee and CommissionEmployee classes in Figure 8-24. Employee contains just two fields and a constructor; CommissionEmployee descends from Employee and contains a constructor as well. The DemoSalesperson4 program in Figure 8-25 contains just one statement; it instantiates a CommissionEmployee. The output in Figure 8-26 shows that this one statement causes both constructors to execute.

Of course, most constructors perform many more tasks than printing a message to inform you that they exist. When constructors initialize variables, you usually want the base class constructor to initialize the data fields that originate in the base class. The derived class constructor needs to initialize only the data fields that are specific to the derived class.

```csharp
public class Employee
{
   private int empNum;
   protected double empSal;
   public Employee()
   {
      Console.WriteLine("Employee constructed");
   }
}
public class CommissionEmployee : Employee
{
   private double commissionRate;
   public CommissionEmployee()
   {
      Console.WriteLine("CommissionEmployee constructed");
   }
}
```

Figure 8-24 `Employee` and `CommissionEmployee` classes with parameterless constructors

```csharp
using System;
public class DemoSalesperson4
{
   public static void Main()
   {
      CommissionEmployee salesperson = new CommissionEmployee();
   }
}
```

Figure 8-25 The `DemoSalesperson4` program

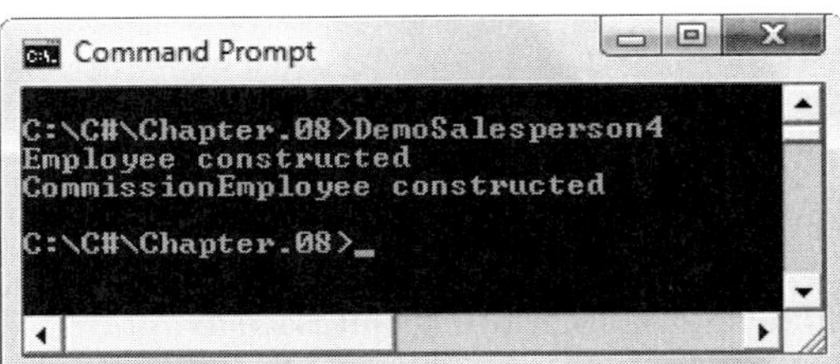

Figure 8-26 Output of the `DemoSalesperson4` program

USING BASE CLASS CONSTRUCTORS
THAT REQUIRE ARGUMENTS

When you create a class and do not provide a constructor, C# automatically supplies one that never requires arguments. When you write your own constructor for a class, you replace the automatically supplied version. Depending on your needs, the constructor you create for a class might require arguments. When you use a class as a base class and the class has a constructor that requires arguments, then you must make sure that any derived classes provide the base class constructor with what it needs.

When a base class constructor requires arguments, you must include a constructor for each derived class you create. Your derived class constructor can contain any number of statements; however, within the header of the constructor, you must provide values for any arguments required by the base class constructor. Even if you have no other reason for creating a derived class constructor, you must write the derived class constructor so it can call its parent's constructor.

The format of the portion of the constructor header that calls a base class constructor is `base(list of arguments)`. The keyword **base** always refers to the superclass of the class in which you use it. For example, if you create an `Employee` class with a constructor that requires two arguments—an integer and a string—and you create a `CommissionEmployee` class that is a subclass of `Employee`, then the following code shows a valid constructor for `CommissionEmployee`:

```
public CommissionEmployee() : base(1234, "XXXX")
{
    // Other statements can go here
}
```

In this example, the `CommissionEmployee` constructor requires no arguments, but it passes two arguments to its base class constructor. Every `CommissionEmployee` passes 1234 and "XXXX" to the `Employee` constructor. A different `CommissionEmployee` constructor might require arguments; then it could pass the appropriate arguments on to the base class constructor, as in the following example:

```
public CommissionEmployee(int id, string name) : base(id, name)
{
  // Other statements can go here
}
```

Yet another `CommissionEmployee` constructor might require three or more arguments. Some arguments might be passed to the base class constructor, and some might be used within `CommissionEmployee`. Consider the following example:

```
public CommissionEmployee(int id, string name, double rate) :
    base(id, name) // two parameters passed to base constructor
{
    CommissionRate = rate;
    // rate is used within child constructor
    // Other statements can go here
}
```

»TWO TRUTHS AND A LIE: WORKING WITH BASE CLASS CONSTRUCTORS

1. When you create any derived class object, the base class constructor executes first, followed by the derived class constructor.
2. When a base class constructor requires arguments, you must include a constructor for each derived class you create.
3. When a derived class's constructor requires arguments, all of the arguments must be passed to the base class constructor.

The false statement is #3. When a derived class's constructor requires arguments, all of the arguments might be needed in the derived class, or perhaps all must be passed to the base class constructor. It also might be possible that some arguments are passed to the base class constructor and others are used within the derived class constructor.

CREATING AND USING ABSTRACT CLASSES

Creating classes is easier after you understand the concept of inheritance. When you create a child class, it inherits all the general attributes you need; you must create only the new, more specific attributes required by the child class. For example, a `Painter` and a `Sculptor` are more specific than an `Artist`. They inherit all the general attributes of `Artists`, but you must add the attributes and methods that are specific to `Painter` and `Sculptor`.

> **»NOTE**
> Nonabstract classes from which objects *can* be instantiated are called **concrete** classes.

Another way to think about a superclass is to notice that it contains the features shared by its subclasses. The derived classes are more specific examples of the base class type; they add features to the shared, general features. Conversely, when you examine a derived class, you notice that its parent is more general. Sometimes you create a parent class to be so general that you never intend to create any specific instances of the class. For example, you might never create "just" an `Artist`; each `Artist` is more specifically a `Painter`, `Sculptor`, `Illustrator`, and so on. A class that you create only to extend from, but not to instantiate from, is an abstract class. An **abstract class** is one from which you cannot create concrete objects, but from which you can inherit. You use the keyword `abstract` when you declare an abstract class.

> **»NOTE**
> If you attempt to instantiate an object from an abstract class, you will receive a compiler error message.

Abstract classes are like regular classes in that they can contain data fields and methods. The difference is that you cannot create instances of abstract classes by using the `new` operator. Rather, you create abstract classes simply to provide a base class from which other objects may be derived. Abstract classes usually contain abstract methods, although methods are not required. An **abstract method** has no method statements; any class derived from a class that contains an abstract method must override the abstract method by providing a body (an implementation) for it. (Alternatively, the derived class can declare the method to be abstract; in that case, the derived class's children must implement the method.)

> **»NOTE**
> An abstract method is a virtual method. A **virtual method** is one whose behavior is determined by the implementation in a child class.

When you create an abstract method, you provide the keyword `abstract` and the intended method type, name, and arguments, but you do not provide statements within the method; you do not even supply curly braces. When you create a derived class that inherits an abstract method from a parent, you must use the keyword **override** in the method header and provide the actions, or implementation, for the inherited method within the derived class. In other words, you are required to code a derived class method to override the empty base class method that is inherited.

For example, suppose you want to create classes to represent different animals. You can create a generic, abstract class named `Animal` so you can provide generic data fields, such as the animal's name, only once. An `Animal` is generic, but each specific `Animal`, such as `Dog` or `Cat`, makes a unique sound that differs from `Animal` to `Animal`. If you code an abstract `Speak()` method in the abstract `Animal` class, then you require all future `Animal` derived classes to override the `Speak()` method and provide an implementation that is specific to the derived class. Figure 8-27 shows an abstract `Animal` class that contains a data field for the name, a constructor that assigns a name, a `Name` property, and an abstract `Speak()` method.

```
abstract class Animal
{
    protected string name;
    public Animal(string name)
    {
        this.name = name;
    }
    public string Name
    {
        get
        {
            return name;
        }
    }
    public abstract string Speak();
}
```

Figure 8-27 `Animal` class

The `Animal` class in Figure 8-27 is declared to be `abstract`. (The keyword is shaded.) You cannot place a statement such as `Animal myPet = new Animal("Murphy");` within a program, because the program will not compile. Because `Animal` is an `abstract` class, no `Animal` objects can exist.

You create an abstract class like `Animal` so that you can extend it. For example, you can create `Dog` and `Cat` classes as shown in Figure 8-28. Because the `Animal` class contains a constructor that requires a `string` argument, both `Dog` and `Cat` must contain constructors that provide `string` arguments for their base class.

The `Dog` and `Cat` constructors perform no tasks other than passing out the name to the `Animal` constructor. The overriding `Speak()` methods within `Dog` and `Cat` are required because the `abstract` parent `Animal` class contains an `abstract` `Speak()` method. The

```
class Dog : Animal
{
  public Dog(string name) : base(name)
  {
  }
  public override string Speak()
  {
     return "woof";
  }
}
class Cat : Animal
{
  public Cat(string name) : base(name)
  {
  }
  public override string Speak()
  {
     return "meow";
  }
}
```

Figure 8-28 Dog and Cat classes

keyword override (shaded) is required in the method header. You can code any statements you want within the Dog and Cat class Speak() methods, but the Speak() methods must exist.

Figure 8-29 shows a program that implements Dog and Cat objects, and Figure 8-30 shows the output. Speak() operates polymorphically; that is, each object acts appropriately using the correct Speak() method.

```
using System;
class DemoAnimals
{
    public static void Main()
    {
        Dog spot = new Dog("Spot");
        Cat puff = new Cat("Puff");
        Console.WriteLine(spot.Name + " says " + spot.Speak());
        Console.WriteLine(puff.Name + " says " + puff.Speak());
    }
}
```

Figure 8-29 DemoAnimals program

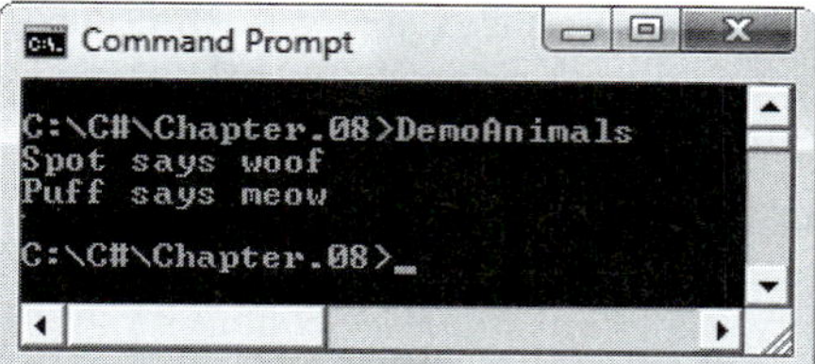

Figure 8-30 Output of the `DemoAnimals` program

»TWO TRUTHS AND A LIE: CREATING AND USING ABSTRACT CLASSES

1. An abstract class is one from which you cannot create concrete objects.
2. Unlike regular classes, abstract classes cannot contain methods.
3. When a base class contains an abstract method, its descendants must override it or declare it to be abstract.

The false statement is #2. Abstract classes are like regular classes in that they can contain data fields and methods. The difference is that you cannot create instances of abstract classes by using the new operator. Rather, you create abstract classes simply to provide a base class from which other objects may be derived.

CREATING AND USING INTERFACES

Some object-oriented programming languages, notably C++, allow a subclass to inherit from more than one parent class. For example, you might create an `Employee` class that contains data fields pertaining to each employee in your organization. You also might create a `Product` class that holds information about each product your organization manufactures. When you create a `Patent` class for each product for which your company holds a patent, you might want to include product information as well as information about the employee who was responsible for the invention. In this situation, it would be convenient to inherit fields and methods from both the `Product` and `Employee` classes. The ability to inherit from more than one class is called **multiple inheritance**.

Multiple inheritance is a difficult concept, and programmers encounter many problems when they use it. For example, variables and methods in the parent classes may have identical names, creating a conflict when the child class uses one of the names. Additionally, as you already have learned, a child class constructor must call its parent class constructor. When two or more parents exist, this becomes a more complicated task: To which class should `base` refer when a child class has multiple parents?

For all of these reasons, multiple inheritance is prohibited in C#. However, C# does provide an alternative to multiple inheritance, known as an interface. Much like an abstract class, an **interface** is a collection of methods (and perhaps other members) that can be used by any

> **»NOTE**
> You first learned about interfaces in Chapter 7 when you used the `IComparable` interface.

class as long as the class provides a definition to override the interface's abstract definitions. Within an abstract class, some methods can be abstract, while others need not be. Within an interface, all methods are abstract.

You create an interface much as you create an abstract class definition, except that you use the keyword `interface` instead of `abstract class`. For example, suppose you create an `IWork` interface as shown in Figure 8-31. For simplicity, the `IWork` interface contains a single method named `Work()`.

>>**NOTE** Although not required, in C# it is customary to start interface names with an uppercase "I". Other languages follow different conventions. Interface names frequently end with "able".

```
public interface IWork
{
    string Work();
}
```

Figure 8-31 The `IWork` interface

When any class implements `IWork`, it must also include a `Work()` method that returns a `string`. Figure 8-32 shows two classes that implement `IWork`: the `Employee` class and the `Animal` class. Because each implements `IWork`, each must declare a `Work()` method. The `Employee` class implements `Work()` to return the "I do my job" `string`. The abstract `Animal` class defines `Work()` as an abstract method, meaning that descendants of `Animal` must implement `Work()`. Figure 8-32 also shows two child classes of `Animal`: `Dog` and `Cat`. Note how `Work()` is defined differently for each.

```
class Employee : IWork
{
    private string name;
    public Employee(string name)
    {
        Name = name;
    }
    public string Name {get; set;}
    public string Work()
    {
        return "I do my job";
    }
}
```

Figure 8-32 Employee, Animal, Cat, and Dog classes with the `IWork` interface (*continued*)

```
abstract class Animal : IWork
{
    protected string name;
    public Animal(string name)
    {
        Name = name;
    }
    public string Name
    {
        get
        {
            return name;
        }
        set
        {
            name = value;
        }
    }
    public abstract string Work();
}
class Dog : Animal
{
    public Dog(string name) : base(name)
    {
    }
    public override string Work()
    {
        return "I watch the house";
    }
}
class Cat : Animal
{
    public Cat(string name) : base(name)
    {
    }
    public override string Work()
    {
        return "I catch mice";
    }
}
```

Figure 8-32 (*continued*)

When you create a program that instantiates an `Employee`, a `Dog`, or a `Cat`, as in the `DemoWorking` program in Figure 8-33, each object type knows how to "`Work()`" appropriately. Figure 8-34 shows the output.

```
using System;
class DemoWorking
{
    public static void Main()
    {
        Employee bob = new Employee("Bob");
        Dog spot = new Dog("Spot");
        Cat puff = new Cat("Puff");
        Console.WriteLine(bob.Name + " says " + bob.Work());
        Console.WriteLine(spot.Name + " says " + spot.Work());
        Console.WriteLine(puff.Name + " says " + puff.Work());
    }
}
```

Figure 8-33 `DemoWorking` program

Figure 8-34 Output of the `DemoWorking` program

Abstract classes and interfaces are similar in that you cannot instantiate concrete objects from either one. Abstract classes differ from interfaces in that abstract classes can contain nonabstract methods, but all methods within an interface must be abstract. A class can inherit from only one base class (whether abstract or not), but it can implement any number of interfaces. For example, if you want to create a `Child` that inherits from a `Parent` class and implements two interfaces, `IWork` and `IPlay`, you would define the class name and list the base class and interfaces separated by commas:

```
class Child : Parent, IWork, IPlay
```


You implement an existing interface because you want a class to be able to use a method that already exists in other applications. For example, suppose you have created a `Payroll` application that uses the `Work()` method in the interface class. Also suppose you create a new class named `BusDriver`. If `BusDriver` implements the `IWork` interface, then `BusDriver` objects can be used by the existing `Payroll` program. As another example, suppose you have written a game program that uses an `IAttack` interface with methods that determine how and when an object can attack. When you create new classes such as `MarsAlien`, `Vampire`, and `CivilWarSoldier`, and each implements the interface, you can define how each one attacks and how each type of object can be added to the game.

Beginning programmers sometimes find it difficult to decide when to create an abstract base class and when to create an interface. Typically, you create an abstract class when you want to provide some data or methods that derived classes can inherit, but you want the subclasses to override some specific methods that you declare to be `abstract`. You create an interface when you want derived classes to override every method. Use a base class when the class you want to create "is a" subtype of another class; use an interface when the class you want to create will act like the interface.

Interfaces provide you with a way to exhibit polymorphic behavior. If diverse classes implement the same interface in unique ways, then you can treat each class type in the same way using the same language. When various classes use the same interface, you know the names of the methods that are available with those classes, and C# classes adopt a more uniform functionality; this consistency helps you to understand new classes you encounter more easily. If you know, for example, the method names contained in the `IWork` interface, and you see that a class implements `IWork`, you have a head start in understanding how the class functions.

> **»NOTE**
> Now that you understand how to construct your own interfaces, you will benefit from rereading the section describing the `IComparable` interface in Chapter 7.

»TWO TRUTHS AND A LIE: CREATING AND USING INTERFACES

1. An interface is a collection of methods (and perhaps other members) that can be used by any class as long as the class provides a definition to override the interface's abstract definitions.
2. Abstract classes and interfaces differ in that all methods in abstract classes must be abstract, but interfaces can contain nonabstract methods.
3. A class can inherit from only one base class, but it can implement any number of interfaces.

The false statement is #2. Abstract classes and interfaces are similar in that you cannot instantiate concrete objects from either one. However, they differ in that abstract classes can contain nonabstract methods, but all methods within an interface must be abstract.

USING EXTENSION METHODS

When you write C# programs you constantly use classes, some that you have written yourself and many more that have been written by others. Sometimes you might wish a class had an additional method that would be useful to you. If you created the original class, you have two options:

» You could revise the existing class, including the new useful method.
» You could derive a child class from the existing class and provide it with a new method.

> **»NOTE**
> Extension methods are a new feature in C# 3.0.

Sometimes, however, classes you use were created by others, and you might not be allowed to either revise or extend them. Of course, you could create an entirely new class that includes your new method, but that would duplicate a lot of the work already done when the first class was created. In these cases, the best option is to write an extension method. **Extension methods** are methods you can write to add to any type.

For example, you have used the prewritten Int32 class throughout this book to declare integers. Suppose you work for a company that frequently uses customer account numbers, and that the company has decided to add an extra digit to each account number. For simplicity, assume all account numbers are two digits and that the new, third number should be the rightmost digit in the sum of the first two digits. You could handle this problem by creating a class named AccountNumber, including a method to produce the extra digit, and redefining every instance of a customer's account number in your applications as an AccountNumber object. However, if you already have a lot of applications that define the account number as an integer, you might prefer to create an extension method that extends the Int32 class.

»NOTE When organizations append extra digits to account numbers, the extra digits are called check digits. **Check digits** help assure that all the digits in account numbers and other numbers are entered correctly. Check digits are calculated using different formulas. If a digit used to calculate the check digit is incorrect, then the resulting check digit is probably incorrect as well.

Figure 8-35 contains a method that extends the Int32 class. The first parameter in an extension method specifies the type extended and must begin with the keyword this. For example, the first (and in this case, only) parameter in the GetCheckDigit() method is this int num, as shown in the shaded portion of the figure. Extension methods must be static methods. Within the GetCheckDigit() method in Figure 8-35, the first digit is extracted from the two-digit account number by dividing by 10 and taking the resulting whole number, and the second digit is extracting by taking the remainder. Those two digits are added, and the last digit of that sum is returned from the method. For example, if 49 is passed into the method, first becomes 4, second becomes 9, and third becomes the last digit of 13, or 3. Then the original number (49) is multiplied by 10 and added to the third digit, resulting in 493.

```
public static int GetCheckDigit(this int num)
{
    int first = num / 10;
    int second = num % 10;
    int third = (first + second) % 10;
    int result = num * 10 + third;
    return result;
}
```

Figure 8-35 The GetCheckDigit() extension method

When you write an extension method, it must be stored in a static class. For example, the DemoExtensionMethod program in Figure 8-36 shows an application that is declared static in the first shaded statement and uses the extension method in the second shaded statement.

The static method `GetCheckDigit()` is used as if it were an instance method of the `Int32` class; in other words, it is attached to an `Int32` object with a dot, just as instance methods are when used with objects. No arguments are passed to the `GetCheckDigit()` method explicitly from the `DemoExtensionMethod` class. The parameter in the method is implied, just as these references are always implied in instance methods. Figure 8-37 shows the execution of the program.

```
using System;
static class DemoExtensionMethod
{
    public static void Main()
    {
        int acctNum = 49;
        int revisedAcctNum = acctNum.GetCheckDigit();
        Console.WriteLine("Original account number was {0}",
            acctNum);
        Console.WriteLine("Revised account number is {0}",
            revisedAcctNum);
    }
    public static int GetCheckDigit(this int num)
    {
        int first = num / 10;
        int second = num % 10;
        int third = (first + second) % 10;
        int result = num * 10 + third;
        return result;
    }
}
```

Figure 8-36 The `DemoExtensionMethod` application

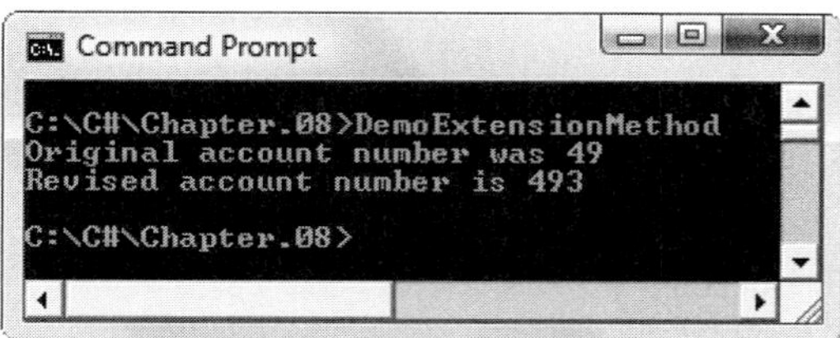

Figure 8-37 Execution of the `DemoExtensionMethod` application

You can create extension methods for your own classes in the same way one was created for the `Int32` class in this example. Just like other outside methods, and unlike ordinary class instance methods, extension methods cannot access any private members of classes they extend. Furthermore, if a class contains an instance method with the same signature as an extension method, the instance method takes priority and will be the one that executes.

»TWO TRUTHS AND A LIE: USING EXTENSION METHODS

1. The first parameter in an extension method specifies the type extended and must begin with the keyword `this`.
2. Extension methods must be static methods.
3. When you write an extension method, it must be stored within the class to which it refers, along with the class's other instance methods.

The false statement is #3. Although you use an extension method like an instance method, any extension method you write must be stored in a static class.

RECAPPING THE BENEFITS OF USING INHERITANCE

When an automobile company designs a new car model, it does not build every component from scratch. The car might include a new feature—for example, some model contained the first air bag—but many of a new car's features are simply modifications of existing features. The manufacturer might create a larger gas tank or a more comfortable seat, but these new features still possess many of the properties of their predecessors from older models. Most features of new car models are not even modified; instead, existing components, such as air filters and windshield wipers, are included on the new model without any changes.

Similarly, you can create powerful computer programs more easily if many of their components are used either "as is" or with slight modifications. Inheritance does not enable you to write any programs that you could not write if inheritance did not exist; you *could* create every part of a program from scratch, but reusing existing classes and interfaces makes your job easier.

You already have used many "as is" classes, such as `Console`, `Int32`, and `String`. Using these classes made it easier to write programs than if you had to invent the classes yourself. Now that you have learned about inheritance, you can extend existing classes as well as just use them. When you create a useful, extendable base class, you and other future programmers gain several advantages:

» Derived class creators save development time because much of the code that is needed for the class already has been written.

» Derived class creators save testing time because the base class code already has been tested and probably used in a variety of situations. In other words, the base class code is reliable.

» Programmers who create or use new derived classes already understand how the base class works, so the time it takes to learn the new class features is reduced.

» When you create a derived class in C#, the base class source code is not changed. Thus, the base class maintains its integrity.

> **» NOTE** Classes that are not intended to be instantiated and that contain only `static` members are declared as `static` classes. You cannot extend `static` classes. For example, `System.Console` is a static class.

When you think about classes, you need to think about the commonalities between them, and then you can create base classes from which to inherit. You might even be rewarded professionally when you see your own superclasses extended by others in the future.

» TWO TRUTHS AND A LIE: RECAPPING THE BENEFITS OF USING INHERITANCE

1. Inheritance enables you to create powerful computer programs more easily.
2. Without inheritance, you *could* create every part of a program from scratch, but reusing existing classes and interfaces makes your job easier.
3. Inheritance is frequently inefficient because base class code is seldom reliable when extended to a derived class.

The false statement is #3. Derived class creators save testing time because the base class code has already been tested and probably used in a variety of situations. In other words, the base class code is reliable.

YOU DO IT

In this section, you will create a working example of inheritance. You will create this example in four parts:

1. You will create a general `BankLoan` class that holds data pertaining to a bank loan—a loan number, a customer name, and the amount borrowed.

2. After you create the general `BankLoan` class, you will write a program to instantiate and use a `BankLoan` object.

3. You will create a more specific `CarLoan` derived class that inherits the attributes of the `BankLoan` class but adds information about the automobile that serves as collateral for the loan.

4. You will modify the `BankLoan` demonstration program to add a `CarLoan` object and demonstrate its use.

To create the BankLoan class:

1. Open a new file in your text editor, then enter the following first few lines for a BankLoan class. The class will host three data fields—the loan number, the last name of the customer, and the value of the loan.

```
public class BankLoan
{
    private int loanNumber;
    private string lastName;
    private double loanAmount;
```

2. Add a property with get and set accessors for each of the three data fields.

```
    public int LoanNumber {get; set;}
    public string LastName {get; set;}
    public double LoanAmount {get; set;}
```

3. Add a closing curly brace for the class. Save the file as **DemoBankLoan.cs**. Compile the file and correct any errors other than the one error you expect, which tells you that the program does not define an entry point. The message means that you cannot execute the file because it doesn't contain a class with a Main() method yet.

4. At the top of the file, enter the following code to add a DemoBankLoan class that contains a Main() method. The class declares a BankLoan object and shows how to set each field and display the results.

```
using System;
public class DemoBankLoan
{
    public static void Main()
    {
        BankLoan aLoan = new BankLoan();
        aLoan.LoanNumber = 2239;
        aLoan.LastName = "Mitchell";
        aLoan.LoanAmount = 1000.00;
        Console.WriteLine("Loan #{0} for {1} is for {2}",
            aLoan.LoanNumber, aLoan.LastName,
            aLoan.LoanAmount.ToString("C2"));
    }
}
```

5. Save the file, then compile the program. (You can safely ignore warnings about fields that are not used.) Execute the program. The output looks like Figure 8-38. There is nothing unusual about this class or how it operates; it is similar to many you saw in Chapter 7.

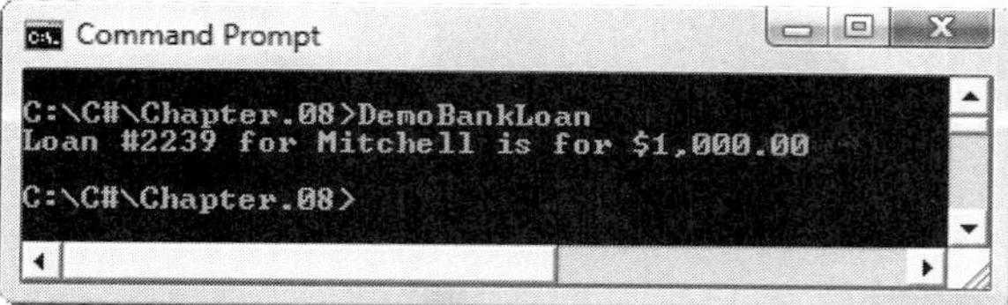

Figure 8-38 Output of the DemoBankLoan program

EXTENDING A CLASS

Next, you will create a class named CarLoan. A CarLoan "is a" type of BankLoan. As such, it has all the attributes of a BankLoan, but it also has the year and make of the car that the customer is using as collateral for the loan. Therefore, CarLoan is a subclass of BankLoan.

To create the CarLoan class that extends the BankLoan class:

1. Save the DemoBankLoan.cs file as **DemoCarLoan.cs**. Change the DemoBankLoan class name to **DemoCarLoan**. Position your cursor after the closing brace for the BankLoan class, press **Enter** to start a new line, and begin the definition of the CarLoan class. It extends BankLoan and contains two fields: year and make.

```
class CarLoan : BankLoan
{
    private int year;
    private string make;
```

2. Include properties for the fields you created in Step 1.

```
    public int Year {get; set;}
    public string Make {get; set;}
```

3. Add a closing curly brace for the class. Save the program, compile it, and correct any errors.

4. Modify the DemoBankLoan class to include a CarLoan object. First, change the name of the class from DemoBankLoan to **DemoCarLoan**.

5. Within the Main() method, just after the declaration of the BankLoan object, declare a CarLoan as follows:

```
CarLoan aCarLoan = new CarLoan();
```

6. After the three property assignments for the BankLoan object, insert five assignment statements for the CarLoan object.

```
aCarLoan.LoanNumber = 3358;
aCarLoan.LastName = "Jansen";
aCarLoan.LoanAmount = 20000.00;
aCarLoan.Make = "Ford";
aCarLoan.Year = 2005;
```

7. Following the `WriteLine()` statement that displays the `BankLoan` object data, insert two `WriteLine()` statements that display the `CarLoan` object's data.

```
Console.WriteLine("Loan #{0} for {1} is for {2}",
   aCarLoan.LoanNumber, aCarLoan.LastName,
   aCarLoan.LoanAmount.ToString("C2"));
Console.WriteLine("Loan #{0} is for a {1} {2}",
   aCarLoan.LoanNumber, aCarLoan.Year,
   aCarLoan.Make);
```

8. Save the program, then compile and execute it. The output looks like Figure 8-39. The `CarLoan` object correctly uses its own fields and properties as well as those of the parent `BankLoan` class.

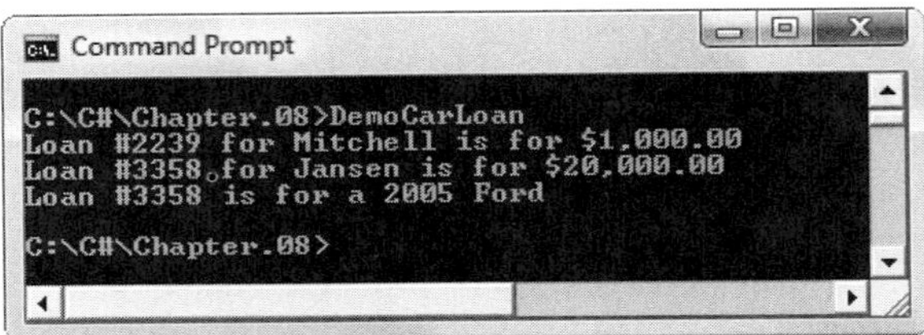

Figure 8-39 Output of the `DemoCarLoan` program

USING BASE CLASS MEMBERS IN A DERIVED CLASS

In the previous sections, you created `BankLoan()` and `CarLoan()` classes and objects. Suppose the bank adopts new rules as follows:

» No regular loan will be made for less than $5000.

» No car loan will be made for any car older than model year 2006.

» Although `BankLoans` might have larger loan numbers, `CarLoans` will have loan numbers that are no more than three digits. If a larger loan number is provided, the program will use only the last three digits for the loan number.

To implement the new `CarLoan` rules:

1. Open the DemoCarLoan.cs file and immediately save it as **DemoCarLoan2.cs**. Also change the class name from `DemoCarLoan` to **DemoCarLoan2**.

2. Within the `BankLoan` class, add a new constant that represents the minimum loan value.

```
public const double MINIMUM_LOAN = 5000;
```

3. Replace the auto-implemented property for `LoanAmount` in the `BankLoan` class with standard `get` and `set` accessors as follows. This change ensures that no loan is made for less than the minimum allowed value.

```
public double LoanAmount
{
    set
    {
        if(value < MINIMUM_LOAN)
            loanAmount = MINIMUM_LOAN;
        else
            loanAmount = value;
    }
    get
    {
        return loanAmount;
    }
}
```

4. Within the `BankLoan` class, change the access modifier of `loanAmount` from `private` to **protected**. You do so to enable the `CarLoan` child class to change the `loanAmount` to 0 if a car year is older than 2006. If the child class had to use the `public` property to change the loan value, the value would become equal to MINIMUM_LOAN instead of 0.

5. Within the `CarLoan` class, add two new constants to hold the earliest year for which car loans will be given and the lowest allowed loan number.

```
private const int EARLIEST_YEAR = 2006;
private const int LOWEST_INVALID_NUM = 1000;
```

6. Also within the `CarLoan` class, replace the existing auto-implemented `Year` property with one that contains coded `get` and `set` accessors. The `Year` property `set` accessor not only sets the `year` field, it sets `loanAmount` to 0 when a car's year is less than 2006.

```
public int Year
{
    set
    {
        if(value < EARLIEST_YEAR)
        {
            year = value;
            loanAmount = 0;
        }
        else
            year = value;
    }
    get
    {
        return year;
    }
}
```

If `loanAmount` was `private` in the parent `BankLoan` class, you would not be able to set its value in the child `CarLoan` class, as you do here. You could use the `public` property

LoanAmount to set the value, but the parent class set accessor would force the value to 5000.

7. Suppose there are unique rules for issuing loan numbers for cars. Within the CarLoan class, just before the closing curly brace, change the inherited LoanNumber property to accommodate the new rules. If a car loan number is three digits or fewer, pass it on to the base class property. If not, obtain the last three digits by calculating the remainder when the loan number is divided by 1000 and pass the new number to the base class property. Add the following property after the definition of the Make property.

```
public new int LoanNumber
{
    get
    {
        return base.LoanNumber;
    }
    set
    {
        if(value < LOWEST_INVALID_NUM)
            base.LoanNumber = value;
        else
            base.LoanNumber = value % LOWEST_INVALID_NUM;
    }
}
```


If you did not use the keyword base to access the LoanNumber property within the CarLoan class, you would be telling this version of the LoanNumber property to call itself. Although the program would compile, it would run continuously in an infinite loop until it ran out of memory and issued an error message.

8. Save the file. Compile it and correct any errors. When you execute the program, the output looks like Figure 8-40. Compare the output to Figure 8-39. Notice that the $1000 bank loan has been forced to $5000. Also notice that the car loan number has been shortened to three digits and the value of the loan is $0 because of the age of the car.

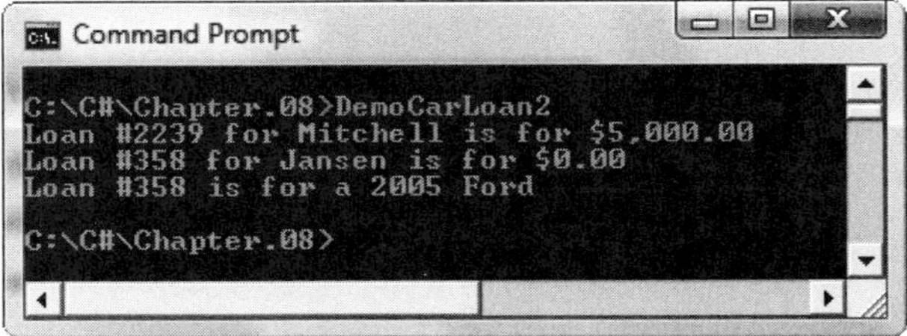

Figure 8-40 Output of the DemoCarLoan2 program

9. Change the assigned values within the `DemoCarLoan2` class to combinations of early and late years and valid and invalid loan numbers. After each change, save the program, compile and execute it, and confirm that the program operates as expected.

ADDING CONSTRUCTORS TO BASE AND DERIVED CLASSES

When a base class contains only constructors that require parameters, then any derived classes must provide for the base class constructor. In the next steps, you will add constructors to the `BankLoan` and `CarLoan` classes and demonstrate that they work as expected.

To add constructors to the classes:

1. Open the `DemoCarLoan2` program and change the class name to `DemoCarLoan3`. Save the file as **DemoCarLoan3.cs**.

2. In the `BankLoan` class, just after the declaration of the fields and constants, add a constructor that requires values for all the `BankLoan`'s fields and assigns them to the properties:

```
public BankLoan(int num, string name, double amount)
{
    LoanNumber = num;
    LastName = name;
    LoanAmount = amount;
}
```

3. In the `CarLoan` class, just after the declaration of the fields and constants, add a constructor that takes five parameters. It passes three of the parameters to the base class constructor and uses the other two to assign values to the properties that are unique to the child class.

```
public CarLoan(int num, string name, double amount,
    int year, string make)  : base(num, name, amount)
{
    Year = year;
    Make = make;
}
```

4. In the `Main()` method of the `DemoCarLoan3` class, remove the existing declarations for `aLoan` and `aCarLoan` and replace them with two declarations that use the arguments passed to the constructors.

```
BankLoan aLoan = new BankLoan(333, "Hanson", 7000.00);
CarLoan aCarLoan = new CarLoan(444, "Carlisle", 30000.00,
    2009, "BMW");
```

5. Remove the eight statements that assigned values to the `BankLoan` and `CarLoan`, but retain the `Console.WriteLine()` statements that display the values.

6. Save the program, then compile and execute it. The output looks like Figure 8-41. Both constructors work as expected. The `CarLoan` constructor has called its parent's constructor to set the necessary fields before executing its own unique statements.

```
C:\C#\Chapter.08>DemoCarLoan3
Loan #333 for Hanson is for $7,000.00
Loan #444 for Carlisle is for $30,000.00
Loan #444 is for a 2009 BMW

C:\C#\Chapter.08>
```

Figure 8-41 Output of the `DemoCarLoan3` program

CHAPTER SUMMARY

» Inheritance is the principle that you can apply your knowledge of a general category to more specific objects. The classes you create in object-oriented programming languages can inherit data and methods from existing classes. The ability to use inheritance makes programs easier to write, easier to understand, and less prone to errors.

» A class that is used as a basis for inheritance is called a base class. When you create a class that inherits from a base class, it is called a derived class or extended class. A derived class always "is a" case or instance of the more general base class. You can use the terms *superclass* and *parent class* as synonyms for base class, and the terms *subclass* and *child class* as synonyms for derived class.

» When you create a class that is an extension or child of another class, you use a single colon between the derived class name and its base class name. The child class inherits all the methods and fields of its parent. Inheritance works only in one direction—a child inherits from a parent, but not the other way around.

» If you could use private data outside of its class, the principle of information hiding would be destroyed. On some occasions, however, you want to access parent class data from within a derived class. For those occasions, you declare parent class fields using the keyword `protected`, which provides you with an intermediate level of security between `public` and `private` access.

» You can declare a child class method with the same name and argument list as a method within its parent class. When you do so, you override the parent class method and allow your class objects to exhibit polymorphic behavior. You can use the keyword `new` or `override` with the derived class method.

» When a derived class overrides a parent class method but you want to access the parent class version of the method, you can use the keyword `base`.

» Every derived class object "is a" specific instance of both the derived class and the base class. Therefore, you can assign a derived class object to an object of any of its base class types. When you do so, C# makes an implicit conversion from derived class to base class.

» Every class you create in C# derives from a single class named `System.Object`. Because all classes inherit from the `Object` class, all classes inherit the `Object` class methods. The `Object` class contains four `public` instance methods: `Equals()`, `GetHashCode()`, `GetType()`, and `ToString()`.

» When you instantiate an object that is a member of a subclass, you actually call two constructors: the constructor for the base class and the constructor for the extended, derived class. When you create any derived class object, the base class constructor must execute first; only then does the derived class constructor execute.

» When you use a class as a base class and the class has a constructor that requires arguments, then within the header of the derived class constructor you must provide values for any arguments required by the base class constructor. Even if you have no other reason for creating a derived class constructor, you must write the subclass constructor so it can call its parent's constructor.

» An abstract class is one from which you cannot create concrete objects, but from which you can inherit. Usually, abstract classes contain abstract methods; an abstract method has no method statements. Any class derived from a class that contains an abstract method must override the abstract method by providing a body (an implementation) for it.

» C# provides an alternative to multiple inheritance, known as an interface. Much like an abstract class, an interface is a collection of methods (and perhaps other members) that can be used by any class as long as the class provides a definition to override the interface's abstract definitions. Within an abstract class, some methods can be abstract, while others need not be. Within an interface, all methods are abstract. A class can inherit from only one abstract base class, but it can implement any number of interfaces.

» Extension methods are methods you can write to add to any type. They are static methods, but they operate like instance methods. Their parameter lists begin with the keyword `this` and the data type being extended.

KEY TERMS

Inheritance is the application of your knowledge of a general category to more specific objects.

Unified Modeling Language (UML) diagrams are graphical tools that programmers and analysts use to describe systems.

A **base class** is a class that is used as a basis for inheritance.

A **derived class** or **extended class** is one that has inherited from a base class.

A **superclass** is a base class.

A **subclass** is a derived class.

A **parent class** is a base class.

A **child class** is a derived class.

The **ancestors** of a derived class are all the superclasses from which the subclass is derived.

Inheritance is **transitive**, which means that a child inherits all the members of all its ancestors.

Using the keyword **protected** provides you with an intermediate level of security between `public` and `private` access. A `protected` data field or method can be used within its own class or in any classes extended from that class, but it cannot be used by "outside" classes.

Classes that depend on field names from parent classes are said to be **fragile** because they are prone to errors—that is, they are easy to "break."

A derived class member that overrides a parent class member **hides** it.

A base class member that is not hidden by the derived class is **visible** in the derived class.

An **implicit conversion** occurs when a type is automatically converted to another upon assignment.

An **implicit reference conversion** occurs when a derived class object is assigned to its ancestor's data type.

The **object** (or `Object`) class type in the `System` namespace is the ultimate base class for all other types.

Reference equality occurs when two reference type objects refer to the same object.

A **hash code** is a number that should uniquely identify an object.

The keyword **base** always refers to the superclass of the class in which you use it.

An **abstract class** is one from which you cannot create concrete objects, but from which you can inherit.

Concrete classes are nonabstract classes from which objects can be instantiated.

An **abstract method** has no method statements; any class derived from a class that contains an abstract method must override the abstract method by providing a body (an implementation) for it.

The keyword **override** is used in method headers when you create a derived class that inherits an abstract method from a parent.

A **virtual method** is one whose behavior is determined by the implementation in a child class.

Multiple inheritance is the ability to inherit from more than one class.

An **interface** is a collection of abstract methods (and perhaps other members) that can be used by any class as long as the class provides a definition to override the interface's abstract definitions.

Extension methods are static methods that act like instance methods. You can write extension methods to add to any type.

A **sealed** class cannot be extended.

A **check digit** is a digit calculated from a formula and appended to a number to help verify the accuracy of the other digits in the number.

A method that calls itself is a **recursive** method.

REVIEW QUESTIONS

1. The principle that you can apply your knowledge of a general category to more specific objects is ___________ .

   a. polymorphism

   b. encapsulation

   c. inheritance

   d. structure

2. Which of the following is *not* a benefit of using inheritance when creating a new class?

   a. You save time, because you need not create fields and methods that already exist in a parent class.

   b. You reduce the chance of errors, because the parent class methods have already been used and tested.

   c. You make it easier for anyone who has used the parent class to understand the new class because the programmer can concentrate on the new features.

   d. You save computer memory because when you create objects of the new class, storage is not required for parent class fields.

3. A child class is also called a(n) ___________ .

   a. extended class

   b. base class

   c. superclass

   d. delineated class

4. Assuming that the following classes are well named, which of the following is a parent class of `House`?

   a. `Apartment`

   b. `Building`

   c. `Victorian`

   d. `myHouse`

5. A derived class usually contains ___________ than its parent.

   a. more fields and methods

   b. the same number of fields but fewer methods

   c. fewer fields but more methods

   d. fewer fields and methods

6. When you create a class that is an extension or child of another class, you use a(n) ___________ between the derived class name and its base class name.

   a. ampersand

   b. colon

   c. dot

   d. hyphen

7. A base class named `Garden` contains a private field `width` and a property `public int Width` that contains `get` and `set` accessors. A child class named `VegetableGarden`

does not contain a `Width` property. When you write a class in which you declare an object as follows, what statement can you use to access the `VegetableGarden`'s `width`?

```
VegetableGarden myGarden = new VegetableGarden();
```

a. `myGarden.Width`

b. `myGarden.base.Width`

c. `VegetableGarden.Width`

d. You cannot use `Width` with a `VegetableGarden` object.

8. When a parent class contains a `private` data field, the field is __________ the child class.

   a. hidden in

   b. not a member of

   c. directly accessible in

   d. `public` in

9. When a base class and a derived class contain a method with the same name and argument list, and you call the method using a derived class object, __________.

   a. you receive an error message

   b. the base class version overrides the derived class version

   c. the derived class version overrides the base class version

   d. both method versions execute

10. Which of the following is an English-language form of polymorphism?

    a. seeing a therapist and seeing the point

    b. moving friends with a compelling story and moving friends to a new apartment

    c. both of these

    d. neither of these

11. When base and derived classes contain a method with the same name and argument list, you can use the base class method within the derived class by using the keyword __________ before the method name.

    a. `new`

    b. `override`

    c. `base`

    d. `super`

12. In a program that declares a derived class object, you __________ assign it to an object of its base class type.

    a. can

    b. cannot

    c. must

    d. should not

13. The ultimate base class for all other class types is ___________ .

    a. `Base`   c. `Parent`

    b. `Super`   d. `Object`

14. All of the following are `Object` class methods *except* ___________ .

    a. `ToString()`   c. `Print()`

    b. `Equals()`   d. `GetHashCode()`

15. When you create any derived class object, ___________ .

    a. the base class and derived class constructors execute simultaneously

    b. the base class constructor must execute first; then the derived class constructor executes

    c. the derived class constructor must execute first; then the base class constructor executes

    d. neither the base class nor the derived class constructor executes

16. When a base class constructor requires arguments, then each derived class ___________ .

    a. must include a constructor

    b. must include a constructor that requires arguments

    c. must include two or more constructors

    d. must not include a constructor

17. When you create an abstract class, ___________ .

    a. you can inherit from it

    b. you can create concrete objects from it

    c. both of these are true

    d. neither of these is true

18. When you create an abstract method, you provide ___________ .

    a. the keyword `abstract`

    b. curly braces

    c. method statements

    d. all of these

19. Within an interface, ___________ .

    a. no methods can be `abstract`

    b. some methods might be `abstract`

    c. some, but not all, methods must be `abstract`

    d. all methods must be `abstract`

20. Abstract classes and interfaces are similar in that __________ .

    a. you can instantiate concrete objects from both

    b. you cannot instantiate concrete objects from either one

    c. all methods in both must be `abstract`

    d. neither can contain nonabstract methods

EXERCISES

1. Create a class named `Game` that contains a string with the name of the `Game` and an integer that holds the maximum number of players. Include properties with `get` and `set` accessors for each field. Also, include a `ToString()` `Game` method that overrides the `Object` class's `ToString()` method and returns a string that contains the name of the class (using `GetType()`), the name of the `Game`, and the number of players. Create a child class named `GameWithTimeLimit` that includes an integer time limit in minutes and a property that contains `get` and `set` accessors for the field. Write a program that instantiates an object of each class and demonstrates all the methods. Save the file as **GameDemo.cs**.

2. Create a class named `Tape` that includes fields for length and width in inches and properties for each field. Also include a `ToString()` method that returns a string constructed from the return value of the object's `GetType()` method and the values of the length and width fields. Derive two subclasses—`VideoCassetteTape` and `AdhesiveTape`. The `VideoCassetteTape` class includes an integer field to hold playing time in minutes and a property for the field. The `AdhesiveTape` class includes an integer field that holds a stickiness factor—a value from 1 to 10—and a property for the field. Write a program that instantiates one object of each of the three classes, and demonstrate that all of each class's methods work correctly. Be sure to use valid and invalid values when testing the numbers you can use to set the `AdhesiveTape` class stickiness factor. Save the file as **TapeDemo.cs**.

3. a. Create a class named `Order` that performs order processing of a single item that sells for $19.95 each. The class has four variable fields: order number, customer name, quantity ordered, and total price. Create a constructor that requires parameters for all the fields except total price. Include `public get` and `set` accessors for each field except the total price field; that field is calculated as quantity ordered times unit price (19.95) whenever the quantity is set, so it needs only a `get` accessor. Also create the following for the class:

    » An `Equals()` method that determines two `Order`s are equal if they have the same order number

    » A `GetHashCode()` method that returns the order number

    » A `ToString()` method that returns a string containing all order information

    Write an application that declares a few `Order` objects and sets their values, making sure to create at least two with the same order number. Display the string from the

`ToString()` method for each order. Write a method that compares two orders at a time and displays a message if they are equal. Send the `Orders` you created to the method two at a time and display the results. Save the file as **OrderDemo.cs.**

b. Using the `Order` class you created in Exercise 3a, write a new application that creates an array of five `Orders`. Prompt the user for values for each `Order`. Do not allow duplicate order numbers; force the user to reenter the order when a duplicate order number is entered. When five valid orders have been entered, display them all, plus a total of all orders. Save the program as **OrderDemo2.cs**.

c. Create a `ShippedOrder` class that derives from `Order`. A `ShippedOrder` has a $4.00 shipping fee (no matter how many items are ordered). Override any methods in the parent class as necessary. Write a new application that creates an array of five `ShippedOrders`. Prompt the user for values for each, and do not allow duplicate order numbers; force the user to reenter the order when a duplicate order number is entered. When five valid orders have been entered, display them all, plus a total of all orders. Save the program as **OrderDemo3.cs**.

d. Make any necessary modifications to the `ShippedOrder` class so that it can be sorted by order number. Modify the `OrderDemo3` application so the displayed orders have been sorted. Save the application as **OrderDemo4.cs**.

4. a. Create a class named `Book` that includes fields for the International Standard Book Number (ISBN), title, author, and price. Include properties for each field. (An ISBN is a unique number assigned to each published book.) Create a child class named `TextBook` that includes a grade level and a `CoffeeTableBook` child class that contains no additional fields. In the child classes, override the accessor that sets a `Book`'s price so that `TextBooks` must be priced between $20.00 and $80.00, inclusive, and `CoffeeTableBooks` must be priced between $35.00 and $100.00, inclusive. Write a program that creates a few objects of each type and demonstrate that all of the methods and properties work correctly. Be sure to use valid and invalid values when testing the child class properties. Save the file as **BookDemo.cs**.

b. In the `Book` class you created in Exercise 4a, overload the `Object` class `Equals()` method to consider two `Books` equal if they have the same ISBN. Create a program that declares three `Books`; two should have the same ISBN and one should have a different one. Demonstrate that the `Equals()` method works correctly to compare the `Books`. Save the program as **BookDemo2.cs**.

c. Write an application that declares two `Book` objects and uses an extension method named `DisplayTitleAndAuthor()` with each. The method displays a `Book`'s title, the word "by", and the author's name. Save the program as **BookDemo3.cs**.

5. a. Create a `Patient` class for the Wrightstown Hospital Billing Department. Include a patient ID number, name, age, and amount due to the hospital. Include properties and any other methods you need. Override the `ToString()` method to return all the details for a patient. Write an application that prompts the user for data for five

`Patient`s. Sort them in patient ID number order and display them all, including a total amount owed. Save the program as **PatientDemo.cs**.

b. Using the `Patient` class as a base, derive an `InsuredPatient` class. An `InsuredPatient` contains all the data of a `Patient`, plus fields to hold an insurance company name and the percentage of the hospital bill the insurance company will pay. Insurance payments are based on the following table:

Insurance Company	Portion of bill paid by insurance (%)
Wrightstown Mutual	80
Red Umbrella	60
All other companies	25

Create an array of five `InsuredPatient` objects. Prompt the user for all the patient data, plus the name of the insurance company; the insurance company `set` accessor determines the percentage paid. Override the parent class `ToString()` method to include the name of the insurance company, the percent paid, and the amount due after the insurance has been applied to the bill. Sort all the records in ID number order and display them with a total amount due from all insured patients. Save the program as **PatientDemo2.cs**.

c. Write an application that uses an extension method for the `Patient` class. The method computes and returns a `Patient`'s quarterly insurance payment (one-fourth of the annual premium). The application should allow the user to enter data for five `Patient`s and then display all the `Patient` data for each, including the quarterly payment. Save the program as **PatientDemo3.cs**.

6. Create an abstract class called `GeometricFigure`. Each figure includes a height, a width, and an area. Provide `get` and `set` accessors for each field except for area; the area is computed and is read-only. Include an abstract method called `ComputeArea()` that computes the area of the `GeometricFigure`. Create three additional classes:

» A `Rectangle` is a `GeometricFigure` whose area is determined by multiplying width by height.

» A `Square` is a `Rectangle` in which the width and height are the same. Provide a constructor that accepts both height and width, forcing them to be equal if they are not. Provide a second constructor that accepts just one dimension and uses it for both height and width. The `Square` class uses the `Rectangle`'s `ComputeArea()` method.

» A `Triangle` is a `GeometricFigure` whose area is determined by multiplying the width by half the height.

Create an application that demonstrates creating objects of each class. After each is created, pass it to a method that accepts a `GeometricFigure` argument in which the figure's data is displayed. Change some dimensions of some of the figures and pass each to the display method again. Save the program as **ShapesDemo.cs**.

7. Create an interface named `IRecoverable`. It contains a single method named `Recover()`. Create classes named `Patient`, `Furniture`, and `Football`; each of these classes implements `IRecoverable`. Create each class's `Recover()` method to display an appropriate message. For example, the `Patient`'s `Recover()` method might display "I am getting better." Write a program that declares an object of each of the three types and uses its `Recover()` method. Save the file as **RecoveringDemo.cs**.

8. Create an interface named `ITurnable`. It contains a single method named `Turn()`. Create classes named `Page`, `Corner`, `Pancake`, and `Leaf`; each of these classes implements `ITurnable`. Create each class's `Turn()` method to display an appropriate message. For example, the `Page`'s `Turn()` method might display "You turn a page in a book." Write a program that declares an object of each of the four types and uses its `Turn()` method. Save the file as **TurningDemo.cs**.

9. Create an abstract class named `Salesperson`. Fields include first and last names; the `Salesperson` constructor requires both these values. Include properties for the fields. Include a method that returns a string that holds the `Salesperson`'s full name—the first and last names separated by a space. Then perform the following tasks:

   » Create two child classes of `Salesperson`: `RealEstateSalesperson` and `GirlScout`. The `RealEstateSalesperson` class contains fields for total value sold in dollars and total commission earned (both of which are initialized to 0), and a commission rate field required by the class constructor. The `GirlScout` class includes a field to hold the number of boxes of cookies sold, which is initialized to 0. Include properties for every field.

   » Create an interface named `ISell` that contains two methods: `SalesSpeech()` and `MakeSale()`. In each `RealEstateSalesperson` and `GirlScout` class, implement `SalesSpeech()` to display an appropriate one- or two-sentence sales speech that the objects of the class could use. In the `RealEstateSalesperson` class, implement the `MakeSale()` method to accept an integer dollar value for a house, add the value to the `RealEstateSalesperson`'s total value sold, and compute the total commission earned. In the `GirlScout` class, implement the `MakeSale()` method to accept an integer representing the number of boxes of cookies sold and add it to the total field.

   » Write a program that instantiates a `RealEstateSalesperson` object and a `GirlScout` object. Demonstrate the `SalesSpeech()` method with each object, then use the `MakeSale()` method two or three times with each object. Display the final contents of each object's data fields. Save the file as **SalespersonDemo.cs**.

DEBUGGING EXERCISES

Each of the following files in the Chapter.08 folder on your Student Disk has syntax and/or logical errors. In each case, determine the problem and fix the program. After you correct the errors, save each file using the same filename preceded with *Fixed*. For example, DebugEight01.cs will become FixedDebugEight01.cs.

a. DebugEight01.cs
b. DebugEight02.cs
c. DebugEight03.cs
d. DebugEight04.cs

UP FOR DISCUSSION

1. In this chapter, you learned the difference between `public`, `private`, and `protected` class members. Why are some programmers opposed to classifying class members as `protected`? Do you agree with them?

2. Playing computer games has been shown to increase the level of dopamine in the human brain. High levels of this substance are associated with addiction to drugs. Suppose you work for a company that manufactures games and it decides to research how its games can produce more dopamine in the brains of players. Would you support the company's decision?

3. If you are completing all the programming exercises at the ends of the chapters in this book, you know that it takes a lot of time to write and test programs that work. Professional programs require even more hours of work. In the workplace, programs frequently must be completed by strict deadlines—for example, a tax-calculating program must be completed by year's end, or an advertising Web site must be completed by the launch of the product. Programmers often find themselves working into the evenings or weekends to complete rush projects at work. How would you feel about having to do this? What types of compensation would make the extra hours worthwhile for you?

4. Suppose your organization asks you to develop a code of ethics for the Information Technology Department. What would you include?

9

EXCEPTION HANDLING

In this chapter you will:

Learn about exceptions and the `Exception` class
Purposely generate a `SystemException`
Learn about traditional error-handling methods
Learn about object-oriented exception-handling methods
Use the `Exception` class's `ToString()` method and `Message` property
Catch multiple `Exceptions`
Use the `finally` block
Handle an `Exception` with a loop
Throw an `Exception`
Trace `Exceptions` through the call stack
Create your own `Exception` classes
Rethrow `Exceptions`

While visiting Web sites, you have probably seen an unexpected and cryptic message that announces an error and then shuts down your browser immediately. Perhaps something similar has happened to you while using a piece of application software. Certainly, if you have worked your way through all of the programming exercises in this book, you have encountered such errors while running your own programs. When a program just stops, it is aggravating, especially when you lose data you have typed and the program error message seems to indicate the program "knows" exactly what is wrong. You might grumble, "If it knows what is wrong, why doesn't it just fix it?" In this chapter, you will learn how to handle these unexpected error conditions so your programs can be more user-friendly than those that simply shut down in the face of errors.

UNDERSTANDING EXCEPTIONS

An **exception** is any error condition or unexpected behavior in an executing program. The programs you write can generate many types of potential exceptions, including when:

» Your program asks for user input, but the user enters invalid data.

» The program attempts to divide a value by zero.

» You attempt to access an array with a subscript that is too large or too small.

» You calculate a value that is too large for the answer's variable type.

These errors are called exceptions because presumably, they are not usual occurrences; they are "exceptional." The object-oriented techniques used to manage such errors make up the group of methods known as **exception handling**.

In C#, all exceptions are objects that are instances of the `Exception` class or one of its derived classes. An exception condition generates an object that encapsulates information about the error. Like all other classes in the C# programming language, the `Exception` class is a descendant of the `Object` class. The `Exception` class has several descendant classes of its own, many with unusual names such as `CodeDomSerializerException`, `SUDSParserException`, and `SoapException`. Others have names that are more easily understood, such as `IOException` (for input and output errors), `InvalidPrinterException` (for when a user requests an invalid printer), and `PathTooLongException` (used when the path to a file contains more characters than a system allows). C# has more than 100 defined `Exceptions`; Table 9-1 lists just a few to give you an idea of the wide variety of circumstances they cover.

Most exceptions you will use derive from three classes:

» The predefined Common Language Runtime exception classes derived from `SystemException`

» The user-defined application exception classes you derive from `ApplicationException`

» The `Exception` class, which is the parent of `SystemException` and `ApplicationException`

Class	Description
System.ArgumentException	Thrown when one of the arguments provided to a method is not valid
System.ArithmeticException	Thrown for errors in an arithmetic, casting, or conversion operation
System.ArrayTypeMismatchException	Thrown when an attempt is made to store an element of the wrong type within an array
System.Data.OperationAbortedException	Thrown when an ongoing operation is aborted by the user
System.Drawing.Printing.InvalidPrinterException	Thrown when you try to access a printer using printer settings that are not valid
System.FormatException	Thrown when the format of an argument does not meet the parameter specifications of the invoked method
System.IndexOutOfRangeException	Thrown when an attempt is made to access an element of an array with an index that is outside the bounds of the array; this class cannot be inherited
System.InvalidCastException	Thrown for an invalid casting or explicit conversion
System.InvalidOperationException	Thrown when a method call is invalid for the object's current state
System.IO.InvalidDataException	Thrown when a data stream is in an invalid format
System.IO.IOException	Thrown when an I/O error occurs
System.MemberAccessException	Thrown when an attempt to access a class member fails
System.NotImplementedException	Thrown when a requested method or operation is not implemented
System.NullReferenceException	Thrown when there is an attempt to dereference a null object reference
System.OperationCanceledException	Thrown in a thread upon cancellation of an operation that the thread was executing
System.OutOfMemoryException	Thrown when there is not enough memory to continue the execution of a program
System.RankException	Thrown when an array with the wrong number of dimensions is passed to a method
System.StackOverflowException	Thrown when the execution stack overflows because it contains too many nested method calls; this class cannot be inherited

Table 9-1 Selected C# Exceptions

> **»NOTE** Microsoft previously advised that you should create your own custom exceptions from the `ApplicationException` class. They have revised their thinking because in practice, they have not found the approach to be of significant value. For updates, visit *http://msdn2.microsoft.com*.

»TWO TRUTHS AND A LIE: UNDERSTANDING EXCEPTIONS

1. An exception is any error condition or unexpected behavior in an executing program.
2. The object-oriented techniques used to manage errors make up the group of methods known as behavior management.
3. In C#, all exceptions are objects that are members of the `Exception` class or one of its derived classes.

The false statement is #2. The object-oriented techniques used to manage errors make up the group of methods known as exception handling.

PURPOSELY GENERATING A `SystemException`

You can deliberately generate a `SystemException` by forcing a program to contain an error. As an example, in every programming language, it is illegal to divide a value by zero because the operation is mathematically undefined. Consider the `MilesPerGallon` program in Figure 9-1. It is a simple program that prompts a user for two values and divides them. If the user enters nonzero integers, the program runs correctly and without incident. However, if the user enters 0 when prompted to enter gallons, division by 0 takes place and an error is generated. Figure 9-2 shows two executions of the program.

```
using System;
public class MilesPerGallon
{
    public static void Main()
    {
        int milesDriven;
        int gallonsOfGas;
        int mpg;
        Console.Write("Enter miles driven ");
        milesDriven = Convert.ToInt32(Console.ReadLine());
        Console.Write("Enter gallons of gas purchased ");
        gallonsOfGas = Convert.ToInt32(Console.ReadLine());
        mpg = milesDriven / gallonsOfGas;
        Console.WriteLine("You got {0} miles per gallon", mpg);
    }
}
```

Figure 9-1 `MilesPerGallon` program

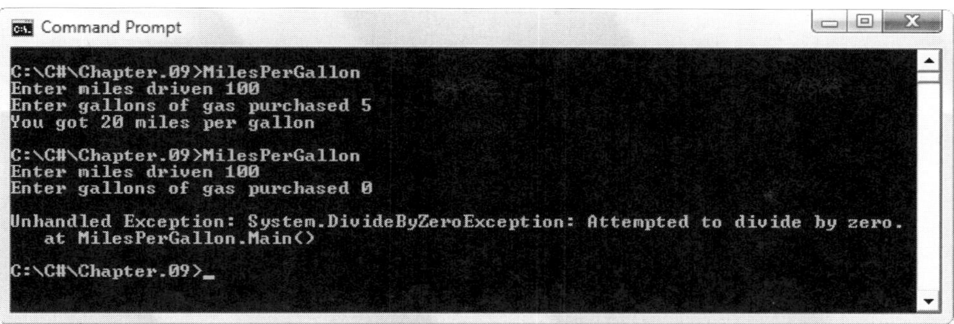

Figure 9-2 Two executions of `MilesPerGallon` program

>> **NOTE** When the user enters a 0 for gallons in the `MilesPerGallon` program, a dialog box reports that the application has stopped working and needs to close. Because this error is intentional for demonstration purposes, you can ignore the message by clicking Close program.

In the first execution of the `MilesPerGallon` program in Figure 9-1, the user entered two usable integers, and division was carried out successfully. However, in the second execution, the user entered 0 for gallons of gas, and the error message indicates that an unhandled exception named `System.DivideByZeroException` was created. The message gives further information ("Attempted to divide by zero."), and shows the method where the exception occurred—in `MilesPerGallon.Main()`.

>> **NOTE** The `DivideByZeroException` object was generated automatically by C#. It is an instance of the `DivideByZeroException` class that has four ancestors. It is a child of the `ArithmeticException` class, which descends from the `SystemException` class. The `SystemException` class derives from the `Exception` class, which is a child of the `Object` class.

Just because an exception occurs and an `Exception` object is created, you don't necessarily have to deal with it. In the `MilesPerGallon` class, you simply let the offending program terminate; that's why the error message in Figure 9-2 indicates that the `Exception` is "Unhandled." However, the termination of the program is abrupt and unforgiving. When a program divides two numbers, or even performs a more trivial task like playing a game, the user might be annoyed if the program ends abruptly. If the program is used for air-traffic control or to monitor a patient's vital statistics during surgery, an abrupt conclusion could be disastrous. Object-oriented error-handling techniques provide more elegant solutions than simply shutting down.

>> **NOTE** Programs that can handle exceptions appropriately are said to be more fault tolerant and robust than those that do not. **Fault-tolerant** applications are designed so that they continue to operate, possibly at a reduced level, when some part of the system fails. **Robustness** represents the degree to which a system is resilient to stress, maintaining correct functioning.

»TWO TRUTHS AND A LIE: PURPOSELY GENERATING A SystemException

1. You can deliberately generate a SystemException by forcing a program to contain an error.
2. A program might automatically generate a System.DivideByZeroException.
3. In C#, when an exception occurs and an Exception object is created, you must employ a specific set of exception-handling techniques in order to manage the problem.

The false answer is #3. Just because an exception occurs and an Exception object is created, you don't necessarily have to deal with it.

UNDERSTANDING TRADITIONAL ERROR-HANDLING METHODS

Programmers had to deal with error conditions long before object-oriented methods were conceived. For example, dividing by zero is an avoidable error for which programmers always have had to plan. If you simply check a variable's value with an `if` statement before attempting to divide it into another number, you can prevent the creation of an `Exception` object. For example, the following code uses a traditional, non-object-oriented method to check a variable to prevent division by zero:

```
if(gallonsOfGas != 0)
   mpg = milesDriven / gallonsOfGas;
else
   mpg = 0;
```

This code successfully prevents division by zero, but it does not really "handle an exception" because no `Exception` class object is created. The example code illustrates a perfectly legal and reasonable method of preventing division by zero, and it represents the most efficient method of handling the error if you think it will be a frequent problem. Because a program that contains this code does not have to instantiate an `Exception` object every time the user enters a 0 for the value of `gallonsOfGas`, the program saves time and computer memory. (Programmers say this program has little "overhead.") On the other hand, if you think dividing by zero will be infrequent—that is, the *exception* to the rule—then the decision will execute many times when it is not needed. In other words, if a user enters 0 for `gallonsOfGas` in only one case out of 1000, then the `if` statement is executed unnecessarily 999 times. In that case, it is more efficient to eliminate the `if` test and instantiate an `Exception` object when needed.

> **» NOTE** The creators of C# define "infrequent" as an event that happens less than 30 percent of the time. That is, if you think an error will occur in less than 30 percent of all program executions, create an `Exception`; if you think the error will occur more often, use traditional error checking. Of course, your boss or instructor might prefer a different percentage.

> **» NOTE** Exception handling is critical in operations that are prone to failure. For example, when you attempt to connect to a remote server, the connection might be down.

»TWO TRUTHS AND A LIE: UNDERSTANDING TRADITIONAL ERROR-HANDLING METHODS

1. Before object-oriented methods were conceived, programmers had no way of handling unexpected conditions.
2. A program that handles potential errors by using `if` statements often saves time and computer memory over one that uses exception-handling methods.
3. Exception handling is most appropriate when an error is expected to occur infrequently.

The false statement is #1. Programmers had to deal with error conditions long before object-oriented methods were conceived.

UNDERSTANDING OBJECT-ORIENTED EXCEPTION-HANDLING METHODS

In object-oriented terminology, you "try" a procedure that may not complete correctly. A method that detects an error condition or `Exception` "throws" an `Exception`, and the block of code that processes the error "catches" the `Exception`.

When you write a block of code in which something can go wrong, you can place the code in a **try block,** which consists of the following elements:

» The keyword `try`
» A pair of curly braces containing statements that might cause `Exceptions`

You must code at least one `catch` block or `finally` block immediately following a `try` block. (You will learn about `finally` blocks later in this chapter.) Each **catch block** can "catch" one type of `Exception`. You create a `catch` block by typing the following elements:

» The keyword `catch`
» Parentheses containing an `Exception` type, and optionally, a name for an instance of the `Exception` type
» A pair of curly braces containing statements that deal with the error condition

Figure 9-3 shows the general format of a `try...catch` pair. The placeholder `XxxException` represents the `Exception` class or any of its more specific subclasses. If an `Exception` occurs during the execution of the `try` block, then the statements in the `catch` block will execute. If no `Exception` occurs within the `try` block, then the `catch` block will not execute. Either way, the statements following the `catch` block execute normally.

```
try
{
    // Statements including some that might cause an Exception
}
catch(XxxException anExceptionInstance)
{
    // Do something about it
}
// Statements here execute whether there was an Exception or not
```

Figure 9-3 General form of a `try...catch` pair

Any one of the statements you place within the `try` block in Figure 9-3 might throw an `Exception`. If one is thrown, it goes to the `catch` block, in which its local identifier is `anExceptionInstance`. A `catch` block looks a lot like a method named `catch()`, which takes an argument that is an instance of `XxxException`. However, it is not a method; it has no return type and you can't call it directly.

For example, Figure 9-4 contains a program in which the statements that prompt for, accept, and use `gallonsOfGas` are encased in a `try` block. Figure 9-5 shows two executions of the program. In the first execution, a usable value is entered for `gallonsOfGas` and the program operates normally, bypassing the `catch` block. In the second execution, however, the user enters 0 for `gallonsOfGas`. When division is attempted, an `Exception` object is automatically created and thrown. The `catch` block catches it, where it becomes known as `e`. The statements in the `catch` block set `mpg` to 0 and display a message. Whether the `catch` block executes or not, the final `WriteLine()` statement that follows the `catch` block's closing curly brace executes.

```
using System;
public class MilesPerGallon2
{
    public static void Main()
    {
        int milesDriven;
        int gallonsOfGas;
        int mpg;
        try
        {
            Console.Write("Enter miles driven ");
            milesDriven = Convert.ToInt32(Console.ReadLine());
            Console.Write("Enter gallons of gas purchased ");
            gallonsOfGas = Convert.ToInt32(Console.ReadLine());
            mpg = milesDriven / gallonsOfGas;
        }
        catch(Exception e)
        {
            mpg = 0;
            Console.WriteLine("You attempted to divide by zero!");
        }
        Console.WriteLine("You got {0} miles per gallon", mpg);
    }
}
```

Figure 9-4 `MilesPerGallon2` program

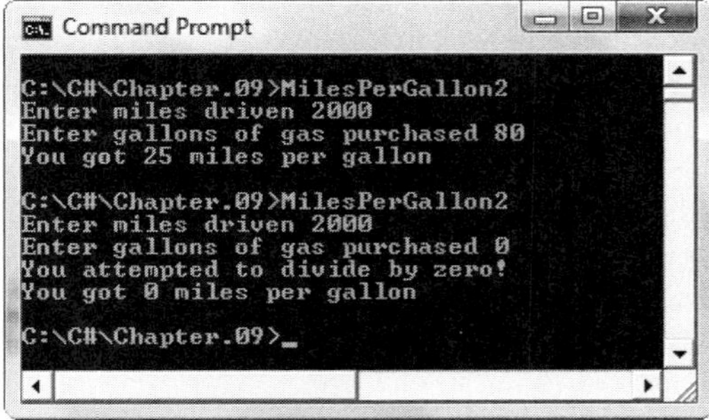

Figure 9-5 Two executions of `MilesPerGallon2` program

In the `MilesPerGallon2` program, you could catch a more specific `DivideByZeroException` object instead of catching an `Exception` object. You will employ this technique later in the chapter. If you are working on a professional project, Microsoft recommends that you never use the general `Exception` class in a `catch` block.

> **» NOTE** In the application in Figure 9-4, the source of the exception and the `catch` block reside in the same method. Later in this chapter, you will learn that exceptions and their corresponding `catch` blocks frequently reside in separate methods.

» TWO TRUTHS AND A LIE: UNDERSTANDING OBJECT-ORIENTED EXCEPTION-HANDLING METHODS

1. Using object-oriented techniques, when you write a block of code in which something can go wrong, you can place the code in a `try` block.
2. If an `Exception` occurs within a `try` block, then the `catch` block that follows it will not execute.
3. If a `catch` block executes, then an `Exception` must have been thrown.

The false statement is #2. If an `Exception` occurs within a `try` block, then the `catch` block that follows it executes. If no `Exception` occurs within a `try` block, then the `catch` block that follows it will not execute.

USING THE Exception CLASS'S ToString() METHOD AND Message PROPERTY

When the `MilesPerGallon2` program prints the error message ("You attempted to divide by zero!"), you actually cannot confirm from the message that division by zero was the source of the error. In reality, any `Exception` generated from within the `try` block in the program would be caught by the `catch` block in the method because the argument in the `catch` block is an `Exception`.

Instead of writing your own message, you can use the `ToString()` method that every `Exception` inherits from the `Object` class. The `Exception` class overrides `ToString()` to provide a descriptive error message so a user can receive precise information about the nature of any `Exception` that is thrown. For example, Figure 9-6 shows a `MilesPerGallon3` program. The only changes from the `MilesPerGallon2` program are shaded: the name of the class and the message that is displayed when an `Exception` is thrown. In this example, the `ToString()` method is used with the caught `Exception` e. Figure 9-7 shows an execution of the program in which the user enters 0 for `gallonsOfGas`.

> **» NOTE**
> You learned about overriding the `Object` class `ToString()` method in Chapter 8.

The error message displayed in Figure 9-7 ("System.DivideByZeroException: Attempted to divide by zero.") is the same message that appeared in Figure 9-2 when you provided no exception handling. Therefore, you can assume that the operating system uses the same `ToString()` method you can use when displaying information about an `Exception`. In the program in which you provided no exception handling, execution simply stopped; in this one, execution continues and the final output statement is displayed whether the user's input was usable or not. Programmers would say this second version ended more "elegantly."

```csharp
using System;
public class MilesPerGallon3
{
    public static void Main()
    {
        int milesDriven;
        int gallonsOfGas;
        int mpg;
        try
        {
            Console.Write("Enter miles driven ");
            milesDriven = Convert.ToInt32(Console.ReadLine());
            Console.Write("Enter gallons of gas purchased ");
            gallonsOfGas = Convert.ToInt32(Console.ReadLine());
            mpg = milesDriven / gallonsOfGas;
        }
        catch(Exception e)
        {
            mpg = 0;
            Console.WriteLine(e.ToString());
        }
        Console.WriteLine("You got {0} miles per gallon", mpg);
    }
}
```

Figure 9-6 `MilesPerGallon3` program

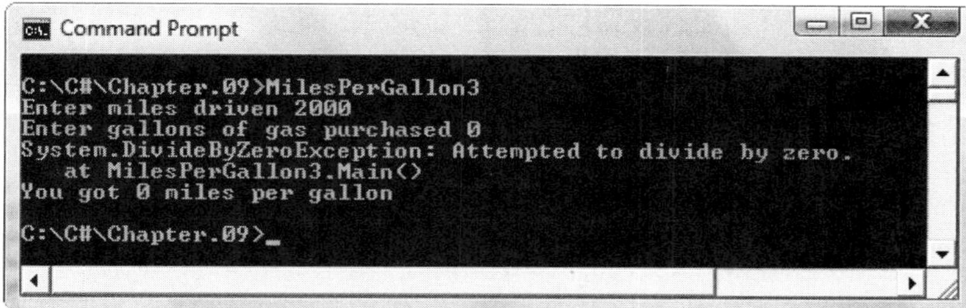

Figure 9-7 Execution of `MilesPerGallon3` program

The `Exception` class also contains a property named `Message` that contains useful information about an `Exception`. For example, the program in Figure 9-8 contains just two shaded changes from the `MilesPerGallon3` program: the class name and the use of the `Message` property in the statement that displays the error message in the `catch` block. The program produces the output shown in Figure 9-9. The value of `e.Message` is a `string` that is identical to the second part of the value returned by the `ToString()` method. You can guess that the `DivideByZeroException` class's `ToString()` method used in `MilesPerGallon3` constructs its string from two parts: the return value of the `getType()` method (that indicates the name of the class) and the return value from the `Message` property.

```
using System;
public class MilesPerGallon4
{
    public static void Main()
    {
        int milesDriven;
        int gallonsOfGas;
        int mpg;
        try
        {
            Console.Write("Enter miles driven ");
            milesDriven = Convert.ToInt32(Console.ReadLine());
            Console.Write("Enter gallons of gas purchased ");
            gallonsOfGas = Convert.ToInt32(Console.ReadLine());
            mpg = milesDriven / gallonsOfGas;
        }
        catch(Exception e)
        {
            mpg = 0;
            Console.WriteLine(e.Message);
        }
        Console.WriteLine("You got {0} miles per gallon", mpg);
    }
}
```

Figure 9-8 `MilesPerGallon4` program

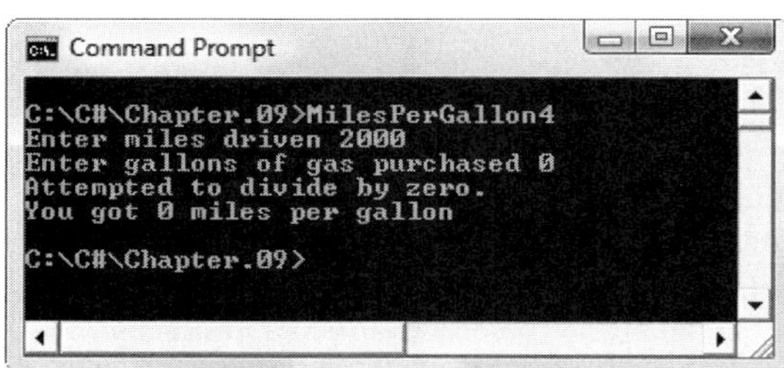

Figure 9-9 Execution of `MilesPerGallon4` program

**»TWO TRUTHS AND A LIE: USING THE Exception CLASS'S ToString()
METHOD AND Message PROPERTY**

1. Any Exception generated from within a try block in a program will be caught by a catch block that has an Exception type argument.

2. The Exception class overrides the Object class Description() method to provide a descriptive error message so a user can receive precise information about the nature of any Exception that is thrown.

3. The Exception class contains a property named Message that contains useful information about an Exception.

The false statement is #2. The Exception class overrides the Object class ToString() method to provide a descriptive error message so a user can receive precise information about the nature of any Exception that is thrown.

CATCHING MULTIPLE ExceptionS

You can place as many statements as you need within a try block, and you can catch as many different Exceptions as you want. If you try more than one statement, only the first error-generating statement throws an Exception. As soon as the Exception occurs, the logic transfers to the catch block, which leaves the rest of the statements in the try block unexecuted.

When multiple catch blocks are present, they are examined in sequence until a match is found for the Exception that occurred. The matching catch block then executes, and each remaining catch block is bypassed.

For example, consider the program in Figure 9-10. The Main() method in the TwoErrors class potentially throws two types of Exceptions—a DivideByZeroException and an IndexOutOfRangeException. (An IndexOutOfRangeException occurs when an array subscript is not within the allowed range. In the TwoErrors program, the array has only three elements, but 13 is used as a subscript.)

The TwoErrors class declares three integers and an integer array with three elements. In the Main() method, the try block executes, and at the first statement within the try block, an Exception occurs because the denom in the division problem is zero. The try block is abandoned, and control transfers to the first catch block. Division by zero causes a DivideByZeroException, and because the first catch block receives that type of Exception, the message "In first catch block" appears along with the Message value of the Exception. In this example, the second try statement is never attempted, and the second catch block is skipped. Figure 9-11 shows the output.

If you reverse the two statements within the try block in the TwoErrors program, the process changes. If you use the following try block, the division by zero does not take place because the invalid array access throws an Exception first:

```
try
{
    result = array[num]; // New first try
    result = num / denom; // Old first try
}
```

```csharp
using System;
public class TwoErrors
{
    public static void Main()
    {
        int num = 13, denom = 0, result;
        int[] array = {22, 33, 44};
        try
        {
            result = num / denom; // First try
            result = array[num]; // Second try
        }
        catch(DivideByZeroException error)
        {
            Console.WriteLine("In first catch block: ");
            Console.WriteLine(error.Message);
        }
        catch(IndexOutOfRangeException error)
        {
            Console.WriteLine("In second catch block: ");
            Console.WriteLine(error.Message);
        }
    }
}
```

Figure 9-10 `TwoErrors` program with two `catch` blocks

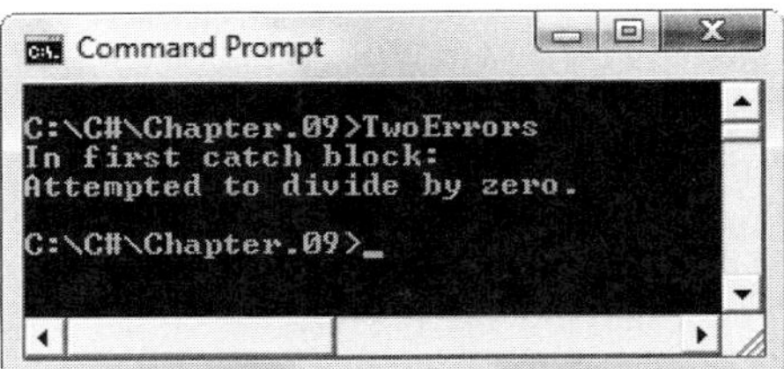

Figure 9-11 Output of `TwoErrors` program

The new first statement within the `try` block attempts to access element 13 of a three-element array, so it throws an `IndexOutOfRangeException`. The `try` block is abandoned, and the first `catch` block is examined and found unsuitable because the `Exception` is of the wrong type—it is not a `DivideByZeroException` object. The program logic proceeds to the second `catch` block, whose `IndexOutOfRangeException` argument type is a match for the thrown `Exception`. The message "In second catch block" and the `Exception`'s `Message` value are therefore displayed. Figure 9-12 shows the output.

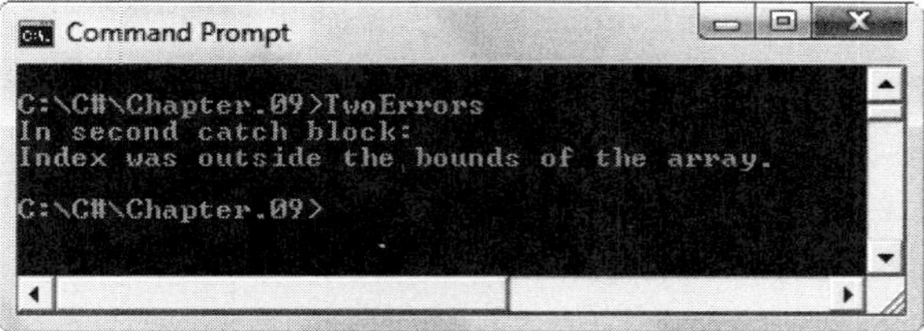

Figure 9-12 Output of `TwoErrors` program when the positions of the statements in the `try` block are reversed

Sometimes you want to execute the same code, no matter which `Exception` type occurs. For example, in the `TwoErrors` program in Figure 9-10, each of the two `catch` blocks prints a unique message. Instead, you might want both the `DivideByZeroException` catch block and the `IndexOutOfRangeException` catch block to simply use the thrown `Exception`'s `Message` field. Because both `DivideByZeroExceptions` and `IndexOutOfRangeExceptions` are subclasses of `Exception`, you can rewrite the `TwoErrors` class as shown in Figure 9-13 and include only one `Exception` catch block that catches any type of `Exception`.

```
using System;
public class TwoErrors2
{
   public static void Main()
   {
      int num = 13, denom = 0, result;
      int[] array = {22, 33, 44};
      try
      {
         result = num / denom; // First try
         result = array[num]; // Second try
      }
      catch(Exception error)
      {
         Console.WriteLine(error.Message);
      }
   }
}
```

Figure 9-13 `TwoErrors2` class with one `catch` block

The `catch` block in Figure 9-13 accepts a more generic `Exception` type than either of the potentially error-causing `try` statements throw, so the generic `catch` block can act as a "catch-all" block. That is, when either a division arithmetic error or an array error occurs, the thrown error is "promoted" to an `Exception` error in the `catch` block. Through inheritance, `DivideByZeroExceptions` and `IndexOutOfRangeExceptions` are `Exceptions`.

> **» NOTE** As stated earlier, Microsoft recommends that a `catch` block should not handle general `Exceptions`. They say that if you cannot predict all possible causes of an exception and ensure that malicious code cannot exploit the resulting application state, you should allow the application to terminate instead of handling the exception.

Although a block of code can throw any number of `Exception` types, many developers believe that it is poor style for a block or method to throw more than three or four types. If it does, one of the following conditions might be true:

» Perhaps the code block or method is trying to accomplish too many diverse tasks and should be broken up into smaller blocks or methods.

» Perhaps the `Exception` types thrown are too specific and should be generalized, as they are in the `TwoErrors2` program in Figure 9-13. As another example, both `DivideByZeroExceptions` and `OverflowExceptions` (which occur in some situations when an arithmetic answer is too large) are children of the `ArithmeticException` class (which, in turn, is a child of the `Exception` class). If a method throws both subclass `Exception` types, and you want (for example) to set a result to 0 in either case, then catching one superclass `Exception` type is sufficient and clearer.

When you list multiple `catch` blocks following a `try` block, you must be careful that some `catch` blocks don't become unreachable. **Unreachable** blocks contain statements that can never execute under any circumstances because the program logic "can't get there." For example, if successive `catch` blocks catch a `DivideByZeroException` and an "ordinary" `Exception`, then `DivideByZeroException` errors will cause the first `catch` to execute and other `Exceptions` will "fall through" to the more general `Exception` catch. However, if you reverse the sequence of the `catch` blocks (so the `catch` block that catches the more general `Exception` objects comes first), then you indicate that even `DivideByZeroExceptions` should be caught by the `Exception` catch. The `DivideByZeroException` catch block is unreachable because the more general `Exception` catch block is in its way, and therefore the class will not compile. Figure 9-14 shows a program in which the second `catch` block is not reachable, and Figure 9-15 shows the error message generated when you try to compile this program.

> **» NOTE**
> Programmers also call unreachable code **dead code**.

```csharp
using System;
public class UnreachableCatch
{
    public static void Main()
    {
        int num = 13, denom = 0, result;
        try
        {
            result = num / denom;
        }
        catch(Exception error)
        {
            Console.WriteLine(error.Message);
        }
        catch(DivideByZeroException error)
        {
            Console.WriteLine(error.Message);
        }
    }
}
```

Figure 9-14 Program with unreachable `catch` block

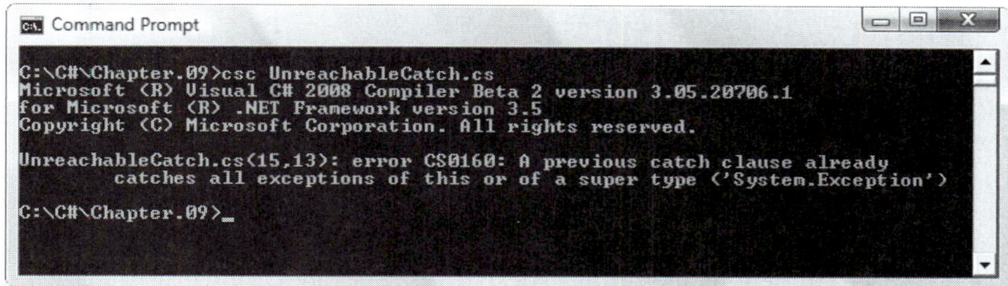

Figure 9-15 Compiler message generated by `UnreachableCatch` program

»TWO TRUTHS AND A LIE: CATCHING MULTIPLE Exception**S**

1. If you `try` more than one statement in a block, each error-generating statement throws an `Exception`.
2. You can write `catch` blocks that catch multiple `Exception` types.
3. When you list multiple `catch` blocks following a `try` block, you must be careful that some `catch` blocks don't become unreachable.

The false statement is #1. If you `try` more than one statement in a block, only the first error-generating statement throws an Exception.

USING THE `finally` BLOCK

When you have actions to perform at the end of a `try...catch` sequence, you can use a **finally block**, which executes whether the `try` block identifies any `Exceptions` or not. Typically, you use the `finally` block to perform clean-up tasks that must occur, regardless of whether any errors occurred or were caught. Figure 9-16 shows the format of a `try...catch` sequence that uses a `finally` block.

```
try
{
    // Statements that might cause an Exception
}
catch(SomeException anExceptionInstance)
{
    // What to do about it
}
finally
{
    // Statements here execute
    // whether an Exception occurred or not
}
```

Figure 9-16 General form of a `try...catch` block with a `finally` block

At first glance, it seems as though the `finally` block serves no purpose. When a `try` block works without error, control passes to the statements that come after the `catch` block. Additionally, if the `try` code fails and throws an `Exception` that is caught, then the `catch` block executes, and control again passes to any statements that are coded after the `catch` block. Therefore, it seems as though the statements after the `catch` block always execute, so there is no need to place any statement within a special `finally` block. However, the last set of statements after the `catch` might never execute for at least two reasons:

» An `Exception` for which you did not plan might occur.

» The `try` or `catch` block might contain a statement that quits the application.

> **» NOTE** You can quit an application with a statement such as `Environment.Exit(0);`. The `Environment.Exit()` method is part of the `System` namespace. It terminates a program and passes the argument (which can be any integer) to the operating system. You also might exit a `catch` block with a `break` statement or a `return` statement. You encountered `break` statements when you learned about the `switch` statement in Chapter 3. You learned about `return` statements and how they return values from methods in Chapter 6.

The possibility exists that your `try` block might throw an `Exception` for which you did not provide a `catch`. After all, `Exceptions` occur all the time without your handling them, as you saw in the first `MilesPerGallon` program at the beginning of this chapter. In case of an unhandled `Exception`, program execution stops immediately, sending the error to the operating system for handling and abandoning the current method. Likewise, if the `try` block contains an exit statement, execution stops immediately. When you include a `finally` block, you are assured that its enclosed statements will execute before the program is abandoned, even if the method concludes prematurely.

For example, the `finally` block is used frequently with file input and output to ensure that open files are closed. You will learn more about writing to and reading from data files in Chapter 13. For now, however, consider the format shown in Figure 9-17, which represents part of the logic for a typical file-handling program. The `catch` block was written to catch an `IOException`, which is the type of exception automatically generated if there is a problem opening a file, reading data from a file, or writing to a file.

```
try
{
    // Open the file
    // Read the file
    // Place the file data in an array
    // Calculate an average from the data
    // Display the average
}
catch (IOException e)
{
    // Issue an error message
    // Exit
}
finally
{
    // If the file is open, close it
}
```

Figure 9-17 Pseudocode that tries reading a file and handles an `Exception`

The pseudocode in Figure 9-17 handles any file problems. However, because the application uses an array (see the statement "Place the file data in an array"), an uncaught `Exception` could occur when using the array or performing the division, even though the file opened successfully. In such an event, you would want to close the file before proceeding. By using the `finally` block, you ensure that the file is closed, because the code in the `finally` block executes before the uncaught exception returns control to the operating system. The code in the `finally` block executes no matter which of the following outcomes of the `try` block occurs:

» The `try` ends normally.

» The `catch` executes.

» The `try` ends abnormally and the `catch` does not execute. For example, an `Exception` might cause the method to abandon prematurely—perhaps the array is not large enough to hold the data, or calculating the average results in division by 0. These `Exceptions` do not allow the `try` block to finish, nor do they cause the `catch` block to execute.

> **»NOTE** If an application might throw several types of exceptions, you can try some code, catch the possible exception, try some more code, catch the possible exception, and so on. Usually, however, the superior approach is to try all the statements that might throw exceptions, then include all the needed `catch` blocks and an optional `finally` block. This is the approach shown in Figure 9-17, and it usually results in logic that is easier to follow.

You often can avoid using a `finally` block, but you would need repetitious code. For example, instead of using the `finally` block in the pseudocode in Figure 9-17, you could insert the statement "If the file is open, close it" as both the last statement in the `try` block and the second-to-last statement in the `catch` block, just before the program exits. However, writing code just once in a `finally` block is clearer and less prone to error.

> **»NOTE** Java and C++ provide `try` and `catch` blocks. Java also provides a `finally` block, but C++ does not.

> **»NOTE** Many well-designed programs that try code do not include any `catch` blocks; instead, they contain only `try-finally` pairs. The `finally` block is used to release resources that other applications might be waiting for, such as database connections.

»TWO TRUTHS AND A LIE: USING THE `finally` BLOCK

1. When a `finally` block follows a `try` block, it executes whether the `try` block identifies any `Exception`s or not.
2. Typically, you use a `finally` block to perform clean-up tasks that must occur after an `Exception` has been thrown and caught.
3. Statements that follow a `try-catch` pair might never execute because an unplanned `Exception` might occur, or the `try` or `catch` block might contain a statement that quits the application.

The false statement is #2. Typically, you use a `finally` block to perform clean-up tasks that must occur, regardless of whether any errors occurred or were caught.

HANDLING AN `Exception` WITH A LOOP

Different programs require different ways of handling `Exception`s. In some programs you write, you simply want to display an error message when an `Exception` occurs. In others, you want to remedy the situation the same way every time, such as setting a result to 0. In yet others, you want to keep trying the offending code until it is correct. In these cases, you can place a `try...catch` block within a loop that continues to execute until the code is successful.

As an example, consider the `HandlingAFormatException` program in Figure 9-18. This program asks a user to input an integer value that will be used as a sports team player's number. A Boolean variable named `isGoodNumber` is initialized to `false`; this variable controls the data entry loop that will continue to execute until the variable's value becomes `true`.

```
using System;
public class HandlingAFormatException
{
   public static void Main()
   {
      int playerNumber = 0;
      string strNumber;
      bool isGoodNumber = false;
      while(!isGoodNumber)
      {
         try
         {
            Console.Write("Enter player's number ");
            strNumber = Console.ReadLine();
            playerNumber = Convert.ToInt32(strNumber);
            isGoodNumber = true;
         }
         catch(FormatException fe)
         {
            Console.WriteLine(fe.Message +
               " Player's number should be an integer.");
         }
      }
      Console.WriteLine("Player's number is " + playerNumber);
   }
}
```

Figure 9-18 `HandlingAFormatException` program

Within the `try` block in Figure 9-18, a `string` value is read from the keyboard and then converted to an integer. However, when users enter values from the keyboard, they don't always enter the correct value types. For example, instead of an integer, a user might enter a floating-point number or a non-numeric character. Any keyboard data will successfully be accepted into a string, but only strings containing all digits (or a + or - sign) will successfully be converted to integers. If the user enters a noninteger, the `Convert.ToInt32()` method throws a `FormatException` and execution continues with the `catch` block at the bottom of the loop. The program "gets past" the `Convert.ToInt32()` method only when the user enters an integer and the `ToInt32()` method is successful. Only then will `isGoodNumber` change to `true`, ending the loop when the `while` statement executes. Figure 9-19 shows a typical execution of the program in which the user enters invalid data twice before "getting it right." Trying and catching the `Exception` in a loop ensures that the input data will be the correct type before the program proceeds.

Figure 9-19 Typical execution of `HandlingAFormatException` program

»NOTE In the `HandlingAFormatException` program, the `Convert.ToInt32()` method fails when a floating-point value is entered. If you use the `Convert.ToDouble()` method, it would not throw an `Exception` if you attempted to convert an integer, because an integer can be automatically promoted to a `double`.

(T) (T) (F)

»TWO TRUTHS AND A LIE: HANDLING AN Exception WITH A LOOP

1. In an object-oriented program, you should not place a `try...catch` block within a loop.

2. If a program attempts to use a string with the `Convert.ToInt32()` method in a `try` block, it throws a `FormatException` and execution continues with an appropriate `catch` block that follows.

3. If a program attempts to use a string with the `Convert.ToInt32()` method without a `try` block, it throws a `FormatException` and execution stops.

The false statement is #1. You can place a `try...catch` block within a loop, and frequently you will want to do so.

THROWING ExceptionS BETWEEN METHODS

An advantage of using object-oriented exception-handling techniques is the ability to deal with `Exceptions` appropriately as you decide how to handle them. When methods from other classes throw `Exceptions`, they don't have to catch them; instead, your calling program can catch them, and you can decide what to do. For example, in the `HandlingAFormatException` program in Figure 9-18, the `Convert.ToInt32()` method threw an `Exception` when the user entered a noninteger value, but the `Convert.ToInt32()` method did not catch the `Exception`. Instead, the `HandlingAFormatException` program caught it and handled it by placing the `catch` in a loop, forcing the user to reenter a value. A different program might force the `playerNumber` to a default value, or it might display an error message and quit the program. This flexibility is an advantage when you need to create specific reactions to thrown `Exception`s.

When a method you write throws an `Exception`, the same method can catch the `Exception`, although it is not required, and in most object-oriented programs, it does not. Often, you don't want a method to handle its own `Exception`. In many cases, you want the method to check for errors, but you do not want to require a method to handle an error if it finds one. An advantage to object-oriented exception handling is that you gain the ability to appropriately deal with `Exception`s in each client program. Just as a police officer can deal with a speeding driver differently depending on circumstances, you can react to `Exception`s specifically for your current purposes.

When you design classes containing methods that have statements that might throw `Exception`s, you most frequently should create the methods so they throw the `Exception`, but not handle it. Handling an `Exception` should be left to the client—the program that uses your class—so the `Exception` can be handled in an appropriate way for the application.

For example, consider the very brief `PriceList` class in Figure 9-20. The class contains a list of prices and a single method that displays one price based on a parameter subscript value. Because the `DisplayPrice()` method uses an array, an `IndexOutOfRangeException` might be thrown. However, the `DisplayPrice()` method does not handle the potential `Exception`.

```csharp
public class PriceList
{
    private static double[] price = {15.99, 27.88, 34.56, 45.89};
    public static void DisplayPrice(int item)
    {
        Console.WriteLine("The price is " +
            price[item].ToString("C"));
    }
}
```

Figure 9-20 The `PriceList` class

Figure 9-21 shows an application that uses the `DisplayPrice()` method. It calls the method in a `try` block and handles an `IndexOutOfRangeException` by displaying a price of $0. Figure 9-22 shows the output when a user enters an invalid item number.

```
using System;
public class PriceListApplication1
{
    public static void Main()
    {
        int item;
        try
        {
            Console.Write("Enter an item number from 0 through 3 ");
            item = Convert.ToInt32(Console.ReadLine());
            PriceList.DisplayPrice(item);
        }
        catch(IndexOutOfRangeException e)
        {
            Console.WriteLine(e.Message + " The price is $0");
        }
    }
}
```

Figure 9-21 The `PriceListApplication1` program

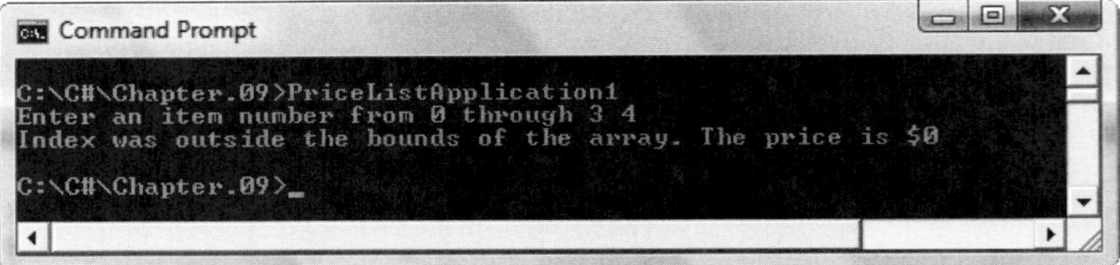

Figure 9-22 Output of `PriceListApplication1` program when user enters invalid item number

Figure 9-23 shows a different application that uses the same `PriceList` class, but handles the exception differently. In this case, the program author wanted the user to keep responding until a correct entry was made. Because the `DisplayPrice()` method in the `PriceList` class was written to throw an `Exception` but not handle it, the programmer of `PriceListApplication2` could handle the `Exception` in a totally different manner from the way it was handled in `PriceListApplication1`. Figure 9-24 shows a typical execution of this program.

```
using System;
public class PriceListApplication2
{
    public static void Main()
    {
        int item = 0;
        bool isGoodItem = false;
        while(!isGoodItem)
        {
            try
            {
                Console.Write("Enter an item number from " +
                    "0 through 3 ");
                item = Convert.ToInt32(Console.ReadLine());
                PriceList.DisplayPrice(item);
                isGoodItem = true;
            }
            catch(IndexOutOfRangeException e)
            {
                Console.WriteLine("You must enter a number less " +
                    "than 4");
                Console.WriteLine("Please reenter item number ");
            }
        }
        Console.WriteLine("Thank you");
    }
}
```

Figure 9-23 The `PriceListApplication2` program

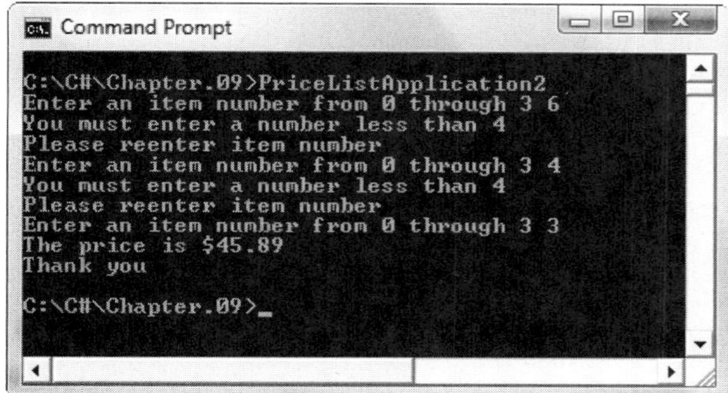

Figure 9-24 Output of `PriceListApplication2` program when user enters invalid
item number several times

»TWO TRUTHS AND A LIE: THROWING ExceptionS BETWEEN METHODS

1. When methods from other classes throw Exceptions, they don't have to catch them; instead, your calling program can catch them, and you can decide what to do.

2. Often, you don't want a method to handle its own Exception; in many cases, you want the method to check for errors, but you do not want to require a method to handle an error if it finds one.

3. When you design classes containing methods that have statements that might throw Exceptions, you should make sure your class handles each Exception appropriately.

The false statement is #3. When you design classes containing methods that have statements that might throw Exceptions, you most frequently should create the methods so they throw the Exception, but not handle it.

TRACING ExceptionS THROUGH THE CALL STACK

When one method calls another, the computer's operating system must keep track of where the method call came from, and program control must return to the calling method when the called method is complete. For example, if MethodA() calls MethodB(), the operating system has to "remember" to return to MethodA() when MethodB() ends. Similarly, if MethodB() calls MethodC(), then while MethodC() is executing, the computer needs to "remember" that it will return to MethodB() and eventually to MethodA(). The memory location where the computer stores the list of locations to which the system must return is known as the **call stack**.

If a method throws an Exception and the same method does not catch it, then the Exception is thrown to the next method "up" the call stack; in other words, it is thrown to the method that called the offending method. Consider this sequence of events:

1. MethodA() calls MethodB().

2. MethodB() calls MethodC().

3. MethodC() throws an Exception.

4. C# looks first for a catch block in MethodC().

5. If none exists, then C# looks for the same thing in MethodB().

6. If MethodB() does not have a catch block for the Exception, then C# looks to MethodA().

7. If MethodA() doesn't catch the Exception, then the program terminates and the operating system displays an error message.

This system of passing Exceptions through the chain of calling methods has great advantages because it allows your methods to handle Exceptions more appropriately. However, a program that uses several classes has the disadvantage of making it very difficult for the programmer to locate the original source of an Exception.

You already have used the Message property to obtain information about an Exception. Another useful Exception property is the StackTrace property. When you catch an Exception, you can print the value of StackTrace to display a list of methods in the call stack so you can determine the location of the Exception.

The StackTrace property can be a useful debugging tool. When your program stops abruptly, it is helpful to discover in which method the Exception occurred. Often, you do not want to display a StackTrace property in a finished program; the typical end user has no interest in the cryptic messages that would be printed. However, while you are developing a program, using StackTrace can help you diagnose your program's problems.

A CASE STUDY: USING StackTrace

As an example of when StackTrace can be useful, consider the Tax class in Figure 9-25. Suppose your company has created or purchased this class to make it easy to calculate tax rates on products sold. For simplicity, assume that only two tax rates are in effect—6% for sales of $20 or less and 7% for sales over $20. The Tax class would be useful for any programmer who wrote a program involving product sales, except for one flaw: in the shaded statement, the subscript is erroneously set to 2 instead of 1 for the higher tax rate. If this subscript is used with the taxRate array in the next statement, it will be out of bounds.

```
public class Tax
{
    private static double[] taxRate = {0.06, 0.07};
    private static double CUTOFF = 20.00;
    public static double DetermineTaxRate(double price)
    {
        int subscript;
        double rate;
        if(price <= CUTOFF)
            subscript = 0;
        else
            subscript = 2;
        rate = taxRate[subscript];
        return rate;
    }
}
```

Figure 9-25 The Tax class

Assume your company has also created a revised PriceList class, as shown in Figure 9-26. This class is similar to the one in Figure 9-20, except that it includes a tax calculation in the shaded statement.

```
public class PriceList
{
    private static double[] price = {15.99, 27.88, 34.56, 45.89};
    public static void DisplayPrice(int item)
    {
        double tax;
        double total;
        double pr;
        pr = price[item];
        tax = pr * Tax.DetermineTaxRate(pr);
        total = pr + tax;
        Console.WriteLine("The total price is " +
            total.ToString("C"));
    }
}
```

Figure 9-26 `PriceList` class that includes call to the `Tax` class method `DetermineTaxRate()`

Suppose you write the application shown in Figure 9-27. Your application is similar to the price list applications earlier in this chapter, including a call to `PriceList.DisplayPrice()`. As in `PriceListApplication1` and `PriceListApplication2`, your new program tries the data entry and display statement and then catches an exception. When you run the program using what you know to be a good item number, as in Figure 9-28, you are surprised to see the shaded "Error!" message you have coded in the `catch` block. In the earlier examples that used `PriceList.DisplayPrice()`, using an item number 1 would have resulted in a successful program execution.

```
using System;
public class PriceListApplication3
{
    public static void Main()
    {
        int item;
        try
        {
            Console.Write("Enter an item number from 0 through 3 ");
            item = Convert.ToInt32(Console.ReadLine());
            PriceList.DisplayPrice(item);
        }
        catch(Exception e)
        {
            Console.WriteLine("Error!");
        }
    }
}
```

Figure 9-27 `PriceListApplication3` class

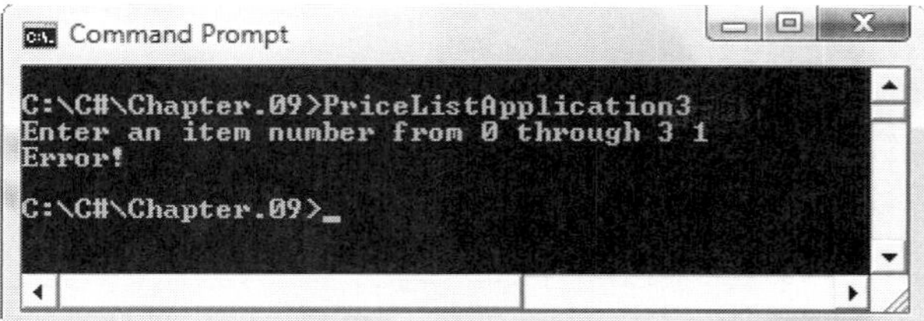

Figure 9-28 Execution of `PriceListApplication3` program when user enters 1 for item number

To attempt to discover what caused the "Error!" message, you can replace the statement that writes it as follows:

```
Console.WriteLine(e.Message);
```

However, when you execute the program with this modification, you receive the output in Figure 9-29, indicating that the index is out of the bounds of the array. You are puzzled because you know 1 is a valid item number for the price array, and it should not be considered out of bounds.

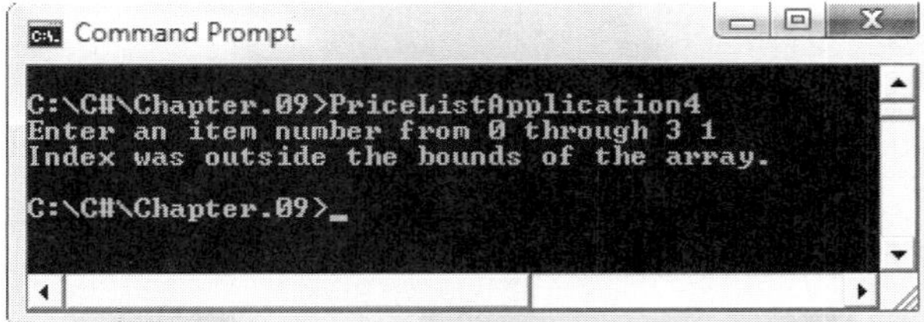

Figure 9-29 Execution of `PriceListApplication4` program in which `e.Message` is displayed in the `catch` block

Finally, you decide to replace the `catch` block statement with a `StackTrace` call, as follows:

```
Console.WriteLine(e.StackTrace);
```

The output is shown in Figure 9-30. You can see from the list of methods that the error in your application came from `PriceList.DisplayPrice()`, which in turn came from `Tax.DetermineTaxRate()`. You had not even considered that the `Tax` class could have been the source of the problem. If you work in a small organization, you can look at the code yourself and fix it. If you work in a larger organization or you purchased the class from an outside vendor, you can contact the programmer who created the class for assistance.

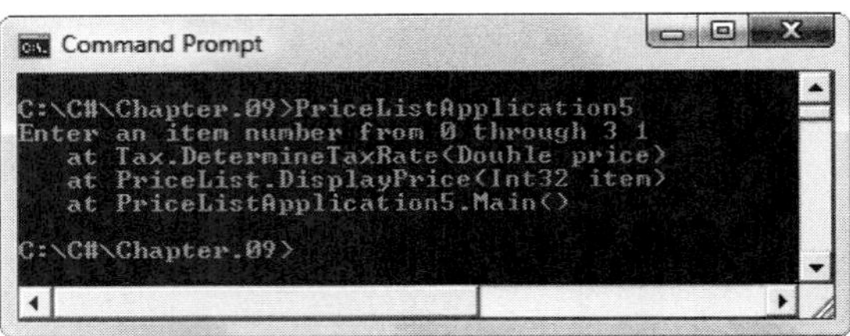

Figure 9-30 Execution of `PriceListApplication5` program in which `e.StackTrace` is displayed in the `catch` block

The classes in this example were small to help you easily follow the discussion. However, a full-blown application might have many more classes that contain many more methods, and so using `StackTrace` would become increasingly beneficial.

>>TWO TRUTHS AND A LIE: TRACING ExceptionS THROUGH THE CALL STACK

1. The memory location where the computer stores the list of locations to which the system must return after a series of method calls is known as the stack trace.

2. If a method throws an `Exception` and the same method does not catch it, then the `Exception` is thrown to the method that called the offending method.

3. When you catch an `Exception`, you can print the value of `StackTrace` to display a list of methods in the call stack so you can determine the location of the `Exception`.

The false statement is #1. The memory location where the computer stores the list of locations to which the system must return after a series of method calls is known as the call stack.

CREATING YOUR OWN Exception CLASSES

C# provides more than 100 categories of `Exceptions` that you can throw in your programs. However, C#'s creators could not predict every condition that might be an `Exception` in the programs you write. For example, you might want to declare an `Exception` when your bank balance is negative or when an outside party attempts to access your e-mail account. Most organizations have specific rules for exceptional data, such as "an employee number must not exceed three digits" or "an hourly salary must not be less than the legal minimum wage." Of course, you can handle these potential error situations with `if` statements, but you also can create your own `Exceptions`.

To create your own `Exception` that you can throw, you can extend the `ApplicationException` class, which is a subclass of `Exception`, or you can extend `Exception`. As you saw earlier in the chapter, Microsoft's advice on this matter has changed over time. Although you might see extensions of `ApplicationException` in classes written by others, the current advice is to simply derive your own classes from `Exception`. Either approach will produce workable programs.

Figure 9-31 shows a `NegativeBalanceException` class that extends `Exception`. This class passes an appropriate `string` message to its parent's constructor. If you create an `Exception` and display its `Message` property, you will see the message "Error in the application." When the `NegativeBalanceException` constructor passes the string "Bank balance is negative." to its parent's constructor, the `Message` property will hold this more descriptive message.


```
public class NegativeBalanceException : Exception
{
   private static string msg = "Bank balance is negative. ";
   public NegativeBalanceException() : base(msg)
   {
   }
}
```

Figure 9-31 The `NegativeBalanceException` class

When you create a `BankAccount` class like the one shown in Figure 9-32, you can create the `Balance` property `set` accessor to throw a `NegativeBalanceException` when a client attempts to set the balance to be negative.

```
public class BankAccount
{
   private int accountNum;
   private double balance;
   public int AccountNum {get; set;}
   public double Balance
   {
      get
      {
         return balance;
      }
      set
      {
         if(value < 0)
         {
            NegativeBalanceException nbe =
               new NegativeBalanceException();
            throw(nbe);
         }
         balance = value;
      }
   }
}
```

Figure 9-32 The `BankAccount` class

```
throw(new NegativeBalanceException());
```

Figure 9-33 shows a program that attempts to set a BankAccount balance to a negative value in the shaded statement. When the BankAccount class's SetBalance() method throws the NegativeBalanceException, the catch block in the TryBankAccount program executes, displaying both the NegativeBalanceException Message and the value of StackTrace. Figure 9-34 shows the output.

```
using System;
public class TryBankAccount
{
    public static void Main()
    {
        BankAccount acct = new BankAccount();
        try
        {
            acct.AccountNum = 1234;
            acct.Balance = -1000;
        }
        catch(NegativeBalanceException e)
        {
            Console.WriteLine(e.Message);
            Console.WriteLine(e.StackTrace);
        }
    }
}
```

Figure 9-33 The TryBankAccount program

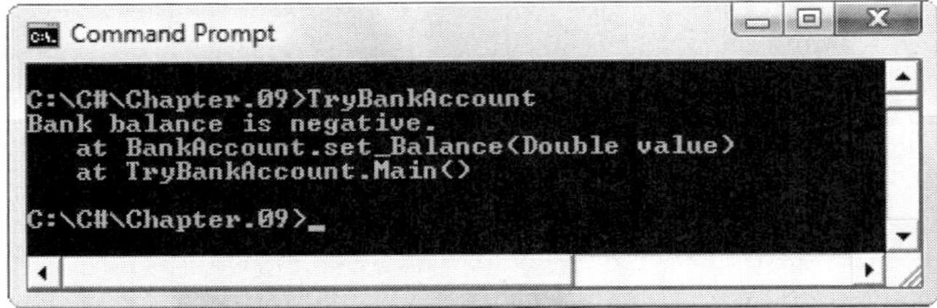

Figure 9-34 Output of TryBankAccount program

In C#, you can't throw an object unless it is an `Exception` or a descendant of the `Exception` class. In other words, you cannot throw a `double` or a `BankAccount`. However, you can throw any type of `Exception` at any time, not just `Exceptions` of your own creation. For example, within any program you can code any of the following:

```
throw(new ApplicationException());
throw(new IndexOutOfRangeException());
throw(new Exception());
```

Of course, you should not throw an `IndexOutOfRangeException` when you encounter division by 0 or data of an incorrect type; you should use it only when an index (subscript) is too high or too low. However, if a built-in `Exception` type is appropriate and suits your needs, you should use it. You should not create an excessive number of special `Exception` types for your classes, especially if the C# development environment already contains an `Exception` that accurately describes the error. Extra `Exception` types add a level of complexity for other programmers who will use your classes. Nevertheless, when appropriate, creating a specialized `Exception` class is an elegant way for you to take care of error situations. They provide you with the capability of separating your error code from the usual, nonexceptional sequence of events. They also allow for errors to be passed up the stack and traced.

> **» NOTE**
> The `StackTrace` begins at the point where an `Exception` is thrown, not where it is created. This consideration makes a difference when you create an `Exception` and throw it from two different methods.

> **» NOTE**
> `Exceptions` can be particularly useful when you throw them from constructors. Constructors do not have a return type, so they have no other way to send information back to the calling method.

»TWO TRUTHS AND A LIE: CREATING YOUR OWN `Exception` **CLASSES**

1. To create your own `Exception` that you can throw, you can extend the `ApplicationException` class or the `Exception` class.
2. In C#, you can throw any object you create if it is appropriate for the application.
3. You can throw any type of `Exception` at any time—both those that are already created as part of C# and those of your own creation.

The false statement is #2. In C#, you can't throw an object unless it is an `Exception` or a descendant of the `Exception` class.

RETHROWING AN `Exception`

When you write a method that catches an `Exception`, your method does not have to handle the `Exception`. Instead, you might choose to **rethrow the `Exception`** to the method that called your method. Then you can let the calling method handle the problem. Within a `catch` block, you can rethrow the `Exception` that was caught by using the keyword `throw` with no object after it. For example, Figure 9-35 shows a class that contains four methods. In this program, the following sequence of events takes place:

1. The `Main()` method calls `MethodA()`.

2. `MethodA()` calls `MethodB()`.

3. `MethodB()` calls `MethodC()`.

```csharp
using System;
public class ReThrow
{
    public static void Main()
    {
        try
        {
            Console.WriteLine("Trying in Main() method");
            MethodA();
        }
        catch(Exception ae)
        {
            Console.Write("Caught in Main() method -- ");
            Console.WriteLine(ae.Message);
        }
        Console.WriteLine("Main() method is done");
    }
    public static void MethodA()
    {
        try
        {
            Console.WriteLine("Trying in method A");
            MethodB();
        }
        catch(Exception)
        {
            Console.WriteLine("Caught in method A");
            throw;
        }
    }
    public static void MethodB()
    {
        try
        {
            Console.WriteLine("Trying in method B");
            MethodC();
        }
        catch(Exception)
        {
            Console.WriteLine("Caught in method B");
            throw;
        }
    }
    public static void MethodC()
    {
        Console.WriteLine("In method C");
        throw(new Exception("This came from method C"));
    }
}
```

Figure 9-35 The `ReThrow` program

4. `MethodC()` throws an `Exception`.

5. When `MethodB()` catches the `Exception`, it does not handle the `Exception`; instead, it throws the `Exception` back to `MethodA()`.

6. `MethodA()` catches the `Exception`, but does not handle it either. Instead, `MethodA()` throws the `Exception` back to the `Main()` method.

7. The `Exception` is caught in the `Main()` method, where the message that was created in `MethodC()` is finally displayed.

Figure 9-36 shows the execution of the program.

NOTE If you name the `Exception` argument to the `catch` block in the preceding figure (for example, `catch(Exception e)`), then you should use that identifier in the `throw` statement at the end of the block (for example, `throw e;`).

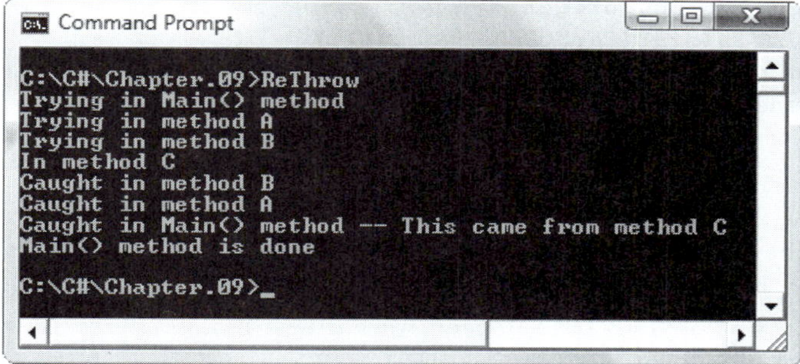

Figure 9-36 Execution of the `ReThrow` program

(T) (T) (F)

»TWO TRUTHS AND A LIE: RETHROWING AN Exception

1. When you write a method that catches an `Exception`, your method must handle the `Exception`.
2. When a method catches an `Exception`, you can rethrow it to a method that called the method.
3. Within a `catch` block, you can rethrow a caught `Exception` by using the keyword `throw` with no object after it.

The false statement is #1. When you write a method that catches an `Exception`, your method does not have to handle the `Exception`.

YOU DO IT

PURPOSELY CAUSING ExceptionS

C# generates `SystemExceptions` automatically under many circumstances. In the next steps, you will purposely generate a `SystemException` by executing a program that provides multiple opportunities for `Exceptions`.

To create a program that purposely generates `Exceptions`:

1. Open a new file in your text editor and type the following program, which allows you to generate several different `Exceptions`.

```
using System;
public class ExceptionsOnPurpose
{
    public static void Main()
    {
        int answer;
        int result;
        int zero = 0;
        Console.Write("Enter an integer ");
        answer = Convert.ToInt32(Console.ReadLine());
        result = answer / zero;
        Console.WriteLine("The answer is " + answer);
    }
}
```


2. The variable `zero` cannot be defined as a constant; if it is, the program will not compile. As a variable, the compiler "trusts" that a legitimate value will be provided for it before division occurs (although in this case, the trust was not warranted). Save the program as **ExceptionsOnPurpose.cs**. Compile the program.

3. Execute the program several times using different values and observe the results. Depending on your operating system, two windows might appear with each execution. The first says that Windows is collecting more information about the problem. This window is soon replaced with the one shown in Figure 9-37, which repeats that ExceptionsOnPurpose.exe has stopped working. If you were executing a professional application, you might be notified of a solution. Because you created this exception on purpose, just click the **Close program** button.

Figure 9-38 shows three executions of the program during which the user typed the following:

» **seven**—This generates a `System.FormatException`, which occurs when the program tries to convert the input value to an integer, because letters are not allowed in integers.

» **7.7**—This also generates a `System.FormatException` because the decimal point is not allowed in an integer.

» **7**—This does not generate a `System.FormatException`, but instead causes a `System.DivideByZero` exception when the result is calculated.

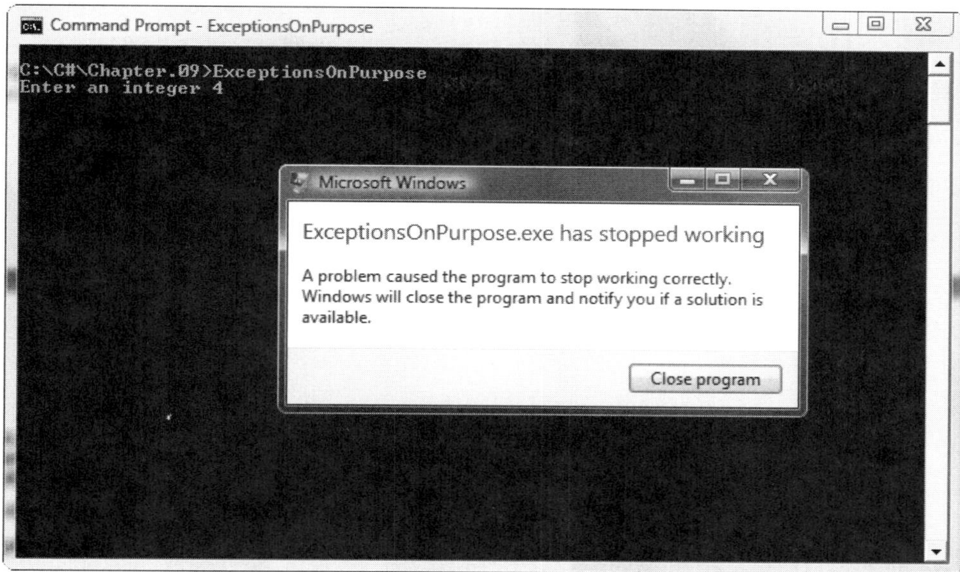

Figure 9-37 Error report window generated by an unhandled `Exception`

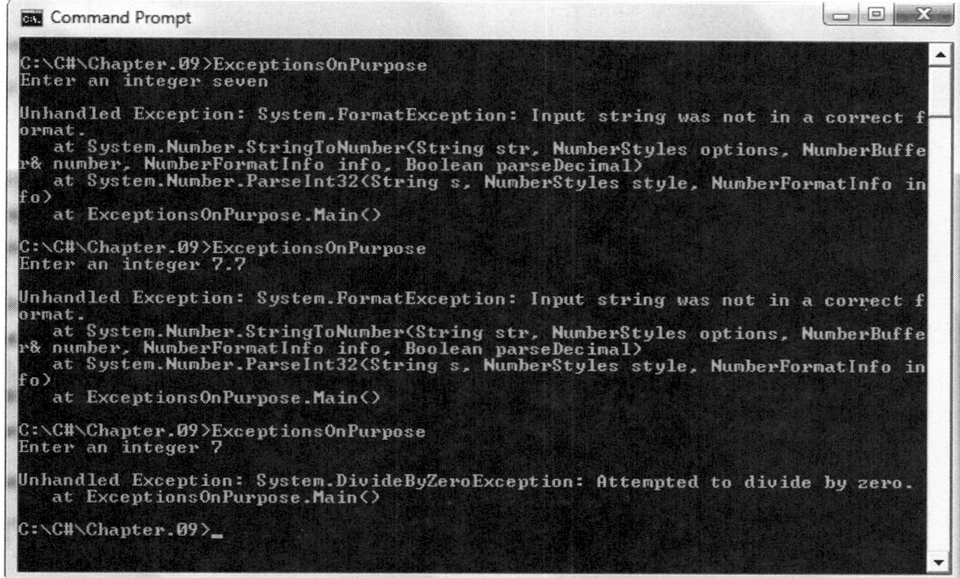

Figure 9-38 Error messages generated by successive executions of `ExceptionsOnPurpose` program

HANDLING ExceptionS

You can handle `Exceptions` by placing them in a `try` block and then catching any `Exceptions` that are thrown from it.

To add a `try...catch` block to your application:

1. Open the ExceptionsOnPurpose.cs file if it is not still open. Change the class name to **ExceptionsOnPurpose2** and immediately save the file as **ExceptionsOnPurpose2.cs**.

2. In the `Main()` method, after the three variable declarations, enclose the next three statements in a `try` block as follows:

```
try
{
    Console.Write("Enter an integer ");
    answer = Convert.ToInt32(Console.ReadLine());
    result = answer / zero;
}
```

3. Following the `try` block (but before the statement that displays the answer), add a `catch` block that catches any thrown `Exception` and displays its `Message` property.

```
catch(Exception e)
{
    Console.WriteLine(e.Message);
}
```

4. Save the program and compile it. You should receive a compiler error that indicates that `answer` is an unassigned local variable. This error occurs at the last line of the program where `answer` is displayed. In the first version of this program, no such message appeared. However, now that the assignment to `answer` is within the `try` block, the compiler understands that an `Exception` might be thrown before a valid value is assigned to `answer`. To eliminate this problem, initialize `answer` at its declaration.

```
int answer = 0;
```

5. Compile and execute the program again. Figure 9-39 shows three executions. The values typed by the user are the same as in Figure 9-38. However, the results are different in several significant ways:

   » No error message window appears (as in Figure 9-37).
   » The error messages displayed are cleaner and "friendlier" than the automatically generated versions in Figure 9-38.
   » The program ends normally in each case, with the `answer` value displayed in a user-friendly manner.

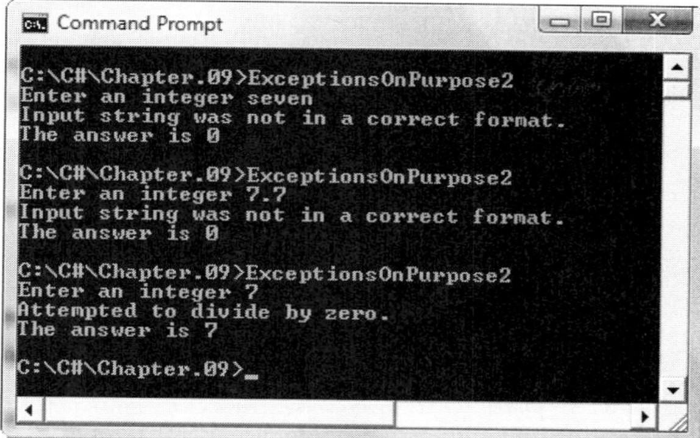

Figure 9-39 Error messages generated by successive executions of
`ExceptionsOnPurpose2` program

CATCHING VARIOUS Exception TYPES

When you want appropriate actions to occur for various `Exceptions`, you can provide multiple
`catch` blocks.

To provide multiple `catch` blocks for the `ExceptionsOnPurpose` program:

1. Open the ExceptionsOnPurpose2.cs file if it is not still open. Change the class
   name to **ExceptionsOnPurpose3** and immediately save the file as
   ExceptionsOnPurpose3.cs.

2. Replace the existing generic `catch` block with two `catch` blocks. (The statement that displays the answer still follows these `catch` blocks.) The first catches any `FormatException`
   and displays a short message. The second catches a `DivideByZeroException` and displays
   a much longer message.

```
catch(FormatException e)
{
    Console.WriteLine("You did not enter an integer");
}
catch(DivideByZeroException e)
{
    Console.WriteLine("This is not your fault.");
    Console.WriteLine("You entered the integer correctly.");
    Console.WriteLine("The program divides by zero.");
}
```

3. Save the program and compile it. When you execute the program and enter an invalid integer, the first `catch` block executes. When you enter an integer so that the program can
   proceed to the statement that divides by 0, the second `catch` block executes. Figure 9-40
   shows two typical executions of the program.

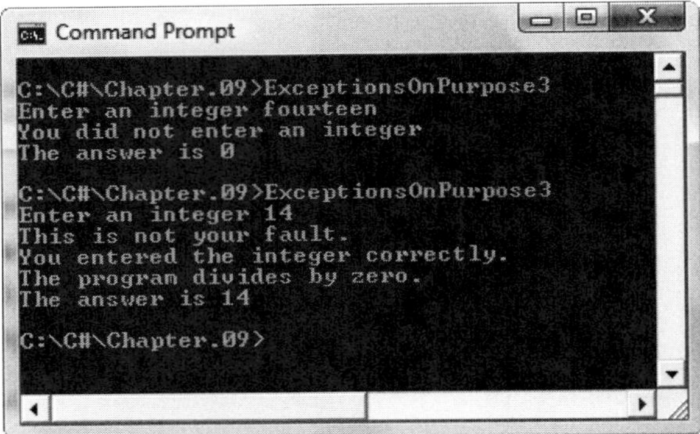

Figure 9-40 Error messages generated by successive executions of `ExceptionsOnPurpose3` program

CHAPTER SUMMARY

» An exception is any error condition or unexpected behavior in an executing program; the object-oriented techniques used to manage such errors make up the group of methods known as exception handling. In C#, all exceptions are objects that are members of the `Exception` class or one of its derived classes. Most exceptions you will use are derived from three classes: `SystemException`, `ApplicationException`, and their parent `Exception`.

» You can purposely generate a `SystemException` by forcing a program to contain an error. Although you are not required to handle `Exceptions`, you can use object-oriented techniques to provide elegant error-handling solutions.

» When you think an error will occur frequently, it is most efficient to handle it in the traditional way, with `if` statements. If an error will occur infrequently, it is more efficient to instantiate an `Exception` object when needed.

» In object-oriented terminology, you "try" a procedure that may not complete correctly. A method that detects an error condition or `Exception` "throws" an `Exception`, and the block of code that processes the error "catches" the `Exception`. You must include at least one `catch` block or `finally` block immediately following a `try` block.

» Every `Exception` object contains a `ToString()` method and a `Message` property that contains useful information about the `Exception`.

» You can place as many statements as you need within a `try` block, and you can `catch` as many different `Exceptions` as you want. If you `try` more than one statement, only the first error-generating statement will throw an `Exception`. When multiple `catch` blocks are present, they are examined in sequence until a match is found for the `Exception` that occurred. When you list multiple `catch` blocks after a `try` block, you must be careful about their order, or some `catch` blocks might become unreachable.

» When you have actions to perform at the end of a `try...catch` sequence, you can use a `finally` block.

» When you want to keep trying a block of code until some value or state within a program is correct, you can place a `try...catch` block within a loop.

» When methods throw `Exceptions`, they don't have to catch them; instead, the program that calls a method that throws an `Exception` can catch it and determine what to do. For the best software design, you should create your classes to throw any `Exceptions` so that various application programs can catch them and handle them appropriately.

» If a method throws an `Exception` and does not catch it, then the `Exception` is thrown to the method that called the offending method. When you catch an `Exception`, you can print the value of the `StackTrace` property to display a list of methods in the call stack, allowing you to determine the location of the `Exception`.

» To create your own `Exception` that you can throw, you can extend the `ApplicationException` class or the `Exception` class. The current advice is to extend `Exception`.

» When you write a method that catches an `Exception`, your method does not have to handle the `Exception`. Instead, you might choose to rethrow the `Exception` to the method that called your method and let that method handle it.

KEY TERMS

An **exception** is any error condition or unexpected behavior in an executing program.

Exception handling is the set of object-oriented techniques used to manage unexpected errors.

Fault-tolerant applications are designed so that they continue to operate, possibly at a reduced level, when some part of the system fails.

Robustness represents the degree to which a system is resilient to stress, maintaining correct functioning even in the presence of errors.

The term **mission critical** refers to any process that is crucial to an organization.

A **try block** contains code that might create exceptions you want to handle.

A **catch block** can catch one type of `Exception`.

Unreachable blocks contain statements that can never execute under any circumstances because the program logic "can't get there."

Dead code is unreachable code.

A **finally block** can follow a `try` block; code within one executes whether the `try` block identifies any `Exceptions` or not.

The **call stack** is the memory location where the computer stores the list of locations to which the system must return after method calls.

A method can catch an `Exception` and **rethrow the Exception** instead of handling it.

REVIEW QUESTIONS

1. Any error condition or unexpected behavior in an executing program is known as an __________ .

   a. exception

   b. anomaly

   c. exclusion

   d. omission

2. Which of the following is *not* treated as a C# `Exception`?

   a. Your program asks the user to input a number, but the user enters a character.

   b. You attempt to execute a C# program, but the C# compiler has not been installed.

   c. You attempt to access an array with a subscript that is too large.

   d. You calculate a value that is too large for the answer's variable type.

3. Most exceptions you will use derive from three classes: __________ .

   a. `Object`, `ObjectException`, and `ObjectApplicationException`

   b. `Exception`, `SystemException`, and `ApplicationException`

   c. `FormatException`, `ApplicationException`, and `IOException`

   d. `SystemException`, `IOException`, and `FormatException`

4. `Exceptions` can be __________ .

   a. generated automatically by C#

   b. created by a program

   c. both of these

   d. neither of these

5. When a program creates an `Exception`, you __________ .

   a. must handle it

   b. can handle it

   c. must not handle it

   d. none of these; programs cannot create `Exceptions`

6. Without using object-oriented techniques, __________ .

   a. there are no error situations

   b. you cannot manage error situations

   c. you can manage error situations, but with great difficulty

   d. you can manage error situations

7. In object-oriented terminology, you ___________ a procedure that may not complete correctly.

    a. circumvent   c. catch

    b. attempt   d. try

8. In object-oriented terminology, a method that detects an error condition ___________ an `Exception`.

    a. throws   c. tries

    b. catches   d. unearths

9. When you write a block of code in which something can go wrong, you can place the code in a ___________ block.

    a. `catch`   c. `system`

    b. `blind`   d. `try`

10. A `catch` block executes when its `try` block ___________ .

    a. completes

    b. throws any `Exception`

    c. throws an `Exception` of an acceptable type

    d. completes without throwing anything

11. Which of the following `catch` blocks will catch any `Exception`?

    a. `catch(Any e){}`

    b. `catch(Exception e){}`

    c. `catch(e)`

    d. All of the above will catch any `Exception`.

12. Which of the following is valid within a `catch` block with the header `catch(Exception error)`?

    a. `Console.WriteLine(error.ToString());`

    b. `Console.WriteLine(error.Message);`

    c. `return(error.ToString());`

    d. two of these

13. You can place ___________ statement(s) within a `try` block.

    a. zero   c. two

    b. one   d. any number of

14. How many `catch` blocks might follow a `try` block within the same method?

    a. only one

    b. any number as long as it is greater than zero

    c. any number as long as it is greater than one

    d. any number, including zero or one

15. Consider the following `try` block. If x is 15, what is the value of a when this code completes?

```
try
{
    a = 99;
    if(x > 10)
        throw(new Exception());
    a = 0;
    ++a;
}
```

    a. 0

    c. 99

    b. 1

    d. undefined

16. Consider the following `catch` blocks. The variable b has been initialized to 0. If a `DivideByZeroException` occurs in a `try` block just before this `catch` block, what is the value of b when this code completes?

```
catch(DivideByZeroException e)
{
    ++b;
}
catch(Exception e)
{
    ++b;
}
```

    a. 0

    c. 2

    b. 1

    d. 3

17. Consider the following `catch` blocks. The variable c has been initialized to 0. If an `IndexOutOfRangeException` occurs in a `try` block just before this `catch` block, what is the value of c when this code completes?

```
catch(IndexOutOfRangeException e)
{
      ++c;
}
catch(Exception e)
{
      ++c;
}
finally
{
      ++c;
}
```

a. 0

c. 2

b. 1

d. 3

18. If your program throws an `IndexOutOfRangeException` and the only available `catch` block catches an `Exception`, __________ .

a. an `IndexOutOfRangeException catch` block is generated automatically

b. the `Exception catch` block executes

c. the `catch` block is bypassed

d. an `Exception` is thrown to the operating system

19. When you design your own classes that might cause `Exceptions`, and other classes will use your classes as clients, you should usually create your methods to __________ .

a. neither throw nor handle `Exceptions`

b. throw `Exceptions` but not handle them

c. handle `Exceptions` but not throw them

d. both throw and handle `Exceptions`

20. When you create an `Exception` of your own, you should extend the __________ class.

a. `SystemException`

b. `PersonalException`

c. `OverloadedException`

d. `Exception`

EXERCISES

1. Write a program in which you declare an array of five integers and store five values in the array. Write a `try` block in which you place a loop that attempts to access each element of the array, incrementing a subscript from 0 to 10. Create a `catch` block that catches the eventual `IndexOutOfRangeException`; within the block, display "Now you've gone too far." on the screen. Save the file as **GoTooFar.cs**.

2. a. The `Convert.ToInt32()` method requires a string argument that can be converted to an `int`. Write a program in which you prompt the user for a stock number and quantity ordered. Accept the strings the user enters and convert them to integers. Catch the `Exception` that is thrown when the user enters noninteger data for either field. Within the `catch` block, display an error message and set both the stock number and quantity values to 0. Save the file as **PlacingOrder.cs**.

    b. Modify the `PlacingOrder` application so that data entry is performed in a `DataEntry()` function that accepts a string parameter to use as a prompt. The function prompts the user, reads a value from the keyboard, attempts to convert it to an integer, and then returns the integer. If an `Exception` is encountered, the function should return 0. Save the file as **PlacingOrder2.cs**.

3. `ArgumentException` is an existing class that derives from `Exception`; you use it when one or more of a method's arguments do not fall within an expected range. Create a class named `CarInsurance` containing variables that can hold a driver's age and state of residence. Within the class, create a method that accepts the two input values and calculates a premium. The premium base price is $100 for residents of Illinois (IL) and $50 for residents of Wisconsin (WI). Additionally, each driver pays $3 times the value of 100 minus his or her age. If the driver is younger than 16, older than 80, or not a resident of IL or WI, throw an `ArgumentException` from the method. In the `Main()` method of the `CarInsurance` class, try code that prompts the user for each value. If the user does not enter a numeric value for age, catch a `FormatException` and display an error message. Call the method that calculates the premium and `catch` the potential `ArgumentException` object. Save the file as **CarInsurance.cs**.

4. The `Math` class contains a static method named `Sqrt()` that accepts a `double` and returns the parameter's square root. Write a program that declares two `double`s: number and sqrt. Accept an input value for `number` from the user. Handle the `FormatException` that is thrown if the input value cannot be converted to a `double` by displaying the message "The input should be a number." and setting the `sqrt` variable to 0. If no `FormatException` is thrown, test the input number's value. If it is negative, throw a `new ApplicationException` to which you pass the message "Number can't be negative." and again set `sqrt` to 0. If `number` is not negative, pass it to the `Math.Sqrt()` method, returning the square root to the `sqrt` variable. As the last program statement, display the value of `sqrt`. Save the file as **FindSquareRoot.cs**.

5. a. Create an `Employee` class with two fields: `IDNum` and `hourlyWage`. The `Employee` constructor requires values for both fields. Upon construction, throw an `ArgumentException` if the `hourlyWage` is less than 6.00 or more than 50.00. Write a program that establishes, one at a time, at least three `Employees` with `hourlyWages` that are above, below, and within the allowed range. Immediately after each instantiation attempt, handle any thrown `Exceptions` by displaying an error message. Save the file as **EmployeeExceptionDemo.cs**.

b. Using the `Employee` class created in Exercise 5a, write an application that creates an array of five `Employee`s. Prompt the user for values for each field for each `Employee`. If the user enters improper or invalid data, handle any exceptions that are thrown by setting the `Employee`'s ID number to 999 and the `Employee`'s pay rate to the $6.00 minimum. At the end of the program, display all the entered, and possibly corrected, records. Save the file as **EmployeeExceptionDemo2.cs**.

6. a. The Peterman Publishing Company has decided that no published book should cost more than 10 cents per page. Create a `BookException` class whose constructor requires three arguments: a `string` Book title, a `double` price, and an `int` number of pages. Create an error message that is passed to the `Exception` class constructor for the `Message` property when a `Book` does not meet the price-to-pages ratio. For example, an error message might be:

```
For Goodnight Moon, ratio is invalid.
...Price is $12.99 for 25 pages.
```

Create a `Book` class that contains fields for title, author, price, and number of pages. Include properties for each field. Throw a `BookException` if a client program tries to construct a `Book` object for which the price is more than 10 cents per page. Create a program that creates at least four `Book` objects—some where the ratio is acceptable and others where it is not. Catch any thrown exceptions and display the `BookException Message`. Save the file as **BookExceptionDemo.cs**.

b. Using the `Book` class created in Exercise 6a, write an application that creates an array of five `Book`s. Prompt the user for values for each `Book`. To handle any exceptions that are thrown because of improper or invalid data entered by the user, set the `Book`'s price to the maximum 10 cents per page. At the end of the program, display all the entered, and possibly corrected, records. Save the file as **BookExceptionDemo2.cs**.

DEBUGGING EXERCISES

Each of the following files in the Chapter.09 folder on your Student Disk has syntax and/or logical errors. In each case, determine the problem and fix the program. After you correct the errors, save each file using the same filename preceded with *Fixed*. For example, DebugNine1.cs will become FixedDebugNine1.cs.

   a. DebugNine1.cs

   b. DebugNine2.cs

   c. DebugNine3.cs

   d. DebugNine4.cs

UP FOR DISCUSSION

1. What do the terms *syntactic sugar* and *syntactic salt* mean? From your knowledge of the C# programming language, list as many syntactic sugar and salt features as you can.

2. Have you ever been victimized by a computer error? For example, were you ever incorrectly denied credit, billed for something you did not purchase, or assigned an incorrect grade in a course? How did you resolve the problem? On the Web, find the most outrageous story you can involving a computer error.

3. Search the Web for information about educational video games in which historical simulations are presented in an effort to teach students about history. For example, Civilization IV is a game in which players control a society as it progresses through time. Do you believe such games are useful to history students? Does the knowledge gained warrant the hours it takes to master the games? Do the makers of the games have any obligations to present history factually? Do they have a right to penalize players who choose options of which the game writers disapprove (such as using nuclear weapons or allowing slavery)? Do game creators have the right to create characters who possess negative stereotypical traits—for example, a person of a specific nationality portrayed as being stupid, weak, or evil? Would you like to take a history course that uses such games?

10

USING GUI OBJECTS AND THE VISUAL STUDIO IDE

In this chapter you will:

Create a `MessageBox`
Add functionality to `MessageBox` buttons
Create a `Form`
Create a `Form` that is a program's main window
Place a `Button` on a `Window`
Use the Visual Studio IDE to design a `Form`
Learn about the code created by the IDE
Add functionality to a `Button` on a `Form`
Use Visual Studio Help

Using the knowledge you have gained so far in this book, you can write many useful C# applications that can accept input, produce output, perform arithmetic, make decisions, handle exceptions, and so on. You also can create classes and instantiate objects from those classes by using the fundamental object-oriented principles of encapsulation, polymorphism, and inheritance. You can create a virtually infinite number of applications that will solve users' problems and provide services for them.

Unfortunately, your applications look dull. When you execute the programs you have written so far, input is accepted from a lackluster command prompt, and output is displayed in the same way. Most modern applications, and certainly most programs you have used on the Internet, use visually pleasing graphic objects to interact with users. These **graphical user interface (GUI)** objects include the buttons, check boxes, and toolbars you are used to controlling with a mouse when you interact with Windows-type programs. You can apply everything you have learned about C# classes and methods to the GUI objects that are built into the .NET environment so you can use Visual Studio to create your own interactive GUI applications.

The programs you have written have also been relatively small. When you start to use graphical objects in your programs, the program size quickly can become daunting. So far, you may have been using a simple text editor, such as Notepad, to write your C# programs. If so, it is time to explore the tools in the Visual Studio integrated development environment (IDE). These tools automatically create much of the code you need to develop appealing and attention-grabbing GUI programs. Of course, if you do not understand the C# code that the tools create, you cannot say you have mastered the C# programming language. In this chapter, you will build some graphical objects "by hand." Then, after you understand the details, you will create the same objects by using the IDE.

CREATING A MessageBox

A **MessageBox** is a GUI object that can contain text, buttons, and symbols that inform and instruct a user. You cannot create a new instance of the `MessageBox` class because its constructor is not `public`. Instead, you use the `static` class method `Show()` to display a `MessageBox`. The `MessageBox` class contains 12 overloaded versions of the `Show()` method; the simplest version accepts a string argument that is displayed within the `MessageBox`. Figure 10-1 shows a program that uses the `MessageBox.Show()` method with the string argument "Hello!". The program must contain the statement `using System.Windows.Forms;` to include the `MessageBox` class. Figure 10-2 shows the output.

```csharp
using System;
using System.Windows.Forms;
public class MessageBox1
{
    public static void Main()
    {
        MessageBox.Show("Hello!");
    }
}
```

Figure 10-1 Program that displays a `MessageBox`

Figure 10-2 Output of `MessageBox1` program

The `MessageBox` in Figure 10-2 is similar to those you have used in many Windows programs. It contains a title bar at the top, a Close button in the upper-right corner, the message "Hello!", and an OK button. When the user clicks either the Close button or the OK button, the `MessageBox` disappears. Because the .NET framework contains the `MessageBox` class, you do not have to design these standard `MessageBox` features and capabilities yourself when you write a program. Instead, you can simply use the `MessageBox` class and concentrate on the message you want to convey within the `MessageBox`. Besides saving development time, the built-in `MessageBox` makes your programs look and feel like others your users usually see.

Besides a `string`, you can pass additional arguments to the `MessageBox.Show()` method. You pass these arguments when you want to display a caption in a `MessageBox`'s title bar or add buttons and an icon. Table 10-1 summarizes the features of six of the 12 versions of the `MessageBox.Show()` method. (The other six versions correspond to the table entries, with the addition of naming a component in front of which you want the `MessageBox` to display.) When you use any version of the `Show()` method, you must provide values in the correct order for each argument listed in the table.

Argument to `MessageBox.Show()`	Explanation
`string`	Displays a message box with the specified text
`string, string`	Displays a message box with the specified text and caption
`string, string, MessageBoxButtons`	Displays a message box with specified text, caption, and buttons
`string, string, MessageBoxButtons, MessageBoxIcon`	Displays a message box with specified text, caption, buttons, and icon
`string, string, MessageBoxButtons, MessageBoxIcon, MessageBoxDefaultButton`	Displays a message box with the specified text, caption, buttons, icon, and default button
`string, string, MessageBoxButtons, MessageBoxIcon, MessageBoxDefaultButton, MessageBoxOptions`	Displays a message box with the specified text, caption, buttons, icon, default button, and options

Table 10-1 Arguments used with the `MessageBox.Show()` method

For example, the program in Figure 10-3 uses two `string` arguments with the `MessageBox.Show()` method. Figure 10-4 shows the execution; notice that the second `string` argument passed to the `Show()` method in the program appears in the title bar of the `MessageBox`.

```
using System;
using System.Windows.Forms;
public class MessageBox2
{
   public static void Main()
   {
      MessageBox.Show("Hello!", "MessageBox2");
   }
}
```

Figure 10-3 Using two `string` parameters with `MessageBox.Show()`

Figure 10-4 Output of `MessageBox2` program

Besides `string` parameters, the `MessageBox.Show()` method can also accept `MessageBoxButtons`, `MessageBoxIcon`, `MessageBoxDefaultButton`, and `MessageBoxOptions` parameters. Tables 10-2 through 10-5 describe all of the possible values for each of the arguments you can send to `MessageBox.Show()`. Using different combinations of these arguments provides you with a wide variety of appearances for your `MessageBox` objects.

> **» NOTE** The `MessageBoxOptions` values are not used frequently. They are listed in Table 10-5 but are not used in this chapter.

Member Name	Description
`AbortRetryIgnore`	The message box contains Abort, Retry, and Ignore buttons
`OK`	The message box contains an OK button
`OKCancel`	The message box contains OK and Cancel buttons
`RetryCancel`	The message box contains Retry and Cancel buttons
`YesNo`	The message box contains Yes and No buttons
`YesNoCancel`	The message box contains Yes, No, and Cancel buttons

Table 10-2 `MessageBoxButtons` values

Member Name	Description
Asterisk	The message box contains a lowercase letter *i* in a circle (the result is the same as `Information`)
Error	The message box contains a white *X* in a circle with a red background
Exclamation	The message box contains an exclamation point in a triangle with a yellow background (the result is the same as `Warning`)
Hand	The message box contains a white *X* in a circle with a red background (the result is the same as `Stop`)
Information	The message box contains a lowercase letter *i* in a circle
None	The message box contains no symbols
Question	The message box contains a question mark in a circle
Stop	The message box contains a white *X* in a circle with a red background
Warning	The message box contains an exclamation point in a triangle with a yellow background

Table 10-3 `MessageBoxIcon` values

Member Name	Description
Button1	The first button on the message box is the default button
Button2	The second button on the message box is the default button
Button3	The third button on the message box is the default button

Table 10-4 `MessageBoxdefaultButton` values

Member Name	Description
DefaultDesktopOnly	The message box appears on the active desktop
RightAlign	The message box text is right-aligned
RtlReading	The message box text is displayed with right-to-left reading order
ServiceNotification	The message box appears on the active desktop even if no user is logged on to the computer

Table 10-5 `MessageBoxOptions` values

Figure 10-5 shows an application that uses a variety of `MessageBox.Show()` options. Figure 10-6 shows how the `MessageBoxes` display in sequence.

```csharp
using System;
using System.Windows.Forms;
public class MessageBoxDemo
{
    public static void Main()
    {
        string message = "This is message ";
        string caption = "Message box experiment ";
        int count = 1;
        MessageBox.Show(message + count);
        ++count;
        MessageBox.Show(message + count, caption + count);
        ++count;
        MessageBox.Show(message + count, caption + count,
            MessageBoxButtons.OKCancel);
        ++count;
        MessageBox.Show(message + count, caption + count,
            MessageBoxButtons.RetryCancel, MessageBoxIcon.Warning);
        ++count;
        MessageBox.Show(message + count, caption + count,
            MessageBoxButtons.YesNoCancel,
            MessageBoxIcon.Information,
            MessageBoxDefaultButton.Button3);
    }
}
```

Figure 10-5 `MessageBoxDemo` program

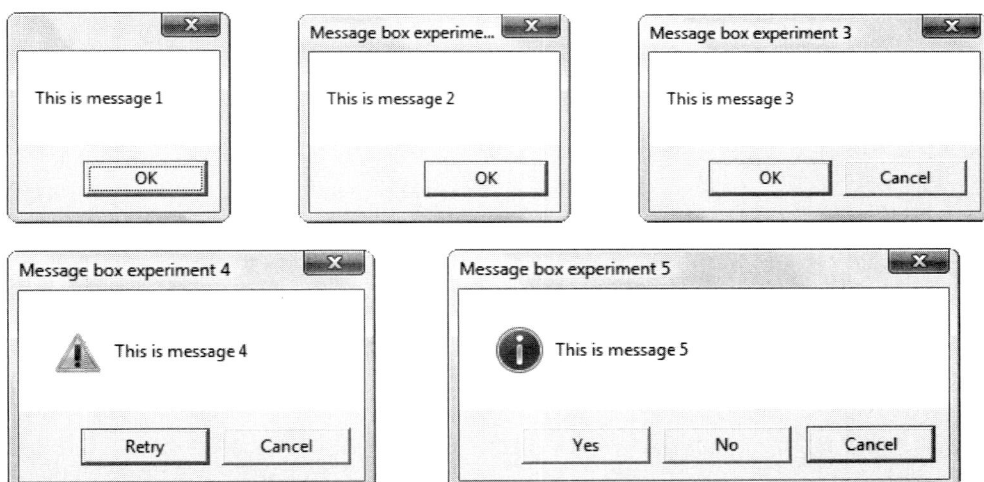

Figure 10-6 Output of `MessageBoxDemo` program

When the first shaded statement in Figure 10-5 executes, the first `MessageBox` in Figure 10-6 appears and a sound is played. The user hears the sound only if the user's system has speakers and they are turned on. This sound calls the user's attention to the `MessageBox`. No caption appears in the first `MessageBox`—just the message "This is message 1". A Close button is available in the upper-right corner. A `MessageBox` is a **modal dialog box**, which means that the program cannot progress until the user dismisses the box. (When you **dismiss** a component, you get rid of it, frequently by pressing its Close button, but in some cases by making some other selection.) When the user clicks OK or Close, the program proceeds; in this case, the second `MessageBox` appears.

The second shaded statement in Figure 10-5 creates a `MessageBox` to which a caption is added. In the second box in Figure 10-6, the message is updated with the new value of `count`, and the `count` is displayed in the caption. This `MessageBox` is automatically wider than the first one to accommodate the title bar caption.

OK and Cancel buttons are added in the third `MessageBox`. The OK button has a darker outline than the Cancel button, which means that the OK button has focus. When a button has **focus**, not only is the user's attention drawn to it visually, but if the user presses the Enter key, the action associated with the button executes, just as it would if the user clicked the button. If you press the Tab key or use the right and left arrow keys on your keyboard, you can change the focus from one button to the other. In this example, whether a user dismisses the third `MessageBox` by pressing the Enter key, closing the box, or clicking one of the two buttons, the fourth `MessageBox` appears.

The fourth `MessageBox` contains Retry and Cancel buttons and the Warning icon—an exclamation point in a triangle. The Warning icon might come with a different sound than a box without a warning. Because you normally would use the Warning icon in a "dangerous" situation, the sound is intended to get the user's attention. For example, you might use the Warning icon if a user leaves a required field blank on an order form or enters a phone number with too few or too many digits.

The last `MessageBox` includes an Information icon and three buttons. When this box appears, the button on the far right has focus because `MessageBoxDefaultButton.Button3` was used as an argument to the `MessageBox.Show()` method.

»TWO TRUTHS AND A LIE: CREATING A `MessageBox`

1. You create a new instance of the `MessageBox` class using the keyword `new` and the `MessageBox` constructor.
2. A `MessageBox` is a modal dialog box, which means a user must dismiss the box before the program continues.
3. When a button has focus and the user presses the Enter key, the action associated with the button executes.

The false statement is #1. You cannot create a new instance of the `MessageBox` class because its constructor is not public. Instead, you use the static class method `Show()` to display a `MessageBox`.

ADDING FUNCTIONALITY
TO MessageBox BUTTONS

`MessageBox` objects provide an easy way to display information to a user in a GUI format. When you use a `MessageBox` to display some text you want the user to read, it makes sense to include only an OK button that the user can click after reading the text. Including multiple `MessageBoxButtons`, all of which dismiss the `MessageBox`, doesn't make sense. Usually you want to determine users' interactions with a `MessageBox`'s buttons and take appropriate action based on the users' choices. **DialogResult** is an **enumeration**, or list of values in which names are substituted for numeric values. Each value corresponds to a user's potential `MessageBox` button selection. Table 10-6 contains `DialogResult` values you can compare to the return value of `MessageBox.Show()`. The `DialogResult` member names correspond to the button labels available within a `MessageBox`.

Member Name	Description
Abort	The dialog box return value is Abort
Cancel	The dialog box return value is Cancel
Ignore	The dialog box return value is Ignore
No	The dialog box return value is No
None	Nothing is returned from the dialog box, which means that the modal dialog box stays open
OK	The dialog box return value is OK
Retry	The dialog box return value is Retry
Yes	The dialog box return value is Yes

Table 10-6 `DialogResult` values

Figure 10-7 shows a program written for a fast-food restaurant. Its `MessageBox` asks the user to click Yes or No in response to a standard fast-food question. If the user clicks the Yes button, then the return value of `MessageBox.Show()` is equivalent to `DialogResult.Yes`, the `choice` string is set to "With fries", and the price increases by 0.75; otherwise, the `choice` string retains its original value "Without fries", and the price remains $3.00. Whatever button the user chooses, a new `MessageBox` displays the final description and meal price. Figure 10-8 shows the `MessageBox` that contains the question and two results: the first occurs when the user clicks Yes, and the second occurs when the user clicks No.

```
using System;
using System.Windows.Forms;
public class HamburgerAddition
{
   public static void Main()
   {
      string question = "Do you want fries with that?";
      string caption = "Hamburger addition";
      string choice = "Without fries";
      double price = 3.00;
      const double FRIES_PRICE = 0.75;
      if(MessageBox.Show(question, caption,
         MessageBoxButtons.YesNo, MessageBoxIcon.Question) ==
         DialogResult.Yes)
      {
         choice = "With fries";
         price += FRIES_PRICE;
      }
      MessageBox.Show(choice + "total is " +
         price.ToString("C"));
   }
}
```

Figure 10-7 `HamburgerAddition` program

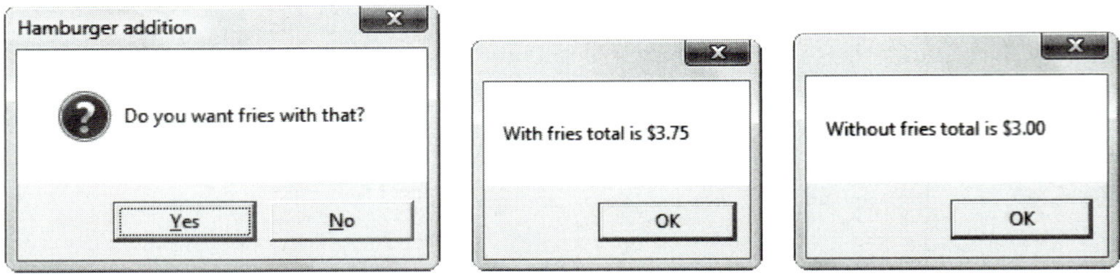

Figure 10-8 `MessageBox` in `HamburgerAddition` program, and results when user clicks Yes and No

> **»NOTE** Instead of the long, shaded `if` statement in Figure 10-7, you could create a `DialogResult` object and assign the result of the `MessageBox.Show()` method to it, as in the following code:
>
> ```
> DialogResult dResult = MessageBox.Show(question, caption,
>        MessageBoxButtons.YesNo, MessageBoxIcon.Question);
> ```
>
> Then the `if` expression becomes simpler:
>
> ```
> if(dResult = DialogResult.Yes)...
> ```
>
> Also, when you use this technique, you can reuse `dResult`, comparing it to different values one at a time.

»TWO TRUTHS AND A LIE: ADDING FUNCTIONALITY TO MessageBox BUTTONS

1. `DialogResult` is an enumeration, or list of values in which names are substituted for numeric values.
2. `DialogResult` values include `Yes`, `No`, `OK`, and `Cancel`.
3. `MessageBox.Show()` is a `void` method.

The false statement is #3. `MessageBox.Show()` returns a `DialogResult` value that you often want to compare with another value such as `DialogResult`.

CREATING A Form

`MessageBox`es offer a large, but not infinite, number of ways to interact with users. They provide information, and several versions can allow a user to select one of two or three button options. However, some applications require more components than a few buttons; for example, they might require an entire grid of buttons, lists of available options from which to select, or text fields in which to type. **Forms** provide an interface for collecting, displaying, and delivering such information; they are key components of GUI programs. You can use a `Form` to represent any window you want to display within your application. Although they are not required, you can include **controls** such as text fields, buttons, and check boxes that users can manipulate to interact with a program.

The `Form` class descends from the `Object` class like all other C# classes, but not directly. It is six generations removed from the `Object` class in the following line of descent:

» `Object`
» `MarshalByRefObject`
» `Component`
» `Control`
» `ScrollableControl`
» `ContainerControl`
» `Form`

You can create an instance of the `Form` class. (This is different from the `MessageBox` class, in which you cannot create an instance but must use the `Show()` method.) Figure 10-9 shows a program that creates the simplest `Form` possible, and Figure 10-10 shows the output.

»NOTE
To use a `Form`, you must include the `using` statement at the top of the program file, as shown in Figure 10-9.

```
using System.Windows.Forms;
public class CreateForm1
{
    public static void Main()
    {
        Form form1 = new Form();
        form1.ShowDialog();
    }
}
```

Figure 10-9 `CreateForm1` program

Figure 10-10 Output of `CreateForm1` program

> **NOTE** If you use a Microsoft product such as Word and open a new, unnamed document, it is called `Document1`. When you open Excel, the first unnamed spreadsheet is called `Sheet1`. Microsoft uses the same naming convention for `Forms`, `WindowsApplications`, and other components in the IDE.

In Figure 10-9, the object `form1` is an instance of the `Form` class. The `ShowDialog()` method displays the `Form` as a modal dialog box, so the user must dismiss the box before the program proceeds. The `Form` contains neither a caption nor components, but it does possess a title bar with an icon. You can use your mouse to minimize, restore, resize (by dragging on the `Form`'s borders), and close the `Form`, just as you can with most of the `Form`s you have encountered when you have used programs written by others.

You can change the appearance, size, color, and window management features of a `Form` by setting its properties. The `Form` class contains approximately 100 properties, many of which it inherits from the `Control` class. Table 10-7 lists just some of them. For example, setting the `Text` property allows you to specify the caption of the `Form` in the title bar. The `Size` and `DesktopLocation` properties allow you to define the size and position of the window when it is displayed.

> **NOTE** You have been creating properties for your own classes since Chapter 7. There, you learned that a property is a member of a class that defines how fields will be set and retrieved. When you use controls in a C# project, you are using properties that have already been created by others.

> **NOTE** If you use the Visual Studio .NET Search option, you can find descriptions for all the `Form` class properties. Additionally, if you highlight a property and press F1 or click a property name, you will see a description of the property at the bottom of the Properties window. Not every property you can use with a `Form` appears in the Properties window in the Visual Studio IDE—only the most frequently used are listed.

Member Name	Description
AcceptButton	Gets or sets the button on the form that is clicked when the user presses the Enter key
AllowDrop	Gets or sets a value indicating whether the control can accept data that the user drags and drops into it
BackColor	Gets or sets the background color for this control
BackgroundImage	Gets or sets the background image displayed in the control
Bottom	Gets the distance between the bottom edge of the control and the top edge of its container's client area
CancelButton	Gets or sets the button control that is clicked when the user presses the Esc key
CanFocus	Gets a value indicating whether the control can receive focus
CanSelect	Gets a value indicating whether the control can be selected
ContainsFocus	Gets a value indicating whether the control or one of its child controls currently has the input focus
ControlBox	Gets or sets a value indicating whether a control box is displayed in the title bar of the form
Cursor	Gets or sets the cursor that is displayed when the user moves the mouse pointer over this control
DesktopBounds	Gets or sets the size and location of the form on the Windows desktop
DesktopLocation	Gets or sets the location of the form on the Windows desktop
DialogResult	Gets or sets the dialog result for the form
Focused	Gets a value indicating whether the control has input focus
Font	Gets or sets the current font for the control
ForeColor	Gets or sets the foreground color of the control
FormBorderStyle	Gets or sets the border style of the form
Height	Gets or sets the height of the control
HelpButton	Gets or sets a value indicating whether a Help button should be displayed in the title bar of the form
Icon	Gets or sets the icon for the form
Left	Gets or sets the x-coordinate of a control's left edge in pixels
Location	Gets or sets the coordinates of the upper-left corner of the control relative to the upper-left corner of its container
MaximizeBox	Gets or sets a value indicating whether the Maximize button is displayed in the title bar of the form
MaximumSize	Gets the maximum size to which the form can be resized
Menu	Gets or sets the main menu that is displayed in the form

Table 10-7 Properties of Forms (*continued*)

Member Name	Description
MinimizeBox	Gets or sets a value indicating whether the Minimize button is displayed in the title bar of the form
MinimumSize	Gets the minimum size to which the form can be resized
Modal	Gets a value indicating whether this form is displayed modally
Name	Gets or sets the name of the control
Opacity	Gets or sets the opacity level of the form
Right	Gets the distance between the right edge of the control and the left edge of its container
RightToLeft	Gets or sets whether the alignment of the control's elements is reversed to support locales using right-to-left fonts
ShowInTaskbar	Gets or sets a value indicating whether the form is displayed in the Windows taskbar
Size	Gets or sets the size of the form
StartPosition	Gets or sets the starting position of the form at run time
TabStop	Gets or sets a value indicating whether the user can give the focus to this control using the Tab key
Text	Gets or sets the text associated with this control
Top	Gets or sets the top coordinate of the control
Visible	Gets or sets a value indicating whether the control is visible
Width	Gets or sets the width of the control

Table 10-7 (*continued*)

Figure 10-11 shows a CreateForm2 class that instantiates a Form object and sets several of its properties: a caption and a Help button with a question mark are set in the title bar, and the Minimize and Maximize buttons that usually appear on a Form are removed. Figure 10-12 shows the output.

```
using System.Windows.Forms;
public class CreateForm2
{
   public static void Main()
   {
      Form form2 = new Form();
      form2.Text = "This is a Form2 Form";
      form2.HelpButton = true;
      form2.MaximizeBox = false;
      form2.MinimizeBox = false;
      form2.ShowDialog();
   }
}
```

Figure 10-11 CreateForm2 class

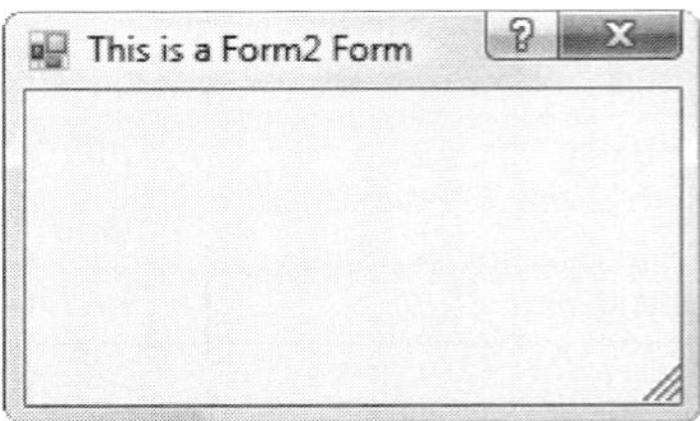

Figure 10-12 Output of CreateForm2 program

>>**TWO TRUTHS AND A LIE: CREATING A** Form

1. You cannot create an instance of the Form class because its constructor is private.
2. By default, a Form contains neither a caption nor components, but it does possess a title bar with an icon.
3. You can change the appearance, size, color, and window management features of a Form by setting its properties.

The false statement is #1. You can create an instance of the Form class. This is different from the MessageBox class, in which you cannot create an instance but must use the Show() method.

CREATING A Form THAT IS A PROGRAM'S MAIN WINDOW

You can instantiate a Form within an application and use the ShowDialog() method to display it, as in Figure 10-11. More frequently, you create a child class from Form that becomes the main window of an application. When you create a new main window, you must complete two steps:

» You must derive a new custom class from the base class
   System.Windows.Forms.Form.

» You must write a Main() method that calls the Application.Run() method, and you must pass an instance of your newly created Form class as an argument. This activity starts the program and makes the form visible.

Figure 10-13 shows the simplest program you can write that creates a new main window for a program. The class name is Window1; it extends the Form class, as you can see by the shaded colon and base class name in the class header.

```
using System.Windows.Forms;
public class Window1 : Form
{
    public static void Main()
    {
        Application.Run(new Window1());
    }
}
```

Figure 10-13 Window1 class

>>**NOTE** Later in this chapter, you will learn to create a Form using the Visual Studio IDE. Here, you learn to create one "by hand" so you better understand what the IDE does automatically.

>>**NOTE** You learned about inheritance and the syntax of using the colon and the base class name in Chapter 8.

>>**NOTE** The statement Application.Run(new Window1()); creates an unnamed instance of the Window1 class. Alternatively, you could instantiate a named Window object using Window1 aWindow = new Window(); and then call Application.Run(aWindow);. However, because this application never needs to use the name aWindow, there is no need to provide the new Window1 object with a unique identifier.

The Window1 class in Figure 10-13 contains a single method: a Main() method that calls the Application.Run() method, passing a new instance of the Window1 class. Figure 10-14 shows the output. The Form created has no title and contains no components, but it has a title bar that displays an icon and Minimize, Restore, and Close buttons in the expected locations.

Figure 10-14 Output of Window1 program

The Application.Run() method processes messages from the operating system to the application. Without the call to Application.Run(), the program would compile and execute, but the program would end without displaying the window.

When you want to add property settings to a program's main window, you can do so within the class constructor. Figure 10-15 shows a Window2 class in which the Size and Text attributes of a Window are set. The keyword this in the constructor method refers to "this Form being constructed"; you could eliminate this, and the constructor would work in the same way. To set the Size property, you must instantiate a System.Drawing.Size object. Its constructor takes two parameters. The first indicates the horizontal size, or width, of a component; the second indicates the vertical size (or height) of a component. Setting the Size to System.Drawing.Size(500, 100) creates a window that is five times wider than it is tall. The Text property supplies the caption that appears in the window's title bar. Figure 10-16 shows the created Window2 object.

```
using System.Windows.Forms;
public class Window2 : Form
{
    public Window2()
    {
        this.Size = new System.Drawing.Size(500, 100);
        this.Text = "This is a Window2 Object";
    }
    public static void Main()
    {
        Application.Run(new Window2());
    }
}
```

Figure 10-15 Window2 class

Figure 10-16 Output of `Window2` program

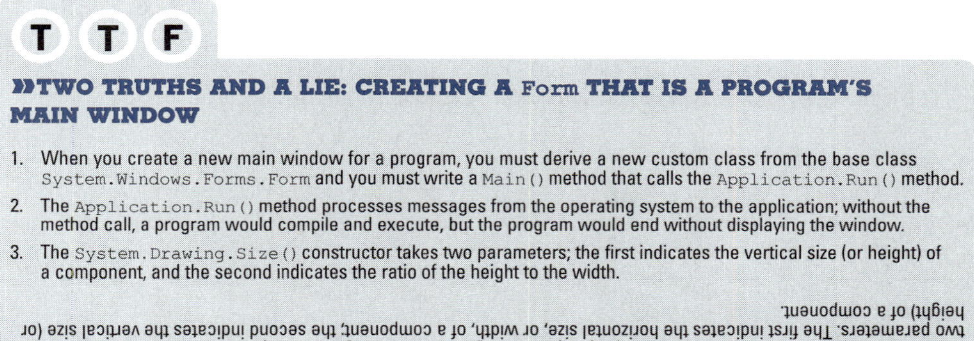

»TWO TRUTHS AND A LIE: CREATING A Form THAT IS A PROGRAM'S MAIN WINDOW

1. When you create a new main window for a program, you must derive a new custom class from the base class `System.Windows.Forms.Form` and you must write a `Main()` method that calls the `Application.Run()` method.

2. The `Application.Run()` method processes messages from the operating system to the application; without the method call, a program would compile and execute, but the program would end without displaying the window.

3. The `System.Drawing.Size()` constructor takes two parameters; the first indicates the vertical size (or height) of a component, and the second indicates the ratio of the height to the width.

The false statement is #3. A window's `Size` property uses a `System.Drawing.Size` object whose constructor takes two parameters. The first indicates the horizontal size, or width, of a component; the second indicates the vertical size (or height) of a component.

PLACING A `Button` ON A `Window`

Although it has interesting dimensions, the window in Figure 10-16 is not yet as useful as a `MessageBox`. However, a window is more flexible than a `MessageBox` because you can place manipulatable `Window` controls wherever you like on the surface of the `Window`.

One type of control the user can manipulate is a `Button`. A **Button** is a GUI object you can click to cause some action. (Alternatively, you can press the Enter key if the `Button` has focus.) You can create your own `Button` objects by using the `Button` class. This class contains more than 60 properties; two of the most useful are its `Text` and `Location` properties. You use the `Text` property to set a `Button`'s label. You can use the `Location` property to position a `Button` relative to the upper-left corner of the `Form` (or any other `ContainerControl` object) that contains it.

When you set the `Location` property, you instantiate a `System.Drawing.Point` object and supply two integer arguments to its constructor. The first argument represents a number of horizontal pixels to the right of the upper-left corner of a `Form` (or other container). The second argument represents the vertical position down from the top. For example, 0, 0 is the upper-left corner, and 10, 200 is a little to the right but much further down.

Figure 10-17 shows a `WindowWithButton` class that descends from `Form`. The class declares a `Button` named `button1`. The class constructor sets the form size to 300 by 150—a size that is twice as wide as it is tall. The `Form`'s `Text` property is set, as is the `Button`'s `Text` property. The `Button` is located at `Point(25, 50)`, not very far from the `Form`'s left side. Figure 10-18 shows the resulting `Form`—a `Window` with `Text` in the title bar and a clickable `Button` with text.

```
using System.Windows.Forms;
public class WindowWithButton : Form
{
    Button button1 = new Button();
    public WindowWithButton()
    {
        this.Size = new System.Drawing.Size(300, 150);
        this.Text = "Window Object With Button";
        button1.Text = "Press";
        this.Controls.AddRange(new System.Windows.Forms.Control[]
            {this.button1});
        this.button1.Location = new System.Drawing.Point(25, 50);
    }
    public static void Main()
    {
        Application.Run(new WindowWithButton());
    }
}
```

Figure 10-17 `WindowWithButton` class

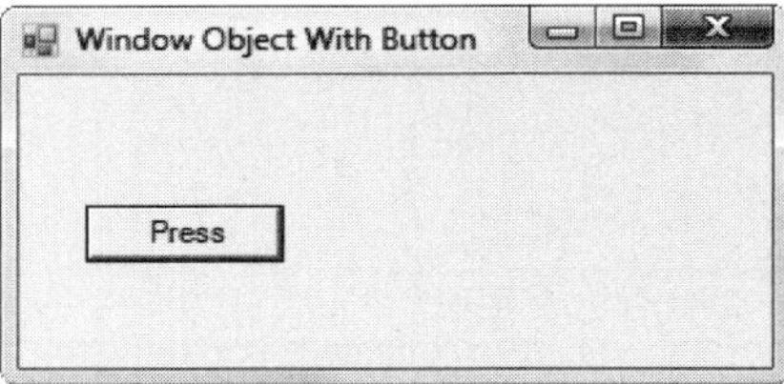

Figure 10-18 Output of `WindowWithButton` program

> **»NOTE** In the `WindowWithButton` class, you could leave out the four instances of `this`. For example, the statement `Text = "Window Object With Button";` would work exactly like the one that uses the `this` reference. Figure 10-17 includes the `this` reference for two reasons. First, it helps you understand that "this" object, the `WindowWithButton` Form, has `Text` that is being altered, and not some other component on the Form. Second, when you create programs visually using the IDE, as you will do later in this chapter, you will see liberal uses of `this` in the automatically generated code. That's because the IDE cannot predict what identifiers you will use for your components, so it fully qualifies its statements to avoid conflicts.

T T F

»TWO TRUTHS AND A LIE: PLACING A Button ON A Window

1. You can use the `Button` class `Text` property to set a `Button`'s label.

2. You use the `Button` class `Location` property to position a `Button` relative to the center of the `Form` that contains it.

3. A `Form` with a `Size` property set to `System.Drawing.Size(200, 400)` is twice as tall as it is wide.

The false statement is #2. The `Button` class `Location` property positions a `Button` relative to the upper-left corner of the `Form` that contains it.

USING THE VISUAL STUDIO
IDE TO DESIGN A Form

The window in Figure 10-18 consists of only a Form and a Button, and even though the Button doesn't do anything yet, scores of additional options are available to you. The program in Figure 10-17 sets only two attributes for the Form (Size and Text), yet Table 10-7 shows dozens of additional properties you can set—and that table lists only half the available properties. Likewise, the program in Figure 10-17 sets only two Button properties (Text and Location); by the time you create a full-blown Windows application, you might want to set several more properties for the existing Button, add more Buttons, and set all their properties. You might want to add other components to the window, supplying locations and appropriate actions for each of them as well. Just determining an attractive and useful layout in which to position all the components on your Form would take many lines of code and a lot of trial and error. A simple but fully functional GUI program might require several hundred statements. Therefore, coding such a program can be tedious.

The Visual Studio IDE provides a wealth of tools to help you design Forms. Rather than having to write multiple assignment statements and guess at appropriate component locations, it allows you to use a visual environment for designing your Forms.

> **» NOTE** Chapter 1 contains instructions for creating and running a console application using the IDE. If you have been using the IDE throughout this book to create programs, you are already familiar with many of the menu options. If you have been using a simple text editor instead of the IDE, you might want to return to the "You Do It" section in Chapter 1 and create, compile, and execute a simple console application, just to get used to the IDE. In the "You Do It" section at the end of this chapter, you will create your own Windows application. Note that when you use the IDE to create Windows applications, you choose the Windows Application option instead of Console Application when starting the new project.

> **» NOTE**
> Designing aesthetically pleasing, functional, and user-friendly Forms is an art; entire books are devoted to the topic.

Figure 10-19 shows the environment in which you can create Windows applications. Some key features in Visual C# include:

» The **main menu**, which includes a File menu from which you open, close, and save projects. It also contains submenus for editing, debugging, and help tasks, among others.

» The **Toolbox tab**, which, when you open it, provides lists of controls you can drag onto a Form so that you can develop programs visually, using a mouse.

» The **Form Designer** and **Code Editor**, which appear in the center of the screen. You can switch back and forth between these two when you want to design an application by dragging components onto the screen or when you want to write or view code statements.

» The **Solution Explorer**, for viewing and managing project files and settings.

» The **Properties window**, for configuring properties and events on controls in your user interface. For example, you can use this window to set the Size property of a Button or the Text property of a Form without writing the necessary C# statements; the IDE will create the statements for you.

> **» NOTE**
> If some of these features are not immediately visible after you start a project in the IDE, you can select them from the View menu.

» The **output tab** and **error list tab**, which display messages about projects you are running and list any compiler errors in your code.

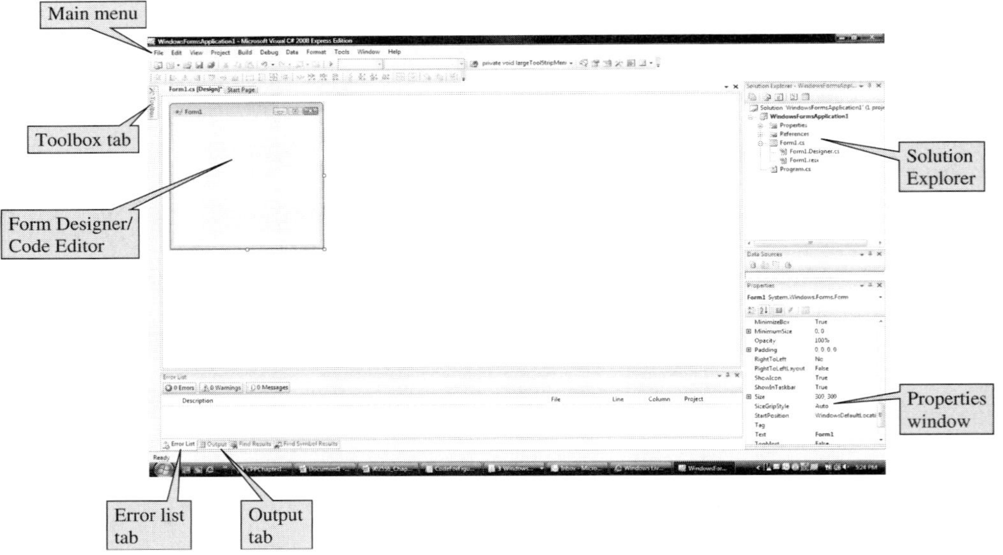

Figure 10-19 Features of the Visual Studio IDE

When you create a Windows Forms project, Visual C# names the project `WindowsFormsApplication1` by default. In Figure 10-19, you see this name in the following locations:

» In the title bar above the main menu

» In the title bar of the Solution Explorer

» In two locations in the Solution Explorer file list

When you create a Windows Forms project, Visual C# adds a form to the project and calls it `Form1`. You can see `Form1` in the following locations in Figure 10-19:

» On the folder tab at the top of the Form Designer area

» In the title bar of the form in the Form Designer area

» In the Solution Explorer file list (with a .cs extension)

» In the Properties window

The Solution Explorer file list shows the files that are part of the current project. If you expand the Form1.cs node by clicking the small plus sign to the left of it, you see two files that represent the form: Form1.Designer.cs and Form1.resx. As you develop an application, you write your code for the form in the Form1.cs file. The Windows Forms Designer automatically writes code in the Designer.cs file; the code created there implements all the actions that are performed when you drag and drop controls from the Toolbox. The Program.cs file contains the `Main()` method of the program.

When you select the Toolbox tab, a list of groups of tools appears. The list will automatically close when you move your mouse off the list, or you can pin the Toolbox to the screen by clicking the pushpin icon at the top of the list. Selecting All Windows Forms displays a complete list of available tools; selecting Common Controls displays a smaller list that is a subset of the original one. As shown in Figure 10-20, this list contains many controls—the GUI objects a user can click or manipulate. The list includes controls you probably have seen when using Windows applications—for example, Button, CheckBox, and Label. You can drag these controls onto the Form. For example, Figure 10-20 contains a pinned Toolbox and a Form onto which a Button has been dragged.

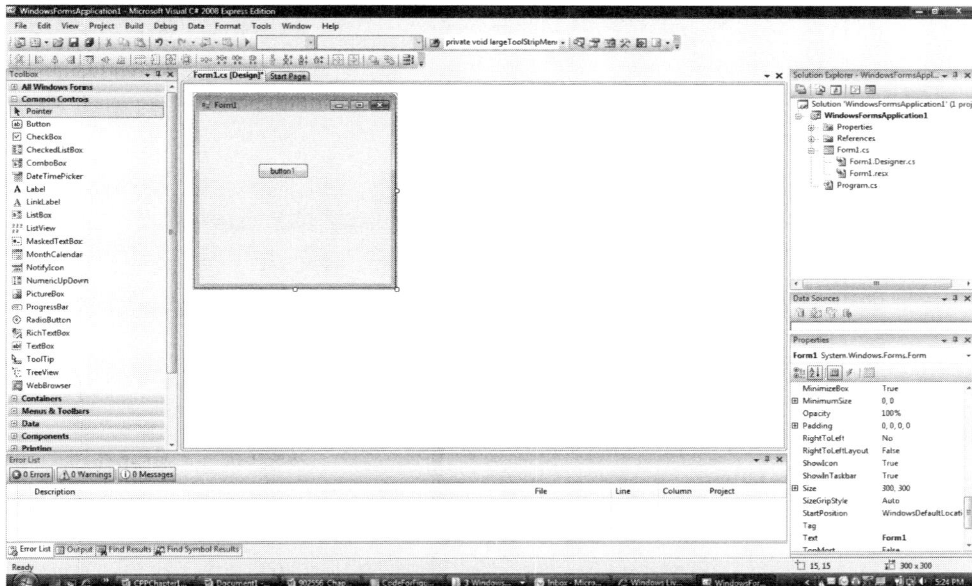

Figure 10-20 The pinned Toolbox and a Form with a Button in the IDE

When you select View from the main menu bar and then select Code, the IDE appears as in Figure 10-21. This code (and more that currently is hidden) was automatically generated for you.

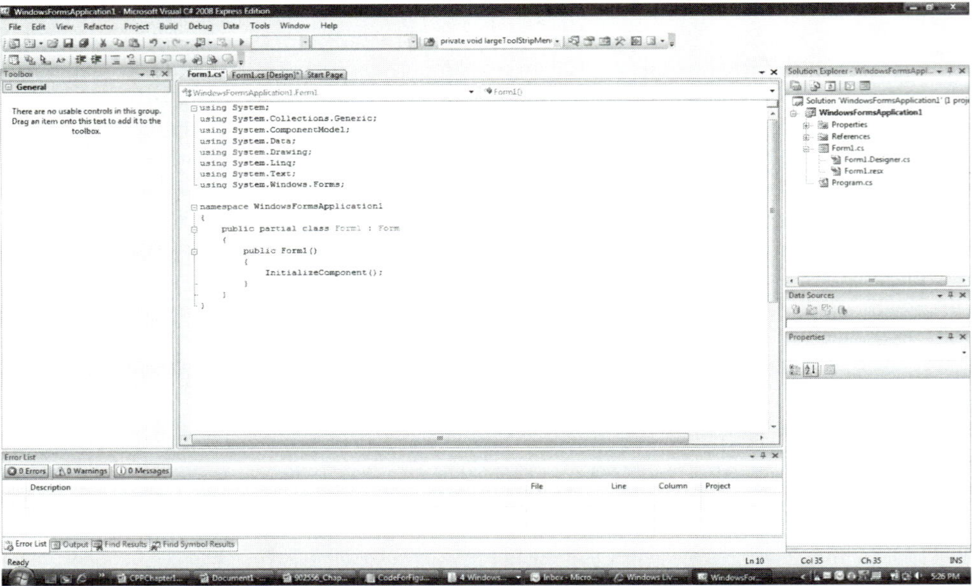

Figure 10-21 Sample code generated by C#

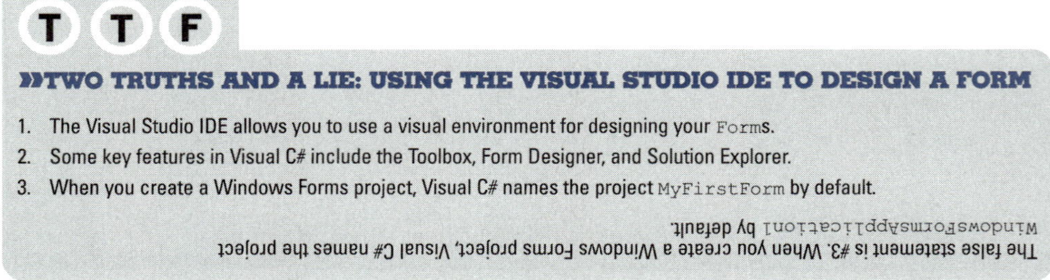

T   T   F

»TWO TRUTHS AND A LIE: USING THE VISUAL STUDIO IDE TO DESIGN A FORM

1. The Visual Studio IDE allows you to use a visual environment for designing your `Form`s.
2. Some key features in Visual C# include the Toolbox, Form Designer, and Solution Explorer.
3. When you create a Windows Forms project, Visual C# names the project `MyFirstForm` by default.

The false statement is #3. When you create a Windows Forms project, Visual C# names the project `WindowsFormsApplication1` by default.

UNDERSTANDING THE CODE CREATED BY THE IDE

Using the Visual Studio IDE, it is easy to create elaborate forms with a few keystrokes. However, if you don't understand the code behind the forms you create, you cannot say you have truly mastered the C# language, and you won't be able to troubleshoot problems as easily. Everything you have learned to this point has prepared you to understand the code

that underlies a visually designed form. The generated code is simply a collection of C#
statements and method calls similar to those you have used throughout this book. When you
use the Designer in the IDE to design your forms, you save a lot of typing, which reduces the
errors you create. As shown in Figure 10-21, it takes quite a bit of code to create even a simple
form with a single button. Examine the code piece by piece.

The code in Figure 10-21 contains a list of `using` statements as follows:

```
using System;
using System.Collections.Generic;
using System.ComponentModel;
using System.Data;
using System.Drawing;
using System.Linq;
using System.Text;
using System.Windows.Forms;
```

You have placed many statements like these within your earlier programs. These statements
simply list the namespaces for the classes the program will use.

The next code segment in Figure 10-21 creates a namespace using the name the
programmer supplied when this C# Windows project was started: `namespace
WindowsFormsApplication1`. You have been using the `System` namespace since
Chapter 1. Using the IDE, C# creates a namespace for you. The namespace declaration is
followed by an opening curly brace and, several statements later, a closing curly brace.

In Figure 10-21, you can see the declaration of the `Form1` class as follows:

```
public partial class Form1 : Form
{
    public Form1()
    {
        InitializeComponent();
    }
}
```

The name `Form1` was supplied by default; you can change this name using the form's `Name`
property if you want. The `Form1` class header shows that the class descends from the `Form`
class. The class header is followed by an opening curly brace, and several lines later, the
matching closing brace.

> **» NOTE** You should change the IDE's automatically supplied identifiers, such as `Form1`, to more meaningful names.
> However, many examples in this book show components with their original names so changes are kept to a minimum and
> you can concentrate on the topic at hand.

The `Form1` class is declared as a `partial` class. As you might imagine, a `partial` class
contains only part of the class; the rest is spread among multiple files. (The rest of the class
will be discussed shortly.)

The `Form1` class contains one method—a constructor. It looks like many other constructors
you have created: it is `public`, has no `return` type, and has the same name as the class. The

> **» NOTE**
> Because the IDE
> generates so much
> code automatically,
> it is often more dif-
> ficult to find and
> correct errors in
> programs created
> using the IDE than
> in programs you
> code by hand.

> **» NOTE**
> In Chapter 7, you
> learned that
> `partial` is a con-
> textual keyword,
> like `get` and `set`.

`Form1()` constructor is parameterless and contains one statement—a call to a method named `InitializeComponent()`.

In Figure 10-21, notice the node for Form1.Designer.cs below Form1.cs. Figure 10-22 shows the IDE after the Form1.Designer.cs icon is selected to reveal more of the partial `Form1()` class.

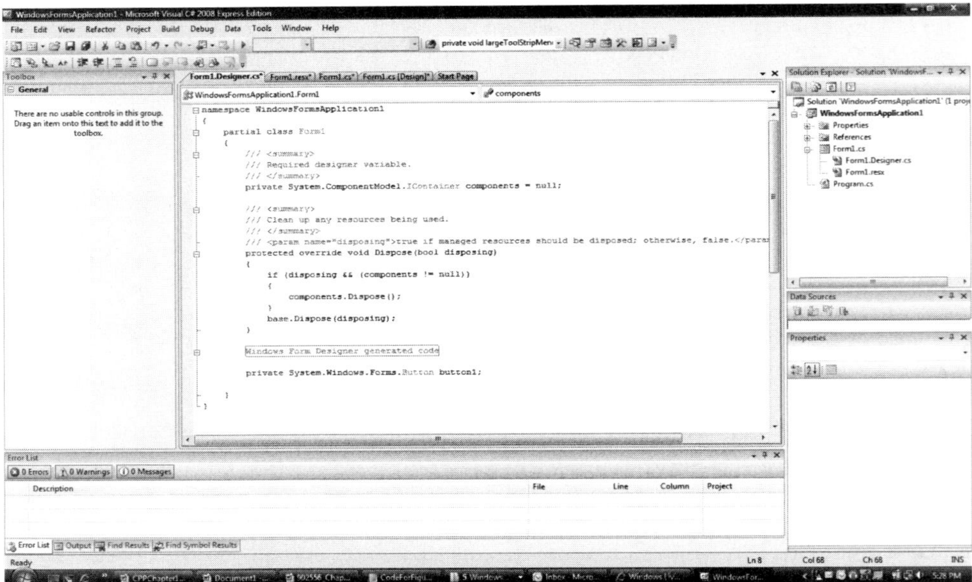

Figure 10-22 Code revealed in the IDE after user double-clicks the Form1.Designer node in the Solution Explorer

The significant parts of the automatically generated code that you can see in Figure 10-22 include:

» Comments
» The `Dispose()` method
» Object declarations

Other parts of the code that you can reveal (and that you will see in later figures) include:

» The `InitializeComponent()` method
» Preprocessor directives
» A `Main()` method

The following sections describe each part of the generated code. Again, you might need to scroll down to see it.

COMMENTS

The code in Figure 10-22 contains many comments, such as the following:

```
/// <summary>
/// Clean up any resources being used.
/// </summary>
```

In other C# programs, you have seen many line comments that begin with two slashes. C# uses three slashes (///) to begin an XML comment. When C# inserts the tag pairs <summary> and </summary> within the code, it allows the IntelliSense feature in Visual Studio to display additional information about the members contained between the tags. The IntelliSense feature automatically completes statements for you within the Visual Studio IDE.

> **NOTE** You first learned about XML comments when you learned about block and line comments in Chapter 1. Recall that XML stands for eXtensible Markup Language. To obtain more information, search for XML in the Visual Studio Help facility; it will direct you to several articles that discuss XML.

THE `Dispose()` METHOD

The code created by C# in Figure 10-22 and visible in the IDE includes a method named `Dispose()`, as follows:

```
protected override void Dispose(bool disposing)
{
    if (disposing && (components != null))
    ⋮
       components.Dispose();
    ⋮
    base.Dispose(disposing);
}
```

By now, you should be familiar and comfortable with most of the elements in the method:

- » This method is `protected`, meaning any descendants can access it.
- » The method header uses the term `override`, meaning it overrides a method with the same name in an interface named `IDisposable`. That interface provides a mechanism for releasing program resources, such as files, that can be used by only one program at a time. This method contains any cleanup activities you need when a `Form` is dismissed. When you write an application that leaves open files or other unfinished business, you might want to add statements to this method. You do not need to understand all the details of the `Dispose()` method in order to create a workable program. C# has created the method for you, and for now, you can let C# take care of the cleanup tasks that are invisible to you.
- » The method's return type is `void`, so the method returns nothing to any method that calls it.
- » The method accepts a `bool` parameter.
- » The method includes an `if` statement and a call to another method that resides in its base class.

OBJECT DECLARATIONS

Within the `Form1` class in Figure 10-22, you can see two object declarations:

```
private System.ComponentModel.IContainer components = null;
private System.Windows.Forms.Button button1;
```

The first statement declares an object named `components` that is used by the designer. The second statement declares an object named `button1`. This object declaration was added to the code when the programmer dragged the `Button` onto the `Form`'s surface. You could change the `Button`'s access from `private` to `public` if you liked, but it is defined as `private` because it will be used only within this class. You also could eliminate the fully qualified `System.Windows.Forms.Button` class name and replace it with `Button` because the `using` statement at the top of the file includes `System.Windows.Forms`. You also can change the name of `button1` to any other legal identifier you choose. However, if you delete `button1` in the declaration and replace it with a new name, then you must be sure to change every instance of `button1` in the program. The safer, and recommended, alternative is to change `button1`'s `Name` property in the IDE. (You change it in the Settings box for the `Name` property, which you can locate in the Properties window of the Designer view. You can see the Properties window in the lower-right corner of Figure 10-19. You will get the opportunity to perform similar steps in the "You Do It" section later in this chapter.) When you change a control's `Name` property in the Properties window, every reference to the control will be replaced with its new identifier.

> **>> NOTE** If you change `button1`'s `Name` property within the code, switch to Designer view and then double-click the button to switch back to Code view. You will find that every instance of `button1` has been changed to the new name you assigned.

When you create more complicated forms that contain additional objects such as `Checkbox`es, `Label`s, or more `Button`s, more objects will be declared in the code.

THE `InitializeComponent()` METHOD

A dimmed rectangle with the label "Windows Form Designer generated code" appears just above the `button1` declaration in Figure 10-22. To its left is a node with a plus sign (+). If you double-click the box, additional code is exposed, as shown in Figure 10-23. A method named `InitializeComponent()` occupies most of the newly exposed code.

The `InitializeComponent()` method contains all of the component initialization tasks. Many of the statements within the method should look familiar to you. These statements reflect the code generated by the properties that have been selected for the `Form`. For example, the `button1.Text` and `Form this.Text` properties contain values like those you would have typed into the code when creating a GUI application "by hand," without using the Visual Studio design environment. Similarly, the following statement sets a drawing size:

```
this.button1.Size = new System.Drawing.Size(75, 23);
```

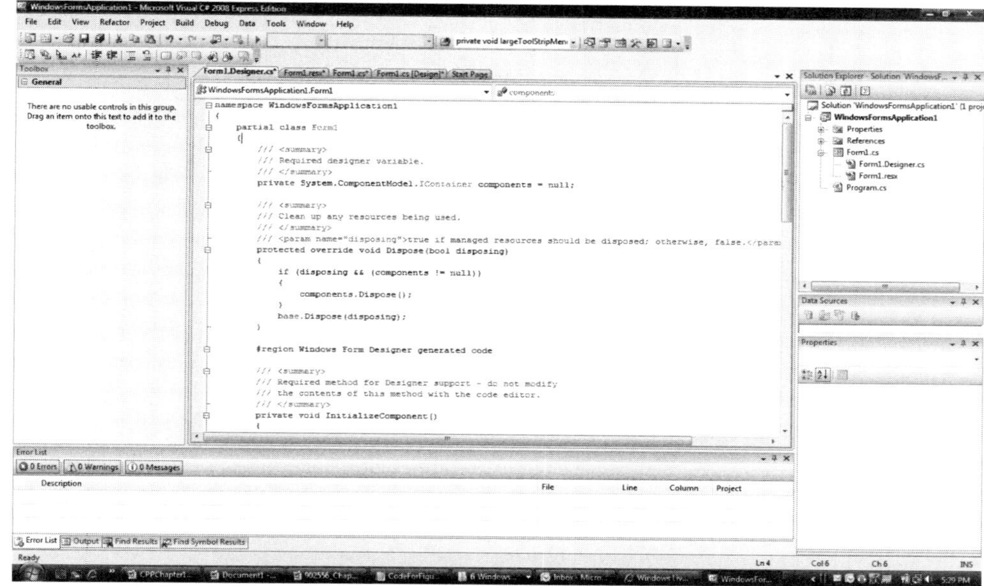

Figure 10-23 The `InitializeComponent()` method

PREPROCESSOR DIRECTIVES

The statements in the code that do not look familiar begin with a pound sign (#). The statements `#region` and `#endregion` are examples of preprocessor directives. **Preprocessor directives** always start with a pound sign (#) and are instructions to a program that executes before the compiler (called the **preprocessor**) to modify the code in some way. Any code placed between the `#region` and `#endregion` directives constitutes a group that can be used by some of the IDE's automated tools.

For example, the Code Editor treats namespaces, classes, and methods as regions that you can collapse. Collapsing regions provides an outline of your code, hiding the details. Using this feature can make parts of your code easier to find. On the vertical line to the left of the code in the Code Editor, you can click a + to expand code and a – to collapse it. You can make your own collapsible code regions by surrounding sections with `#region` and `#endregion`. The `#region` and `#endregion` statements do not affect the way the code operates; they help you navigate the editor.

THE PROJECT'S `Main()` METHOD

At the right side of Figure 10-22, the Solution Explorer screen contains a file named Program.cs. This file contains the `Main()` method for the `WindowsFormsApplication1` application, as shown in Figure 10-24. You can see that the last line of code calls `Application.Run()` for this `Form`, just as you did manually for the `Windows` in Figures 10-13, 10-15, and 10-17 earlier in this chapter.

> **» NOTE**
> You can see the `#region` pre-processor directive in Figure 10-23. You would have to scroll down to see the `#endregion` directive.

> **» NOTE**
> Other preprocessor directives in C# include `#if`, `#else`, `#elif`, `#endif`, `#define`, `#undef`, `#warning`, `#error`, and `#line`.

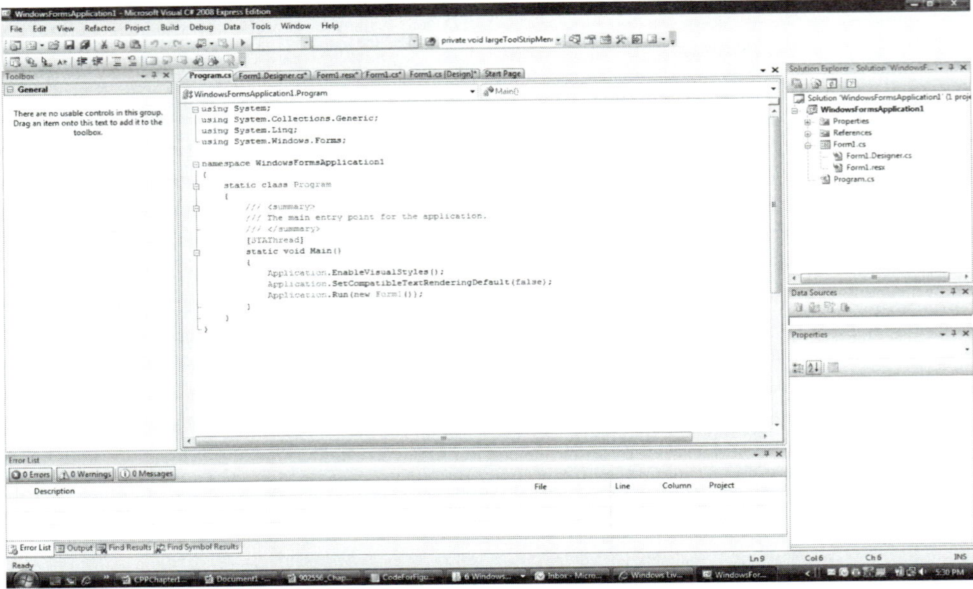

Figure 10-24 Program.cs file

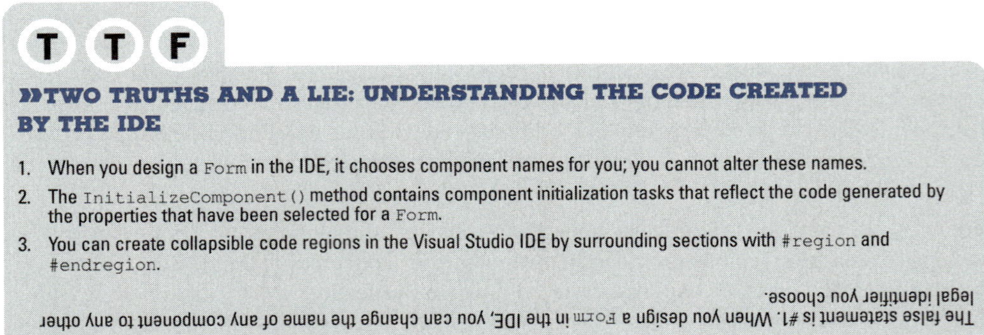

»TWO TRUTHS AND A LIE: UNDERSTANDING THE CODE CREATED BY THE IDE

1. When you design a `Form` in the IDE, it chooses component names for you; you cannot alter these names.
2. The `InitializeComponent()` method contains component initialization tasks that reflect the code generated by the properties that have been selected for a `Form`.
3. You can create collapsible code regions in the Visual Studio IDE by surrounding sections with `#region` and `#endregion`.

The false statement is #1. When you design a `Form` in the IDE, you can change the name of any component to any other legal identifier you choose.

ADDING FUNCTIONALITY TO A Button ON A Form

In most cases, it is easier to design a `Form` using the IDE than it is to write by hand all the code a `Form` requires. Adding functionality to a `Button` is particularly easy when you use the IDE. After you have dragged a `Button` onto a `Form`, you can double-click it. Figure 10-25 shows the generated code. The class contains a constructor that performs a single task—it calls the

```
using System.Text;
using System.Windows.Forms;

namespace WindowsFormsApplication1
{
    public partial class Form1 : Form
    {
        public Form1()
        {
            InitializeComponent();
        }

        private void button1_Click(object sender, EventArgs e)
        {

        }
    }
}
```

Figure 10-25 Partial `Form1` class that contains a constructor and `Click()` method

`InitializeComponent()` method. Following the constructor is a shell of a method named `button1_Click()`. In Figure 10-25, you can see that the method is `private` and `void`.

When a user interacts with a GUI object, an **event** is generated that causes the program to perform a task. When a user clicks a `Button`, the action fires a **click event**. This event causes the `Button`'s `Click()` method to execute. You might guess that if you placed a second button on the form, its method would be named `button2_Click()`. You might also guess that if you changed the `Name` property of the `button1` object in the IDE, the name of this method should also change. For example, if you renamed the `Button` `acceptLicenseAgreement`, the name of the method should become:

```
acceptLicenseAgreement_Click()
```

> **» NOTE**
> Actually, the click event indirectly causes the `Button`'s `Click()` method to execute. Event handler code is operating "behind the scenes."

> **» NOTE**
> Using a process called refactoring, C# can automatically change a method name when its associated object's name changes. See Appendix C.

> **» NOTE** You are not required to create a `Click()` method for a `Button`. If, for some reason, you did not want to take any action when a user clicked a button, you simply would not include the method in your program. Alternatively, you could create an empty method that contains no statements between its curly braces and thus does nothing. However, these choices would be unusual—you usually place a `Button` on a `Form` because you expect it to be clicked at some point. You will frustrate users if you do not allow your `Controls` to act in expected ways.

You can write any statements you want between the curly braces of the `button1_Click()` method. For example, if you write the following statement, a `MessageBox` will be displayed when the user clicks the `Button`:

```
MessageBox.Show("You clicked the button");
```

> **» NOTE**
> Chapter 12 describes event handling in detail.

Alternatively, you could declare a string that contains a message and use it within the class (see Figure 10-26).

```csharp
using System.Text;
using System.Windows.Forms;

namespace WindowsFormsApplication1
{
    public partial class Form1 : Form
    {
        const string MESSAGE = "You clicked the button";
        public Form1()
        {
            InitializeComponent();
        }

        private void button1_Click(object sender, EventArgs e)
        {
            MessageBox.Show(MESSAGE);
        }
    }
}
```

Figure 10-26 `Form1` class that contains a declaration

> **» NOTE**
> In Chapter 11, you will learn to place additional statements within your application's `Click()` methods.

> **» NOTE** If you see a code screen in the IDE, you can return to the visual view of the `Form` by double-clicking Form1.cs in the Solution Explorer panel at the right side of the screen. Alternatively, you can right-click in the Code window and click View Designer.

»TWO TRUTHS AND A LIE: ADDING FUNCTIONALITY TO A Button **ON A** Form

1. When a user clicks a `Button`, the action fires a click event that causes the `Button`'s `Click()` method to execute.
2. If a `Button`'s identifier is `myButton`, then the name of its `Click()` method is `myButton.Click()`.
3. You can write any statements you want between the curly braces of a `Button`'s `Click()` method.

The false statement is #2. If a `Button`'s identifier is `myButton`, then the name of its `Click()` method is `myButton_Click()`.

USING VISUAL STUDIO HELP

When you are working with a class that is new to you, such as `Button` or `Form`, no book can answer all of your questions. The ultimate authority on C# classes is the Visual Studio Help documentation. You should use this tool often as you continue to learn about C# in particular and the Visual Studio products in general.

The Help documentation for Visual Studio is in the MSDN Library, which you can install locally on your own computer. It is also available at *http://msdn.microsoft.com/library*. You can install all or part of the library on your machine; the complete MSDN installation is close to 2 GB in size, and includes documentation for many Microsoft technologies besides C#.

There are multiple ways to access Help while working in Visual C#:

» *F1 Search*—In the Code Editor, you can position the cursor on or just after a keyword or class member and press F1. The Help provided is context-sensitive, which means the screen you see depends on where your cursor is located.

» *Search*—On the main menu, you can click Help, click Search, and type in a topic.

» *Index*—You can select Help from the main menu and click Index. The index provides a quick way to locate documents in your local MSDN library. It searches only the index keywords that have been assigned to each document.

» *Table of Contents*—The MSDN library table of contents shows all the topics in the library in a hierarchical tree structure. It is a useful tool for browsing through the documentation to see what is in the library, and for exploring documents that you might not find through the Index or Search tools. Often, when you find a document using F1, Index, or Search, it is useful to know where the document is located in the table of contents so you can see other related documentation.

» *How Do I*—How Do I provides a view of MSDN documents called How-to's or Walkthroughs. These documents show you how to perform a specific task.

» *Dynamic Help*—Dynamic Help provides a way to get information about the IDE. To open the Dynamic Help window, select Help from the main menu, and then click Dynamic Help. Then, when you click a word in the code, help topics are displayed accordingly.

You will learn much more about creating Windows applications using the IDE in the next two chapters.

»TWO TRUTHS AND A LIE: USING VISUAL STUDIO HELP

1. To get help in the Visual Studio IDE, you can position the cursor on or just after a keyword or class member in the Code Editor and press F10.

2. To get help in the Visual Studio IDE, you can click Help on the main menu, click Search, and type in a topic.

3. To get help in the Visual Studio IDE Index, you can select Help from the main menu and click Index.

The false statement is #1. As is the convention with most Microsoft products, you can get help in the Visual Studio IDE by positioning the cursor on or just after a keyword or class member in the Code Editor and pressing F1.

YOU DO IT

CREATING MessageBoxES

In the following steps, you will create GUI objects using the `MessageBox` class, and you will experiment with `MessageBox.Show()` method arguments.

To create MessageBoxes:

1. Open a new file in your text editor. Enter the first few lines of a program that will instantiate several `MessageBox` objects.

```
using System;
using System.Windows.Forms;
public class MessageBoxExperiment
{
```

2. Add a `Main()` method that declares two constant strings to serve as the `MessageBox` messages and captions.

```
public static void Main()
{
    const string MESSAGE = "Hello";
    const string CAPTION = "Message box experiment";
```

3. Create three `MessageBox` objects. The first has a single string argument that is the `MessageBox`'s message. The second `MessageBox` adds a caption, and the third adds two buttons.

```
MessageBox.Show(MESSAGE);
MessageBox.Show(MESSAGE, CAPTION);
MessageBox.Show(MESSAGE, CAPTION,
    MessageBoxButtons.OKCancel);
```

4. Add two closing curly braces—one for the `Main()` method and one for the class.

5. Save the file as **MessageBoxExperiment.cs**. Compile and execute the program. The first `MessageBox` appears on the left in Figure 10-27. Notice that the string "Hello" appears as the message, but no caption appears in the `MessageBox` title bar. A Close button is available in the upper-right corner of the `MessageBox`. Whether you click **OK** or **Close**, the second `MessageBox` appears, including the caption. Notice that this `MessageBox` is slightly wider than the first one to accommodate the title bar caption.

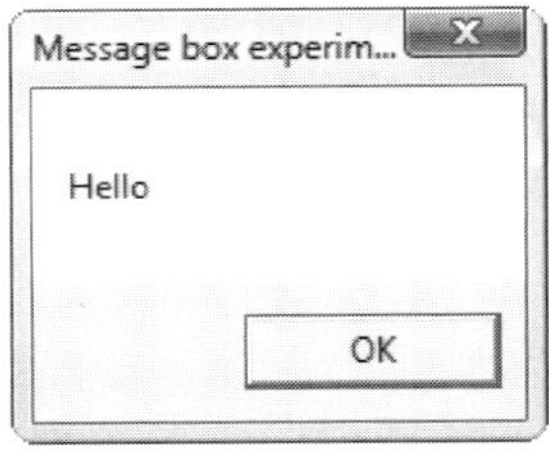

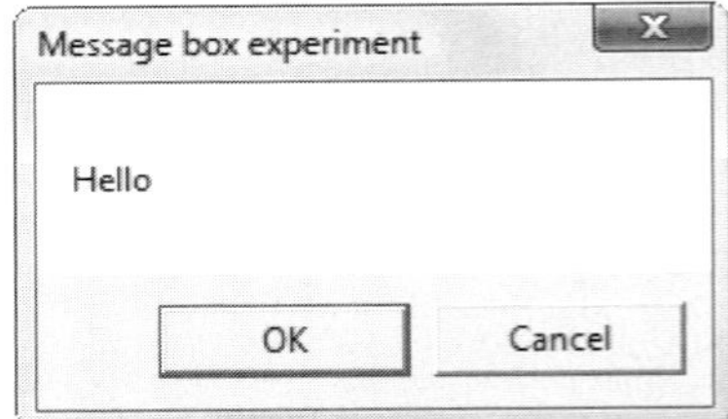

Figure 10-27 The three `MessageBox` objects created by `MessageBoxExperiment`

6. Whether you click **OK** or **Close** in the second MessageBox, the third MessageBox appears; it contains OK and Cancel buttons (see Figure 10-27). The OK button has a darker outline than the Cancel button, which means that the OK button has focus. If you press the Tab key or use the right and left arrow keys on your keyboard, you can change the focus from one button to the other. Whether you dismiss this MessageBox by pressing the Enter key, closing the box, or clicking one of the two buttons, the program ends.

7. Run the program several times and experiment by dismissing the MessageBoxes using the various options (the Enter key, the Buttons, or the Close button.).

8. Resave the program as **MessageBoxExperiment2.cs**, then experiment by using different values for the message, caption, MessageBoxButtons, MessageBoxIcon, MessageBoxDefaultButton, and MessageBoxOptions for the individual MessageBoxes.

WORKING WITH THE VISUAL STUDIO IDE

You can most easily understand the Visual Studio environment by using it. In the next steps, you will use the IDE to create a Form with a Button.

To use the IDE:

1. Open Microsoft Visual C# 2008 Express Edition. You might have a desktop shortcut you can double-click, or you might click **Start** on the taskbar, point to **All Programs**, and then click **Microsoft Visual C# 2008 Express Edition**. If you are using a school network, you might be able to select Visual Studio from the school's computing menu. Figure 10-28 shows the Visual C# Start Page.

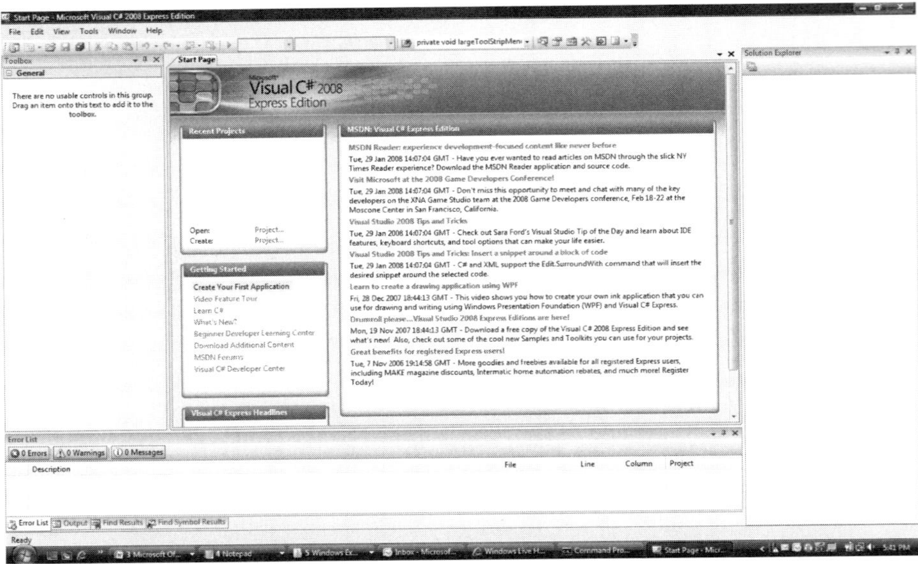

Figure 10-28 Visual C# Start Page

2. Click **File** on the menu bar and click **New Project**, as shown in Figure 10-29.

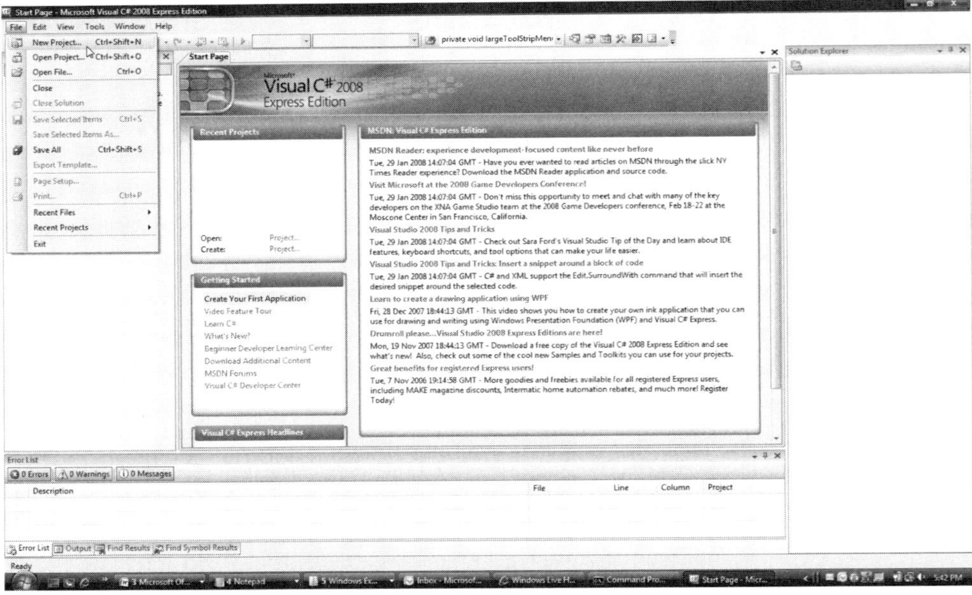

Figure 10-29 Opening a new project

3. A New Project window (see Figure 10-30) appears. Click **Windows Forms Application**. Near the bottom of the New Project window, click in the **Name** text box and replace the default name there (WindowsFormsApplication1) with **WindowCreatedWithIDE** as the name for your application. Figure 10-31 shows the design screen that appears.

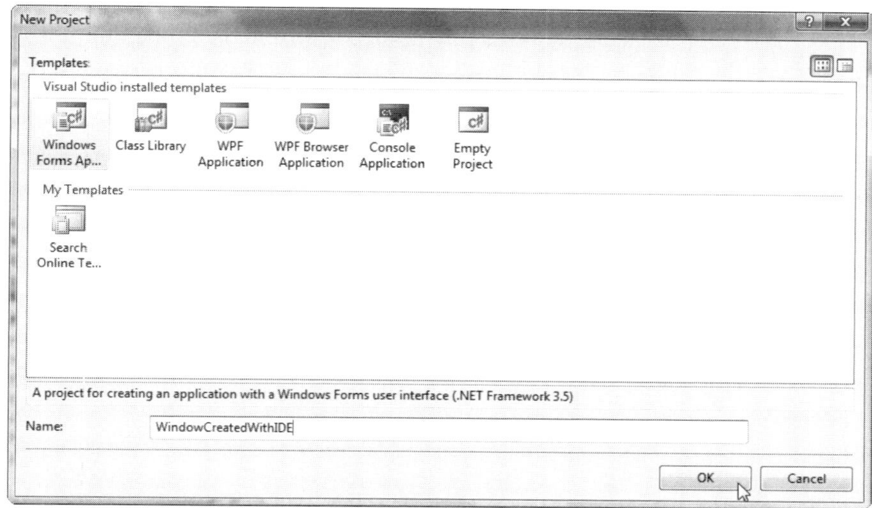

Figure 10-30 The New Project window

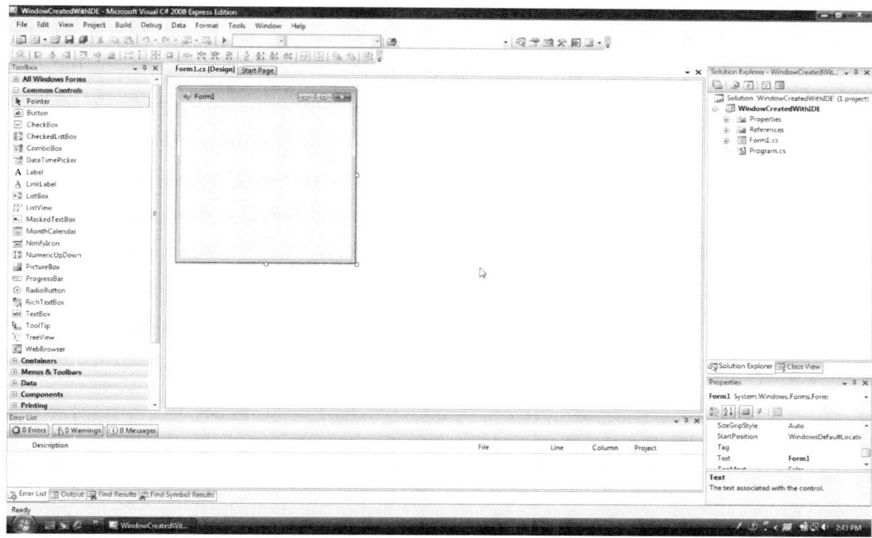

Figure 10-31 The `WindowCreatedWithIDE` project environment

4. The text in the title bar of the blank Form contains the default name Form1. In the Properties window in the lower-right portion of the screen, you can see that the Text property is set to Form1. Take a moment to scroll through the list in the Properties window, examining the values of other properties of the Form. For example, the value of the Size property is 300, 300.

5. In the Properties window, click the description **Form1** in the Settings box for the Text property. Delete Form1 and type **My First Form**. Press **Enter**; the title of the Form in the center of the screen changes to "My First Form". See Figure 10-32.

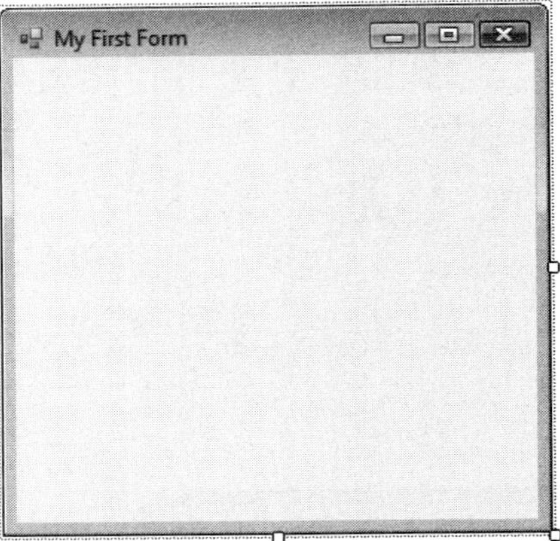

Figure 10-32 My First Form window

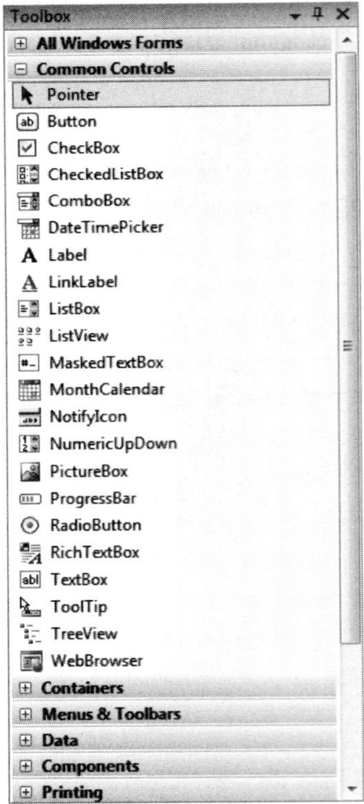

Figure 10-33 The Toolbox

6. Examine the Toolbox on the left side of the screen. Select **Common Controls** if it is not already selected. As shown in Figure 10-33, the Common Controls listed in the Toolbox are components that can be added to a Form, including Pointer, Button, CheckBox, and many others.

7. In the Toolbox, click **Button**. As you move your mouse off the Toolbox and onto the form, the mouse pointer changes so that it appears to carry a Button . Position your mouse anywhere on the form, then click and drag down and to the right. When you release the mouse button, the Button appears on the Form and contains the text "button1" (see Figure 10-34). When you click the Button, it displays handles that you can drag to resize the Button . When you click off the Button on the Form, the handles disappear.

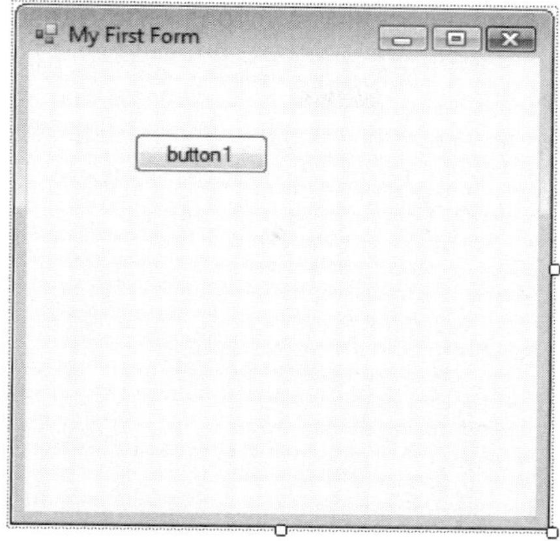

Figure 10-34 A Button on a Form

8. If you click the Form, the list box on the right side of the screen under Properties shows that you are viewing the properties for Form1. If you click the Button, the list displays the properties for button1. Change the Text property of button1 to **Click here**, then press **Enter**. The text of the Button on the Form changes to "Click here". See Figure 10-35.

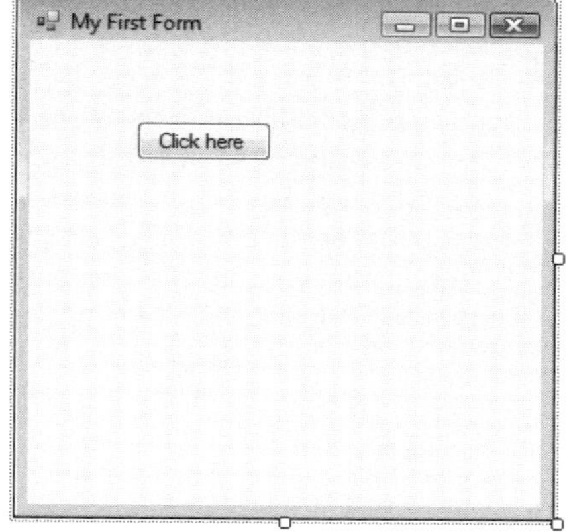

Figure 10-35 A Button with changed Text

9. Scroll through the other button1 properties. The value in the Settings box for the Location property of the Button in Figure 10-35 is 59, 46. Your Location property might be different, depending on where you released the Button when you dragged it onto the Form. Drag the Button across the Form to a new position. Each time you release your mouse button, the value of the Form Button's Location property is updated to reflect the new location. Try to drag the Button to location 80, 64. Alternatively, delete the contents of the Location property field and type **80, 64**. The Button moves to the requested location on the Form.

10. Save your form by clicking **File** on the menu bar, then clicking **Save All**. Alternatively, you can click the **Save All** button on the toolbar; its icon is a stack of diskettes. A Save Project dialog box appears, as in Figure 10-36. Confirm that the program name and disk location are correct. (You can click the **Browse** button to choose another storage location, or you can just type in the location.)

Figure 10-36 The Save Project dialog box

11. Although the Form you have designed doesn't do much yet, you can execute the program anyway. Click **Debug** on the menu bar and then click **Start Without Debugging**, or press **Ctrl+F5**. The Form appears. (See Figure 10-37.) You can drag, minimize, and restore it, and you can click its Button. The Button has not yet been programmed to do anything, but it appears to be pressed when you click it. Click the Form's **Close** button to dismiss the Form.

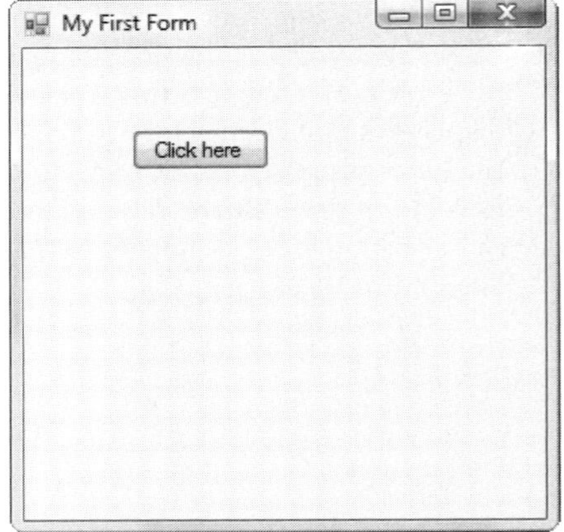

Figure 10-37 My First Form with a "Click here" button

12. Click **View** on the menu bar, click **Code**, and then view some of the code for the Form. In the Solution Explorer window at the right of the screen, click **Form1.Designer.cs** and view that code. (You might have to expand the Form1.cs node to see Form1.Designer.cs.) Finally, click **Program.cs** in the Solution Explorer window and view that part of the code. Based on the descriptions of the code presented in this chapter, how many components of the code do you recognize? For example, you should be able to identify comments, method calls, and the Form1 constructor. Make some modifications to the properties. For example, if you want to change the location of the Button on the Form, return to Designer View

by choosing **View** on the menu bar and then **Designer**. (You can also click the **Form1.cs [Design]** page tab at the top of the code area.) Click on the Button so its Properties window is displayed in the lower-right corner of the screen. Next, change the Location values in the Properties window.

> **» NOTE**   Recall that after any changes, an asterisk appears on the tab for Form1.Designer.cs. The asterisk means that changes have been made but not yet saved. When you save the project, the asterisk disappears.

Also experiment by changing the Font, Forecolor, and Text of the Button. Click on the Form so its properties are displayed, and modify its Text and Size. You can preview any changes by clicking the **Form1.Design** tab, or you can save the program and execute it again; the Button's appearance will be modified.

13. Exit Visual Studio by clicking the **Close** button in the upper-right corner of the screen, or by clicking **File** on the menu bar and then clicking **Exit**. If you have made more changes since the last time you saved, you will be prompted to save again. When you choose **Yes**, the program closes.

PROVIDING FUNCTIONALITY FOR A Button

In the next steps, you will make the Button on the WindowCreatedWithIDE Form functional; it will display a MessageBox when the user clicks it.

To make a Button functional:

1. Start Visual Studio. Click **File** on the menu bar and then click **Open Project**. In the Open Project window, navigate to the folder where you stored the WindowCreatedWithIDE project.

2. Double-click the **WindowCreatedWithIDE** folder. Double-click the **WindowCreatedWithIDE.sln** file. In the Solution Explorer window, double-click the **Form1.cs** entry. The Form you created should appear in Designer View.

3. Double-click the Button on the Form. A new window that contains program code appears, revealing a newly created button1_Click method with no statements:

```
private void button1_Click(object sender, EventArgs e)
{
}
```

4. The method named button1_Click() will contain the code that identifies the actions you want to perform when a user clicks button1. The method receives two arguments— an object named sender and an EventArgs object named e. You will examine these objects more thoroughly in Chapter 11. For now, add some code that will display a MessageBox when the user clicks button1. Place your insertion point between the curly braces of the button1_Click() method, if necessary, and add the following:

```
MessageBox.Show("Thank you");
```

5. Save the file, then run the program by clicking **Debug** on the menu bar and clicking **Start Without Debugging**, or press **Ctrl+F5**. When My First Form appears, click the **Click here** button. The `MessageBox` that contains "Thank you" is displayed, as shown in Figure 10-38.

Figure 10-38 The `MessageBox` displayed after the user clicks the `Button` on My First Form

6. Dismiss the `MessageBox`, then close the `Form`.

7. In the Solution Explorer, click **Form1.Designer.cs** and expand the **Windows Form Designer generated code**. In the twelfth line of the `InitializeComponent()` method, a new statement has been added:

```
this.button1.Click += new System.EventHandler(this.button1_Click);
```

This statement associates the `button1_Click()` method with the `button1.Click` event that is generated when a user clicks the `button1` `Button`. In Chapter 12, you will learn more about events. Fortunately, the IDE allows you to use an event without understanding all the details of how one operates.

8. Select **Save All**, then close the IDE.

ADDING A SECOND Button TO A Form

`Forms` often contain multiple `Button` objects; a `Form` can contain as many `Buttons` as you need. Because each `Button` has a unique identifier, you can provide unique methods that execute when a user clicks each `Button`.

When you first use the IDE, the generated code appears intimidating. However, it is just C# code. You are already familiar with many of the statements you need to create useful and interesting programs. In the next steps, you will create a form that allows a customer to select one of two `Buttons` that identify two types of pizza—Cheese or Sausage. The form will then display one of two pizza prices—$10 or $12, depending on the user's selection.

1. Start Visual Studio. Click **File** on the menu bar, click **New Project**, and then click **Windows Forms Application**. Change the name of the project to **WindowWithTwoButtons**, as shown in Figure 10-39. Click **OK**.

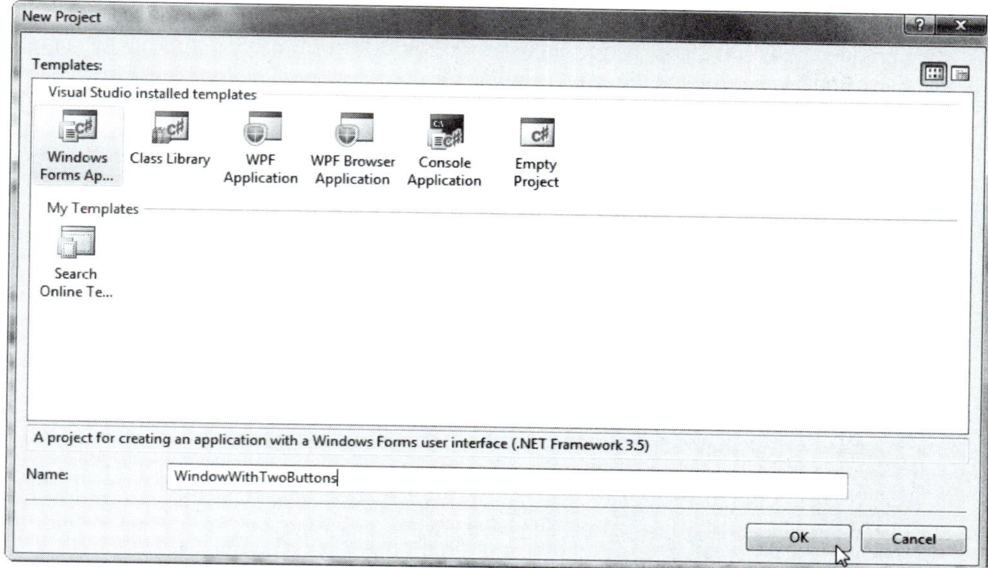

Figure 10-39 Opening a project

2. Click the title bar of the Form Designer that appears. In the `Form`'s Properties window, change the `Text` property of the form from Form1 to **Make a Choice**. When you press **Enter**, "Make a Choice" appears in the `Form`'s title bar. Drag a `Button` onto the `Form`. Release your mouse button to place the `Button` on the `Form`, then drag a second `Button` onto the `Form`. The `Button`s automatically contain text labels `button1` and `button2`, as shown in Figure 10-40.

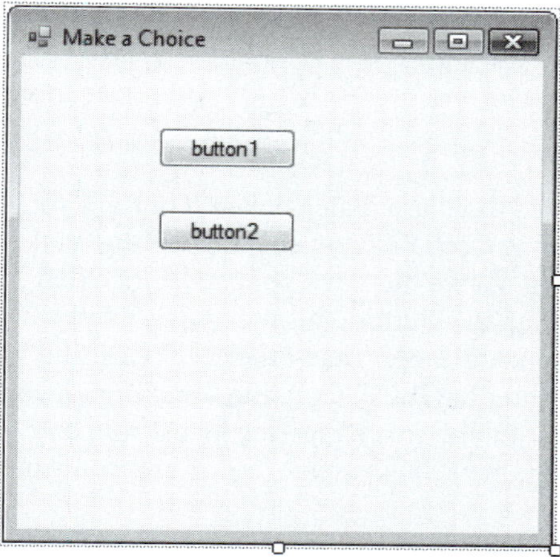

Figure 10-40 Two `Button`s on a `Form`

3. In the Properties window, click the list box and click **button1**. Alternatively, click button1 on the Form. Either way, the Properties window for button1 appears. Change its Text property setting to **Cheese**. In the Properties window, click **button2**. Change its Text property to **Sausage**. See Figure 10-41.

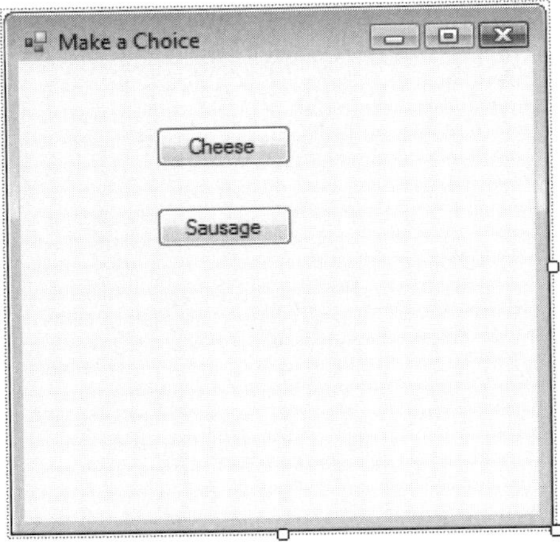

Figure 10-41 Two Buttons on a Form with altered Text properties

4. Double-click the **Cheese** button to view the code for the button1_Click() method. Between the curly braces, type the following:

```
MessageBox.Show("Price is $10");
```

5. Return to Designer View. Double-click the **Sausage** button. Between the curly braces of the method, add the following:

```
MessageBox.Show("Price is $12");
```

6. Save the file. (If this is the first time you have saved the file, a dialog box will prompt you for a storage location.) Run the program by pressing **Ctrl+F5** or by clicking **Debug** on the menu bar and clicking **Start Without Debugging**. When the Form appears, notice that the Cheese button has a darker outline than the Sausage button; this means the Cheese button has focus. When a Button has focus, it appears darker than other Buttons, and you can activate it by clicking it or pressing the Enter key. By default, the first Button you place on a Form has focus. The user can press the Tab key to change the focus from one Button to the next. Experiment with the **Tab** key, then click either Button and confirm that the correct price message is displayed.

7. Dismiss the `MessageBox` and click the other `Button`. Again, the correct price is displayed. Figure 10-42 shows the result when the user clicks **Sausage**.

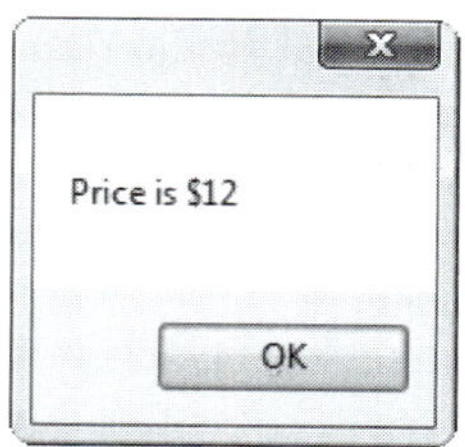

Figure 10-42 A `MessageBox` displayed by the `WindowWithTwoButtons` project

8. Dismiss the `MessageBox` and close the `Form`.

9. If you want, you can experiment with the `Size` and `Location` properties of the `Buttons`. For example, when you dragged them onto the `Form`, you might not have created the `Button` objects to be exactly the same size or distance from the top of the `Form`. Correct this in the Properties window if necessary. Remember to save the project after you make any changes you want to keep.

10. Close Visual Studio.

CHAPTER SUMMARY

» A `MessageBox` is a GUI object that can contain text, buttons, and icons that inform and instruct a user. You use the `static` class method `Show()` to display a `MessageBox`; the method can accept strings as text or as a title for the `MessageBox`, and it can also accept arguments for buttons, icons, and other options.

» Usually you want to determine users' interactions with a `MessageBox`'s buttons and take appropriate action based on the users' choices. `DialogResult` is an enumeration, or list of values, that correspond to a user's potential `MessageBox` button selections.

» `Forms` provide an interface for collecting, displaying, and delivering information; they are key components of GUI programs. `Forms` often contain controls such as text fields, buttons, and check boxes that users can manipulate to interact with a program. You can change the appearance, size, color, and window management features of a `Form` by setting its properties.

» You can create a child class from `Form` that becomes the main window of an application. You must derive a new custom class from the base class `System.Windows.Forms.Form` and write a `Main()` method that calls the `Application.Run()` method, passing an instance of your newly created `Form` class as an argument. This activity starts the program and makes the form visible.

» A window is more flexible than a `MessageBox` because you can place manipulatable `Window` controls wherever you like on the surface of the window. For example, you can create `Button` objects.

» The Visual Studio IDE provides a wealth of tools to help you design `Forms`. It allows you to use a visual environment rather than having to write multiple assignment statements and guess at appropriate component locations.

» Using the Visual Studio IDE, it is easy to create elaborate forms with a few keystrokes. The generated code is simply a collection of C# statements. When you use the Designer in the IDE to design your forms, you save a lot of typing, which reduces the errors you create. The IDE creates a `Form` onto which you can drag controls. The generated code contains familiar components such as comments, object declarations, and methods.

» Adding functionality to a `Button` is particularly easy using the IDE. After you have dragged a `Button` onto a `Form`, you can double-click it to generate a shell method into which you can place statements.

» The ultimate authority on C# classes is the Visual Studio Help documentation. You should use this tool often as you continue to learn about C# in particular and the Visual Studio products in general. The Help documentation for Visual Studio is in the MSDN Library, which you can install locally on your own computer or view online.

KEY TERMS

A **graphical user interface (GUI)** employs graphical images that the user manipulates. GUI objects include the buttons, check boxes, and toolbars you are used to controlling with a mouse when you interact with Windows-type programs.

A **MessageBox** is a GUI object that can contain text, buttons, and icons that inform and instruct a user.

A **modal dialog box** prevents a program from further progress until the user dismisses the box.

When you **dismiss** a component, you get rid of it, frequently by pressing its Close button, but in some cases by making some other selection.

When a button has **focus**, not only is the user's attention drawn to it visually, but if the user presses the Enter key, the action associated with the button executes, just as it would if the user clicked the button.

DialogResult is an enumeration that contains a user's potential `MessageBox` button selections.

An **enumeration** is a list of values in which names are substituted for numeric values.

Forms provide an interface for collecting, displaying, and delivering information; they are key components of GUI programs.

Controls are GUI components such as text fields, buttons, and check boxes that users can manipulate to interact with a program.

A **Button** is a GUI object you can click to cause some action.

The **main menu** of the IDE runs horizontally across the top of the screen; it includes a File menu from which you open, close, and save projects.

The **Toolbox tab** of the IDE contains controls you can drag onto a `Form` so that you can develop programs visually, using a mouse.

The **Form Designer** and **Code Editor** of the IDE appear in the center of the Visual Studio screen. You can switch back and forth between these two when you want to design an application by dragging components onto the screen or you want to write or view code statements.

The **Solution Explorer** of the IDE allows you to view and manage project files and settings.

The **Properties window** of the IDE allows you to configure properties and events on controls in your user interface.

The **output tab** and **error list tab** of the IDE display any compiler errors.

In Visual Studio, a **node** is a box that appears on a vertical tree to the left of a list or a section of code and that can be expanded or condensed.

Preprocessor directives always start with a pound sign (#) and are instructions to the preprocessor to modify the code in some way.

The **preprocessor** is a program that executes before the compiler and looks for preprocessor directives for instructions on how to modify code.

When a user interacts with a GUI object, an **event** is generated that causes the program to perform a task.

When a user clicks a button, the action fires a **click event**.

REVIEW QUESTIONS

1. Which is true of the `MessageBox` class?

   a. You cannot create a new instance of this class.

   b. Its constructor is `public`.

   c. Its methods cannot be overloaded.

   d. Its `Show()` method is not overloaded.

2. A programmer who uses a `MessageBox` must __________ .

   a. determine the message that will appear on the OK button

   b. write the message that will appear in the `MessageBox`

   c. write an overloaded version of the `Show()` method

   d. select an icon to be displayed within the `MessageBox`

3. A programmer can select all of the following for a `MessageBox` except __________ .

   a. a message within it   c. its default button

   b. a caption in its title bar   d. its modality

4. A `MessageBox` is modal, meaning __________ .

   a. it can appear in several different styles

   b. the program will not progress until a user dismisses the `MessageBox`

   c. it is always rectangular with a title bar

   d. it appears in the Windows style so that all components have the same look and feel

5. An enumeration is a __________ in a program.

    a. list of values you can use

    b. sum or total of values used

    c. count of the number of values used

    d. list of values that cannot be used

6. Which of the following is not a possible `DialogResult`?

    a. Cancel

    b. OK

    c. End

    d. Retry

7. The `Form` class descends from the __________ class.

    a. `Object`

    b. `Component`

    c. `Control`

    d. all of these

8. The `Form` class differs from the `MessageBox` class in that __________ .

    a. you can create an instance of the `Form` class, but not the `MessageBox` class

    b. you can create an instance of the `MessageBox` class, but not the `Form` class

    c. `Form`s can contain `Button`s, but `MessageBox`es cannot

    d. `MessageBox`es can contain `Button`s, but `Form`s cannot

9. The `Form` class contains __________ properties.

    a. 2

    b. 5

    c. about 100

    d. more than 4000

10. Which of the following is not a `Form` property?

    a. `BackColor`

    b. `DesktopLocation`

    c. `Invisible`

    d. `Size`

11. When you create a new main window, you must __________ .

    a. derive a new custom class from the base class `System.Windows.Forms.Form`

    b. write a `Main()` method that calls the `Application.Run()` method

    c. either a or b, but not both

    d. both a and b

12. When used with a component, the `System.Drawing.Size` constructor takes two parameters representing __________ .

    a. width and height

    b. line thickness and horizontal position

    c. height and degrees of rotation

    d. horizontal position and width

13. A `Form`'s `Controls` are its __________ .

    a. `static` methods

    b. nonstatic methods

    c. manipulatable components

    d. parents

14. For a `Button` to appear to be pressed when a user clicks it, you __________ .

    a. need only to add the `Button` to a `Form`

    b. use the `System.Windows.Forms.Control` class

    c. include a `GUIImplement()` method within your program

    d. write a method named `ClickButton()`

15. The main reason to use the Visual Studio integrated development environment is to __________ .

    a. use methods that are not available when you write code by hand

    b. have access to the Studio's private data types

    c. make programs easier to design

    d. all of these

16. When you begin to create a `Form` using the Visual Studio IDE, the default `Form` name is __________ .

    a. `MyForm`

    b. `IDEForm`

    c. `Form1`

    d. `null`

17. When you design a `Form` using the IDE, __________ .

    a. much less code is generated than when you design a `Form` by hand

    b. the generated code is written in machine language so you cannot read it

    c. you cannot alter the generated code

    d. none of these

18. If you do not like the default name the IDE gives to a `Button`, you should __________ .

    a. change the `Name` property in the code

    b. change the `Name` property in the Properties window in the IDE

    c. either of these

    d. none of these

19. A partial class __________ .

    a. exists as an outline into which you must add statements

    b. is still being written

    c. has been saved, but not yet compiled

    d. is spread among multiple files

20. If a `Form` contains a `Button` named `agreeButton`, then you should code the actions to be performed when the user clicks the `Button` in a method named __________ .

    a. `ButtonClick()`   c. `agreeButtonClick()`

    b. `Button_Click()`   d. `agreeButton_Click()`

EXERCISES

1. Write a program that displays a `MessageBox` that contains contact information for your company. Save the program as **Contact.cs**.

2. Write a program for an Internet provider that displays a `MessageBox` asking users whether they want Internet access. If they do not, their total price is $0. If they do, display a second `MessageBox` asking whether they want limited access (at $10.95 per month) or unlimited access (at $19.95 per month). Display the total price in a third `MessageBox`. Save the program as **InternetAccess.cs**.

3. Write a program for an Internet provider that displays a `MessageBox` asking users whether they want to read the company's usage policy. Include a question icon. If the user chooses Yes, display a `MessageBox` that contains a short usage policy. If the user chooses No, display a `MessageBox` reminding the user to read the policy later. If the user chooses Cancel, end the program. Save the program as **Policy.cs**.

4. Write a program that simulates an Internet connection error. Display a `MessageBox` that notifies the user of the error and provide three buttons: Abort, Retry, and Ignore. If the user chooses Retry, display a message indicating that the connection succeeded. If the user chooses Ignore, display a message indicating that the user will work off-line. If the user chooses Abort, end the program. Save the program as **Connection.cs**.

5. Using the Visual Studio IDE, create a `Form` that contains a button labeled "About". When a user clicks the button, display a `MessageBox` that contains your personal copyright statement for the program. Save the project as **About**.

6. Create a `Form` that contains two buttons for a book publisher. If a user clicks the Paperback button, display a `MessageBox` that contains a book price of $6.99. If the user clicks the Hardback button, display $24.99. Save the project as **Book**.

7. Create a game `Form` that contains six buttons. Display different prizes depending on the button the user selects. Save the project as **Game**.

DEBUGGING EXERCISES

Each of the following files or projects in the Chapter.10 folder on your Student Disk has syntax and/or logical errors. In each case, determine the problem and fix the program. After you correct the errors, save each file or project using the same filename preceded with *Fixed*. For example, the file DebugTen1.cs will become FixedDebugTen1.cs and the project folder for DebugTen3 will become FixedDebugTen3.

   a. DebugTen1.cs

   b. DebugTen2.cs

   c. DebugTen3

   d. DebugTen4

»NOTE
Immediately save the two project folders with their new names before you correct their errors.

UP FOR DISCUSSION

1. Think of some practice or position to which you are opposed. For example, you might have objections to organizations on the far right or left politically. Now suppose that such an organization offered you twice your annual salary to create Web sites for them. Would you do it? Is there a price at which you would do it? What if the organization was not so extreme, but featured products you found distasteful? What if the Web site you designed was not objectionable, but the parent company's policies were objection-able? For example, if you are opposed to smoking, would you design a Web site for a tobacco company? At what price? What if the site just displayed sports scores without promoting smoking directly?

2. Suppose you have learned a lot about programming from your employer. Is it ethical for you to use this knowledge to start your own home-based programming business on the side? Does it matter whether you are in competition for the same clients as your employer? Does it matter whether you use just your programming expertise or whether you also use information about clients' preferences and needs gathered from your regular job?

11

USING CONTROLS

In this chapter you will:

Learn about `Controls`
Create a `Form` that contains `Labels`
Set a `Label`'s `Font`
Create a `Form` that contains `LinkLabels`
Add color to a `Form`
Add `CheckBox` and `RadioButton` objects to a `Form`
Add a `PictureBox` to a `Form`
Add `ListBox`, `ComboBox`, and `CheckedListBox` items
  to a `Form`
Add a `MonthCalendar` and `DateTimePicker`
  to a `Form`
Work with a `Form`'s layout
Add a `MenuStrip` to a `Form`
Learn to use other controls

In Chapter 10, you learned to create `Forms` by hand using an ordinary text editor and by using the Visual Studio IDE. Both approaches yield the same results, but the IDE provides you with an easy-to-use design environment. Additionally, by examining the IDE-generated program code, you can learn more about code you want to write by hand.

The `Form` and `Button` objects you created in Chapter 10 represent only a tiny fraction of the types of objects that are available to you in C#. When using programs or visiting Internet sites, you have encountered and used many other interactive **widgets**—elements of graphical interfaces that allow you to interact with programs—such as labels, scroll bars, check boxes, and radio buttons. C# has many classes that represent these GUI objects, and the Visual Studio IDE makes it easy to add them to your programs. In this chapter, you will learn to incorporate some of the most common and useful widgets into your programs. Additionally, you will see how these components work in general so you can use other widgets that are not covered in this book or that become available to programmers in future releases of C#.

> **»»NOTE** GUI components are referred to as *widgets*, which some sources claim is a combination of the terms *window* and *gadgets*. Originally, "widget" comes from the 1924 play "Beggar on Horseback," by George Kaufman and Marc Connelly. In the play, a young composer gets engaged to the daughter of a rich businessman, and foresees spending his life doing pointless work in a bureaucratic big business that manufactures widgets, which represent a useless item whose purpose is never explained.

UNDERSTANDING ControlS

When you design a `Form`, you can place `Button`s and other controls on the `Form` surface. The **Control** class provides the definitions for these GUI objects. `Control` objects such as `Form`s and `Button`s, like all other objects in C#, ultimately derive from the `Object` class. Figure 11-1 shows where the `Control` class fits into the inheritance hierarchy.

```
System.Object
    System.MarshalByRefObject
        System.ComponentModel.Component
            System.Windows.Forms.Control
                26 Derived classes
```

Figure 11-1 `Control` class inheritance hierarchy

Figure 11-1 shows that all `Control`s are `Object`s, of course. They are also all `MarshalByRefObject`s. (A `MarshalByRefObject` is one you can instantiate on a remote computer so that you can manipulate a reference to the object rather than a local copy of the object.) `Control`s also descend from `Component`. (The **Component** class provides containment and cleanup for other objects—inheriting from `Component` allows `Control`s to be contained in objects such as `Form`s, and provides for disposal of `Control`s when they are destroyed. The `Control` class adds visual representation to `Component`s.) The `Control` class implements very basic functionality required by classes that appear to the user—in other words, the GUI objects the user sees on the screen. This class handles user input through the keyboard and pointing devices as well as message routing and security. It defines the bounds of a `Control` by determining its position and size.

Table 11-1 shows the 26 direct descendants of `Control` and some commonly used descendants of those classes. It does not show all the descendants that exist; rather, it shows only the descendants covered in this chapter. For example, the `ButtonBase` class is the parent of `Button`, a class you used in Chapter 10. In this chapter, you will use two other `ButtonBase` children—`CheckBox` and `RadioButton`. This chapter cannot cover every `Control` that has been invented; however, after you learn to use some `Control`s, you will find that others work in much the same way. You also can read more about them in the Visual Studio Help documentation.

Class	Commonly Used Descendants
`Microsoft.WindowsCE.Forms.DocumentList`	
`System.Windows.Forms.AxHost`	
`System.Windows.Forms.ButtonBase`	`Button, CheckBox, RadioButton`
`System.Windows.Forms.DataGrid`	
`System.Windows.Forms.DataGridView`	
`System.Windows.Forms.DateTimePicker`	
`System.Windows.Forms.GroupBox`	
`System.Windows.Forms.Integration.ElementHost`	
`System.Windows.Forms.Label`	`LinkLabel`
`System.Windows.Forms.ListControl`	`ListBox, ComboBox, CheckedListBox`
`System.Windows.Forms.ListView`	
`System.Windows.Forms.MdiClient`	
`System.Windows.Forms.MonthCalendar`	
`System.Windows.Forms.PictureBox`	
`System.Windows.Forms.PrintPreviewControl`	
`System.Windows.Forms.ProgressBar`	
`System.Windows.Forms.ScrollableControl`	
`System.Windows.Forms.ScrollBar`	
`System.Windows.Forms.Splitter`	
`System.Windows.Forms.StatusBar`	
`System.Windows.Forms.TabControl`	
`System.Windows.Forms.TextBoxBase`	
`System.Windows.Forms.ToolBar`	
`System.Windows.Forms.TrackBar`	
`System.Windows.Forms.TreeView`	
`System.Windows.Forms.WebBrowserBase`	

Table 11-1 Classes derived from `System.Windows.Forms.Control`

Because Controls are all relatives, they share many of the same attributes. Each Control has more than 80 public properties and 20 protected ones. For example, each Control has a Font and a ForeColor that dictate how its text is displayed, and each Control has a Width and Height. Table 11-2 shows just some of the public properties associated with Controls in general; reading through them will give you an idea of the Control attributes that you can change.

Property	Description
AllowDrop	Gets or sets a value indicating whether the control can accept data that the user drags onto it
Anchor	Gets or sets the edges of the container to which a control is bound and determines how a control is resized with its parent
BackColor	Gets or sets the background color for the control
BackgroundImage	Gets or sets the background image displayed in the control
Bottom	Gets the distance, in pixels, between the bottom edge of the control and the top edge of its container's client area
Bounds	Gets or sets the size and location of the control, including its nonclient elements, in pixels, relative to the parent control
CanFocus	Gets a value indicating whether the control can receive focus
CanSelect	Gets a value indicating whether the control can be selected
Capture	Gets or sets a value indicating whether the control has captured the mouse
Container	Gets the IContainer that contains the Component (inherited from Component)
ContainsFocus	Gets a value indicating whether the control or one of its child controls currently has the input focus
Cursor	Gets or sets the cursor that is displayed when the mouse pointer is over the control
Disposing	Gets a value indicating whether the base Control class is in the process of disposing
Dock	Gets or sets which control borders are docked to its parent control and determines how a control is resized with its parent
Enabled	Gets or sets a value indicating whether the control can respond to user interaction
Focused	Gets a value indicating whether the control has input focus
Font	Gets or sets the font of the text displayed by the control
ForeColor	Gets or sets the foreground color of the control
HasChildren	Gets a value indicating whether the control contains one or more child controls
Height	Gets or sets the height of the control

Table 11-2 Selected public Control properties (*continued*)

Property	Description
IsDisposed	Gets a value indicating whether the control has been disposed of
Left	Gets or sets the distance, in pixels, between the left edge of the control and the left edge of its container's client area
Location	Gets or sets the coordinates of the upper-left corner of the control relative to the upper-left corner of its container
Margin	Gets or sets the space between controls
ModifierKeys	Gets a value indicating which of the modifier keys (Shift, Ctrl, and Alt) is in a pressed state
MouseButtons	Gets a value indicating which of the mouse buttons is in a pressed state
MousePosition	Gets the position of the mouse cursor in screen coordinates
Name	Gets or sets the name of the control
Parent	Gets or sets the parent container of the control
Right	Gets the distance, in pixels, between the right edge of the control and the left edge of its container's client area
Size	Gets or sets the height and width of the control
TabIndex	Gets or sets the tab order of the control within its container
TabStop	Gets or sets a value indicating whether the user can give focus to the control using the Tab key
Text	Gets or sets the text associated with this control
Top	Gets or sets the distance, in pixels, between the top edge of the control and the top edge of its container's client area
TopLevelControl	Gets the parent control that is not parented by another Windows Forms control; typically, this is the outermost Form in which the control is contained
Visible	Gets or sets a value indicating whether the control and all its parent controls are displayed
Width	Gets or sets the width of the control

Table 11-2 (*continued*)

» NOTE   The description of each property in Table 11-2 indicates whether the property is read-only; such properties only get values and do not set them.

» NOTE   In Chapter 10, you learned about the Button Control and how to declare a Button. You learned that you could change Button properties such as its Text either by typing statements or using the Properties window in Visual Studio. All the other Controls you learn about in this chapter can be manipulated in the same ways.

»TWO TRUTHS AND A LIE: UNDERSTANDING Controls

1. The `Control` class implements basic functionality required by GUI objects that a user sees on the screen.
2. Most `Controls` have `Font` and `ForeColor` properties.
3. Every `Control` has `Width` and `Height` properties.

The false statement is #2. Every `Control` has `Font` and `ForeColor` properties.

CREATING A `Form` WITH `Label`S

A **Label** is one of the simplest GUI `Control` objects you can place on a `Form`. The `Label` class descends directly from `Control`. Typically, you use a `Label` to provide descriptive text for another `Control` object (for example, to tell the user what pressing a `Button` will accomplish). You can also use a `Label` to display other text information on a `Form`.

Creating a `Label` is very similar to creating a `Button`. You can manually create a `Label` by using the class name and an identifier and then calling the class constructor. For example:

```
private Label label1;
label1 = new Label();
```

Alternatively, you could use the fully qualified class name and the `this` reference with the `label1` object, as in the following:

```
private System.Windows.Forms.Label label1;
this.label1 = new System.Windows.Forms.Label();
```

As when you created `Button` objects in Chapter 10, it is almost always more convenient to use the Visual Studio IDE to design `Form`s than it is to write the code statements. Figure 11-2

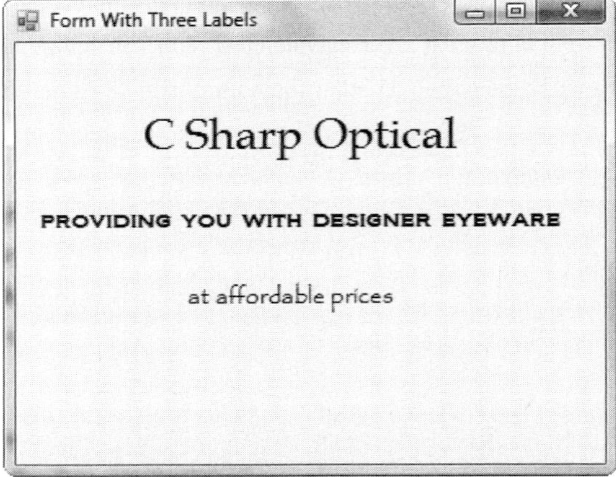

Figure 11-2 `Form` generated by `FormWithThreeLabels` program

shows a `Form` created in the IDE. Three `Label`s have been dragged onto a `Form`. The `Text` property of the `Form` has been set to "Form With Three Labels", and the `Text` property of each `Label` has been set. Additionally, a different `Font` has been selected for each `Label`.

Within the Form1.Designer.cs file in Visual Studio, three lines of code are generated as follows:

```
private System.Windows.Forms.Label label1;
private System.Windows.Forms.Label label2;
private System.Windows.Forms.Label label3;
```

These lines declare the three `Label`s just as you could have by typing the statements yourself.

To create this `Form`, the programmer only had to drag three objects and type four `string`s—one for the `Form` caption and three for the contents of the `Label`s. Then the programmer selected a font for each `Label` from a drop-down list in the Properties window. These actions generate all the code in Figure 11-3. (You must expand the code to see it. To do so, you can click the + in the **method node** to the left of the gray box that contains Windows Form Designer generated code, or you can double-click the gray box.) More than 30 statements are generated. By using the Visual Studio Designer, you save lots of time and eliminate many chances for error.

When you hover your mouse over the gray box, you can preview the collapsed code.

```
private void InitializeComponent()
{
    this.label1 = new System.Windows.Forms.Label();
    this.label2 = new System.Windows.Forms.Label();
    this.label3 = new System.Windows.Forms.Label();
    this.SuspendLayout();
    //
    // label1
    //
    this.label1.AutoSize = true;
    this.label1.Font = new System.Drawing.Font
        ("Book Antiqua", 20.25F,
        System.Drawing.FontStyle.Regular,
        System.Drawing.GraphicsUnit.Point, ((byte)(0)));
    this.label1.Location = new
        System.Drawing.Point(72, 42);
    this.label1.Name = "label1";
    this.label1.Size = new System.Drawing.Size(207, 32);
    this.label1.TabIndex = 0;
    this.label1.Text = "C Sharp Optical";
    //
    // label2
    //
```

Figure 11-3 `InitializeComponent()` method for `FormWithThreeLabels` (*continued*)

```csharp
            this.label2.AutoSize = true;
            this.label2.Font = new System.Drawing.Font
                ("Biondi", 11.25F,
                System.Drawing.FontStyle.Regular,
                System.Drawing.GraphicsUnit.Point, ((byte)(0)));
            this.label2.Location = new
                System.Drawing.Point(12, 101);
            this.label2.Name = "label2";
            this.label2.Size = new System.Drawing.Size(326, 18);
            this.label2.TabIndex = 1;
            this.label2.Text =
                "providing you with designer eyeware";
            //
            // label3
            //
            this.label3.AutoSize = true;
            this.label3.Font = new System.Drawing.Font
                ("Papyrus", 11.25F,
                System.Drawing.FontStyle.Regular,
                System.Drawing.GraphicsUnit.Point, ((byte)(0)));
            this.label3.Location = new
                System.Drawing.Point(101, 148);
            this.label3.Name = "label3";
            this.label3.Size = new System.Drawing.Size(136, 24);
            this.label3.TabIndex = 2;
            this.label3.Text = "at affordable prices";
            //
            // Form1
            //
            this.AutoScaleDimensions = new
                System.Drawing.SizeF(6F, 13F);
            this.AutoScaleMode =
                System.Windows.Forms.AutoScaleMode.Font;
            this.ClientSize = new
                System.Drawing.Size(360, 264);
            this.Controls.Add(this.label3);
            this.Controls.Add(this.label2);
            this.Controls.Add(this.label1);
            this.Name = "Form1";
            this.Text = "Form With Three Labels";
            this.ResumeLayout(false);
            this.PerformLayout();

        }
```


Figure 11-3 (*continued*)

Do not be intimidated by the amount of code generated in Figure 11-3. You can easily understand most of it.

» After the `InitializeComponent()` method header and opening brace, the next three statements call the `Label` constructor for each `Label`.

» `SuspendLayout()` is a method that prevents conflicts when you are placing `Controls` on a form. Its counterparts are `ResumeLayout()` and `PerformLayout()`, which appear at the bottom of the method. If you remove these method calls from small applications, you won't notice the difference. However, in large applications, suspending the layout logic while you adjust the appearance of components improves performance.

» Comments serve to separate the `label1` code from other code in the method. Following the `label1` comment lines, seven statements set properties of the `Label`. For example, you can see that the `Font`, `Location`, `Size`, and `Text` have been assigned values based on the programmer's choices in the IDE.

» The property statements for `label2` and `label3` are similar to those for `label1`. The `TabIndex` for `label1` is 0 by default, the `TabIndex` for `label2` is 1, and so on. The `TabIndex` values determine the order in which `Controls` receive focus when the user presses the Tab key. This property is typically more useful for selectable items like `Buttons`.

» The `InitializeComponent()` method ends with statements that set the properties of the `Form`, such as its drawing size and text. You can also see the statements that add the three `Labels` to the `Form` using the `Add()` method.

If you wanted to add a fourth label to the form while designing it, you *could* code a statement to declare it, code another statement to call its constructor, write all the statements to set all the properties, and insert a new `Add()` method call into the code for the `Form`. However, you should not design programs in this way. Instead, you should return to the Design view of the `Form` in the IDE, drag a new `Label` onto the form, and make changes in the Properties window. It is far easier this way, and you are less likely to generate errors.

»TWO TRUTHS AND A LIE: CREATING A Form WITH LabelS

1. By using the Visual Studio Designer, you save lots of time and eliminate many chances for error.
2. When you use the Visual Studio IDE to drag a `Label` onto a `Form`, no constructor call is needed for the `Label`.
3. You can use the Visual Studio IDE to set properties for a `Label` such as `Font`, `Location`, `Size`, and `Text`.

The false statement is #2. When you use the Visual Studio IDE to drag a Label onto a Form, you do not have to write a constructor call, but one is generated for you.

SETTING A Label'S Font

You use the **Font** class to change the appearance of printed text on your `Forms`. When designing a `Label` or other `Control` on a `Form`, it is easiest to select a `Font` from the Properties list. After you place a `Control` on a `Form` in the IDE, you can select the ellipsis (three dots) that follows the current `Font` property name in the Properties list. (See Figure 11-4.) This selection displays a `Font` window in which you can choose a `Font` name, size, style, and other effects. (See Figure 11-5.)

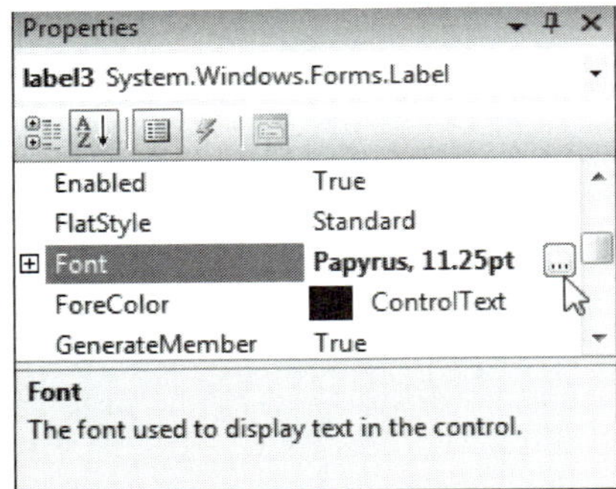

Figure 11-4 Clicking the ellipsis following the `Font` property

However, if you wanted to change a `Font` later in a program—for example, after a user clicks a button—you might want to create your own instance of the `Font` class. As another example, suppose you want to create multiple controls that use the same `Font`. In that case, it makes sense to declare a named instance of the `Font` class. For example, you can declare the following `Font`:

```
System.Drawing.Font myFont = new
    System.Drawing.Font("Courier New", 16f);
```

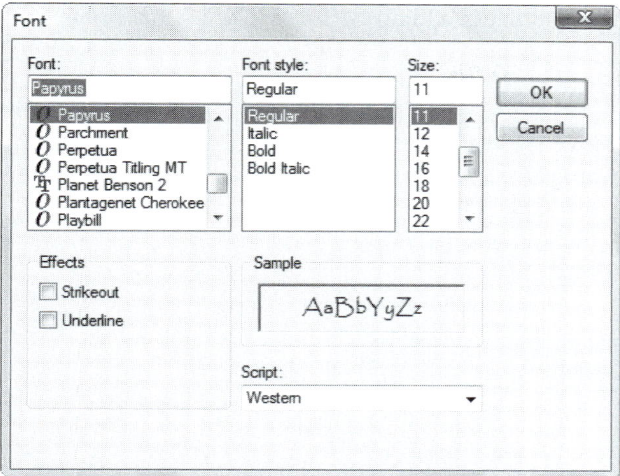

Figure 11-5 The `Font` window

Then, in the three statements that set the `Font` in the `InitializeComponent()` method in Figure 11-3, you can code the following:

```
this.label1.Font = myFont;
this.label2.Font = myFont;
this.label3.Font = myFont;
```

All three labels will display the same font: size 16 Courier New. If you want to change the font size or style later, you change it only in the one location where it is defined.

The `Font` class includes a number of overloaded constructors. For example, you can create a `Font` using two arguments (a type and a size) as follows:

```
System.Drawing.Font myFavoriteFont = new
    System.Drawing.Font("Courier New", 12.5F);
```

The string you pass to the `Font` constructor is the name of the font. If you use a font name that does not exist in your system, the `Font` defaults to Microsoft Sans Serif. The second value is a `float` that represents the font size. Notice that you must use an *F* (or an *f*) following the `Font` size value constant when it contains a decimal point to ensure that the constant will be recognized as a `float` and not a `double`. The `Font` constructor parameter list contains a `float` for size; using a `double` will generate a compiler error indicating that the `double` cannot be converted to a `float`. (If you use an `int` as the font size, you do not need the *f*, because the `int` will automatically be cast to a `float`, but a numeric constant such as 12.5 is a `double` by default.) An alternative would be to instantiate a `float` constant or variable, as in the following example, and use its name in the argument to the `Font` constructor:

```
const float PREFERRED_SIZE = 12.5f;
```

»» NOTE
If you want to change the properties of several objects at once in the IDE, you can drag your mouse around them to create a temporary group, and then change the property for all of them with one entry in the Properties list.

»» NOTE
In Chapter 2, you learned to use an `f` following a floating-point constant to indicate the `float` type.

You also can create a `Font` using three arguments, adding a `FontStyle`, as in the following example:

```
Font aFancyFont = new Font("Arial", 24, FontStyle.Italic);
```

Table 11-3 lists the available `FontStyle`s. You can combine multiple styles using the pipe (|), which is also called the logical OR. For example, the following code creates a `Font` that is bold and underlined:

```
Font boldAndUnderlined = new Font("Helvetica",
    10, FontStyle.Bold | FontStyle.Underline);
```

Member Name	Description
Bold	Bold text
Italic	Italic text
Regular	Normal text
Strikeout	Text with a line through the middle
Underline	Underlined text

Table 11-3 `FontStyle` enumeration

Once you have defined a `Font`, you can set a `Label`'s `Font` with a statement like the following:

```
this.label1.Font = myFavoriteFont;
```

Alternatively, you can create and assign an anonymous `Font` in one step. In other words, you do not provide an identifier for the `Font`, as in this example:

```
this.label1.Font = new
    System.DrawingFont("Courier New", 12.5F);
```

>> **NOTE** If you don't provide an identifier for a `Font`, you can't reuse it. You will have to create it again to use it with additional `Control`s.

>>TWO TRUTHS AND A LIE: SETTING A `Label`'S `Font`

1. You use the `Font` class to change the appearance of printed text on `Control`s in your `Form`s.
2. When designing a `Label` or other `Control` on a `Form`, you must select a `Font` from the Properties list in the IDE.
3. The `Font` class includes several overloaded constructors.

The false statement is #2. When designing a `Label` or other `Control` on a `Form`, it is easiest to select a `Font` from the Properties list, but you also can create your own instance of the `Font` class.

USING A LinkLabel

A **LinkLabel** is similar to a Label; it is a child of Label. Therefore, you can use it like a Label, but it provides the additional capability to link the user to other sources, such as Web pages or files. Table 11-4 summarizes the properties and lists the default event method for a LinkLabel. The **default event** for a Control is:

» The method whose shell is automatically created when you double-click the Control while designing a project in the IDE

» The method that you are most likely to alter when you use the Control

» The event that users most likely expect to generate when they encounter the Control in a working application

With many Controls, including a LinkLabel, a mouse click by the user triggers the default event. When designing a program, you can double-click a Control in the IDE to generate a method shell, and then write any necessary statements within the shell.

Property or Method	Description
ActiveLinkColor	The color of the link when it is clicked
LinkColor	The original color of links before they have been visited; usually blue by default
LinkVisited	If true, the link's color is changed to the VisitedLinkColor
VisitedLinkColor	The color of a link after it has been visited; usually purple by default
LinkClicked()	Default event that is generated when the link is clicked by the user

Table 11-4 Commonly used LinkLabel properties and default event

» NOTE The default event for many Controls, such as Buttons and LinkLabels, occurs when the user clicks the Control. However, the default event for a Form is the Load() method. In other words, if you double-click a Form in the IDE, you generate this method. In it, you can place statements that execute as soon as a Form is loaded.

When you create a LinkLabel, it appears as underlined text. The text is blue by default, but you can change the color in the LinkLabel Properties list in the IDE. When you pass the mouse pointer over a LinkLabel, the pointer changes to a hand; you have seen similar behavior while using hyperlinks in Web pages. When a user clicks a LinkLabel, it generates a click event, just as clicking a Button does. When a click event is fired from a LinkLabel, a LinkClicked() method is executed, similar to how clicking a Button can execute a Clicked() method.

» NOTE You can create a program so that a user generates an event by clicking many types of objects. For example, for a Label named label1, you could write statements in a label1_Click() method. However, users do not usually expect to click Labels, but they do expect to click LinkLabels.

Figure 11-6 shows a `Form` onto which two `LinkLabel`s have been dragged from the Toolbox in the IDE. The `Text` properties of the `LinkLabel`s have been changed to "Course Technology Website" and "Read Our Policy".

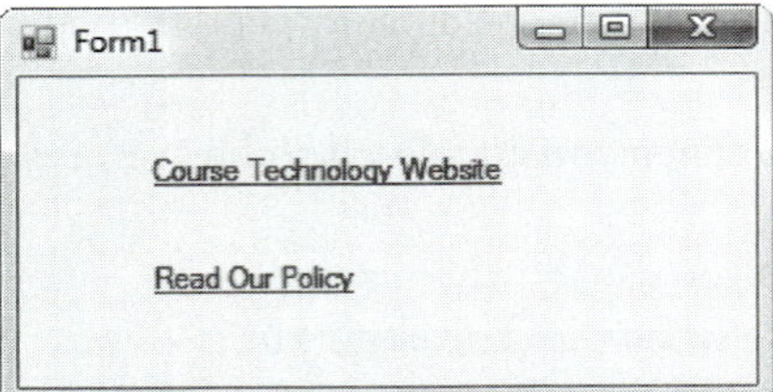

Figure 11-6 A `Form` with two `LinkLabel`s

If you double-click a `LinkLabel` in the IDE, a method shell is created for you in the format `xxx_LinkClicked()`, where `xxx` is the value of the `Name` property assigned to the `LinkLabel`. (This corresponds to what happens when you double-click a `Button` in the IDE.) For example, Figure 11-7 shows the two generated methods for the `Form` in Figure 11-6 when the default `LinkLabel` identifiers `linkLabel1` and `linkLabel2` are used. In Figure 11-7, all the code was automatically generated except for the two shaded lines. The programmer added those lines to indicate which actions should occur when a user clicks the corresponding `LinkLabel` in a running application.

```
public partial class Form1 : Form
{
    public Form1()
    {
        InitializeComponent();
    }

    private void linkLabel1_LinkClicked(object sender,
        LinkLabelLinkClickedEventArgs e)
    {
        System.Diagnostics.Process.Start("IExplore",
            "http://www.course.com");
    }

    private void linkLabel2_LinkClicked(object sender,
        LinkLabelLinkClickedEventArgs e)
    {
        System.Diagnostics.Process.Start
            (@"C:\C#\Chapter.11\Policy.txt");
    }
}
```

Figure 11-7 Two `LinkClicked()` methods

In each of the `LinkClicked()` methods in Figure 11-7, the programmer has added a call to `System.Diagnostics.Process.Start()`. This method allows you to run other programs from within an application. The `Start()` method has two overloaded versions:

» When you use one `string` argument, you open the named file.
» When you use two arguments, you open an application and provide its needed arguments.

In the `linkLabel1_LinkClicked()` method, the two arguments open Internet Explorer ("`IExplore`") and pass it the address of the Course Technology Web site. If an Internet connection is active, control transfers to the Web site.

In the `linkLabel2_LinkClicked()` method, only one argument is provided. It opens a file stored on the local disk. Figure 11-8 shows the text file that opens when the user clicks the link. By default, Notepad opens to display the policy because Notepad is the default application for a file with a .txt extension. Alternatively, you could code the following, which explicitly names Notepad as the application:

```
System.Diagnostics.Process.Start("Notepad",
    @"C:\C#\Chapter.11\Policy.txt");
```

Figure 11-8 Text file opened by `linkLabel2_LinkClicked()` method

»NOTE In the `linkLabel2_LinkClicked()` method, an at sign (@) appears in front of the filename to be opened. This symbol indicates that all characters in the string should be interpreted literally. Therefore, the backslashes in the path are not interpreted as escape sequence characters.

The `LinkVisited` property can be set to `true` when you determine that a user has clicked a link, as shown in Figure 11-9. This setting indicates that the link should be displayed in a different color so the user can see the link has been visited. By default, the visited link color is purple, but you can change this setting in the Properties list for the `LinkLabel`.

```
private void linkLabel1_LinkClicked(object sender,
    LinkLabelLinkClickedEventArgs e)
{
    System.Diagnostics.Process.Start("IExplore",
        "http://www.course.com");
    linkLabel1.LinkVisited = true;
}
```

Figure 11-9 Setting the `LinkVisited` property

»TWO TRUTHS AND A LIE: USING A LinkLabel

1. A LinkLabel is similar to a child class of Label and it provides the additional capability to link the user to other sources.
2. The default event for a Control is the method whose shell is automatically created when you double-click the Control while designing a project in the IDE. Users most likely expect to generate this event when they encounter the Control in a working application.
3. When you create a LinkLabel, it appears as italicized underlined text, and when you pass the mouse pointer over a LinkLabel, the pointer changes to an hourglass.

The false statement is #3. When you create a LinkLabel, it appears as underlined text, and when you pass the mouse pointer over a LinkLabel, the pointer changes to a hand.

ADDING COLOR TO A Form

The **Color** class contains a wide variety of predefined Colors that you can use with your Controls (see Table 11-5).

»NOTE C# also allows you to create custom colors. If no color in Table 11-5 suits your needs, search for "custom color" in the Visual Studio Help to obtain more information.

AliceBlue	Chocolate	DarkOrchid	Fuchsia
AntiqueWhite	Coral	DarkRed	Gainsboro
Aqua	CornflowerBlue	DarkSalmon	GhostWhite
Aquamarine	Cornsilk	DarkSeaGreen	Gold
Azure	Crimson	DarkSlateBlue	Goldenrod
Beige	Cyan	DarkSlateGray	Gray
Bisque	DarkBlue	DarkTurquoise	Green
Black	DarkCyan	DarkViolet	GreenYellow
BlanchedAlmond	DarkGoldenrod	DeepPink	Honeydew
Blue	DarkGray	DeepSkyBlue	HotPink
BlueViolet	DarkGreen	DimGray	IndianRed
Brown	DarkKhaki	DodgerBlue	Indigo
BurlyWood	DarkMagenta	Firebrick	Ivory
CadetBlue	DarkOliveGreen	FloralWhite	Khaki
Chartreuse	DarkOrange	ForestGreen	Lavender

Table 11-5 Color properties (*continued*)

LavenderBlush	MediumAquamarine	PaleGoldenrod	SkyBlue
LawnGreen	MediumBlue	PaleGreen	SlateBlue
LemonChiffon	MediumOrchid	PaleTurquoise	SlateGray
LightBlue	MediumPurple	PaleVioletRed	Snow
LightCoral	MediumSeaGreen	PapayaWhip	SpringGreen
LightCyan	MediumSlateBlue	PeachPuff	SteelBlue
LightGoldenrodYellow	MediumSpringGreen	Peru	Tan
LightGray	MediumTurquoise	Pink	Teal
LightGreen	MediumVioletRed	Plum	Thistle
LightPink	MidnightBlue	PowderBlue	Tomato
LightSalmon	MintCream	Purple	Transparent
LightSeaGreen	MistyRose	Red	Turquoise
LightSkyBlue	Moccasin	RosyBrown	Violet
LightSlateGray	NavajoWhite	RoyalBlue	Wheat
LightSteelBlue	Navy	SaddleBrown	White
LightYellow	OldLace	Salmon	WhiteSmoke
Lime	Olive	SandyBrown	Yellow
LimeGreen	OliveDrab	SeaGreen	YellowGreen
Linen	Orange	SeaShell	
Magenta	OrangeRed	Sienna	
Maroon	Orchid	Silver	

Table 11-5 (*continued*)

When you are designing a Form, you can choose colors from a list next to the BackColor and ForeColor properties in the IDE's Properties list. The statements created will be similar to the following:

```
this.label1.BackColor = System.Drawing.Color.Blue;
this.label1.ForeColor = System.Drawing.Color.Gold;
```

»NOTE If you add using System.Drawing; at the top of your file, you can eliminate the references in the preceding lines and refer to the colors simply as Color.Blue and Color.Gold.

»NOTE For professional-looking results when you prepare a resume or most other business documents, business executives recommend that you only use one or two fonts and colors, even though your word-processing program allows many such selections. The same is true when you design interactive GUI applications. Although many fonts and colors are available, you probably should stick with a few choices in a single project.

»TWO TRUTHS AND A LIE: ADDING COLOR TO A Form

1. Because the choice of colors in C# is limited, you are required to create custom colors for many GUI applications.
2. When you are designing a Form, color choices appear in a list next to the BackColor and ForeColor properties in the IDE's Properties list.
3. The complete name of the color pink in C# is System.Drawing.Color.Pink.

The false statement is #1. The Color class contains a wide variety of predefined Colors that you can use with your controls.

USING CheckBox AND RadioButton OBJECTS

In Chapter 10, you placed Button objects on a Form. The Button class derives from the ButtonBase class. The ButtonBase class has two other descendants: CheckBox and RadioButton.

CheckBox objects are GUI widgets the user can click to select or deselect an option. When a Form contains multiple CheckBoxes, any number of them can be checked or unchecked at the same time. **RadioButtons** are similar to CheckBoxes, except that when they are placed on a Form, only one RadioButton can be selected at a time—selecting any RadioButton automatically deselects the others. Table 11-6 contains commonly used CheckBox properties and the default event for which a method shell is generated when you double-click a CheckBox in the IDE. Table 11-7 contains the properties and default event for RadioButtons.

Property or Method	Description
Checked	Indicates whether the CheckBox is checked
CheckState	Indicates whether the CheckBox is checked, with a value for the CheckState enumeration (Checked, Unchecked, or Indeterminate)
Text	The text displayed to the right of the CheckBox
CheckedChanged()	Default event that is generated when the Checked property changes

Table 11-6 Commonly used CheckBox properties and default event

»NOTE If you precede a letter in the Text property value of a ButtonBase object with an ampersand (&), that letter acts as an access key. For example, if a Button's text is defined as &Press, then typing Alt + P has the same effect as clicking the Button. Access keys are also called hot keys.

Property or Method	Description
Checked	Indicates whether the RadioButton is checked
Text	The text displayed to the right of the RadioButton
CheckedChanged()	Default event that is generated when the Checked property changes

Table 11-7 Commonly used RadioButton properties and default event

» NOTE You can place multiple groups of RadioButtons on a Form by using a GroupBox or Panel. For example, if you place several GroupBox Controls on a Form and you place several RadioButtons in each GroupBox, then one RadioButton can be selected from each GroupBox at any point in time; in other words, each GroupBox operates independently. You will learn more about GroupBoxes and Panels later in this chapter.

Figure 11-10 shows an example of a Form that contains several Labels, four CheckBox objects, and three RadioButton objects. It makes sense for the pizza topping choices to be displayed using CheckBoxes because a user might select multiple toppings. However, options for delivery, pick-up, and dining in the restaurant are mutually exclusive, so they are presented using RadioButton objects.

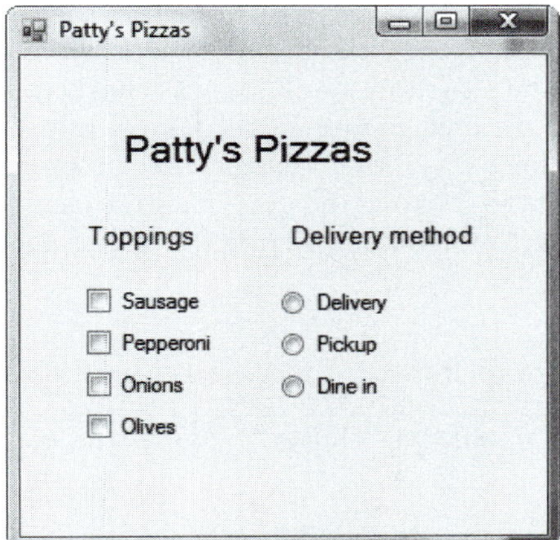

Figure 11-10 A Form with Labels, CheckBoxes, and RadioButtons

When you add CheckBox and RadioButton objects to a form, they automatically are named using the same conventions you have seen with Buttons and Labels. That is, the first CheckBox is named checkBox1 by default, the second is named checkBox2, and so on. Using the Properties list, you can assign more meaningful names such as sausageCheckBox and `pepperoniCheckBox`. Naming objects appropriately makes your code more understandable to others, and makes your programming job easier.

Both `CheckBox` and `RadioButton` objects have a `Checked` property whose value is `true` or `false`. For example, if you create a `CheckBox` named `sausageCheckBox` and you want to add $1.00 to a `pizzaPrice` value when the user checks the box, you can write the following:

```
if(sausageCheckBox.Checked)
    pizzaPrice = pizzaPrice + 1.00;
```

Both `CheckBox` and `RadioButton` objects also have a `CheckedChanged()` method that is called when a user clicks any `CheckBox` or `RadioButton`.

Suppose the total price of a pizza should be altered based on a user's selections. In this example, the base price for a pizza is $12.00, and $1.25 is added for each selected topping. You can declare constants for the `BASE_PRICE` and `TOPPING_PRICE` of a pizza and declare a variable that is initialized to the pizza base price as follows:

```
private const double BASE_PRICE = 12.00;
private const double TOPPING_PRICE = 1.25;
private double price = BASE_PRICE;
```

Figure 11-11 shows some of the code you would add to the Form.cs file for the application. The `sausageCheckBox_CheckedChanged()` method changes the pizza price. The shaded statements in the method were written by a programmer; the unshaded statements were generated by the IDE. If a change occurs because the `sausageCheckBox` was checked, then the `TOPPING_PRICE` is added to the price. If the change to the `checkBox` was to uncheck it, the `TOPPING_PRICE` is subtracted from the price. Either way, the `Text` property of a `Label` is changed to reflect the new price. Figure 11-12 shows the `Form` after the user has checked a box, checked another box, and then unchecked a box. Figure 11-13 shows the entire Form.cs file.

```
private void sausageCheckBox_CheckedChanged(object sender, EventArgs e)
{
    if (sausageCheckBox.Checked)
        price += TOPPING_PRICE;
    else
        price -= TOPPING_PRICE;
    totalLabel.Text = "Total is " + price.ToString("C");
}
```

Figure 11-11 The `sausageCheckBox_CheckedChanged()` method

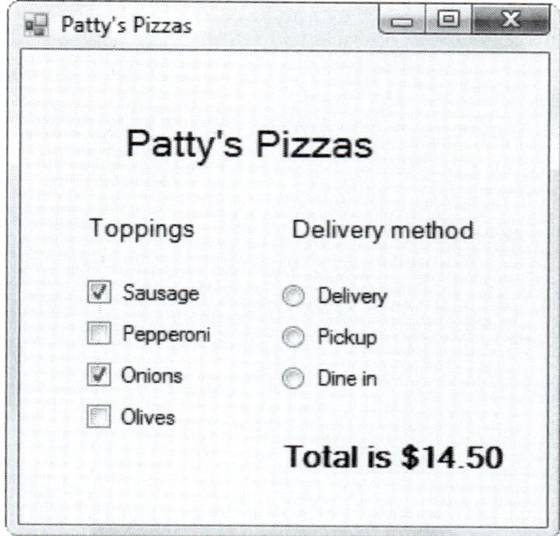

Figure 11-12 Typical execution of `PattysPizza` program after code is added for `CheckBox`es

```csharp
using System;
using System.Collections.Generic;
using System.ComponentModel;
using System.Data;
using System.Drawing;
using System.Linq;
using System.Text;
using System.Windows.Forms;

namespace PattysPizza
{
    public partial class Form1 : Form
    {
        private const double BASE_PRICE = 12.00;
        private const double TOPPING_PRICE = 1.25;
        private double price = BASE_PRICE;

        public Form1()
        {
            InitializeComponent();
        }
```

Figure 11-13 The Form1.cs file of the `PattysPizza` application showing `CheckBox CheckedChanged` methods (*continued*)

```
        private void sausageCheckBox_CheckedChanged(object sender, EventArgs e)
        {
            if (sausageCheckBox.Checked)
                price += TOPPING_PRICE;
            else
                price -= TOPPING_PRICE;
            totalLabel.Text = "Total is " + price.ToString("C");
        }

        private void pepperoniCheckBox_CheckedChanged(object sender, EventArgs e)
        {
            if (pepperoniCheckBox.Checked)
                price += TOPPING_PRICE;
            else
                price -= TOPPING_PRICE;
            totalLabel.Text = "Total is " + price.ToString("C");
        }

        private void onionCheckBox_CheckedChanged(object sender, EventArgs e)
        {
            if (onionCheckBox.Checked)
                price += TOPPING_PRICE;
            else
                price -= TOPPING_PRICE;
            totalLabel.Text = "Total is " + price.ToString("C");
        }

        private void oliveCheckBox_CheckedChanged(object sender, EventArgs e)
        {
            if (oliveCheckBox.Checked)
                price += TOPPING_PRICE;
            else
                price -= TOPPING_PRICE;
            totalLabel.Text = "Total is " + price.ToString("C");
        }
    }
}
```

Figure 11-13 (*continued*)

In a similar fashion, you can add appropriate code for `RadioButton` objects. For example, assume that a $2.00 delivery charge is in effect, but there is no extra charge for customers who pick up a pizza or dine in. The code for `deliverRadioButton_CheckedChanged()` appears in Figure 11-14. When the user selects the `deliverRadioButton`, $2.00 is added to the total. When the user selects either of the other `RadioButton`s, the `deliverRadioButton` becomes unchecked, and the $2.00 charge is removed from the total.

```
private void deliverRadioButton_CheckedChanged(object sender, EventArgs e)
{
    const double DELIVERY_CHARGE = 2.00;
    if (deliverRadioButton.Checked)
        price += DELIVERY_CHARGE;
    else
        price -= DELIVERY_CHARGE;
    totalLabel.Text = "Total is " + price.ToString("C");
}
```

Figure 11-14 The `deliverRadioButton_CheckedChanged()` method

TWO TRUTHS AND A LIE: USING CheckBox AND RadioButton OBJECTS

1. `CheckBox` objects are GUI widgets that the user can click to select or deselect an option; when a `Form` contains multiple `CheckBox`es, any number of them can be checked or unchecked at the same time.

2. `RadioButton`s are similar to `CheckBox`es, except that when they are placed on a `Form`, only one `RadioButton` can be selected at a time—selecting any `RadioButton` automatically deselects the others.

3. The default event for a `CheckBox` is `CheckBoxChanged()` and the default event for a `RadioButton` is `RadioButtonChanged()`.

The false statement is #3. The default event for both `CheckBox` and `RadioButton` objects is `CheckedChanged()`.

> **NOTE**
> When an application starts, sometimes you want a `CheckBox` or `RadioButton` to be selected by default. If so, you can set the `CheckBox` or `RadioButton`'s `Checked` property to `true`.

ADDING A PictureBox TO A Form

A **PictureBox** is a `Control` in which you can display graphics from a bitmap, icon, JPEG, GIF, or other image file type. Just as with a `Button` or a `Label`, you can easily drag a `PictureBox Control` onto a `Form` in the Visual Studio IDE. Table 11-8 shows the common properties and default event for a `PictureBox`.

Property or Method	Description
`Image`	Sets the image that appears in the `PictureBox`
`SizeMode`	Controls the size and position of the image in the `PictureBox`; values are `Normal`, `StretchImage` (which resizes the image to fit the `PictureBox`), `AutoSize` (which resizes the `PictureBox` to fit the image), and `CenterImage` (which centers the image in the `PictureBox`)
`Click()`	Default event that is generated when the user clicks the `PictureBox`

Table 11-8 Commonly used `PictureBox` properties and default event

Figure 11-15 shows a new project in the IDE. The following tasks have been completed:

- » A project was started.
- » The `Form Text` property was changed to "Save Money".
- » The `Form BackColor` property was changed to white.
- » A `Label` was dragged onto the `Form`, and its `Text` and `Font` were changed.
- » A `PictureBox` was dragged onto the `Form`.

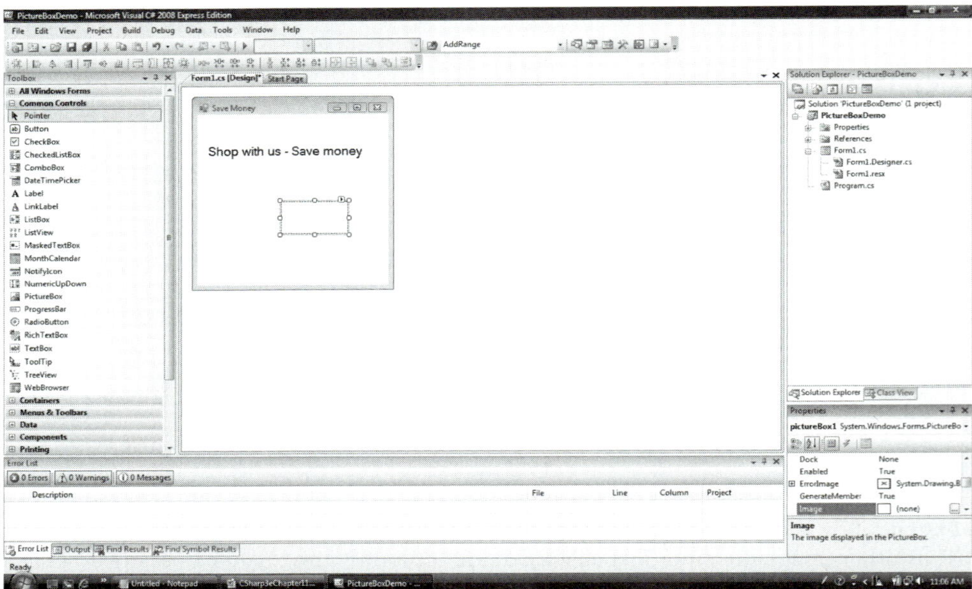

Figure 11-15 The IDE with a `Form` that contains a `PictureBox`

In Figure 11-15, in the Properties list at the right of the screen, the `Image` property is set to *none*. If you click the button with the ellipsis, a Select Resource window appears, as shown on the left in Figure 11-16. When you click the Import button, you can browse for stored images. When you select one, you see a preview in the Select Resource window, as shown on the right in Figure 11-16.

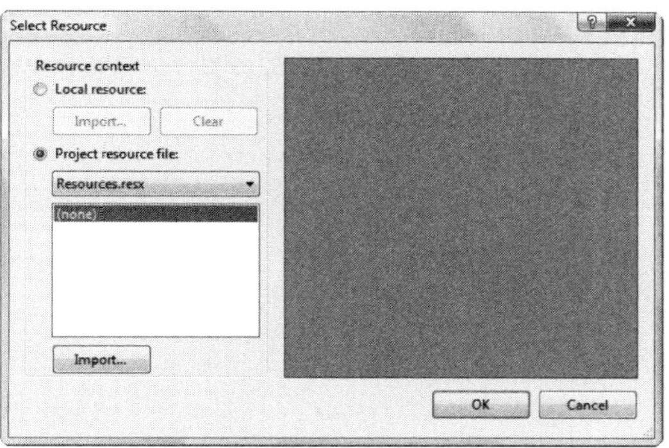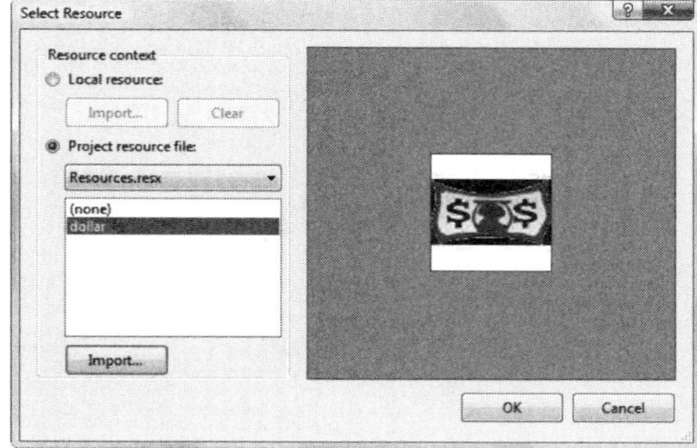

Figure 11-16 Select Resource window before and after image is selected

After you click OK, the image appears in the `PictureBox`, as in Figure 11-17. In the Solution Explorer on the right side of the IDE, notice that the dollar.jpg file has been added to the project. (You can resize the `PictureBox` so the image displays clearly.)

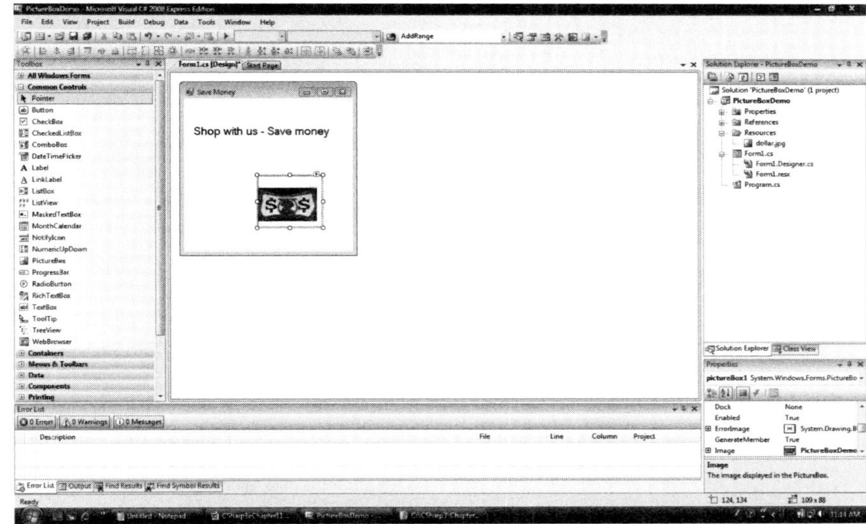

Figure 11-17 The `SaveMoney` project with an inserted image

If you examine the generated code, you can find the statements that instantiate a `PictureBox` (named `pictureBox1` by default) and statements that set its properties, such as `Size` and `Location`.

»TWO TRUTHS AND A LIE: ADDING A `PictureBox` TO A Form

1. A `PictureBox` is a `Control` in which you can display graphics from a bitmap, icon, JPEG, GIF, or other image file type.
2. The default event for a `PictureBox` is `LoadImage()`.
3. The `Image` property of a `PictureBox` holds the name of a file where a picture is stored.

The false statement is #2. The default event for a `PictureBox` is `Click()`.

ADDING `ListBox`, `CheckedListBox`, AND `ComboBox` Control`S` TO A Form

`Buttons`, `RadioButtons`, and `CheckBoxes` represent a GUI family because they all descend from the `ButtonBase` class and they all share certain characteristics. Similarly, `ListBox`, `ComboBox`, and `CheckedListBox` objects descend from the same family—they all are list-type widgets that descend from `ListControl`. Of course, they are also `Controls` and so inherit properties such as `Text` and `BackColor` from the `Control` class. Other properties are more specific to list-type objects. Table 11-9 describes some commonly used `ListBox` properties.

Property or Method	Description
Items	The collection of items in the `ListBox`; frequently, these are `strings`, but they can also be other types of objects
MultiColumn	Indicates whether display can be in multiple columns
SelectedIndex	Returns the index of the selected item. It no item has been selected, the value is -1. Otherwise, it is a value from 0 through $n - 1$, where n is the number of items in the `ListBox`.
SelectedIndices	Returns a collection of all the selected indices (when `SelectionMode` is more than `One`)
SelectedItem	Returns a reference to the selected item
SelectedItems	Returns a collection of the selected items (when `SelectionMode` is more than `One`)
SelectionMode	Determines how many items can be selected (see Table 11-10)
Sorted	Sorts the items when set to `true`
SelectedIndexChanged()	Default event that is generated when the selected index changes

Table 11-9 Commonly used `ListBox` properties and default event

Figure 11-18 shows a typical `ListBox` on a `Form`. The **ListBox** `Control` enables you to display a list of items that the user can select by clicking. After you drag a `ListBox` onto a `Form`, you can select its `Items` property and type a list into a String Collection Editor, as shown on the right in Figure 11-18.

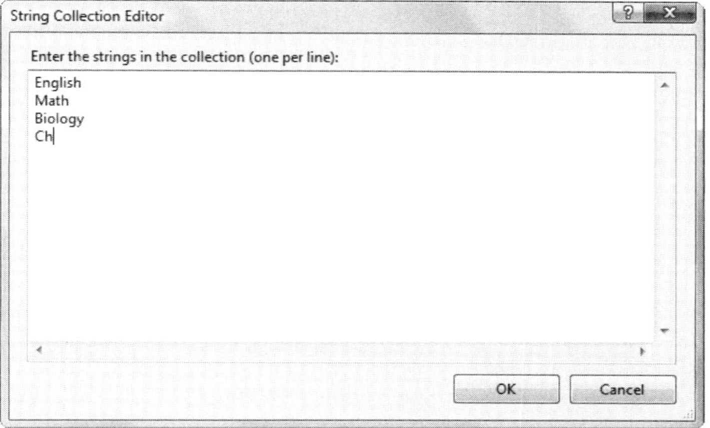

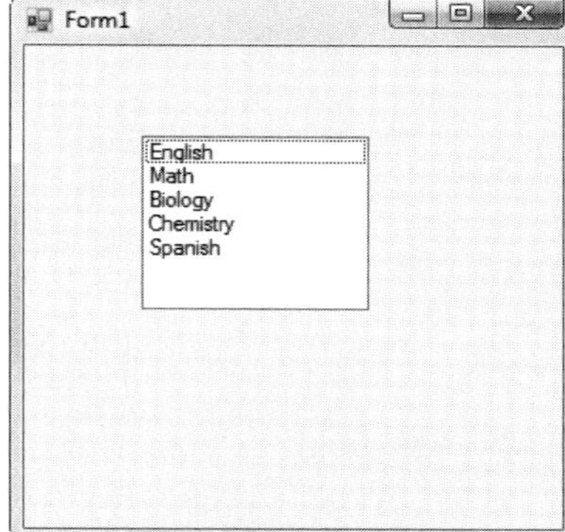

Figure 11-18 The String Collection Editor filling a `ListBox` and the completed `ListBox` on a `Form`

When you fill the String Collection Editor with the strings in Figure 11-18, the following code is generated in the `InitializeComponent()` method:

```
this.listBox1.Items.AddRange(new object[] {
        "English",
        "Math",
        "Biology",
        "Chemistry",
        "Spanish",
        ""});
```

With a `ListBox`, you allow the user to make a single selection or multiple selections by setting the `SelectionMode` property appropriately. For example, when the `SelectionMode` property is set to `One`, the user can make only a single selection from the `ListBox`. When the `SelectionMode` is set to `MultiExtended`, pressing Shift and clicking the mouse or pressing Shift and one of the arrow keys (up, down, left, or right) extends the selection to span from the previously selected item to the current item. Pressing Ctrl and clicking the mouse selects or deselects an item in the list. Table 11-10 lists the possible `SelectionMode` values.

>> **NOTE** When the `SelectionMode` property is set to `SelectionMode.MultiSimple`, click the mouse or press the spacebar to select or deselect an item in the list.

Member Name	Description
MultiExtended	Multiple items can be selected, and the user can press the Shift, Ctrl, and arrow keys to make selections
MultiSimple	Multiple items can be selected
None	No items can be selected
One	Only one item can be selected

Table 11-10 SelectionMode enumeration list

For example, within a Form's Load() method (the one that executes when a Form is first loaded), you could add the following:

```
this.listBox1.SelectionMode =
    System.Windows.Forms.SelectionMode.MultiExtended;
```

As the example in Figure 11-19 shows, when you size a ListBox so that all the items cannot be displayed at the same time, a scroll bar is provided automatically on the side. The ListBox also provides the Boolean MultiColumn property, which you can set to display items in columns instead of a straight vertical list. This approach allows the control to display more items and avoids the need for the user to scroll down to an item. See Figure 11-20.

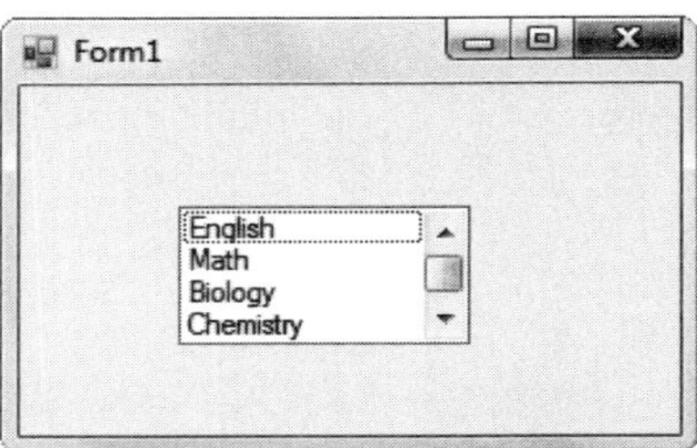

Figure 11-19 A ListBox with a scroll bar

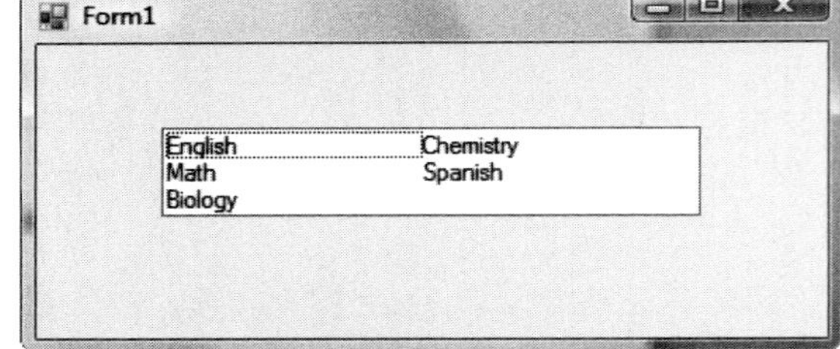

Figure 11-20 A multicolumn ListBox

The SelectedItem property of a ListBox contains the value of the item a user has selected. For example, if you create a Label with the Text property "You selected: ", you can modify the label's Text property in the majorListBox_SelectedIndexChanged() method with a statement such as the following:

```
private void majorListBox_SelectedIndexChanged
    (object sender, EventArgs e)
{
    majorLabel.Text += majorListBox1.SelectedItem;
}
```

The SelectedItem is appended to the label. Figure 11-21 shows a typical result.

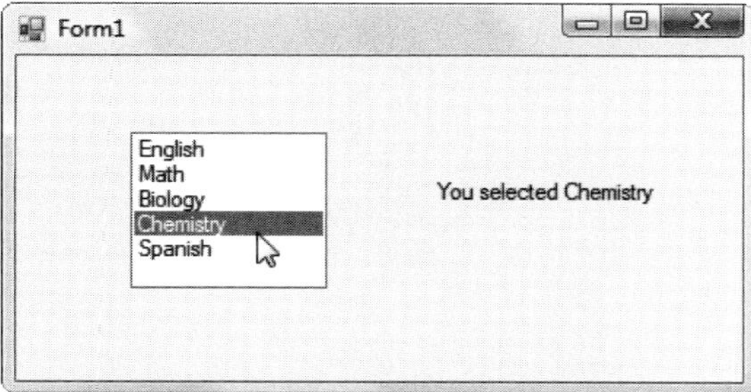

Figure 11-21 `ListBoxDemo` application after user has chosen *Chemistry*

The `Items.Count` property of a `ListBox` object holds the number of items in the `ListBox`. The `GetSelected()` method accepts an integer argument representing the array position of an item in the list. The method returns `true` if an item is selected and `false` if it is not. Therefore, code like the following could be used to count the number of selections a user makes from `listbox1`:

```
int count = 0;
for(int x = 0; x < majorListBox.Items.Count; ++x)
    if(majorListBox.GetSelected(x))
        ++count;
```


The `SetSelected()` method can be used to set a `ListBox` item to be automatically selected by default. For example, the following statement causes the first item in `majorListBox` to be the selected one:

```
majorListBox.SetSelected(0, true);
```

A **ComboBox** is similar to a `ListBox`, except that it displays an additional editing field to allow the user to select from the list or to enter new text. The default `ComboBox` displays an editing field with a hidden list box. The application in Figure 11-22 contains a `ComboBox` for selecting an airline. A **CheckedListBox** is also similar to a `ListBox`, with check boxes appearing to the left of each desired item. The application in Figure 11-22 uses a `CheckedListBox` for flight options.

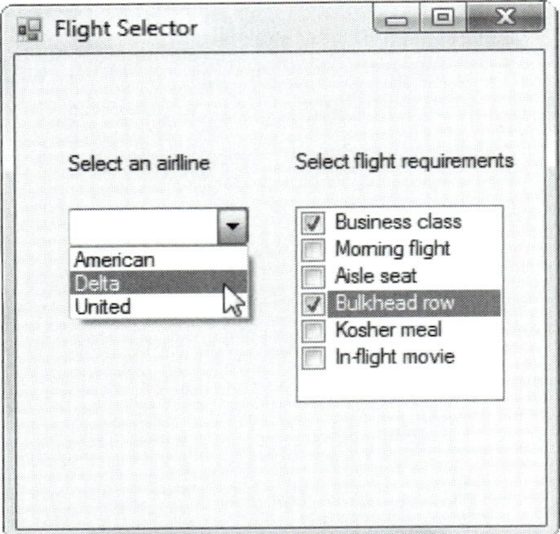

Figure 11-22 `ComboBoxAndCheckedListBoxDemo` application after user has made some selections

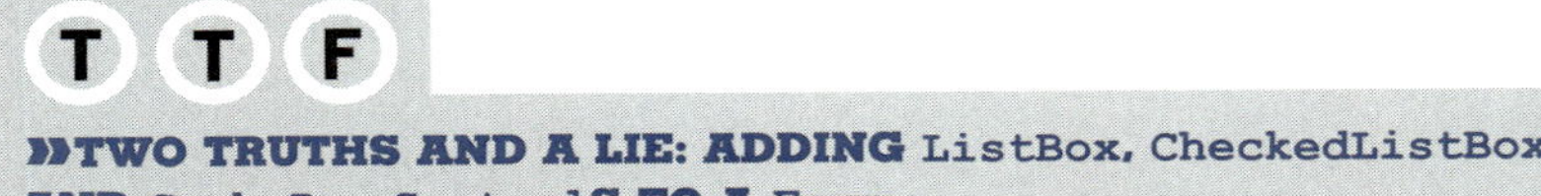

»TWO TRUTHS AND A LIE: ADDING `ListBox`, `CheckedListBox`, AND `ComboBox` ControlS TO A Form

1. The `ListBox Control` enables you to display a list of items that the user can select by clicking; the user can select only one option at a time.

2. A `ComboBox` is similar to a `ListBox`, except that it displays an additional editing field that allows users to select from the list or to enter new text.

3. A `CheckedListBox` is also similar to a `ListBox`, with check boxes appearing to the left of each desired item.

The false statement is #1. With a `ListBox`, you allow the user to make a single selection or multiple selections by setting the `SelectionMode` property appropriately.

ADDING `MonthCalendar` AND `DateTimePicker` ControlS TO A Form

The **MonthCalendar** and **DateTimePicker** `Control`s allow you to retrieve date and time information. Figure 11-23 shows a `MonthCalendar` that has been placed on a `Form`. The current date is contained in a rectangle by default, and the date that the user clicked is shaded. `Control`s at the top of the calendar allow the user to go forward or back one month at a time. Table 11-11 describes common `MonthCalendar` properties and the default event.

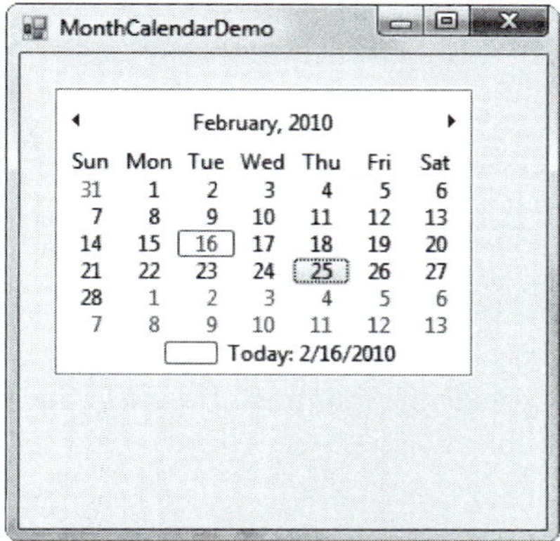

Figure 11-23 Typical execution of `MonthCalendarDemo`

Property or Method	Description
`MaxDate`	Sets the last day that can be selected (the default is 12/31/9998)
`MaxSelectionCount`	Sets the maximum number of dates that can be selected at once (the default is 7)
`MinDate`	Sets the first day that can be selected (the default is 1/1/1753)
`MonthlyBoldedDates`	An array of dates that appear in boldface in the calendar; for example, holidays
`SelectionEnd`	The last of a range of dates selected by the user
`SelectionRange`	The dates selected by the user
`SelectionStart`	The first of a range of dates selected by the user
`ShowToday`	If `true`, the date displays in text at the bottom of the calendar
`ShowTodayCircle`	If `true`, today's date is circled (the "circle" appears as a square)
`DateChanged()`	Default event that is generated when the user selects a date

Table 11-11 Commonly used `MonthCalendar` properties and default event

» NOTE If you set the `MinDate` value to the `MonthCalendar`'s `TodayDate` property, the user cannot select a date before today. For example, you cannot make appointments or schedule deliveries to happen in the past, so you might code the following:

```
monthCalendar1.MinDate = monthCalendar1.TodayDate;
```

Conversely, you might want to prevent users from selecting a date in the future—for example, if the user is entering the date he placed an outstanding order. In that case, you could code a statement similar to the following:

```
monthCalendar1.MaxDate = monthCalendar1.TodayDate;
```

You can use several useful methods with the `SelectionStart` and `SelectionEnd` properties of `MonthCalendar`, including the following:

- » `ToShortDateString()`, which displays the date in the format 2/16/2010
- » `ToLongDateString()`, which displays the date in the format Tuesday, February 16, 2010
- » `AddDays()`, which takes a `double` argument and adds a specified number of days to the date
- » `AddMonths()`, which takes an `int` argument and adds a specified number of months to the date
- » `AddYears()`, which takes an `int` argument and adds a specified number of years to the date

>> **NOTE** The format in which dates are displayed depends on the operating system's regional settings. For example, using United Kingdom settings, the short string format would use the day first, followed by the month, as in 16/02/2010. The examples in the preceding list assume United States settings.

>> **NOTE** The `AddDays()` method accepts a `double` argument because you can add fractional days to `SelectionStart` and `SelectionEnd`.

>> **NOTE** `SelectionStart` and `SelectionEnd` are structures of the `DateTime` type. Chapter 13 contains additional information about using `DateTime` objects to determine when files were created, modified, or accessed.

Many business and financial applications use `AddDays()`, `AddMonths()`, and `AddYears()` to calculate dates for events, such as payment for a bill (perhaps due in 10 days from an order) or scheduling a salesperson's callback to a customer (perhaps two months after initial contact). The default event for `MonthCalendar` is `DateChanged()`. For example, Figure 11-24 shows a method that executes when the user clicks a `MonthCalendar` named `cal`. A `string` is created from the literal text "You selected " and the start of the user's selection is converted to a short `string`. The message is placed on a `Label` that has been named `messageLabel`. Figure 11-25 shows the output when the user selects February 26, 2010. The date that is 10 days in the future is correctly calculated as March 8.

```
private void cal_DateChanged(object sender, DateRangeEventArgs e)
{
    const int DAYS_TO_ADD = 10;
    string newDate = "You selected " +
       calendar.SelectionStart.ToShortDateString();
    messageLabel.Text = newDate + "\nTen days from now is " +
       calendar.SelectionStart.AddDays(DAYS_TO_ADD).ToShortDateString();
}
```

Figure 11-24 `MonthCalendarDemo` application `cal_DateChanged()` method

Figure 11-25 Typical execution of `MonthCalendarDemo`

The `DateTimePicker Control` displays a month calendar when the down arrow is selected. For example, Figure 11-26 shows a `DateTimePicker` before and after the user clicks the down arrow.

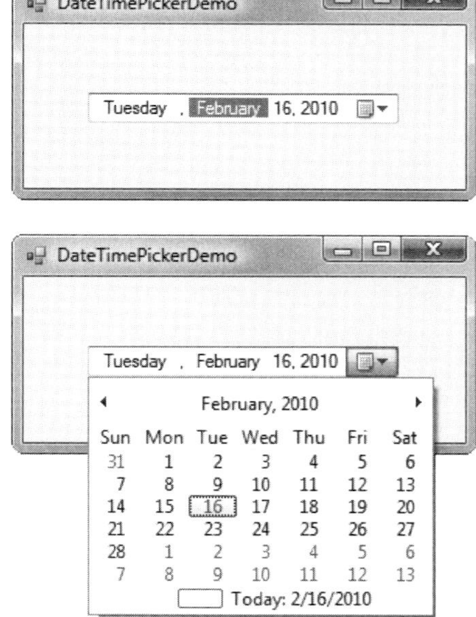

Figure 11-26 The `DateTimePicker Control`

When you use the `CustomFormat` property, the date displayed in a `DateTimePicker` `Control` is more customizable than the one in a `MonthCalendar`. Table 11-12 describes some commonly used `DateTimePicker` properties and the default event.

Property or Method	Description
`CalendarForeColor`	Sets the calendar text color
`CalendarMonthBackground`	Sets the calendar background color
`CustomFormat`	A string value that uses codes to set a custom date and time format. For example, to display the date and time as `02/16/2010 12:00 PM - Friday`, set this property to `"MM'/'dd'/'yyyy hh':'mm tt - dddd"`. See the C# documentation for a complete set of format string characters.
`Format`	Sets the format for the date or time. Options are `Long` (for example, Tuesday, February 16, 2010), `Short` (2/16/2010), and `Time` (for example, 3:15:01 PM). You can also create a `CustomFormat`.
`Value`	The data selected by the user
`ValueChanged()`	Default event that is generated when the `Value` property changes

Table 11-12 Commonly used `DateTimePicker` properties and default event

»TWO TRUTHS AND A LIE: ADDING `MonthCalendar` **AND** `DateTimePicker` `Control`**S TO A** `Form`

1. The `MonthCalendar` and `DateTimePicker` `Control`s allow you to retrieve date and time information.
2. The default event for `MonthCalendar` is `DateChanged()`.
3. The `DateTimePicker` `Control` displays a small clock when you click it.

The false statement is #3. The `DateTimePicker` `Control` displays a month calendar when the down arrow is selected.

WORKING WITH A `Form`'S LAYOUT

When you place `Control`s on a `Form` in the IDE, you can drag them to any location to achieve the effect you want.

When you drag multiple `Controls` onto a `Form`, blue **snap lines** appear and help you align new `Controls` with others already in place. Figure 11-27 shows two snap lines that you can use to align a second label below the first one. Snap lines also appear when you place a control closer to the edge of a container than is recommended.

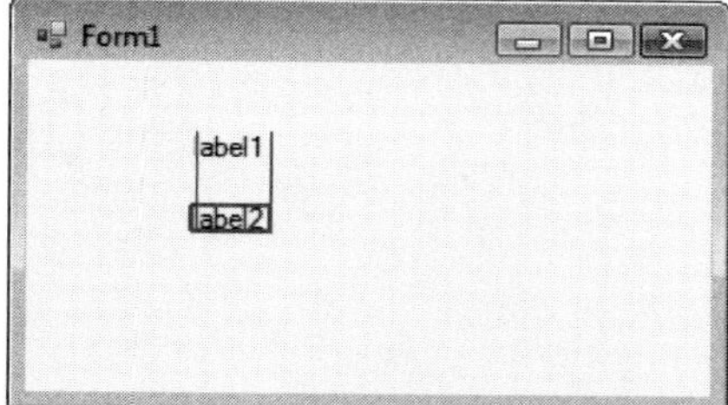

Figure 11-27 Snap lines in the Visual Studio Designer

You also can use the `Location` property in a `Control`'s Properties list to specify a location. With either technique, code like the following is generated:

```
this.label1.Location = new System.Drawing.Point(23, 19);
```

Several other properties can help you to manage the appearance of a `Form` (or other `ContainerControl`). For example, setting the **Anchor property** causes a `Control` to remain at a fixed distance from the side of a container when the user resizes it. Figure 11-28 shows the Properties window for a `Label` that has been placed on a `Form`. The `Anchor` property has a drop-down window that lets you select or deselect the sides to which the label should be anchored. For most `Controls`, the default setting for `Anchor` is `Top, Left`.

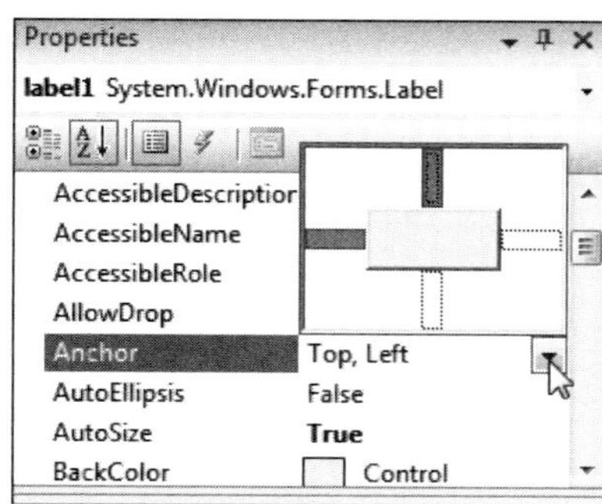

Figure 11-28 Selecting an `Anchor` property

Figure 11-29 shows a `Form` with two `Labels`. On the `Form`, `label1` has been anchored to the top left and `label2` has been anchored to the bottom right. The left side of the figure shows the `Form` as it first appears to the user, and the right side shows the `Form` after the user has resized it. Notice that in the resized `Form`, `label1` is still the same distance from the top left as it originally was, and `label2` is still the same distance from the bottom right as it originally was. Anchoring is useful when users expect a specific control to always be in the same general location in a container.

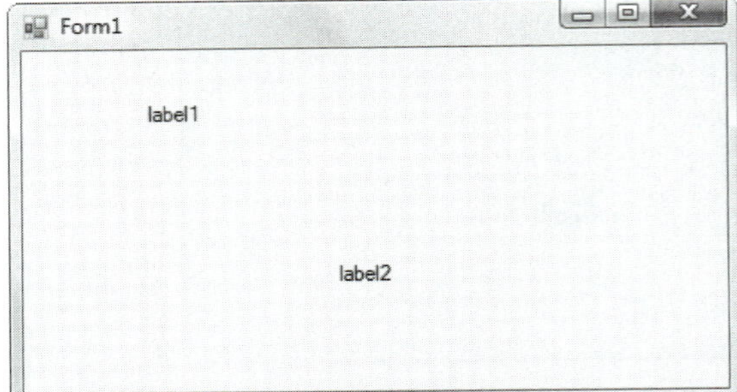
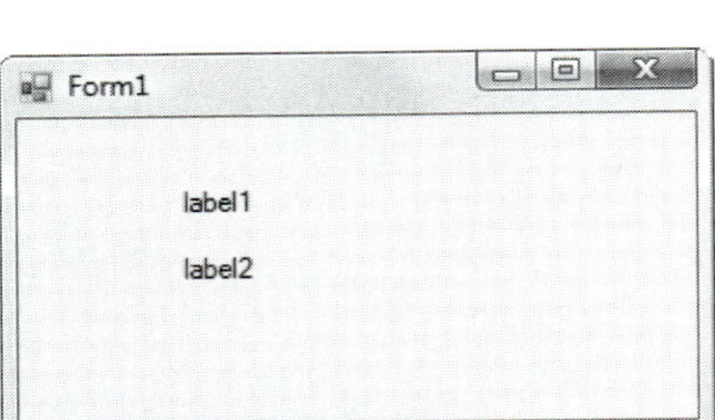

Figure 11-29 A `Form` with two `Label`s anchored to opposite corners

Setting the **Dock property** attaches a `Control` to the side of a container so that the `Control` stretches when the container's size is adjusted. Figure 11-30 shows the drop-down `Dock` Properties window for a `Button`. You can select any region in the window. Figure 11-31 shows a `Button` docked to the bottom of a `Form` before and after the `Form` has been resized.

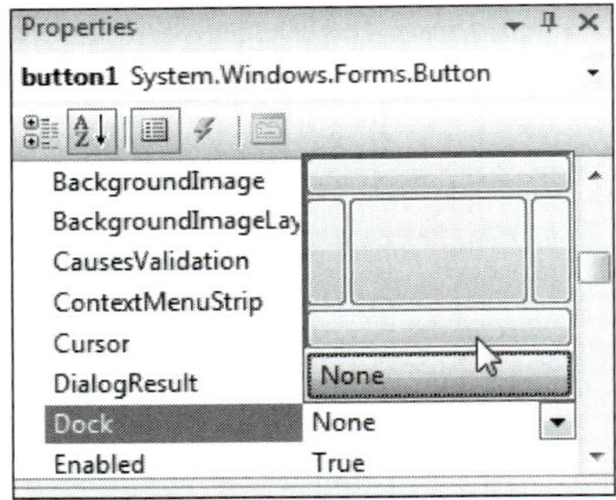

Figure 11-30 The `Dock` Properties window

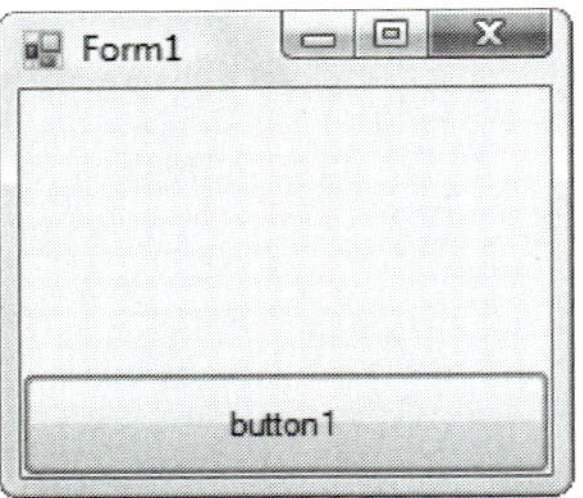
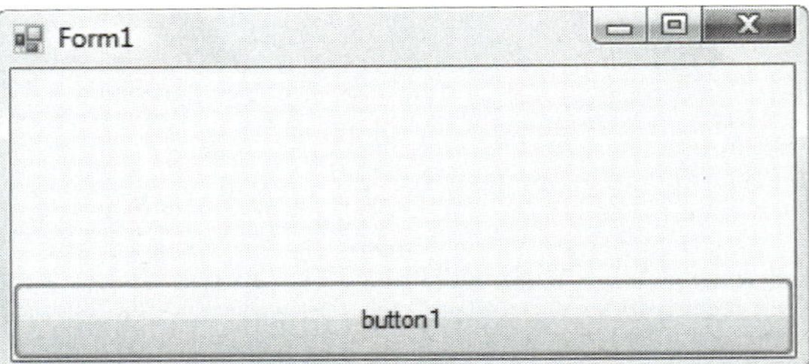

Figure 11-31 A `Form` with a docked `Button`

A `Form` has a **Padding property** that specifies the distance between docked `Controls` and the edges of the `Form`. The `Padding` property has four values—one for each side of the `Form` (left, top, right, and bottom). They are set to 0 by default. Figure 11-32 shows the docked button from Figure 11-31 when the padding values have been set to 0, 0, 30, and 10. The `Button` is three times further from the right edge of the `Form` than it is from the bottom.

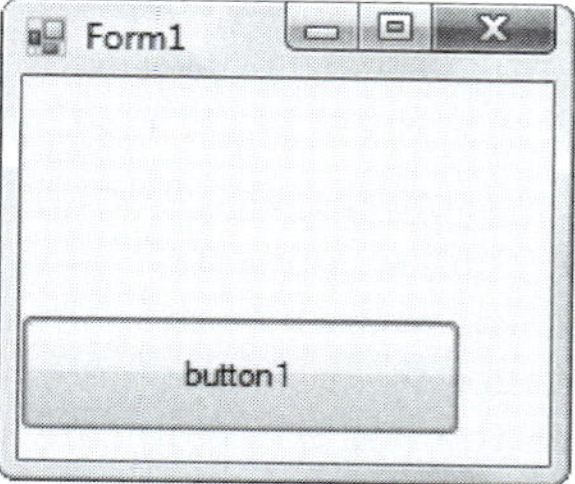

Figure 11-32 A docked button on a `Form` with padding

A `Form` also has a **MinimumSize property** and a **MaximumSize property**. Each has two values—`Width` and `Height`. If you set these properties, the user cannot make the `Form` smaller or larger than you have specified. If you do not want the user to be able to adjust a `Form`'s size at all, set the `MinimumSize` and `MaximumSize` properties to be equal.

UNDERSTANDING GROUPBOXES AND PANELS

Many types of `ContainerControls` are available to hold `Controls`. For example, you can use a **GroupBox** or **Panel** to group related `Controls` on a `Form`. When you move a `GroupBox` or `Panel`, all its `Controls` are moved as a group. To create either of these `Controls`, you drag it from the Toolbox in the IDE, and then drag the `Controls` you want on top of it. `GroupBoxes` can display a caption, but `Panels` cannot. `Panels` can include a scroll bar that the user can manipulate to view `Controls`; `GroupBoxes` do not have scroll bars. You can anchor or dock `Controls` inside a `GroupBox` or `Panel`, and you can anchor or dock a `GroupBox` or `Panel` inside a `Form`. Doing this provides `Control` groups that easily can be arranged.

»TWO TRUTHS AND A LIE: WORKING WITH A Form'S LAYOUT

1. Setting the `Anchor` property causes a `Control` to remain at a fixed distance from the side of a container when the user resizes it.

2. Setting the `Dock` property attaches a `Control` to the side of a container so that the `Control`'s size does not change when the container's size is adjusted.

3. A `Form` has a `Padding` property that specifies the distance between docked `Controls` and the edges of the `Form`.

The false statement is #2. Setting the `Dock` property attaches a `Control` to the side of a container so that the `Control` stretches when the container's size is adjusted.

ADDING A MenuStrip TO A Form

Most programs you use in a Windows environment contain a **menu strip,** which is a horizontal list of general options that appears under the title bar of a Form or Window. When you click an item in a menu strip, you might initiate an action. More frequently, you see a list box that contains more specific options. Each of these might initiate an action, or it might lead to another menu. For example, the Visual Studio IDE contains a horizontal main menu strip that begins with the options File, Edit, and View. You have used word-processing, spreadsheet, and even game programs with similar menus.

You can add a **MenuStrip** Control object to any Form you create. Using the Visual Studio IDE, you can add a MenuStrip to a Form by dragging it from the Toolbox onto the Form. This creates a menu bar horizontally across the top of the Form, just below the title bar. Figure 11-33 shows a MenuStrip dragged onto a Form. The strip extends across the width of the Form and contains a "Type Here" text box. When you click the text box, you can enter a menu item. New text boxes appear below and to the right of the first one. Each time you add a menu item, new boxes are created so you can see where your next options will go.

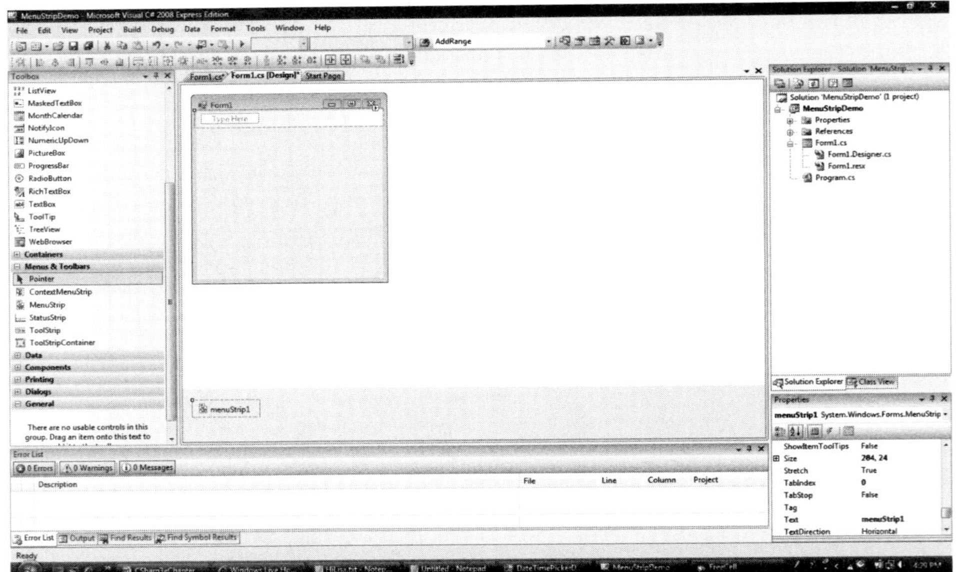

Figure 11-33 Form with MenuStrip

Figure 11-34 shows a `MenuStrip` in which the programmer has typed *Font*, and beneath it, *Large* and *Small*. New boxes are available to the right of Font and beneath Small. Figure 11-35 shows that the programmer continued by entering *Color* and three choices beneath it.

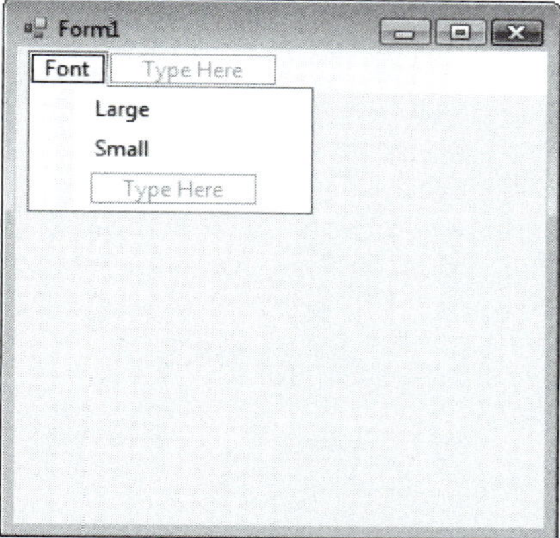

Figure 11-34 `Form` that contains `MenuStrip` with a few entries

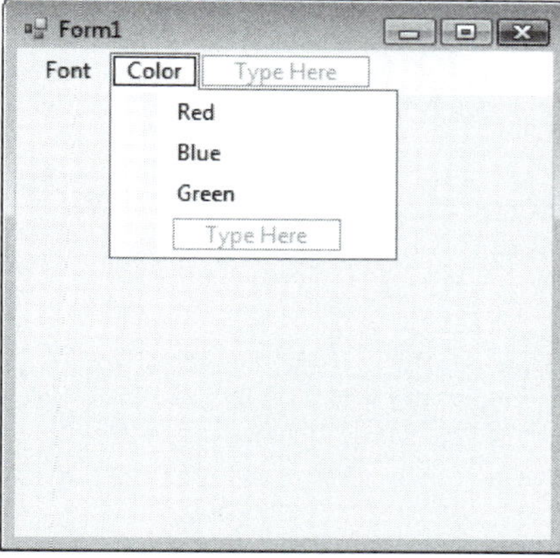

Figure 11-35 `Form` that contains `MenuStrip` with more entries

>> **NOTE**
If possible, your main menu selections should be single words. That way, a user will not mistakenly think that a single menu item represents multiple items.

>> **NOTE**
If you create each main menu item with an ampersand (&) in front of a unique letter, then the user can press Alt and the letter to activate the menu choice, besides clicking it with the mouse.

When you double-click an entry in the `MenuStrip`, a `Click()` method is generated. For example, if you click Large in the menu shown in Figure 11-36, the method generated is `largeToolStripMenuItem_Click()`, as follows:

```
private void largeToolStripMenuItem_Click
    (object sender, EventArgs e)
{
}
```

As with all the other controls you have learned about, you can write any code statements you like within the method. For example, suppose a `Label` named `helloLabel` has been dragged onto the `Form`. If choosing the Large menu option should result in a larger font for the label, you might code the method as follows:

```
private void largeToolStripMenuItem_Click
   (object sender, EventArgs e)
{
    helloLabel.Font = new Font("Courier New", 34);
}
```

With the addition of this method, the `Form` operates as shown in Figure 11-36. If the `Label` appears in a small font and the user clicks the Large menu option, the font changes.

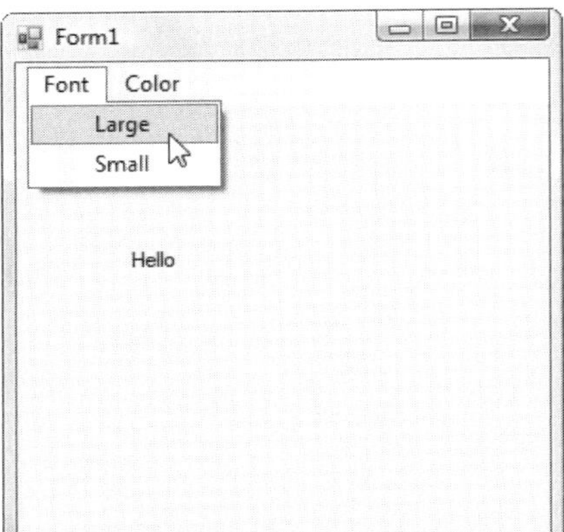

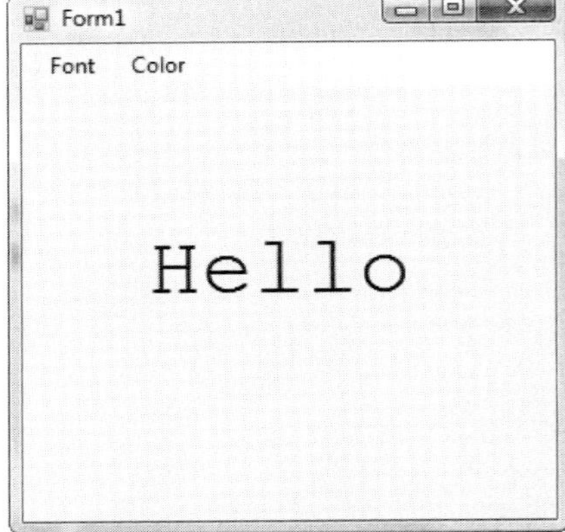

Figure 11-36 Executing the `MenuStripDemo` program

NOTE
You can work with the other menu items in this program in an exercise at the end of this chapter.

T T F

▶▶TWO TRUTHS AND A LIE: ADDING A `MenuStrip` TO A `Form`

1. When you click an item in a menu strip, the most common result is to initiate an action.
2. When you drag a `MenuStrip` Control object onto a `Form` using the Visual Studio IDE, the `MenuStrip` is added horizontally across the top of the `Form`, just below the title bar.
3. The default event for `MenuStrip` is `Click()`.

The false statement is #1. When you click an item in a menu strip, you might initiate an action. More frequently, you see a list box that contains more specific options.

USING OTHER Controls

If you examine the Visual Studio IDE or search through the Visual Studio documentation, you will find many other Controls that are not covered in this chapter. If you click Project on the main menu and click Add New Item, you can add extra Forms, Files, Controls, and other elements to your project. New controls and containers will be developed in the future, and you might even design new controls of your own. Still, all controls will contain properties and methods, and your solid foundation in C# will prepare you to use new controls effectively.

YOU DO IT

ADDING Labels TO A Form AND CHANGING THEIR PROPERTIES

In the next steps, you will begin to create an application for Bailey's Bed and Breakfast. The main Form allows the user to select one of two suites and discover the amenities and price associated with each choice. You will start by placing two Labels on a Form and setting several of their properties.

The screen images in the next steps represent a typical Visual Studio environment. Based on options you selected in your installation, your screen might look different.

To create a Form with Labels:

1. Open Microsoft Visual Studio. You might be able to use a desktop shortcut, or you might click the **Start button**, point to **All Programs**, and click the version of C# you have installed (for example, **Microsoft Visual C# Express Edition**).

2. Click **File** on the menu bar and click **New Project**. A New Project window appears. In the window under Templates, click **Windows Forms Application**. Near the bottom of the New Project window, click in the **Name** text box and replace the default name with **BedAndBreakfast**. See Figure 11-37.

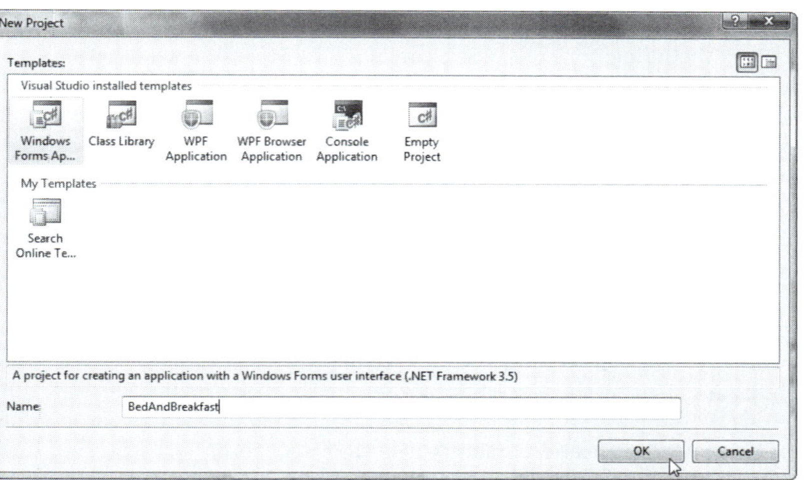

Figure 11-37 The New Project window for the BedAndBreakfast application

3. Click **OK**. The design screen appears. The blank Form in the center of the screen has an empty title bar. Click the Form. The lower-right corner of the screen contains a Properties window that lists the Form's properties. (If you do not see the Properties window, you can click **View** on the main menu and then click **Properties Window**. Another option is to press **Ctrl+W**, followed by **P**.)

4. In the Properties list, click the **Name** property and change the Name of the Form to **BaileysForm**. Click the **Text** property and change it to **Bailey's Bed and Breakfast.** Press **Enter**; the title of the Form in the center of the screen changes to *Bailey's Bed and Breakfast*. (See Figure 11-38.)

Figure 11-38 Form with revised Text property

5. On the left side of the design screen, the Toolbox contains a list of components that can be added to a Form, including Buttons, CheckBoxes, Labels, and many others. Click **Label** and drag a Label onto the Form. When you release your mouse button, the Label appears on the Form and contains the default text "label1". On the right side of the screen under Properties, make sure the list box shows that you are viewing the properties for label1. If not, click label1 on the Form on the design screen.

> **NOTE** If you do not see the Toolbox, click the **Toolbox tab** at the left side of the screen and pin it to the screen by clicking the pushpin. Alternatively, you can select **View** from the main menu and then click **Toolbox**.

6. Change the Name of label1 to **welcomeLabel** and change the Text property to **Welcome to Bailey's**, then press **Enter**; the text of the Label on the Form changes. Drag and resize the Label so it is close to the position of the Label in Figure 11-39. (If you prefer to set the Label's Location property manually in the Properties list, the Location should be **60, 30**.)

Figure 11-39 A `Label` placed on the `Form` in the
`BedAndBreakfast` project

7. Make sure the Properties list still shows the properties for `welcomeLabel`; if not, click the `Label` on the design screen. Locate the `Font` property in the Properties list. Currently, it lists the default font: Microsoft Sans Serif, 8.25 pt. Notice the ellipsis (three dots) at the right of the `Font` property name. (You might have to click in the Property to see the button.) Click the ellipsis to display the `Font` dialog box. Make selections to change the font to **Microsoft Sans Serif**, **18 point**, and **Italic**. Click **OK**. When you enlarge the `Font` for the `Label`, it is too close to the right edge of the `Form`. Drag it to change its `Location` property to approximately **30, 25**, or type the new `Location` value in the Properties window.

8. Drag a second `Label` onto the `Form` beneath the first one, and then set its `Name` property to `rateLabel` and its `Text` property to **Check our rates**. Change its `Location` to approximately **80, 80** and its `Font` to **Microsoft Sans Serif, 12 point, Regular**.

9. Save the project using one of the following methods: Click **File** on the menu bar and then click **Save All**, click the **Save All** button (which resembles a stack of diskettes), or press **Ctrl+Shift+S**. The project name (BedAndBreakfast) should already appear in the dialog box. You can browse for the location where you want to save the project. For example, you can choose the Chapter.11 folder on your Student Disk.

10. Click **Debug** on the menu bar and then click **Start Without Debugging**, or press **Ctrl+F5**. The `Form` appears, as shown in Figure 11-40.

Figure 11-40 The `BedAndBreakfast` Form with two `Label`s

11. Dismiss the `Form` by clicking the **Close** button in its upper-right corner.

EXAMINING THE CODE GENERATED BY THE IDE

In the next steps, you will examine the code generated by the IDE for at least two reasons:

» To gain an understanding of the types of statements created by the IDE.

» To lose any intimidation you might have about the code generated. You will recognize many of the C# statements from what you have already learned in this book.

To examine the generated code:

1. Click **View** on the menu bar and then click **Code** (or press **F7**) to view the code. As shown in Figure 11-41, you see several `using` statements, the `BedAndBreakfast` namespace header, the `BaileysForm` class header, and the constructor for `Form1` that calls the `InitializeComponent()` method.

```
BedAndBreakfast.BaileysForm                              BaileysForm()

using System;
using System.Collections.Generic;
using System.ComponentModel;
using System.Data;
using System.Drawing;
using System.Linq;
using System.Text;
using System.Windows.Forms;

namespace BedAndBreakfast
{
    public partial class BaileysForm : Form
    {
        public BaileysForm()
        {
            InitializeComponent();
        }
    }
}
```

Figure 11-41 The Form1.cs code

2. In the Solution Explorer at the right side of the screen, double-click the **Form1.Designer.cs** filename. Scroll to the gray rectangle that contains **Windows Form Designer generated code** and click the node to its left to expose the hidden code. (You can drag the bottom border of the code window to expose more of the code or you can scroll to see all of it.) As Figure 11-42 shows, `welcomeLabel`, `rateLabel`, and `BaileysForm` objects have been declared and assigned the attributes you provided for them.

```
BedAndBreakfast.BaileysForm                              InitializeComponent()

        private void InitializeComponent()
        {
            this.welcomeLabel = new System.Windows.Forms.Label();
            this.rateLabel = new System.Windows.Forms.Label();
            this.SuspendLayout();
            //
            // welcomeLabel
            //
            this.welcomeLabel.AutoSize = true;
            this.welcomeLabel.Font = new System.Drawing.Font("Microsoft Sans Serif", 18F, System.Drawing.
            this.welcomeLabel.Location = new System.Drawing.Point(30, 25);
            this.welcomeLabel.Name = "welcomeLabel";
            this.welcomeLabel.Size = new System.Drawing.Size(229, 29);
            this.welcomeLabel.TabIndex = 0;
            this.welcomeLabel.Text = "Welcome to Bailey\'s";
            //
            // rateLabel
            //
            this.rateLabel.AutoSize = true;
            this.rateLabel.Font = new System.Drawing.Font("Microsoft Sans Serif", 12F, System.Drawing.Fon
            this.rateLabel.Location = new System.Drawing.Point(80, 80);
            this.rateLabel.Name = "rateLabel";
            this.rateLabel.Size = new System.Drawing.Size(121, 20);
            this.rateLabel.TabIndex = 1;
            this.rateLabel.Text = "Check our rates";
            //
            // BaileysForm
            //
            this.AutoScaleDimensions = new System.Drawing.SizeF(6F, 13F);
            this.AutoScaleMode = System.Windows.Forms.AutoScaleMode.Font;
            this.BackColor = System.Drawing.Color.Yellow;
            this.ClientSize = new System.Drawing.Size(284, 264);
            this.Controls.Add(this.mealButton);
            this.Controls.Add(this.lincolnBox);
            this.Controls.Add(this.belleAireBox);
            this.Controls.Add(this.rateLabel);
```

Figure 11-42 Part of the Form1.Designer.cs code

3. In the Solution Explorer, double-click the **Program.cs** filename to view the `Main()` method for the application. The method contains just three statements; each is a method call. Click the **Form1.cs [Design] tab** to return to the Design view for the `Form`.

4. Next, change the `BackColor` property of the Bailey's Bed and Breakfast `Form`. Click the **Form** or click the list box of components at the top of the Properties window and select **BaileysForm**. In the Properties list, click the **BackColor** property to see its list of choices. Choose the **Custom** tab and select **Yellow** in the third row of available colors. Click the **Form**, notice the color change, and then view the code in the Form1.Designer.cs file. Locate the statement that changes the `BackColor` of the `Form` to `Yellow`. As you continue to design `Form`s, periodically check the code to confirm your changes and better learn C#.

5. Save the project.

6. If you want to take a break at this point, close Visual Studio.

ADDING CheckBoxES TO A Form

In the next steps, you will add two CheckBoxes to the BedAndBreakfast Form. These controls allow the user to select an available room and view information about it.

To add CheckBoxes to a Form:

1. Open the BedAndBreakfast project in Visual Studio, if it is not still open on your screen.

2. In the Design view of the Bed And Breakfast project in the Visual Studio IDE, drag a CheckBox onto the Form below the "Check our rates" Label. (See Figure 11-43 for its approximate placement.)

3. Change the Text property of the CheckBox to **BelleAire Suite**. Change the Name of the property to **belleAireBox**. Drag a second CheckBox onto the Form beneath the first one. Change its Text property to **Lincoln Room** and its Name to **lincolnBox**.

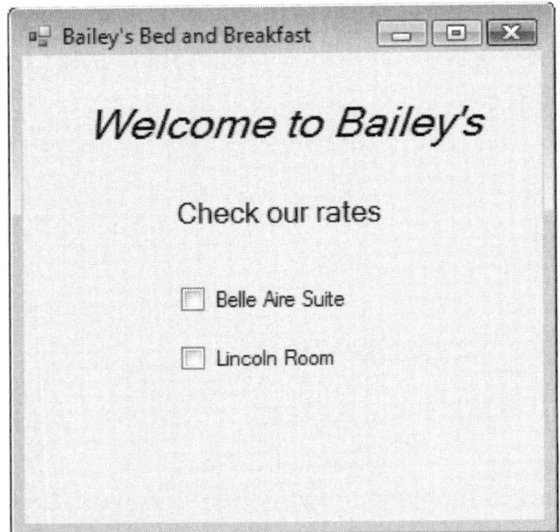

Figure 11-43 BedAndBreakfast Form with two CheckBoxes

4. Next, you will create two new Forms: one that appears when the user selects the BelleAire CheckBox and one that appears when the user selects the Lincoln CheckBox. Click **Project** on the menu bar, then click **Add New Item**. In the Add New Item window, click **Windows Form**. In the Name text box at the bottom of the window, type **BelleAireForm**. See Figure 11-44.

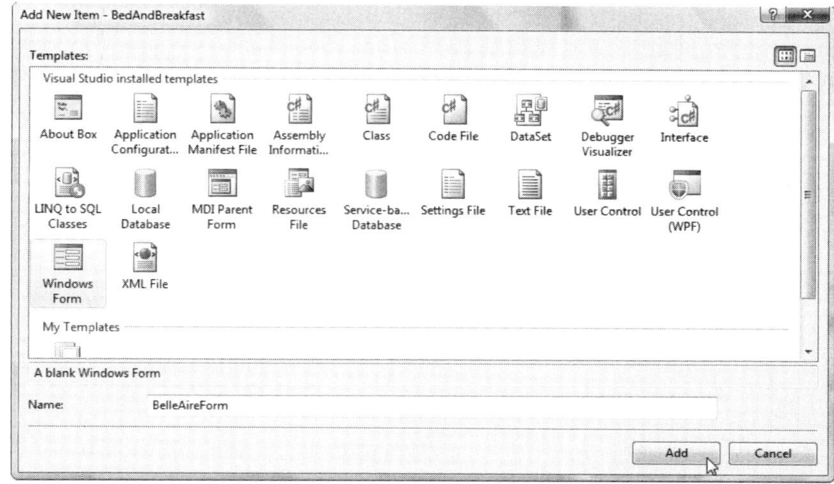

Figure 11-44 The Add New Item window

5. Click the **Add** button. A new `Form` is added to the project, and its title bar contains *BelleAireForm*. Save the project (and continue to do so periodically).

6. Change the `BackColor` property of the `Form` to `Yellow` to match the `welcomeForm`.

7. Drag a `Label` onto the `Form`, using Figure 11-45 as a guide to approximate its placement. Change the `Name` of the `Label` to **belleAireDescriptionLabel**. Change the `Text` property of the `Label` to contain the following: **The BelleAire Suite has two bedrooms, two baths and a private balcony**. Click the arrow on the text property to type the long label message on two lines. Adjust the size of the `Label` if necessary to resemble Figure 11-45. Drag a second `Label` onto the `Form`, name it **belleAirePriceLabel**, and type the price as the `Text` property: **$199.95 per night**.

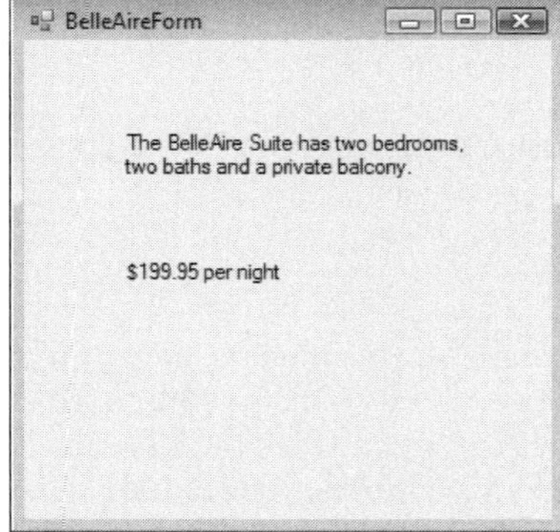

Figure 11-45 `BelleAireForm` with two `Label`s

8. Select the **Pointer** tool from the Toolbox at the left of the screen. Drag it to encompass both Labels. In the Properties list, select the **Font** property to change the Font for both Controls at once. Choose a pleasing Font. Figure 11-46 shows **10-point Regular Papyrus**; you might choose a different font. Adjust the positions of the Labels if necessary to achieve a pleasing effect.

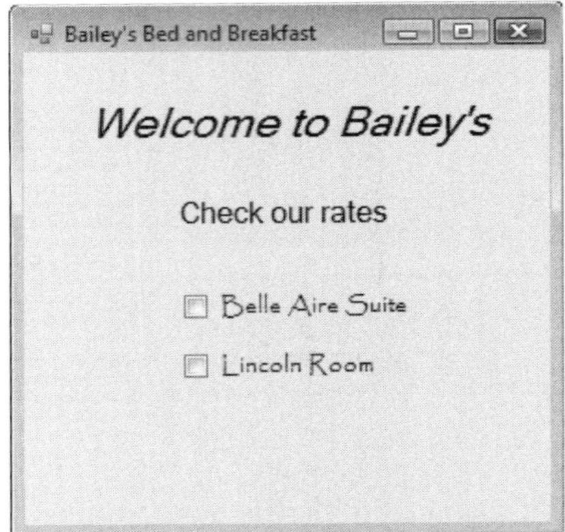

Figure 11-46 Font changed for the Labels

9. In the Solution Explorer at the right side of the screen, double-click **Form1.cs**. Alternatively, click the **Form1** tab at the top of the Designer screen. Double-click the **BelleAire Suite CheckBox**. The program code (the method shell for the default event of a CheckBox) appears in the IDE main window. Within the belleAireBox_CheckedChanged() method, add an if statement that determines whether the BelleAire CheckBox is checked. If it is checked, create a new instance of BelleAireForm and display it.

```
private void belleAireBox_CheckedChanged(object sender,
   EventArgs e)
{
    if (belleAireBox.Checked)
    {
        BelleAireForm belleAireForm = new BelleAireForm();
        belleAireForm.ShowDialog();
    }
}
```

10. Save and then execute the program by selecting **Debug** from the main menu, then **Start Without Debugging**. The main Bed and Breakfast Form appears. Click the **BelleAire Suite CheckBox**. The BelleAire Form appears. Dismiss the Form. Click the **Lincoln Room CheckBox**. Nothing happens because you have not yet written event code for this CheckBox. When you click the **BelleAire Suite CheckBox** again, the BelleAire form reappears. Dismiss the BelleAire Form.

11. When you dismiss the BelleAire `Form`, the BelleAire `CheckBox` remains checked. To see it appear as unchecked after its `Form` is dismissed, dismiss the program's main form (Bailey's Bed and Breakfast) and add a third statement within the `if` block in the `CheckedChanged()` message as follows:

```
belleAireBox.Checked = false;
```

That way, whenever the `CheckedChanged()` method executes because the `belleAireBox` was checked, it will become unchecked.

12. Save the project, then execute it again. When you select the BelleAire `CheckBox`, view the `Form`, and dismiss it, the `CheckBox` appears unchecked and is ready to check again. Dismiss the BedAndBreakfast `Form`.

13. Click **Project** on the menu bar and then click **Add New Item**. Click **Windows Form** and enter its `Name`: **LincolnForm**. When the new `Form` appears, change its `Name` property to **LincolnForm** and its `Text` property to **Lincoln Room**. Then add two `Label`s to the `Form` and provide appropriate `Name` properties for them. Change the `Text` on the first `Label` to: **Return to the 1850s in this lovely room with private bath**. The second should be: **$110.00 per night**. Change the `Form`'s `BackColor` property to **White**. Change the `Font` to match the `Font` on the BelleAire `Form`. See Figure 11-47.

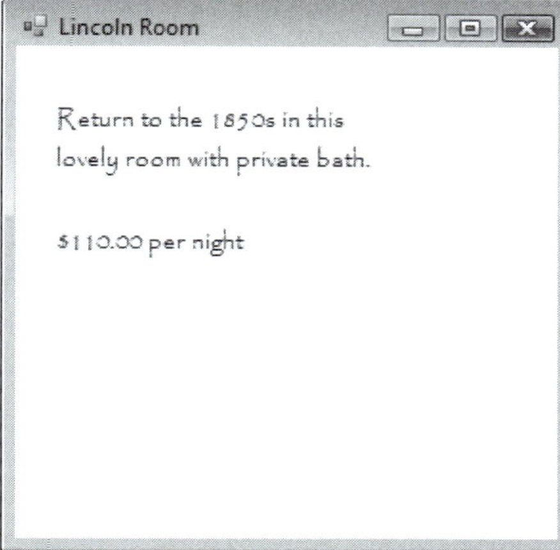

Figure 11-47 The `LincolnForm`

14. From the Toolbox, drag a `PictureBox` onto the `Form`. Select its **Image** property. A dialog box allows you to browse for an image. Find the AbeLincoln file on your Student Disk and select **Import**. Adjust the size of the `Form` and the sizes and positions of the labels and picture box so that everything looks attractive on the `Form`. See Figure 11-48.

Figure 11-48 `LincolnForm` with `Image` in `PictureBox`

> **NOTE** The AbeLincoln file was obtained at *www.free-graphics.com*. You can visit the site and download other images to use in your own applications. You should also search the Web for "free clip art" and similar phrases.

15. In the Solution Explorer, double-click **Form1.cs** or click the **Form1.cs[Design] tab** at the top of the design screen. On the Bed and Breakfast `Form`, double-click the Lincoln Room `CheckBox`, and add the following `if` statement to the `lincolnBox_CheckedChanged()` method:

```csharp
private void lincolnBox_CheckedChanged(object sender,
    EventArgs e)
{
    if (lincolnBox.Checked)
    {
        LincolnForm lincolnForm = new LincolnForm();
        lincolnForm.ShowDialog();
        lincolnBox.Checked = false;
    }
}
```

16. Save the project and then execute it. When the Bed and Breakfast `Form` appears, click either `CheckBox`—the appropriate informational `Form` appears. Close it and then click the other `CheckBox`. Again, the appropriate `Form` appears.

17. Close all forms. If you are taking a break, exit Visual Studio.

ADDING RadioButtons TO A Form

Next you will add more Controls to the Bed And Breakfast Form. You generally use RadioButtons when a user must select from mutually exclusive options.

To add RadioButtons to the project:

1. Open the BedAndBreakfast project if it is not still open. In the Design view of the main Form, add a Button to the Form, using Figure 11-49 as a general guide to locations. Change the Button's Name property to **mealButton** and the Button's Text to **Click for meal options**.

Figure 11-49 BedAndBreakfast Form with an added Button

2. From the main menu, select **Project**, click **Add New Item**, and click **Windows Form**. Name the Form **BreakfastOptionForm** and click **Add**. On the new Form, make the following changes:

   » Drag a Label onto the Form. Name it appropriately and set its Text to **Select your breakfast option**.

   » Drag three RadioButtons onto the Form. Set their respective Text properties to **Continental**, **Full**, and **Deluxe**. Set their respective Names to **contBreakfastButton**, **fullBreakfastButton**, and **deluxeBreakfastButton**.

   » Drag a Label onto the Form, then set its Text to **Price:** and its Name to **priceLabel**. Make its Font property a little larger than the Font for the other Form components.

See Figure 11-50 for approximate placement of all these Controls.

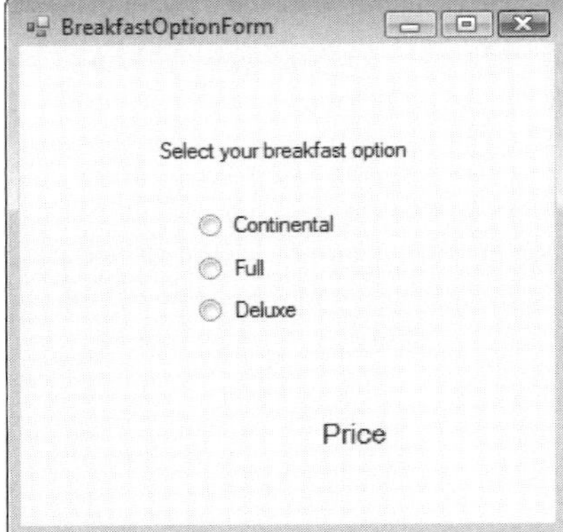

Figure 11-50 Developing the `BreakfastOptionForm`

3. Double-click the title bar of the `BreakfastOptionForm`. You generate a method named `BreakfastOptionForm_Load()`. Within this method, you can type statements that execute each time the `Form` is created. Add the following statements within the `BreakfastOptionForm` class, which declare three constants representing prices for different breakfast options. Within the `BreakfastOptionForm_Load()` method, set the `priceLabel Text` to the lowest price by default when the `Form` loads.

```
public partial class BreakfastOptionForm : Form
{
    private const double CONT_BREAKFAST_PRICE = 6.00;
    private const double FULL_BREAKFAST_PRICE = 9.95;
    private const double DELUXE_BREAKFAST_PRICE = 16.50;
    public BreakfastOptionForm()
    {
        InitializeComponent();
    }

    private void BreakfastOptionForm_Load
      (object sender, EventArgs e)
    {
        priceLabel.Text = "Price: " +
            CONT_BREAKFAST_PRICE .ToString("C");
    }
}
```

4. Return to the Design view for the BreakfastOption `Form` and double-click the **Continental breakfast** `RadioButton`. When you see the generated `CheckedChanged()` method, add a statement that sets `priceLabel` to the continental breakfast price when the user makes that selection.

```
private void contBreakfastButton _CheckedChanged
    (object sender, EventArgs e)
{
    priceLabel.Text = "Price: " +
        CONT_BREAKFAST_PRICE.ToString("C");
}
```

5. Return to the Design view for the `BreakfastOptionForm`, double-click the **Full breakfast** `RadioButton`, and add a statement to the generated method that sets the `priceLabel` to the full breakfast price when the user makes that selection.

```
private void fullBreakfastButton_CheckedChanged
    (object sender, EventArgs e)
{
    priceLabel.Text = "Price: " +
        FULL_BREAKFAST_PRICE.ToString("C");
}
```

6. Return to the Design view for the `BreakfastOptionForm`, double-click the **Deluxe breakfast** `RadioButton`, and add a statement to the generated method that sets the `priceLabel` to the deluxe breakfast price when the user makes that selection.

```
private void deluxeBreakfastButton_CheckedChanged
    (object sender, EventArgs e)
{
    priceLabel.Text = "Price: " +
        DELUXE_BREAKFAST_PRICE.ToString("C");
}
```

7. In the Solution Explorer, double-click the **Form1.cs file** to view the original `Form`. Double-click the **Click for meal options** `Button`; when the `Click()` method is generated, add the following code so that the `BreakfastOptionForm` is loaded when a user clicks the `Button`:

```
private void mealButton_Click(object sender,
    EventArgs e)
{
    BreakfastOptionForm breakfastForm = new
        BreakfastOptionForm();
    breakfastForm.ShowDialog();
}
```

8. Save the project and execute it. When the `BedAndBreakfast Form` appears, confirm that the BelleAire Suite and Lincoln Room `CheckBoxes` still work correctly, displaying their information `Forms` when they are clicked. Then click the **Click for meal options** `Button`. By default, the Continental breakfast option is chosen, as shown in Figure 11-51, so the price is $6.00. Click the other `RadioButton` options to confirm that each correctly changes the breakfast price.

Figure 11-51 The `BreakfastOptionForm` with Continental breakfast `RadioButton` selected

9. Dismiss all the `Forms` and close Visual Studio.

CHAPTER SUMMARY

» The `Control` class provides definitions for GUI objects such as `Forms` and `Buttons`. There are 26 direct descendants of `Control` and additional descendants of those classes. Each `Control` has more than 80 `public` properties and 20 `protected` ones. For example, each `Control` has a `Font` and a `ForeColor` that dictate how its text is displayed, and each `Control` has a `Width` and `Height`.

» A `Label` is one of the simplest GUI `Control` objects you can place on a `Form`. The `Label` class descends directly from `Control`. Typically, you use a `Label` to provide descriptive text for another `Control` object or to display other text information on a `Form`. You can create a `Label` by writing code or by using the Visual Studio IDE.

» You use the `Font` class to change the appearance of printed text on your `Forms`. When designing a `Label` or other `Control` on a `Form`, it is easiest to select a `Font` from the Properties list. The `Font` class includes a number of overloaded constructors.

» A `LinkLabel` is similar to a `Label`; it is a child of `Label`, but it provides the additional capability to link the user to other sources, such as Web pages or files.

» The `Color` class contains a wide variety of predefined `Color`s that you can use with your `Control`s.

» `CheckBox` objects are GUI widgets the user can click to select or deselect an option. When a `Form` contains multiple `CheckBoxes`, any number of them can be checked or unchecked at the same time. `RadioButtons` are similar to `CheckBoxes`, except that when they are placed on a `Form`, only one `RadioButton` can be selected at a time—selecting any `RadioButton` automatically deselects the others. `CheckBox` and `RadioButton` objects both have a `Checked` property whose value is `true` or `false`.

» A `PictureBox` is a `Control` in which you can display graphics from a bitmap, icon, JPEG, GIF, or other image file type. Just as with a `Button` or a `Label`, you can easily add a `PictureBox` by dragging its `Control` onto the `Form` in the Visual Studio IDE.

» `ListBox`, `ComboBox`, and `CheckedListBox` objects descend from `ListControl`. The `ListBox Control` enables you to display a list of items that the user can select by clicking. With a `ListBox`, you allow the user to make a single selection or multiple selections by setting the `SelectionMode` property appropriately. A `ComboBox` is similar to a `ListBox`, except that it displays an additional editing field to allow the user to select from the list or to enter new text. A `CheckedListBox` is also similar to a `ListBox`, with check boxes appearing to the left of each desired item.

» The `MonthCalendar` and `DateTimePicker Controls` allow you to retrieve date and time information.

» When you place `Controls` on a `Form` in the IDE, you can drag them to any location to achieve the effect you want. When you drag multiple `Controls` onto a `Form`, blue snap lines appear and help you align new `Controls` with others already in place. You also can use the `Location` property in the Properties list to specify a location. `Anchor`, `Dock`, and `Padding` properties help you determine a `Control`'s size and position in the `Form`. A `Form` also has a `MinimumSize` property and a `MaximumSize` property. Each has two values—`Width` and `Height`. Many types of `ContainerControls` are available to hold `Controls`. For example, you can use a `GroupBox` or `Panel` to group related `Controls` on a `Form`. When you move a `GroupBox` or `Panel`, all its `Controls` are moved as a group.

» Most programs you use in a Windows environment contain a menu strip, which is a horizontal list of general options that appears under the title bar of a `Form` or `Window`. When you click an item in a menu strip, you might initiate an action. More frequently, you see a list box that contains more specific options. Each of these might initiate an action, or it might lead to another menu. You can add a `MenuStrip Control` object to any `Form` you create.

» If you examine the Visual Studio IDE or search through the Visual Studio documentation, you will find many other `Controls` you can use. If you click Project on the main menu and click Add New Item, you can add extra `Forms`, `Files`, `Controls`, and other elements to a project.

KEY TERMS

Widgets are interactive controls such as labels, scroll bars, check boxes, and radio buttons.

The **Control** class provides the definitions for GUI objects.

The **Component** class provides containment and cleanup for other objects.

A **Label** is a `Control` object that typically provides descriptive text for another `Control` object or displays other text information on a `Form`.

In Visual Studio, a **method node** is a small box that appears to the left of code; you use it to expand or collapse code.

The **Font** class is used to change the appearance of printed text on Forms.

A **LinkLabel** is similar to a Label, but it provides the additional capability to link the user to other sources, such as Web pages or files.

The **default event** for a Control is the one generated when you double-click it while designing it in the IDE. It is the method you are most likely to alter when you use the Control, as well as the event that users most likely expect to generate when they encounter the Control in a working application.

The **Color** class contains a wide variety of predefined colors to use with Controls.

CheckBox objects are GUI widgets the user can click to select or deselect an option. When a Form contains multiple CheckBoxes, any number of them can be checked or unchecked at the same time.

RadioButtons are similar to CheckBoxes, except that when they are placed on a Form, only one RadioButton can be selected at a time—selecting any RadioButton automatically deselects the others.

A **PictureBox** is a Control in which you can display graphics from a bitmap, icon, JPEG, GIF, or other image file type.

The **ListBox** Control enables you to display a list of items that the user can select by clicking.

A **ComboBox** is similar to a ListBox, except that it displays an additional editing field that allows a user to select from the list or enter new text.

A **CheckedListBox** is also similar to a ListBox, with check boxes appearing to the left of each desired item.

The **MonthCalendar** and **DateTimePicker** Controls allow you to retrieve date and time information.

Snap lines appear in a design environment to help you align new Controls with others already in place.

Setting the **Anchor property** causes a Control to remain at a fixed distance from the side of a container when the user resizes it.

Setting the **Dock property** attaches a Control to the side of a container so that the Control stretches when the container's size is adjusted.

A Form has a **Padding property** that specifies the distance between docked Controls and the edges of the Form.

A Form also has a **MinimumSize property** and a **MaximumSize property**. Each has two values—Width and Height.

A **GroupBox** or **Panel** can be used to group related Controls on a Form.

A **menu strip** is a horizontal list of general options that appears under the title bar of a Form or Window. When you click an item in a menu strip, you might initiate an action. More frequently, you see a list box that contains more specific options.

You can add a **MenuStrip** Control object to any Form you create.

REVIEW QUESTIONS

1. `Labels`, `Buttons`, and `CheckBoxes` are all ___________ .

   a. GUI objects

   b. `Controls`

   c. widgets

   d. all of these

2. All `Control` objects descend from ___________ .

   a. `Form`

   b. `Component`

   c. `ButtonBase`

   d. all of these

3. Which of the following is most like a `RadioButton`?

   a. `ListControl`

   b. `CheckedListBox`

   c. `PictureBox`

   d. `Button`

4. Which of the following is not a commonly used `Control` property?

   a. `BackColor`

   b. `Language`

   c. `Location`

   d. `Size`

5. The `Control` you frequently use to provide descriptive text for another `Control` object is a ___________ .

   a. `Form`

   b. `Label`

   c. `CheckBox`

   d. `MessageBox`

6. Which of the following creates a `Label` named `firstLabel`?

   a. `firstLabel = new firstLabel();`

   b. `Label = new firstLabel();`

   c. `Label firstLabel = new Label();`

   d. `Label firstLabel = Label();`

7. The property that determines what the user reads on a `Label` is the ___________ property.

   a. `Text`

   b. `Label`

   c. `Phrase`

   d. `Setting`

8. Which of the following correctly creates a `Font`?

   a. `Font myFont = new Font("Arial", 14F, FontStyle.Bold);`

   b. `Font myFont = new Font("Courier", 13.6);`

   c. `myFont = Font new Font("TimesRoman", FontStyle.Italic);`

   d. `Font myFont = Font(20, "Helvetica", Underlined);`

9. The default event for a `Control` is the one that ___________ .

    a. occurs automatically whether a user manipulates the `Control` or not

    b. is generated when you double-click the `Control` while designing it in the IDE

    c. requires no parameters

    d. occurs when a user clicks the `Control` with a mouse

10. Assume you have created a `Label` named `myLabel`. Which of the following sets `myLabel`'s background color to green?

    a. `myLabel = BackColor.System.Drawing.Color.Green;`

    b. `myLabel.BackColor = System.Drawing.Color.Green;`

    c. `myLabel.Green = System.DrawingColor;`

    d. `myLabel.Background = new Color.Green;`

11. A difference between `CheckBox` and `RadioButton` objects is ___________ .

    a. `RadioButtons` descend from `ButtonBase`; `CheckBoxes` do not

    b. only one `RadioButton` can be selected at a time

    c. only one `CheckBox` can appear on a `Form` at a time

    d. `RadioButtons` cannot be placed in a `GroupBox`; `CheckBoxes` can

12. The `Checked` property of a `RadioButton` can hold the values ___________ .

    a. `true` and `false`   c. 0 and 1

    b. `Checked` and `Unchecked`   d. `Yes`, `No`, and `Undetermined`

13. The `Control` in which you can display a bitmap or JPEG image is a(n) ___________ .

    a. `DisplayModule`   c. `BitmapControl`

    b. `ImageHolder`   d. `PictureBox`

14. `ListBox`, `ComboBox`, and `CheckedListBox` objects descend from the same family: ___________ .

    a. `ListControl`   c. `ButtonBase`

    b. `List`   d. `ListBase`

15. Which of the following properties is associated with a `ListBox` but not a `Button`?

    a. `BackColor`   c. `Location`

    b. `SelectedItem`   d. `IsSelected`

16. With a `ListBox` you can allow the user to choose __________ .

    a. only a single option   c. either of these

    b. multiple selections   d. none of these

17. You can add items to a `ListBox` by using the __________ method.

    a. `Add()`   c. `List()`

    b. `Append()`   d. `AddRange()`

18. A `ListBox`'s `SelectedItem` property contains __________ .

    a. the position of the currently selected item

    b. the value of the currently selected item

    c. a Boolean value indicating whether an item is currently selected

    d. a count of the number of currently selected items

19. When you create a `ListBox`, by default its `SelectionMode` is __________ .

    a. `Simple`   c. `One`

    b. `MultiExtended` d. `false`

20. A horizontal list of general options that appears under the title bar of a `Form` or `Window` is a __________ .

    a. task bar   c. menu strip

    b. subtitle bar d. list box

EXERCISES

1. Create a `Form` that contains two `Buttons`, one labeled Stop and one labeled Go. Add a `Label` telling the user to click a button. When the user clicks Stop, change the `BackColor` of the `Form` to Red; when the user clicks Go, change the `BackColor` of the `Form` to Green. Save the project as **StopGo**.

2. Create a `Form` that contains at least five `Button` objects, each labeled with a color. When the user clicks a `Button`, change the `BackColor` of the `Form` appropriately. Save the project as **FiveColors**.

3. Create a `Form` that contains at least five `RadioButton` objects, each labeled with a color. When the user clicks a `RadioButton`, change the `BackColor` of the `Form` appropriately. Save the project as **FiveColors2**.

4. Create a `Form` for a video store that contains a `ListBox` with the titles of at least eight videos available to rent. Provide directions that tell users they can choose as many videos as they want by holding down the Ctrl key while making selections. When the user clicks a `Button` to indicate the choices are final, display the total rental price, which is $2.50 per video. If the user selects or deselects items and clicks the button again, make sure the total is updated correctly. Save the project as **Video**.

5. Create a `Form` with two `ListBoxes`—one contains at least four `Font` names and the other contains at least four `Font` sizes. Let the first item in each list be the default selection if the user fails to make a selection. Allow only one selection per `ListBox`. After the user clicks a `Button`, display "Hello" in the selected `Font` and size. Save the project as **FontSelector**.

6. Create a `Form` for a car rental company. Allow the user to choose a car style (compact, standard, or luxury) and a number of days (1 through 7). After the user makes selections, display the total rental charge, which is $19.95 per day for a compact car, $24.95 per day for a standard car, and $39 per day for a luxury car. Use the `Controls` that you think are best for each function. Label items appropriately and use fonts and colors to achieve an attractive design. Save the project as **CarRental**.

7. Create a `Form` for a restaurant. Allow the user to choose one item from at least three options in each of the following categories—appetizer, entrée, and dessert. Assign a different price to each selection and display the total when the user clicks a `Button`. Use the `Controls` that you think are best for each function. Label items appropriately and use fonts and colors to achieve an attractive design. Save the project as **Restaurant**.

8. Create a `Form` for an automobile dealer. Include options for at least three car models. After users make a selection, proceed to a new `Form` that contains information about the selected model. Use the `Controls` that you decide are best for each function. Label items on the `Form` appropriately and use fonts and colors to achieve an attractive design. Save the project as **CarDealer**.

9. Create a spreadsheet and then include a few numbers in it that represent an annual budget. Create a `Form` that includes two `LinkLabels`. One opens the spreadsheet for viewing, and the other visits your favorite Web site. Include `Labels` on the `Form` to explain each link. Save the project as **AnnualBudget**.

10. Create a `Form` for Nina's Cookie Source. Allow the user to select from at least three types of cookies, each with a different price per dozen. Allow the user to select 1/2, 1, 2, or 3 dozen cookies. Adjust the final displayed price as the user chooses cookie types and quantities. Also allow the user to select an order date from a `MonthCalendar`. Assuming that shipping takes three days, display the estimated arrival date for the order. Include as many labels as necessary so the user understands how to use the `Form`. Save the project as **NinasCookieSource**.

11. Using the `MenuStripDemo` project on your Student Disk (see Figure 11-36), add appropriate functionality to the currently unprogrammed menu options (Small in the Font menu and the three options in the Color menu). Add at least three other menu options to the program, either vertically, horizontally, or both. Save the modified project as **MenuStripDemo2**.

DEBUGGING EXERCISES

Each of the following projects in the Chapter.11 folder on your Student Disk has syntax and/or logical errors. In each case, determine the problem and fix the program. After you correct the errors, save each project using the same name preceded with *Fixed*. For example, DebugEleven1 will become FixedDebugEleven1.

    a. DebugEleven1

    b. DebugEleven2

    c. DebugEleven3

    d. DebugEleven4

UP FOR DISCUSSION

1. Making exciting, entertaining, professional-looking GUI applications becomes easier once you learn to include graphics images, as you did when you learned about `PictureBox` objects in this chapter. You can copy graphics images from many locations on the Web. Should there be any restrictions on what graphics you use? Does it make a difference if you are writing programs for your own enjoyment, as opposed to putting them on the Web where others can see them? Should restrictions be different for using photographs versus using drawings? Does it matter if the photographs contain recognizable people? Would you impose any restrictions on images posted to your organization's Web site?

2. Should you be allowed to store computer games on your computer at work? If so, should you be allowed to play the games at work? If so, should there be any restrictions on when you can play them?

3. Suppose you discover a way to breach security in a Web site so that visitors might access information that belongs to the company. Should you be allowed to publish your findings? Should you notify the organization? Should the organization pay you a reward for discovering the breach? If they do, would this encourage you to search for more potential security violations? Suppose the newly available information on the Web site is relatively innocuous—for example, office telephone numbers of company executives. Suppose it is not—for example, home telephone numbers for the same executives. Does this make a difference?

12

HANDLING EVENTS

In this chapter you will:

Learn about event handling
Learn about delegates
Create composed delegates
Declare your own events and handlers
Use the built-in `EventHandler`
Handle `Control` component events
Handle mouse events
Handle keyboard events
Manage multiple `Controls`
Learn how to continue your exploration of `Controls`
  and events

Throughout this book, you have learned how to create C# programs that perform a variety of tasks. In the last few chapters, you expanded your repertoire from creating functional but dull-looking command-line applications to creating attractive and interactive GUI programs.

The aspect of Windows widgets that makes them useful is their ability to cause events when a user interacts with them. In the last two chapters, you have seen `Controls` that respond to a user-initiated event—for example, a mouse click. In those chapters, you provided actions for `Controls`' default events. In this chapter, you will expand your understanding of the event-handling process. You will learn more about the object that triggers an event and the object that captures and responds to that event. You also will learn about delegates—objects that act as intermediaries in transferring messages from senders to receivers. You will create delegates and manage interactive events. You will learn to manage multiple events for a single `Control` and to manage multiple `Controls` for a project.

EVENT HANDLING

In C#, an event occurs when something interesting happens to an object. When you create a class, you decide exactly what is considered "interesting." For example, when you create a `Form`, you might decide to respond to a user clicking a `Button` but ignore a user who clicks a `Label`—clicking the `Label` is just not "interesting" to the `Form`.

You use an event to notify a client program when something happens to a class object the program is using. Events are used frequently in GUI programs—for example, you notify a program when the user clicks a `Button` or chooses an option from a `ListBox`. In addition, you can use events with ordinary classes that do not represent GUI controls. When an object's client might want to know about any changes that occur in the object, events enable the object to signal the client.

In Chapter 10, you learned that when a user interacts with a GUI object, an event is generated that causes the program to perform a task. GUI programs are **event driven**—an event such as a button click "drives" the program to perform a task. Programmers also say that a button click **raises an event**, **fires an event**, or **triggers an event**. A method that performs a task in response to an event is an **event handler**.

For example, Figure 12-1 shows a `Form` that contains a `Label` and a `Button`. The following changes are the only ones that have been made to the default `Form` in the IDE:

» The `Size` property has been adjusted to 500, 120.

» A `Label` has been dragged onto the `Form`, its `Name` property has been set to `helloLabel`, its `Text` property has been set to "Hello", and its `Font` has been increased to 9.75.

» A `Button` has been dragged onto the `Form`, its `Name` property has been set to `changeButton`, and its `Text` property has been set to "Change Label".

Figure 12-1 A Form with a Label and a Button

If you double-click the button on the form in the IDE, you generate the following empty method in the program code:

```
private void changeButton_Click(object sender, EventArgs e)
{
}
```

The changeButton_Click() method is an event handler. Conventionally, event handlers are named using the identifier of the Control (in this case, changeButton), an underscore, and the name of the event type (in this case, Click). You can create your own methods to handle events and provide any names for them, but the names should follow these conventions.

Suppose that when a user clicks the button, you want the text on the label to change from "Hello" to "Goodbye". You can write the following code within the event handler:

```
private void changeButton_Click(object sender, EventArgs e)
{
    helloLabel.Text = "Goodbye";
}
```

Then, when you run the application and click the button, the output appears as shown in Figure 12-2.

Figure 12-2 Output of EventDemo application after user clicks button

The event-handler method is also known as an **event receiver**. The control that generates an event is an **event sender**. The first parameter in the list for the event receiver method is an object named `sender`; it is a reference to the object that generated the event. For example, if you code the event handler as follows, the output appears as in Figure 12-3.

```
private void changeButton_Click(object sender, EventArgs e)
{
    helloLabel.Text = sender.ToString();
}
```

Figure 12-3 `EventDemo` application modified to display sender information

The label in Figure 12-3 shows that the sender of the event is an instance of `System.Windows.Forms.Button`, whose `Text` property is "Change Label".

The second parameter in the event-handler parameter list is a reference to an event arguments object of type `EventArgs`; in this method, the `EventArgs` argument is named e. **EventArgs** is a C# class designed for holding event information. If you change the code in the event handler to the following, then run the program and click the button, you see the output in Figure 12-4:

```
private void changeButton_Click(object sender, EventArgs e)
{
    helloLabel.Text = e.ToString();
}
```

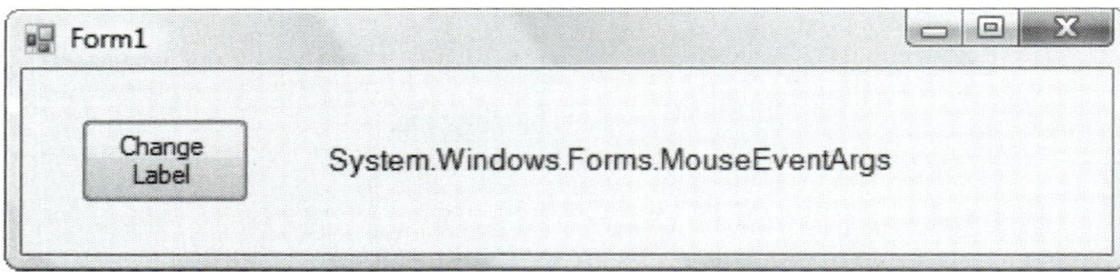

Figure 12-4 `EventDemo` application modified to display `EventArgs` information

In Figure 12-4, you can see that the e object is a `MouseEventArgs` object. That makes sense, because the user used the mouse to click the `Button`.

As you learned in Chapter 10, you can examine all the code generated for the application that creates the `Form` shown in Figure 12-4. When you open the Designer.cs file in the IDE and expand the Windows Form Designer generated code, you see comments as well as statements

```
//
//  changeButton
//
this.changeButton.Location = new System.Drawing.Point(21, 33);
this.changeButton.Name = "changeButton";
this.changeButton.Size = new System.Drawing.Size(75, 23);
this.changeButton.TabIndex = 1;
this.changeButton.Text = "Change Label";
this.changeButton.UseVisualStyleBackColor = true;
this.changeButton.Click += new
    System.EventHandler(this.changeButton_Click);
```

Figure 12-5 Code involving `changeButton` generated by Visual Studio

that set the `Controls`' properties. For example, the code generated for `changeButton` appears in Figure 12-5. You can recognize that such features as the button's `Location`, `Name`, and `Size` have been set.

The most unusual statement in the section of `changeButton` code is shaded in Figure 12-5; this statement concerns the **Click event**, which is generated when `changeButton` is clicked by a user. This statement is necessary because `changeButton` does not automatically "know" what method will handle its events—C# and all other .NET languages allow you to choose your own names for event-handling methods for events generated by GUI objects. In other words, there is no requirement that the event-handling method be named `changeButton_Click()`. You *could* create your program so that when the user clicks the button, the event-handling method is named `calculatePayroll()`, `changeLabel()`, or any other identifier for a method you could then write. Of course, you do not want to make such a change; it is clearest if the method that executes when `changeButton` is clicked is named `changeButton_Click()`. However, that convention is not required by the compiler, so the shaded statement in Figure 12-5 is necessary to identify the method that will handle the `Click` event. The shaded statement indicates that, for this program, the method named `changeButton_Click()` is the receiver for `changeButton`'s `Click` event. Programmers say the shaded method creates a delegate, or more specifically, a composed delegate. You will learn about these terms in the next two sections of this chapter.

》NOTE
The code generated in Design mode in the IDE is not meant to be altered by typing. You should modify `Control` properties through the Properties window in the IDE, not by typing in the Designer.cs file.

》NOTE
Connecting an event to its resulting actions is called **event wiring**.

》TWO TRUTHS AND A LIE: EVENT HANDLING

1. An action such as a key press or button click raises an event.
2. A method that performs a task in response to an event is an event handler.
3. The control that generates an event is an event receiver.

The false statement is #3. The control that generates an event is an event sender.

UNDERSTANDING DELEGATES

A **delegate** is an object that contains a reference to a method; object-oriented programmers would say that a delegate encapsulates a method. In government, a delegate is a representative that you authorize to make choices for you. For example, you select a delegate to a presidential nominating convention. When human delegates arrive at a convention, they are free to make choices based on current conditions. Similarly, C# delegates provide a way for a program to take alternative courses when running. When you write a method, you don't always know which actions will occur, so you give your delegates authority to run the correct methods.

> **»NOTE** In Chapter 1, you learned that encapsulation is a basic feature of object-oriented programming. Recall that encapsulation is the technique of packaging an object's attributes and methods into a cohesive unit that can then be used as an undivided entity.

After you have instantiated a C# delegate, you can pass this object to a method, which then can call the method referenced within the delegate. In other words, a delegate provides a way to pass a reference to a method as an argument to another method. For example, if `del` is a delegate that contains a reference to the method `M1()`, you can pass `del` to a new method named `MyMethod()`. Alternatively, you could create a delegate named `del` that contains a reference to a method named `M2()` and then pass this version to `MyMethod()`. When you write `MyMethod()`, you don't have to know whether it will call `M1()` or `M2()`; you only need to know that it will call whatever method is referenced within `del`.

> **»NOTE** A C# delegate is similar to a function pointer in C++. A function pointer is a variable that holds a method's memory address. In the C++ programming language, you pass a method's address to another method using a pointer variable. Java does not allow function pointers because they are dangerous—if the program alters the address, you might inadvertently execute the wrong method. C# provides a compromise between the dangers of C++ pointers and the Java ban on passing functions. Delegates allow flexible method calls but remain secure because you cannot alter the method addresses.

You declare a delegate using the keyword `delegate`, followed by an ordinary method declaration that includes a return type, method name, and argument list. For example, by entering the following statement, you can declare a delegate named `GreetingDelegate()`, which accepts a `string` argument and returns nothing:

```
delegate void GreetingDelegate(string s);
```

The `GreetingDelegate` can encapsulate any method as long as it has a `void` return type and a single `string` parameter. Any delegate can encapsulate any method that has the same return type and parameter list as the delegate. If you declare the delegate and then write a method with the same return type and parameter list, you can assign an instance of the delegate to represent it. For example, the following `Hello()` method is a `void` method that takes a `string` parameter:

```
public static void Hello(string s)
{
    Console.WriteLine("Hello, {0}!", s);
}
```

Because the `Hello()` method matches the `GreetingDelegate` definition, you can assign a reference to the `Hello()` method to a new instance of `GreetingDelegate`, as follows:

```
GreetingDelegate myDel = new GreetingDelegate(Hello);
```

Once the reference to the `Hello()` method is encapsulated in the delegate `myDel`, each of the following statements will result in the same output: "Hello, Kim!":

```
Hello("Kim");
myDel("Kim");
```

In this example, the ability to use the delegate `myDel` does not seem to provide any benefits over using a regular method call to `Hello()`. If you have a program in which you pass the delegate to a method, however, the method becomes more flexible; you gain the ability to send a reference to an appropriate method you want to execute at the time.

For example, Figure 12-6 shows a `Greeting` class that contains `Hello()` and `Goodbye()` methods. The `Main()` method declares two delegates named `firstDel` and `secondDel`.

```
using System;
delegate void GreetingDelegate(string s);
class Greeting
{
    public static void Hello(string s)
    {
        Console.WriteLine("Hello, {0}!", s);
    }
    public static void Goodbye(string s)
    {
        Console.WriteLine("Goodbye, {0}!", s);
    }
    public static void Main()
    {
        GreetingDelegate firstDel, secondDel;
        firstDel = new GreetingDelegate(Hello);
        secondDel = new GreetingDelegate(Goodbye);
        GreetMethod(firstDel, "Cathy");
        GreetMethod(secondDel, "Bob");
    }
    public static void GreetMethod
        (GreetingDelegate gd, string name)
    {
        Console.WriteLine("The greeting is:");
        gd(name);
    }
}
```

Figure 12-6 The `Greeting` program

One is instantiated using the `Hello()` method, and the other is instantiated using the `Goodbye()` method. When the `Main()` method calls `GreetMethod()` two times, it passes a different method and string each time. Figure 12-7 shows the output.

Figure 12-7 Output of the `Greeting` program

»TWO TRUTHS AND A LIE: UNDERSTANDING DELEGATES

1. A delegate is an object that contains a reference to a method.
2. A delegate provides a way to pass a reference to a method as an argument to another method.
3. Once you have created a delegate, it can encapsulate any method with the same identifier as the delegate.

The false statement is #3. Once you have created a delegate, it can encapsulate any method with the same return type and parameter list as the delegate.

CREATING COMPOSED DELEGATES

You can assign one delegate to another using the = operator. You also can use the + and += operators to combine delegates into a **composed delegate** that calls the delegates from which it is built. As an example, assume that you declare three delegates named del1, del2, and del3, and that you assign a reference to the method M1() to del1 and a reference to method M2() to del2. When the statement del3 = del1 + del2; executes, del3 becomes a delegate that executes both M1() and M2(), in that order. Only delegates with the same parameter list can be composed, and the delegates used must have a void return type. Additionally, you can use the − and −= operators to remove a delegate from a composed delegate.

Figure 12-8 shows a program that contains a composed delegate. This program contains only two changes from the Greeting program in Figure 12-6—the class name (Greeting2) and the shaded statement that creates the composed delegate. The delegate firstDel now executes two methods, Hello() and Goodbye(), whereas secondDel still executes only Goodbye(). Figure 12-9 shows the output; "Cathy" is used with two methods, but "Bob" is used with only one.

```csharp
using System;
delegate void GreetingDelegate(string s);
class Greeting2
{
   public static void Hello(string s)
   {
      Console.WriteLine("Hello, {0}!", s);
   }
   public static void Goodbye(string s)
   {
      Console.WriteLine("Goodbye, {0}!", s);
   }
   public static void Main()
   {
      GreetingDelegate firstDel, secondDel;
      firstDel = new GreetingDelegate(Hello);
      secondDel = new GreetingDelegate(Goodbye);
      firstDel += secondDel;
      GreetMethod(firstDel, "Cathy");
      GreetMethod(secondDel, "Bob");
   }
   public static void GreetMethod
      (GreetingDelegate gd, string name)
   {
      Console.WriteLine("The greeting is:");
      gd(name);
   }
}
```

Figure 12-8 The Greeting2 program

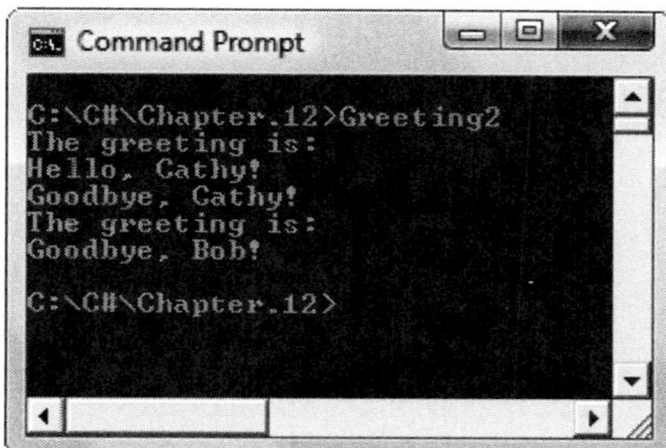

Figure 12-9 Output of the Greeting2 program

DECLARING YOUR OWN EVENTS AND HANDLERS

To declare your own event, you use a delegate. An event provides a way for a class's clients to dictate methods that should execute when an event occurs. The clients identify methods to execute by providing delegates. When an event occurs, any delegate that a client has given or passed to the event is invoked. Just like the event handlers automatically created in the IDE, each of your own event handler `delegates` requires two arguments—the object where the event was initiated (the sender) and an `EventArgs` argument. You can create an `EventArgs` object that contains event information, or you can use the `EventArgs` class static field named `Empty`, which represents an event that contains no event data. In other words, using the `Empty` field simply tells the client that an event has occurred, without specifying details. For example, you can declare a `delegate` event handler named `ChangedEventHandler`, as follows:

```
public delegate void ChangedEventHandler
    (object sender, EventArgs e);
```

The identifier `ChangedEventHandler` can be any legal identifier you choose. This delegate defines the set of arguments that will be passed to the method that handles the event. It can be used in a program that handles events.

> **»NOTE** The value of `Empty` is a read-only instance of `EventArgs`. You can pass it to a method that accepts an `EventArgs` parameter.

For example, Figure 12-10 contains a simple `Student` class that is similar to many classes you already have created. The `Student` class contains just two data fields and will generate an event when the data in either field changes.

The `Student` class in Figure 12-10 contains fields that will hold an ID number and grade point average (GPA) for a `Student`. The first shaded statement in the

```
public class Student
{
    private int idNum;
    private double gpa;
    public event ChangedEventHandler Changed;
    public int IdNum
    {
        get
        {
            return idNum;
        }
        set
        {
            idNum = value;
            OnChanged(EventArgs.Empty);
        }
    }
    public double Gpa
    {
        get
        {
            return gpa;
        }
        set
        {
            gpa = value;
            OnChanged(EventArgs.Empty);
        }
    }
    public void OnChanged(EventArgs e)
    {
        Changed(this, e);
    }
}
```

Figure 12-10 The Student class

figure defines a third Student class attribute—an event named Changed. The declaration for an event looks like a field, but instead of being an int or a double, it is a ChangedEventHandler.

The Student class event (Changed) looks like an ordinary field. However, you cannot assign values to the event as easily as you can to ordinary data fields. You can take only two actions on an event: you can compose a new delegate onto it using the += operator, and you can remove a delegate from it using the -= operator. For example, to add

>> **NOTE**
Events usually are declared as public, but you can use any accessibility modifier.

`StudentChanged` to the `Changed` event of a `Student` object named `stu`, you would write the following:

```
stu.Changed += new ChangedEventHandler(StudentChanged);
```

In the `Student` class, each `set` accessor assigns a value to the appropriate class instance field. However, when either the `idNum` or the `gpa` changes, the method in the `Student` class named `OnChanged()` is also called, using `EventArgs.Empty` as the argument. The `OnChanged()` method calls `Changed()` using two arguments—a reference to the `Student` object that was changed and the empty `EventArgs` object. Calling `Changed()` is also known as **invoking the event**.

> **»NOTE** If no client has wired a delegate to the event, the `Changed` field will be `null`, rather than referring to the delegate that should be called when the event is invoked. Therefore, programmers often check for `null` before invoking the event, as in the following example:
>
> ```
> if(Changed != null)
>     Changed(this, e);
> ```
>
> For simplicity, the example in Figure 12-10 does not bother checking for `null`.

Figure 12-11 shows an `EventListener` class that listens for `Student` events. This class contains a `Student` object that is assigned a value using the parameter to the `EventListener` class constructor. The `StudentChanged()` method is added to the `Student`'s event delegate using the `+=` operator. The `StudentChanged()` method displays a message and `Student` data.

```
class EventListener
{
    private Student stu;
    public EventListener(Student student)
    {
        stu = student;
        stu.Changed += new ChangedEventHandler
            (StudentChanged);
    }
    private void StudentChanged(object sender, EventArgs e)
    {
        Console.WriteLine("The student has changed.");
        Console.WriteLine("   ID# {0}   GPA {1}",
            stu.IdNum, stu.Gpa);
    }
}
```

Figure 12-11 The `EventListener` class

Figure 12-12 shows a program that demonstrates the `Student` and `EventListener` classes. The program contains a single `Main()` method, which declares one `Student` and registers the program to listen for events from the `Student` class. Then three assignments are made.

```
using System;
class DemoStudentEvent
{
    public static void Main()
    {
        Student oneStu = new Student();
        EventListener listener = new EventListener(oneStu);
        oneStu.IdNum = 2345;
        oneStu.IdNum = 4567;
        oneStu.Gpa = 3.2;
    }
}
```

Figure 12-12 The DemoStudentEvent program

Because this program is registered to listen for events from the Student, each change in a data field triggers an event. That is, each assignment not only changes the value of the data field, it also executes the StudentChanged() method that displays two lines of explanation. In Figure 12-13, the program output shows that an event occurs three times—once when the ID becomes 2345 (and the GPA is still 0), again when the ID becomes 4567 (and the GPA still has not changed), and a third time when the GPA becomes 3.2.

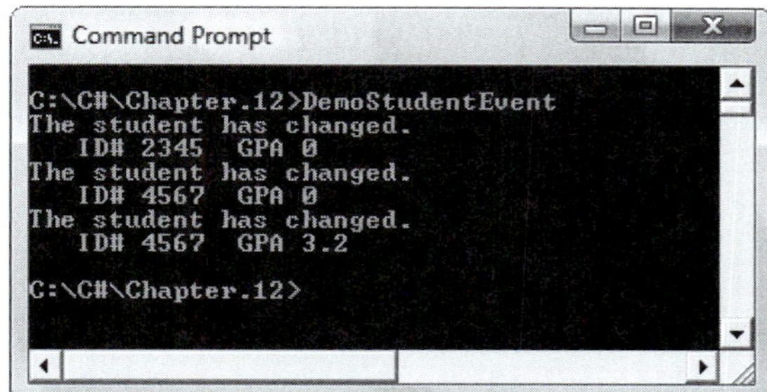

Figure 12-13 Output of the DemoStudentEvent program

»TWO TRUTHS AND A LIE: DECLARING YOUR OWN EVENTS AND HANDLERS

1. When an event occurs, any delegate that a client has given or passed to the event is invoked.
2. Built-in event handler delegates have two arguments, but those you create yourself have only one.
3. You can take only two actions on an event field: you can compose a new delegate onto the field using the += operator, and you can remove a delegate from the field using the -= operator.

The false statement is #2. Every event handler delegate requires two arguments—the object where the event was initiated (the sender) and an EventArgs argument.

USING THE BUILT-IN EventHandler

The C# language allows you to create events using any delegate type. However, the .NET Framework provides guidelines you should follow if you are developing a class that others will use. These guidelines indicate that the delegate type for an event should take exactly two parameters: a parameter indicating the source of the event, and an EventArgs parameter that encapsulates any additional information about the event. For events that do not use additional information, the .NET Framework has already defined an appropriate delegate type named **EventHandler**.

Figure 12-14 shows all the code necessary to demonstrate an EventHandler. Note the following changes from the classes used in the DemoStudentEvent program:

> » No delegate named ChangedEventHandler is declared.
> » In the first statement with shading in the Student class, the event is associated with the built-in delegate EventHandler.
> » In the second statement with shading, which appears in the EventListener class, the delegate composition uses EventHandler.

```
using System;
public class Student
{
    private int idNum;
    private double gpa;
    public event EventHandler Changed;
    public int IdNum
    {
        get
        {
            return idNum;
        }
        set
        {
            idNum = value;
            OnChanged(EventArgs.Empty);
        }
    }
    public double Gpa
    {
        get
        {
            return gpa;
        }
```

Figure 12-14 The Student, EventListener, and DemoStudentEvent2 classes (*continued*)

```csharp
      set
      {
         gpa = value;
         OnChanged(EventArgs.Empty);
      }
   }
   public void OnChanged(EventArgs e)
   {
      Changed(this, e);
   }
}
class EventListener
{
   private Student stu;
   public EventListener(Student student)
   {
      stu = student;
      stu.Changed += new EventHandler(StudentChanged);
   }
   private void StudentChanged(object sender, EventArgs e)
   {
      Console.WriteLine("The student has changed.");
      Console.WriteLine("   ID# {0}   GPA {1}",
        stu.IdNum, stu.Gpa);
   }
}
class DemoStudentEvent2
{
   public static void Main()
   {
      Student oneStu = new Student();
      EventListener listener = new EventListener(oneStu);
      oneStu.IdNum = 2345;
      oneStu.IdNum = 4567;
      oneStu.Gpa = 3.2;
   }
}
```

Figure 12-14 (*continued*)

When you compile and execute the program in Figure 12-14, the output is identical to that in
Figure 12-13.

»TWO TRUTHS AND A LIE: USING THE BUILT-IN EventHandler

1. The .NET Framework guidelines indicate that the delegate type for an event should take exactly two parameters.
2. The EventArgs parameter for an event handler holds the source of an event.
3. For events that do not require custom code for information about the event, the .NET Framework has already defined an appropriate type named EventHandler.

The false statement is #2. An object that is the first parameter to an event handler holds the source of the event. The EventArgs parameter for an event handler (the second parameter) encapsulates information about an event.

HANDLING Control
COMPONENT EVENTS

Handling events requires understanding several difficult concepts. Fortunately, you most frequently will want to handle events in GUI environments when the user will manipulate Controls, and the good news is that these events have already been defined for you. When you want to handle events generated by GUI Controls, you use the same techniques as when you handle events that are not generated by Controls. The major difference is that when you create your own classes, like Student, you must define both the data fields and events you want to manage; but existing Control components, like Buttons and ListBoxes, already contain fields and public properties, like Text, as well as events with names, like Click. Table 12-1 lists just some of the more commonly used Control events.

»NOTE You can consult the Visual Studio Help feature to discover additional Control events as well as more specific events assigned to individual Control child classes.

You have already used the IDE to create some event-handling methods. These methods have been the default events generated when you double-click a Control in the IDE. For example, in Chapter 10 you created a Click() method for a Button, and in Chapter 11 you created a LinkClicked() method for a LinkLabel. A Form can contain any number of Controls that might have events associated with them. Additionally, a single Control might be able to raise any number of events. For example, besides creating a Button's default Click event, you might want to define various actions when the user's mouse rolls over the button. Table 12-1 lists only a few of the many events available with Controls; any Control could conceivably raise many of those events.

Event	Description
BackColorChanged	Occurs when the value of the BackColor property has changed
Click	Occurs when a control is clicked
ControlAdded	Occurs when a new control is added
ControlRemoved	Occurs when a control is removed
CursorChanged	Occurs when the Cursor property value has changed
DragDrop	Occurs when a drag-and-drop operation is completed
DragEnter	Occurs when an object is dragged into a control's bounds
DragLeave	Occurs when an object has been dragged into and out of a control's bounds
DragOver	Occurs when an object has been dragged over a control's bounds
EnabledChanged	Occurs when the Enabled property value has changed
Enter	Occurs when a control is entered
FontChanged	Occurs when the Font property value has changed
ForeColorChanged	Occurs when the ForeColor property value has changed
GotFocus	Occurs when a control receives focus
HelpRequested	Occurs when a user requests help for a control
KeyDown	Occurs when a key is pressed while a control has focus
KeyPress	Occurs when a key is pressed while a control has focus
KeyUp	Occurs when a key is released while a control has focus
Leave	Occurs when a control is left
LocationChanged	Occurs when the Location property value has changed
LostFocus	Occurs when a control loses focus
MouseDown	Occurs when the mouse pointer hovers over a control and a mouse button is pressed
MouseEnter	Occurs when the mouse pointer enters a control
MouseHover	Occurs when the mouse pointer hovers over a control
MouseLeave	Occurs when the mouse pointer leaves a control
MouseMove	Occurs when the mouse pointer moves over a control
MouseUp	Occurs when the mouse pointer hovers over a control and a mouse button is released
MouseWheel	Occurs when the mouse wheel moves while a control has focus
Move	Occurs when a control is moved
Resize	Occurs when a control is resized
TextChanged	Occurs when the Text property value has changed
VisibleChanged	Occurs when the Visible property value has changed

Table 12-1 Some Control class public instance events

Suppose you want to create a project that takes a different set of actions when the mouse is over a `Button` than when the mouse is clicked. Figure 12-15 shows a project that has been started in the IDE. The following actions have been taken:

» A `Button` was dragged onto the `Form` and its `Text` was set to "Click me".

» A `Label` was added to the `Form`, its `Text` was set to "Hello", and its `Font` was increased.

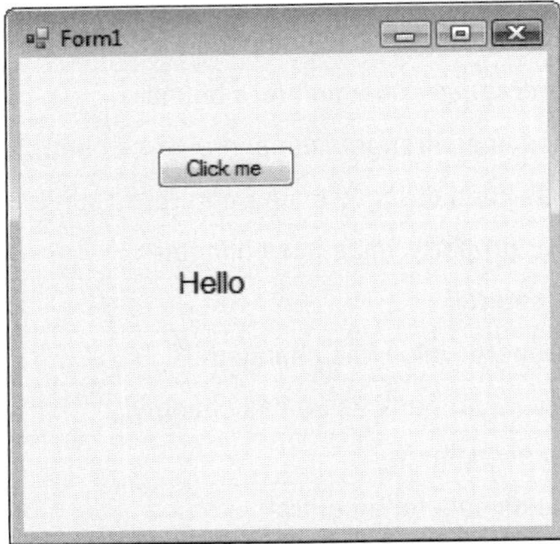

Figure 12-15 Start of `OneButtonTwoEvents` project in the IDE

When you double-click the `Button` on the `Form` in the IDE, you generate the shell of a `Click()` method into which you can type a command to change the `Label`'s text and its color, as follows:

```
private void button1_Click(object sender, EventArgs e)
{
    label1.Text = "Button was clicked";
    label1.BackColor = Color.CornflowerBlue;
}
```

» **NOTE** `Color.CornflowerBlue` is one of C#'s predefined `Color` properties. A complete list appears in Table 11-5 in Chapter 11.

With the `Button` selected on the design `Form`, you can click the Events icon in the Properties window at the right side of the screen. The Events icon looks like a lightning bolt. Figure 12-16 shows that the Properties window displays events instead of properties and that the `Click` event has an associated method.

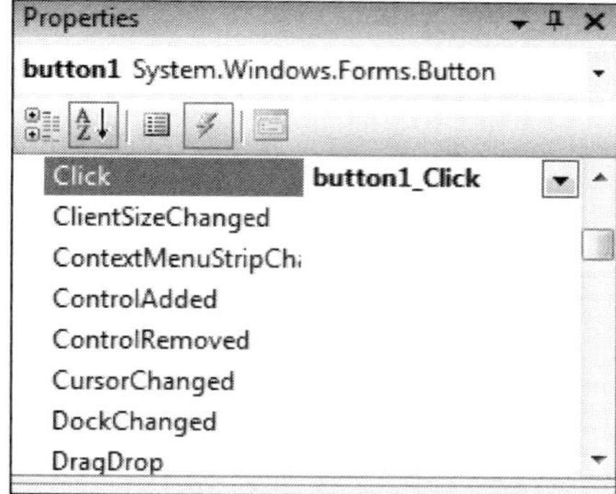

Figure 12-16 Properties window displaying events

If you scroll through the Events listed in the Properties window, you can see a wide variety of Event choices. If you scroll down to MouseEnter and double-click, you can see the code for an event handler as follows:

```
private void button1_MouseEnter(object sender, EventArgs e)
{
}
```

>> **NOTE** When you are viewing events in the Properties window, you can return to the list of properties by clicking the Properties icon. This icon is to the immediate left of the Events icon.

You can type any statements you want within this method. For example:

```
private void button1_MouseEnter(object sender, EventArgs e)
{
    label1.Text = "Go ahead";
    button1.BackColor = Color.Red;
}
```

When you run the program with the two new methods, two different events can occur:

» When you enter the button with the mouse (that is, pass the mouse over it), the Label's Text changes to "Go ahead" and the button turns red, as shown on the left in Figure 12-17.

» After the button is clicked, the Label's Text changes again and the Label becomes blue, as shown on the right in Figure 12-17.

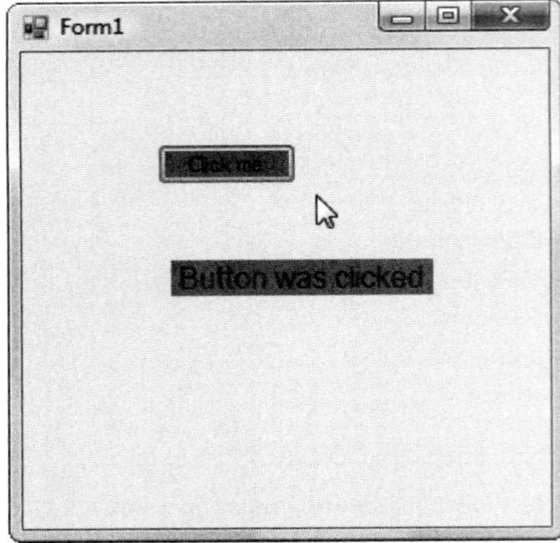

Figure 12-17 OneButtonTwoEvents program when mouse enters button and after button is clicked

If you examine the code generated by the Windows Form Designer, you will find the following two statements:

```
this.button1.Click += new System.EventHandler(this.button1_Click);
this.button1.MouseEnter += new System.EventHandler
   (this.button1_MouseEnter);
```

These EventHandler statements are similar to those in the Student class in Figure 12-14. The Click and MouseEnter delegates have been set to handle events appropriately for this application. You could have used the IDE to create these events just by selecting them from the Properties list and writing the action statements you want. The IDE saves you time by automatically entering the needed statement correctly. However, by knowing how to manually create a GUI program that contains events, you gain a greater understanding of how event handling works. This knowledge helps you troubleshoot problems and helps you create your own new events and handlers when necessary.

»TWO TRUTHS AND A LIE: HANDLING Control COMPONENT EVENTS

1. The default methods generated when you double-click a Control in the IDE are known as procedures.

2. A Form can contain any number of Controls that might have events associated with them, and a single Control might be able to raise any number of events.

3. You can type any statements you want within an automatically generated event method.

The false statement is #1. The default methods generated when you double-click a Control in the IDE are known as event handlers.

HANDLING MOUSE EVENTS

Mouse events include all the actions a user takes with a mouse, including clicking, pointing, and dragging. Mouse events can be handled for any `Control` through an object of the class `MouseEventArgs`. The delegate used to create mouse event handlers is `MouseEventHandler`. Every mouse event-handling method must have two parameters: an object representing the sender and an object representing the event. Depending on the event, the type of the second parameter is `EventArgs` or `MouseEventArgs`. Table 12-2 describes several common mouse events, and Table 12-3 lists some properties of the `MouseEventArgs` class.

Mouse Event	Description	Event Argument Type
MouseClick	Occurs when the user clicks the mouse within the `Control`'s boundaries	MouseEventArgs
MouseDoubleClick	Occurs when the user double-clicks the mouse within the `Control`'s boundaries	MouseEventArgs
MouseEnter	Occurs when the mouse cursor enters the `Control`'s boundaries	EventArgs
MouseLeave	Occurs when the mouse cursor leaves the `Control`'s boundaries	EventArgs
MouseDown	Occurs when a mouse button is pressed while the mouse is within the `Control`'s boundaries	MouseEventArgs
MouseHover	Occurs when the mouse cursor is within the `Control`'s boundaries	MouseEventArgs
MouseMove	Occurs when the mouse is moved while within the `Control`'s boundaries	MouseEventArgs
MouseUp	Occurs when a mouse button is released while the mouse is within the `Control`'s boundaries	MouseEventArgs

Table 12-2 Common mouse events

》NOTE A `MouseDown` event can occur without a corresponding `MouseUp` if the user presses the mouse but switches focus to another control or application before releasing the mouse button.

MouseEventArgs Property	Description
Button	Specifies which mouse button triggered the event; the value can be Left, Right, Middle, or none
Clicks	Specifies the number of times the mouse was clicked
X	The x-coordinate where the event occurred on the control that generated the event
Y	The y-coordinate where the event occurred on the control that generated the event

Table 12-3 Properties of the MouseEventArgs class

>> **NOTE** MouseClick and Click are separate events. The Click event takes an EventArgs parameter, but MouseClick takes a MouseEventArgs parameter. For example, if you define a Click event, you do not have the MouseEventArgs class properties.

Each part of Figure 12-18 contains a Form with a single Label named clickLocationLabel that changes as the user continues to click the mouse on it. The figure shows how the Label changes in response to a series of user clicks. Initially, the Label is empty (that is, the default Text property has been deleted and not replaced), but the following code was added to the Form.cs file:

```
private void Form1_MouseClick(object sender, MouseEventArgs e)
{
    clickLocationLabel.Text += "\nClicked at " + e.X +
        ", " + e.Y;
}
```

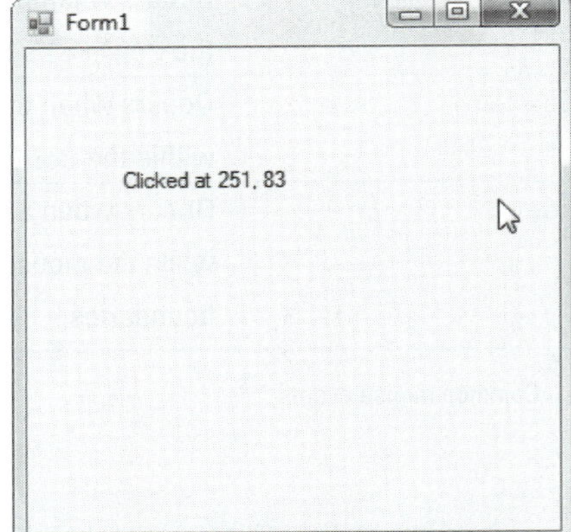

Figure 12-18 A Form that responds to clicks (*continued*)

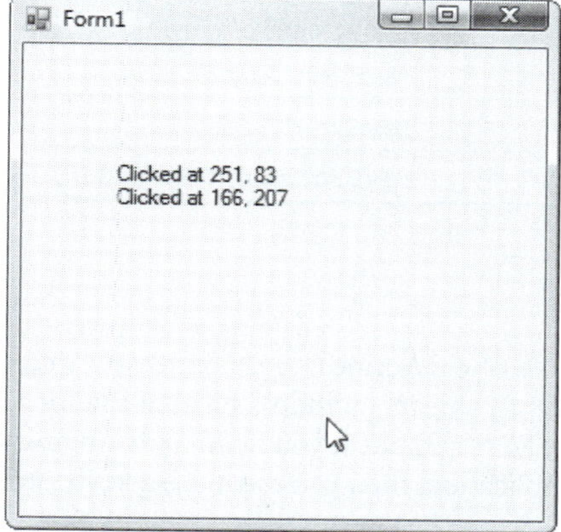 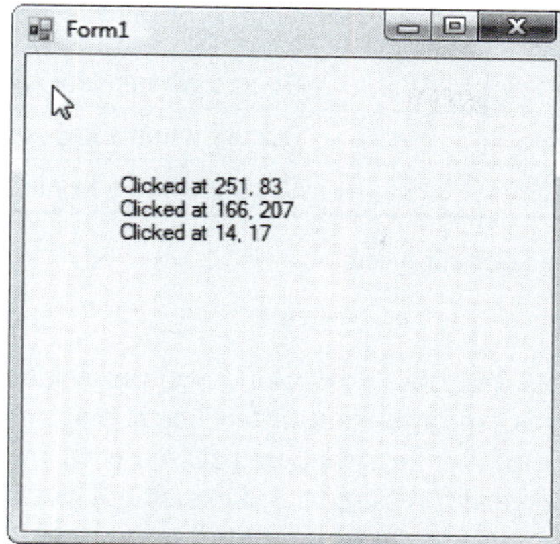

Figure 12-18 (*continued*)

Every time the mouse is clicked on the Form, the Label is appended with the words "Clicked at" on a new line and the x- and y-coordinate position where the click occurred on the Form.

When the programmer selects the MouseClick() event for Form1 from the Event list in the IDE, the following code is generated in the Designer.cs file. This code instantiates the MouseClick delegate.

```
this.MouseClick += new System.Windows.Forms.MouseEventHandler
    (this.Form1_MouseClick);
```

»TWO TRUTHS AND A LIE: HANDLING MOUSE EVENTS

1. The delegate used to create mouse event handlers is MouseEventHandler.
2. Depending on the event, the type of the second parameter to a mouse-handling method is EventArgs or MouseEventArgs.
3. Commonly used mouse events include ClickMouse(), DoubleClickMouse(), and MoveMouse().

The false statement is #3. ClickMouse(), DoubleClickMouse(), and MoveMouse() are not mouse events. Commonly used mouse events include MouseClick(), MouseDoubleClick(), and MouseMove().

HANDLING KEYBOARD EVENTS

Keyboard events, also known as **key events**, occur when a user presses and releases keyboard keys. Table 12-4 lists some common keyboard events. Similar to the way mouse events work, every keyboard event-handling method must have two parameters: an object representing the sender and an object representing the event. Depending on the event, the delegate used to create the keyboard event handler is either KeyEventHandler or KeyPressEventHandler, and the type of the second parameter is KeyEventArgs or KeyPressEventArgs.

Keyboard Event	Description	Event Argument Type
`KeyDown`	Occurs when a key is first pressed	`KeyEventArgs`
`KeyUp`	Occurs when a key is released	`KeyEventArgs`
`KeyPress`	Occurs when a key is pressed	`KeyPressEventArgs`

Table 12-4 Keyboard events

Table 12-5 describes `KeyEventArgs` properties, and Table 12-6 describes `KeyPressEventArgs` properties. An important difference is that `KeyEventArgs` objects include data about helper keys or modifier keys that are pressed with another key. For example, if you need to distinguish between a user pressing *A* and pressing *Alt+A* in your application, then you must use a keyboard event that uses an argument of type `KeyEventArgs`.

Property	Description
`Alt`	Indicates whether the Alt key was pressed
`Control`	Indicates whether the Control (Ctrl) key was pressed
`Shift`	Indicates whether the Shift key was pressed
`KeyCode`	Returns the code for the key
`KeyData`	Returns the key code along with any modifier key
`KeyValue`	Returns a numeric representation of the key (this number is known as the Windows virtual key code)

Table 12-5 Some properties of `KeyEventArgs` class

Property	Description
`KeyChar`	Returns the ASCII character for the key pressed

Table 12-6 A property of `KeyPressEventArgs` class

For example, suppose you create a `Form` with an empty `Label`, like the first `Form` in the series in Figure 12-18. From the Properties window for the `Form`, you can double-click the `KeyUp` event to generate the shell for a method named `Form1KeyUp()`. Suppose you then insert the statements into the method in the Form1.cs file, as shown in Figure 12-19. When the user runs the program and presses and releases a keyboard key, the `Label` is filled with information about the key. Figure 12-20 shows four executions of this modified program. During the first execution, the user typed *a*. You can see on the form that the `KeyCode` is "A" (not "a"), but you also can see that the user did not press the Shift key.

```csharp
private void Form1_KeyUp(object sender,
    KeyEventArgs e)
{
    label1.Text += "Key Code " + e.KeyCode;
    label1.Text += "\nAlt " + e.Alt;
    label1.Text += "\nShift " + e.Shift;
    label1.Text += "\nControl " + e.Control;
    label1.Text += "\nKey Data " + e.KeyData;
    label1.Text += "\nKey Value " + e.KeyValue;
}
```

Figure 12-19 `KeyUp()` method

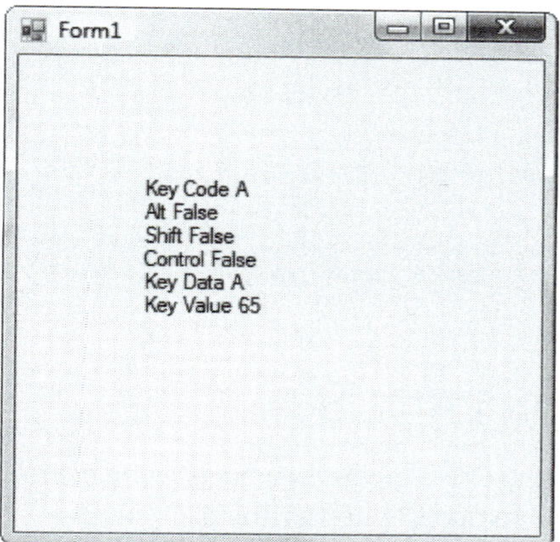

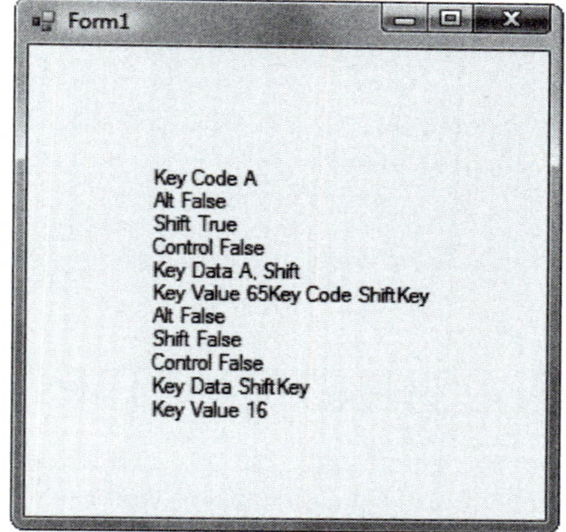

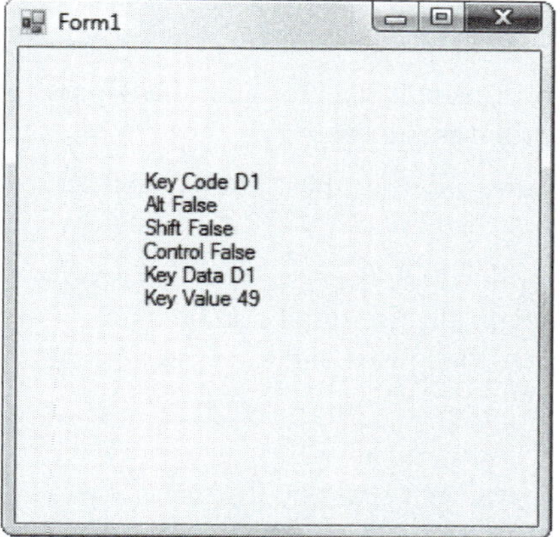

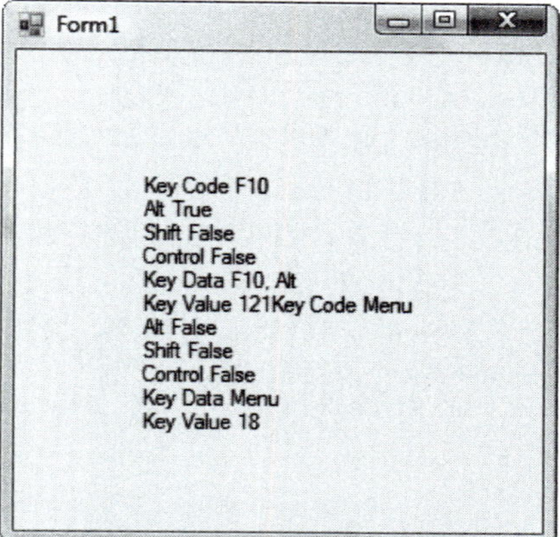

Figure 12-20 Four executions of `KeyDemo` program

In the second execution in Figure 12-20, the user held down Shift, pressed *a*, and then released the Shift key. This causes two separate KeyUp events. The first has KeyCode "A" with Shift true, and the second has KeyCode ShiftKey. Notice that the Key values generated after typing *a*, *A*, and Shift are all different.

In the third execution in Figure 12-20, the user pressed the number 1, whose code is D1. In the final execution, the user pressed Alt+F10 and released the F10 key first. When you view the Form1.Designer.cs file for the KeyDemo program, you see the following automatically created statement, which defines the composed delegate:

```
this.KeyUp += new System.Windows.Forms.KeyEventHandler
    (this.Form1_KeyUp);
```

»TWO TRUTHS AND A LIE: HANDLING KEYBOARD EVENTS

1. Keyboard events, also known as key events, occur when a user presses and releases keyboard keys.
2. Unlike mouse events, every keyboard event-handling method must be parameterless.
3. Depending on the event, the delegate used to create the keyboard event handler is either KeyEventHandler or KeyPressEventHandler.

The false statement is #2. Like mouse events, every keyboard event-handling method must have two parameters: an object representing the sender and an object representing the event.

MANAGING MULTIPLE CONTROLS

When Forms contain multiple Controls, you often want several actions to have a single consequence. For example, you might want the same action to occur whether the user clicks a button or presses the Enter key, or you might want multiple buttons to generate the same event when they are clicked.

DEFINING FOCUS

When users encounter multiple GUI Controls on a Form, usually one Control has **focus**. That is, if the user presses the Enter key, the Control will raise an event.

TabStop is a Boolean property of a Control that identifies whether the Control will serve as a stopping place in a sequence of Tab key presses.

TabIndex is a numeric property that indicates the order in which the Control will receive focus when the user presses the Tab key. Programmers typically use small numbers for TabIndex values, beginning with 0. When a Control has the lowest TabIndex of a Form's Controls, it receives focus when the Form is initialized.

»NOTE Setting two or more Controls' TabIndex values to 0 does not cause an error. Only one Control will receive focus, however.

Figure 12-21 shows a `Form` that contains three `Button`s and a `Label`. The `Button` labeled "1" has focus because the `TabStop` value has been set to `true` for each of the `Button`s, and they have been assigned `TabIndex` values in ascending order. When the application starts, the first `Button` has focus; whether the user clicks that button or presses Enter, the message appears as shown on the second view of the `Form` in the figure. In the third part of the figure, the user has pressed Tab and Enter to select `button2`, so it has focus and the `Label`'s `Text` property has changed. Alternatively, the user could have clicked `button2` to achieve the same result. The user could then select either of the other `Button`s by clicking them as usual, or by pressing Tab until the desired button has focus and then pressing Enter.

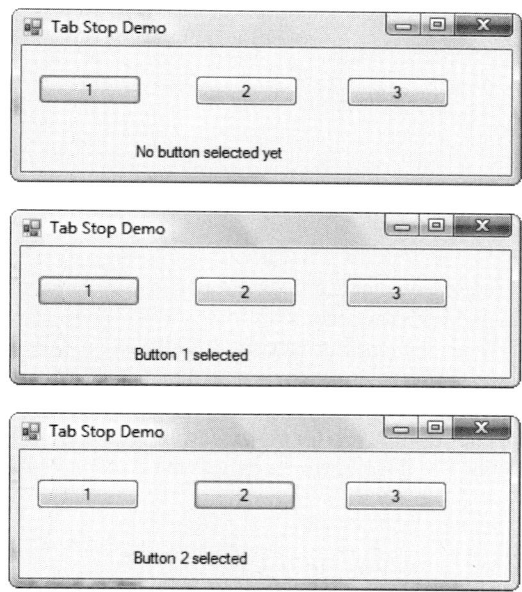

Figure 12-21 The `TabStopDemo` application

In the application that generates the results shown in Figure 12-21, each button was associated with a `Click()` event such as the following:

```
private void button1_Click(object sender, EventArgs e)
{
    buttonInfoLabel.Text = "Button 1 selected";
}
```

HANDLING MULTIPLE EVENTS
WITH A SINGLE HANDLER

When a `Form` contains multiple `Control`s, you can create a separate event handler for each `Control`. However, you can also associate the same event handler with multiple `Control`s. For example, Figure 12-22 shows a `Form` that contains three `Buttons` and a `Label`. The buttons have been labeled "A", "B", and "3". Suppose you want to display one message when the user clicks a letter button and a different message when the user clicks a number button. In the IDE, you can double-click the first `Button` and create an associated method such as the following:

```
private void button1_Click(object sender, EventArgs e)
{
    buttonInfoLabel.Text += "You clicked a letter button";
}
```

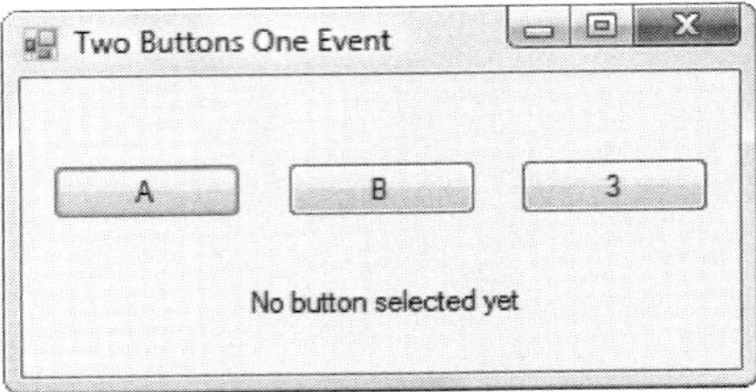

Figure 12-22 `Form` displayed by `TwoButtonsOneEvent` program

If you click the second button so its properties are displayed in the IDE's Properties list, you can click the Events icon to see a list of events associated with the second button. In Figure 12-23, no `Click` event has been chosen yet, but a list box is available. This list contains all the existing events that have the correct signature to be the event handler for the event. The list shows that the `button1_Click()` handler can also handle a `button2_Click` event, so you can select it. When you run the program, clicking either button produces the output shown in Figure 12-24. When you run the program and click the third button, no message is displayed.

» NOTE If you run the application in Figure 12-24 and click a letter button, the label changes. If you subsequently click the "3" button, nothing happens because no event has been associated with the third button, so the `Label`'s `Text` property remains "You clicked a letter button." Most likely, you would want to associate an event with the "3" button to modify the `Label`'s `Text` to "You clicked a number button".

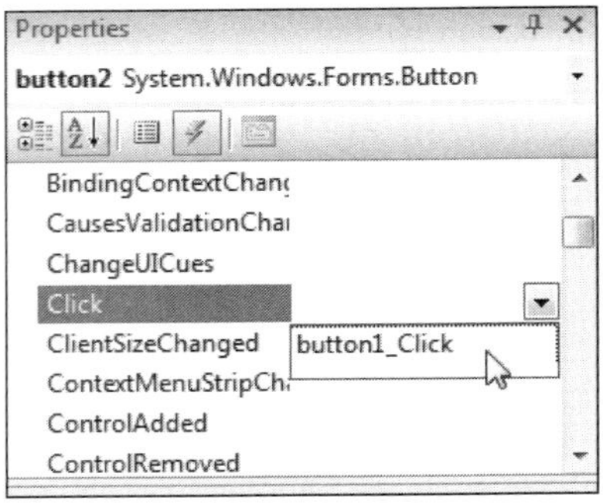

Figure 12-23 `Event` properties for `button2`

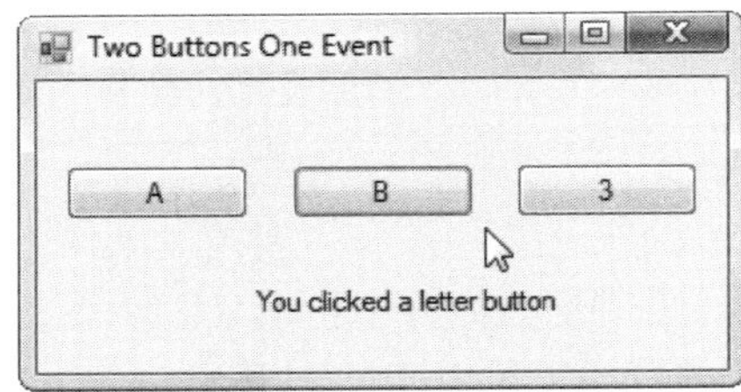

Figure 12-24 Output of `TwoButtonsOneEvent` program after either letter button is clicked

»NOTE When two or more `Control`s generate the same event, many programmers prefer to generalize the event method name. For example, if `button1` and `button2` call the same method when clicked, it makes sense to name the event method `button_Click()` instead of `button1_Click()`.

»TWO TRUTHS AND A LIE: MANAGING MULTIPLE `Control`**s**

1. The `Control TabStop` property can be set to true or false; it identifies whether the `Control` will serve as a stopping place in a sequence of Tab key presses.
2. On a `Form` with multiple `Control`s, one `Control` must have a `TabIndex` value of 0.
3. When a `Form` contains multiple `Control`s, you can associate the same event with all of them.

The false statement is #2. `TabIndex` is a numeric property that indicates the order in which the `Control` will receive focus when the user presses the Tab key. Programmers typically use small numbers for `TabIndex` values, beginning with 0. However, you might choose not to use any `TabIndex` values, or if you do, you might choose not to start with 0.

CONTINUING TO LEARN ABOUT CONTROLS AND EVENTS

If you examine the Visual Studio IDE, you will discover many additional `Control`s that contain hundreds of properties and events. No single book or programming course can demonstrate all of them for you. However, if you understand good programming principles and the syntax and structure of C# programs, learning about each new C# feature becomes progressively easier. When you encounter a new control in the IDE, you probably can use it without understanding all the code generated in the background, but when you do understand the background, your knowledge of C# is more complete.

Continue to explore the Help facility in the Visual Studio IDE. Particularly, read the brief tutorials there. Also, you should search the Internet for C# discussion groups. C# is a new, dynamic language, and programmers pose many questions to each other online. Reading these discussions can provide you with valuable information and suggest new approaches to resolving problems.

»TWO TRUTHS AND A LIE: CONTINUING TO LEARN ABOUT `Control`**s AND EVENTS**

1. Now that you have completed this chapter, you are aware of all the available C# `Control`s in the Visual Studio IDE.
2. When you encounter a new control in the IDE, you probably can use it without understanding all the code generated in the background.
3. C# is a new, dynamic language, and programmers pose many questions to each other about C# online.

The false statement is #1. If you examine the Visual Studio IDE, you will discover many additional `Control`s that contain hundreds of properties and events.

YOU DO IT

CREATING DELEGATES

To demonstrate how delegates work, you will create two delegate instances in the next steps and assign different method references to them.

To demonstrate delegates:

1. Open a new file in your text editor. Type the necessary `using` statement, then create a delegate that encapsulates a `void` method that accepts a `double` argument:

```
using System;
delegate void DiscountDelegate(ref double saleAmount);
```

2. Begin creating a `Discount` class that contains a `StandardDiscount()` method. The method accepts a reference parameter that represents an amount of a sale. If the sale amount is at least $1000.00, a discount of 5% is calculated and subtracted from the sale amount; if the sale amount is not at least $1000, nothing is subtracted.

```
class Discount
{
    public static void StandardDiscount
        (ref double saleAmount)
    {
        const double DISCOUNT_RATE = 0.05;
        const double CUTOFF = 1000.00;
        double discount;
        if(saleAmount >= CUTOFF)
            discount = saleAmount * DISCOUNT_RATE;
        else
            discount = 0;
        saleAmount -= discount;
    }
```

3. Add a `PreferredDiscount()` method. The method also accepts a reference parameter that represents the amount of a sale and calculates a discount of 10% on every sale.

```
    public static void PreferredDiscount(ref double saleAmount)
    {
        const double SPECIAL_DISCOUNT = 0.10;
        double discount = saleAmount * SPECIAL_DISCOUNT;
        saleAmount -= discount;
    }
```

4. Start a `Main()` method that declares variables whose values will be supplied by the user—a sale amount and a code. Declare two `DiscountDelegate` objects named `firstDel` and `secondDel`. Assign a reference to the `StandardDiscount()` method to one `DiscountDelegate` object and a reference to the `PreferredDiscount()` method to the other `DiscountDelegate` object.

```csharp
public static void Main()
{
    double saleAmount;
    char code;
    DiscountDelegate firstDel, secondDel;
    firstDel = new DiscountDelegate(StandardDiscount);
    secondDel = new DiscountDelegate(PreferredDiscount);
```

5. Continue the Main() method with prompts to the user to enter a sale amount and a code indicating whether the standard or preferred discount should apply. Then, depending on the code, use the appropriate delegate to calculate the correct new value for saleAmount. Display the value and add closing curly braces for the Main() method and the class.

```csharp
        Console.Write("Enter amount of sale ");
        saleAmount = Convert.ToDouble(Console.ReadLine());
        Console.Write("Enter S for standard discount, " +
            "or P for preferred discount ");
        code = Convert.ToChar(Console.ReadLine());
        if(code == 'S')
            firstDel(ref saleAmount);
        else
            secondDel(ref saleAmount);
        Console.WriteLine("New sale amount is {0}",
            saleAmount.ToString("C2"));
    }
}
```

6. Save the file as **DiscountDelegateDemo.cs**, then compile and execute it. Figure 12-25 shows the results when the program is executed several times.

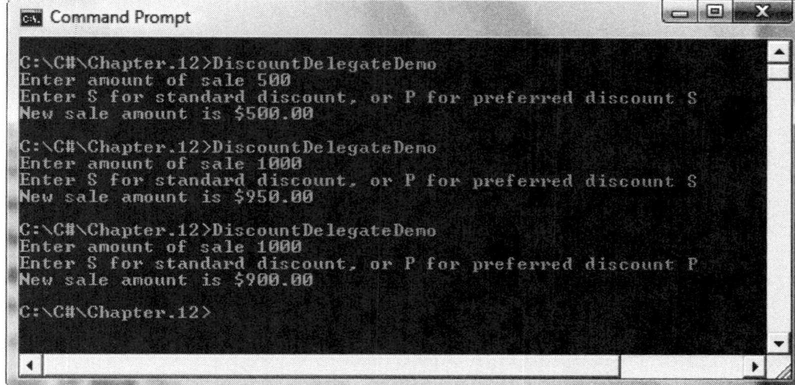

Figure 12-25 Sample executions of DiscountDelegateDemo program

CREATING A COMPOSED DELEGATE

When you compose delegates, you can invoke multiple method calls using a single statement. In the next steps, you will create a composed delegate to demonstrate how composition works.

To create a composed delegate:

1. Open the **DiscountDelegateDemo.cs** file in your text editor. Immediately save it as **DiscountDelegateDemo2.cs**.

2. Within the `Main()` method, add a third `DiscountDelegate` object to the statement that declares the two existing versions, as follows:

```
DiscountDelegate firstDel, secondDel, thirdDel;
```

3. After the statements that assign values to the existing `DiscountDelegate` objects, add statements that assign the `firstDel` object to `thirdDel` and then add `secondDel` to it through composition.

```
thirdDel = firstDel;
thirdDel += secondDel;
```

4. Change the prompt for the code, as follows, to reflect three options. The standard and preferred discounts remain the same, but the extreme discount (supposedly for special customers) provides both types of discounts, first subtracting 5% for any sale equal to or greater than $1000, and then providing a discount of 10% more.

```
Console.Write("Enter S for standard discount, " +
   "P for preferred discount, " +
   "\nor X for eXtreme discount ");
```

5. Change the `if` statement so that if the user does not enter *S* or *P*, then the extreme discount applies.

```
if(code == 'S')
   firstDel(ref saleAmount);
else
   if(code == 'P')
      secondDel(ref saleAmount);
   else
      thirdDel(ref saleAmount);
```

6. Save the program, then compile and execute it. For reference, Figure 12-26 shows the complete program. Figure 12-27 shows the output when the program is executed several times. When the user enters a sale amount of $1000 and an *S*, a 5% discount is applied. When the user enters a *P* for the same amount, a 10% discount is applied. When the user enters *X* with the same amount, a 5% discount is applied, followed by a 10% discount, which produces a net result of a 14.5% discount.

```csharp
using System;
delegate void DiscountDelegate(ref double saleAmount);
class Discount
{
   public static void StandardDiscount(ref double saleAmount)
   {
      const double DISCOUNT_RATE = 0.05;
      const double CUTOFF = 1000.00;
      double discount;
      if(saleAmount >= CUTOFF)
         discount = saleAmount * DISCOUNT_RATE;
      else
         discount = 0;
      saleAmount -= discount;
   }

   public static void PreferredDiscount(ref double saleAmount)
   {
      const double SPECIAL_DISCOUNT = 0.10;
      double discount = saleAmount * SPECIAL_DISCOUNT;
      saleAmount -= discount;
   }
   public static void Main()
   {
      double saleAmount;
      char code;
      DiscountDelegate firstDel, secondDel, thirdDel;
      firstDel = new DiscountDelegate(StandardDiscount);
      secondDel = new DiscountDelegate(PreferredDiscount);
      thirdDel = firstDel;
      thirdDel += secondDel;
      Console.Write("Enter amount of sale ");
      saleAmount = Convert.ToDouble(Console.ReadLine());
      Console.Write("Enter S for standard discount, " +
         "P for preferred discount, " +
         "\nor X for eXtreme discount ");
      code = Convert.ToChar(Console.ReadLine());
      if(code == 'S')
         firstDel(ref saleAmount);
      else
         if(code == 'P')
            secondDel(ref saleAmount);
         else
            thirdDel(ref saleAmount);
      Console.WriteLine("New sale amount is {0}",
         saleAmount.ToString("C2"));
   }
}
```

Figure 12-26 DiscountDelegateDemo2 program

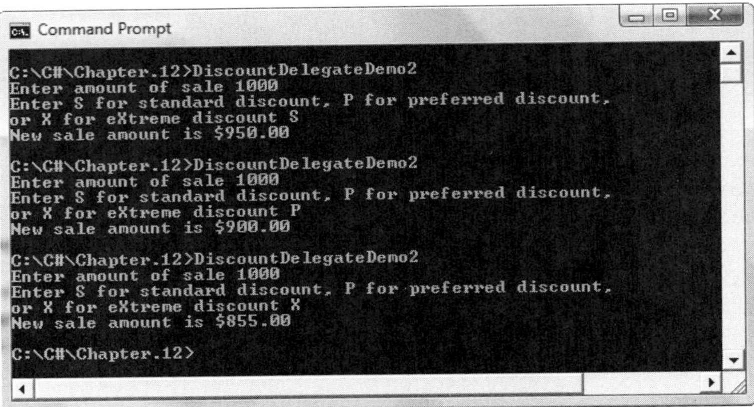

Figure 12-27 Three executions of `DiscountDelegateDemo2` program

> **» NOTE** For `static` methods, like `StandardDiscount` and `PreferredDiscount`, a `delegate` object encapsulates the method to be called. When creating a class that contains instance methods, you create `delegate` objects that encapsulate both an instance of the class and a method of the instance. You will create this type of `delegate` in the next section.

CREATING A DELEGATE THAT ENCAPSULATES INSTANCE METHODS

In the next set of steps, you will create a simple `BankAccount` class that is similar to many classes you already have created. The `BankAccount` class will contain just two data fields—an account number and a balance. It also will contain methods to make withdrawals and deposits. An event will be generated after any withdrawal or deposit.

To create the `BankAccount` class:

1. Open a new file in your text editor. Type the `using System;` statement, then begin a class named `BankAccount`. The class contains an account number, a balance, and an event that executes when an account's balance is adjusted.

```
using System;
public class BankAccount
{
    private int acctNum;
    private double balance;
    public event EventHandler BalanceAdjusted;
```

2. Add a constructor that accepts an account number parameter and initializes the balance to 0.

```
public BankAccount(int acct)
{
    acctNum = acct;
    balance = 0;
}
```

3. Add read-only properties for both the account number and the account balance.

```csharp
public int AcctNum
{
   get
   {
      return acctNum;
   }
}
public double Balance
{
   get
   {
      return balance;
   }
}
```

4. Add two methods. One makes account deposits by adding the parameter to the account balance, and the other makes withdrawals by subtracting the parameter value from the bank balance. Each uses the `OnBalanceAdjusted` event handler that reacts to all deposit and withdrawal events by displaying the new balance.

```csharp
public void MakeDeposit(double amt)
{
   balance += amt;
   OnBalanceAdjusted(EventArgs.Empty);
}
public void MakeWithdrawal(double amt)
{
   balance -= amt;
   OnBalanceAdjusted(EventArgs.Empty);
}
```

5. Add the `OnBalanceAdjusted()` method that accepts an `EventArgs` parameter and calls `BalanceAdjusted`, passing it a reference to the current `BankAccount` object that was adjusted and to the `EventArgs` object. Include a closing curly brace for the class.

```csharp
public void OnBalanceAdjusted(EventArgs e)
{
   BalanceAdjusted(this, e);
}
}
```

> **»NOTE** Earlier in the chapter, you learned that calling a method such as `OnBalanceAdjusted()` is also known as invoking the event.

6. Save the file as **DemoBankEvent.cs**.

CREATING AN EVENT LISTENER

When you write an application that declares a BankAccount, you might want the client program to listen for BankAccount events. To do so, you create an EventListener class.

To create an EventListener class:

1. After the closing curly brace of the BankAccount class, type the following EventListener class that contains a BankAccount object. When the EventListener constructor executes, the BankAccount field is initialized with the constructor parameter. Using the += operator, add the BankAccountBalanceAdjusted() method to the event delegate. Next, write the BankAccountBalanceAdjusted() method to display a message and information about the BankAccount.

```
class EventListener
{
    private BankAccount acct;
    public EventListener(BankAccount account)
    {
        acct = account;
        acct.BalanceAdjusted += new EventHandler
           (BankAccountBalanceAdjusted);
    }
    private void BankAccountBalanceAdjusted(object sender,
        EventArgs e)
    {
        Console.WriteLine
           ("The account balance has been adjusted.");
        Console.WriteLine("   Account# {0}   balance {1}",
           acct.AcctNum, acct.Balance.ToString("C2"));
    }
}
```

2. Create a class to test the BankAccount and EventListener classes. Below the closing curly brace for the EventListener class, start a DemoBankAccountEvent class that contains a Main() method. Declare an integer to hold the number of transactions that will occur in the demonstration program. Also declare two variables: one can hold a code that indicates whether a transaction is a deposit or withdrawal, and one is the amount of the transaction.

```
class DemoBankAccountEvent
{
    public static void Main()
    {
        const int TRANSACTIONS = 5;
        char code;
        double amt;
```

3. Declare a BankAccount object that is assigned an arbitrary account number and declare an EventListener object so this program is registered to listen for events from the BankAccount. Each change in the BankAccount balance will not only

change the balance data field, it will execute the `BankAccountBalanceAdjusted()` method that displays two lines of explanation.

```
BankAccount acct = new BankAccount(334455);
EventListener listener = new EventListener (acct);
```

4. Add a loop that executes five times (the value of `TRANSACTIONS`). On each iteration, prompt the user to indicate whether the current transaction is a deposit or withdrawal and to enter the transaction amount. Call the `MakeDeposit()` or `MakeWithdrawal()` method accordingly. At the end of the `for` loop, add a closing curly brace for the `Main()` method and another one for the class.

```
        for(int x = 0; x < TRANSACTIONS; ++x)
        {
            Console.Write
                ("Enter D for deposit or W for withdrawal ");
            code = Convert.ToChar(Console.ReadLine());
            Console.Write("Enter dollar amount ");
            amt = Convert.ToDouble(Console.ReadLine());
            if(code == 'D')
                acct.MakeDeposit(amt);
            else
                acct.MakeWithdrawal(amt);
        }
    }
}
```

5. Save the file, then compile and execute it. For reference, Figure 12-28 shows a typical execution in which five transactions modify the account. The output shows that an event occurs five times—twice for deposits and three times for withdrawals.

USING `TabStop` AND `TabIndex`

In the next steps, you will create a `Form` in the Visual Studio IDE and add four `Buttons` so you can demonstrate how to manipulate the `TabStop` and `TabIndex` properties.

To demonstrate `TabStop` and `TabIndex`:

1. Open the Visual Studio IDE and start a new project. Define it to be a **Windows Forms Application** named **ManyButtons**.

2. Change the `Text` property of `Form1` to **Many Buttons**.

3. Drag four `Buttons` onto the `Form` and place them so that they are similar to the layout shown in Figure 12-29. Change the `Name` properties of the buttons to `redButton`, `whiteButton`, `blueButton`, and `favoriteButton`. Change the `Text` on the `Buttons` to **Red**, **White**, **Blue**, and **My Favorite Color**, respectively. Adjust the size of the last button so its longer `Text` is fully displayed.

4. Examine the Properties list for the Red button. The `TabStop` property has been set to `True`, and the `TabIndex` is 0. Examine the properties for the White, Blue, and My Favorite Color buttons. The IDE has set their `TabIndex` values to 1, 2, and 3, respectively.

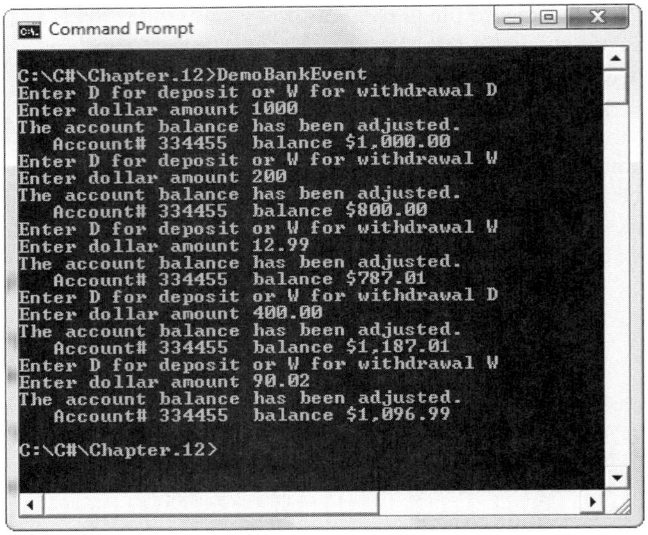

Figure 12-28 Typical execution of `DemoBankEvent` program

Figure 12-29 Four `Button`s on the Many Buttons `Form`

5. Click the **Save All** button and then run the program. When the `Form` appears, the Red button has focus. Press the **Tab** key, and notice that focus changes to the White button. When you press **Tab** again, focus changes to the Blue button. Press **Tab** several more times and observe that the focus rotates among the four `Button`s.

6. Dismiss the `Form`.

7. Change the `TabIndex` property of the Blue button to **0**, and change the `TabIndex` of the Red button to **2**. (The `TabIndex` of the White button remains 1 and the `TabIndex` of the My Favorite Color button remains 3.) Save the program again and then run it. This time, the Blue button begins with focus. When you press Tab, the order in which the `Buttons` receive focus is Blue, then White, then Red, then My Favorite Color. (Clicking the `Buttons` or pressing Enter raises no event because you have not assigned events to the `Buttons`.)

8. Dismiss the `Form`. Select the White button and change its `TabStop` property to **False**. Save the program and then execute it. This time, the Blue button has focus when the `Form` appears. When you press **Tab**, focus alternates among the Blue, Red, and My Favorite Color buttons, bypassing the White button, which is no longer part of the tabbing sequence.

9. Change the White button's `TabStop` value back to `True`. Change the `TabIndex` property for the Red button back to **0** and the `TabIndex` property for the Blue button back to **2**. Click the **Save All** button.

ASSOCIATING ONE METHOD WITH MULTIPLE EVENTS

In the next steps, you will add three methods to the Many Buttons `Form` and cause one of the methods to execute each time the user clicks one of the four `Buttons`.

To associate methods with the application's events:

1. If it is not still open, open the **Many Buttons** project in the Visual Studio IDE. Drag a `Label` onto the `Form` and place it at the approximate location of the `Label` in Figure 12-30. Change the `Label`'s `Text` property to **Click a button** and change its `Font` to **12**.

Figure 12-30 Many Buttons `Form` with `Label`

2. Double-click the **Red** button on the `Form` to view the code for the shell of a `button1_Click()` method. Between the method's curly braces, insert a statement that will change the `Form`'s background color to red as follows:

```
this.BackColor = Color.Red;
```

> **» NOTE** At first glance, you might think `this` refers to the `Button` that is clicked. However, if you examine the `redButton_Click()` code in the Form1.cs file in the IDE, you will discover that the method is part of the `Form1` class. Therefore, `this.BackColor` refers to the `Form`'s `BackColor` property.

3. Select the **Form1.cs [Design]** tab and then double-click the **White** button. Add the following code to the `whiteButton_Click()` method that is generated:

```
this.BackColor = Color.White;
```

4. On the `Form`, double-click the **Blue** button. In its `Click()` method, add the following statement:

```
this.BackColor = Color.Blue;
```

5. On the form, click the **My Favorite Color** button. In its Properties list, click the **Events** button (the lightning bolt). Select the **Click** event. From the list box next to the `Click` event, select one of the three events to correspond to your favorite color of the three.

6. Click the **Save All** button and then execute the program. As you click `Buttons`, the `Form`'s background color changes appropriately.

7. Dismiss the form and exit Visual Studio.

CHAPTER SUMMARY

- » You use an event to notify a client program when something happens to a class object the program is using. GUI programs are event driven—an event such as a button click "drives" the program to perform a task. Programmers also say a button click raises an event, fires an event, or triggers an event. A method that performs a task in response to an event is an event handler. The `Click` event is the event generated when a button is clicked.

- » A delegate is an object that contains a reference to a method. C# delegates provide a way for a program to take alternative courses when running; a delegate provides a way to pass a reference to a method as an argument to another method.

- » You can assign one delegate to another using the = operator. You also can use the + and += operators to combine delegates into a composed delegate that calls the delegates from which it is built.

- » To declare your own event, you use a delegate. An event provides a way for a class's clients to dictate methods that should execute when an event occurs. The clients identify methods to execute by providing delegates. When an event occurs, any delegate that a client has given or passed to the event is invoked.

» The .NET Framework provides guidelines you should follow if you are developing a class that others will use. These guidelines indicate that the delegate type for an event should take exactly two parameters: a parameter indicating the source of the event, and an `EventArgs` parameter that encapsulates any additional information about the event. For events that do not use additional information, the .NET Framework has already defined an appropriate type named `EventHandler`.

» When you use existing `Control` components like `Buttons` and `ListBoxes`, they contain fields and `public` properties like `Text`, as well as events with names like `Click`. A `Form` can contain any number of `Controls` that might have events associated with them. Additionally, a single control might be able to raise any number of events.

» Mouse events include all the actions a user takes with a mouse, including clicking, pointing, and dragging. Mouse events can be handled for any `Control` through an object of the class `MouseEventArgs`. The delegate used to create mouse event handlers is `MouseEventHandler`. Every mouse event-handling method must have two parameters: an object representing the sender and an object representing the event. Depending on the event, the type of the second parameter is `EventArgs` or `MouseEventArgs`.

» Keyboard events, also known as key events, occur when a user presses and releases keyboard keys. Every keyboard event-handling method must have two parameters: an object representing the sender and an object representing the event. Depending on the event, the type of the second parameter is `KeyEventArgs` or `KeyPressEventArgs`.

» When users encounter multiple GUI `Controls` on a `Form`, usually one `Control` has focus. That is, if the user presses Enter, the `Control` will raise an event. When a `Form` contains multiple `Controls`, you can create a separate event for each `Control`. However, you can also associate the same event with multiple `Controls`.

» When you encounter a new control in the IDE, you probably can use it without understanding all the code generated in the background. However, when you do understand the background, your knowledge of C# is more complete.

KEY TERMS

Event-driven programs contain code that causes an event such as a button click to drive the program to perform a task.

A button click **raises an event**, **fires an event**, or **triggers an event**.

An **event handler** is a method that performs a task in response to an event.

An **event receiver** is another name for an event handler.

An **event sender** is the control that generates an event.

EventArgs is a C# class designed for holding event information.

The **Click event** is the event generated when a `Control` is clicked.

Event wiring is the act of connecting an event to its resulting actions.

A **delegate** is an object that contains a reference to a method.

A **composed delegate** calls the delegates from which it is built.

Invoking the event occurs when you call an event method.

EventHandler is an appropriate type for events that do not use any information besides the source of the event and the EventArgs parameter.

Key events are keyboard events that occur when a user presses and releases keyboard keys.

When a Control has **focus** and the user presses Enter, the Control will raise an event.

REVIEW QUESTIONS

1. A delegate is an object that contains a reference to a(n) _________ .

   a. object

   b. class

   c. method

   d. Control

2. C# delegates provide a way for a program to _________ .

   a. take alternative courses when running

   b. include multiple methods

   c. include methods from other classes

   d. include multiple Controls that use the same method

3. Which of the following correctly declares a delegate type?

   a. `void aDelegate(int num);`

   b. `delegate void aDelegate(num);`

   c. `delegate void aDelegate(int num);`

   d. `delegate aDelegate(int num);`

4. If you have declared a delegate instance, you can assign it a reference to a method as long as the method has the same _________ as the delegate.

   a. return type

   b. identifier

   c. parameter list

   d. two of the above

5. You can combine two delegates to create a(n) _________ delegate.

   a. assembled

   b. classified

   c. artificial

   d. composed

6. To combine two delegates using the + operator, the `delegate` objects must __________ .
    a. have the same parameter list   c. both of these
    b. have the same return type   d. neither of these

7. In C#, a(n) __________ occurs when something interesting happens to an object.
    a. delegate   c. notification
    b. event   d. instantiation

8. In C#, an event provides a way for a class to allow clients to provide __________ .
    a. GUI objects that other classes can use
    b. delegates to methods
    c. arguments to other classes
    d. widgets to `Forms`

9. An event handler `delegate` requires __________ arguments.
    a. zero   c. two
    b. one   d. any number greater than zero

10. Using an event handler, the sender is the __________ .
    a. delegate associated with the event
    b. method called by the event
    c. object where the event was initiated
    d. class containing the method that the event invokes

11. The `EventArgs` class contains a static field named __________ .
    a. `Empty`   c. `Location`
    b. `Text`   d. `Source`

12. When creating events, you can use a predefined delegate type named __________ that is automatically provided by the .NET Framework.
    a. `EventArgs`   c. `EventType`
    b. `EventHandler`   d. `Event`

13. Which of the following is not a predefined `Control` event?
    a. `MouseEnter`   c. `Destroy`
    b. `Click`   d. `TextChanged`

14. A single `Control` can raise ___________ event(s).

    a. one
    c. five

    b. two
    d. any number of

15. When you create `Forms` with `Controls` that raise events, an advantage to creating the code by hand over using the Visual Studio IDE is ___________ .

    a. you are less likely to make typing errors

    b. you save a lot of repetitious typing

    c. you are less likely to forget to set a property

    d. you gain a clearer understanding of the C# language

16. When a `Form` contains three `Controls` and one has focus, you can raise an event by ___________ .

    a. clicking any `Control`
    c. either of these

    b. pressing Enter
    d. none of these

17. The `TabStop` property of a `Control` is a(n) ___________ .

    a. integer value indicating the tab order

    b. Boolean value indicating whether the `Control` has a position in the tab sequence

    c. string value indicating the name of the method executed when the `Control` raises an event

    d. `delegate` name indicating the event raised when the user tabs to the `Control`

18. The `TabIndex` property of a `Control` is a(n) ___________ .

    a. integer value indicating the tab order

    b. Boolean value indicating whether the `Control` has a position in the tab sequence

    c. string value indicating the name of the method executed when the `Control` raises an event

    d. `delegate` name indicating the event raised when the user tabs to the `Control`

19. The `Control` that causes an event is the ___________ argument to an event method.

    a. first
    c. third

    b. second
    d. fourth

20. Which of the following is true?

    a. You can generate a single event from multiple `Controls`.

    b. You can generate multiple events from a single `Control`.

    c. Both of the above are true.

    d. None of the above are true.

EXERCISES

1. Create a `Form` that contains three `Label`s that hold famous quotes of your choice. When the program starts, the background color of the `Form` and each `Label` should be black. When the user passes a mouse over a `Label`, change its `BackColor` to white, revealing the text of the quote. Save the project as **DisplayQuotes**.

2. Create a `Form` with a list of three `LinkLabel`s that link to any three Web sites you choose. When a user clicks a `LinkLabel`, link to that site. When a user's mouse hovers over a `LinkLabel`, display a brief message that explains the site's purpose. After a user clicks a link, move the most recently selected link to the top of the list and move the other two links down, making sure to retain the correct explanation with each link. Save the project as **RecentlyVisitedSites**.

3. Create a `Form` with a `ListBox` that lists at least four sports teams of your choice. When the user places the mouse over the `ListBox`, display a `Label` that contains single-game ticket prices for each team. The `Label` disappears when the user's mouse leaves the `ListBox` area. When the user clicks a team name in the `ListBox`, display another `Label` that contains the correct ticket price. Also change the `BackColor` of the `Form` to the selected team's color. Save the project as **TeamSelector**.

4. Locate an animated .gif file on the Web or use the one stored in the Chapter.12 folder on your Student Disk. Create a `Form` that contains a `PictureBox`. Display three different messages on a `Label`—one when the user's mouse is over the `PictureBox`, one when the mouse is not over the `PictureBox`, and one when the user clicks the `PictureBox`. Save the project as **Animated**.

5. The Sunshine Subdivision allows users to select siding for their new homes, but they allow only specific trim colors with each siding color. Create a `Form` for Sunshine Subdivision that allows a user to choose one of three siding colors from a `ListBox`—white, gray, or blue. When the user selects a siding color, the program should display a second `ListBox` that contains only the following choices:

   » White siding—black, red, green, or dark blue trim
   » Gray siding—black or white trim
   » Blue siding—white or dark blue trim

   After the user selects a trim color, the program should display a congratulatory message on a `Label` indicating that the choice is a good one. The trim `ListBox` also becomes invisible. If the user makes a new selection from the siding `ListBox`, the congratulatory message is invisible until the user selects a complementary trim.

   Hint: You can remove the entire contents of a `ListBox` using the `Items.Clear()` method, as in `this.listBox2.Items.Clear();`.

   Save the project as **SunshineSubdivision**.

6. Create a `Form` that contains a guessing game with five `RadioButtons` numbered 1 through 5. Randomly choose one of the `RadioButtons` as the winning button. When the user clicks a `RadioButton`, display a message indicating whether the user is right.

   Add a `Label` to the `Form` that provides a hint. When the user's mouse hovers over the label, notify the user of one `RadioButton` that is incorrect. After the user makes a selection, disable all the `RadioButtons`. Save the project as **GuessANumber**.

>> **NOTE** You can create a random number that is at least `min` but less than `max` using the following statements:

```
Random RandomClass = new Random();
int randomNumber;
randomNumber = RandomClass.Next(min, max);
```

7. Create a `Form` that contains two randomly generated arrays, each containing 100 numbers. Include two `Buttons` labeled "1" and "2". Starting with position 0 in each array, ask the user to guess which of the two arrays contains the higher number and to click one of the two buttons to indicate the guess. After each button click, the program displays the values of the two compared numbers, as well as running counts of the number of correct and incorrect guesses. After the user makes a guess, disable the `Buttons` while the user views the results. After clicking a Next `Button`, the user can make another guess using the next two array values. If the user makes more than 100 guesses, the program should reset the array subscript to 0 so the comparisons start over, but continue to keep a running score. Save the project as **PickLarger**.

DEBUGGING EXERCISES

>> **NOTE**
Immediately save the two project folders with their new names before starting to correct their errors.

Each of the following files or projects in the Chapter.12 folder on your Student Disk has syntax and/or logical errors. In each case, determine the problem and fix the program. After you correct the errors, save each file or project using the same filename preceded with *Fixed*. For example, the file DebugTwelve1.cs will become FixedDebugTwelve1.cs and the project folder for DebugTwelve3 will become FixedDebugTwelve3.

   a. DebugTwelve1.cs

   b. DebugTwelve2.cs

   c. DebugTwelve3.cs

   d. DebugTwelve4.cs

UP FOR DISCUSSION

1. Programming is a job that can be done from a remote location. For example, as a professional programmer, you might be able to work from home. Does this appeal to you? What are the advantages and disadvantages? If you have other programmers working for you, would you allow them to work from home? Would you require any "face time"—that is, time in the office with you or other workers?

2. Programming is a job that can be done from a remote location. For example, your organization might contact programmers who live in another country where wages are considerably lower than in the United States. Do you have any objections to employers using these workers? If so, what are they? If not, what objections might others have?

3. Suppose your organization hires programmers to work in another country. Suppose you also discover that working conditions there are not the same as in your country. For example, the buildings in which the workers do their jobs might not be subject to the same standards for ventilation and fire codes as the building where you work. Is your company under any obligation to change the working conditions?

4. Would you ever participate in a computer dating site? Would you go on a date with someone you met over the Web? What precautions would you take before such a date?

13

FILES AND STREAMS

In this chapter you will:

Understand computer files and how they are stored
Use the `File` and `Directory` classes
Understand data organization within a file
Understand streams
Write to a sequential access text file
Read from a sequential access text file
Search a sequential file
Understand serialization and deserialization

In the early chapters of this book, you learned that storing values in variables provides programs with flexibility—a program that uses variables to replace constants can manipulate different values each time the program executes. However, when data values in a program are stored in variables, they are lost when the program ends. To retain data values for future use, you must store them in files. In this chapter, you will learn to create and manage files in C#.

UNDERSTANDING COMPUTER FILES AND HOW THEY ARE STORED

When data items are stored in a computer system, they can be stored for varying periods of time—temporarily or permanently.

Temporary storage is usually called computer memory or **random access memory** (RAM). When you write a C# program that stores a value in a variable, you are using temporary storage; the value you store is lost when the program ends or the computer loses power. This type of storage is **volatile**.

Permanent storage, on the other hand, is not lost when a computer loses power; it is **nonvolatile**. When you write a program and save it to a disk, you are using permanent storage.

> **▶▶ NOTE** When discussing computer storage, *temporary* and *permanent* refer to volatility, not length of time. For example, a *temporary* variable might exist for several hours in a large program or one that the user forgets to end, but a *permanent* piece of data might be saved and then deleted within a few seconds.

A **computer file** is a collection of information stored on a nonvolatile device in a computer system. Files exist on **permanent storage devices**, such as hard disks, floppy disks, Zip disks, USB drives, reels or cassettes of magnetic tape, and optical disks, which include CDs and DVDs. Some files are **data files** that contain facts and figures, such as a payroll file that contains employee numbers, names, and salaries; some files are **program files** or **application files** that store software instructions. (You have created many such files throughout this book.) Other files can store graphics, text, or operating system instructions (such as the files with an .exe extension that your compiler has created for every .cs project you compile). Although their contents vary, files have many common characteristics—each file occupies space on a section of a storage device, and each has a name and a specific time of creation.

When you use data, you never directly use the copy that is stored in a file. Instead, you use a copy that is in memory. Especially when data items are stored on a hard disk, their location might not be clear to you—data just seems to be "in the computer." However, when you work with stored data, you must transfer a copy from the storage device into memory. When you store data in a computer file on a persistent storage device, you **write to the file**. This means you copy data from RAM to the file. When you copy data from a file on a storage device into RAM, you **read from the file**.

> **NOTE** Because you can erase data from files, some programmers prefer the term *persistent* storage to permanent storage. In other words, you can remove data from a file stored on a device such as a disk drive, so it is not technically permanent. However, the data remains in the file even when the computer loses power, so, unlike RAM, the data persists, or perseveres.

Computer files are the electronic equivalent of paper documents stored in file cabinets. In a physical file cabinet, the easiest way to store a document is to toss it into a drawer without a folder. When storing computer files, this is the equivalent of placing a file in the main or **root directory** of your storage device. However, for better organization, most office clerks place documents in folders; most computer users also organize their files into **folders** or **directories**. Users also can place folders within folders to form a hierarchy. The combination of the disk drive plus the complete hierarchy of directories in which a file resides is its **path**. For example, in the Windows operating system, the following line would be the complete path for a file named Data.txt on the C drive in a folder named Chapter.13 within the C# folder:

```
C:\C#\Chapter.13\Data.txt
```

> **NOTE** The terms *directory* and *folder* are used synonymously to mean an entity that is used to organize files. *Directory* is the more general term; the term *folder* came into use in graphical systems. For example, Microsoft began calling directories *folders* with the introduction of Windows 95.

C# provides built-in classes named `File` and `Directory` that contain methods to help you manipulate files and their directories, respectively.

» TWO TRUTHS AND A LIE: UNDERSTANDING COMPUTER FILES AND HOW THEY ARE STORED

1. Temporary storage is nonvolatile and permanent storage is volatile.
2. When you write to a file, you copy data from RAM to a permanent storage device.
3. Most computer users organize their files into directories; the complete hierarchy of directories in which a file resides is its path.

The false statement is #1. Temporary storage is volatile and permanent storage is nonvolatile.

USING THE `File` AND `Directory` CLASSES

The **File class** contains methods that allow you to access information about files. Some of the methods are listed in Table 13-1.

Method	Description
`Create()`	Creates a file
`CreateText()`	Creates a text file
`Delete()`	Deletes a file
`Exists()`	Returns `true` if the specified file exists
`GetCreationTime()`	Returns a `DateTime` object specifying when a file was created
`GetLastAccessTime()`	Returns a `DateTime` object specifying when a file was last accessed
`GetLastWriteTime()`	Returns a `DateTime` object specifying when a file was last modified
`Move()`	Moves a file to the specified location

Table 13-1 Selected `File` class methods

> **»NOTE** `DateTime` is a structure that contains data about a date and time. In Chapter 11, you used the date data from `DateTime` structures with `MonthCalendar` and `DateTimePicker` GUI objects. `DateTime` values can be expressed using Coordinated Universal Time (UTC), which is the internationally recognized name for Greenwich Mean Time (GMT). By default, `DateTime` values are expressed using the local time set on your computer. The property `DateTime.Now` returns the current local time. The property `DateTime.UtcNow` returns the current UTC time.

The `File` class is contained in the `System.IO` namespace. So, to use the `File` class, you can use its fully qualified name, `System.IO.File`, or you can add the statement `using System.IO;` at the top of your file. Figure 13-1 shows a program that includes the `using` statement and demonstrates several of the `File` class methods. The program prompts the user for a filename and then tests the file's existence. If the file exists, the last creation time, write time, and access time are displayed. If the file does not exist, a message is displayed. Figure 13-2 shows two executions of the program. In the first execution, the user enters a filename that is not found. In the second execution, the file is found and the three significant dates are displayed.

> **»NOTE** The `System.IO.FileInfo` class also allows you to access information about a file. See the Microsoft documentation at *http://msdn2.microsoft.com* for more information.

```
using System;
using System.IO;
public class FileStatistics
{
    public static void Main()
    {
        string fileName;
        Console.Write("Enter a filename ");
        fileName = Console.ReadLine();
        if(File.Exists(fileName))
        {
            Console.WriteLine("File exists");
            Console.WriteLine("File was created " +
                File.GetCreationTime(fileName));
            Console.WriteLine("File was last accessed " +
                File.GetLastAccessTime(fileName));
            Console.WriteLine("File was last written to " +
                File.GetLastWriteTime(fileName));
        }
        else
        {
            Console.WriteLine("File does not exist");
        }
    }
}
```

Figure 13-1 The `FileStatistics` program

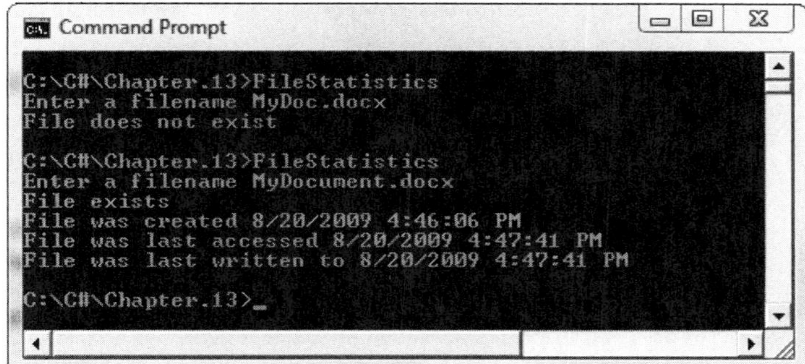

Figure 13-2 Two typical executions of the `FileStatistics` program

The **Directory class** provides you with information about directories or folders. Table 13-2 lists some available methods in the `Directory` class.

Figure 13-3 contains a program that prompts a user for a directory and then displays a list of the files stored within it. Figure 13-4 shows two typical executions of the program.

Method	Description
`CreateDirectory()`	Creates a directory
`Delete()`	Deletes a directory
`Exists()`	Returns `true` if the specified directory exists
`GetCreationTime()`	Returns a `DateTime` object specifying when a directory was created
`GetDirectories()`	Returns a `string` array that contains the names of the subdirectories in the specified directory
`GetFiles()`	Returns a `string` array that contains the names of the files in the specified directory
`GetLastAccessTime()`	Returns a `DateTime` object specifying when a directory was last accessed
`GetLastWriteTime()`	Returns a `DateTime` object specifying when a directory was last modified
`Move()`	Moves a directory to the specified location

Table 13-2 Selected `Directory` class methods

```
using System;
using System.IO;
public class DirectoryInformation
{
    public static void Main()
    {
        string directoryName;
        string[] listOfFiles;
        Console.Write("Enter a folder ");
        directoryName = Console.ReadLine();
        if(Directory.Exists(directoryName))
        {
            Console.WriteLine("Directory exists");
            listOfFiles = Directory.GetFiles(directoryName);
            for(int x = 0; x < listOfFiles.Length; ++x)
                Console.WriteLine(listOfFiles[x]);
        }
        else
        {
            Console.WriteLine("Directory does not exist");
        }
    }
}
```

Figure 13-3 The `DirectoryInformation` program

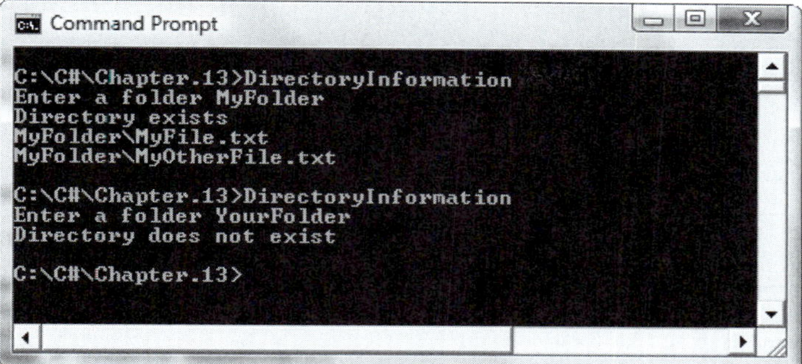

Figure 13-4 Two typical executions of the `DirectoryInformation` program

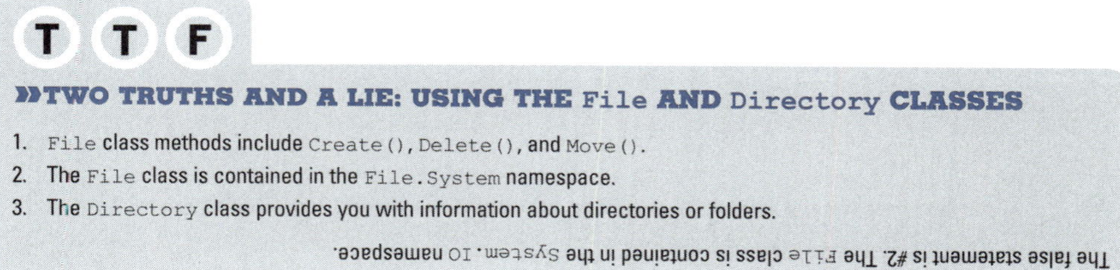

»TWO TRUTHS AND A LIE: USING THE `File` AND `Directory` CLASSES

1. `File` class methods include `Create()`, `Delete()`, and `Move()`.
2. The `File` class is contained in the `File.System` namespace.
3. The `Directory` class provides you with information about directories or folders.

The false statement is #2. The `File` class is contained in the `System.IO` namespace.

UNDERSTANDING DATA ORGANIZATION WITHIN A FILE

Most businesses generate and use large quantities of data every day. You can store data in variables within a program, but this type of storage is temporary. When the application ends, the variables no longer exist, and the data is lost. Variables are stored in the computer's main or primary memory (RAM). When you need to retain data for any significant amount of time, you must save the data on a permanent, secondary storage device.

Businesses store data in a relationship known as the **data hierarchy**, as shown in Figure 13-5. The smallest useful piece of data to most people is the character. A **character** is any one of the letters, numbers, or other special symbols (such as punctuation marks) that comprise data. Characters are made up of bits (the zeros and ones that represent computer circuitry), but people who use data do not care whether the internal representation for an 'A' is 01000001 or 10111110; rather, they are concerned with the meaning of 'A'—for example, it might represent a grade in a course, a person's initial, or a company code.

» NOTE C# uses Unicode to represent its characters. You first learned about Unicode in Chapter 1.

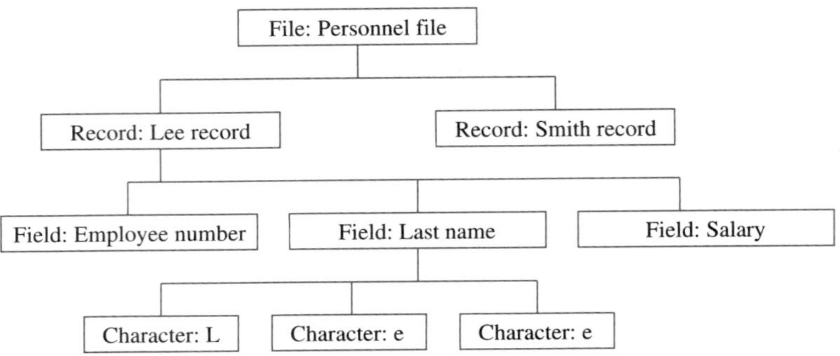

Figure 13-5 Data hierarchy

> **NOTE** In computer terminology, a character can be any group of bits, and it does not necessarily represent a letter or number. Some of these do not correspond to characters in natural language; for example, some "characters" produce a sound or control your display. You also have used the '\n' character to start a new line.

> **NOTE** You can think of a character as a unit of information instead of data with a particular appearance. For example, the mathematical character *pi* (π) and the Greek letter *pi* look the same, but have two different Unicode values.

> **NOTE**
> The set of all the characters used to represent data on a particular computer is that computer's **character set**.

> **NOTE**
> The field used to uniquely identify each record in a sequential file is the **key field**. Frequently, records are sorted based on the key field.

> **NOTE**
> When records are not used in sequence, the file is used as a random access file, which means that records can be accessed in any order.

When businesses use data, they group characters into fields. A **field** is a character or group of characters that has some meaning. For example, the characters *T*, *o*, and *m* might represent your first name. Other data fields might represent items such as last name, Social Security number, zip code, and salary.

Fields are grouped together to form records. A **record** is a collection of fields that contain data about an entity. For example, a person's first and last names, Social Security number, zip code, and salary represent that person's record. When programming in C#, you have created many classes, such as an `Employee` class or a `Student` class. You can think of the data typically stored in each of these classes as a record. These classes contain individual variables that represent data fields. A business's data records usually represent a person, item, sales transaction, or some other concrete object or event.

Records are grouped to create files. **Data files** consist of related records, such as a company's personnel file that contains one record for each company employee. Some files have only a few records; perhaps your professor maintains a file for your class with 25 records—one record for each student. Other files contain thousands or even millions of records. For example, a large insurance company maintains a file of policyholders, and a mail-order catalog company maintains a file of available items. A data file is a **sequential access file** when each record is read in order of its position in the file. Usually, the records are stored in order based on the value in some field; for example, employees might be stored in Social Security number order, or inventory items might be stored in item number order.

Before an application can use a data file, it must open the file. A C# application **opens a file** by creating an object and associating a stream of bytes with that object. When you finish using a file, the program should **close the file**—that is, make the file no longer available to your application. If you fail to close an input file (a file from which you are reading data), there usually are no serious consequences; the data still exists in the file. However, if you fail to close an output file (a file to which you are writing data), the data might become inaccessible. You should always close every file you open, and you should close the file as soon as you no longer need it. When you leave a file open for no reason, you use computer resources and your computer's performance suffers. Also, particularly within a network, another program might be waiting to use the file.

»TWO TRUTHS AND A LIE: UNDERSTANDING DATA ORGANIZATION WITHIN A FILE

1. A field is a character or group of characters that has some meaning.
2. A record is a collection of data files that contain information about an entity.
3. A data file that is used as a sequential access file frequently contains records stored in order based on the value in some field.

The false statement is #2. A record is a collection of fields that contain data about an entity. Data files consist of related records.

UNDERSTANDING STREAMS

Whereas people view files as a series of records, with each record containing data fields, C# views files as just a series of bytes. When you perform an input operation in an application, you can picture bytes flowing into your program from an input device through a **stream**, which functions as a pipeline or channel. When you perform output, some bytes flow out of your application through another stream to an output device, as shown in Figure 13-6. A stream is an object, and like all objects, streams have data and methods. The methods allow you to perform actions such as opening, closing, and flushing (clearing) the stream.

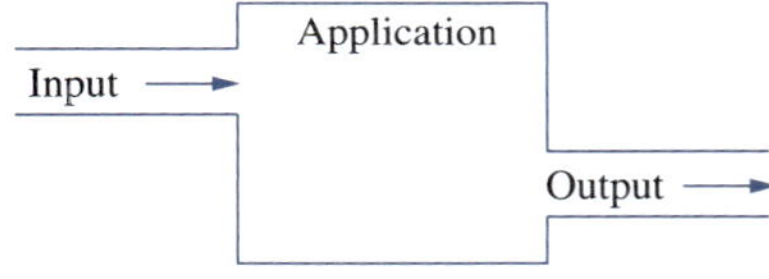

Figure 13-6 File streams

When a file is opened, an object is created and a stream is associated with that object. When a C# program executes, three stream objects are created:

- » `Console.In` refers to the standard input stream object, which accepts data from the keyboard.
- » `Console.Out` refers to the standard output stream object, which allows a program to produce output on the screen.
- » `Console.Error` refers to the standard error stream object, which allows a program to write error messages to the screen.

You have been using `Console.Out` and its `WriteLine()` and `Write()` methods throughout this book. However, you may have forgotten about the `Out` reference because in Chapter 1 you learned to eliminate it by including `using System;` at the top of your program files. Likewise, you have used `Console.In` with the `ReadLine()` and `Read()` methods.

Most streams flow in only one direction; each stream is either an input or output stream. You might open several streams at once within an application. For example, an application that reads a data disk and separates valid records from invalid ones might require three streams. The data arrives via an input stream, and as the program checks the data for invalid values, one output stream writes some records to a file of valid records, and another output stream writes other records to a file of invalid records.

Many file processing classes are available to you, including:

- » `StreamReader` for text input from a file
- » `StreamWriter` for text output to a file
- » `FileStream` (which is used alone and with both `StreamReader` and `StreamWriter`) for both input from and output to a file

> **» NOTE** `StreamReader` and `StreamWriter` inherit from `TextReader` and `TextWriter`, respectively. `Console.In` and `Console.Out` are properties of `TextReader` and `TextWriter`, respectively.

When you write a program that stores data in a file, you create a `FileStream` object. Table 13-3 lists some `FileStream` properties.

Property	Description
CanRead	Gets a value indicating whether current `FileStream` supports reading
CanSeek	Gets a value indicating whether current `FileStream` supports seeking
CanWrite	Gets a value indicating whether current `FileStream` supports writing
Length	Gets the length of the `FileStream` in bytes
Name	Gets the name of the `FileStream`
Position	Gets or sets the current position of the `FileStream`

Table 13-3 Selected `FileStream` properties

The `FileStream` class has 15 overloaded constructors. One that is used frequently includes the filename (or complete path), mode, and type of access. For example, you might construct a `FileStream` object using the following statement:

```
FileStream outFile = new FileStream("SomeText.txt",
    FileMode.Create, FileAccess.Write);
```

> **NOTE** Another of `FileStream`'s overloaded constructors requires only a filename and mode. If you use this version and the mode is set to `Append`, then the default access is `Write`; otherwise, the access is set to `ReadWrite`.

In this example, the filename is "SomeText.txt" and the mode is `Create`, which means a new file will be created even if one with the same name already exists. Also, the access is `Write`, which means you can write data to the file, but not read from it. Table 13-4 describes the available file modes and Table 13-5 describes the access types.

> **NOTE**
> Programmers say `FileStream` **exposes** a stream around a file.

Member	Description
`Append`	Opens the file if it exists and seeks the end of the file to append new data
`Create`	Creates a new file; if the file already exists, it is overwritten
`CreateNew`	Creates a new file; if the file already exists, an `IOException` is thrown
`Open`	Opens an existing file; if the file does not exist, a `System.IO.FileNotFoundException` is thrown
`OpenOrCreate`	Opens an existing file; if the file does not exist, it is created
`Truncate`	Opens an existing file; once opened, the file is truncated so its size is zero bytes

Table 13-4 `FileMode` enumeration

Member	Description
`Read`	Data can be read from the file.
`ReadWrite`	Data can be read from and written to the file.
`Write`	Data can be written to the file.

Table 13-5 `FileAccess` enumeration

When you create a `FileStream` object, you associate the object with a `StreamWriter`. Then you use `WriteLine()` or `Write()` with the `StreamWriter` object in much the same way you use it with `Console.Out`. For example, Figure 13-7 shows an application in which a `FileStream` object named `outFile` is created, then associated with a `StreamWriter` named `writer` in the first shaded line. The `writer` object then uses `WriteLine()` to send a `string` to the `FileStream` file instead of sending it to the `Console`. Figure 13-8 shows a typical execution of the program, and Figure 13-9 shows the file as it appears in Notepad.

```
using System;
using System.IO;
public class WriteSomeText
{
    public static void Main()
    {
        FileStream outFile = new
            FileStream("SomeText.txt", FileMode.Create,
                FileAccess.Write);
        StreamWriter writer = new StreamWriter(outFile);
        Console.Write("Enter some text >> ");
        string text = Console.ReadLine();
        writer.WriteLine(text);
        // Error occurs if the next two statements are reversed
        writer.Close();
        outFile.Close();
    }
}
```

Figure 13-7 WriteSomeText program

>> **NOTE** Although the WriteSomeText application uses Console.ReadLine() to accept user input, you could also create a GUI Form to accept input. You will create an application that writes to and reads from files using a GUI environment in the "You Do It" exercises at the end of this chapter.

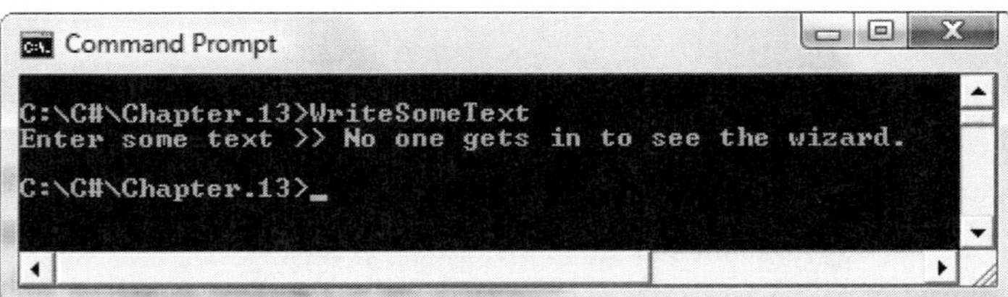

Figure 13-8 Typical execution of WriteSomeText program

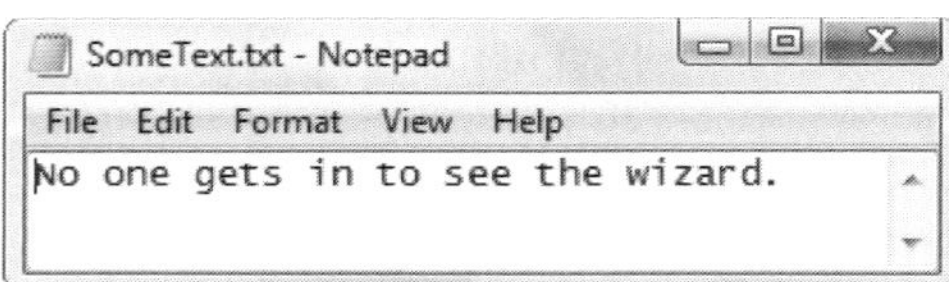

Figure 13-9 File created by WriteSomeText program

> **» NOTE** In Chapter 9, you learned about exception handling with `try` and `catch` blocks. In most applications that use files, you will want to place all the statements that open, write to, read from, and close files in a `try` block and then catch any `IOException`s that are thrown. Exception handling is eliminated from many examples in this chapter so that you can concentrate on the details of handling files without extra statements. In the "You Do It" section at the end of this chapter, you will add exception handling to an application.

> **» NOTE** The classes `BinaryReader` and `BinaryWriter` exist for working with binary files. **Binary files** can store any of the 256 combinations of bits in any byte instead of just those combinations that form readable text. For example, photographs and music are stored in binary files.

> **» NOTE** The classes `XmlTextReader` and `XmlTextWriter` exist for working with XML files. **XML** is an abbreviation of eXtensible Markup Language, which is a standard for exchanging data over the Internet.

» TWO TRUTHS AND A LIE: UNDERSTANDING STREAMS

1. When a file is opened in C#, an object is created and a stream is associated with that object.
2. Most streams flow in only one direction; each stream is either an input or output stream.
3. You can open one stream at a time within a C# application.

The false statement is #3. You might open several streams at once within an application.

WRITING TO A SEQUENTIAL ACCESS TEXT FILE

Although people think of data files as consisting of records that contain fields, C# uses files only as streams of bytes. Therefore, when you write a program to store a data file, you must dictate the form in which the program will handle the file.

For example, suppose you want to store `Employee` data in a file. Assume an `Employee` contains an ID number, a name, and a salary. You could write stand-alone data for each of the three types to a file, or you could create an `Employee` class that is similar to many you have seen throughout this book. Figure 13-10 shows a typical `Employee` class that contains three fields and properties for each.

```
public class Employee
{
    private int empNum;
    private string name;
    private double salary;
    public int EmpNum {get; set;}
    public string Name {get; set;}
    public double Salary {get; set;}
}
```

Figure 13-10 An `Employee` class

> **NOTE** In Chapter 7, you learned that the concise form of `{get; set;}` is new to C# 3.0. If you want to use the `Employee` class with an earlier version of C#, you must explicitly code implementations for the methods.

To store `Employee` data to a persistent storage device, you declare a `FileStream` object. For example:

```
FileStream outFile = new FileStream(FILENAME,
    FileMode.Create, FileAccess.Write);
```

The object is then associated with a `StreamWriter` object. For example:

```
StreamWriter writer = new StreamWriter(outFile);
```

After the `outFile` is associated with the `writer` object, `Employee` data can be written to the `writer` object using the `WriteLine()` method. When you write `Employee` data to a file, the fields should be separated by a delimiter. A **delimiter** is a character used to specify the boundary between data items in text files. Without a delimiter, the process of separating and interpreting data fields on a storage device is more difficult. For example, suppose you define a delimiter as follows:

```
const string DELIM = ",";
```

> **NOTE** A comma is a commonly used delimiter, but a delimiter can be any character that is not needed as part of the data in a file. A file that contains comma-separated values is often called a **CSV file**. When commas are needed as part of the data, sometimes either the Tab character, the pipe character (|), or a comma within quotes is used as a delimiter.

Then, when you write data to a file, you can separate the fields with a comma using a statement such as the following:

```
writer.WriteLine(emp.EmpNum + DELIM + emp.Name + DELIM + emp.Salary);
```

> **NOTE** Because `WriteLine()` is used for writing data to the file, the carriage return becomes the *record delimiter*.

> **NOTE**
> A block of text within a string that represents an entity or field is a **token**.

Figure 13-11 contains a complete program that opens a file and continuously prompts the user for `Employee` data. When all three fields have been entered for an employee, the fields are written to the file, separated by commas. When the user enters the sentinel value 999 for an `Employee` ID number, the data entry loop ends and the file is closed. Figure 13-12 shows a typical execution and Figure 13-13 shows the contents of the sequential data file that is created.

```csharp
using System;
using System.IO;
public class WriteSequentialFile
{
    public static void Main()
    {
        const int END = 999;
        const string DELIM = ",";
        const string FILENAME = "EmployeeData.txt";
        Employee emp = new Employee();
        FileStream outFile = new FileStream(FILENAME,
            FileMode.Create, FileAccess.Write);
        StreamWriter writer = new StreamWriter(outFile);
        Console.Write("Enter employee number or " + END + " to quit ");
        emp.EmpNum = Convert.ToInt32(Console.ReadLine());
        while(emp.EmpNum != END)
        {
            Console.Write("Enter last name ");
            emp.Name = Console.ReadLine();
            Console.Write("Enter salary ");
            emp.Salary = Convert.ToDouble(Console.ReadLine());
            writer.WriteLine(emp.EmpNum + DELIM + emp.Name +
                DELIM + emp.Salary);
            Console.Write("Enter next employee number or " +
                END + " to quit ");
            emp.EmpNum = Convert.ToInt32(Console.ReadLine());
        }
        writer.Close();
        outFile.Close();
    }
}
```

Figure 13-11 WriteSequentialFile class

> **NOTE** In the WriteSequentialFile class, the delimiter is defined to be a string instead of a char to force the composed argument to WriteLine() to be a string. If the first data field sent to WriteLine() was a string, then DELIM could have been declared as a char.

> **NOTE** In the WriteSequentialFile program in Figure 13-11, the constant END is defined to be 999 so it can be used to check for the sentinel value. You first learned to use named constants in Chapter 2. Defining a named constant eliminates using a magic number in a program. The term **magic number** refers to the bad programming practice of hard-coding numbers (unnamed, literal constants) in code without explanation. In most cases, this makes programs harder to read, understand, and maintain.

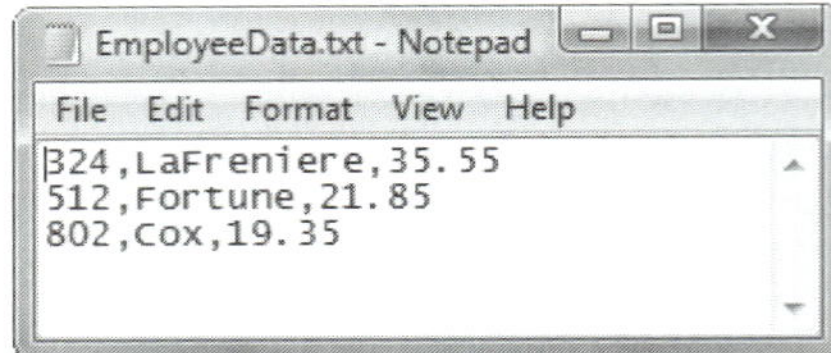

Figure 13-12 Typical execution of `WriteSequentialFile` program

Figure 13-13 Contents of file created by `WriteSequentialFile` program

»TWO TRUTHS AND A LIE: WRITING TO A SEQUENTIAL ACCESS TEXT FILE

1. Although people think of data files as consisting of records that contain fields, C# uses files only as streams of bytes.
2. Data can be written to a `StreamWriter` object using the `WriteLine()` method.
3. A comma is the default C# delimiter.

The false statement is #3. A delimiter is any character used to specify the boundary between characters in text files. Although a comma is commonly used for this purpose, there is no default C# delimiter, and any character could be used.

READING FROM A SEQUENTIAL ACCESS TEXT FILE

A program that reads from a sequential access data file contains many similar components to one that writes to a file. For example, a `FileStream` object is created, as in a program that writes a file. However, the access must be `FileAccess.Read` (or `ReadWrite`), as in the following statement:

```
FileStream inFile = new FileStream(FILENAME,
     FileMode.Open, FileAccess.Read);
```

Then, as when data is being written, the `FileStream` object is associated with a `StreamReader` object, as in the following statement:

```
StreamReader reader = new StreamReader(inFile);
```


After the `StreamReader` has been defined, the `ReadLine()` method can be used to retrieve one line at a time from the data file. For example, the following statement gets one line of data from the file and stores it in a string named `recordIn`:

```
string recordIn = reader.ReadLine();
```

If the value of `recordIn` is `null`, then no more data exists in the file. Therefore, a loop that begins `while(recordIn != null)` can be used to control the data entry loop.

After a record (line of data) is read in, the `Split()` method can be used to separate the data fields into an array of strings. The `Split()` method takes a character parameter and separates a string into substrings at each occurrence of the character delimiter. For example, the following code splits `recordIn` into the `fields` array at each `DELIM` occurrence. Then the three array elements can be stored as an `int`, `string`, and `double`, respectively.

```csharp
string[] fields;
fields = recordIn.Split(DELIM);
emp.EmpNum = Convert.ToInt32(fields[0]);
emp.Name = fields[1];
emp.Salary = Convert.ToDouble(fields[2]);
```

Figure 13-14 contains a complete `ReadSequentialFile` application that uses the data file created in Figure 13-12. The records stored in the EmployeeData.txt file are read in

```csharp
using System;
using System.IO;
public class ReadSequentialFile
{
    public static void Main()
    {
        const char DELIM = ',';
        const string FILENAME = "EmployeeData.txt";
        Employee emp = new Employee();
        FileStream inFile = new FileStream(FILENAME,
            FileMode.Open, FileAccess.Read);
        StreamReader reader = new StreamReader(inFile);
        string recordIn;
        string[] fields;
        Console.WriteLine("\n{0,-5}{1,-12}{2,8}\n",
            "Num", "Name", "Salary");
        recordIn = reader.ReadLine();
        while(recordIn != null)
        {
            fields = recordIn.Split(DELIM);
            emp.EmpNum = Convert.ToInt32(fields[0]);
            emp.Name = fields[1];
            emp.Salary = Convert.ToDouble(fields[2]);
            Console.WriteLine("{0,-5}{1,-12}{2,8}",
                emp.EmpNum, emp.Name, emp.Salary.ToString("C"));
            recordIn = reader.ReadLine();
        }
        reader.Close();
        inFile.Close();
    }
}
```

Figure 13-14 ReadSequentialFile program

one at a time, split into their `Employee` record components, and displayed. Figure 13-15 shows the output.

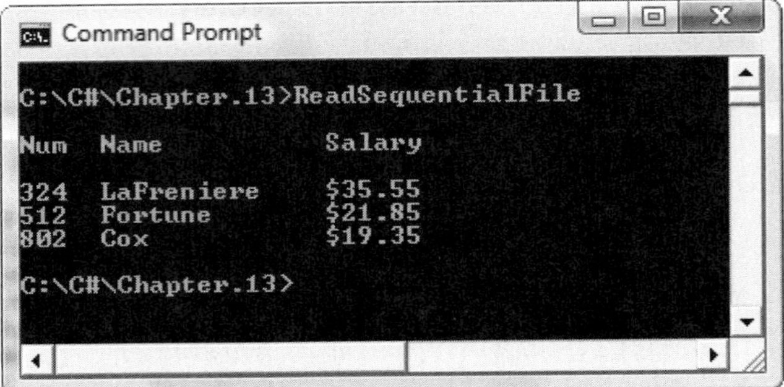

Figure 13-15 Output of `ReadSequentialFile` program

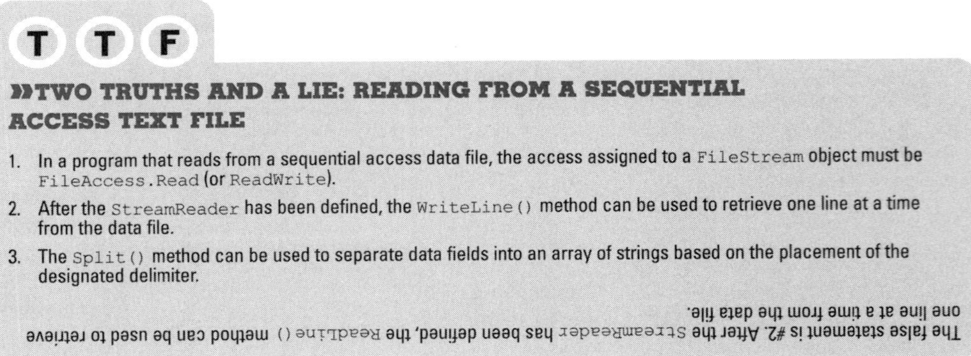

»TWO TRUTHS AND A LIE: READING FROM A SEQUENTIAL ACCESS TEXT FILE

1. In a program that reads from a sequential access data file, the access assigned to a `FileStream` object must be `FileAccess.Read` (or `ReadWrite`).
2. After the `StreamReader` has been defined, the `WriteLine()` method can be used to retrieve one line at a time from the data file.
3. The `Split()` method can be used to separate data fields into an array of strings based on the placement of the designated delimiter.

The false statement is #2. After the `StreamReader` has been defined, the `ReadLine()` method can be used to retrieve one line at a time from the data file.

SEARCHING A SEQUENTIAL FILE

When you read data from a sequential file, as in the `ReadSequentialFile` program in Figure 13-14, the program starts at the beginning of the file and reads each record in turn until all the records have been read. Subsequent records are read in order because a file's **file position pointer** holds the byte number of the next byte to be read. For example, if each record in a file is 32 bytes long, then the file position pointer holds 0, 32, 64, and so on in sequence during the execution of the program.

Sometimes it is necessary to process a file multiple times from the beginning during a program's execution. For example, suppose you want to continue to prompt a user for a minimum salary and then search through a file for `Employee`s who make at least that salary.

You can compare the user's entered minimum with each salary in the data file and list those employees who meet the requirement. However, after one list is produced, the file pointer is at the end of the file and no more records can be read. To reread the file, you could close it and reopen it, but that requires unnecessary overhead. Instead, you can just reposition the file pointer using the `Seek()` method and the `SeekOrigin` enumeration. For example, the following statement repositions the pointer of a file named `inFile` to 0 bytes away from the `Begin` position of the file:

```
inFile.Seek(0, SeekOrigin.Begin);
```

Table 13-6 lists the values in the `SeekOrigin` enumeration that you can use.

Member	Description
Begin	Specifies the beginning of a stream
Current	Specifies the current position of a stream
End	Specifies the end of a stream

Table 13-6 The `SeekOrigin` enumeration

Figure 13-16 contains a program that repeatedly searches a file to produce lists of employees who meet a minimum salary requirement. The shaded portions of the program represent differences from the `ReadSequentialFile` application in Figure 13-14. In this program, each time the user enters a minimum salary that does not equal 999, the file position pointer is set to the beginning of the file, and then each record is read and compared to the minimum. Figure 13-17 shows a typical execution of the program.

```
using System;
using System.IO;
public class FindEmployees
{
    public static void Main()
    {
        const char DELIM = ',';
        const int END = 999;
        const string FILENAME = "EmployeeData.txt";
        Employee emp = new Employee();
        FileStream inFile = new FileStream(FILENAME,
            FileMode.Open, FileAccess.Read);
        StreamReader reader = new StreamReader(inFile);
        string recordIn;
        string[] fields;
        double minSalary;
```

Figure 13-16 `FindEmployees` program (*continued*)

```csharp
         Console.Write("Enter minimum salary to find or " +
            END + " to quit ");
         minSalary = Convert.ToDouble(Console.ReadLine());
         while(minSalary != END)
         {
            Console.WriteLine("\n{0,-5}{1,-12}{2,8}\n",
               "Num", "Name", "Salary");
            inFile.Seek(0, SeekOrigin.Begin);
            recordIn = reader.ReadLine();
            while(recordIn != null)
            {
               fields = recordIn.Split(DELIM);
               emp.EmpNum = Convert.ToInt32(fields[0]);
               emp.Name = fields[1];
               emp.Salary = Convert.ToDouble(fields[2]);
               if(emp.Salary >= minSalary)
                  Console.WriteLine("{0,-5}{1,-12}{2,8}",
                     emp.EmpNum, emp.Name,
                        emp.Salary.ToString("C"));
               recordIn = reader.ReadLine();
            }
            Console.Write("\nEnter minimum salary to find or " +
               END + " to quit ");
            minSalary = Convert.ToDouble(Console.ReadLine());
         }
         reader.Close();  // Error occurs if
         inFile.Close(); //  these two statements are reversed
      }
}
```

Figure 13-16 (*continued*)

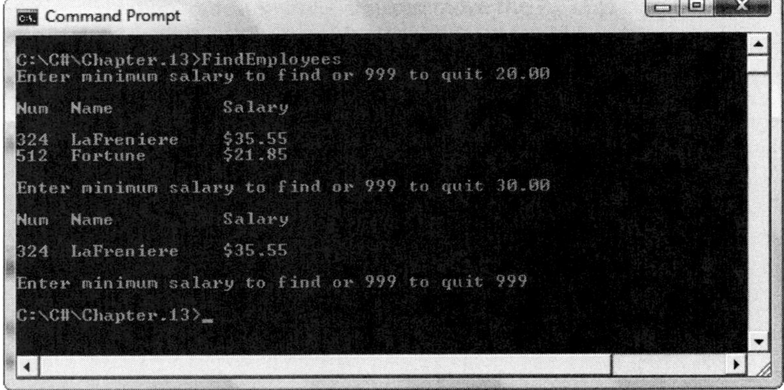

Figure 13-17 Typical execution of FindEmployees program

»NOTE The program in Figure 13-16 is intended to demonstrate using the `Seek()` method. In a business setting, you might prefer not to leave a file open in one application if other users might be waiting for it. As an alternative, you could load all the records into an array and then search the array for desired records.

»NOTE When you seek beyond the length of the file, you do not cause an error. Instead, the file size grows. In Microsoft Windows NT and later, any data added to the end of a file is set to zero. In Microsoft Windows 98 or earlier, any data added to the end of the file is not set to zero. This means that previously deleted data might become visible to the stream.

»TWO TRUTHS AND A LIE: SEARCHING A SEQUENTIAL FILE

1. When you read data from a sequential file, the program starts at the beginning of the file and reads each record in turn until all the records have been read.
2. When you read from a sequential file, its file position pointer holds the number of the record to be read.
3. To reread a file, you can close it and reopen it, or you can reposition the file pointer to the beginning of the file.

The false statement is #2. When you read from a sequential file, its file position pointer holds the byte number of the next byte to be read.

UNDERSTANDING SERIALIZATION AND DESERIALIZATION

Writing to a text file allows you to store data for later use. However, there are two disadvantages to writing to a text file:

» Data in a text file is easily readable in a text editor such as Notepad. Although this feature is useful to developers when they test programs, it is not a very secure way to store data.

» When a record in a data file contains many fields, it is cumbersome to convert each field to text and combine the fields with delimiters before storing the record on a disk. Similarly, when you read a text file, it is somewhat unwieldy to eliminate the delimiters, split the text into tokens, and convert each token to the proper data type. It would be more convenient to write an entire object to a file at once.

C# provides a technique called serialization that can be used for writing objects to and reading objects from data files. **Serialization** is the process of converting objects into streams of bytes. **Deserialization** is the reverse process; it converts streams of bytes back into objects.

To create a class that can be serialized, you mark it with the `[Serializable]` attribute, as shown in the shaded statement in Figure 13-18. The `Employee` class in the figure is identical to the one in Figure 13-10 except for the `[Serializable]` attribute.

In a class marked with the `[Serializable]` attribute, every instance variable must also be serializable. By default, all C# simple data types are serializable, including `strings`. However, if your class contains fields that are more complex data types, you must check the declaration of those classes to ensure they are serializable. By default, array objects are serializable.

```
[Serializable]
public class Employee
{
    private int empNum;
    private string name;
    private double salary;
    public int EmpNum {get; set;}
    public string Name {get; set;}
    public double Salary {get; set;}

}
```

Figure 13-18 Serializable `Employee` class

However, if the array contains references to other objects, such as `Dates` or `Students`, those objects must be serializable.

> **NOTE** If you want to be able to write class objects to a file, you can implement the `ISerializable` interface instead of marking a class with the `[Serializable]` attribute. When you use this approach, you must write a method named `GetObjectData()`. Marking the class with the attribute is the simpler format.

Two namespaces are included in programs that employ serialization:

» `System.Runtime.Serialization.Formatters.Binary;`
» `System.Runtime.Serialization;`

When you create a program that writes objects to files, you declare an instance of the `BinaryFormatter` class with a statement such as the following:

```
BinaryFormatter bFormatter = new BinaryFormatter();
```

Then, after you fill a class object with data, you can write it to an output file named `outFile` with a statement such as the following:

```
bFormatter.Serialize(outFile, objectFilledWithData);
```

The `Serialize()` method takes two arguments—the name of the file and a complete object that might contain any number of data fields. The entire object is written to the data file with this single statement.

Similarly, when you read an object from a data file, you use a statement like the following:

```
objectInstance = (TypeOfObject)bFormatter.Deserialize(inFile);
```

This statement uses the `Deserialize()` method with a `BinaryFormatter` object to read in one object from the file. The object is cast to the appropriate type and can be assigned to an instance of the object. Then you can access individual fields. An entire object is read with this single statement, no matter how many data fields it contains.

Figure 13-19 shows a program that writes `Employee` class objects to a file and later reads them in. After the `FileStream` is declared for an output file, a `BinaryFormatter` is declared in the first shaded statement. The user enters an ID number, name, and salary for an `Employee`, and the completed object is written to a file in the second shaded statement. When the user enters 999, the output file is closed.

```
using System;
using System.IO;
using System.Runtime.Serialization.Formatters.Binary;
using System.Runtime.Serialization;
public class SerializableDemonstration
{
   public static void Main()
   {
      const int END = 999;
      const string FILENAME = "Data.ser";
      Employee emp = new Employee();
      FileStream outFile = new FileStream(FILENAME,
         FileMode.Create, FileAccess.Write);
      BinaryFormatter bFormatter = new BinaryFormatter();
      Console.Write("Enter employee number or " + END +
         " to quit ");
      emp.EmpNum = Convert.ToInt32(Console.ReadLine());
      while(emp.EmpNum != END)
      {
         Console.Write("Enter last name ");
         emp.Name = Console.ReadLine();
         Console.Write("Enter salary ");
         emp.Salary = Convert.ToDouble(Console.ReadLine());
         bFormatter.Serialize(outFile, emp);
         Console.Write("Enter employee number or " + END +
            " to quit ");
         emp.EmpNum = Convert.ToInt32(Console.ReadLine());
      }
      outFile.Close();
      FileStream inFile = new FileStream(FILENAME,
         FileMode.Open, FileAccess.Read);
      Console.WriteLine("\n{0,-5}{1,-12}{2,8}\n",
         "Num", "Name", "Salary");
      while(inFile.Position < inFile.Length)
      {
         emp = (Employee)bFormatter.Deserialize(inFile);
         Console.WriteLine("{0,-5}{1,-12}{2,8}",
            emp.EmpNum, emp.Name, emp.Salary.ToString("C"));
      }
      inFile.Close();
   }
}
```

Figure 13-19 SerializableDemonstration program

After the output file closes in the `SerializableDemonstration` program in Figure 13-19, it is reopened for reading. A loop is executed while the `Position` property of the input file is less than its `Length` property. In other words, the loop executes while there is more data in the file. The last shaded statement in the figure deserializes data from the file and casts it to an `Employee` object, where the individual fields can be accessed. Figure 13-20 shows a typical execution of the program.

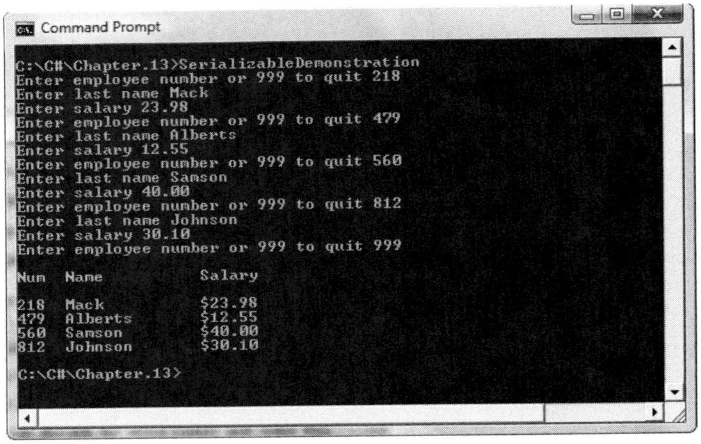

```
Command Prompt
C:\C#\Chapter.13>SerializableDemonstration
Enter employee number or 999 to quit 218
Enter last name Mack
Enter salary 23.98
Enter employee number or 999 to quit 479
Enter last name Alberts
Enter salary 12.55
Enter employee number or 999 to quit 560
Enter last name Samson
Enter salary 40.00
Enter employee number or 999 to quit 812
Enter last name Johnson
Enter salary 30.10
Enter employee number or 999 to quit 999

Num   Name        Salary

218   Mack        $23.98
479   Alberts     $12.55
560   Samson      $40.00
812   Johnson     $30.10

C:\C#\Chapter.13>
```

Figure 13-20 Typical execution of `SerializableDemonstration` program

The file created by the `SerializableDemonstration` program is not as easy to read as the text file created by the `WriteSequentialFile` program earlier in the chapter (in Figure 13-13). Figure 13-21 shows the file contents displayed in Notepad. If you examine the file carefully, you can discern the string names and some `Employee` class information, but the rest of the file is not easy to read.

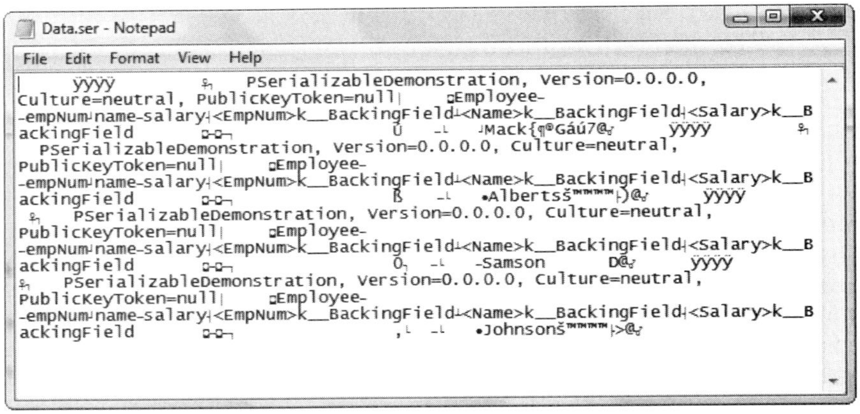

Figure 13-21 Data file created using `SerializableDemonstration` program

»TWO TRUTHS AND A LIE: UNDERSTANDING SERIALIZATION AND DESERIALIZATION

1. An advantage of writing data to a text file is that the data is easily readable in a text editor such as Notepad.
2. Serialization is the process of converting objects into streams of bytes and deserialization is the reverse process; it converts streams of bytes back into objects.
3. By default, all C# classes are serializable.

The false statement is #3. By default, all C# simple data types are serializable, including `strings`. However, if your class contains fields that are more complex data types, you must check the declaration of those classes to ensure they are serializable.

YOU DO IT

CREATING A FILE

In the next steps, you will create a file that contains a list of names.

To create a file:

1. Open a new file in your editor and write the first lines needed for a program that creates a file of names.

```
using System;
using System.IO;
public class CreateNameFile
{
```

2. Start a `Main()` method that declares a `FileStream` you can use to create a file named Names.txt that is open for writing. Also create a `StreamWriter` to which you associate the file.

```
public static void Main()
{
    FileStream file = new FileStream("Names.txt",
        FileMode.Create, FileAccess.Write);
    StreamWriter writer = new StreamWriter(file);
```

3. Add an array of names as follows. Each name is 10 characters long.

```
string[] names =    {"Anthony    ",
                     "Belle      ",
                     "Carolyn    ",
                     "David      ",
                     "Edwin      ",
                     "Frannie    ",
                     "Gina       ",
                     "Hannah     ",
                     "Inez       ",
                     "Juan       "};
```

»NOTE
Add spaces to make each new name the same length so that they can demonstrate the `Seek()` method in a later exercise.

4. Declare a variable to use as an array subscript, then write each name to the output file.

```
int x;
for(x = 0; x < names.Length; ++x)
    writer.WriteLine(names[x]);
```

5. Close the `StreamWriter` and the `FileStream`. Also add two closing curly braces—one for the `Main()` method and one for the class.

```
        writer.Close();
        file.Close();
    }
}
```

6. Save the file as **CreateNameFile.cs**. Compile and execute it. Using My Computer or Windows Explorer, open the newly created **Names.txt** file in a text editor. The file contents appear in Figure 13-22.

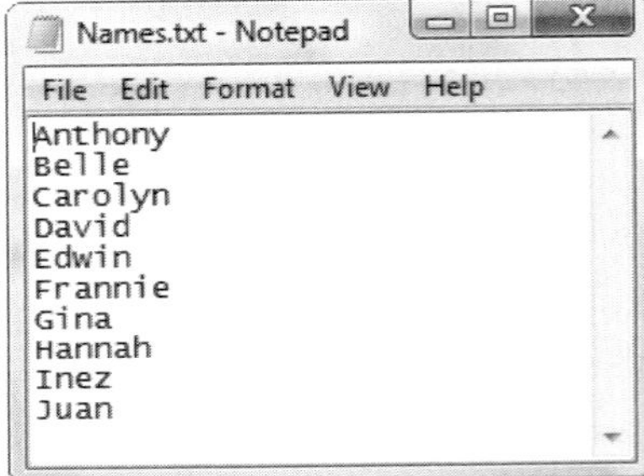

Figure 13-22 File created by `CreateNameFile` program

READING FROM A FILE

In the next steps, you will read the text from the file created by the `CreateNameFile` program.

To read text from a file:

1. Start a new file in your text editor as follows:

```
using System;
using System.IO;
public class ReadNameFile
{
```

2. Start a `Main()` method that declares a `FileStream` that uses the same filename as the one created by the `CreateNameFile` program. Declare the file mode to be `Open` and the access to be `Read`. Declare a `StreamReader` with which to associate the file. Also declare an integer that counts the names read and a `string` that holds the names.

```
public static void Main()
{
    FileStream file = new FileStream("Names.txt",
        FileMode.Open, FileAccess.Read);
    StreamReader reader = new StreamReader(file);
    int count = 1;
    string name;
```

3. Display a heading and read the first line from the file. While a name is not `null`, display a count and a name, and increment the count.

```
Console.WriteLine("Displaying all names");
name = reader.ReadLine();
while(name != null)
{
    Console.WriteLine("" + count + " " + name);
    name = reader.ReadLine();
    ++count;
}
```

4. Close the `StreamReader` and the `File`, and add closing curly braces for the method and the class.

```
        reader.Close();
        file.Close();
    }
}
```

5. Save the file as **ReadNameFile.cs**. Compile and execute it. The output appears in Figure 13-23.

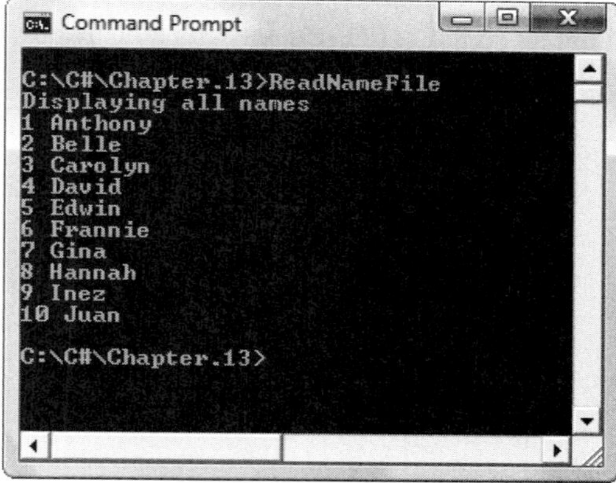

Figure 13-23 Output produced by `ReadNameFile` program

USING THE `Seek()` METHOD

In the next steps, you will use the `Seek()` method to reposition a file pointer so you can access a file from any location. The user will be prompted to enter a number representing a starting point to list the names in the Names.txt file. Names from that point forward will be listed, and then the user will be prompted for another selection.

To demonstrate the `Seek()` method:

1. Open a new file in your editor and start a program that will demonstrate how to access certain names from the Names.txt file. You created this file in the `CreateNameFile` application.

```csharp
using System;
using System.IO;
public class AccessSomeNames
{
    public static void Main()
    {
        FileStream file = new FileStream("Names.txt",
            FileMode.Open, FileAccess.Read);
        StreamReader reader = new StreamReader(file);
```

2. Declare a constant named END that represents an input value that allows the user to exit the program. Then declare other variables that the program will use.

```csharp
const int END = 999;
int count = 0;
int num;
int size;
string name;
```

3. Read a line from the input file. While names are available, continue to read and count them. Then compute the size of each name by dividing the file length by the number of strings stored in it.

```csharp
name = reader.ReadLine();
while(name != null)
{
    ++count;
    name = reader.ReadLine();
}
size = (int)file.Length / count;
```

4. Prompt the user for the number of the first record to read, and read the value from the Console.

```csharp
Console.Write("\nWith which number do you want to start? ");
num = Convert.ToInt32(Console.ReadLine());
```

5. As long as the user does not enter the sentinel END value, display the number and then use the Seek() method to position the file pointer at the correct file location. Because users enter numbers starting with 1, you calculate the file position by first subtracting 1 from the user's entry. For example, when a user enters 1 as the number of the first record to view, the file should start at position 0. The calculated record number is then multiplied by the size of each name in the file. For example, if each name is 12 bytes long, then the calculated starting position should be 0, 12, 24, 36, or some other multiple of the record size. Read and write the name at the calculated location. Then, in a loop, read and write all the remaining names until the end of the file. Finally, prompt the user for the next starting value for a new list and inform the user how to quit the application.

```
while(num != END)
{
   Console.WriteLine("Starting with name " + num +": ");
   file.Seek((num - 1) * size, SeekOrigin.Begin);
   name = reader.ReadLine();
   Console.WriteLine("   " + name);
   while(name != null)
   {
      name = reader.ReadLine();
      Console.WriteLine("   " + name);
   }
   Console.Write("\nWith which number do you " +
      "want to start? (Enter " + END + " to quit) ");
   num = Convert.ToInt32(Console.ReadLine());
}
```

6. Close the `StreamReader` and `File` objects and add closing braces for the method and the class.

```
      reader.Close();
      file.Close();
   }
}
```

7. Save the file as **AccessSomeNames.cs**. Compile and execute it. Figure 13-24 shows a typical execution during which the user displays three sets of names starting at a different point each time.

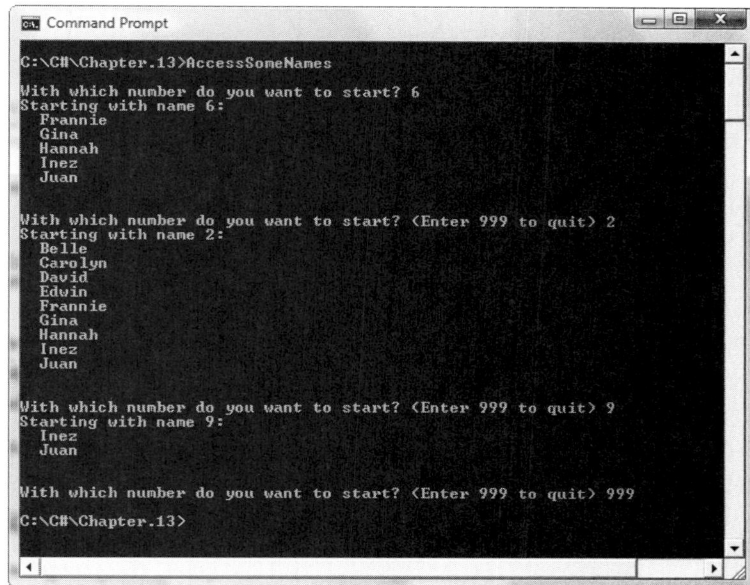

Figure 13-24 Typical execution of `AccessSomeNames` program

CREATING A FILE IN A GUI ENVIRONMENT

The file writing and reading examples in this chapter have used console applications so that you could concentrate on the features of files in the simplest environment. However, you can write and read files in GUI environments as well. In the next steps, you will create two applications. The first allows a user to enter invoice records using a `Form` and to store them in a file. The second application allows a user to view stored records using a `Form`.

To write a GUI application that creates a file:

1. Open the Visual Studio IDE and start a new Windows Forms Application project named **EnterInvoices**.

2. Create a `Form` like the one shown in Figure 13-25 by making the following changes:

   » Change the `Text` property of the `Form` to **Invoice Data**.

   » Drag a `Label` onto the `Form` and change its `Text` property to **Enter invoice data**. Increase the `Label`'s `Font` to **12**.

   » Drag three more `Label`s onto the `Form` and change their `Text` properties to **Invoice number**, **Last name**, and **Amount**, respectively.

   » Drag three `TextBox`es onto the `Form` next to the three descriptive `Label`s. Change the `Name` properties of the three `TextBox`es to **invoiceBox**, **nameBox**, and **amountBox**, respectively.

   » Drag a `Button` onto the `Form`, change its `Name` to **enterButton**, and change its `Text` to **Enter record**. If necessary, resize **enterButton** so that all of its text is visible.

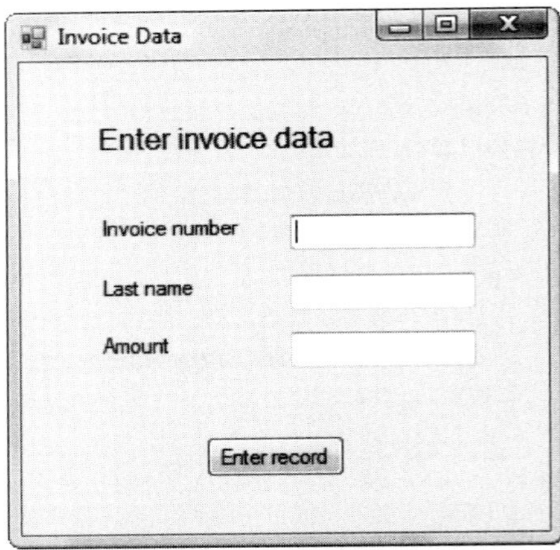

Figure 13-25 Designing the `EnterInvoices` Form

3. View the code for the `Form`. At the start of the class, before the `Form1()` constructor, add the shaded code shown in Figure 13-26. The new code contains statements that perform the following:

   » Declare a delimiter that will be used to separate records in the output file.

   » Declare a path and filename. You can change the path if you want to store the file in a different location on your system.

   » Declare variables for the number, name, and amount of each invoice.

   » Open the file and associate it with a `StreamWriter`.

```
namespace EnterInvoices
{
    public partial class Form1 : Form
    {
        const string DELIM = ",";
        const string FILENAME =
            @"C:\C#\Chapter.13\Invoices.txt";
        int num;
        string name;
        double amount;
        static FileStream outFile = new
            FileStream(FILENAME, FileMode.Create,
            FileAccess.Write);
        StreamWriter writer = new StreamWriter(outFile);
        public Form1()
        {
            InitializeComponent();
        }
```

Figure 13-26 Partial code for `EnterInvoices` program with typed statements shaded

> **» NOTE**
> In Chapter 11, you learned that placing an at sign (@) in front of a filename indicates that all characters in the string should be interpreted literally. This means that the backslashes in the path will not be interpreted as escape sequence characters.

4. At the top of the file, with the other `using` statements, add the following so that the `FileStream` can be declared:

   using System.IO;

5. Click **Save All** (and continue to do so periodically as you work). Return to Design view and double-click the **Enter record** button. As shown in the shaded portions of Figure 13-27, add statements within the method to accept data from each of the three `TextBox`es and convert each field to the appropriate type. Then write each field to a text file, separated by delimiting commas. Finally, clear the `TextBox` fields to be ready for the user to enter a new set of data.

```
private void enterButton_Click(object sender, EventArgs e)
{
    num = Convert.ToInt32(invoiceBox.Text);
    name = nameBox.Text;
    amount = Convert.ToDouble(amountBox.Text);
    writer.WriteLine(num + DELIM + name + DELIM + amount);
    invoiceBox.Clear();
    nameBox.Clear();
    amountBox.Clear();
}
```

Figure 13-27 Code for `enterButton_Click()` method of `EnterInvoices` program

6. Locate the `Dispose()` method, which executes when the user clicks the Close button to dismiss the `Form`. A quick way to locate the method in the Visual Studio IDE is to select **Edit** from the main menu, click **Find and Replace**, click **Quick Find**, and type **Dispose** in the Find What: box. (The Look in: setting can be either Entire Solution or Current Project.) The method appears on the screen. Add two statements to close `writer` and `outFile`, as shown in the shaded statements in Figure 13-28.

```csharp
protected override void Dispose(bool disposing)
  {
     writer.Close();
     outFile.Close();
     if (disposing && (components != null))
     {
         components.Dispose();
     }
     base.Dispose(disposing);
  }
```

Figure 13-28 The `Dispose()` method in the `EnterInvoices` program

7. Click **Save All**. Execute the program. When the `Form` appears, enter data in each `TextBox` and then click the **Enter record** button when you finish. The `TextBox`es clear in preparation for you to enter another record. Enter at least three records before dismissing the `Form`. Figure 13-29 shows data entry in progress.

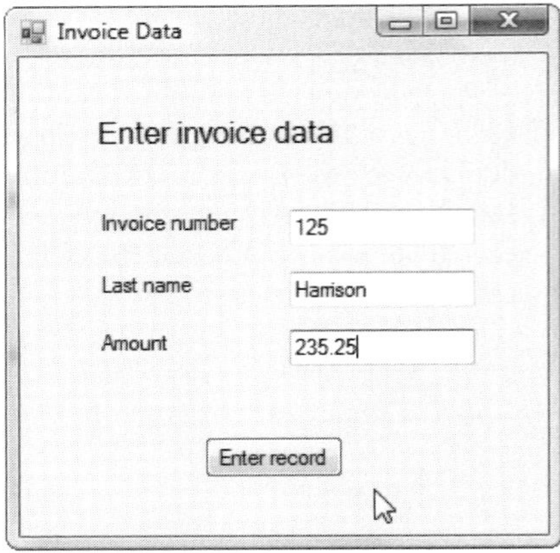

Figure 13-29 Entering data in the `EnterInvoices` application

READING DATA FROM A FILE INTO A Form

In the next steps, you will create a `Form` that you can use to read records from a `File`.

To read data into a Form:

1. Open a new Windows project in Visual Studio and name it **ViewInvoices**.

2. Create a `Form` like the one shown in Figure 13-30 by making the following changes:

» Change the `Text` of `Form1` to **Invoice Data**.

» Add four `Label`s with the text, font, and approximate locations shown in Figure 13-30. (You can click the down arrow next to the `Text` property of a component and then type multiple lines of text.)

» Add a `Button` with the `Text` **View records**.

» Add three `TextBox`es. Name them `invoiceBox`, `nameBox`, and `amountBox`, respectively.

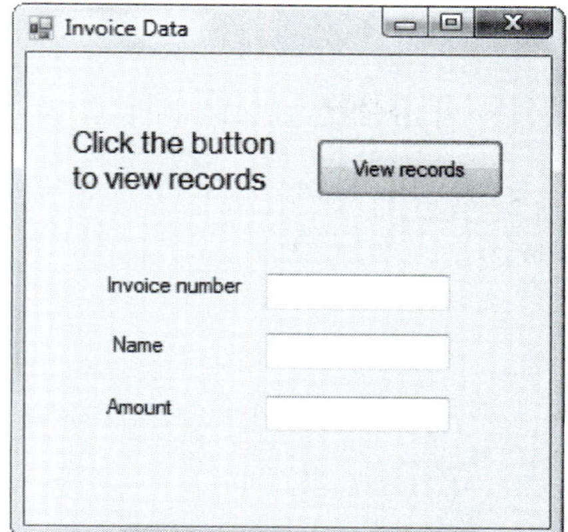

Figure 13-30 The `ViewInvoices` Form

3. In the IDE, double-click the **View records** `Button` to view the code.

4. Add the shaded statements in 13-31. They include:

» A `using System.IO` statement

» Constants for the file delimiter character and the filename

» A `string` into which records can be read and an array of `string`s into which to separate the string read in

» A `FileStream` and `StreamReader` to handle the input file

» Within the `button1_Click()` method, statements to read in a line from the file and split it into three components

> **» NOTE** If you used a different path for the Invoices.txt file in the `EnterInvoices` program, then change this file's path accordingly.

```csharp
using System;
using System.Collections.Generic;
using System.ComponentModel;
using System.Data;
using System.Drawing;
using System.Text;
using System.Windows.Forms;
using System.IO;
```

Figure 13-31 Partial code for the `ViewInvoices` application (*continued*)

```csharp
namespace ViewInvoices
{
    public partial class Form1 : Form
    {
        const char DELIM = ',';
        const string FILENAME = @"C:\C#\Chapter.13\Invoices.txt";
        string recordIn;
        string[] fields;
        static FileStream file = new FileStream(FILENAME,
            FileMode.Open, FileAccess.Read);
        StreamReader reader = new StreamReader(file);
        public Form1()
        {
            InitializeComponent();
        }

        private void button1_Click(object sender, EventArgs e)
        {
            recordIn = reader.ReadLine();
            fields = recordIn.Split(DELIM);
            invoiceBox.Text = fields[0];
            nameBox.Text = fields[1];
            amountBox.Text = fields[2];
        }
    }
}
```

Figure 13-31 (*continued*)

5. Add two `Close()` statements to the `Dispose()` method in the Form1Designer.cs file, as shown in Figure 13-32.

```csharp
protected override void Dispose(bool disposing)
{
    reader.Close();
    file.Close();
    if (disposing && (components != null))
    {
        components.Dispose();
    }
    base.Dispose(disposing);
}
```

Figure 13-32 The `Dispose()` method for the `ViewInvoices` program

6. Save the project and then execute it. When the `Form` appears, click the `Button` to view records. You see the data for the first record you entered when you ran the `EnterInvoices` application; your `Form` should look like the one in Figure 13-33. Click the `Button` again to display the next record.

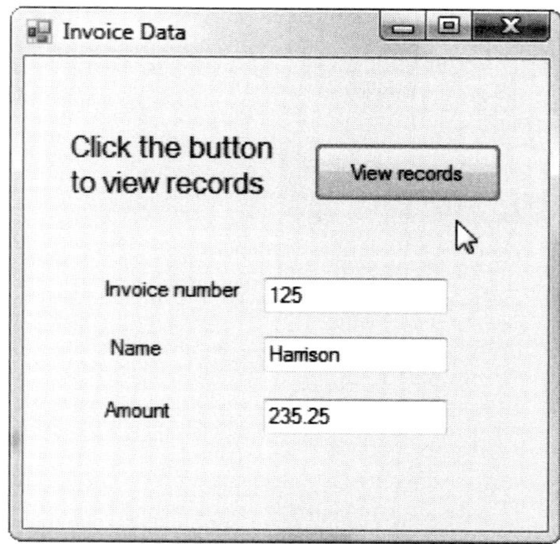

Figure 13-33 Typical execution of `ViewInvoices` program

7. Continue to click the `Button` to view each record. After you view the last record you entered, click the `Button` again. An unhandled exception is generated, as shown in Figure 13-34, because you attempted to read data past the end of the input file.

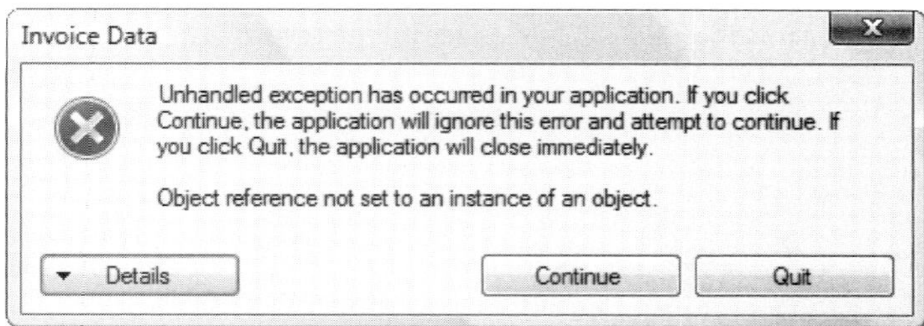

Figure 13-34 Error message window displayed after user attempts to read past the end of the file

8. Click the **Details** button in the `UnhandledException` window to view details of the error. Figure 13-35 shows that a `System.NullReferenceException` was thrown and not handled.

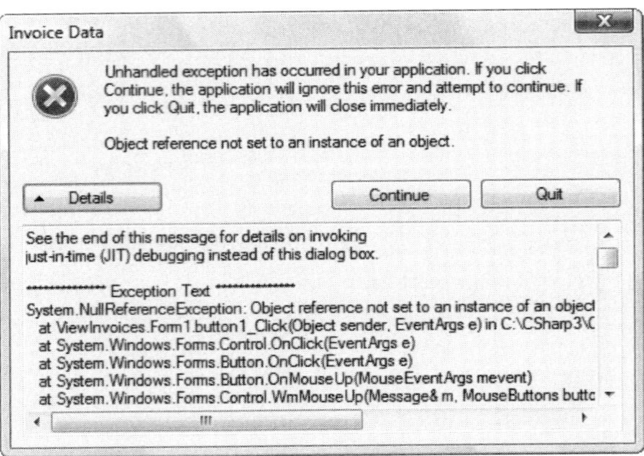

Figure 13-35 Details displayed by unhandled exception window

9. Click **Quit** to close the unhandled exception window.

10. To remedy the unhandled `NullReferenceException` problem, you could take any number of actions. Depending on the application, you might want to do one or more of the following:

    » Display a message.
    » Disallow any more button clicks.
    » End the program.
    » Reposition the file pointer to the file's beginning so the user can view the records again.

    For this example, you will take the first two actions: display a message and disallow further button clicks. Return to Visual Studio and locate the code for the `button1_Click()` method. Add a `try...catch` block, as shown in Figure 13-36. Place all the record-handling code

```
private void button1_Click(object sender, EventArgs e)
{
    try
    {
        recordIn = reader.ReadLine();
        fields = recordIn.Split(DELIM);
        invoiceBox.Text = fields[0];
        nameBox.Text = fields[1];
        amountBox.Text = fields[2];
    }
    catch (NullReferenceException)
    {
        label1.Text = "You have viewed\nall the records";
        button1.Enabled = false;
    }
}
```


Figure 13-36 The `button1_Click()` method modified to handle an exception

in a `try` block, and if a `NullReferenceException` is thrown, change the `Text` in `label1` and disable the View records `Button`.

11. Save the project and then execute it. This time, after you have viewed all the available records, an appropriate message is displayed and the button is disabled, as shown in Figure 13-37.

Figure 13-37 `ViewInvoices Form` after user has viewed last record

12. Dismiss the `Form`. Close Visual Studio.

CHAPTER SUMMARY

» Temporary storage is usually called computer memory or random access memory (RAM). This type of storage is volatile. Permanent storage, on the other hand, is nonvolatile. A computer file is a collection of information stored on a nonvolatile device in a computer system. Files exist on permanent storage devices. When you store data in a computer file on a persistent storage device, you write to the file. When you copy data from a file on a storage device into RAM, you read from the file. Computer users organize their files into folders or directories.

» The `File` class contains methods that allow you to access information about files. The `Directory` class provides you with information about directories or folders.

» A character can be any one of the letters, numbers, or other special symbols (such as punctuation marks) that comprise data. A field is a group of characters that has some meaning. Fields are grouped together to form records. A record is a collection of fields that contain data about an entity. Records are grouped to create files. A data file is a sequential access file when each record is read in order of its position in the file. Usually, the records are stored in order based on the value in some field. Before an application can use a data file, it must open the file by creating an object and associating a stream of bytes with that object. When you close a file, it is no longer available to your application.

» C# views files as a series of bytes that flow into a program from an input device or out of a program to an output device through an object called a stream, which functions as a pipeline or channel. When a C# program executes, three stream objects are created: `Console.In`, `Console.Out`, and `Console.Error`. When you write a program that stores data in a file, you create a `FileStream` object.

» Data can be written to a `StreamWriter` object using the `WriteLine()` method. Fields should be separated by a delimiter, which is a character used to specify the boundary between data items in text files.

» Data can be read from a `StreamReader` object using the `ReadLine()` method. The return value is a string. If the value of the returned string is `null`, then no more data exists in the file. After a record (line of data) is read in, the `Split()` method can be used to separate the data fields into an array of strings. The `Split()` method takes a character parameter and separates a string into substrings at each occurrence of the character delimiter.

» When you read data from a sequential file, subsequent records are read in order because a file's position pointer holds the byte number of the next byte to be read. To reread a file, you could close it and reopen it, or you can just reposition the file pointer using the `Seek()` method and the `SeekOrigin` enumeration.

» Serialization is the process of converting objects into streams of bytes. Deserialization is the reverse process; it converts streams of bytes back into objects. To create a class that can be serialized, you mark it with the `[Serializable]` attribute. An entire object can be written to or read from a data file with a single statement.

KEY TERMS

Random access memory (RAM) is temporary storage in a computer.

Volatile storage is the type that is lost when power is lost.

Nonvolatile storage is permanent storage; it is not lost when a computer loses power.

A **computer file** is a collection of information stored on a nonvolatile device in a computer system.

Permanent storage devices, such as hard disks, floppy disks, Zip disks, USB drives, reels or cassettes of magnetic tape, and optical disks, are used to store files.

Data files contain facts and figures.

Program files or **application files** store software instructions.

When you store data in a computer file on a permanent storage device, you **write to the file**.

When you copy data from a file on a storage device into RAM, you **read from the file**.

Persistent storage is nonvolatile storage.

The **root directory** is the main directory of a storage device.

Folders or **directories** are structures used to organize files on a storage device.

A **path** is composed of the disk drive in which a file resides plus the complete hierarchy of directories.

The **File class** contains methods that allow you to access information about files.

The **Directory class** provides information about directories or folders.

The **data hierarchy** is the relationship of characters, fields, records, and files.

A **character** is any one of the letters, numbers, or other special symbols (such as punctuation marks) that comprise data.

A computer's **character set** is the group of all the characters used to represent data on a particular computer.

A **field** is a character or group of characters that has some meaning.

A **record** is a collection of fields that contain data about an entity.

Data files consist of related records.

A **sequential access file** is a data file in which each record is read in order based on its position in the file; usually the records are stored in order based on the value in some field.

The **key field** is the field used to control the order of records in a sequential file.

Opening a file involves creating an object and associating a stream of bytes with it.

Closing a file means it is no longer available to an application.

A **stream** is a pipeline or channel through which bytes are input from and output to a file.

Programmers say `FileStream` **exposes** a stream around a file.

Binary files are files that can store any of the 256 combinations of bits in any byte instead of just those combinations that form readable text.

XML is an abbreviation of eXtensible Markup Language, which is a standard for exchanging data over the Internet.

A **delimiter** is a character used to specify the boundary between characters in text files.

A **CSV file** is one that contains comma-separated values.

A **token** is a block of text within a string that represents an entity or field.

The term **magic number** refers to the bad programming practice of hard-coding numbers in code without explanation.

A file's **file position pointer** holds the byte number of the next byte to be read.

Serialization is the process of converting objects into streams of bytes.

Deserialization is the process of converting streams of bytes back into objects.

REVIEW QUESTIONS

1. Random access memory is ___________ .
    a. persistent
    b. volatile
    c. permanent
    d. sequential

2. A collection of facts and figures stored on a nonvolatile device in a computer system is a(n) ___________ .
    a. data file
    b. application file
    c. operating system
    d. memory map

3. Which of the following is not permanent storage?
    a. RAM
    b. a hard disk
    c. a USB drive
    d. all of these

4. When you store data in a computer file on a persistent storage device, you are ___________ .

    a. reading   c. writing

    b. directing   d. rooting

5. Which of the following is not a `File` class method?

    a. `Create()`   c. `Exists()`

    b. `Delete()`   d. `End()`

6. In the data hierarchy, a group of characters that has some meaning, such as a last name or ID number, is a ___________ .

    a. byte   c. file

    b. field   d. record

7. When each record in a file is stored in order based on the value in some field, the file is a(n) ___________ file.

    a. random access   c. formatted

    b. application   d. sequential

8. When you open a file, you create an object and associate a ___________ of bytes with it.

    a. path   c. stream

    b. folder   d. directory

9. Which of the following is not part of a `FileStream` constructor?

    a. the file size   c. the filename

    b. the file mode   d. the type of access

10. When a file's mode is `Create`, a new file will be created ___________ .

    a. even if one with the same name already exists

    b. only if one with the same name does not already exist

    c. only if one with the same name already exists

    d. only if the access is `Read`

11. Which of the following is not a `FileStream` property?

    a. `CanRead`   c. `CanSeek`

    b. `CanExist`   d. `CanWrite`

12. Which of the following is not a file `Access` enumeration?

    a. `Read`   c. `WriteRead`

    b. `Write`   d. `ReadWrite`

13. A character used to specify the boundary between data items in text files is a ____________ .
    a. sentinel   c. delimiter
    b. stopgap   d. margin

14. Which character can be used to specify a boundary between characters in text files?
    a. a comma   c. either of these
    b. a semicolon   d. neither of these

15. After a `StreamReader` has been defined and associated with a file, the `ReadLine()` method can be used to ____________ .
    a. retrieve one line at a time from the file
    b. retrieve one character at a time from the file
    c. store one line at a time in a file
    d. split a `string` into tokens

16. The argument to the `Split()` method is ____________ .
    a. `void`
    b. the number of fields into which to split a record
    c. the character that identifies a new field in a `string`
    d. a `string` that can be split into tokens

17. The `Split()` method stores its results in ____________ .
    a. a `string`
    b. an array of `strings`
    c. an appropriate data type for each token
    d. an array of bytes

18. A file's ____________ holds the byte number of the next byte to be read.
    a. index indicator   c. header file
    b. position pointer   d. key field

19. The process of converting objects into streams of bytes is ____________ .
    a. extrication   c. mapping
    b. splitting   d. serialization

20. Which of the following is serializable?
    a. an `int`   c. a `string`
    b. an array of `ints`   d. all of the above

EXERCISES

1. Create a program that allows a user to continually enter directory names until the user types "end". If the directory name exists, display a list of the files in it; otherwise, display a message indicating the directory does not exist. If the directory exists and files are listed, prompt the user to enter one of the filenames. If the file exists, display its creation date and time; otherwise, display a message indicating the file does not exist. Save the program as **TestFileAndDirectory.cs**. Create as many test directories and files as necessary to test your program. Figure 13-38 shows a typical execution.

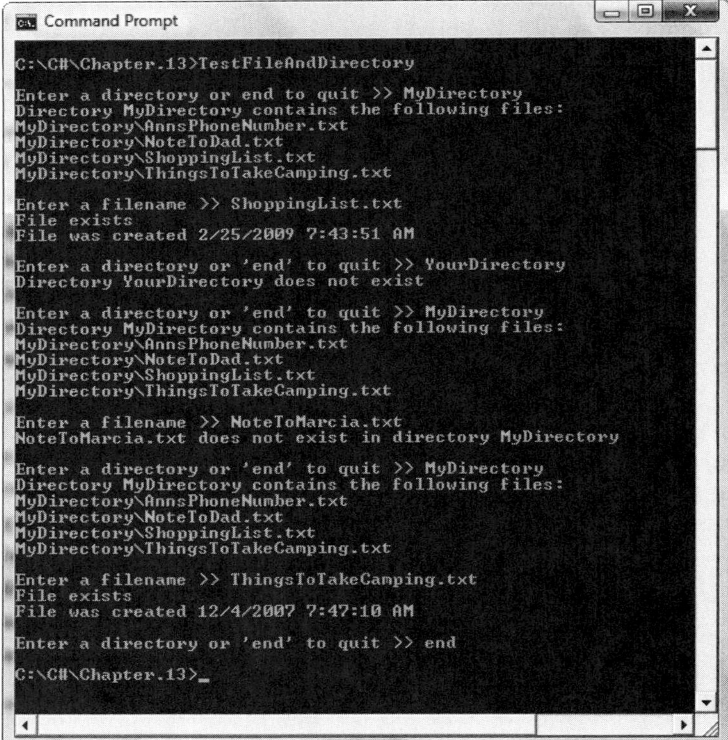

Figure 13-38 Typical execution of `TestFileAndDirectory` program

2. Create a file that contains your favorite movie quote. Use a text editor such as Notepad and save the file as **Quote.txt**. Copy the file contents and paste them into a word-processing program such as Word. Save the file as **Quote.doc**. Write an application that displays the sizes of the two files as well as the ratio of their sizes to each other. To discover a file's

size, you can create a `System.IO.FileInfo` object using a statement such as the following, where `FILE_NAME` is a string that contains the name of the file:

```
FileInfo wordInfo = new FileInfo(FILE_NAME);
```

Save the file as **FileComparison.cs**.

3. Using Visual Studio, create a `Form` like the one shown in Figure 13-39. Specify a directory on your system, and when the `Form` loads, list the files it contains in a `CheckedListBox`. Allow the user to click a file's check box and display the file's creation date and time. (Each time the user checks a new filename, display its creation date in place of the original selection.) Save the project as **TestFileAndDirectory2**. Create as many files as necessary to test your program. Figure 13-39 shows a typical execution.

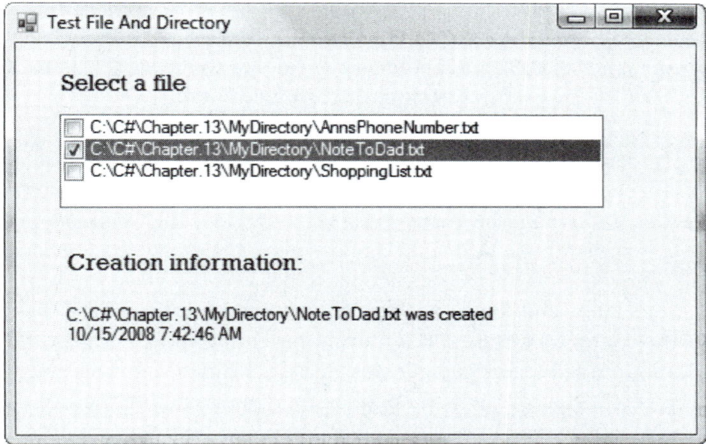

Figure 13-39 Typical execution of `TestFileAndDirectory2` program

4. a. Create a `Friend` class in which you can store your friends' first and last names, phone numbers, and the month and day of your friends' birthdays. Write a program that prompts you to enter friends' data and saves each record to a file. Save the program as **WriteFriendRecords.cs**.

   b. Create a program that reads the file created in Exercise 4a and displays each friend's data to the screen. Save the programs as **ReadFriendRecords.cs**.

   c. Create a program that prompts you for a birth month, reads the file created in Exercise 4a, and displays data for each friend who has a birthday in the specified month. Save the programs as **FriendBirthdayReminder.cs**.

5. a. In the Visual Studio IDE, design a `Form` that allows a user to select options for the background color and size and to give the `Form` a title. The `Form` should look like the one shown in Figure 13-40. Change each feature of the `Form` as the user makes selections. After the user clicks the "Save form settings" `Button`, save the color, size, and title as strings to a file and disable the button. Save the project as **CustomizeAForm**.

    b. In the Visual Studio IDE, design a `Form` like the one in Figure 13-40, except include a `Button` to retrieve the `Form` settings. When the user clicks the "Retrieve form settings" `Button`, read the settings from the file saved in the `CustomizeAForm` project, and set the `Form`'s color, size, and title to the values that were saved previously. Save the project as **RetrieveCustomizedForm**.

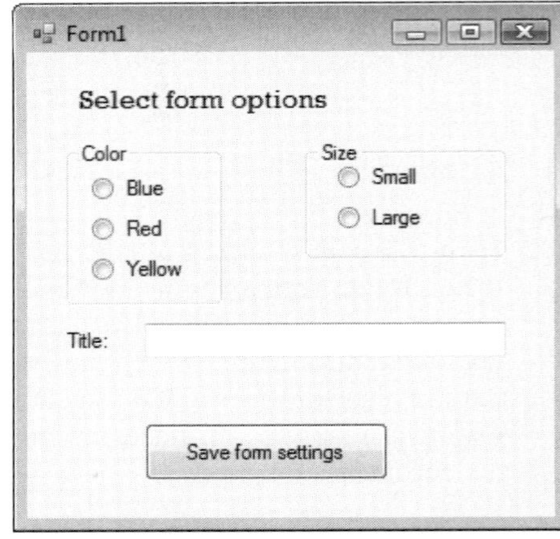

Figure 13-40 Form in `CustomizeAForm` project

6. Using the Visual Studio IDE, create a `Form` that contains a game in which the computer randomly selects one of three letters (A, B, or C) 10 times, and the user tries to guess which letter was selected. At the start of the game, read in the previous high score from a data file. (Create this file to hold "0" the first time the game is played.) Display the previous high score on the `Form` to show the player the score to try to beat. As the player makes each guess, show the player's guess and the computer's choice, and award a point if the player correctly guesses the computer's choice. Keep a running count of the number of correct guesses. After 10 random selections and guesses, disable the game controls and create a file that holds the new high score, which might be the same as before the game or a new higher number. When the player begins a new game, the high score will be displayed on the `Form` as the new score to beat. Save the project as **HighScore**.

DEBUGGING EXERCISES

Each of the following files in the Chapter.13 folder on your Student Disk has syntax and/or logical errors. In each case, determine the problem and fix the program. After you correct the errors, save each file using the same filename preceded with *Fixed*. For example, save DebugThirteen1.cs as **FixedDebugThirteen1.cs**.

   a. DebugThirteen1.cs

   b. DebugThirteen2.cs

   c. DebugThirteen3.cs

   d. DebugThirteen4.cs

UP FOR DISCUSSION

1. In Exercise 2 earlier in this chapter, what did you discover about the size difference between files that hold the same contents but were created using different software (such as Word and Notepad)? Why do you think the file sizes are so different, even though the files contain the same data?

2. Suppose your employer asks you to write a program that lists all the company's employees, their salaries, and their ages. You are provided with the company personnel file to use as input. You decide to take the file home so you can create the program over the weekend. Is this acceptable? What if the file contained only employees' names and departments, but not more sensitive data such as salaries and ages?

14

USING LINQ TO ACCESS DATA IN C# PROGRAMS

In this chapter you will:

Understand relational database fundamentals
Create databases and table descriptions
Be able to identify primary keys
Understand database structure notation
Create SQL queries
Create an Access database
Understand implicitly typed variables
Understand LINQ
Retrieve data from an Access database in C#
Use LINQ queries with an Access database table
Use LINQ operators to sort and group data

Businesses run by using data. Most businesses would be damaged severely if their data was lost—for example, customers could not be contacted, employees could not be paid, and orders could not be shipped. Well-run businesses do not just possess a lot of data; the data must be organized to be useful. When a business's data is structured in a useful manner, the business can improve its performance. For example, salespeople can discover which customers prefer which products or services, and administrators can discover which employees are the most productive. Businesses can determine which products and services produce the most profit and which should be dropped. Relational databases provide a means to accomplish all these tasks.

In this chapter you will learn about databases. You also will learn about LINQ, which is a Visual Studio tool for accessing data stored in databases and other collections, and you will learn how to incorporate LINQ into your C# programs. This chapter is only a brief introduction to these topics. You can buy entire books on database construction and theory, and other books on every detail of LINQ. This chapter covers only the fundamentals of each topic so you can begin to appreciate how your C# programs have the potential to satisfy important business data needs.

UNDERSTANDING RELATIONAL DATABASE FUNDAMENTALS

When you store data items for use within computer systems, they are often stored in what is known as a data hierarchy, where the smallest usable unit of data is the character, often a letter or number. Characters are grouped together to form fields, such as `firstName`, `lastName`, and `socialSecurityNumber`. Related fields are often grouped together to form records—groups of fields that go together because they represent attributes of some entity, such as an employee, a customer, an inventory item, or a bank account. Files are composed of related records; for example, a file might contain a record for each employee in a company or each account at a bank.

Most organizations store many files that contain the data they need to operate their businesses. For example, businesses often need to maintain files that contain data about employees, customers, inventory items, and orders. Many organizations use database software to organize the information in these files. A **database** holds a file, or more frequently, a group of files that an organization needs to support its applications. In a database, the files often are called **tables** because you can arrange their contents in rows and columns. Real-life examples of database-like tables abound. For example, consider the listings in a telephone book. Each listing in a city directory might contain four columns, as shown in Figure 14-1—last name, first name, street address, and phone number. Although your local phone directory might not store its data in the rigid columnar format shown in the figure, it could. You can see that each column represents a field and that each row represents one record. You can picture a table within a database in the same way.

Last Name	First Name	Address	Phone
Abbott	William	123 Oak Lane	490-8920
Ackerman	Kimberly	467 Elm Drive	787-2781
Adams	Stanley	8120 Pine Street	787-0129
Adams	Violet	347 Oak Lane	490-8912
Adams	William	12 Second Street	490-3667

Figure 14-1 A telephone book table

» NOTE In Chapter 6, you learned that arrays also are sometimes referred to as tables. Arrays (stored in memory) and tables (stored in databases) are similar in that both contain rows and columns. When an array has multiple columns, all must have the same data type. The same is not true for tables stored in databases.

Figure 14-1 includes five records, each representing a unique person. It is relatively easy to scan this short list of names to find a person's phone number; of course, telephone books contain many more records. Some telephone book users, such as telemarketers or even the phone company, might prefer to use a book in which the records are organized in telephone-number order. Others, such as door-to-door salespeople, might prefer a telephone book in which the records are organized in street-address order. Most people, however, prefer a telephone book in which the records are organized as shown, in alphabetical order by last name. It is most convenient for different users when computerized databases can sort records in various orders based on the contents of different columns.

Unless you are reading a telephone book for a very small town, a last name alone often is not sufficient to identify a person. In the example in Figure 14-1, three people have the last name of Adams. For these records, you need to examine the first name before you can determine the correct phone number. In a large city, many people might have the same first and last names; in that case, you might also need to examine the street address to identify a person. As with the telephone book, most computerized database tables require a way to identify each record uniquely, even if it means using multiple columns. A value that uniquely identifies a record is called a **primary key**, or a **key** for short. Key fields often are defined as a single column, but as with the telephone book, keys can be constructed from multiple columns. A key constructed from multiple columns is a **compound key**, also known as a **composite key**.

Telephone books are republished periodically because changes have occurred—new people have moved into the city and become telephone customers, and others have left, canceled service, or changed phone numbers. With computerized database tables, you also need to add, delete, and modify records, although usually far more frequently than phone books are published.

As with telephone books, computerized database tables frequently contain thousands of records, or rows, and each row might contain entries in dozens of columns. Handling and organizing all the data contained in an organization's tables requires sophisticated software.

Database management software, also known as a **database management system (DBMS)**, is a set of programs that allows users to:

» Create table descriptions.

» Identify keys.

» Add, delete, and update records within a table.

» Arrange records within a table so they are sorted by different fields.

» Write questions that select specific records from a table for viewing.

» Write questions that combine information from multiple tables. This is possible because the database management software establishes and maintains relationships between the columns in the tables. A group of database tables from which you can make these connections is a **relational database**.

» Create reports that allow users to easily interpret your data, and create forms that allow users to view and enter data using an easy-to-manage interactive screen.

» Keep data secure by employing sophisticated security measures.

If you have used different word-processing or spreadsheet programs, you know that each version works a little differently, although each carries out the same types of tasks. Like other computer programs, each database management software package operates differently; however, with each, you need to perform the same types of tasks.

» TWO TRUTHS AND A LIE: UNDERSTANDING RELATIONAL DATABASE FUNDAMENTALS

1. Files are composed of related records, and records are composed of fields.
2. In a database, files often are called tables because you can arrange their contents in rows and columns.
3. Key fields always are defined as a single table column.

The false statement is #3. Key fields often are defined as a single table column, but keys can be constructed from multiple columns. A key constructed from multiple columns is a compound or composite key.

CREATING DATABASES AND TABLE DESCRIPTIONS

Creating a useful database requires a lot of planning and analysis. You must decide what data will be stored, how that data will be divided between tables, and how the tables will interrelate. Before you create any tables, you must create the database itself. With most database software packages, creating the database that will hold the tables requires nothing more than providing a name for the database and indicating the physical location, perhaps a hard disk drive, where the database will be stored. When you save a table, one convention recommends that you use a name that begins with the prefix "tbl"—for example, `tblCustomers`. Your databases often become filled with a variety of objects—tables, forms that users can use for data entry, reports that organize the data for viewing, queries that select subsets of data for viewing, and so on. Using naming conventions, such as beginning each table name with a prefix that identifies it as a table, helps you to keep track of the various objects in your system.

»NOTE When you save a table description, many database management programs suggest a default, generic name such as `Table1`. Usually, a more descriptive name is more useful to you as you continue to create objects.

»NOTE Beginning table names with the `tbl` prefix is part of the **Leszynski naming convention** (LNC). This convention is most popular with Microsoft Access users and Visual Basic programmers. This format is just a convention, and is not required by any database. Your instructor or supervisor might approve of a different convention.

Before you can enter any data into a database table, you must design the table. At minimum, this involves two tasks:

» You must decide what columns your table needs, and provide names for them.

» You must provide a data type for each column.

For example, assume you are designing a customer database table. Figure 14-2 shows some column names and data types you might use.

Column	Data Type
customerID	Text
lastName	Text
firstName	Text
streetAddress	Text
balanceOwed	Numeric

Figure 14-2 Customer table description

»NOTE
A table description closely resembles the list of variables that you have used with every program throughout this book.

»NOTE It is important to think carefully about the original design of a database. After the database has been created and data has been entered, it could be difficult and time consuming to make changes.

The table description in Figure 14-2 uses just two data types—text and numeric. Text columns can hold any type of characters—letters or digits. Numeric columns can hold numbers only. Depending on the database management software you use, you might have many more sophisticated data types at your disposal. For example, some database software divides the numeric data type into several subcategories such as integers (whole number only) and double-precision numbers (numbers that contain decimals). Other options might include special categories for currency numbers (representing dollars and cents), dates, and Boolean columns (representing true or false). At the least, all database software recognizes the distinction between text and numeric data.

> **» NOTE** Throughout this book, you have been aware of the distinction that computers make between text and numeric data. Because of the way computers handle data, every type of software observes this distinction. Throughout this book, the term "string" has been used to describe text fields. The term "text" is used in this chapter only because popular database packages use it.

> **» NOTE** Unassigned variables within computer programs might be empty (containing a null value), or might contain unknown or garbage values. Similarly, columns in database tables might also contain null or unknown values. When a field in a database contains a null value, it does not mean that the field holds a 0 or a space; it means that no data has been entered for the field at all. Although "null" and "empty" are used synonymously by many database developers, the terms have slightly different meanings to some programming professionals such as Visual Basic programmers.

The table description in Figure 14-2 uses one-word column names and camel casing, in the same way that variable names have been defined throughout this book. Many database software packages do not require that data column names be single words without embedded spaces, but many database table designers prefer single-word names because they resemble variable names in programs. In addition, when you write programs that access a database table, the single-word field names can be used "as is," without special syntax to indicate the names that represent a single field. As a further advantage, when you use a single word to label each database column, it is easier to understand whether just one column is being referenced, or several.

The `customerID` column in Figure 14-2 is defined as a text field or text column. If `customerID` numbers are composed entirely of digits, this column could also be defined as numeric. Some database designers feel that key fields should usually be numeric. However, some database designers feel that columns should be defined as numeric only if they need to be—that is, only if they might be used in arithmetic calculations. The description in Figure 14-2 follows this convention by declaring `customerID` to be a text column, but it would also be reasonable to declare it as a numeric column.

> **» NOTE** Among database designers, there is controversy about the best data type for key fields. As you continue to study database creation, you will learn more about the relevant issues and be able to establish your own opinions about them.

Many database management software packages allow you to add a narrative description of each data column of a table. This allows you to make comments that become part of the table. These comments do not affect the way the table operates; they simply serve as documentation for those who are reading a table description. For example, you might want to make a note that `customerID` should consist of five digits, or that `balanceOwed` should not exceed a given limit. Some software allows you to specify that values for a certain column are required—the user cannot create a record without providing data for these columns. In addition, you might be able to indicate value limits for a column—high and low numbers between which the column contents must fall.

»TWO TRUTHS AND A LIE: CREATING DATABASES AND TABLE DESCRIPTIONS

1. Databases are often filled with multiple objects such as tables, forms, and queries.

2. Designing a table involves deciding how many rows your table needs and filling them with appropriate data.

3. Many database table designers prefer single-word column names because they resemble variable names in programs, because the names can be easily used in programs, and because people can more easily understand whether one or several columns are being referenced.

The false statement is # 2. Designing a table involves deciding what columns your table needs, providing names for them, and providing a data type for each column.

IDENTIFYING PRIMARY KEYS

In most tables you create for a database, you want to identify a column, or possibly a combination of columns, as the table's key column or field, also called the primary key. The primary key in a table is the column that makes each record different from all others. For example, in the customer table in Figure 14-2, the logical choice for a primary key is the `customerID` column—each customer record that is entered into the customer table has a unique value in this column. Many customers might have the same first name or last name (or both), and multiple customers also might have the same street address or balance due. However, each customer possesses a unique ID number.

Other typical examples of primary keys include:

» A student ID number in a table that contains college student information

» A part number in a table that contains inventory items

» A Social Security number in a table that contains employee information

In each of these examples, the primary key uniquely identifies the row. For example, each student has a unique ID number assigned by the college. Other columns in a student table would not be adequate keys—many students have the same last name, first name, hometown, or major.

»NOTE In some database software packages, such as Microsoft Access, you indicate a primary key simply by selecting a column name and clicking a button that is labeled with a key icon.

»NOTE A primary key should be immutable, meaning that a value does not change during normal operation.

»NOTE Even if a database table contains only one employee named Smith, for example, or only one employee with the job title of Salesperson, those fields are still not good primary key candidates because more Smiths and salespeople could be added later. Analyzing existing data is not a foolproof way to select a good key; you must also consider likely future data.

»NOTE It is no coincidence that each of the preceding examples of a key is a number, such as a student ID number or item number. Often, assigning a number to each row in a table is the simplest and most efficient method of obtaining a useful key. However, it is possible that a table's key could be a text field.

>> **NOTE** Sometimes, several columns could serve as the key. For example, if an employee record contains both a company-assigned employee ID and a Social Security number, then both columns are candidate keys. After you choose a primary key from among candidate keys, the remaining candidate keys become alternate keys.

The primary key is important for several reasons:

>> You can configure your database software to prevent multiple records from containing the same value in this column, thus avoiding data-entry errors.

>> You might want to sort your records in this order before displaying or printing them.

>> You use this column when setting up relationships between this table and others that will become part of the same database.

In addition, you need to understand the concept of the primary key when you normalize a database. **Normalization** is the process of designing and creating a set of database tables that satisfies users' needs and avoids many potential problems such as data redundancies and anomalies. **Data redundancy** is the unnecessary repetition of data. An **anomaly** is an irregularity in a database's design that causes problems and inconveniences. To keep the examples in this chapter simple, only single database tables are used. However, as you grow proficient in database use and constructions, you will want to create databases with relationships between multiple tables, which requires a more thorough understanding of normalization.

>> **NOTE** As an example of data redundancy, consider a table of names and addresses in which many addresses are in the same zip code. Instead of storing the same city and state name with each record, it is more efficient to store only the zip code with each record, and then to associate the table with another table that contains a list of zip codes and the corresponding cities and states.

>> **NOTE** There are many types of anomalies. For example, an anomaly occurs when the same data is stored in multiple locations. For example, if a database contains a table of items in stock and their prices, and another table contains customer orders, including items and prices, then any price changes must be made in multiple locations, increasing the chance for error.

Usually, after you have identified the necessary fields and their data types and identified the primary key, you are ready to save your table description and begin to enter data.

>>TWO TRUTHS AND A LIE: IDENTIFYING PRIMARY KEYS

1. The primary key in a table is the record that appears first in a sorted list.
2. Normalization is the process of designing and creating a set of database tables that satisfies users' needs and avoids many potential problems.
3. Data redundancy is the unnecessary repetition of data.

The false statement is #1. The primary key in a table is the column that makes each record different from all others.

UNDERSTANDING DATABASE STRUCTURE NOTATION

A shorthand way to describe a table is to use the table name followed by parentheses that contain all the field names, with the primary key underlined. Thus, when a table is named `tblStudents` and contains columns named `idNumber`, `lastName`, `firstName`, and `gradePointAverage`, and `idNumber` is the key, you can reference the table using the following notation:

```
tblStudents(idNumber, lastName, firstName, gradePointAverage)
```

Although this shorthand notation does not provide information about data types or range limits on values, it does provide a quick overview of the table's structure.

» TWO TRUTHS AND A LIE: UNDERSTANDING DATABASE STRUCTURE NOTATION

1. A shorthand way to describe a table is to use the table name followed by parentheses that contain all the field names.
2. Typically, when you describe a table using database structure notation, the primary key is underlined.
3. Database structure notation provides you with information about column names, their data types, and their range limits.

The false statement is #3. Although this shorthand notation does not provide information about data types or range limits on values, it does provide a quick overview of the structure of a table.

CREATING SQL QUERIES

Data tables often contain hundreds or thousands of rows; making sense out of that much information is a daunting task. Frequently, you want to cull subsets of data from a table you have created. For example, you might want to view only those customers with an address in a specific state, only inventory items whose quantity in stock has fallen below the normal reorder point, or only employees who participate in an insurance plan. Besides limiting records, you might also want to limit the columns that you view. For example, student records might contain dozens of fields, but a school administrator might only be interested in looking at names and grade point averages (GPAs). The questions that cause the database software to extract the appropriate records from a table and specify the fields to be viewed are called queries; a **query** is simply a request using syntax that the database software can understand.

Depending on the software you use, you might create a query by filling in blanks (using a language called **query by example**) or by writing statements similar to those in many programming languages. The most common language that database administrators use to access data in their tables is **Structured Query Language**, or **SQL**. The basic form of the SQL command that retrieves selected records from a table is **SELECT-FROM-WHERE**. The SELECT-FROM-WHERE SQL statement:

- » *Selects* the columns you want to view
- » *From* a specific table
- » *Where* one or more conditions are met

> **»»NOTE** "SQL" frequently is pronounced "sequel"; however, several SQL product Web sites insist that the official pronunciation is "S-Q-L." Similarly, some people pronounce GUI as "gooey" and others insist that it should be "G-U-I." In general, a preferred pronunciation evolves in an organization. The **TLA**, which is a three-letter abbreviation for *three-letter abbreviation*, is the most popular type of abbreviation in technical terminology.

For example, suppose a customer table named `tblCustomer` contains data about your business customers and that the structure of the table is `tblCustomer(`<u>`custId`</u>`, lastName, state)`. Then, a statement such as:

```
SELECT custId, lastName FROM tblCustomer WHERE state = "WI"
```

> **»»NOTE**
> Conventionally, SQL keywords such as `SELECT` appear entirely in uppercase; this book follows that convention.

would display a new table that contains two columns—`custId` and `lastName`—and only as many rows as needed to hold customers whose state column contains "WI". Besides using = to mean "equal to," you can use the comparison conditions > (greater than), < (less than), >= (greater than or equal to), and <= (less than or equal to). As you have already learned from working with programming variables throughout this book, text field values are always contained within quotes, whereas numeric values are not.

> **»»NOTE** In database management systems, a particular way of looking at a database is sometimes called a **view**. Typically, a view arranges records in some order and makes only certain fields visible. The different views provided by database software are virtual; that is, they do not affect the physical organization of the database.

To select all fields for each record in a table, you can use the asterisk as a wildcard; a **wildcard** is a symbol that means "any" or "all." For example, `SELECT * FROM tblCustomer WHERE state = " WI "` would select all columns for every customer whose state is "WI", not just specifically named columns. To select all customers from a table, you can omit the `WHERE` clause in a `SELECT-FROM-WHERE` statement. In other words, `SELECT * FROM tblCustomer` selects all columns for all customers. You learned about making selections in computer programs much earlier in this book, and you have probably noticed that `SELECT-FROM-WHERE` statements serve the same purpose as programming decisions. As with decision statements in programs, SQL allows you to create compound conditions using `AND` or `OR` operators. In addition, you can precede any condition with a `NOT` operator to achieve a negative result. In summary, Figure 14-3 shows a database table named `tblInventory` with the following structure:

```
tblInventory(itemNumber, description, quantityInStock, price)
```

The table contains five records. Figure 14-4 lists several typical SQL SELECT statements you might use with tblInventory, and explains each.

itemNumber	description	quantityInStock	price
144	Pkg 12 party plates	250	$14.99
231	Helium balloons	180	$2.50
267	Paper streamers	68	$1.89
312	Disposable tablecloth	20	$6.99
383	Pkg 20 napkins	315	$2.39

Figure 14-3 The tblInventory table

SQL Statement	Explanation
SELECT itemNumber, price FROM tblInventory	Shows only the item number and price for all five records.
SELECT * FROM tblInventory WHERE price > 5.00	Shows all fields from only those records in which price is greater than $5.00—items 144 and 312.
SELECT itemNumber FROM tblInventory WHERE quantityInStock > 200 AND price > 10.00	Shows item number 144—the only record that has a quantity greater than 200 as well as a price greater than $10.00.
SELECT description, price FROM tblInventory WHERE description = "Pkg 20 napkins" OR itemNumber < 200	Shows the description and price fields for the package of 12 party plates and the package of 20 napkins. Each selected record only needs to satisfy one of the two criteria.
SELECT itemNumber FROM tblInventory WHERE NOT price < 14.00	Shows the item number for the only record in which the price is not less than $14.00—item 144.

Figure 14-4 Sample SQL statements and explanations

»TWO TRUTHS AND A LIE: CREATING SQL QUERIES

1. A query is a question that causes database software to extract appropriate fields and records from a table.
2. The most common language that database administrators use to access data in their tables is Structured Query Language, or SQL.
3. The basic form of the SQL command that retrieves selected records from a table is RETRIEVE-FROM-SELECTION.

The false statement is # 3. The basic form of the SQL command that retrieves selected records from a table is SELECT-FROM-WHERE.

CREATING AN ACCESS DATABASE

Microsoft Office Access is a relational database that is part of some versions of the Microsoft Office 2007 system. It combines the relational Microsoft Jet Database Engine with a GUI user interface and other tools. Access is not the only database on the market, but it is convenient for many users because it comes packaged with some versions of Microsoft Office. Using Access correctly and efficiently can take some time to learn; at most colleges, you can take at least a two-semester course to learn Access thoroughly. This section introduces you to Access as an example of a typical database.

Figure 14-5 shows the environment in which a database table is designed in Access. Suppose Cartman College wants to keep track of some student data in a database. To keep the example simple, suppose the college wants to store only an ID number, first and last names, and a GPA for each student. In Access, a database developer can type field names for the data that will be stored and can assign an appropriate data type for each. In Figure 14-5, a `tblStudents` table is defined, including fields for `ID`, `LastName`, `FirstName`, and `GradePointAverage`.

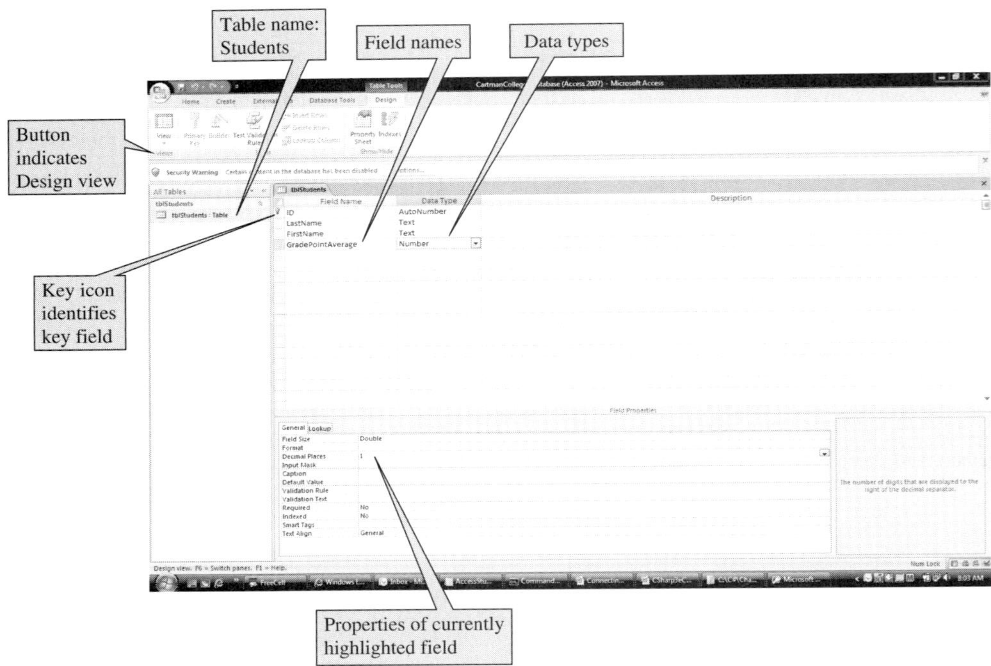

Figure 14-5 The Design view of the `tblStudents` table in Access

> **NOTE** Figure 14-5 shows that the ID field type was chosen to be `AutoNumber`, which means Access will automatically assign consecutive numbers to each new record as it is entered.

> **NOTE**
> Access was the name of an earlier failed Microsoft communications program. The corporation reused the name when it developed its database software in 1992.

> **NOTE**
> Other popular database packages include Microsoft SQL, MySQL, Borland Paradox, FileMaker Pro, Lotus Approach, Oracle XE, and Sun StarBase.

> **NOTE**
> In the "You Do It" section at the end of this chapter, you can walk through the specific steps to create your own database.

> **NOTE**
> When you open the Cartman College database file that is provided with your Student files, if you do not immediately see the Design View as shown in Figure 14-5, you can click the Home tab, click the down arrow under View, and click Design View.

After a table's design has been completed, a user can enter data into the table. Figure 14-6 shows the `tblStudents` table in Access's Datasheet view, in which a user can type data like it would be typed into a spreadsheet. The column headings in the datasheet are provided automatically based on the names that were selected in the Design view.

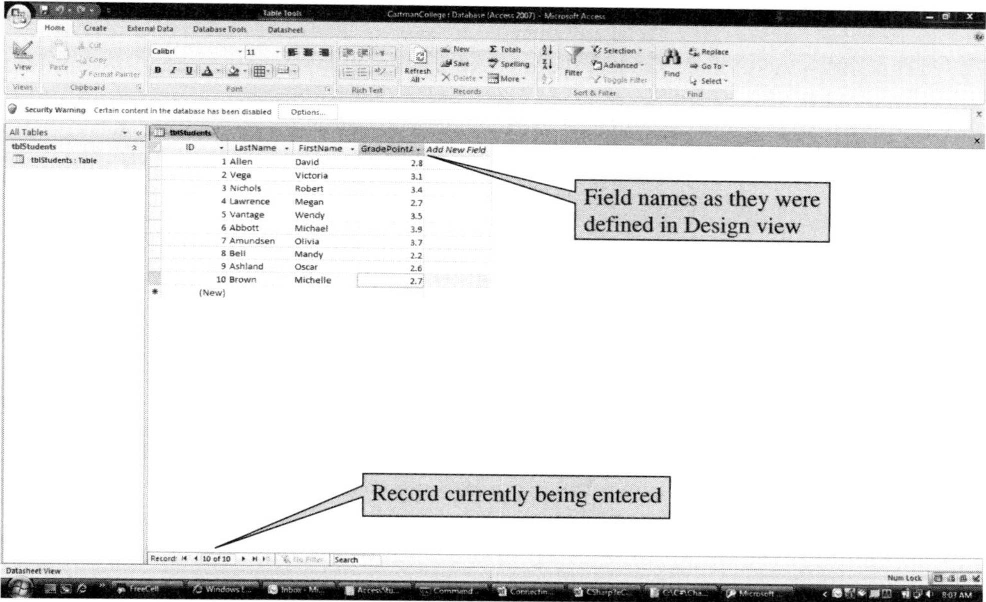

Figure 14-6 The Datasheet view of the `tblStudents` table in Access

In a database actually used by a college, many more fields would be stored for each student and additional tables would be created for courses, faculty, and so on. However, this small database provides enough data to demonstrate using C# to access the stored data.

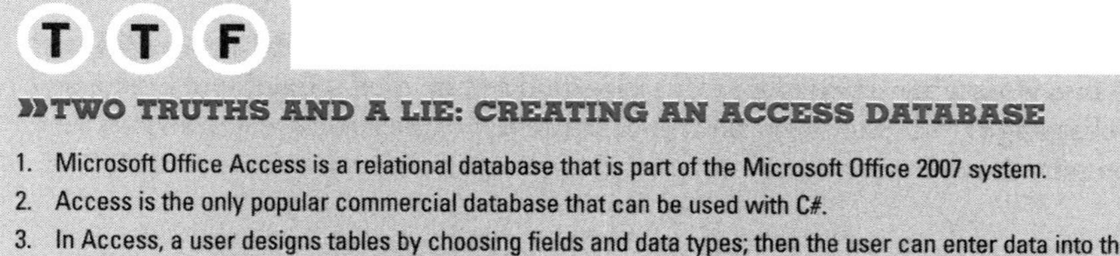

⟩⟩TWO TRUTHS AND A LIE: CREATING AN ACCESS DATABASE

1. Microsoft Office Access is a relational database that is part of the Microsoft Office 2007 system.
2. Access is the only popular commercial database that can be used with C#.
3. In Access, a user designs tables by choosing fields and data types; then the user can enter data into the tables.

The false statement is #2. Access is not the only one on the market, and is not the only one that can be accessed in C#, but it is convenient for many users because it comes packaged with Microsoft Office.

UNDERSTANDING IMPLICITLY TYPED VARIABLES

Implicitly typed variables are a new feature in C# 3. An **implicitly typed variable** has a data type that is inferred from the expression used to initialize the variable. To create an implicitly typed variable, you use a variable declaration with **var** as the data type. When you use an implicitly typed variable, the C# compiler decides on a data type for you. This process is called **type inference**. When you use an implicitly typed variable, an object's set of allowed properties and methods is not fixed when the code is written but is determined when the program executes.

> **» NOTE** Using var to create implicitly typed variables is also called **duck typing** because it fits the phrase, "If it walks like a duck and quacks like a duck, I would call it a duck." The phrase is attributed to an American writer and poet, James Whitcomb Riley, who lived from 1849 to 1916.

For example, in the following statement, money is implicitly typed as a double because the value assigned to the variable is a double:

```
var money = 1.99;
```

Because money is a double, you can, for example, perform arithmetic with it. If the declaration had been var money = "a dollar ninety-nine";, then money would be a string and you could not perform arithmetic with it. The statement var money = 1.99; has exactly the same meaning as the following:

```
double money = 1.99;
```

> **» NOTE**
> Although each of these uses of var is a valid C# statement, you should not use var simply to avoid declaring a data type for an item. The var keyword should be used only in specific situations, such as with LINQ statements.

Other examples of assigning values to implicitly typed variables include the following:

- » var age = 30; has the same meaning as int age = 30;
- » var name = "Roxy"; has the same meaning as string name = "Roxy";
- » var book = new Book(); has the same meaning as Book book = new Book();
- » var emp = new Employee(101, "Smith", 15.00); has the same meaning as Employee emp = new Employee(101, "Smith", 15.00);

In Chapter 5 you learned to use the foreach statement to process array elements. For example, the following code displays each double in the payRate array:

```
double[] payRate = {6.00, 7.35, 8.12, 12.45, 22.22};
foreach(double money in payRate)
    Console.WriteLine("{0}", money.ToString("C"));
```

In this example, money is declared as a double and is used as the **iteration variable**—the variable that is used to hold each successive value in the array. Alternatively, you can declare the iteration variable in a foreach statement to be an implicitly typed local variable. In this case, the iteration variable's type is inferred from the collection type it uses. For example, the same results can be achieved with the following:

```
double[] payRate = {6.00, 7.35, 8.12, 12.45, 22.22};
foreach(var money in payRate)
    Console.WriteLine("{0}", money.ToString("C"));
```

In this example, money is implied to be a double because payRate is an array of doubles. In Figure 14-7, the implicitly typed variable n is an int because numbers is an int array. Figure 14-8 shows the program's output.

```
using System;
public class ImplicitVariableDemo
{
    public static void Main()
    {
        int[] numbers = { 6, 4, 2, 1, 8, 3, 7, 5, 2, 0 };
        Console.WriteLine("Numbers List");
        foreach (var n in numbers)
            Console.WriteLine(n);
    }
}
```

Figure 14-7 The ImplicitVariableDemo class

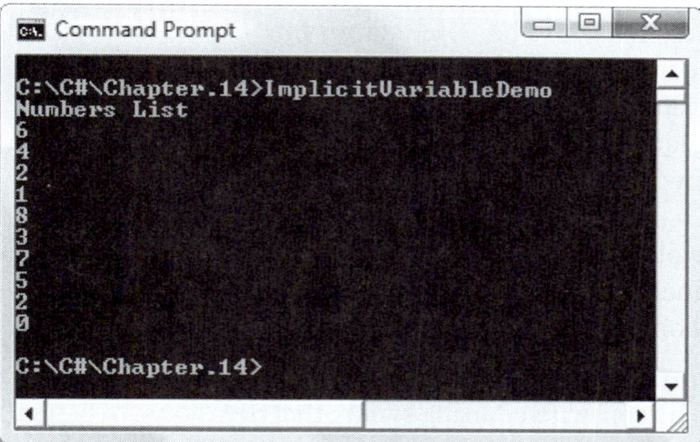

Figure 14-8 Output of the ImplicitVariableDemo program

When you declare a variable, usually you want to assign a data type. One advantage of a modern programming language like C# is that it is **strongly typed**. When a language is strongly typed, severe restrictions are placed on what data types can be mixed. Strong typing prevents certain errors—for example, the loss of data that might occur if you inadvertently assigned a double to an integer. However, you will use implicitly typed variables frequently in LINQ statements, which you will use to access data stored in a database.

»TWO TRUTHS AND A LIE: UNDERSTANDING IMPLICITLY TYPED VARIABLES

1. An implicitly typed variable has a data type that is inferred from the expression used to initialize the variable.
2. To create an implicitly typed variable, you use a variable declaration with `implicit` as the data type.
3. When you use an implicitly typed variable, the C# compiler decides on a data type for you.

The false statement is #2. To create an implicitly typed variable, you use a variable declaration with `var` as the data type.

UNDERSTANDING LINQ

As you have studied C#, you have become comfortable with the ideas of objects and classes. However, businesses operate using data that frequently is stored in relational databases. Applications that tried to bridge the gap between modern languages and traditional databases have been difficult to build and maintain. To reduce the complexity of accessing and integrating data that is stored in databases and other collections, Microsoft Corporation developed the **LINQ** (Language INtegrated Query) Project to provide queries that can be used in C# and Visual Basic.

In older versions of C#, you could access database data by passing an SQL string to a database object (and you still *can* do so in C# 3.0). For example, if you want to select all the fields in records in a table named `tblStudents` for which the field `GradePointAverage` was greater than 3.0, you could create a string such as "`SELECT * from tblStudents WHERE GradePointAverage > 3.00`" and pass it to an object of type `OleDbCommand`, which is a built-in type used to access databases. (The "Ole" stands for "Object linking and embedding.") You also would be required to type a few other statements that performed tasks like establishing a connection to the database and opening the database, and the select command would then select all the fields for all the records in the table that met the GPA criterion. The drawback to using a string command is that C# does not provide any syntax checking for characters stored within a string. For example, if you misspelled `SELECT` or `GradePointAverage`, the compiler would not issue an error message, but the program would fail when you executed it. Obviously, this feature is good when you want to store people's names or addresses, but it is a shortcoming when you want to issue a correct command.

LINQ was created to help solve these problems. LINQ provides a set of general-purpose standard operators that allow queries to be constructed using syntax that is easy to understand. This syntax is similar to SQL's, and the compiler can check it for errors. The operators defined in LINQ can be used to query arrays, enumerable classes, XML, relational databases, and other sources. This chapter concentrates on arrays and databases, but the LINQ queries you learn can be used with many types of data.

Some keywords in the LINQ vocabulary include the following:

» **select** indicates what to select
» **from** indicates the collection or sequence from which data will be drawn
» **where** indicates conditions for selecting records

It is no accident that these are the same words you learned about in the discussion of SQL earlier in this chapter.

Figure 14-9 shows an example of LINQ in action. In the first shaded section, an implicitly typed collection, `highNums`, is constructed from each variable `x` in the `numbers` array where the value of `x` is greater than 3. The `foreach` loop uses the sequence which is a subset of the original array to display all the records that meet the selection criteria—that is, all the integers greater than 3. Figure 14-10 shows the output.


```csharp
using System;
using System.Linq;
public class LinqDemo1
{
   public static void Main()
   {
      int[] numbers = { 6, 4, 2, 1, 8, 3, 7, 5, 2, 0 };
      const int CUTOFF = 3;
      var highNums =
            from x in numbers
            where x > CUTOFF
            select x;

      Console.WriteLine("Numbers > " + CUTOFF);
      foreach (var n in highNums)
      {
            Console.WriteLine(n);
      }
   }
}
```

Figure 14-9 `LinqDemo1` program

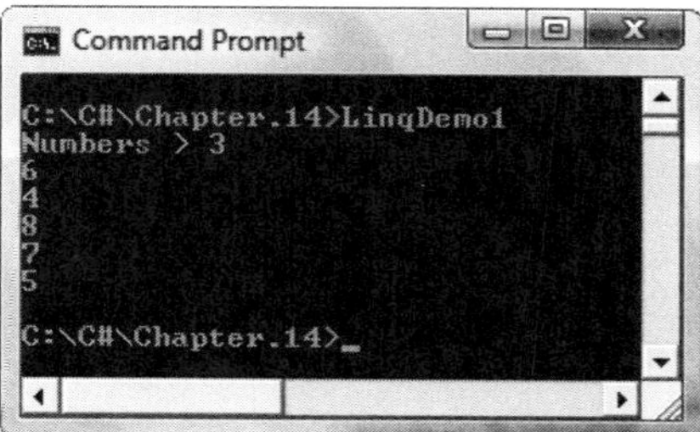

Figure 14-10 Output of the `LinqDemo1` application

You can use LINQ with more complicated sequences, such as a list of objects. Figure 14-11 shows a `Student` class that is similar to many you have seen throughout this book. The class contains three fields, a constructor that requires three parameters, and auto-implemented properties for each field. Figure 14-12 provides an example of how LINQ can select specific `Students` from an array. Figure 14-13 shows this output.

```csharp
public class Student
{
    private int idNumber;
    private string name;
    private double gradePointAverage;
    public Student(int num, string name, double avg)
    {
        IdNumber = num;
        Name = name;
        GradePointAverage = avg;
    }
    public int IdNumber {get; set;}
    public string Name {get; set;}
    public double GradePointAverage {get; set;}
}
```

Figure 14-11 Student class

```csharp
using System;
using System.Linq;
public class LinqDemo2
{
    public static void Main()
    {
        Student[] stus = {  new Student(1,   "Jones",     3.1),
                            new Student(2,   "Kimball",   2.9),
                            new Student(5,   "Oliver",    2.6),
                            new Student(6,   "Mitchell",  3.0),
                            new Student(8,   "Lee",       4.0),
                            new Student(10,  "Cooper",    3.5) };
        const double CUTOFF = 3.0;
        var goodStudents =
            from s in stus
            where s.GradePointAverage > CUTOFF
            select s;

        Console.WriteLine("Students with GPA > " + CUTOFF);
        foreach (var s in goodStudents)
        {
            Console.WriteLine("{0,3} {1,-8} {2,5}", s.IdNumber,
                s.Name, s.GradePointAverage.ToString("F1"));
        }
    }
}
```

Figure 14-12 LinqDemo2 program

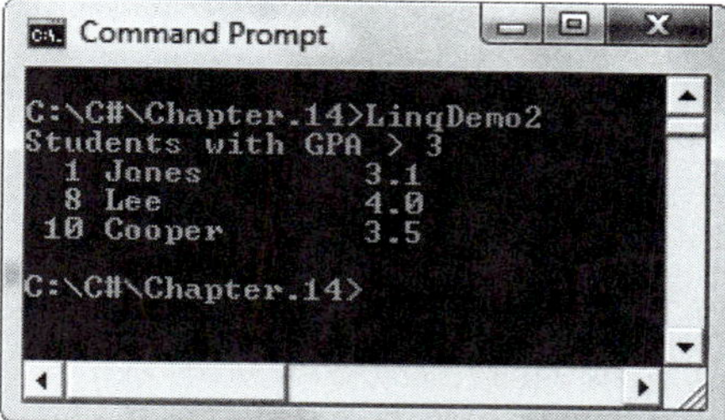

Figure 14-13 Output of the `LinqDemo2` program

Although LINQ statements work well to select specific records from an array, you could have used traditional C# statements to achieve the same results. However, few businesses can operate with all their data hard coded and stored in arrays within programs. The true power of LINQ becomes available when you can access an external database.

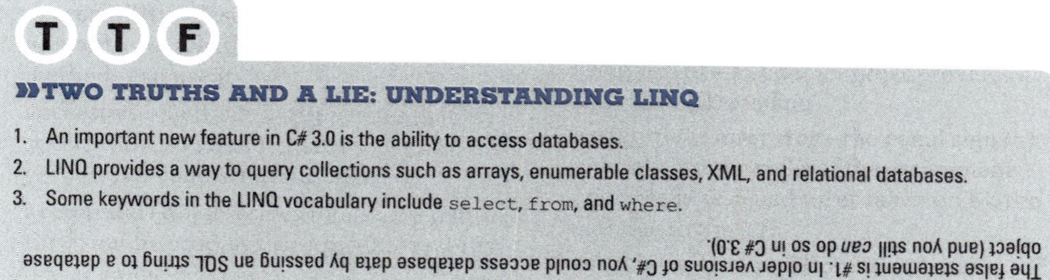

»TWO TRUTHS AND A LIE: UNDERSTANDING LINQ

1. An important new feature in C# 3.0 is the ability to access databases.
2. LINQ provides a way to query collections such as arrays, enumerable classes, XML, and relational databases.
3. Some keywords in the LINQ vocabulary include `select`, `from`, and `where`.

The false statement is #1. In older versions of C#, you could access database data by passing an SQL string to a database object (and you still *can* do so in C# 3.0).

RETRIEVING DATA FROM AN ACCESS DATABASE IN C#

As with many features of C#, you can write code to access a database table by hand, but you save time and reduce the chance for error by using the built-in tools of the Visual Studio IDE.

Adding a database to a Windows Forms project requires making only a few menu selections and browsing for a stored database. (In the "You Do It" section later in this chapter, you can walk through instructions that add a database to your project.) To add a database table to a Windows Forms project, you must perform two sets of tasks:

» From a project's main menu, you choose Data and then Add a New Data Source. Next, you browse for the database and answer a few questions.

» Then you drag a table onto your form. The table's data is bound to the form and you are supplied with a grid in which you can view the data. The grid is an instance of the `DataGridView` class.

Figure 14-14 shows a new Windows Forms project named `StudentsDemo` in which only these two steps have been taken. The Cartman College database depicted in Figures 14-5 and 14-6 earlier in this chapter has been added to the project. You can see the data grid on the `Form`. At the right of the screen, the Solution Explorer contains the `CartmanCollege` database. In the Data Sources window at the lower right, you can see that the `cartmanCollegeDataSet` contains just one table, named `tblStudents`. The bottom of the screen displays icons for several objects that were added to the project automatically when the data source was added and the table was dragged onto the form. These include:

» `cartmanCollegeDataSet`

» `tblStudentsBindingSource`

» `tblStudentsTableAdapter`

» `tblAdapterManager`

» `tblStudentsBindingNavigator`

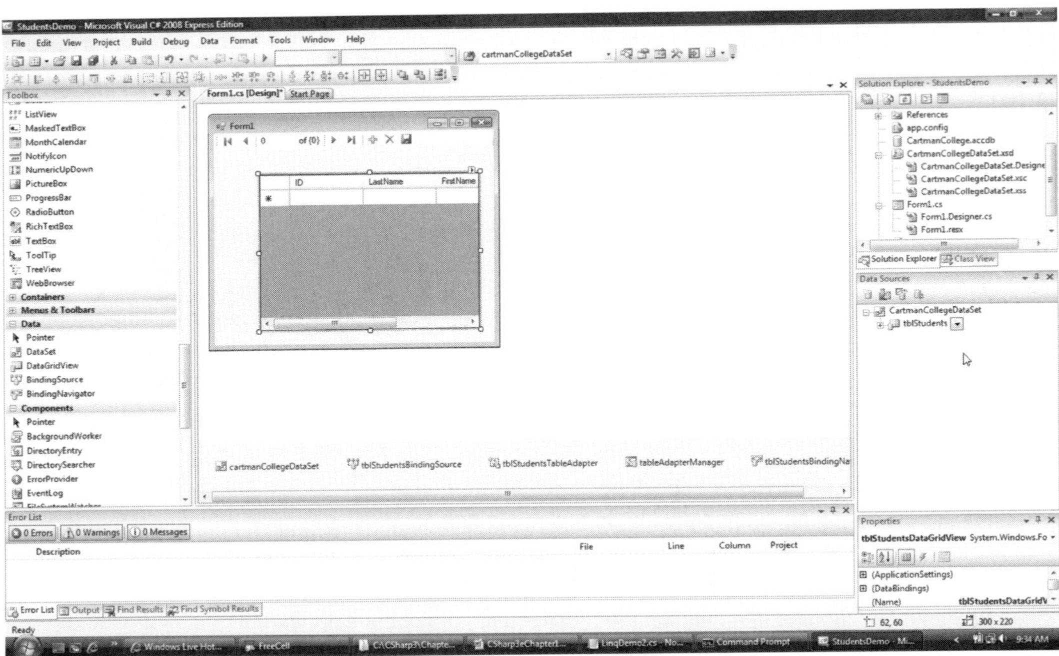

Figure 14-14 A project to which a data source has been added and in which a table has been dragged onto the `Form`

When you view the code behind the `Form` in Figure 14-14, you can see that one comment and one statement have been added to the `Form1_Load()` method, the method that executes when a Windows application starts and the main form is initialized. Figure 14-15 shows the method.

```
private void Form1_Load(object sender, EventArgs e)
{
    // TODO: This line of code loads data
    // into the 'cartmanCollegeDataSet.tblStudents' table.
    // You can move, or remove it, as needed.

    this.tblStudentsTableAdapter.Fill
      (this.cartmanCollegeDataSet.tblStudents);
}
```

Figure 14-15 `Form1_Load()` method with automatically generated code after `CartmanCollege` database is added to the `Form`

»NOTE The line breaks in Figure 14-15 have been altered from the way they appear in Visual Studio to better fit this page.

The comment in the `Form1_Load()` method indicates that you can move the `Fill()` method statement or delete it. The `Fill()` method fills the table adapter with the data from `tblStudents` in the `cartmanCollegeDataSet`.

When you execute the program that contains the method in Figure 14-15, the data from `tblStudents` in the database is loaded into the `Form`, as shown in Figure 14-16. The grid that holds the data is not wide enough to display all the fields in each record, but if you compare the figure to Figure 14-6, you should be able to confirm that the exposed data comes from the database.

»NOTE If you search the code for the project, you will find 18 references to `cartmanCollegeDataSet`. All this code was automatically generated when you added the data to the project and added the table to the `Form`, saving you many chances for error.

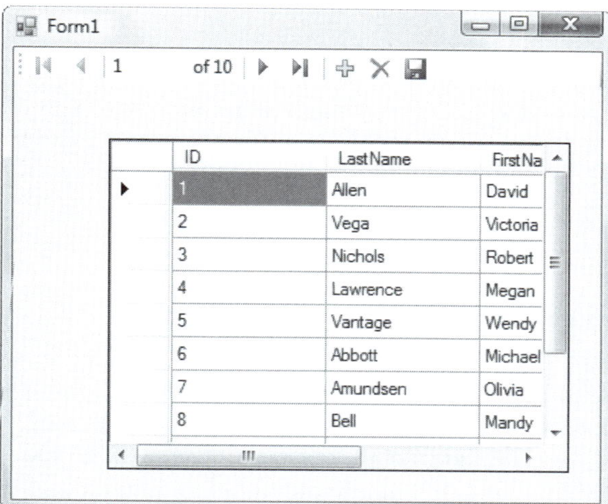

Figure 14-16 A `Form` that contains loaded data

You could return to Design view and increase the size of both the form and the grid to make the display easier to read. Figure 14-17 shows the larger view in which you can see all the data. In Figure 14-17, notice the controls that are provided for you automatically at the top of the `Form`. You can use these controls to navigate through the records, add a new record, delete the current record, and save the changes. When you exit the program and restart it, changes to the data will have been retained.

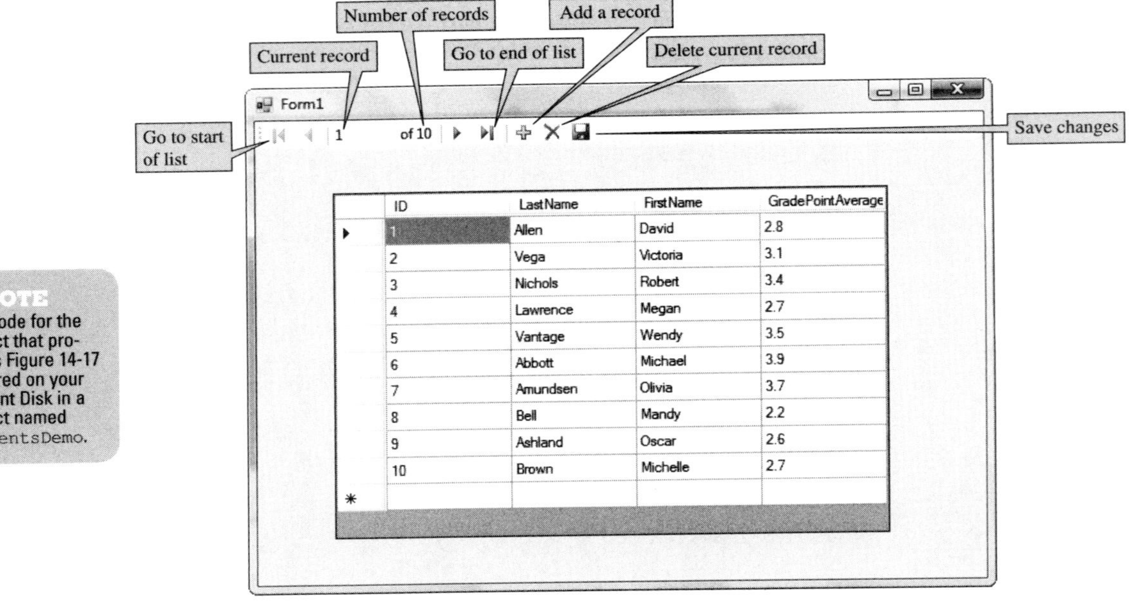

Figure 14-17 A larger `Form` that contains loaded data

You do not have to load the data into the viewing grid when the `Form` loads. For example, you could add a button to the `Form` and move the `Fill()` statement to the button's `Click()` method. Then, when the `Form` loads, no data would be visible, but after the user clicks the button, the data fills the table.

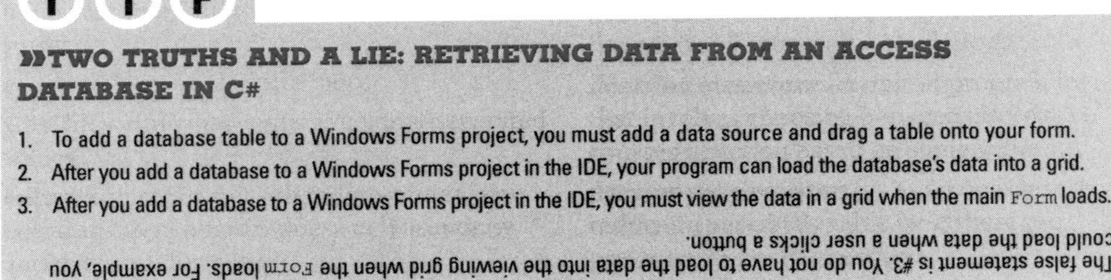

»TWO TRUTHS AND A LIE: RETRIEVING DATA FROM AN ACCESS DATABASE IN C#

1. To add a database table to a Windows Forms project, you must add a data source and drag a table onto your form.
2. After you add a database to a Windows Forms project in the IDE, your program can load the database's data into a grid.
3. After you add a database to a Windows Forms project in the IDE, you must view the data in a grid when the main `Form` loads.

The false statement is #3. You do not have to load the data into the viewing grid when the `Form` loads. For example, you could load the data when a user clicks a button.

USING LINQ QUERIES WITH AN ACCESS DATABASE TABLE

You are not required to use the data grid to view database records. You also are not required to view all the records in the database table or to view all the fields for each record. Instead, you can use a LINQ query to select a collection of data from a table when specific criteria are met. For example, Figure 14-18 shows a `button1_Click()` method that could be used to fill a list box with only the last names of students who have a GPA greater than 3.0. The shaded code in the figure is a copy of the shaded code used with the array in Figure 14-12. Instead of using `Console.WriteLine()` to display students, this method adds them to a `ListBox` named `listBox1`.

```
private void button1_Click(object sender, EventArgs e)
{
    const double CUTOFF = 3.0;
    this.tblStudentsTableAdapter.Fill
       (this.cartmanCollegeDataSet.tblStudents);
    var goodStudents =
        from s in this.cartmanCollegeDataSet.tblStudents
        where s.GradePointAverage > CUTOFF
        select s;
    foreach (var s in goodStudents)
        listBox1.Items.Add(s.LastName);
}
```

Figure 14-18 The `button1_Click()` method that uses a `ListBox` to display the last names of students with high GPAs

> **»NOTE**
> The method in Figure 14-18 is part of the project named `StudentsDemo2`, which is available on your Student Disk.

> **»NOTE** In a completed project, you would want to change the `Name` properties of `button1` and `listBox1` to better reflect their purposes. However, this example was created with the fewest possible changes to a project so you could more quickly replicate the results for yourself.

> **»NOTE** The `from-where-select` combination is a single statement. Conventionally, its parts are written on separate lines for clarity, but that is not required. However, be careful not to use a semicolon until the entire statement is complete.

In the example in Figure 14-18, `goodStudents` is an implicitly typed collection of students with high GPAs. In this case, `goodStudents` is the following type (where `StudentsDemo2` is the name of the current project):

```
System.Data.EnumerableRowCollection<StudentsDemo2.cartmanCollegeDataSet.
tblStudentsRow>
```

This means that `goodStudents` is a collection of rows from the `tblStudents` database table. However, it is easier to use `var` and to have the type inferred than to use this lengthy type name.

Assume that you start a C# Windows Forms project and take the following steps:

» Add the `CartmanCollege` database `tblStudents` table to the project.
» Delete the automatically added grid from the `Form`.
» Drag a button onto the `Form` and change its `Text` property.
» Drag a `ListBox` onto the `Form`.
» Add the `button1_Click()` method from Figure 14-18.

Figure 14-19 shows the results when you execute the program and click the button. Although 10 student records are stored in the table, the figure lists only the last names of the five students who have GPA values over 3.0. You can confirm that these are the correct students by referring back to the complete listing in Figure 14-6.

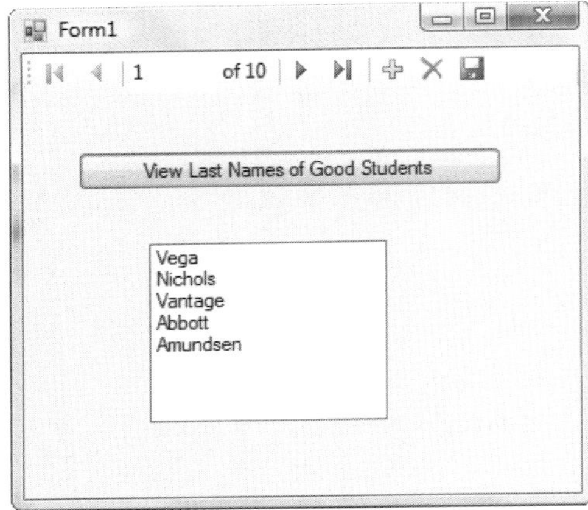

Figure 14-19 Execution of the program containing the method in Figure 14-18

In the method in Figure 14-18, `goodStudents` is a collection of student records gathered from the `tblStudents` table in the `CartmanCollege` database, as indicated in the `from` clause. The `where` clause specifies the condition for selection—a GPA greater than `CUTOFF`. The `select` clause indicates what to select—a record. The `foreach` statement that follows the shaded portion of the method selects each record in the collection, and adds its `LastName` field to the `ListBox`.

As an alternative to the code in Figure 14-18, instead of creating a collection of records, you could create a collection of last names. Figure 14-20 shows an example in which only last names are selected to be added to the collection (see the first shaded expression in the figure). That is, in this example `goodStudents` is a collection of `strings`, and not a collection of records. When each `s` is added to the `ListBox` in the second expression, it is a `string` that is added. In other words, in this example, you do not write `s.LastName` because each `s` *is* a last name. The results are identical to those shown in Figure 14-19.

```csharp
var goodStudents =
    from s in this.cartmanCollegeDataSet.tblStudents
    where s.GradePointAverage > CUTOFF
    select s.LastName;
foreach (var s in goodStudents)
    listBox1.Items.Add(s);
```

Figure 14-20 Collecting strings from a database table

Figure 14-21 contains a `button1_Click()` method from a different application in which a constant GPA cutoff is not used. Instead, the user can enter a cutoff GPA value into a `TextBox` that has been named `gpaTextBox` (see the first shaded expression). In this example, a student's GPA must be greater than the user-supplied value to qualify for the list. The last name, a comma, and the first name of each qualifying student (see the last shaded expression in Figure 14-21) are shown in the `ListBox`. Figure 14-22 shows the output.

```csharp
private void button1_Click(object sender, EventArgs e)
{
    double minGpa = Convert.ToDouble(gpaTextBox.Text);
    this.tblStudentsTableAdapter.Fill
       (this.cartmanCollegeDataSet.tblStudents);
    var goodStudents =
        from s in this.cartmanCollegeDataSet.tblStudents
        where s.GradePointAverage > minGpa
        select s;
    foreach (var s in goodStudents)
        listBox1.Items.Add(s.LastName + ", " + s.FirstName);
}
```

Figure 14-21 The `button1_Click()` method that displays students with a minimum GPA entered by the user

> **▶▶ NOTE** The method in Figure 14-21 is part of the project named `StudentsDemo3`, which is available on your Student Disk. In the example in Figure 14-21, instead of using a `button1_Click()` method, you might prefer to add the code to a `gpaTextBox_TextChanged()` method so that it executes each time the user enters a new value as a minimum GPA instead of when the user clicks a button. You might also prefer to add some error checking in case the user enters a non-numeric value. Error checking was omitted from this example to keep it short.

When you execute an application that contains the method in Figure 14-21, the list of items in `listBox1` is appended each time the user clicks `button1`. In other words, if a user clicks the button twice without changing the selection criterion, the `ListBox` contains a second set of the same records. To prevent the list from growing and to see only the students who meet the current criteria, add the following statement near the beginning of the `Click()` method:

```csharp
listBox1.Items.Clear();
```

With the inclusion of this statement, `listBox1` is emptied before each new group is added to it.

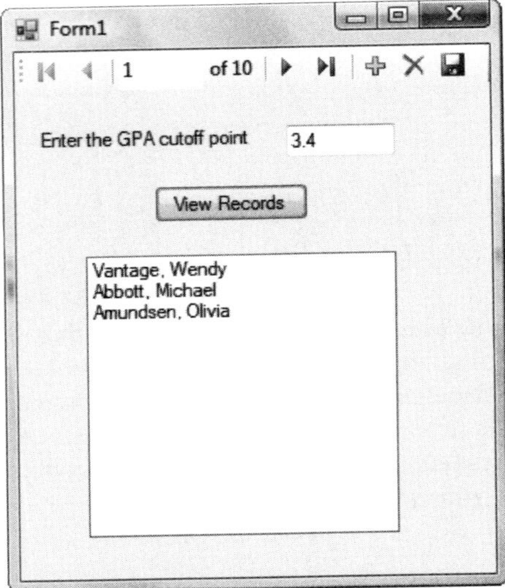

Figure 14-22 Typical execution of an application containing the `button1_Click()` method in Figure 14-21

Many other options are available when you use LINQ expressions. For example, you can use AND and OR expressions in your LINQ statements. The following code selects all students with GPAs between 2.5 and 3.0:

```
var someStudents =
    from s in this.cartmanCollegeDataSet.tblStudents
    where s.GradePointAverage > 2.5 && s.GradePointAverage < 3.0
    select s;
```

With text values, you can use `StartsWith()`, `EndsWith()`, and `Contains()`. For example, the following code selects all students whose first name starts with "M":

```
var someStudents =
    from s in this.cartmanCollegeDataSet.tblStudents
    where s.FirstName.StartsWith("M")
    select s;
```

You can use several **aggregate operators**, or operators that produce statistics for groups of data. The aggregate operators include `Average()`, `Count()`, `Sum()`, `Max()`, and `Min()`. For example, the method in Figure 14-23 assembles a collection of `GradePointAverage` values named `gpas`. Then several aggregate operators are applied to the collection and the results are assigned to `Label`s. Figure 14-24 shows the output when this method is used with `tblStudents`. You can confirm the accuracy of these statistics by referring to the complete data set in Figure 14-6.

```csharp
private void button1_Click(object sender, EventArgs e)
{
    var gpas =
        from s in this.cartmanCollegeDataSet.tblStudents
            select s.GradePointAverage;
    countLabel.Text = "Count is " + gpas.Count();
    minLabel.Text = "Lowest GPA is " + gpas.Min();
    maxLabel.Text = "Highest GPA is " + gpas.Max();
    avgLabel.Text = "Average of all GPAs is " + gpas.Average();
}
```

Figure 14-23 Method that uses some aggregate operators

>>**NOTE**
The method in Figure 14-23 is part of the project named `StudentsDemo4`, which is available on your Student Disk.

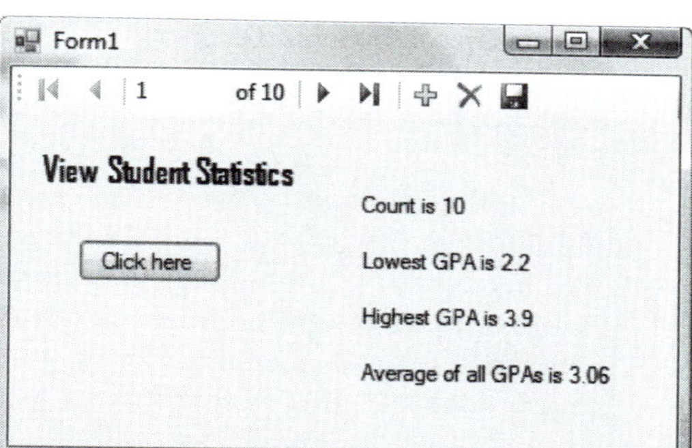

Figure 14-24 Output of program that uses the method in Figure 14-23

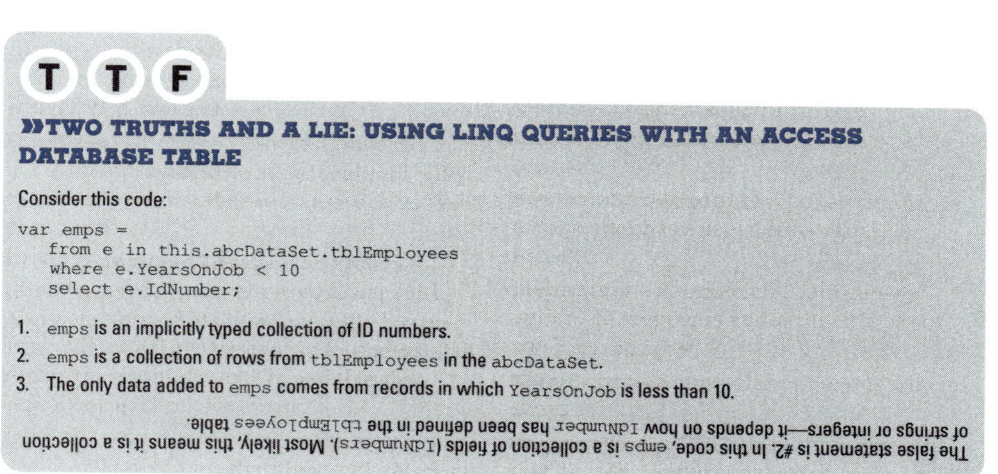

T T F

>>TWO TRUTHS AND A LIE: USING LINQ QUERIES WITH AN ACCESS DATABASE TABLE

Consider this code:

```
var emps =
    from e in this.abcDataSet.tblEmployees
    where e.YearsOnJob < 10
    select e.IdNumber;
```

1. `emps` is an implicitly typed collection of ID numbers.

2. `emps` is a collection of rows from `tblEmployees` in the `abcDataSet`.

3. The only data added to `emps` comes from records in which `YearsOnJob` is less than 10.

The false statement is #2. In this code, emps is a collection of fields (IdNumbers). Most likely, this means it is a collection of strings or integers—it depends on how IdNumber has been defined in the tblEmployees table.

USING LINQ OPERATORS TO SORT AND GROUP DATA

You can use the **orderby operator** to sort a collection of data based on a field or fields. For example, the method in Figure 14-25 produces the output in Figure 14-26. The shaded statement causes the list of students to be ordered by GPA.


```csharp
private void button1_Click(object sender, EventArgs e)
{
    listBox1.Items.Add("GPA    LastName");
    var students =
        from s in this.cartmanCollegeDataSet.tblStudents
            orderby s.GradePointAverage
            select s;
    foreach (var s in students)
        listBox1.Items.Add(" " + s.GradePointAverage + "     " +
            s.LastName);
}
```

Figure 14-25 Method that uses `orderby`

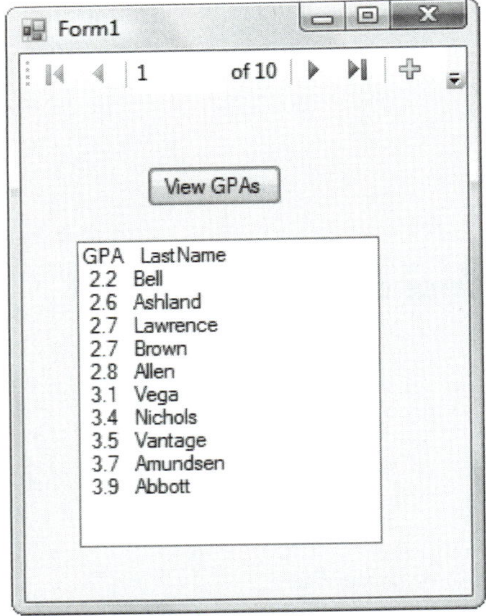

Figure 14-26 Output of project that uses the method in Figure 14-25

The default order for sorting is ascending; that is, from lowest to highest. You can explicitly indicate an ascending sort by using the following phrase:

```
orderby s.GradePointAverage ascending
```

To view the students in the reverse order, from the highest GPA to the lowest, you would write the following:

```
orderby s.GradePointAverage descending
```

You can use compound conditions for ordering. For example, the following would sort students by last name, and then by first name when last names are the same:

```
orderby s.LastName, s.FirstName
```

Data items also can be grouped; the **group operator** groups data by specified criteria. For example, Figure 14-27 shows a `Click()` method that groups students by the integer part of the `GradePointAverage` field. In other words, all students with GPAs between 2 and 3 are in one group, and students with GPAs between 3 and 4 are in another group. (Additional groups would be formed if students had higher or lower GPAs.) The example in Figure 14-27 uses nested `foreach` loops. In the outer loop, which executes one time for each group, the group `Key` is displayed as a heading. The `Key` is not required to be the key field in the database table, although it might be; the `Key` is the value used to determine the groups, which in this case is determined by the integer part of the GPA. In the inner `foreach` loop in Figure 14-27, the GPA and last name for each record in the group are added to the `ListBox`. Figure 14-28 shows the results.

```
private void button1_Click(object sender, EventArgs e)
{
    var stus = from s in cartmanCollegeDataSet.tblStudents
        group s by (int)s.GradePointAverage;

    foreach (var groupByGpa in stus)
    {
        listBox1.Items.Add("GPA: " + groupByGpa.Key);
        foreach (var s in groupByGpa)
          listBox1.Items.Add("   " + s.GradePointAverage +
             "   " + s.LastName);
    }
}
```

Figure 14-27 A method that groups records

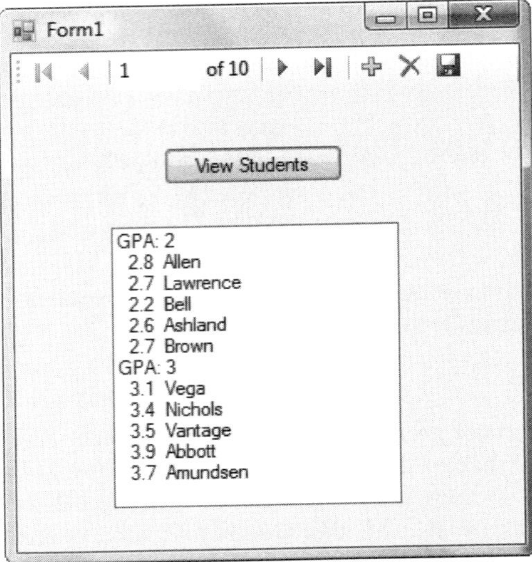

Figure 14-28 Output of application that contains the method in Figure 14-27

When you use the `group` operator, the number of possible values in the criterion determines the number of possible groups. For example, if a company has five departments and you group employees with an expression such as the following, you form five groups:

```
group e by e.Department
```

However, if you use a Boolean expression in the `by` clause, then only two groups are possible because the `by` expression has only two possible values—true or false:

```
group e by e.Department == 1
```

That is, every `e` is part of the group for which `e.Department == 1` is true, or the group for which `e.Department == 1` is false.

A query body must end with a `select` clause or a `group` clause. Therefore, if you combine `orderby` and `group`, `orderby` must come first. For example, to view the students in each GPA category in alphabetical order by last name, you would write the following:

```
var stus = from s in cartmanCollegeDataSet.tblStudents
    orderby s.LastName
    group s by (int)s.GradePointAverage;
```

Many more LINQ operations are available than can be covered in this chapter. More than 50 operators are available, and they can be combined in practically an infinite number of ways. For example, you can insert and delete records from a database. Additionally, a key feature of normalized relational databases is the ability to make relationships between tables. LINQ allows you to join multiple object collections together using a relatively simple syntax that is familiar to those who already know SQL. As you learn more about databases, C#, and LINQ, you will discover many possibilities and learn to create useful applications that access data and provide business clients with powerful ways to view and use their information.

>> **NOTE** For more good ideas on working with LINQ, see "101 LINQ Samples" at *http://msdn2.microsoft.com/en-us/vcsharp/aa336746.aspx*.

>> TWO TRUTHS AND A LIE: USING LINQ OPERATORS TO SORT AND GROUP DATA

Consider the following code:

```
var emps =
    from e in this.abcDataSet.tblEmployees
        orderby e.LastName
        group e by e.Department;
```

1. In the collection `emps`, Brown in Department 1 would come before Adams in Department 3.

2. In the collection `emps`, Graham in Department 4 would come before Lee in Department 7.

3. In the collection `emps`, Kimball in Department 5 would come before Thompson in Department 3.

The false statement is #3. Each lower-numbered department group would precede any higher-numbered group. Within the groups, the employees would be in alphabetical order.

YOU DO IT

ADDING A DATASET TO A PROJECT

In the next steps, you will add a previously created database table to a C# project and retrieve data from the table so you can display it in a `Form`.

To add a dataset to a project:

1. Your Student Disk contains a Microsoft Office Access Database file named **HonestRalphsUsedCars**. If Access is installed on your computer, open the database file by double-clicking its name. When Access opens, double-click `tblCars : Table` under All Tables. (See Figure 14-29.) Examine the data in the table. The fields are `ID`, `ModelYear`, `Make`, `Price`, and `Color`. Ten records have been entered into the table.

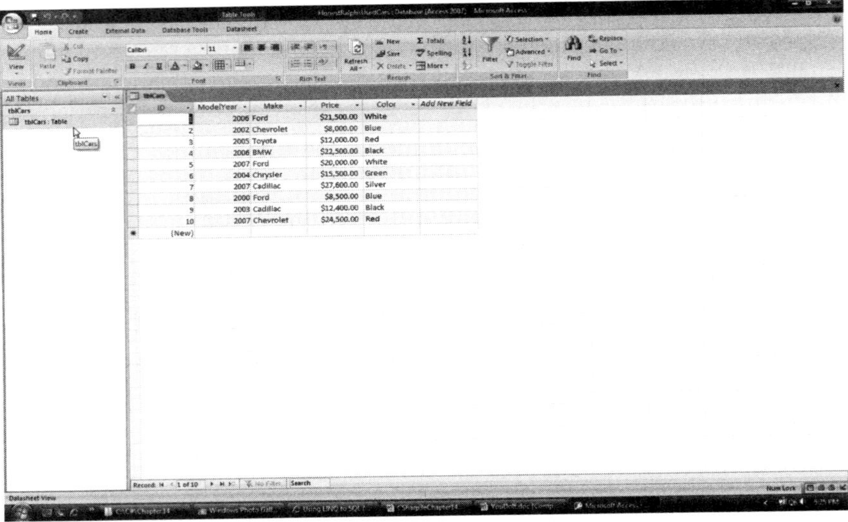

Figure 14-29 HonestRalphsUsedCars `tblCars` table in Access

2. Close Access. Open Visual Studio and start a new Windows Forms Application named `AccessCars`. Change the `Text` property of the `Form` to **Honest Ralph's Used Cars**.

3. In the main menu at the top of the screen, click **Data**. From the drop-down list, click **Add New Data Source** to start the Data Source Configuration Wizard. In the Choose a Data Source Type window, select **Database** and then click **Next**. See Figure 14-30.

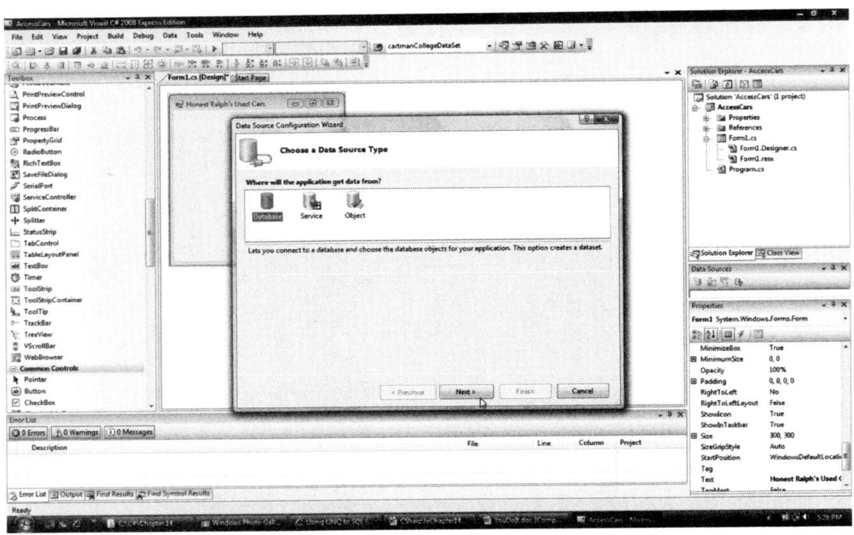

Figure 14-30 The Data Source Configuration Wizard

4. In the Choose Your Data Connection window, click **New Connection**. In the Add Connection dialog box, select **Microsoft Access Database file** as the Data Source, and then click Browse to find the file to use. Select **HonestRalphsUsedCars.accdb** from the folder where the file is stored. Then click **Next**. A dialog box appears and asks if you want to add the file to your project. See Figure 14-31. Click **Yes**.

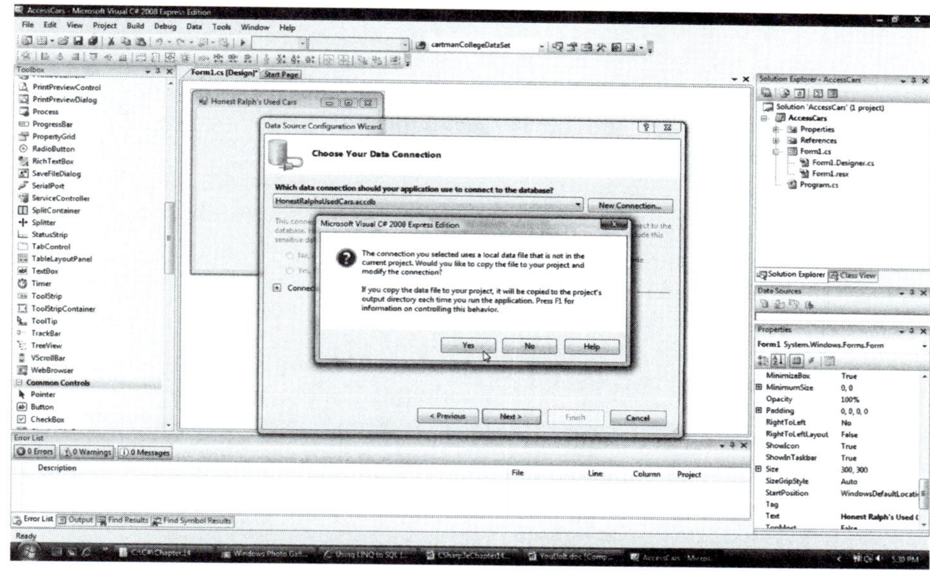

Figure 14-31 Dialog box asking to add a data file to a project

5. In the Data Source Connection window, click **Next**. In the next window that appears, select **Tables**. Then click the **Finish** button.

6. In the Solution Explorer, confirm that the HonestRalphsUsedCars database has been added to the project. See Figure 14-32.

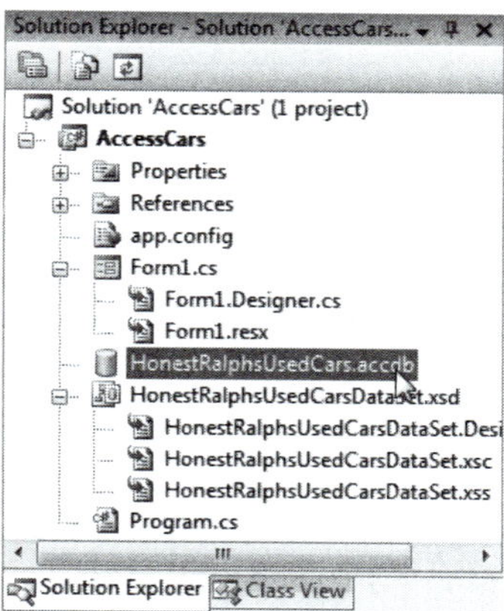

Figure 14-32 Database added to project

7. From Visual Studio's main menu, click **Data** and then click **Show Data Sources**. A Data Sources window should appear under the Solution Explorer. (Drag its borders if it is too narrow to read the contents.) See Figure 14-33.

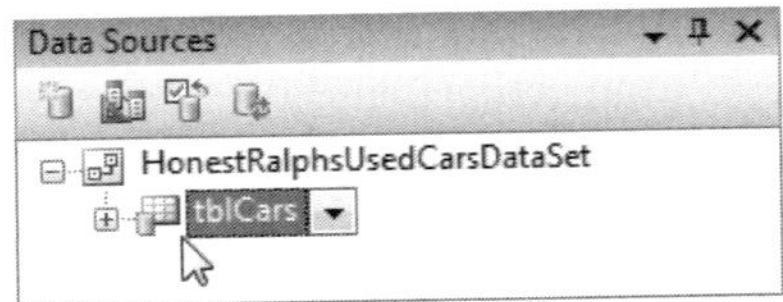

Figure 14-33 The Data Sources window

8. Drag `tblCars` onto the `Form` in the Designer. Several changes occur in the `Form`: a large data grid appears and several icons for scrolling through records appear at the top of the `Form`. Additionally, five new objects appear:

   `honestRalphsUsedCarsDataSet`, `tblCarsBindingSource`, `tblCarsTableAdapter`, `tableAdapterManager`, and `tblCarsBindingNavigator`

   Together, these objects make the connection between the database and your application. See Figure 14-34.

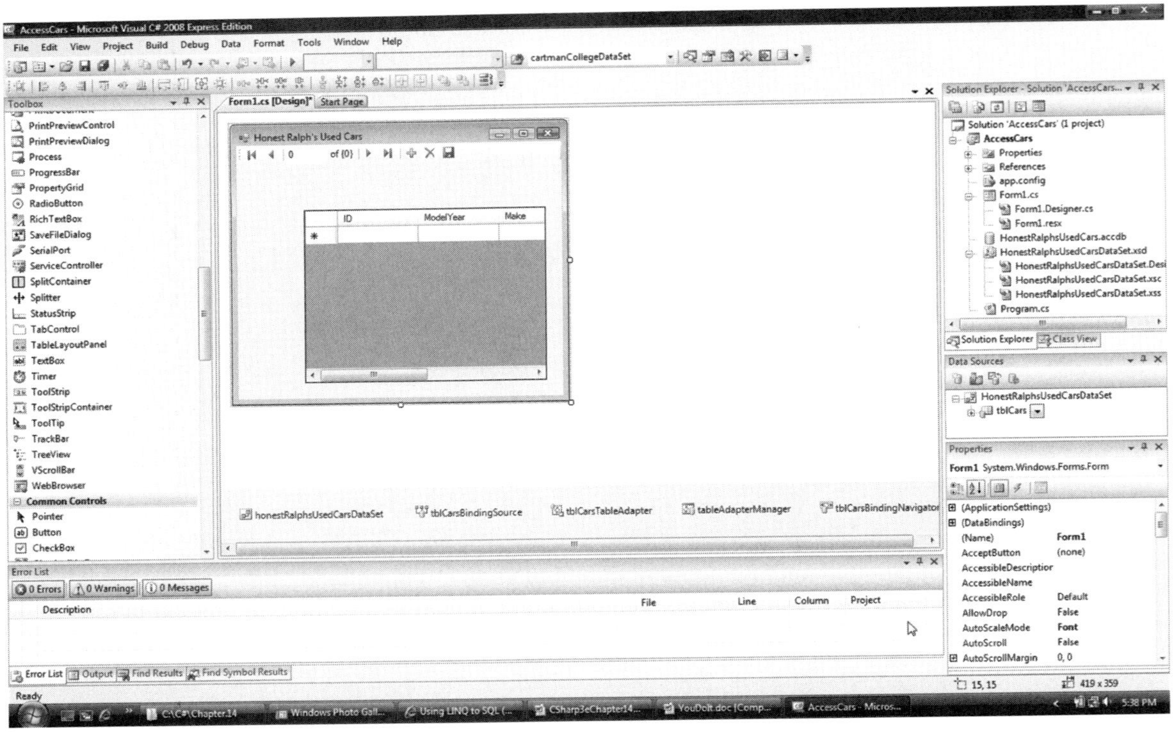

Figure 14-34 The `Form` after `tblCars` has been dragged onto it

9. Save the project, then click **Debug** from the main menu and click **Start without Debugging**. The data appears in the table grid, as shown in Figure 14-35.

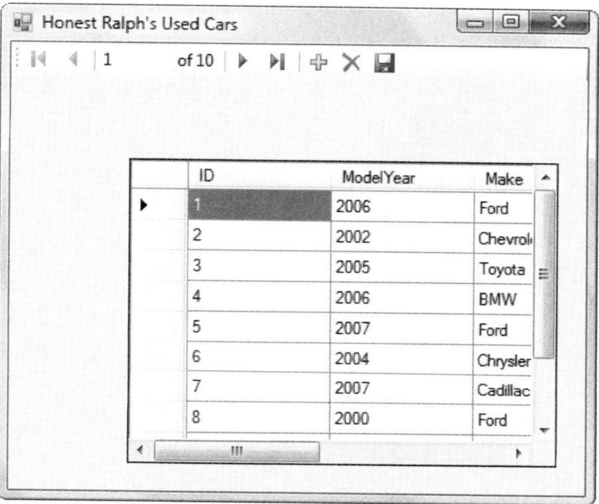

Figure 14-35 Ralph's Used Cars data as it appears in the grid

10. Dismiss the `Form`. In Design view, reposition the grid and widen both the table and the grid to see all the records' fields. Save the project, then click **Debug** and **Start without Debugging**. The data appears in the table grid, as shown in Figure 14-36. Use the scroll bar to view the hidden records at the bottom of the list. Use the arrows at the top of the form to navigate through the records.

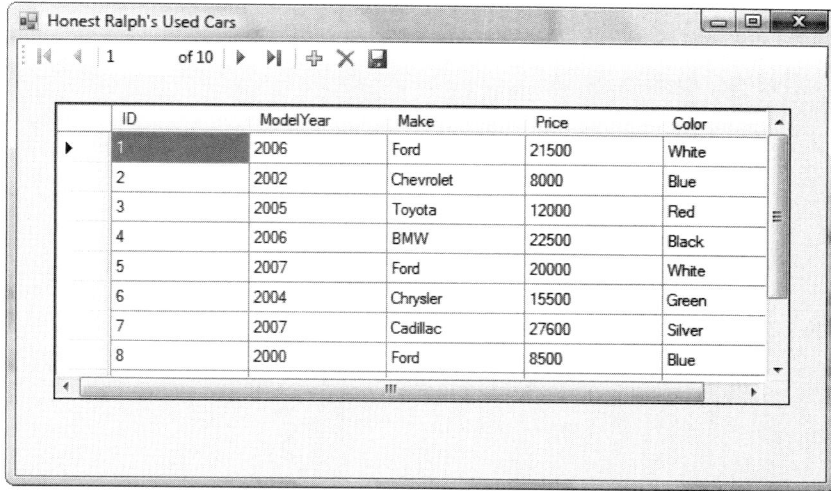

Figure 14-36 Ralph's Used Cars data as it appears in a wider grid

11. Dismiss the `Form`. In the IDE, double-click the `Form` title bar. The `Form1_Load()` method appears as follows. (Note that the comment has been divided into three comments and the `Fill()` method has been divided into two lines so the code fits better on this page.)

```
private void Form1_Load(object sender, EventArgs e)
{
    // TODO: This line of code loads data into the
    // 'honestRalphsUsedCarsDataSet.tblCars' table.
    // You can move, or remove it, as needed.

    this.tblCarsTableAdapter.Fill
       (this.honestRalphsUsedCarsDataSet.tblCars);
}
```

12. Return to Design view. Drag a `Button` onto the `Form`, as shown in Figure 14-37. Change its `Name` property to **`recordsButton`** and its `Text` property to **Retrieve Records**. Double-click the `Button` to generate a `recordsButton_Click()` method and view its code. Cut the `Fill()` method call from the `Form1_Load()` method and paste it into the `recordsButton_Click()` method. Save the project and then execute the program again. This time the grid is empty. When you click the button, the grid fills with data.

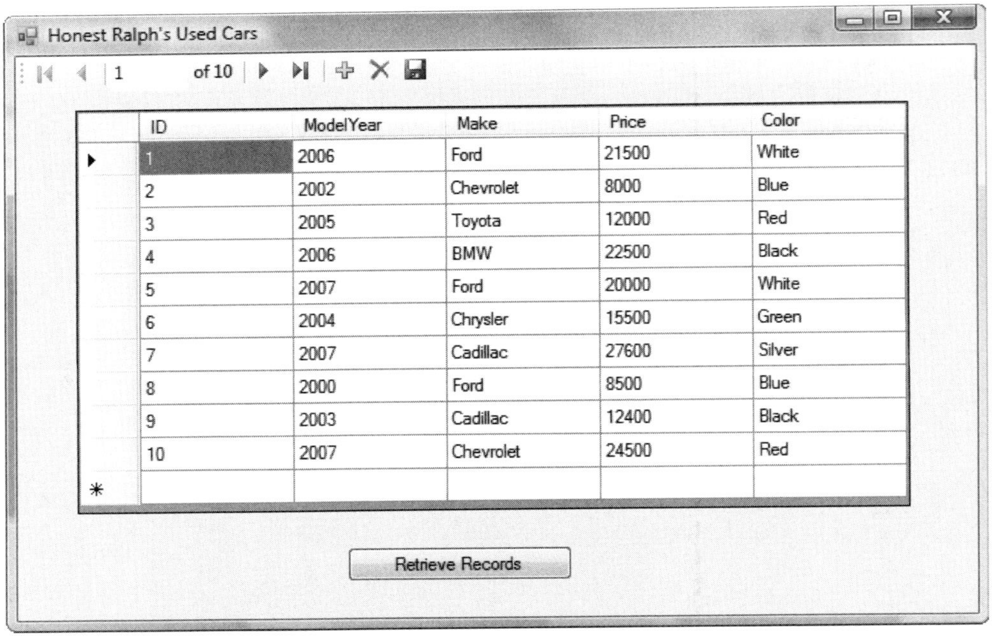
Honest Ralph's Used Cars
1
of 10
ID
ModelYear
Make
Price
Color
1 2006 Ford 21500 White
2 2002 Chevrolet 8000 Blue
3 2005 Toyota 12000 Red
4 2006 BMW 22500 Black
5 2007 Ford 20000 White
6 2004 Chrysler 15500 Green
7 2007 Cadillac 27600 Silver
8 2000 Ford 8500 Blue
9 2003 Cadillac 12400 Black
10 2007 Chevrolet 24500 Red
Retrieve Records

Figure 14-37 Ralph's Used Cars data accessed after user clicks a button

QUERYING A DATASET

In the next steps, you will write LINQ queries that demonstrate how to access subsets of the data stored in the `tblCars` table.

To query a dataset:

1. In Visual Studio, in the `AccessCars` project, go to Form1.cs[Design] view. Delete the data grid from the `Form`. Drag a `Label` and a `ListBox` onto the `Form`, as shown in Figure 14-38. Change the `Label`'s `Text` to **Inexpensive Cars**. Change the `ListBox`'s name to **inexpensiveCarsBox**. Reduce the width of the `Form` appropriately.

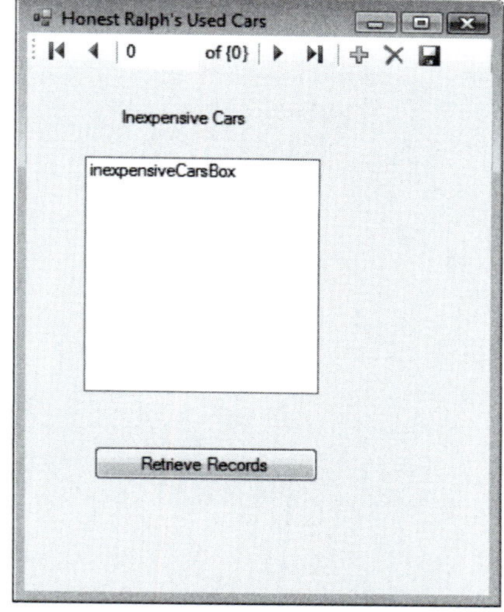

Figure 14-38 Adding a `Label` and `ListBox` to the `AccessCars` project

2. Double-click the button on the `Form` and revise the `recordsButton_Click()` method, as shown in the shaded portions of Figure 14-39. The LINQ code selects all the records in the table in which `Price` is less than $20,000 and then adds the ID number, model year, and make of those cars to the `ListBox`.

```
private void recordsButton_Click(object sender, EventArgs e)
{
    const int HIGHPRICE = 20000;
    this.tblCarsTableAdapter.Fill
        (this.honestRalphsUsedCarsDataSet.tblCars);
    var inexpensiveCars =
        from c in this.honestRalphsUsedCarsDataSet.tblCars
        where c.Price < HIGHPRICE
        select c;
    foreach (var c in inexpensiveCars)
        inexpensiveCarsBox.Items.Add
            (c.ID + " - " + c.ModelYear + " " + c.Make);
}
```

Figure 14-39 The `recordsButton_Click()` method

3. Execute the project. When the `Form` appears, click the `Button`. The output looks like Figure 14-40. Five cars appear in the list.

4. Dismiss the `Form`.

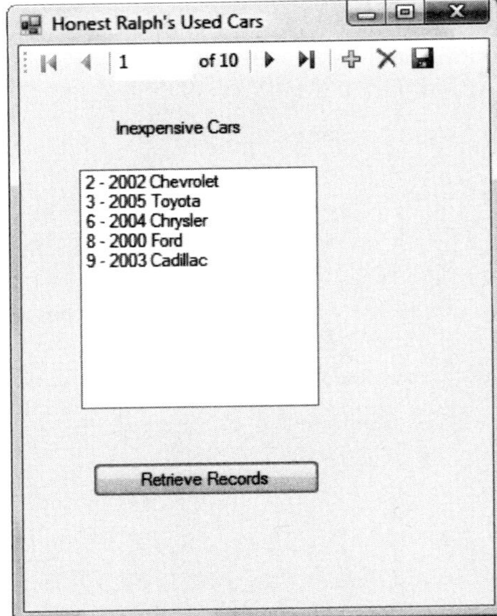

Figure 14-40 Execution of `AccessCars` project

ALLOWING THE USER TO PROVIDE SELECTION CRITERIA

In the next steps, you will provide a `TextBox` to make the application more flexible. Instead of listing cars priced under $20,000, the user will be able to enter a cutoff price.

To provide selection criteria for the user:

1. In the Form1.cs Design view, rearrange the existing components and add a new `Label` and `TextBox`, as shown in Figure 14-41. Name the `TextBox` **priceTextBox**.

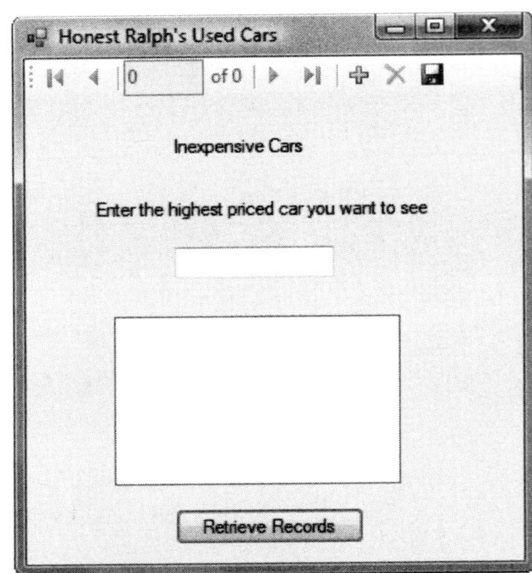

Figure 14-41 Form with `Label` and `TextBox` for data entry

2. Modify the `recordsButton_Click()` method, as shown in the shaded sections of Figure 14-42. Delete the declaration of the constant `HIGHPRICE` and replace it with a statement that accepts entered text from the `TextBox` and converts it to an `int`. Change the selection criterion from less than the constant `HIGHPRICE` to less than or equal to the value entered by the user. Also, add the price to the output in the `ListBox`, which will make it easier for you to confirm that the correct cars were selected for the `inexpensiveCars` collection.

```csharp
private void recordsButton_Click(object sender, EventArgs e)
{
    int highprice = Convert.ToInt32(priceTextBox.Text);
    this.tblCarsTableAdapter.Fill
        (this.honestRalphsUsedCarsDataSet.tblCars);
    var inexpensiveCars =
        from c in this.honestRalphsUsedCarsDataSet.tblCars
        where c.Price <= highprice
        select c;
    foreach (var c in inexpensiveCars)
        inexpensiveCarsBox.Items.Add
            (c.ID + " - " + c.ModelYear + " " + c.Make +
                " $" + c.Price);
}
```

Figure 14-42 The `recordsButton_Click()` method that allows user data entry

3. Save and execute the program. Depending on the value you type into the `TextBox`, the output will look similar to Figure 14-43.

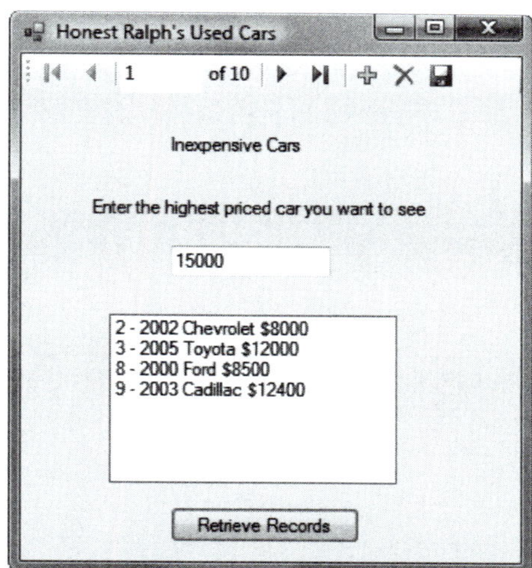

Figure 14-43 Typical execution of application that contains the method in Figure 14-42

4. If you click the button more than once in the current project, the `ListBox` list is appended rather than replaced. To remedy the problem, dismiss the `Form` and return to the code. Add the following statement near the beginning of the `recordsButton_Click()` method, before any items are added to the `inexpensiveCarsBox`:

```
inexpensiveCarsBox.Items.Clear();
```

5. Save and run the application again. If you enter different values and click the `Button` multiple times, now the list of cars is replaced with each new selection.

6. Dismiss the `Form` and run the application again, entering a low value such as $3500 for the maximum price in the search. When you click the `Button`, the `ListBox` is empty, as it should be, because no cars in the table are priced below that value. However, providing no feedback can confuse or frustrate a user, who might think the application is not working properly. To remedy the problem, you can add a message that appears when no cars meet the search criteria. Just before the closing curly brace of the `recordsButton_Click()` method, add the following:

```
if (inexpensiveCars.Count() == 0)
{
    inexpensiveCarsBox.Items.Add("Sorry - there are no cars");
    inexpensiveCarsBox.Items.Add
        ("less than or equal to $" + highprice);
}
```

This code uses the `Count()` aggregate operator to determine the number of records in the `inexpensiveCars` collection. When the count is 0, the user sees an appropriate message.

7. Save and execute the program. When the entered price is too low, the user sees a message confirming that the program works, but that no records meet the search criterion. See Figure 14-44.

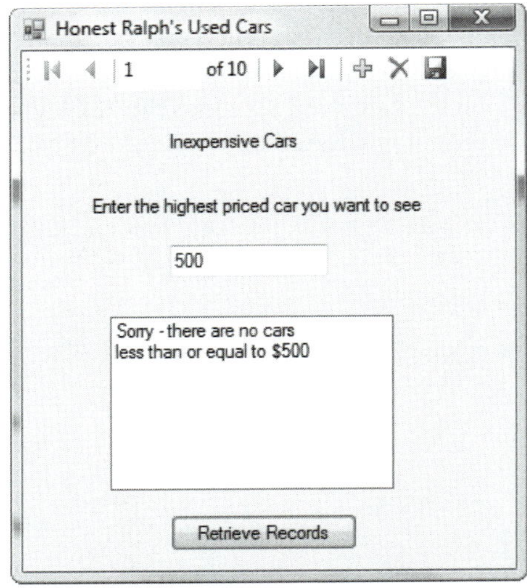

Figure 14-44 Output of `AccessCars` application when no cars meet the selection criterion

GROUPING DATA

In the next steps, you will group output records to make them easier for users to view and inspect.

1. Open a new Visual Studio C# project named **CarsGroupByMake**.

2. As shown in Figure 14-45, change the Form's Text property to **Honest Ralph's Used Cars**. Add a Button to the Form, change its Name to **carsButton**, and change its Text property to **View Cars**. Add a ListBox to the Form and change its name to **carsList**.

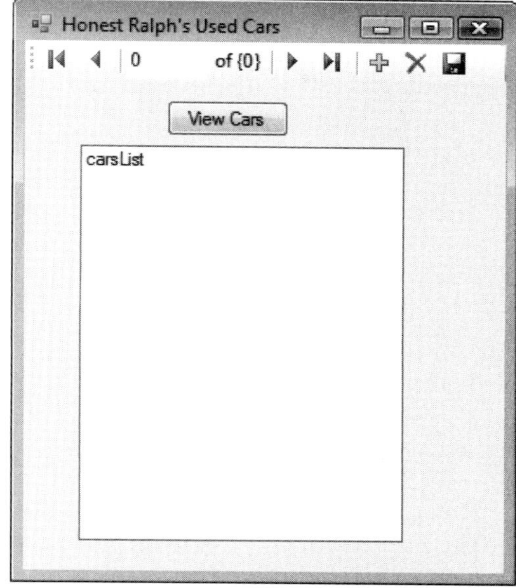

Figure 14-45 Form design for CarsGroupByMake project

3. Add HonestRalphsUsedCars.accdb to the project, drag the tblCars table onto the Form, and delete the automatically supplied grid from the Form.

4. Double-click the Button and add the following LINQ query within the automatically generated Click() method:

```
var cars =
    from c in this.honestRalphsUsedCarsDataSet.tblCars
    group c by c.Make;
```

This statement groups the cars by the value in each Make field.

5. Following the LINQ query, add a nested foreach loop that displays a car make for each group, then lists the year and price for each car within each group.

```
foreach(var group in cars)
{
    carsList.Items.Add("Make: " + group.Key);
    foreach(var c in group)
        carsList.Items.Add("      " + c.ModelYear + " $" + c.Price);
}
```

6. Save and execute the project. Click the `Button` on the `Form`. The output appears as in Figure 14-46. The year and price for each of the 10 cars in the table is displayed. Each car is grouped with others of the same make, and each group is preceded by a heading that shows the make.

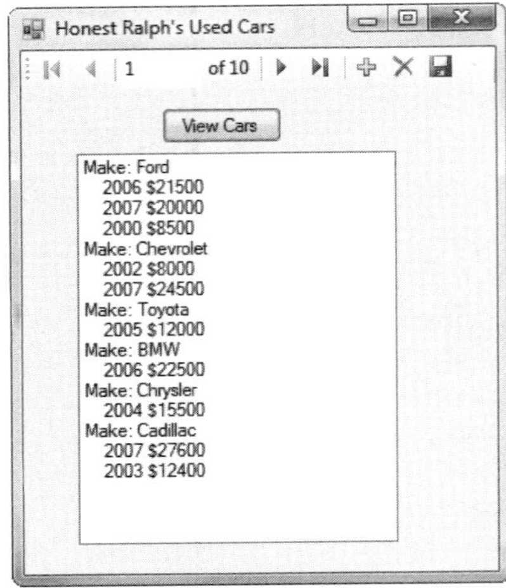

Figure 14-46 Output of `CarsGroupByMake` project

7. In Figure 14-46, the order in which cars are listed in each group is inconsistent. For example, the Chevrolets are listed from oldest to newest but the Cadillacs are listed from newest to oldest. To consistently display the cars in each group in order from newest to oldest, insert an `orderby` clause in the LINQ query as follows:

```
var cars =
    from c in this.honestRalphsUsedCarsDataSet.tblCars
    orderby c.ModelYear descending
    group c by c.Make;
```

8. Save the project and execute it again. When you click the `Button`, the output appears as shown in Figure 14-47. The cars are listed in order by model year within each group.

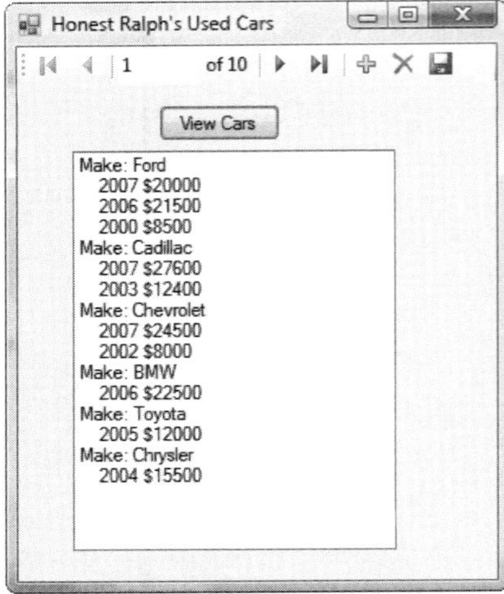

Figure 14-47 Output of `CarsGroupByMake` project ordered by `ModelYear`

9. The output in Figure 14-47 contains only 10 cars in only six different groupings by make. However, if there were more cars, it might be difficult to locate a specific car. To show the `Make` groups in alphabetical order, add a condition to the sort order specified in the LINQ query, as follows:

```
var cars =
    from c in this.honestRalphsUsedCarsDataSet.tblCars
    orderby c.Make, c.ModelYear descending
    group c by c.Make;
```

10. Save and execute the program. When you click the `Button` on the `Form`, the output appears as shown in Figure 14-48. Each make is listed in alphabetical order and each car is listed in descending model-year order within its `Make` group.

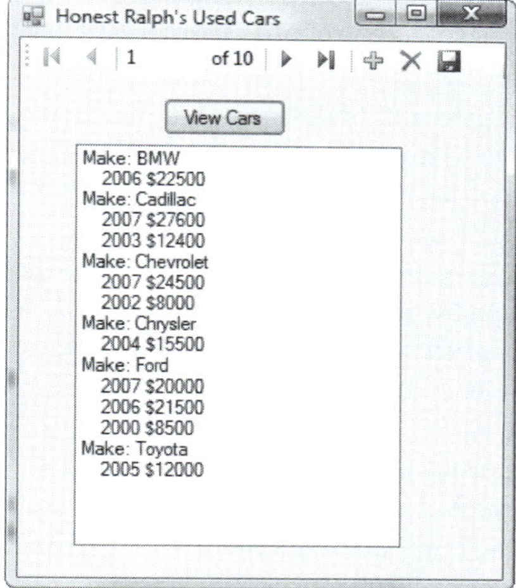

Figure 14-48 Output of `CarsGroupByMake` project ordered by `ModelYear` within alphabetized `Make`

11. Dismiss the `Form` and exit Visual Studio.

CHAPTER SUMMARY

» A database holds a group of files that an organization needs to support its applications. In a database, the files often are called tables because you can arrange their contents in rows and columns. A value that uniquely identifies a record is called a primary key, or a key for short. Database management software, or a database management system, is a set of programs that allows users to create table descriptions, identify keys, add, delete, and update records within a table, arrange records within a table so they are sorted by different fields, write questions that select specific records from a table for viewing, and perform other tasks.

» Creating a useful database requires a lot of planning and analysis. You must decide what data will be stored, how that data will be divided between tables, and how the tables will interrelate. For each table you must decide what columns are needed, provide names for them, and enter data.

» In most tables you create for a database, you want to identify a column, or possibly a combination of columns, as the table's key column or field (also called the primary key). The primary key in a table is the column that makes each record different from all others.

» A shorthand way to describe a table is to use the table name followed by parentheses that contain all the field names, with the primary key underlined.

» Queries are questions that cause database software to extract the appropriate records from a table and specify the fields to be viewed. The most common language that database administrators use to access data in their tables is Structured Query Language, or SQL. The basic form of the SQL command that retrieves selected records from a table is SELECT-FROM-WHERE.

» Microsoft Office Access is a relational database that is part of the Microsoft Office 2007 system. In Access, a database developer can type field names for the data that will be stored and can assign an appropriate data type for each. After a table's design has been completed, a user can enter data into the table.

» An implicitly typed variable has a data type that is inferred from the expression used to initialize the variable. When you use an implicitly typed variable, an object's set of allowed properties and methods is not fixed when the code is written, but is determined when the program executes. Implicitly typed variables are used frequently in LINQ statements, which access data stored in a database.

» The LINQ (Language INtegrated Query) Project provides a set of general-purpose standard operators that allow queries to be constructed using syntax that is easy to understand. This syntax is similar to SQL's, and the compiler can check it for errors. The operators defined in LINQ can be used to query arrays, enumerable classes, XML, relational databases, and other sources. Some keywords in the LINQ vocabulary include `select`, `from`, and `where`.

» To add a database table to a Windows Forms project, you must perform two sets of tasks. From a project's main menu, you choose Data and then Add a New Data Source. Next, you browse for the database and answer a few questions. Then you drag a table onto your form. The table's data is bound to the form and you are supplied with a grid in which you can view the data.

» You can use a LINQ query to select a collection of data from a table when specific criteria are met. You can use AND and OR expressions to limit criteria in your LINQ statements. With text values, you can use `StartsWith()`, `EndsWith()`, and `Contains()`. You can use several aggregate operators, or operators that produce statistics for groups of data, including `Average()`, `Count()`, `Sum()`, `Max()`, and `Min()`.

» You can use the `orderby` operator to sort a collection of data based on a field or fields. Data items also can be grouped. A query body must end with a `select` clause or a `group` clause.

KEY TERMS

A **database** holds a group of files that an organization needs to support its applications.

Tables are database files. They are called *tables* because their contents are arranged in rows and columns.

A **primary key**, or **key** for short, is a value that uniquely identifies a record.

A **compound key** or **composite key** is constructed from multiple columns.

Database management software, also known as a **database management system (DBMS)**, is a set of programs that allows users to create table descriptions, identify keys, add, delete, and update records within a table, arrange records within a table so they are sorted by different fields, write questions that select specific records from a table for viewing, write questions that combine information from multiple tables, create reports, and keep data secure.

A **relational database** is one in which you can establish and maintain relationships between columns in the tables.

The **Leszynski naming convention** (LNC) is a convention for naming database elements that is most popular with Microsoft Access users and Visual Basic programmers.

Normalization is the process of designing and creating a set of database tables that satisfies users' needs and avoids many potential problems such as data redundancies and anomalies.

Data redundancy is the unnecessary repetition of data.

An **anomaly** is an irregularity in a database's design that causes problems and inconveniences.

A **query** is a request to retrieve information from a database using syntax that the database software can understand.

Query by example is a language that allows you to query relational databases by filling in blanks.

Structured Query Language, or **SQL**, is the most common language that database administrators use to access data in their tables.

SELECT-FROM-WHERE is the basic form of the SQL command that retrieves selected records from a table.

TLA is a three-letter abbreviation for *three-letter abbreviation*; it is the most popular type of abbreviation in technical terminology.

A **view** is a particular way of looking at a database in database management systems.

A **wildcard** is a symbol that means "any" or "all."

Microsoft Office Access is a relational database that is part of the Microsoft Office 2007 system.

An **implicitly typed variable** has a data type that is inferred from the expression used to initialize the variable.

The **var** data type creates an implicitly typed variable.

Type inference is the process of implicitly typing a variable; it is also called **duck typing**.

An **iteration variable** is used to hold each successive value in an array.

When a language is **strongly typed**, severe restrictions are placed on what data types can be mixed.

The **LINQ** (Language INtegrated Query) Project provides a set of general-purpose standard operators that allow queries to be constructed in C# using syntax that is easy to understand. This syntax is similar to SQL's, and the compiler can check it for errors.

The LINQ keyword `select` indicates what to select from a collection.

The LINQ keyword `from` indicates the collection or sequence from which data will be drawn.

The LINQ keyword `where` indicates conditions for selecting records.

A **restriction operator** places a restriction on which data is added to a collection.

A **projection operator** is one that projects, or sends off, specific data from a collection.

Aggregate operators are operators that produce statistics for groups of data.

The `orderby` **operator** sorts a collection of data based on a field or fields.

The `group` **operator** groups data by specified criteria.

REVIEW QUESTIONS

1. A database's files often are called _____________ .

   a. records

   b. tables

   c. catalogs

   d. registers

2. A value that uniquely identifies a record is a(n) _____________ .

   a. source

   b. ID

   c. key

   d. prime

3. Database management software is a set of programs that allows users to do all of the following except _____________ .

   a. add, delete, and update records within a table

   b. sort records in a table

   c. verify that all entered data is correct

   d. write queries

4. When you design a database table, you must do all of the following except _____________ .

   a. decide how many columns the table needs

   b. decide how many rows the table needs

   c. provide names for the columns

   d. provide a data type for each column

5. Which of the following would not be a good candidate for a primary key?

    a. The number of seats on a bus in a table that stores data about a city's fleet of buses

    b. A bus pass number in a table of a city's bus service customers

    c. A bus driver's ID number in a table that stores data about bus drivers

    d. A bus route number in a table that stores bus route data

6. Normalization __________ .

    a. is the process of entering data into database tables

    b. is a design process that reduces redundancy and anomalies in databases

    c. is a flaw in database design that results in the repetition of data

    d. is a flaw in database design that causes anomalies

7. Which of the following do you know based on this database notation?

    ```
    tblProducts(itemNum, description, price, quantity)
    ```

    a. The table name is `Products`.

    b. `itemNum` is the key field.

    c. No two descriptions hold the same value.

    d. `price` is a numeric field.

8. A question asked using syntax that database software can understand is a(n) __________ .

    a. query   c. request

    b. anomaly   d. redundancy

9. The basic form of the SQL command that retrieves selected records from a table is __________ .

    a. QUERY-BY-EXAMPLE   c. RETRIEVE-FROM-SOURCE

    b. SELECT-FROM-WHERE   d. STRUCTURED-QUERY-LIST

10. Based on the following SQL statement, you know that __________ will be displayed.

    ```
    SELECT itemNum, price FROM tblProducts WHERE quantity <= 0
    ```

    a. two rows   c. more than two columns

    b. two columns   d. more than two rows

11. Microsoft Office Access is __________ .

    a. a spreadsheet as well as a database

    b. no longer used by professional information specialists

    c. part of Visual Studio

    d. a typical database program

12. Which of the following is not true of implicitly typed variables?

    a. Their data types are inferred from the expression used to initialize the variable.

    b. They are declared using `var` as the data type.

    c. They use a process called type inference.

    d. They use a process called static typing.

13. Which of the following is true?

    a. `var product = new Product();` has the same meaning as `Product product = new Product();`

    b. `var x = 3;` has the same meaning as `double x = 3.0;`

    c. `var a = 17;` has the same meaning as `var b = 17;`

    d. `var Item();` has the same meaning as `var item = Item();`

14. C# is ___________ .

    a. strongly typed, like Visual Basic

    b. strongly typed, unlike Visual Basic

    c. weakly typed, like Visual Basic

    d. weakly typed, unlike Visual Basic

15. In ___________ you can access database data.

    a. C# 3.0

    d. older versions of C#

    c. both of the above

    d. none of the above

16. The operators defined in LINQ can be used to query ___________ .

    a. arrays

    b. relational databases

    c. both of these

    d. none of the above

17. Consider the following code. In this example, `nums` is ___________ .

```
var nums =
    from n in numbers
    where n > 5
    select n;
```

    a. an array of integers

    b. a database

    c. an implicitly typed collection

    d. a single record in the collection numbers

18. Consider the following code. In this example, `numbers` is ___________ .

```
var nums =
    from n in numbers
    where n > 5
    select n;
```

a. an array of integers

c. a database

b. a record in a database

d. an implicitly typed collection

19. Consider the following code. In this example, x is __________ .

```
var cheapProducts =
    from p in this.abcCompany.tblProducts
    where p.Price < MAX
    select p.Description;
foreach(var x in cheapProducts)
    listBox1.Items.Add(x);
```

a. a row in `tblProducts`

c. a price

b. a column in `tblProducts`

d. a description

20. Which of the following is not true of LINQ?

a. `Average()` is an aggregate operator.

b. `Max()` is an aggregate operator.

c. You can use the `orderby` operator to sort data.

d. You can use the `groupby` operator to group data.

EXERCISES

1. Create a program that holds an array of 10 integers. Prompt the user for and accept a value for each integer. Use LINQ statements to sort the integers in descending order and display them. Save the program as **LinqIntegersDemo.cs**.

2. Create a program that holds an array of eight integers. Prompt the user for and accept a value for each integer. Use LINQ statements to group the integers into two groups (even and odd), and then display each group. Figure 14-49 shows a typical execution. Save the program as **EvenAndOdd.cs**.

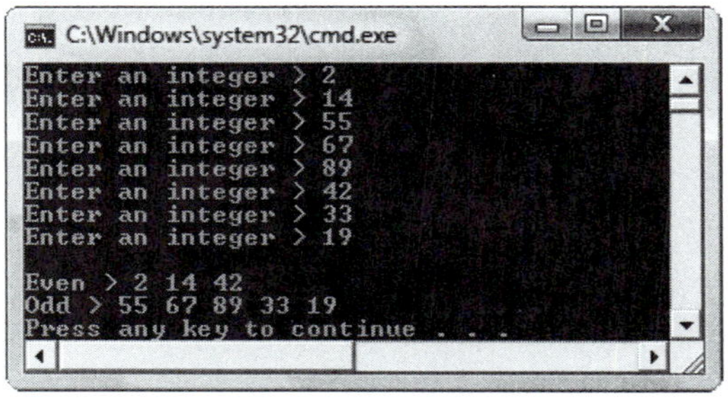

Figure 14-49 Typical execution of `EvenAndOdd` program

3. Create a program that contains an array of 12 strings. Prompt the user to enter a minimum string length and use LINQ statements to display all the strings that are at least as long as the value entered by the user. If no strings meet the criterion, display an appropriate message. Save the program as **LongWords.cs**.

4. Create a program that contains an array of 20 words of your choice. Use LINQ statements to display separate lists: One shows words that begin with letters in the first half of the alphabet (A through M), and the other list shows words that begin with letters in the second half (N through Z). Display a count of the number of words in each group. Save the program as **SplitAlphabet.cs**.

5. Create a `Book` class that contains `Title`, `Author`, and `Price` properties and a constructor that requires data for all three. Create a program that declares an array of at least eight `Books`. Prompt the user for an author. Display all the books written by that author, or an appropriate message if no such books exist. Save the program as **BookQuery.cs**.

6. Create a `Book` class that contains `Title`, `Author`, and `Price` properties and a constructor that requires data for all three. Create a program that declares an array of at least eight `Books`. Display the `Book` titles alphabetically by title and grouped by author. For an example, see Figure 14-50. Save the program as **BookQuery2.cs**.

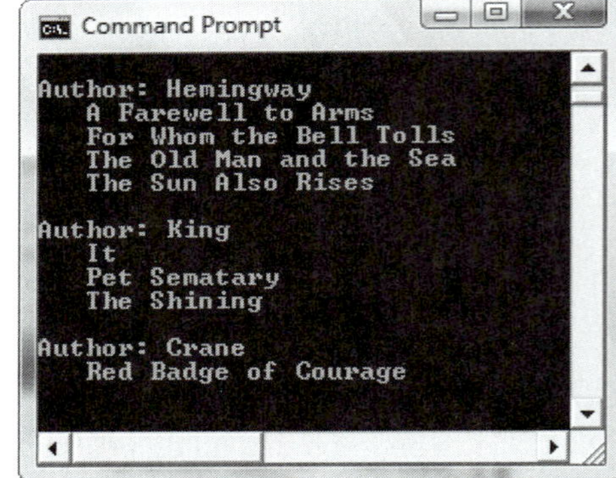

Figure 14-50 Typical execution of `BookQuery` program

7. Create an application that displays statistics about a database table when a user clicks various buttons. Use the HonestRalphsUsedCars database in the Student Files folder of your Student Disk, and display a count of the records, the most expensive car, and the least expensive car. Figure 14-51 shows the program before the user has clicked any buttons and after the user has clicked two of the buttons. Save the project as **CarStatistics**.

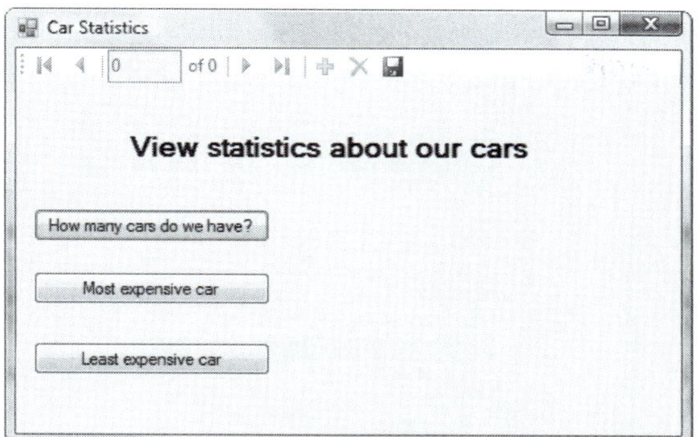
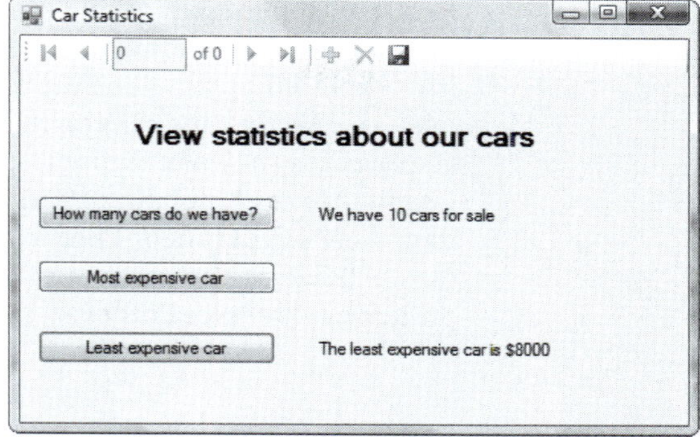

Figure 14-51 Typical execution of `CarStatistics` program before the user clicks any buttons and after the user has clicked two buttons

8. Create an application that allows a user to display cars of different makes. Use the HonestRalphsUsedCars database in the Student Files folder of your Student Disk. Your application should contain four check boxes labeled "Ford", "Chevrolet", "Cadillac", and "All". The user should be able to click any combination of check boxes to see the color, year, make, and price for each car with the desired make. For example, when the user clicks "Cadillac" and "Chevrolet", as in Figure 14-52, only those cars are displayed. Make sure that when the user changes selections, only the newly appropriate cars are visible. Save the project as **CarFinderByMake**.

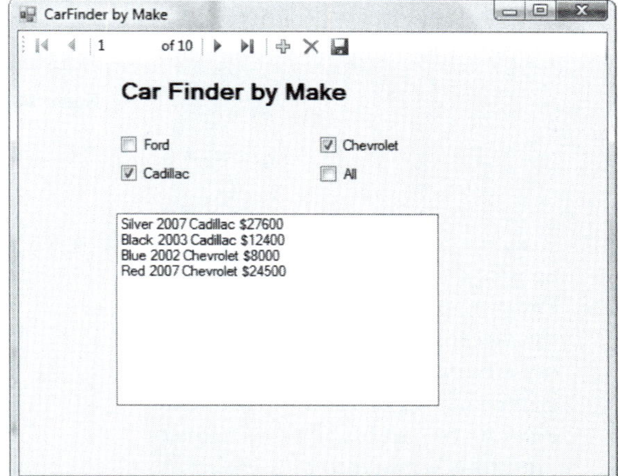

Figure 14-52 Execution of `CarFinderByMake` project

9. Create an application in which all of the cars in a database are displayed in a checked list box. When the user makes a selection, the car's price is displayed, as shown in Figure 14-53. Use the HonestRalphsUsedCars database in the Student Files folder of your Student Disk. Save the project as **CarPriceFinder**.

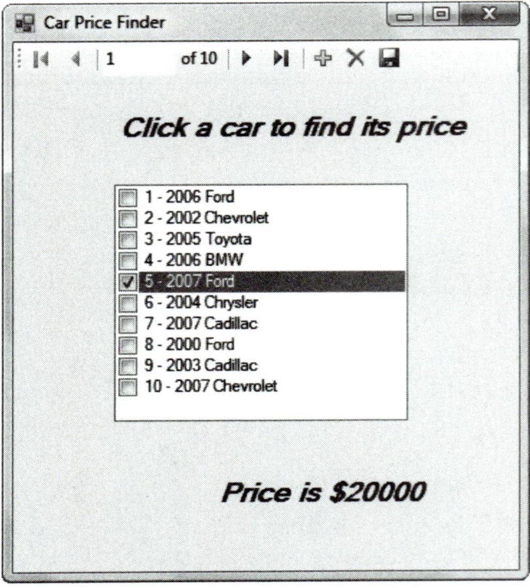

Figure 14-53 Execution of `CarPriceFinder` project

10. Create an application in which the user can select movies to view by entering part of the title or part of the director's name. The user clicks a radio button to choose which type of criterion is used. Then the user can enter all or part of the title's name or director's name into a `TextBox`. Allow the user to find matches regardless of case. See Figure 14-54 for a typical execution. Use the Movies database in the Student Files folder of your Student Disk. Save the project as **MovieFinder**.

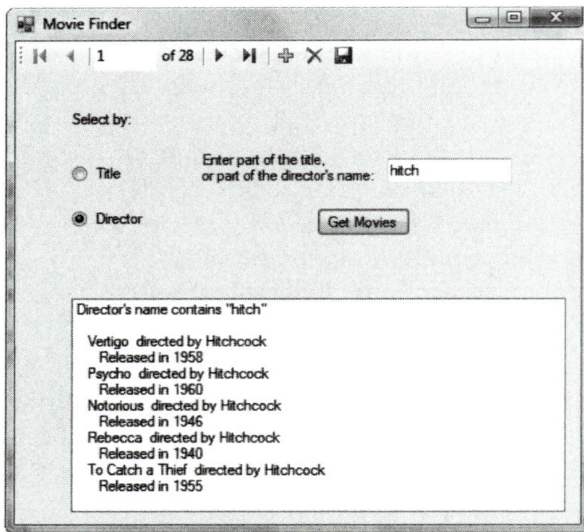

Figure 14-54 Typical execution of `MovieFinder` project

11. Create an application in which the user can enter a year to split a list of movies into those released before the indicated year and those released in the indicated year or afterward. Labels above each list should reflect the user's chosen cutoff year. Each list should be in order by release year. See Figure 14-55 for a typical execution. Use the Movies database in the Student Files folder of your Student Disk. Save the project as **MovieFinder2**.

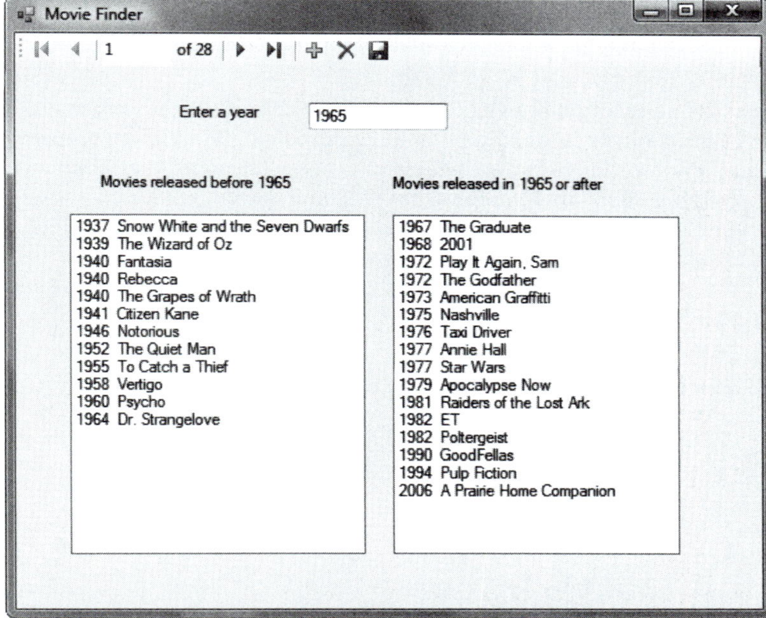

Figure 14-55 Typical execution of `MovieFinder2` project

DEBUGGING EXERCISES

Each of the following files in the Chapter.14 folder on your Student Disk has syntax and/or logical errors. In each case, determine the problem and fix the program. After you correct the errors, save each file using the same filename preceded with *Fixed*. For example, save DebugFourteen1.cs as **FixedDebugFourteen1.cs**.

    a. DebugFourteen1.cs

    b. DebugFourteen2.cs

    c. DebugFourteen3.cs

    d. DebugFourteen4.cs

UP FOR DISCUSSION

1. In this chapter, a phone book was mentioned as an example of a database you use frequently. Name some other examples.

2. Suppose you have authority to browse your company's database. The company keeps information on each employee's past jobs, health insurance claims, and any criminal records. Also suppose that you want to ask one of your co-workers out on a date. Should you use the database to obtain information about the person? If so, are there any limits on the data you should use? If not, should you be allowed to pay a private detective to discover similar data?

3. The FBI's National Crime Information Center (NCIC) is a computerized database of criminal justice information, including data on criminal histories, fugitives, stolen property, and missing persons. It is available to law enforcement and other criminal justice agencies 24 hours a day. Inevitably, such large systems contain some inaccuracies, and various studies have indicated that perhaps less than half the records in this database are complete, accurate, and unambiguous. Do you approve of this system or object to it? Would you change your mind if there were no inaccuracies? Is there a level of inaccuracy you would find acceptable to realize the benefits such a system provides?

4. What type of data might be useful to a community in the wake of a natural disaster? Who should pay for the expense of gathering, storing, and maintaining this data?

OPERATOR PRECEDENCE AND ASSOCIATIVITY

When an expression contains multiple operators, their **precedence** controls the order in which the individual operators are evaluated. For example, multiplication has a higher precedence than addition, so the expression 2 + 3 * 4 evaluates as 14 because the value of 3 * 4 is calculated before adding 2. Table A-1 summarizes all operators in order of precedence from highest to lowest.

When you use two operators with the same precedence, the **associativity** of the operators controls the order in which the operations are performed:

» Except for the assignment and conditional operators, all binary operators (those that take two arguments) are **left-associative**, meaning that operations are performed from left to right. For example, 5 + 6 + 7 is evaluated first as 5 + 6, or 11; then 7 is added, bringing the value to 18.

» The assignment operators and the conditional operator (?:) are **right-associative**, meaning that operations are performed from right to left. For example, x = y = z is evaluated as y = z first, and then x is set to the result.

» All unary operators (those that take one argument) are right-associative. If b is 5, the value of –++b is determined by evaluating ++b first (6), then taking its negative value (–6).

Category	Operators	Associativity
Primary	x.y f(x) a[x] x++ x-- new typeof checked unchecked	left
Unary	+ - ! ~ ++x --x (T)x	right
Multiplicative	* / %	left
Additive	+ -	left
Shift	<< >>	right
Relational	< > <= >= is as	left
Equality	== !=	left
Logical AND	&	left
Logical XOR	^	left
Logical OR	|	left
Conditional AND	&&	left
Conditional OR	||	left
Conditional	?:	right
Assignment	= *= /= %= += = <<= >>= &= ^= |=	right

Table A-1 Operator precedence

You can control precedence and associativity by using parentheses. For example, a + b * c first multiplies b by c and then adds the result to a. The expression (a + b) * c, however, forces the sum of a and b to be calculated first; then the result is multiplied by c.

KEY TERMS

The **precedence** of operators controls the order in which individual operators are evaluated in an expression.

The **associativity** of operators controls the order in which operations of equal precedence are performed in an expression.

With **left-associative** operators, operations are performed from left to right.

With **right-associative** operators, operations are performed from right to left.

B

CREATING A MULTIFILE ASSEMBLY

When you write a program that contains a `Main()` method and other methods, you can contain all the methods in a single file, as shown in the program in Figure B-1.

```csharp
using System;
public class ProgramThatCallsAMethod
{
    public static void Main()
    {
        DisplayMessage();
    }
    public static void DisplayMessage()
    {
        Console.WriteLine("Hello");
    }
}
```

Figure B-1 A class that contains a `Main()` method and a `DisplayMessage()` method

Instead of including the `DisplayMessage()` method in the `ProgramThatCallsAMethod` class, as shown in Figure B-1, you might want to write the method in its own class. That way, it can more easily be used by any application. To be able to use `DisplayMessage()` from its own class, you can create a multifile assembly. In the Microsoft .NET Framework, an **assembly** is a partially compiled code library; a **multifile assembly** is one composed from multiple files. As you become more proficient using C#, you will find additional reasons to create multifile assemblies besides including methods stored in separate files. Probably the most common reason is to combine modules written in different languages, such as Visual C++ or Visual Basic. To create a multifile assembly, you need to create a namespace and use some additional command-line options when you compile your program.

Suppose you want to include the `DisplayMessage()` method in its own class. Figure B-2 shows how the class should be constructed. The `DisplayMessage()` method has been copied from Figure B-1, and the shaded statements have been added.

```
namespace MessageNamespace
{
    using System;
    class Message
    {
        public static void DisplayMessage()
        {
            Console.WriteLine("Hello");
        }
    }
}
```

Figure B-2 The `MessageNamespace` namespace, stored in a file named DisplayMessage.cs

A namespace is created, using any identifier you choose. In Figure B-2, the name is `MessageNamespace`. Normally, you do not include *Namespace* within the name of a namespace; a more conventional name would be *Message*. This example uses *MessageNamespace* to help you remember that the name refers to a namespace rather than a class or a file. The `using System;` command is used in the DisplayMessage.cs file because the method uses `Console.WriteLine()`. The `DisplayMessage()` method is enclosed in its own class. The class might have any legal C# identifier; in this case, it is named `Message`.

When the file in Figure B-2 is saved as DisplayMessage.cs and compiled using the `csc` command, an error message is issued, as shown in Figure B-3. The message indicates that the file does not have a `Main()` method and cannot be compiled as a regular program. Your intention is not to have the class act as a stand-alone program; rather, you want the class to contain a method that other programs can use. To compile the class file, you must use a command that tells the compiler to create a **netmodule file**—that is, a file that contains modules to be used as part of another program rather than one that contains an executable program.

When you compile the program that contains the `Main()` method for the multifile assembly, you must include a command that adds the netmodule to the `Main()` program.

```
C:\C#\AppendixB>csc DisplayMessage.cs
Microsoft (R) Visual C# 2008 Compiler Beta 2 version 3.05.20706.1
for Microsoft (R) .NET Framework version 3.5
Copyright (C) Microsoft Corporation. All rights reserved.

error CS5001: Program 'c:\C#\AppendixB\DisplayMessage.exe' does not contain a
        static 'Main' method suitable for an entry point

C:\C#\AppendixB>
```

Figure B-3 Error message issued when DisplayMessage.cs is compiled using the `csc` command

To compile the DisplayMessage.cs file as a netmodule, use the following command:

```
csc /t:module DisplayMessage.cs
```

This command creates a file named DisplayMessage.netmodule. The file can now be used by a client program. For example, Figure B-4 shows a class named `Test`. Because the shaded statement `using MessageNamespace;` is included at the top of the file, the program has access to the methods stored in the `MessageNamespace` namespace. The method there can be called with the class-dot-method command `Message.DisplayMessage()`, as shown in the second shaded line.

```csharp
using MessageNamespace;
public class Test
{
    public static void Main()
    {
        Message.DisplayMessage();
    }
}
```

Figure B-4 The `Test` class

After the client program in Figure B-4 is stored in a file named Test.cs, you can use the `addmodule` command to associate the netmodule file with the program.

```
csc Test.cs /addmodule:DisplayMessage.netmodule
```

Figure B-5 shows the command that compiles the program and the subsequent execution. The output "Hello" comes from the `DisplayMessage()` method within the `MessageNamespace` namespace.

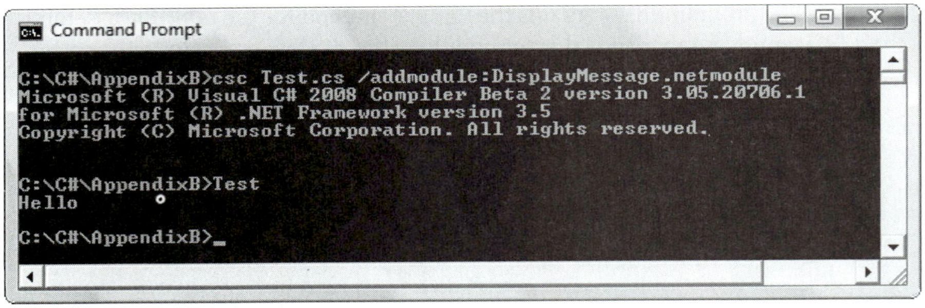

Figure B-5 Compiling and executing Test.cs

KEY TERMS

An **assembly** is a partially compiled code library.

A **multifile assembly** is an assembly composed from multiple files.

A **netmodule file** contains modules to be used as part of another program rather than containing an executable program.

C

USING THE IDE EDITOR

The Visual C# Code Editor is like a word processor for writing source code. Just as a word-processing program provides support for spelling and grammar, the C# Code Editor helps ensure that your C# syntax is free of spelling and grammar errors. This support can be grouped into five main categories:

» IntelliSense
» Refactoring
» Code snippets
» Wavy underlines
» Readability aids

INTELLISENSE

IntelliSense is Microsoft's name for the set of features designed to minimize the time you spend looking for help and to help you enter code more accurately and efficiently. The IntelliSense features provide basic information about C# language keywords, .NET Framework types, and method signatures as you type them in the editor.

The information is displayed in ToolTips, list boxes, and Smart Tags. Features of IntelliSense include:

» Providing completion lists
» Providing quick information
» Listing members
» Providing parameter information
» Adding `using` statements

PROVIDING COMPLETION LISTS

As you enter source code in the editor, IntelliSense displays a list box that contains all the C# keywords, .NET Framework classes, and names you have defined in your program that fit the current circumstances. For example, Figure C-1 shows a list box that makes suggestions based on what the programmer has typed in the Code Editor. If you find a match in the list box for the name you intend to type, you can select the item. Alternatively, you can press the Tab key to have IntelliSense finish entering the name or keyword for you.

Figure C-1 A list displayed by IntelliSense

PROVIDING QUICK INFORMATION

When you hover the cursor over a .NET Framework type, IntelliSense displays a Quick Info ToolTip that contains basic documentation about that type.

LISTING MEMBERS

When you enter a .NET Framework type or an identifier of a specific type into the Code Editor, and then type the dot operator (.), IntelliSense displays a list box that contains the members of that type. When you make a selection and then press the Tab key, IntelliSense enters the member's name. For example, Figure C-2 shows the list displayed when the user types button1, which is an identifier of type Button. When you don't know what method or property you want for an object, typing its identifier and a dot can direct you to the appropriate choice. This technique sometimes teaches you about features you did not even realize were available.

```
WindowsFormsApplication1.Form1                              button1_Click(object sender, EventArgs e)

    using System.Text;
    using System.Windows.Forms;

    namespace WindowsFormsApplication1
    {
        public partial class Form1 : Form
        {
            public Form1()
            {
                InitializeComponent();
            }

            private void button1_Click(object sender, EventArgs e)
            {
                if(button1.
            }                  AccessibilityObject
        }                      AccessibleDefaultActionDescription
    }                          AccessibleDescription
                               AccessibleName
                               AccessibleRole
                               AllowDrop
                               Anchor
```

Figure C-2 List displayed after programmer types an object and a dot

PROVIDING PARAMETER INFORMATION

When you enter a method name in the Code Editor and then type an opening parenthesis, IntelliSense displays a Parameter Info ToolTip that shows the method's parameter list. If the method is overloaded, multiple method signatures are displayed and you can scroll through them.

ADDING using STATEMENTS

If you attempt to create an instance of a .NET Framework class without a sufficiently qualified name, IntelliSense displays a Smart Tag after the unresolved identifier. When you click the Smart Tag, IntelliSense displays a list of using statements to help you resolve the identifier. When you select one from the list, IntelliSense adds the directive to the top of your source code file, and you can continue coding at your current location.

REFACTORING

As a project grows during development, you sometimes need to make changes to make it more readable, better organized, or more portable. For example, you might want to divide methods into smaller methods, change the number or types of a method's parameters, or rename identifiers. **Refactoring** is the process of rewriting a computer program to improve its structure, readability, or performance without changing its function. The IDE's refactoring tool is accessible by right-clicking in the Code Editor. The tool helps you restructure code much more conveniently and thoroughly than traditional approaches, such as searching and replacing every instance of a variable name. For more information, see the C# documentation.

CODE SNIPPETS

Code snippets are small units of commonly used C# source code that you can enter accurately and quickly with only a couple of keystrokes. To access the code snippet menu, right-click in the Code Editor. You can browse from the many snippets provided with Visual C#, and you can also create your own.

WAVY UNDERLINES

Wavy underlines give you instant feedback about errors in your code as you type. A red wavy underline identifies a syntax error, such as a missing semicolon or mismatched braces. A green wavy underline identifies a potential compiler warning, and blue identifies an Edit and Continue issue. In Figure C-3, two wavy underlines appear because the code in the last statement is not yet complete.

```csharp
using System.Text;
using System.Windows.Forms;

namespace WindowsFormsApplication1
{
    public partial class Form1 : Form
    {
        public Form1()
        {
            InitializeComponent();
        }

        private void button1_Click(object sender, EventArgs e)
        {
            if(button1.Text
        }
    }
}
```

Figure C-3 Wavy underlines in Code Editor

READABILITY AIDS

The editor assigns different colors to various categories of identifiers in a C# source code file to make the code easier to read. For example, C# keywords are bright blue, classes are blue-green, and comments are green.

KEY TERMS

IntelliSense is Microsoft's name for the set of features designed to minimize the time you spend looking for help and to help you enter code more accurately and efficiently.

Refactoring is the process of rewriting a computer program to improve its structure, readability, or performance without changing its function.

Code snippets are small units of commonly used C# source code that you can enter accurately and quickly with only a couple of keystrokes.

GLOSSARY

A

abstract class—a class from which you cannot create concrete objects, but from which you can inherit. Contrast with *concrete*.

abstract method—a method that contains no statements; any class derived from a class that contains an abstract method must override the abstract method by providing a body (an implementation) for it.

access modifier—a keyword that defines the circumstances under which a method or class can be accessed; `public` access is the most liberal type of access.

accessibility—describes limits set for a method as to whether and how other methods can use it.

accessors—methods in properties that specify how a class's fields are accessed. See *get accessors* and *set accessors*.

accumulated—describes totals added into a final sum by processing individual records one at a time in a loop.

actual parameters—arguments within a method call.

add and assign operator (+=)—an operator that adds the operand on the right to the operand on the left and assigns it to the operand on the left in one step.

aggregate operators—in LINQ, operators that produce statistics for groups of data.

alias—an alternative name or pseudonym.

ambiguous—describes overloaded methods between which the compiler cannot distinguish.

ancestors—all the superclasses from which a subclass is derived.

Anchor property—an attribute that causes a `Control` to remain at a fixed distance from the side of a container when the user resizes it.

AND operator—determines whether two expressions are both true; it is written using two ampersands (&&). Also called the *conditional AND operator*. Contrast with *Boolean logical AND*.

anomaly—an irregularity in a database's design that causes problems and inconveniences.

application files—files that store software instructions; program files. Contrast with *data files*.

argument—the expression passed to a method.

array—a list of data items that all have the same data type and the same name, but are distinguished from each other by a subscript or index.

array element—one object in an array.

assignment—a statement that provides a variable with a value.

assignment operator—the equal sign (=); any value to the right of the assignment operator is assigned to, or taken on by, the variable to the left.

associativity—specifies the order in which a sequence of operations with the same precedence are evaluated.

attributes—the characteristics of an object.

auto-implemented property—a property in which the code within the accessors is created automatically and the only action in the set accessor is to assign a value to the associated field. The only action in the get accessor is to return the associated field value.

B

base—a keyword that refers to the superclass of the class in which you use it.

base 16—a mathematical system that uses 16 symbols to represent numbers; hexadecimal.

base class—a class that is used as a basis for inheritance.

binary files—files that can store any of the 256 combinations of bits in any byte instead of just those combinations that form readable text.

binary operators—operators that use two arguments: one value to the left of the operator and another value to the right of it.

`BinarySearch()` **method**—a member of the `System.Array` class that finds a requested value in a sorted array.

black box—any device you can use without knowing how it works internally.

block—a collection of one or more statements contained within a pair of curly braces.

block comments—comments that start with a forward slash and an asterisk (/*) and end with an asterisk and a forward slash (*/). Block comments can appear on a line by themselves, on a line before executable code, or after executable code. They can also extend across as many lines as needed. Compare with *line comments*.

`bool`—data type that holds a Boolean value.

Boolean logical AND—an operator that determines whether two expressions are both true; it is written using a single ampersand (&). Unlike the conditional AND operator, it does not use short-circuit evaluation.

Boolean logical inclusive OR—an operator that determines whether at least one of two conditions is true; it is written using a single pipe (|). Unlike the conditional OR operator, it does not use short-circuit evaluation.

Boolean variable—a variable that can hold only one of two values—true or false.

break—a keyword that optionally terminates a `switch` structure at the end of each case.

`Button`—a GUI object you can click to cause some action.

`byte`—an integral data type that can hold an unsigned numeric value from 0 through 155.

C

C# programming language—a computer programming language developed as an object-oriented and component-oriented language. It exists as part of Visual Studio 2008, a package used for developing applications for the Windows family of operating systems.

call—to invoke a method.

call stack—the memory location where the computer stores the list of locations to which the system must return after method calls.

called—describes a method that has been invoked.

called method—a method that has been invoked by another method.

calling method—a method that calls another method.

camel casing—a style of creating identifiers in which the first letter is not capitalized, but each new word is. Contrast with *Pascal casing*.

case—a keyword in a switch structure that is followed by one of the possible values that might equal the `switch` expression.

case label—identifies a course of action in a `switch` structure.

`catch` **block**—a block of code that can catch one type of `Exception`.

`char`—an integral data type that can store a character such as 'A', '4', or '$'.

character—any one of the letters, numbers, or other special symbols (such as punctuation marks) that comprise data.

character set—the group of all the characters used to represent data on a particular computer.

check digit—a digit calculated from a formula and appended to a number to help verify the accuracy of the other digits in the number.

`CheckBox`—a GUI widget that a user can click to select or deselect an option. When a `Form` contains multiple `CheckBoxes`, any number of them can be checked or unchecked at the same time.

CheckedListBox—a `Control` similar to a `ListBox`, with check boxes appearing to the left of each desired item.

child class—a derived class; a subclass; a class that has inherited from a base class.

class—a category of objects or a type of object.

class access modifier—describes access to a class.

class client—a program or class that instantiates objects of another prewritten class. Also called a *class user*.

class definition—the first class line that describes a class; it contains an optional access modifier, the keyword `class`, and any legal identifier for the name of the class.

class header—the first class line that describes a class; it contains an optional access modifier, the keyword `class`, and any legal identifier for the name of the class.

class user—a program or class that instantiates objects of another prewritten class. Also called a *class client*.

Click event—the action fired and the event generated when a `Control` is clicked in a GUI environment.

client—a method that uses another method.

closing a file—the process of making a file no longer available to an application.

code bloat—a term that describes unnecessarily long or repetitive program statements.

Code Editor—the portion of the Visual Studio IDE in which you can write or view code statements.

Color—a class that contains a wide variety of predefined colors to use with `Control`s.

ComboBox—a `Control` similar to a `ListBox`, except that it displays an additional editing field that allows a user to select from the list or enter new text.

command line—the line on which you type a command in a system that uses a text interface.

command prompt—a request for input that appears at the beginning of the command line.

comment out—to turn a statement into a comment so that the compiler will not execute its command.

Compare()—a method that compares two values. In the `String` class, it is a method that requires two `string` arguments; when it returns 0, the two `strings` are equivalent; when it returns a positive number, the first `string` is greater than the second; and when it returns a negative value, the first `string` is less than the second.

CompareTo()—a method that compares objects. In the `String` class, it is a method used with a `string` and a dot before the method name, with another `string` as an argument. When the method returns 0, the two `strings` are equivalent; when it returns a positive number, the first `string` is greater than the second; and when it returns a negative value, the first `string` is less than the second. In the `IComparable` interface, `CompareTo()` is a method that compares one object to another and returns an integer.

comparison operator(= =)—an operator that compares two items; an expression that contains a comparison operator has a Boolean value.

compiler—a computer program that translates high-level language statements into machine code.

Component—a class that provides containment and cleanup for other objects.

composed delegate—a delegate that calls the delegates from which it is built.

composite key—a key constructed from multiple columns; a compound key.

composition—the technique of using an object within another object.

compound key—a key constructed from multiple columns; a composite key.

computer file—a collection of information stored on a nonvolatile device in a computer system.

concatenate—to join strings together in a chain.

concrete—nonabstract; describes classes from which objects can be instantiated.

conditional AND operator—determines whether two expressions are both true; it is written using two ampersands (&&). Also called the *AND operator*. Contrast with *Boolean logical AND*.

conditional operator—a ternary operator that is used as an abbreviated version of the `if-else` statement; it requires three expressions separated by a question mark and a colon.

conditional OR operator—determines whether at least one of two conditions is true; it is written using two pipes (||). Also called the *OR operator*. Contrast with *Boolean logical inclusive OR*.

`Console.ReadLine()`—a method that accepts user input from the keyboard.

constant—describes a data item when it cannot be changed after a program is compiled—in other words, when it cannot vary.

constructor—a method that instantiates (creates an instance of) an object.

constructor initializer—a clause that indicates another instance of a class constructor should be executed before any statements in the current constructor body.

contextual keywords—identifiers that act like keywords in specific circumstances.

`Control`—a class that provides the definitions for GUI objects.

`Controls`—GUI components such as text fields, buttons, and check boxes that users can manipulate to interact with a program.

counted loop—a definite loop.

CSV file—a file that contains comma-separated values.

culture—a set of rules that determines how culturally dependent values such as money and dates are formatted.

D

data files—files that contain facts and figures; persistent collections of related records. Contrast with *program files* and *application files*.

data hierarchy—the relationship of characters, fields, records, and files.

data redundancy—the unnecessary repetition of data.

data type—a description of the format and size of a data item as well as the operations that can be performed on it.

database—a collection of files that an organization needs to support its applications.

database management software or **database management system (DBMS)**—a set of programs that allows users to create table descriptions, identify keys, add, delete, and update records within a table, arrange records within a table so they are sorted by different fields, write questions that select specific records from a table for viewing, write questions that combine information from multiple tables, create reports, and keep data secure.

`DateTimePicker`—a `Control` that retrieves date and time information.

dead code—describes code statements that can never execute under any circumstances because the program logic "can't get there." Also see *unreachable*.

debugging—the process of removing all syntax and logical errors from a program.

`decimal`—a floating-point data type that has a greater precision and a smaller range than a `float` or `double`, which makes it suitable for financial and monetary calculations.

decision structure—a unit of program logic that involves choosing between alternative courses of action based on some value.

decrement operator (--)—an operator that reduces a variable's value by 1; there is a prefix and a postfix version.

decrementing—the act of decreasing the value of a variable, often by 1.

default—a keyword that optionally is used prior to any action that should occur if the test expression in a case structure does not match any case.

default constructor—a constructor that requires no parameters; the automatically supplied parameterless constructor for a class is a default constructor, but you can also create a default constructor.

default event—for a `Control`, the event or method generated when you double-click it while designing it in the IDE. It is the method you are most likely to alter when you use the `Control`, as well as the event that users most likely expect to generate when they encounter the `Control` in a working application.

default value of an object—the value initialized with a default constructor.

definite loop—a loop in which the number of iterations is predetermined. Also a *counted loop*. Contrast with *indefinite loop*.

delegate—an object that contains a reference to a method.

delimiter—a character used to specify the boundary between characters in text files.

derived class—a subclass; a class that has inherited from a base class.

deserialization—the process of converting streams of bytes back into objects.

destructor—a method that contains the actions performed when an instance of a class is destroyed.

DialogResult—an enumeration that contains a user's potential `MessageBox` button selections.

directories—structures used to organize files on a storage device; folders.

Directory class—a class that provides information about directories or folders.

dismiss—to get rid of a component, frequently by pressing its Close button, but in some cases by making some other selection.

do loop—a type of posttest loop; a loop that is tested at the bottom of the loop after one repetition has occurred.

Dock property—an attribute that attaches a `Control` to the side of a container so that the `Control` stretches when the container's size is adjusted.

double—a data type that can hold a floating-point number with 15 or 16 significant digits of accuracy.

dual-alternative decisions—decisions that have two possible outcomes.

duck typing—the process of implicitly typing a variable.

E

empty body—a block that has no statements in it.

encapsulation—the technique of packaging an object's attributes and methods into a cohesive unit that can be used as an undivided entity.

enum—an enumeration; a programmer-defined type that declares a set of constants.

enumeration—a list of values in which names are substituted for numeric values.

Equals()—a method that determines equivalency; in the `String()` class, it is the method that determines if two `strings` have the same value; it requires two `string` arguments that you place within its parentheses, separated by a comma.

error list tab—a portion of the Visual Studio IDE that displays compiler errors.

escape sequence—a single character composed of two symbols beginning with a backslash that represents a nonprinting character such as a tab.

event—an object generated when a user interacts with a GUI object, causing the program to perform a task.

event handler—a method that performs a task in response to an event; an event receiver.

event receiver—a method that performs a task in response to an event; an event handler.

event sender—the control that generates an event.

event wiring—the act of connecting an event to its resulting actions.

EventArgs—a C# class designed for holding event information.

event-driven—describes programs that contain code that causes an event such as a button click to drive the program to perform a task.

EventHandler—a class for events that do not use any information besides the source of the event and the `EventArgs` parameter.

exception—an error condition or unexpected behavior in an executing program.

exception handling—the set of object-oriented techniques used to manage unexpected errors.

explicit cast—purposefully assigns a value to a different data type; it involves placing the desired result type in parentheses followed by the variable or constant to be cast.

explicitly—purposefully. Contrast with *implicitly*.

exposes—a term used to associate a `FileStream` with a file.

extended class—a derived class; a child class; a subclass; a class that has inherited from a base class.

extension methods—static methods that act like instance methods. You can write extension methods to add to any type.

F

fault-tolerant—describes applications that are designed so that they continue to operate, possibly at a reduced level, when some part of the system fails.

field—in a class, an instance variable. In a file or database, a character or group of characters that has some meaning.

File class—a class that contains methods that allow you to access information about files.

file position pointer—a variable that holds the byte number of the next byte to be read from a file.

finally block—a block of code that optionally follows a `try` block; the code within one executes whether the `try` block identifies any `Exceptions` or not.

fires an event—causes an event to occur. Also see *raises an event* and *triggers an event*.

float—a data type that can hold a floating-point number with as many as seven significant digits of accuracy.

floating-point—describes a number that contains decimal positions.

flowchart—a tool that helps programmers plan a program's logic by writing program steps in diagram form, as a series of shapes connected by arrows.

focus—refers to the "ready" state of a GUI component, in which its action is executed if the user presses the Enter key. When a component has focus, the user's attention is drawn to it visually.

folders—structures used to organize files on a storage device; directories.

Font—a class used to change the appearance of printed text on `Forms`.

for loop—a loop that contains the starting value for the loop control variable, the test condition that controls loop entry, and the expression that alters the loop control variable, all in one statement.

foreach statement—statements used to cycle through every array element without using a subscript.

Form Designer—a portion of the Visual Studio IDE in which you visually design applications.

formal parameter—a parameter within a method header that accepts a value.

format specifier—one of nine built-in format characters in a format string that defines the most commonly used numeric format types.

format string—a string of characters that contains one or more placeholders for variable values.

Forms—a GUI interface for collecting, displaying, and delivering information.

fragile—describes classes that depend on field names from parent classes because they are prone to errors—that is, they are easy to "break."

from—a LINQ keyword that indicates the collection or sequence from which data will be drawn.

G

garbage—an unknown memory value.

get accessors—methods in properties that allow retrieval of a field value by using a property name.

getter—another term for a class property's get accessor.

governing type—in a `switch` statement, the type that is established by the `switch` expression. The governing type can be `sbyte`, `byte`, `short`, `ushort`, `int`, `uint`, `long`, `ulong`, `char`, `string`, or `enum`.

graphical user interface (GUI)—an interface that employs graphical images that the user manipulates. GUI objects include the buttons, check boxes, and toolbars you are used to controlling with a mouse when you interact with Windows-type programs.

group operator—in LINQ, the operator that groups data by specified criteria.

GroupBox—a `Control` that can be used to group other `Controls` on a `Form`; similar to a `Panel`, but it has a `Title` property.

H

has-a relationship—the relationship created using composition, so-called because one class "has an" instance of another.

hash code—a number that should uniquely identify an object.

hexadecimal—a mathematical system that uses 16 symbols to represent numbers; base 16.

hides—overrides so as to make invisible.

high-level programming language—allows you to use a vocabulary of reasonable terms such as "read," "write," or "add" instead of the sequence of on/off switches that perform these tasks.

I

IComparable interface—an interface that contains the definition for the `CompareTo()` method.

identifier—the name of a program component such as a variable, class, or method.

if statement—a program statement used to make a single-alternative decision.

if-else statement—a statement that performs a dual-alternative decision.

immutable—unchangeable.

implementation hiding—the technique of keeping the details of a method's operations hidden.

implicit cast—the automatic transformation that occurs when a value is assigned to a type with higher precedence.

implicit conversion—the conversion that occurs when a type is automatically changed to another upon assignment.

implicit parameter—an undeclared parameter that gets its value automatically.

implicit reference conversion—a type of conversion that occurs when a derived class object is assigned to its ancestor's data type.

implicitly—automatically. Contrast with *explicitly*.

implicitly typed variable—a variable that has a data type that is inferred from the expression used to initialize the variable.

incrementing—the act of increasing the value of a variable, often by 1.

indefinite loop—a loop in which the number of iterations is not predetermined. Contrast with *definite loop*.

index—an integer contained within square brackets that indicates the position of one of an array's elements. Also see *subscript*.

infinite loop—a loop that (theoretically) never ends.

information hiding—a feature found in all object-oriented languages, in which a class's data is private and changed or manipulated only by its own methods.

inheritance—the ability to extend a class so as to create a more specific class that contains all the attributes and methods of a more general class; the extended class usually contains new attributes or methods as well. Inheritance also refers to the application of your knowledge of a general category to more specific objects.

initialization—an assignment made when a variable is declared.

initializer list—the list of values provided for an array.

inner loop—the loop in a pair of nested loops that is entirely contained within another loop.

instance—an object; one specific occurrence of a class. Often used as "instance of a class."

instance methods—methods that are used with object instantiations.

instance variables—data components of a class that exist separately for each instantiation. Also called *fields*.

instantiation—a created object.

`int`—an integral data type that can hold a signed numeric value in four bytes.

integers—whole numbers.

integral data types—data types that store whole numbers; the nine integral types are `byte`, `sbyte`, `short`, `ushort`, `int`, `uint`, `long`, `ulong`, and `char`.

interactive program—a program that allows user input.

interface—a collection of abstract methods (and perhaps other members) that can be used by any class as long as the class provides a definition to override the interface's abstract definitions. An interface is also the interaction between a method and an object.

intermediate language (IL)—the language into which source code statements are compiled.

`internal`—a class access modifier that means access is limited to the assembly to which the class belongs.

`internal access`—a level of method accessibility that limits method access to the containing program.

intrinsic types—basic, built-in data types; C# provides 14 intrinsic types.

invoked—described a method that has been called.

invokes—to call a method.

invoking object—the object referenced by `this` in an instance method.

invoking the event—calling an event method.

is-a relationships—object-class relationships.

iteration—one execution of any loop.

iteration variable—a temporary variable that holds each array value in turn in a `foreach` statement.

J

jagged array—a one-dimensional array in which each element is another array.

jump statements—a statement that causes program logic to "jump" out of the normal flow in a control structure. Jump statements include `break` and `continue`.

just in time (JIT)—the C# compiler that translates intermediate code into executable code.

K

key—a value that uniquely identifies a record.

key events—keyboard events that occur when a user presses and releases keyboard keys.

key field—the field used to control the order of records in a sequential file.

keywords—predefined and reserved identifiers that have special meaning to the compiler.

L

Label—a `Control` object that typically provides descriptive text for another `Control` object or displays other text information on a `Form`.

Length property—a member of the `System.Array` class that automatically holds an array's length.

Leszynski naming convention (LNC)—a convention for naming database elements that is most popular with Microsoft Access users and Visual Basic programmers.

lexically—alphabetically.

line comments—comments that start with two forward slashes (//) and continue to the end of the current line. Line comments can appear on a line by themselves, or at the end of a line following executable code. Compare with *block comments*.

LinkLabel—a `Control` that is similar to a `Label`, but provides the additional capability to link the user to other sources, such as Web pages or files.

LINQ (Language INtegrated Query)—provides a set of general-purpose standard query operators that allow queries to be constructed in C#. LINQ uses easy-to-understand syntax that is similar to SQL and that the compiler can check for errors.

ListBox—a `Control` that enables you to display a list of items that the user can select by clicking.

literal constant—a value that is taken literally at each use.

literal string—a series of characters that is used exactly as entered.

local variable—a variable that is declared in the current method.

logic—the sequence of statements and methods that produce the desired results in a computer program.

long—an integral data type that can hold a signed numeric value in eight bytes.

loop—a structure that allows repeated execution of a block of statements.

loop body—the block of statements executed in a loop.

loop control variable—a variable that determines whether loop execution will continue on each iteration.

M

machine language—the most basic circuitry-level language.

magic number—a hard-coded number.

main menu—in the Visual Studio IDE, the list of choices that run horizontally across the top of the screen; it includes a File menu from which you open, close, and save projects.

matrix—a name frequently used by mathematicians when referring to an array. Also see *table*.

MaximumSize property—an attribute of a `Form` that has two values—`Width` and `Height`.

menu strip—a horizontal list of general options that appears under the title bar of a `Form` or `Window`.

MenuStrip—a control that creates a menu strip.

MessageBox—a GUI object that can contain text, buttons, and icons that inform and instruct a user.

method—an encapsulated series of statements that carry out a task.

method body—the block of statements that carry out a method's work; all the instructions contained within a pair of curly braces ({ }) following a method header.

method declaration—a method header or definition; it precedes a method and includes a `return` type, identifier, and an optional parameter list.

method definition—a method header or declaration; it precedes a method and includes a `return` type, identifier, and an optional parameter list.

method header—the first line of a method; it includes the method name and information about what will pass into and be returned from a method.

method node—in Visual Studio, a small box that appears to the left of code; you use it to expand or collapse code.

method's type—a method's `return` type.

Microsoft Office Access—a relational database that is part of the 2007 Microsoft Office system.

`MinimumSize` property—an attribute of a `Form` that has two values—`Width` and `Height`.

mission critical—describes any process that is crucial to an organization.

modal dialog box—a dialog box that prevents a program from further progress until the user dismisses it.

`MonthCalendar`—a `Control` that retrieves date and time information.

multidimensional arrays—arrays that require multiple subscripts to access the array elements.

multifile assembly—a group of files containing methods that work together to create an application.

multiple inheritance—the ability to inherit from more than one class.

N

named constant—an identifier whose contents cannot change.

namespace—a scheme that provides a way to group similar classes.

nested `if`—a statement in which one decision structure is contained within another.

nested method calls—method calls placed inside other method calls.

new—a keyword used to create objects; also known as the `new` operator.

node—in the Visual Studio IDE, a box that appears on a vertical tree to the left of a list or a section of code and that can be expanded or condensed.

`nonstatic`—describes a method that requires an object reference.

nonvolatile—the type of computer storage that is permanent; it is not lost when a computer loses power.

normalization—the process of designing and creating a set of database tables that satisfies the users' needs and avoids many potential problems such as data redundancies and anomalies.

NOT operator (!)—negates the result of any Boolean expression.

O

object (or `Object`)—a class type in the `System` namespace that is the ultimate base class for all other types.

object initializer—a clause that allows you to assign values to any accessible members or properties of a class at the time of instantiation without calling a constructor with parameters.

object-oriented programming—a programming technique that features objects, classes, encapsulation, interfaces, polymorphism, and inheritance.

objects—program elements that are instances of a class.

one-dimensional array—an array whose elements you can access using a single subscript. Also see *single-dimensional array*.

opening a file—the process of creating an object and associating a stream of bytes with it.

operands—the values that operators use in expressions.

operator precedence—rules that determine the order in which parts of a mathematical expression are evaluated. Also called *order of operation*.

OR operator—determines whether at least one of two conditions is true; it is written using two pipes (‖). Also called the *conditional OR operator*. Contrast with *Boolean logical inclusive OR*.

order of operation—rules that determine the order in which parts of a mathematical expression are evaluated. Also called *operator precedence*.

`orderby` **operator**—in LINQ, the operator that sorts a collection of data based on a field or fields.

out of scope—describes a variable that is not usable because it has ceased to exist.

outer loop—the loop in a pair of nested loops that contains another loop.

output parameter—a parameter to a method that receives the argument's address; it is not required to have an initial value. Contrast with *value parameter* and *reference parameter*.

output tab—a portion of the Visual Studio IDE that displays compiler errors.

overloading—using one term to indicate diverse meanings. When you overload a C# method, you write multiple methods with the same name but different parameter lists.

`override`—a keyword used in method headers when you create a derived class that inherits an abstract method from a parent.

`override`—the action that occurs when a method takes precedence over another method, hiding the original version.

P

`Padding` **property**—an attribute of a `Form` that specifies the distance between docked `Control`s and the edges of the `Form`.

`Panel`—a `Control` that can be used to group other `Control`s on a `Form`; similar to a `GroupBox`, but it does not have a `Title` property.

parallel array—an array that has the same number of elements as another array and holds corresponding data.

parameter—an object or reference that is declared in a method definition; that is, where the method instructions are written.

parameter array—a local array declared within a method header.

parameterless constructor—a constructor that takes no parameters; one that is called using no arguments.

`params`—a keyword used to declare a local array in a method so the method can receive any number of arguments.

parent class—a base class; a superclass; a class that is used as a basis for inheritance.

Pascal casing—a style of creating identifiers in which the first letter of all new words in a variable name, even the first one, is capitalized. Contrast with *camel casing*.

passed by reference—describes how data is passed to a method when the method receives the memory address of the argument passed to it.

path—the disk drive in which a file resides plus the complete hierarchy of directories.

permanent storage devices—hardware such as hard disks, floppy disks, Zip disks, USB drives, reels or cassettes of magnetic tape, and compact discs, that are used to store files.

persistent—describes storage that is nonvolatile.

`PictureBox`—a `Control` in which you can display graphics from a bitmap, icon, JPEG, GIF, or other image file type.

placeholder—in a format string, it consists of a pair of curly braces containing a number that indicates the desired variable's position in a list that follows the string.

polymorphism—the ability to create methods that act appropriately depending on the context.

postfix increment operator (++)—an operator placed after a variable that evaluates the variable and then adds 1 to it.

posttest loop—a loop in which the loop control variable is tested after the loop body executes. Contrast with *pretest loop*.

precision specifier—controls the number of significant digits or zeros to the right of the decimal point in a format string.

prefix increment operator (++)—an operator placed before a variable that increases the variable's value by 1 and then evaluates it.

preprocessor—a program that executes before the compiler and looks for preprocessor directives for instructions on how to modify code.

preprocessor directives—statements that always start with a pound sign (#) and are instructions to the preprocessor to modify the code in some way.

pretest loop—a loop in which the loop control variable is tested before the loop body executes. Contrast with *posttest loop*.

primary key—a value that uniquely identifies a record; the term is often used in databases.

primitive data—simple data, such as a number.

private—an access modifier that indicates other classes may not use the method or variable that it modifies. When used as a class access modifier, it means access is limited to another class to which the class belongs.

private access—a level of method accessibility that limits method access to the containing class.

procedural program—a program created by writing a series of steps or operations to manipulate values.

procedures—compartmentalized program units that accomplish tasks. Also see *methods*.

program—a set of instructions that you write to tell a computer what to do.

program comments—nonexecuting statements that document a program.

program files—files that store software instructions; application files. Contrast with *data files*.

projection operator—in LINQ, an operator that projects, or sends off, specific data from a collection.

prompt—an instruction to the user to enter data.

Properties window—a portion of the Visual Studio IDE that allows you to configure properties and events on controls in your user interface.

property—a member of a class that provides access to a field of a class; properties define how fields will be set and retrieved. The value of an object.

protected—a keyword that provides an intermediate level of security between `public` and `private` access. A `protected` data field or method can be used within its own class or in any classes extended from that class, but it cannot be used by "outside" classes. As a class access modifier, it means access to the class is limited to the class and to any classes derived from the class.

protected access—a level of method accessibility that limits method access to the containing class or types derived from the containing class.

protected internal access—a level of method accessibility that limits method access to the containing program, containing class, or types derived from the containing class.

pseudocode—a tool that helps programmers plan a program's logic by writing plain English statements.

`public`—an access modifier that indicates other classes may use the method or variable that it modifies. As a class access modifier, it means access to the class is not limited.

`public access`—a level of method accessibility that allows unlimited access to a method.

Q

query—a question asked to retrieve information from a database using the syntax that the database software can understand.

query by example—a language that allows you to query relational databases by filling in blanks.

R

`RadioButtons`—GUI widgets, similar to `CheckBoxes`, except that when they are placed on a `Form`, only one `RadioButton` can be selected at a time—selecting any `RadioButton` automatically deselects the others.

raises an event—causes an event to occur. Also see *fires an event* and *triggers an event*.

random access memory (RAM)—temporary storage in a computer.

range check—a series of statements that determine whether a value falls within a specified range.

range match—a process that determines whether a value falls between a pair of limiting values.

read from the file—to copy data from a file on a storage device into RAM.

read-only property—a property that has only a get accessor, and not a set accessor.

record—a collection of fields that contain data about an entity.

rectangular array—an array in which each row has the same number of columns.

recursive—describes a method that calls itself.

reference equality—a type of equality that occurs when two reference type objects refer to the same object.

reference parameter—a parameter to a method that receives the argument's address; it is required to have an initial value. Contrast with *value parameter* and *output parameter*.

reference type—a data type that holds a memory address. Contrast with *value types*.

relational database—a database in which you can establish and maintain relationships between columns in the tables.

restriction operator—in LINQ, an operator that places a restriction on which data is added to a collection.

rethrowing the `Exception`—the act of throwing a caught `Exception` instead of handling it.

`return` statement—a method statement that causes a value to be sent back from a method to its calling method.

`return` type—the data type of the value a method will return to any other method that calls it.

`Reverse()` method—a member of the `System.Array` class that reverses the order of items in an array.

robustness—describes the degree to which a system is resilient to stress, maintaining correct functioning even in the presence of errors.

root directory—the main directory of a storage device.

S

`sbyte`—an integral data type that can hold a signed numeric value from –128 through 127.

scientific notation—a numeric expression format that includes an *E* (for exponent) that specifies a number of implied decimal places.

scope—the area where a variable or constant is known and can be used.

sealed—a keyword that describes a class that cannot be extended.

select—a LINQ keyword that indicates what to select from a collection.

SELECT-FROM-WHERE—the basic form of the SQL command that retrieves selected records from a table.

self-documenting—describes a program element that is self-explanatory.

semantic errors—the type of logical errors that occur when you use a correct word in the wrong context.

sentinel value—a value that a user must supply to stop a loop.

sequence structure—a unit of program logic in which one step follows another unconditionally.

sequential access file—a data file in which each record is read in order based on its position in the file; usually the records are stored in order based on the value in some field.

serialization—the process of converting objects into streams of bytes.

set accessors—methods in properties that allow use of the assignment operator with a property name.

setter—another term for a class property's set accessor.

short—an integral data type that can hold a signed numeric value in two bytes.

short-circuit evaluation—the C# feature in which parts of an AND or OR expression are evaluated only as far as necessary to determine whether the entire expression is true or false.

side effect—an unintended consequence of an operation.

signature—a method's name and parameter list.

significant digits—specifies the mathematical accuracy of the value.

single-dimensional array—an array whose elements you can access using a single subscript. Also see *one-dimensional array*.

snap lines—lines that appear in a design environment to help you align new `Controls` with others already in place.

Solution Explorer—a portion of the Visual Studio IDE that allows you to view and manage project files and settings.

Sort() method—a member of the `System.Array` class that arranges array items in ascending order.

source code—the statements you write when you create a program.

standard numeric format strings—strings of characters expressed within double quotation marks that indicate a format for output.

StartsWith()—a `String` method that returns true if the object `string` starts with the characters contained in the argument `string`.

state of an object—the collective value of all an object's attributes at any point in time.

static—a keyword that indicates that a method will be executed through a class and not by an object.

step value—the amount by which a loop control variable is altered on each iteration, especially in a `for` loop.

stream—a pipeline or channel through which bytes are input from and output to a file.

string—a data type that can hold a series of characters.

strongly typed—describes a language in which severe restrictions are placed on what data types can be mixed.

Structured Query Language (SQL)—the most common language that database administrators use to access data in their tables.

subclass—a derived class; a child class; a class that has inherited from a base class.

subscript—an integer contained within square brackets that indicates the position of one of an array's elements. Also see *index*.

superclass—a base class; a parent class; a class that is the basis for inheritance.

switch—a keyword that starts a switch structure.

`switch` expression—a condition in a `switch` statement enclosed in parentheses.

`switch` structure—tests a single variable against a series of exact matches.

syntax—the set of grammar rules in a programming language.

syntax error—an error that occurs when a programming language is used incorrectly.

`System` namespace—a scheme built into the C# compiler that holds commonly used classes.

`System.Array`—a built-in class that defines fields and methods that belong to every array.

T

table—a name frequently used by mathematicians when referring to an array. Also see *matrix*.

tables—database files, so-called because their contents are arranged in rows and columns.

ternary—describes an operator that requires three arguments.

`this` reference—the reference to an object that is implicitly passed to an instance method of its class.

TLA—a three-letter abbreviation for *three-letter abbreviation*; it is the most popular type of abbreviation in technical terminology.

token—a block of text within a string that represents an entity or field.

Toolbox tab—a portion of the Visual Studio IDE that contains controls you can drag onto a `Form` so that you can develop programs visually, using a mouse.

transitive—inheriting all the members of one's ancestors.

triggers an event—causes an event to occur. Also see *fires an event* and *raises an event*.

`try` block—a block that contains code that might create exceptions you want to handle.

two-dimensional arrays—multidimensional arrays that have two or more columns of values for each row.

type inference—the process of implicitly typing a variable.

type precedence—a hierarchy of data types used to determine the unifying type in arithmetic expressions containing dissimilar data types.

U

`uint`—an integral data type that can hold an unsigned numeric value in four bytes.

`ulong`—an integral data type that can hold an unsigned numeric value in eight bytes.

unary operators—operators used with one operand.

Unicode—a 16-bit coding scheme for characters.

Unified Modeling Language (UML) diagrams—graphical tools that programmers and analysts use to describe systems.

unifying type—the type chosen for an arithmetic result when operands are of dissimilar types.

unreachable—describes code statements that can never execute under any circumstances because the program logic "can't get there." Also see *dead code*.

`ushort`—an integral data type that can hold an unsigned numeric value in two bytes.

using clause, or **using directive**—code that declares a `namespace`.

V

value parameter—a parameter to a method that receives a copy of the value passed to it. Contrast with *reference parameter* and *output parameter*.

value types—data types that hold a value; they are predefined types such as `int`, `double`, and `char`. Contrast with *reference type*.

var—a data type that creates an implicitly typed variable.

variable—a named location in computer memory that can hold different values at different points in time.

variable declaration—the statement that names a variable; it includes the data type that the variable will store, an identifier that is the variable's name, an optional assignment operator and assigned value when you want a variable to contain an initial value, and an ending semicolon.

verbatim identifier—an identifier with an @ prefix.

virtual method—a method whose behavior is determined by the implementation in a child class.

visible—describes a class member that has not been hidden.

void—a keyword that indicates that a method does not return any value when called.

volatile—the type of computer storage that is lost when power is lost.

W

where—a LINQ keyword that indicates conditions for selecting records.

while loop—a structure that executes a body of statements continuously while some condition continues to be true; it uses the keyword `while`.

whitespace—any combination of spaces, tabs, and carriage returns (blank lines) in a program.

widgets—interactive controls such as labels, scroll bars, check boxes, and radio buttons.

wildcard—a symbol that means "any" or "all."

write to the file—to store data in a computer file on a permanent storage device.

Write() method—a method that displays a line of output on the screen, but the cursor does not advance to a new line; it remains on the same line as the output.

WriteLine() method—a method that displays a line of output on the screen, positions the cursor on the next line, and waits for additional output.

XML—an abbreviation of eXtensible Markup Language, which is a standard for exchanging data over the Internet.

XML-documentation format comments—comments that use a special set of tags within angle brackets to create documentation from within a program.

INDEX

E

empty body, 135
encapsulation, 6
enum, 110
enumeration, 423
equal sign (=), assignment operator, 48, 60
equal to operator (==), 63
Equals() method, 69
object class, 332
error(s). *See also* exception handling
semantic, 3
syntax, 3, 21
error list tab, 433
escape sequences, 66, 67, 78–79
event(s), 443
event handlers, 528
event handling, 527–568
associating one method with multiple events, 565–566
Control component events, 542–546
declaring your own events and handlers, 536–539
delegates, 532–536, 556–561
EventHandler, 540–542
EventListeners, 562–563
keyboard events, 549–552
mouse events, 547–549
multiple Controls, 552–555
TabStop and TabUndex, 563–565
event receivers, 529–530
event senders, 529–530
event wiring, 531
EventArgs class, 530
event-driven programs, 528
EventHandler, 540–542
EventListener, 562–563
exact matches, searching arrays for, 169–174
exception(s)
definition, 368
list, 368–369

Exception class
Message property, 376–378
ToString method, 376–378
exception handling, 367–407
creating Exception classes, 396–399
Exception class's ToString() method and Message property, 376–378
finally block, 384–386
generating a SystemException purposely, 370–372, 402–403
loops, 386–388
multiple Exceptions, 379–383
object-oriented, 373–376, 404–406
rethrowing Exceptions, 399–401
throwing Exceptions between methods, 388–391
tracing Exceptions through call stack, 392–396
traditional methods, 372–373
explicit cast, 65
explicit overriding, 65
exposing steams around a file, 585
extended classes, 314–315, 318
extending classes, 316–318, 351–352
extension methods, 345–348

F

fault-tolerant applications, 371
fields, 249, 582
key, 582
file(s), 575–613
binary, 587
closing, 583
computer, 576
creating, 599–600
creating in GUI environment, 604–606

CSV, 588
data, 576, 582
data organization, 581–583
Directory class, 580–581
File class, 577–579
opening, 583
organization, 577
program (application), 576
reading from. *See* reading from files
Seek() method, 601–603
sequential access. *See* sequential access files
serialization and deserialization, 595–599
streams, 583–587
writing to, 576, 587–590
File class, 577–579
file position pointer, 592
finally block, 384–386
firing events, 528
float data type, 47, 55
floating-point data types, 55–56
floating-point numbers, 55
formatting, 56–58
flowcharts, 92–93
focus, buttons, 422, 552–553
folders, 577
following conventions, 14
Font, Labels, 474–476
for loops, 138–140, 150–153
arrays, 186–187
searching arrays for exact matches, 170–172
foreach statements, 169
Form(s)
adding functionality to Buttons, 442–444, 453–454
CheckBox objects, 482–487, 510–514
CheckedListBox controls, 493–494
color, 480–482
ComboBox controls, 493–494
creating, 425–429
DatePicker controls, 494–498